Narrative of the Expedition of an American Squadron to the China Seas and Japan

Performed in the years 1852, 1853, and 1854, under the command of Commodore M.C. Perry, United States Navy, by order of the Government of the United States

M. C. Perry, Francis L. Hawks

Alpha Editions

This edition published in 2020

ISBN : 9789354010408

Design and Setting By
Alpha Editions
email - alphaedis@gmail.com

As per information held with us this book is in Public Domain.
This book is a reproduction of an important historical work. Alpha Editions uses the best technology to reproduce historical work in the same manner it was first published to preserve its original nature. Any marks or number seen are left intentionally to preserve its true form.

NARRATIVE

OF

THE EXPEDITION OF AN AMERICAN SQUADRON

TO

THE CHINA SEAS AND JAPAN,

PERFORMED IN THE YEARS 1852, 1853, AND 1854,

UNDER THE COMMAND OF

COMMODORE M. C. PERRY, UNITED STATES NAVY,

BY ORDER OF THE GOVERNMENT OF THE UNITED STATES.

COMPILED FROM THE ORIGINAL NOTES AND JOURNALS OF COMMODORE PERRY AND HIS OFFICERS, AT HIS REQUEST, AND UNDER HIS SUPERVISION,

BY FRANCIS L. HAWKS, D. D. L. L. D.

WITH NUMEROUS ILLUSTRATIONS.

PUBLISHED BY ORDER OF THE CONGRESS OF THE UNITED STATES.

WASHINGTON:
BEVERLEY TUCKER, SENATE PRINTER.
1856.

PREFATORY NOTE.

PROMPTED in a great degree by feelings of personal friendship for Commodore Perry, the compiler of the following pages yielded to his earnest request, enforced as it was by that of other friends, and consented to undertake the task of preparing this Narrative of the United States' Expedition to Japan.

And here it is proper to mention, that among the expressed motives which induced the Commander of the Expedition to desire the execution of the work by other hands than his own, none seemed more prominent than this consideration: that, as the facts here embodied were to be gathered not merely from the pages of his own journal, but from those also of several of his officers, as well as from their official reports to him, he thought it better to confide the compilation to a disinterested third party, who might weave the various materials into a connected narrative of all the important events, uninfluenced by that partiality for his own words or acts, from which, owing to the infirmities of human nature, the most honest and best of men are not always entirely exempt.

As the sole object on the part of the Commander was to afford to his government and countrymen the most ample account he could of what had been done by himself, his officers, and men—as in this respect he had nothing to conceal, as he wished to present truly all of interest that had been observed either by himself or others, and to do justice to the deserving officers who had so effectually sustained him in his plans for carrying out a new, delicate, and arduous work—he deemed it best to place in the hands of the compiler, without reserve, *all* the materials in his possession, whether from his own pen, or furnished by the labor of others, and to request nothing more than that the preparation of the work might be conducted in a spirit conformable to the ends and wishes just expressed.

The materials were abundant and varied. Beside the manuscript journal of the Commodore, in three large folios, and his official correspondence; the journals of his secretary and other officers, the diaries of the fleet captain and flag-lieutenants, the official reports of gentlemen detailed for special duties, and the public documents connected with the Expedition, were all placed in the hands of the writer. Of these, the Commodore's journal and official correspondence form much the larger part.*

The work to be performed was that of a compiler merely. With no responsibility as to the facts related, the writer believed his appropriate duty to be simply to weave into a connected narrative all of interest or importance that could be gathered from these various materials, and to present, in chronological order, the incidents of the Expedition. Eminently suggestive, as were many portions of the story, the compiler felt that it was his business to deal with the *facts* only, and spare the reader the infliction of his reflections on them.

The book, therefore, is but little encumbered with the writer's observations or conjectures on the incidents related. Where a momentary digression from the story does occur, the remarks it embodies are generally those of the Commodore himself. In many instances, the language of the Narrative is a *verbatim* copy from his journal. Wherever it was possible thus to use his manuscript, it was done, as being the course most likely to avoid error. Every word of the work was read to the Commodore in manuscript, and received his correction before it went into the printer's hands; every proof sheet also was read by him before it was sent back to the press. In order to expedite the preparation and publication of the work as much as possible, and place it, at an early period, in the hands of Congress, as the labor was that of compilation only, the present writer, with the approbation of Commodore Perry, availed himself of the kindness of a competent literary gentleman,† who assisted him in the work of comparing the various journals, documents, &c., arranging chronologically the incidents gathered from all sources, and presenting them in a connected form. Some portions of the story were also, in the first instance, sketched by this gentleman, and after undergoing the revision of the present writer, were incorporated by him into the Narrative, and then submitted to the Commodore for his corrections and suggestions. Some of the descriptions of scenery were thus prepared, as well as portions of the Narrative relating to the two vistis to Japan. By means of this valuable aid, the whole story was written out in less than a twelvemonth from the time its publication was ordered by Congress, a result which would otherwise have been unattainable. The

---

* The Commodore, unwilling to appropriate what may belong to others, desires here to acknowledge the use of the *journals* of the captain of the fleet, Commander Adams, of the flag-lieutenants, Mr. Contee and Mr. Bent, those of Purser Harris, Mr. Perry, (Commodore's secretary,) Mr. Bayard Taylor and Chaplain Jones; the *reports* of Captains Abbot, Buchanan, and Adams, Commandants Boyle, Kelly, and Glasson, Chaplain Jones, Mr. Williams, Chinese interpreter, and Doctors Green and Fahs; the *services* of Mr. Portman, Dutch interpreter, and of the artists, Mr. W. Heine and Mr. E. Brown, jr. In the hydrographical department he would specially acknowledge the accurate and laborious work of Lieutenants W. L. Maury and S. Bent. Nor would he pass by without notice minor contributions from any under his command; to all he would render due credit and thanks.

† Robert Tomes, Esq., M.D.

compiler makes this statement, not only to acknowledge the kindness of a friend, but also to guard himself against the suspicion of being willing to appropriate, without recognition, the labors of another.

As to the Narrative itself, the highest ambition of the writer was to tell the story, if he could, in such manner as would not only present a true picture, but also keep alive the interest of the reader; his wish was to make a book that might furnish information without being wearisome. If in this he has succeeded, he has attained all to which he aspired. If he has not, he has only to say that he will feel more of regret than surprise.

In some instances he may be thought to be needlessly minute, and especially in describing the pageantry of receptions, entertainments, &c. In this matter he felt obliged to consult something beside his own taste merely; he was looking to the natural curiosity of his countrymen to know *every particular* of the story, and therefore preferred to tell too much rather than too little. Beside, the pageantry was often an important part of the history of the negotiation itself, with a people so ceremonious as the Japanese.

Nor did the compiler hesitate to use freely the materials placed before him in the shape of journals, &c., even though the substance of some portions of them is already in the hands of the public. They were originally prepared for just such use as is here made of them; the report was designed to tell the incidents of the whole story from beginning to end; and the compiler was directed simply to use the materials that had been furnished him. It was not for him to omit facts because others had already related them.

In but one respect did he venture to exercise any discretion. His duty required that he should tell *all* that occurred from the moment the Mississippi left the Capes of the Chesapeake. As, however, the chief interest of the Expedition was to be found in events that occurred in China, Lew Chew, the Bonin Islands, and Japan, he endeavored to make as brief as duty would permit the incidents of the earlier part of the outward voyage, sensible that but little new remained to be said in passing over a track so often traversed and so well known by intelligent Europeans and Americans. Still he believes he has omitted nothing, which his materials furnished, that is likely to interest the general reader.

Distance from the press has occasioned some typographical errors, which the intelligent reader will readily correct for himself; there are probably other errors; for these the other duties of the compiler and the circumstances of his position will, he hopes, be accepted as an apology.*

---

* This volume will be followed by three others, as soon as the labors of the government press can produce them. They are prepared. Appendix, vol. 1, will contain the Natural History and Illustrations, with various reports; vol. 2 will embrace the Astronomical Observations; and vol. 3 the Hydrography of the Expedition.

AUTHENTICATION OF THE NARRATIVE.

The Narrative here presented of the Japan Expedition has been prepared under my supervision and at my request, from materials furnished by me, and is authentic. I present it as my official report, and am alone responsible for the statement of facts it contains.

M. C. PERRY, *Late Commander-in-chief*
of the United States Expedition to the China Seas and Japan.

NEW YORK, *January* 1, 1856.

CONTENTS.

	Page.
INTRODUCTION	3—74

CHAPTER I.

Probabilities of a successful mission from the United States to Japan.—Such a mission proposed to the Government by Commodore Perry.—Expedition resolved on.—Vessels selected for the squadron.—Vexatious delay in their equipment.—Commodore Perry sent in the Mississippi to the Gulf of St. Lawrence.—Applications of scientific men to join the expedition refused.—Causes of such refusal.—Dr. Von Siebold.—Visit of the President and Secretary of the Navy to Annapolis to take leave of the expedition.—Failure of the machinery of the steamship Princeton on the passage down Chesapeake Bay.—Substitution of steamer Powhatan in place of the Princeton.—Final departure of Commodore Perry on the mission with the Mississippi alone.. 75—80

CHAPTER II.

Voyage from the capes of the Chesapeake to Madeira.—View of the island.—Funchal.—Hospitality of the inhabitants.—Salubrity of the climate.—Exports of the island.—Novel mode of conveyance.—Departure from Madeira and arrival at the Canaries.—Early failure of northeast trades.—Extraordinary swell from the northwest.—General order as to private journals and communications to public prints.—General order as to scientific investigations by officers.—The "Harmattan," consideration of hypotheses as to its origin.—Southeast trades.—Ship steered for St. Helena.—Observations on the currents.—Chaplain's observations on the zodiacal lights.—Arrival at St. Helena.—Description of the island.—Jamestown.—Longwood.—Tomb of Napoleon.—The calculating hospitality of the inhabitants of the island.—Adventure of Lieutenant ———.—Fortifications of the island.—Their sufficiency against sailing vessels.—Probable insufficiency against an approach from the west by steam.—Departure from St. Helena 81—96

CHAPTER III.

Passage to the cape.—Fuel for steamers.—Table rock and Cape Town.—Description of Cape Town.—Climate.—Annoyance from dust.—Violence of winds and difficulty of holding to anchorage.—Supplies at the cape.—Caffre war and its effects.—Mode of transporting produce on land.—Vineyards of Constantia.—Effects of emancipation of slaves on agricultural labor.—Mode of cultivating the vine.—Population of Cape Colony.—Bushmen.—The Caffres.—Physical characteristics.—Fingoes.—Military organization of Caffres.—Condition of the emancipated slaves.—Departure from Table Bay.—Passage to, and arrival at, Mauritius.—Harbor of Port Louis.—Dangers of the harbor.—Skill of port officers in mooring vessels 97—106

CHAPTER IV.

Mauritius, its discovery.—Geological formation and physical aspect.—Production of sugar.—Effect on agriculture of the abolition of slavery.—Coolies.—Population of the island.—State of feeling between English and French residents.—Hospitable treatment of the expedition.—Description of Port Louis.—Grand Port.—Paul and Virginia.—Facts on which St. Pierre founded his story.—Tombs of Paul and Virginia.—Built by an eccentric Frenchman.—Cyclones.—Their probable causes.—Interest felt in them at Mauritius.—Departure of the Mississippi from Port Louis.—Her course thence to Point de Galle, island of Ceylon.—Reasons for taking it.—Point de Galle, description of.—Great rendezvous of steamers.—Difficulty of procuring fuel there.—American consul.—Thoughts on consular system.—Early knowledge of Ceylon.—Its several European possessors.—Climate.—Salubrity.—Causes of its diminished prosperity.—Productions.—Value of cocoanut palm.—Pearl fishery.—Immense numbers of elephants.—Great slaughter of them.—Boa constrictor.—Population of Ceylon.—Physique of Cingalese, Malabars, and Mahomedans in the island.—Religious condition.—Buddhism.—Pilgrimage to the temples.—Intercourse with a Siamese naval officer at Ceylon.—Commodore's letter to the second king of Siam.—Departure from Ceylon.—Passage through the Straits of Malacca.—Arrival at Singapore 107—124

viii   CONTENTS.

                                                                                                               Page.
                                                    CHAPTER V.

Singapore.—Its great commerce.—Population.—Rapid increase.—Hospitality of a wealthy Chinese merchant.—
    Importance of Singapore to England.—Coal depot at Singapore.—Physical aspect of the country.—Agricul-
    tural products.—Animals.—Ferocity of the tiger.—Water buffalo.—Passage from Singapore to Hong Kong.—
    Currents, rocks, tides.—Chinese fishing boats.—Arrival at Hong Kong.—Finding there sloops-of-war Sara-
    toga and Plymouth and store-ship Supply.—Susquehanna gone to Shanghai.—Disappointment of the Com-
    modore.—Condition and prosperity of Hong Kong.—Run to Macao, thence to Whampoa on Canton river.—
    Navigation of the river.—First impressions made by the city.—Disappointed expectations.—Hospitality of
    American consul at Canton.—The hongs or factories.—Streets in Canton.—Proper name of the city.—Bocca
    Tigris.—Chinese forts.—Pirates on the river.—Attempt to rob one of the officers.—Canton market place.—
    Trade of Canton with Europe and America... 125—138

                                                   CHAPTER VI.

Hospitable treatment at Macao.—Usages of the foreign merchants toward visitors.—Depressed condition of
    Macao.—Description of the place.—Tanka boats, and girls who manage them.—Cave of Camoens.—De-
    parture of Mississippi from Macao.—Saratoga left to bring Mr. Williams, the interpreter.—Difficulties of
    navigation from Hong Kong to the mouth of Yang-tse-keang.—Entrance of the river dangerous.—Susque-
    hanna, Plymouth, and Supply all aground.—Mississippi saved by the power of her engines only.—Descrip-
    tion of Shanghai.—Its immense trade.—Cultivation of the country.—Population of the city.—Visit of the
    Commodore to the governor of the city.—Chinese rebellion.—Its effects.—Plymouth left at Shanghai to
    protect American interests.—Departure for Great Lew Chew.—Arrival of the squadron at the capital, Na-
    pha, the Saratoga having joined at the entrance to the harbor.. 139—150

                                                   CHAPTER VII.

Number and position of islands of Lew Chew.—Their supposed political relations to Japan and China.—Descrip-
    tion of the island of Great Lew Chew, as seen on the first approach to it.—Visit of officials to the Susque-
    hanna.—Visit of Dr. Bettelheim.—Refusal of presents, and consequent mortification of the Lew Chewans.—
    Exploration of the island resolved on by the Commodore.—Daguerreotyping on shore.—Coral insect and its
    formations.—Second visit of the authorities of Lew Chew.—Regent of the island received by the Commo-
    dore.—Friendly nature of the interview.—Surprise of the Lew Chewans at sight of the steam-engine.—
    Commodore announces to them his intention of returning the visit at the palace of Shui.—Their evident
    embarrassment thereat.—Leave to go on shore.—Description of Napha and its vicinity, by one of the offi-
    cers.—Exploring party sets out, placed under the command of the chaplain, Mr. Jones.—Mr. Bayard Taylor
    attached to it, with orders to take notes and furnish a detailed report of the journey.—Negotiations with
    the Lew Chew authorities to obtain a house on shore.—Their manifest opposition.—Commodore persists
    and succeeds.—Officers, when on shore, continually watched by spies.—Captain Basil Hall's account of the
    Lew Chewans somewhat exaggerated.—Impressions made on the officers as to the character of the natives.—
    Hydrographic surveys.—Boat exercise of the crews, and drilling on land of the marines..................... 151—161

                                                  CHAPTER VIII.

Report of an inland exploration of Great Lew Chew, by a party from the squadron, under the command of
    Commodore Perry.. 162—186

                                                   CHAPTER IX.

Efforts of authorities of Lew Chew to prevent a visit to the palace.—All unsuccessful.—Landing for the visit.—
    Procession.—Appearance of the country.—Reception at the palace.—Embarrassment of the regent.—Enter-
    tainment at the regent's house.—Saki.—New dishes.—Commodore invites authorities to a dinner on board
    the Susquehanna.—General impressions produced by the visit.—Espionage still kept up.—Daily exercise of
    sailors and marines.—Settlement of accounts with Lew Chew authorities.—Mississippi and Supply remain
    at Lew Chew.—Susquehanna and Saratoga leave for the Bonin islands.—Death of an opium smoker on the
    passage.—Inhumanity of Chinese.—Sunday on board.—Arrival at Port Lloyd............................... 187—196

                                                    CHAPTER X.

Situation of Bonin islands.—First discovery of them.—Europeans have no claim as the discoverers.—Mixed
    character of present settlers.—External appearance of Peel island.—Geological formation.—Harbor of Port
    Lloyd.—Productions of the island, animal and vegetable.—Resort of whalers.—Condition of present in-
    habitants.—Commodore causes the island to be explored.—Reports of exploring parties.—Kanakas.—Ex-
    amination of Stapleton island, and report thereon.—Survey of harbor of Port Lloyd.—Land purchased for
    a coal depot.—Departure from Bonin islands on the return to Lew Chew.—Disappointment island.—Its
    true position.—Borodinos.—Arrival at Napha... 197—214

CONTENTS.

CHAPTER XI.

Changes at Napha.—New regent.—Banquet on board of the Susquehanna.—Excessive dignity of the new regent.—Stateliness of Lew Chewans thawed out by the dinner.—Guests sent home.—Bamboo village.—Interior of Lew Chew houses.—Men indolent.—Gossipping at Lew Chew.—Lew Chew loom.—Different classes of the people.—Their fear of spies.—Slavery of peasants.—Causes of degradation.—Excellence of agricultural cultivation.—Origin of population of Lew Chew.—Former kingdoms on the island.—Relation of Lew Chew to China and Japan, respectively.—Education in Lew Chew.—Religion of the inhabitants.—Christian mission in Lew Chew.—Distinctions of dress.—People sell themselves as slaves.—Clanship.—Coin in Lew Chew.—Sugar making.—Natural products of the island... 215—227

CHAPTER XII.

Departure from Napha for Japan.—Course of the ships.—Oho-Sima.—Island seen by Commander Glynn, probably Oho-Sima.—Cleopatra islands.—Currents.—Fourth of July on board.—Approach to Cape Idzu.—Squadron, led by the Susquehanna, enters the bay of Yedo.—Rock island.—Hazy atmosphere of Japan.—Surprise of the Japanese at sight of the steamers moving against wind and tide.—Bay of Sagami.—Appearance of the coast and country inland.—Fusi-Jama.—Ships made ready for action.—Fleet of Japanese boats put off from the shore.—Left behind by squadron.—Bay of Uraga.—Opposite coast of Awa.—Japanese forts.—Squadron comes to anchor in the bay of Uraga.—Soundings on approaching the anchorage.—Japanese guard-boats put off.—No one permitted to come on board the ships.—Appearance of guard-boats and crews.—Skill of the Japanese in managing their boats.—Guard-boat comes alongside of the Mississippi, and Japanese functionary demands to come on board.—Not permitted.—Notice in the French language, ordering the ships away, held up to be read.—Interpreters directed to inform the Japanese that the Commodore would confer with no one but the highest official in Uraga.—Japanese replied that they had the vice governor on board.—This officer and his interpreter allowed to come on board the Susquehanna.—Not permitted to see the Commodore.—Conference with Lieutenant Contee, who explains that the Americans have come on a friendly mission, and that the Commodore bears a letter from the President of the United States to the Emperor.—Desires the appointment of an officer of suitable rank to receive it from the Commodore.—Commodore refuses to go to Nagasaki.—Informs the Japanese officials that if the guard-boats are not immediately removed he will disperse them by force.—The boats are withdrawn.—Vice governor returns to the shore, promising further communication on the morrow.—Policy resolved on by the Commodore.—Meteorological phenomenon.—Visit on the next day from the governor of Uraga.—Conference between him and Commanders Buchanan and Adams.—Second refusal of the Commodore to go to Nagasaki.—Determination expressed to deliver the letter there, and, if necessary, in the city of Yedo itself.—Governor proposes to refer the matter to Yedo.—Commodore assents and allows three days for an answer.—Survey by the squadron's boats of the bay of Uraga, and ultimately of the bay of Yedo........................ 228—242

CHAPTER XIII.

Reply from the court at Yedo.—Efforts of the Japanese to get the squadron out of the bay of Yedo.—Commodore's firm refusal to leave Uraga.—Agreement of the Emperor to receive, through a commissioner, the President's letter.—High breeding of the Japanese gentlemen; not ill-informed.—Survey of the bay of Yedo.—Fogs of Japan.—Second visit from the governor of Uraga.—He brings a letter from the Emperor, authorizing a prince of the empire to receive, in his name, the President's letter.—Arrangements made for the Commodore's reception on shore to deliver the letter.—Minute attention of the Japanese to etiquette and ceremonials.—Preparations in the squadron for the visit on shore at the reception.—Ships brought near the land, so as to command the place of meeting.—Landing and reception, and delivery of the letter and other documents.—Princes of Idsu and Iwami.—Contents of President's letter.—Commodore's letter of credence, and his letters to the Emperor.—Receipt given by the Japanese for the papers.—Return to the ships .... 243—261

CHAPTER XIV.

Concessions of the Japanese.—Relaxation of their restrictive laws.—Satisfaction of both Japanese and Americans at the result of the visit on shore and delivery of the President's letter.—Visit of Keyama Yezaimen to the ships.—Impudence of the interpreter Saboroske.—The squadron goes further up the bay towards the capital.—Policy of this movement.—Alarm of the Japanese gradually quieted.—Beautiful scenery up the bay.—Survey of the bay continued.—Conviviality on board.—Surveying boats enter a small river.—Cordial greeting of the inhabitants.—Crowd dispersed by a Japanese official.—Commodore transfers his pennant from the Susquehanna to the Mississippi.—The last-named vessel goes up in sight of the shipping place of Yedo.—Sinagawa.—Yedo about ten miles distant from the point where the ships turned about.—Good depth of water in Yedo bay, probably almost up to the city.—The bay pretty thoroughly explored and sounded by the surveying parties.—Interchange of presents with the Japanese officers.—Avowed sorrow of Japanese officials on bidding farewell to the Americans.—Commodore's reasons for not waiting for a reply to the President's letter.—Leaves Yedo bay declaring his intention to return in the ensuing spring.—The Saratoga sent to Shanghai to look after American interests.—The Plymouth ordered to Lew Chew.—Oho-Sima.—Ships encounter a storm.—General results of the first visit of the squadron to the bay of Yedo. 262—273

CHAPTER XV.

Amakirima islands.—State of feeling in Lew Chew.—Commodore's measures for permanent arrangements with the authorities.—Coal depot.—Protest against espionage.—Trade in open market.—Letter to the regent.—Interview with the regent.—Entertainments of the Commodore.—During dinner the regent's answer is brought.—Unsatisfactory to the Commodore.—Letter handed back to the regent, and the Commodore prepares to leave the house.—Informs the regent that he must have a satisfactory answer on the next day, otherwise he will land and take possession of the palace at Shui and retain it until matters are adjusted.—Probable effects of hunting up the old sedan chair on shore.—Commodore's propositions all accepted.—Coal depot built.—Visit to the castle of Timi-Gusko.—Purchases in the bazaar.—Departure from Napha for China.—Plymouth left behind with orders to visit Bonin islands and make further surveys.—Captain Kelly's report of the visit and surveys.—Form of government and constitution of the settlers on Peel island.—General effect of this last visit to Lew Chew.—Arrival of the Vandalia; of the Powhatan.—Overhauling of the vessels of the squadron at Hong Kong.. 274—285

CHAPTER XVI.

Alarm of Americans in China.—Request to Commodore that he would send a ship to Canton.—Supply sent.—The rest of the squadron at Cum-sing-moon.—Hospital established and house taken at Macao.—Sickness in the squadron.—Work kept up in all departments, notwithstanding.—Healthiness of Canton.—Gluttony of the Chinese.—Chinese servants.—Chinese English, or "pigeon."—Male dressmakers, chamber servants, etc.—Chinese female feet.—Chinese guilds.—Beggars.—Charitable institutions.—Thieves.—Boatmen.—Laboring classes.—Domestic servants.—Polygamy and its moral results.—Decadence of Macao.—Humbled condition of the Portuguese.—Harbor of Macao.—Commodore establishes his depot for the squadron at Hong Kong.—Pleasant society of Macao.—Powhatan stationed at Whampoa to relieve the Susquehanna.—Supply still at Canton.—Chinese peaceable towards foreigners.—Steamer "Queen" chartered to protect American interests in China while the squadron should go to Yedo.—Suspicious movements of Russians and French induce the Commodore to hasten his return to Japan.—Lexington arrives.—The squadron ordered to rendezvous at Napha, Lew Chew.—Orders received, just as the squadron leaves China, to detach a steamer for the use of Mr. McLane, American Commissioner to China.—Embarrassment of the Commodore in consequence.—His mode of proceeding to accomplish both the objects of the government.—Correspondence with Sir George Bonham touching the Bonin islands.—Courtesy of the English Admiral Pellew.—Squadron assembles at Napha.. 287—308

CHAPTER XVII.

Increased cordiality and friendly intercourse on the part of the Lew Chewans.—Second visit of the Commodore to the palace at Shui.—Entertainment by the regent.—No metallic coin of Lew Chew to be obtained.—Rev. Mr. Jones' second exploration in search of coal.—Finds it at Shah bay.—The mineral not valued by the natives.—Additional geological observations in Lew Chew.—Remarkable salubrity of the island.—Tenure of lands.—Agriculture.—Rice, potatoes, sugar, cotton, wheat, barley, millet, sago, beans, peas, tobacco, edible roots, fruits, trees, flowers, etc.—Sugar mills.—Grain mills and granaries.—Population.—Ethnology.—Costume.—Politeness of manner.—General intelligence.—Architecture.—Rude attempts in painting and sculpture.—Amusements.—Government.—Religion.—Funeral rites.—Japanese spies in Lew Chew.—Departure for the bay of Yedo... 309—329

CHAPTER XVIII.

Letter from Dutch Governor General of India announcing the death of the Japanese Emperor.—Commodore's reply.—Enumeration of the several objects in view.—Prospects of their attainment by the mission.—Officers and men left in Lew Chew.—Arrival of the Saratoga.—Run to Yedo bay.—Oho-Sima.—Cleopatra isles.—Mijako-Sima.—All belong to Lew Chew group.—Entrance of gulf or outer bay of Yedo.—Japanese charts of little value; made for mere coasting.—Wintry aspect of Japan.—Macedonian aground.—Hauled off by the Mississippi.—Friendly offers of the Japanese to assist the Macedonian.—Squadron proceeds up the bay and anchors at the "American anchorage."—Japanese officials come alongside.—Received by Captain Adams on the Powhatan, pursuant to the Commodore's orders.—They attempt to prevail on the Commodore to return to Uraga, stating that the high Japanese functionaries were there awaiting his arrival, by appointment of the Emperor.—Commodore declines on account of safety of the ships.—Visit on the next

CONTENTS.

xi

Page.

day from the officials, who reiterate their request, with an assurance that the commissioners were ordered to receive the Commodore at Uraga with distinguished consideration.—Commodore again declines.—Japanese ask that an officer may be sent to Uraga to confer with the commissioners as to a place of meeting.—Commodore consents that Captain Adams may hold such a conference, but that the commissioners must come there to hold it.—Japanese become alarmed as to the friendly feelings of the Americans. Their fears allayed.—Survey of the bay resumed without interruption by the Japanese.—Our boats forbidden by the Commodore to land.—Japanese persist for several days in desiring the Commodore to go to Uraga with the ships. Commodore invariably refuses. At length the Japanese are informed that the Commodore will allow Captain Adams to meet a commissioner on shore near the ships, or that he will proceed up the bay to Yedo.—Note from the commissioners to the Commodore. His reply. Captain Adams sent down to Uraga to communicate to the commissioners the Commodore's reasons for declining to take the ships to Uraga.—Some of the Japanese accompany him in the Vandalia. Interview of Captain Adams with the commissioners at Uraga.—Visit to Captain Adams from Yezaimon on board the Vandalia. Assures Captain Adams of the friendly disposition of the Emperor.—Vandalia returns, and perceives ahead the squadron standing up the bay toward Yedo.—The Japanese no longer urge going to Uraga, but suddenly propose Yoku-Hama, where the ships then were, about eight miles from Yedo.—Commodore immediately assents.—Buildings constructed at Yoku-Hama.—A Japanese seaman in the squadron sends a letter to his family ashore, by Yezaimon.—Yezaimon desires an interview with him.—The interview.—Ceremonials settled as to the conferences on shore for negotiation.. 321—342

CHAPTER XIX.

Ships anchored in Yoku-Hama bay so as to command the shore.—Kanagawa "treaty house."—Imperial barge.—Landing of the Commodore.—Description of the Japanese commissioners.—Interpreters.—Servility to superiors.—Negotiations commenced.—Commodore submits a copy of the treaty of the United States with China for consideration.—Death of one of our men.—Commodore proposes to buy a burial ground for Americans.—Commissioners propose to send the body of the deceased to Nagasaki for interment.—Commodore refuses, and proposes to bury the dead on Webster's island.—Commissioners consent to the interment at Yoku-Hama.—The burial by Chaplain Jones.—Interest of the Japanese in the ceremony.—They afterwards perform their own rites over the covered grave.—The Japanese build an enclosure around the spot.—Japanese artists attempt the portraits of our officers.—Answer to the President's letter.—Informal conference between Captain Adams and Yenoske.—Landing and delivery of the presents.—Japanese workmen assist the Americans in preparing for their exhibition.—Negotiations continued.—Surprise and delight of the Japanese at the telegraph and railroad.—Curiosity of the Japanese in examining mechanism.—Passion for buttons.—Note-taking of everything strange to them.—Love of pictures.—Drawings.—Common people disposed to social intercourse with the Americans.—Excitement on Chaplain Bittinger's attempt to reach Yedo by land.—Written reply of commissioners, declining to make a treaty like that of the United States with China.—Further negotiations.—Accuracy of the Japanese in noting all the discussions.—Ports of Simoda and Hakodadi agreed to, but with great difficulty on the part of the Japanese..................... 343—366

CHAPTER XX.

Cordiality between Japanese and Americans.—Presents from the Japanese.—Coins.—Singular custom of including rice, charcoal, and dogs, in a royal Japanese present.—Japanese wrestlers.—Their immense size and strength.—Exhibition in the ring.—Contrast in the exhibition of the telegraph and locomotive.—Parade of the marines.—Yenoske visits the flag-ship, and seeks to draw the Commodore out.—Failure.—Entertainment of the Chinese commissioners on board the flag-ship. Great cordiality. Peformance on ship-board of "Ethiopian minstrels," to the great amusement of the Japanese.—Negotiations continued. Japanese object to the immediate opening of the ports. Finally concede the point to a certain extent.—Absolute and persistent refusal to allow Americans permanently to abide in Japan.—Reluctant consent, after much discussion, to allow one consul to reside at Simoda.—Treaty finally agreed on and signed.—Presents by Commodore to the commissioners, that to the chief being the American flag.—Entertainment of the Commodore and his officers by the commissioners. Peculiarities of the mission to Japan. Obstacles to making any treaty at all.—Disposition of the Japanese shown in the conferences.—Particular refusal to make a treaty allowing American families or females to live in Japan.—Analysis of the treaty. Commodore careful to secure for the United States all privileges that might thereafter be granted by treaty to other nations. Case of the American schooner Foote.. 367—392

CHAPTER XXI.

Departure of Commander Adams for the United States, with the treaty.—Visits of the Commodore and officers on shore.—Imperturbable composure of Yenoske when charged with falsehood.—Call upon the Mayor of Yoku-Hama.—The ladies of his household.—Disgusting fashion of dyeing their teeth.—Use of rouge.—En-

xii   CONTENTS.

Page.

tertainment of the Commodore.—The Mayor's baby.—The common people very comfortable.—Field labors shared by the women.—Straw great-coat for rainy weather.—Paper umbrellas.—People not indisposed to intercourse with foreigners.—Respectful treatment of the female sex.—Japanese un-oriental in this respect.—Polygamy not practised.—Japanese women naturally good-looking.—Some strikingly handsome.—Girls have great vivacity, yet dignified and modest.—Social habits.—Visits.—Tea parties.—Squadron, after notice to the Japanese authorities, proceeds up the bay with some of the officials on board.—Powhatan and Mississippi go within sight of the capital.—Its immense size.—Sea front protected by high palisades.—Change of Japanese policy on the second visit to Yedo.—All show of military resistance studiously avoided.—The Commodore assures the Japanese officials that he will not anchor the steamers near the city, and, after a glance, at their request, returns.—Great joy of the officials thereat.—Preparations for departure.—Macedonian ordered to Peel island.—Southampton, Supply, Vandalia, and Lexington sent to Simoda.—Webster island.—Departure of the Commodore for Simoda.—Harbor examined.—The town and adjacent country.—Shops and dwellings.—Public baths.—Food.—Mode of cultivation.—Buddhist temples.—Grave-yards and tombs.—Statues of Buddha.—Offerings of flowers on the graves.—Epitaphs or inscriptions.—Charms for keeping away from the dead malignant demons.—A temple appropriated for the occupancy of our officers.—A Sintoo temple.—Mariner's temple.—Salubrity of Simoda.—Made an imperial city since the treaty...... 393—414

CHAPTER XXII.

Survey and description of the harbor of Simoda.—Discipline in the squadron.—Intercourse with the authorities of Simoda.—Kura-kawa-kahei, the prefect.—His disposition to produce trouble.—Treatment of the American officers.—Remonstrances of the Commodore.—Equivocation of the prefect.—He is frightened into propriety.—Efforts of two Japanese gentlemen clandestinely to leave their country in the squadron.—Commodore's conduct.—Buddhist temples at Simoda.—Prefect again shows his petty hostility.—His prevarications and falsehoods.—Funeral of an American on shore.—Insult offered to American officers on shore.—Prefect's further falsehoods.—Compelled to apologize, and informed that his insolence would not be borne in future.—Friendly intercourse with the people.—Departure for Hakodadi.—Volcano of Oho-Sima.—The Kuro-siwo, or Japanese "gulf stream."—Straits of Sangar.—Fogs.—Harbor of Hakodadi.—Directions for entering.. 415—432

CHAPTER XXIII.

Visit from the authorities at Hakodadi.—Their ignorance that a treaty had been made.—Visit to authorities and explanation of affairs to the Japanese.—Answer of the officials at Hakodadi.—Their friendliness and courtesy.—Visits and rambles of the Americans on shore.—Houses allotted for their temporary accommodation.—Description of Hakodadi.—Resemblance to Gibraltar.—Cleanliness of streets.—Pavements and sewers.—Division into districts under Ottonas.—Pack-horses used; no wheel-carriages.—Town very thriving.—Buildings described.—Preparations against fires in the city.—Skill of carpenters and house-joiners.—Shops, their construction and goods.—Carvings in wood.—Furniture.—Chairs and tables.—Fashion in eating.—Tea, how prepared; fire for boiling the kettle.—Kitchens, stables, and gardens.—Fire-proof warehouses.—Traffic at the shops.—Buddhist temples.—Grave-yards.—Praying by machinery.—Inscriptions on tombs.—Sintoo temples.—Shrines by the way-side.—Gateways on the roads.—Prospects for Christianity in Japan.—Weak military defences of Hakodadi.—Surrounding country.—Look-out for ships approaching.—Japanese telescope.—Geology of the country.—Mineral spring.—Natural cave.—Culinary vegetables.—Commerce and fisheries.—Japanese junks.—Ship-yards.—Few birds.—Fish abundant.—Wild quadrupeds.—Fox considered as the devil.—Horses much used.—Kagos.—Climate of Hakodadi.—Population and physical characteristics of the people.—Ainos or hairy kuriles.—Mechanical skill of the Japanese.—Carpentry and masonry.—Coopers.—Iron ore workers.—Blacksmiths, their bellows.—Copper much used in junk building.—Spinning and weaving.—Dyed cottons.—Silk fabrics.—Lacquered ware.—Printing, drawing, and painting.—Sculpture.—Architecture.—General intelligence.—Information, derived through the Dutch at Nagasaki, from European publications.—Japanese game of chess.—Cards.—Loto.—Ball and jackstraws among the children.. 433—466

CHAPTER XXIV.

Interview between the Commodore and the representative of the prince of Matsmai.—Southampton sent to explore Volcano bay, including Endermo harbor.—Report of the survey.—Poverty of the region around the bay.—Eruption of a volcano at midnight.—Ainos.—Boundaries of Americans at Hakodadi left to be settled with the imperial commissioners.—Good understanding between the Americans and people of Hakodadi.—Japanese delighted with the exhibition of the "Ethiopian minstrels" on board ship.—Squadron theatricals.—Interest of Japanese in the machinery and fire-arms of the ships.—Answer of Hakodadi authorities to Commodore's inquiries as to European or American vessels wrecked in Japan during the last ten years.—Answer of the imperial commissioners to similar inquiries.—Macedonian sails for Simoda.—Vandalia des-

CONTENTS.

xiii

Page.

patched for China by the western passage.—Japanese officers desire a conference with the Commodore.—Flag-lieutenant sent ashore to bring them on board.—Disrespectful conduct of the officers.—Flag-lieutenant returns without them.—Japanese officers finally come off in their own boat.—Not allowed to see the Commodore until they apologize for their behavior.—Apology accepted.—Conference results in nothing but a further illustration of Japanese finesse.—Burials of Americans at Hakodadi.—Respect shown for the ceremonies by the Japanese.—Buddhist priest performs his funeral ceremonies after the Americans retire.—Services in a Buddhist temple.—Japanese erect a fence around the American graves.—Sailor's epitaph composed by his shipmates.—Block of granite presented by the Japanese at Hakodadi for the Washington monument.—Volcano of Oho-Sima.—Arrival at Simoda.—Meeting with the commissioners.—Boundaries at Hakodadi settled.—Appointment of pilots and harbor-master agreed on.—Value of Japanese and American money respectively fixed.—Additional regulations between the commissioners and Commodore agreed to and signed.—Coal supplied at Simoda.—Its comparative quality and value.—Cost of various articles furnished to the ships.—Another block of stone for the Washington monument presented by the imperial commissioners at Simoda.—Japanese present of dogs to the President.—Sam Patch has an interview with the officials of his country.—Refuses to go on shore or leave the ship.—Praiseworthy conduct of a marine towards Sam.—"Dan Ketch."—Japanese punishment of crucifixion.—Practice of the "Hari-kari" or "Happy-despatch."—Departure from Simoda.—Macedonian and supply sent to Formosa and Philippines.—Redfield rocks.—Party sent on shore for observation of Oho-Sima.—Arrival at Lew Chew.—Southampton ordered to Hong Kong.—Powhatan and Mississippi come to anchor at Napha................................. 467—490

CHAPTER XXV.

Preparations for final departure from the Japanese waters.—Macedonian and Supply ordered to Formosa.—Instructions to Captain Abbot, of the Macedonian, to touch at the Philippines on his way from Formosa to China.—Mississippi, Powhatan, and Southampton proceed to Lew Chew.—State of affairs in Lew Chew.—Supposed murder of an American by Lew Chewans.—Trial of Lew Chewans for murder by their own authorities on the Commodore's demand.—Description of a Lew Chew court of justice.—Accused made to plead by punches in the ribs.—Accused convicted and brought to the Commodore for punishment.—He hands them over to their own authorities.—They are banished.—New Year's customs.—Coal removed from the depot to the ships.—Compact or treaty made with Lew Chew.—Present from the Lew Chewans to the Commodore.—A stone for the Washington monument.—Effort of a Japanese to come off in the squadron to the United States.—Parting entertainment to Lew Chew authorities.—Departure of the squadron for China.—Macedonian's visit to Formosa.—Unavailing search for Americans supposed to have been wrecked on the island.—Explorations by Chaplain Jones for coal.—Found in abundance and of good quality.—Survey of the harbor of Kelung.—Lying and cunning of the Formosans.—Run to Manilla.—Very stormy passage.—Marine volcanoes in the neighborhood of Formosa.—Inquiries at Manilla into the murder of certain Americans.—Satisfactory conduct of the Spanish authorities in the matter.—Delivery by Captain Abbot to the Governor of six Sillibaboos that had been picked up at sea by Lieutenant Commanding Boyle, of the Southampton, floating in an open boat.—Remarkable distance that they had drifted.—Physical appearance of the Sillibaboos.—Voyage of Macedonian to Hong Kong.—Captain Kelly's handling of the Chinese pirates and imperial troops; forces them to make reparation.—Chastisement of the Chinese by the joint action of the officers and men of the Plymouth and of those of her Britannic Majesty's ships Encounter and Grecian.—The Commodore, by leave from the Navy Department, turns over the command to Captain Abbot, and returns home by the overland route.—On the arrival of the Mississippi in New York, on the 23d of April, the Commodore repairs on board, and formally hauling down his flag, terminates the expedition... 491—508

SUPPLEMENTARY CHAPTER.

Commander Adams arrives in the United States with the treaty.—Submitted by the President and ratified by the Senate.—Commander Adams sent back with authority to exchange ratifications.—Arrives at Simoda after an absence of little more than nine months.—Altered aspect of the place from the effects of an earthquake.—Japanese account of the calamity.—Loss of Russian ship-of-war Diana.—Russians make a treaty exactly like ours, with a substitution merely of Nagasaki for Napha as one of the three ports.—French ship brings in two shipwrecked Japanese.—Authorities refuse to receive them except from under our flag, having no treaty with France.—Men taken on board the Powhatan, and then received by their countrymen.—Energy of Japanese in rebuilding Simoda.—Freedom of intercourse with the people.—No more espionage.—Brisk traffic at the shops.—Delivery to Captain Adams of some religious tracts left at Simoda by Mr. Bittinger.—Japanese had learned to manage the locomotive, but not the telegraph.—Moryama Yenoske promoted.—Message from the commissioners to Commodore Perry.—Ratifications exchanged.... 509—512

LIST OF ILLUSTRATIONS.

LITHOGRAPHS.

		Page.
"Mississippi" passing Point Atristow	Heine & Brown	81
Loo Rock and Pontinha, Madeira	Heine & Brown	82
Funchal, Madeira, from the Curral	Heine & Brown	84
Jamestown, St. Helena	Heine & Brown	90
Valley of the Tomb, near Longwood	Heine & Brown	92
Longwood, from the gate	Heine & Brown	94
Cape Town and Table mountain	Heine & Brown	98
Mauritius, from the "Ponce"	Heine & Brown	105
Hindoo ablutions, Mauritius	Heine & Brown	112
Light-house, Point de Galle, Ceylon	Heine & Brown	114
Buddhist temple, Ceylon	Heine & Brown	120
Rajah of Jahore, Singapore—from life	Brown	129
River Jurong, Singapore	Heine & Brown	130
View of Hong Kong from East Point	Heine & Brown	133
Chinese temple, Hong Kong	Heine & Brown	134
Whampoa Pagoda and anchorage	Heine & Brown	135
Fish market, Canton	Heine	138
Chinese temple, Macao	Heine	144
Chief magistrate, Napha—from a daguerreotype	Brown	155
Street in Napha, Lew Chew	Heine	156
Napha, from Bamboo village	Heine	164
Ancient castle, Nagagusko, Lew Chew	Heine & Brown	170
Village near Napha, Lew Chew	Heine & Brown	173
Ancient castle, Nagagusko, Lew Chew	Heine & Brown	174
Lew Chew exploring party	Heine & Brown	176
Tshandicoosah, Lew Chew	Heine & Brown	182
Bridge and causeway, Machinatoo, Lew Chew	Heine & Brown	184
Commodore Perry's visit to Shui, Lew Chew	Heine	189
Reception at the castle, Shui, Lew Chew	Heine	190
Dinner at the Regent's, Lew Chew	Heine	191
Court interpreter, Shin, Lew Chew—from a daguerreotype	Brown	192
Temple at Tumai, Lew Chew	Heine & Brown	194
Kanaka village, Bonin Islands	Heine & Brown	204
Regent of Lew Chew—from a daguerreotype	Brown	215
Afternoon gossip, Lew Chew—from a daguerreotype	Brown	219
Lew Chew costumes, middle class—from a daguerreotype	Brown	226
View of Uraga, Yedo bay	Heine	233
First landing at Gorahama	Heine	256
Delivery of the President's letter	Heine	261
Torigasaki, Yedo bay	Heine	268
Inner harbor and ruins, Timagusko	Heine & Brown	281
China girl, sycee head-dress—from a daguerreotype	Brown	296
Macao, from Penha Hill	Heine	298
Jesuit convent, Macao	Heine	300
Napha, from the sea	Heine	309
Market-place in Napha	Heine	317
Bay of Wodowara	Heine & Walke	325
Commodore meeting commissioners at Yokuhama	Peters	346
Yenoske and Takojuro, interpreters	Brown	348
View from Webster island	Heine	353
Temple at Yokuhama	Heine	355

		Page
Delivery of presents	Peters	357
Japanese soldiers, Yokuhama	Heine	359
Wrestlers at Yokuhama	Peters	371
Dinner on board the Powhatan	Heine	375
Simoda, from Vandalia Bluff	Heine	401
Bridge of cut-stone, &c., Simoda	Heine	403
Japanese woman, Simoda	Brown	404
Mother and child, Simoda—daguerreotype	Brown	405
Temple of Hat-chi-man-ya-chu-ro	Heine	406
Devotions in great temple, Simoda	Heine	407
Buddhist priest, Simoda, in costume	Brown	408
Buddhist priest, Simoda—likeness	Brown	409
Bell-house, Simoda—daguerreotype	Brown	410
Mariner's temple, Simoda	Heine	411
Japanese rice-mill, Simoda	Kellogg	414
Kura-Kawa-Kakei, prefect of Simoda—daguerreotype	Brown	417
Japanese women—daguerreotype	Brown	418
Simoda, from the American grave yard	Heine	425
Japanese funeral, Simoda	Heine	426
Hakodadi, from Snow Peak	Heine	430
Prefect of Hakodadi—daguerreotype	Brown	433
Chief temple, Hakodadi	Heine	442
Street in Hakodadi	Heine	443
Entrance to a temple, Hakodadi	Brown	445
Hakodadi, from Telegraph Hill	Heine	447
Japanese junk, section	Kellogg	448
Japanese junk, cross-section	Kellogg	449
Japanese boat	Kellogg	450
Japanese junk, view complete	Meffert	451
Fire company's house and engine	Heine	459
Fac simile, Japanese painting		462
Japanese painting—crossing the Oho-e-ga-wa		462
Deputy of Prince of Matsmai—daguerreotype	Brown	468
Conference-room, Hakodadi	Heine	470
Governor of Simoda—daguerreotype	Brown	477
Tatsnoske, second interpreter—daguerreotype	Brown	485
Farewell visit at Simoda	Heine	486
Japanese fac simile, crucifixion		487

WOOD-CUTS.

View of Funchal, Madeira	Heine & Brown	82
Funchal Cathedral, Madeira	Heine & Brown	83
Ox sledge, Madeira	Heine	84
Old house, Longwood, St. Helena	Heine & Brown	93
Travellers in South Africa	Heine	100
Kaffir chief and Fingo woman	C. Town, artist	102
Kaffir chief "Seyolo" and wife—from life	E. Brown	102
Port Louis, Mauritius	Heine & Brown	108
Costumes of Mauritius	Heine	110
Public square, Port Louis	Heine	111
Point de galle, Ceylon	Heine	115
Buddhist temple near Point de galle, Ceylon	Heine	121
Mississippi saluted by an English frigate, straits of Malacca	E. Brown	123
Malay Proa	E. Brown	126
Mosque in Singapore	Portman	127
Malay tombs near Singapore	Heine	131
Barber boy, Hong Kong	Heine	134
View of Old China street, Canton	Heine	137
Tanka boat, Macao	E. Brown	141
Tanka boat girl	E. Brown	141
Chinese woman and child	E. Brown	141

ILLUSTRATIONS.

xvii

		Page.
Camoen's cave, Macao, (front)	HEINE	142
Do. do. (rear)	HEINE	143
American consulate and Port of Shanghai	HEINE	145
Lew Chew peasant—daguerreotype	E. BROWN	157
Lew Chew merchant—daguerreotype	E. BROWN	164
Night camp of exploring party, Lew Chew	HEINE	166
Banner Rock, Lew Chew	HEINE	168
Tombs in Lew Chew	HEINE	169
Ground plan of Nagagusko, Lew Chew	HEINE	170
Nagagusko interior	HEINE	171
Ruins of Nagagusko north	HEINE	172
Rice-houses in the valley of On-na, Lew Chew	BAYARD TAYLOR	178
Kung-Kwa of On-na	HEINE & BROWN	180
Cave at Port Lloyd, Bonin	HEINE	204
Valley near Southeast bay, Peel island	BAYARD TAYLOR	207
Southeast bay, Peel island	HEINE	208
Stapleton island	HEINE	210
Dinner to the Regent of Lew Chew on board U. S. S. Susquehanna	HEINE	216
Sugar mill, Lew Chew	HEINE	227
China girl showing head-dress—daguerreotype	BROWN	291
Chinese beggar, Macao—daguerreotype	BROWN	293
Chinese fruit-seller—daguerreotype	BROWN	295
Dress of Chinese lady of rank—daguerreotype	BROWN	296
Chinese barber, Macao—daguerreotype	BROWN	297
Protestant grave yard, Macao	HEINE	300
Salt flats, Napha	HEINE	317
Americans landing at Uraga	HEINE	334
Imperial barge, Yokuhama	HEINE	345
Buddhist priest, full dress	BROWN	354
Namoura, third interpreter	BROWN	373
Farm yard, Yokuhama	HEINE	384
Japanese women—daguerreotype	BROWN	397
Mia at Yokuhama	HEINE	400
Simoda, from the creek	HEINE	400
Landing place, Simoda	HEINE	402
Street and entrance to great temple, Simoda	HEINE	403
Grave yard of chief temple, Simoda	HEINE	407
Valley above Simoda	HEINE	412
Japanese women, Simoda	BROWN	418
Hakodadi from the bay	HEINE	431
Kitchen at Hakodadi	HEINE	441
Fishing at Hakodadi	HEINE	451
Japanese Kago	BROWN	452
Sub-prefect, Hakodadi	BROWN	453
Water boats and junks, Hakodadi	HEINE	454
Japanese cooper	BROWN	455
Blacksmiths' shop	HEINE	456
Ship yard	HEINE	457
Spinning and weaving	HEINE	458
Fac similes of horses, Japanese drawing		459, 460, 461
Japanese women	BROWN	471
Boat with Sillibaboos	BROWN	502
Chinese rice-hulling machine	HEINE	507
Cotton whipping, Hong Kong	HEINE	508
Temple of Ben-Ting, Simoda	HEINE	510

[All the initial letters and tail-pieces of the several chapters are from the pencil of Mr. HEINE.]

ERRATA.

Page 264, 4th paragraph: "while" for "with."
    308, 1st line: "Hong Kong" for "Canton."
    325, 2d paragraph, 4th line: "infer that these" for "infer that this."
    357, (List of presents:) "ship's breakers" for "beakers."
    415, 1st paragraph, 9th line: omit "lower" or "gulf of," and read "of the bay of Yedo."
    461, 1st line: illustration referred to not published.

LETTER

OF

THE SECRETARY OF THE NAVY,

COMMUNICATING,

IN COMPLIANCE WITH A RESOLUTION OF THE SENATE,

THE

REPORT OF COMMODORE M. C. PERRY,

OF THE

NAVAL EXPEDITION TO JAPAN.

JANUARY 22, 1855.—Ordered to be printed, and that 5,000 additional copies be printed; five hundred of which for the use of Commodore Perry.

JANUARY 29, 1855.—*Ordered*, That 500 copies be for the use of the Navy Department.

NAVY DEPARTMENT, *August* 28, 1855.

SIR: In compliance with the resolution of the Senate of the United States, passed on the 22d January last, calling upon the Secretary of the Navy "to communicate to the Senate a copy of the report of Commodore Perry of the Naval Expedition to Japan," I have the honor to enclose herewith a copy of the letter of Commodore Perry to the Department transmitting the manuscript, &c., of said report.

I am sir, very respectfully,

Your obedient servant,

J. C. DOBBIN.

ASBURY DICKINS, Esq.,
Secretary of the Senate of the United States, Washington, D. C.

NEW YORK, *August* 27, 1855.

SIR: In compliance with a resolution of the United States Senate, bearing date January 22, 1855, calling upon the Secretary of the Navy "to communicate to the Senate a copy of the report of Commodore Perry of the Naval Expedition to Japan, and that the same, with the maps, charts and drawings, be printed," I have now the honor of transmitting the manuscript of said report, together with drawings, maps, charts, &c., illustrative of the same.

With great respect, I am, sir,

Your most obedient servant,

M. C. PERRY.

Hon. J. C. DOBBIN.
Secretary of the Navy, Washington, D. C.

INTRODUCTION.

VIEWED in any of its aspects, the Empire of Japan has long presented to the thoughtful mind an object of uncommon interest. And this interest has been greatly increased by the mystery with which, for the last two centuries, an exclusive policy has sought to surround the institutions of this remarkable country. The curiosity of Christendom has been on the alert; and the several votaries of various pursuits have naturally longed to add more to the little that is known of this self-isolated Kingdom.

The political inquirer, for instance, has wished to study in detail the form of government, the administration of laws, and the domestic institutions, under which a nation systematically prohibiting intercourse with the rest of the world has attained to a state of civilization, refinement, and intelligence, the mere glimpses of which so strongly invite further investigation.

The student of physical geography, aware how much national characteristics are formed or modified by peculiarities of physical structure in every country, would fain know more of the lands and the seas, the mountains and the rivers, the forests and the fields, which fall within the limits of this almost *terra incognita*.

The naturalist asks, what is its geology, what are its flora and fauna?

The navigator seeks to find out its rocks and shoals, its winds and currents, its coasts and harbors.

The man of commerce asks to be told of its products and its trade, its skill in manufactures, the commodities it needs, and the returns it can supply.

The ethnologist is curious to pry into the physical appearance of its inhabitants; to dig, if possible, from its language the fossil remains of long buried history: and in the affiliation of its people to supply, perchance, a gap in the story of man's early wanderings over the globe.

The scholar asks to be introduced to its literature that he may contemplate in historians, poets, and dramatists, (for Japan has them all,) a picture of the national mind.

The Christian desires to know the varied phases of their superstition and idolatry: and longs for the dawn of that day when a purer faith and more enlightened worship shall bring them within the circle of Christendom.

Amid such a diversity of pursuits as we have enumerated, a common interest unites all in a common sympathy; and hence, the divine and the philosopher, the navigator and the naturalist, the man of business and the man of letters, have alike joined in a desire for the thorough exploration of a field at once so extensive and so inviting.

With so much to allure, it is not at all wonderful that the attempt to explore should have been repeatedly made. Scarce a maritime nation in the civilized world has been wanting in effort. The Portuguese, Spaniards, Dutch, English, French, and Russians have, each in turn, sought to establish commercial relations with Japan. The Portuguese and English have both so far succeeded, that, but for themselves, they might permanently have retained their positions. The first were expelled; the latter voluntarily abandoned the field. The Dutch alone, of all Christian nations, were allowed to remain for purposes of traffic, and they purchased the privilege at the price of national humiliation and personal imprisonment, for which all the profits of gainful barter offer but an inadequate compensation.

Limited, however, as have been their sources of information, it is to the Dutch chiefly that the world, until within a very recent period, has been indebted for the knowledge it has had of the Japanese. Nor is that knowledge quite as circumscribed as has sometimes been supposed. Kæmpfer, Thunberg, Titsingh, Doeff, Fischer, Meylan, Siebold, and others, have certainly told us something about Japan. But they could not tell us *all* it is desirable to know. All were connected with the factory at Dezima, and were watched, of course, with suspicious jealousy. Their only opportunities for seeing anything beyond the town of Nagasaki were afforded at their periodical visits to the court; and Kæmpfer, the first in the list, has so fully related all that an European could learn from this source, that very little has been added to our stock of knowledge by his successors, with the single exception of Siebold. He has collected new facts and materials, and the result of his observations and researches has been given to the world in his "NIPPON, *Archiv sur Beschreibung von Japan,*" (NIPPON, an Archive toward the Description of Japan.) While, therefore, it is not quite correct to say that the civilized world knows nothing of Japan, it may truly be asserted that what is known is very much less than what is unknown.

Notwithstanding, however, the national efforts at exploration to which we have alluded, it was reserved for our own, the youngest of the nations, to break down at last the barriers with which this singular people had surrounded themselves; and to be the first, in modern times, to establish with them a treaty of friendship and trade which (already copied as far as was possible by other governments) is to form, as we hope, the initiatory step in the introduction of Japan into the circle of commercial nations.

May we not be permitted here to add that it seems not altogether inappropriate that the United States should be the instrument of breaking down these barriers, and of opening Japan to the rest of the world.

When, in 1295, Marco Polo returned to Venice from his long sojourn in Asia, he spake to Europeans, among other marvels which shocked their credulity, but which have since been fully verified, of the existence of a large island off the coast of Cathay, (China,) which he called *Zipangu*. That island is the modern Nippon of the Japanese Kingdom. He told, also, the story of the indomitable courage of the people of Zipangu, and related how they had successfully resisted the armies of the powerful Kublai Khan, the conquerors, at that day, of all Asia, and the terror of Europe. He laid before them the map which he had made and brought home, with an inscription written upon the shore-line of the Yellow sea: "*There is a great island to the east.*" Years rolled on; Marco Polo's written story and maps had found their way to Genoa, and probably had been forgotten. At length, in the sixteenth century, they fell into the hands of a man who did not cast them idly by: that man was Christopher Columbus, whose strong mind was then travelling to the overruling conviction of his life that there must be, to the westward of Europe, great bodies of land at that time utterly unknown. It was Marco Polo's map, and his statements concerning Zipangu particularly, which confirmed his conjectures; and when he sailed, it was Zipangu, or, as the Italian manuscript of Marco Polo had it, *Cipango*, on which he hoped and expected to find the termination of his voyage. Accordingly, (as we know,) when he landed on Cuba he believed that he had reached the goal of his long cherished hopes. He knew not that a continent barred his way between Europe and Zipangu; nor that, still further westward, beyond that continent a mighty ocean rolled its waters, which must be traversed before Zipangu could be reached.

But though not destined himself to find and open Japan to Christendom, it has so happened, in the order of Providence, that on the continent which he discovered, and which barred his way to the land he sought, has grown up a nation which has performed a part of his contemplated work, and fulfilled a portion, at least, of the plan which lured him westward; a nation which, if it did not discover Zipangu, has, we trust, been the instrument of bringing it into full and free communication with the rest of the world; a nation which has, as it were, taken the end of the thread which, on the shores of America, broke in the hands of Columbus, and fastening it again to the ball of destiny, has rolled it onward until, as it has unwound itself, it has led the native and civilized inhabitants of the land discovered by the great Genoese to plant their feet on the far distant region of his search, and thus fulfil his wish to bring Zipangu within the influence of European civilization.

It is the story of the American entrance into Japan that we propose to relate; and it is hoped it will aid in the better understanding of the narrative, as well as show what additions, if any, have been made to our previous knowledge, briefly to present, in a rapid sketch, the outlines of such information as the world possessed before the American expedition left our shores. On this work we now enter.

SECTION I.

NAME, EXTENT, AND GEOGRAPHY.

THERE can be no doubt that Japan was unknown to the Greeks and Romans, and that it was first brought to the knowledge of the European world by the celebrated traveller, Marco Polo. His family was Venetian, and devoted to commercial pursuits. In the year 1275, at the age of eighteen, he accompanied his father and uncle into Asia on mercantile business; and there, mastering the languages of Tartary, on the return of his relatives to Europe, he remained, and entered into the service of Kublai Khan, the then reigning monarch. In this situation he continued for seventeen years. Possessed of a good mind, he was a close observer of what he saw around him, and rendered the most important services, both military and diplomatic, to the monarch, with whom he became not merely a favorite, but in some degree a necessity. At length, in 1295, after an absence of some twenty years, he returned to Venice, and was the first European traveller who made known the existence of Japan to the inhabitants of the west. He had not visited it in person, (as he is careful to state,) but he had traversed the greater part of China, and had there heard what he related concerning Japan. We may remark, in passing, that his statements of what he had seen and heard so far surpassed the experience and knowledge of his countrymen that he shared the fate of some modern travellers, and was not believed. Nothing, however, is more sure than that modern research has impressed with the character of truth all that he related on his personal observation, and much of that which he gathered from the statements of others. He, as we have already said, called Japan *Zipangu*; it was the name which he had heard in China. The Japanese themselves call their country *Dai Nippon*, which means "Great Nippon." As to the origin of the latter word, it is a compound of two others; *nitsu*, "the sun," and *pon* or *fon*, "origin;" these, according to the Japanese rule of combination, become Nippon or Nifon, signifying "origin of the sun;" in other words, the East. In the Chinese language, Nippon, by the usual change of pronunciation, becomes *Jih-pun*, to which *Kone* is added, meaning "country" or "Kingdom." The whole Chinese word, *Jih-pun-kone*, therefore, is, in English, "Kingdom of the origin of the sun," or "Eastern Kingdom." The reader will readily perceive how, on the lips of an European, the name would become *Zi-pun-gu*. We thus have the derivation, *Nippon, Jih-pun, Japan*.

As to the extent of the Kingdom: it consists of a great number of islands, said to be 3,850, lying off the eastern coast of Asia, and spread over that part of the ocean which extends from the 129th to the 146th degree of east longitude from Greenwich, and is between the 31st and 46th degrees of north latitude. The chain to which they belong may be traced on the map from the Loo-Choo islands to the southern extremity of Kamtschatka, and from this latter peninsula, through the Kurile islands, to the promontory of Alaska, on our own continent. They are in the line of that immense circle of volcanic development which surrounds the shores of the Pacific from Tierra del Fuego around to the Moluccas.

The Kingdom is divided into Japan proper and the dependent islands. The first named division consists of the three large islands, Kin-siu, Sitkokf, and Nippon, and the whole Empire contains about 160,000 square miles. Of many of the islands we know nothing. Their coasts are so difficult of access, and shallow seas and channels, with sunken rocks and dangerous whirlpools, added to winds as variable as they are violent, have interposed most serious obstacles to nautical exploration, so that we have yet much to learn of the navigation of the waters around the islands of Japan.

Those of which we have as yet most information are Kin-siu, Nippon, and Yesso, or Jesso. On the first of these is the town of Nagasaki, and this is the port to which the Dutch have been most rigorously confined, in all their commercial transactions, for two hundred years. Indeed, they have not been permitted to live within the town itself, but have been literally imprisoned on a very small island in the harbor, called Dezima, where they have been most closely watched, and many rigid restrictions have been imposed on their intercourse with the people. Under certain circumstances, they have been at times permitted to go into the town, but not to remain for any long period, nor have they ever been allowed to explore the island. Their opportunities, therefore, except in the case of Siebold, have been very limited for acquiring, from personal observation, a knowledge of anything on the island of Kin-siu beyond what they could see from their prison.

As to Nippon, on which is Yeddo, the capital of the Kingdom, they have had the opportunity of seeing more. This has resulted from the fact that periodical visits, with presents, have been made to the Emperor at the capital by the chief Dutch commissioner at the factory on Dezima; and on these visits he has been accompanied by his physician and a small number of his subordinate officers. It is, therefore, to the chief commissioners and their medical attendants that we have been indebted for all we have been told since the establishment of commercial relations with the Dutch. Titsingh, Doeff, Fischer, Meylan, were all chiefs of the factory, while Kæmpfer, Thunberg, and Siebold have all been the physicians. These visits were formerly annual, latterly they have been less frequent, and a more jealous surveillance has been exercised over the European travellers. Still they have evaded restrictions as far as was possible, have seen all they could, and told all they saw. But they were, of necessity, obliged to gather much of what they relate from the information of the Japanese; how far it is to be considered as in all respects accurate neither they nor we are able to say. Yet the Dutch residents undoubtedly knew for themselves more about the island of Nippon than they did concerning Kiu-siu, in one of the harbors of which was their prison.

As to Yesso, or Jesso, it is confessedly very imperfectly known. One of its ports is Matsmai, and here Captain Golownin, of the Russian navy, was kept as a prisoner for two years. In an effort which he made to escape he wandered over a part of the island; but as he was not seeking on this excursion materials for description, nor studying at his leisure the habits of the people, his statements are, as might be expected, altogether unsatisfactory, and yet we have none better from an European eye-witness. Kæmpfer, Thunberg, and Siebold are our most valuable sources of information since the days of the Dutch commerce.

At an earlier period, and before Japanese jealousy of foreign influence had prompted them to adopt their system of exclusion, the opportunity was far more favorable for the acquisition of information by the personal observation of strangers. The Portuguese missionaries and some early English navigators, therefore, afford us on some points a knowledge such as no European during the last two hundred years could possibly have procured.

Of the physical aspect of these principal islands former writers give different accounts. Thunberg represents them as composed of a succession of mountains, hills, and valleys, while Kæmpfer says that he travelled over several plains of considerable extent. The country is undoubtedly very hilly, and in general the hills come down near to the seashore, leaving but narrow strips of land between the water and their bases; it is, however, not improbable that level plains of some extent may be found in the interior. The hills, however, are not sterile; and covered, as most of them seem to be, with the fruits of cultivation up to their summits, bear witness alike to the numbers and industry of the population. Mountains, however, are to be found as well as hills, nor is it surprising that some of them should be volcanic.

Westward of the bay of Yeddo rises to the height of some twelve thousand feet the Fudsi Jamma, with its summit whitened by perpetual snow; it was once an active volcano. The northern part of Nippon also is known to be traversed by a chain of mountains, from which rise several isolated peaks, the craters, in some instances, of extinct volcanoes, while others, still burning, are to be seen on the islands scattered in the gulfs of Corea and Yeddo.

In such a country the rivers cannot probably be long; while the rapidity of their currents indicates that their sources must be considerably elevated. It is said that over some of them no bridges can be built, as none would resist the force of the stream fed by the waters of the mountain torrents. Some of the rivers, however, are navigable by small boats for several miles from the sea into the interior. The Japanese, from the nature and position of their country, ought to be a maritime people; they can have but few natural facilities for inland trade. Their ingenuity and industry have, however, been taxed to open modes of communication with the interior; roads and bridges have been constructed, and in some instances canals have been made to unite their rivers and lakes.

Of the climate of Japan it is not possible to speak with much certainty. In the southern part of the Kingdom it is said to be not unlike that of England. Some winters are remarkably mild, without any frost or snow, though generally such is not the case; when however these occur, they last but for a few days. The heat in summer is said to average 98° of Fahrenheit at Nagasaki. This, which would otherwise be excessive, is much moderated by the breeze which, in the day time, blows from the south, and at night from the east. There is what the Japanese call *satkasi*, or the rainy season, in June and July; by this, however, it is only meant that the rains are then most abundant; for, in point of fact, they are frequent all the year round, and the weather appears to be variable. No part of the ocean is subject to heavier gales than the sea around Japan, and the hurricanes are terrific; fogs also are, as might be expected, very prevalent, thunder storms are common, and earthquakes have more than once destroyed a great part of the most populous towns. Kæmpfer remarked, also, that water-spouts were of very frequent occurrence in the seas around Japan. Yet, notwithstanding all these things, the country cannot, we think, be deemed insalubrious; for the Japanese are in general a healthful people, and the country is very thickly inhabited.

SECTION II.

ORIGIN OF THE JAPANESE PEOPLE.

An opinion has been expressed by several writers that Japan was colonized by the Chinese. Such an opinion, founded on very superficial observation, was advanced long before comparative philology had been resorted to by the learned, as one of the safest and best tests of truth in tracing the relationship of nations. But since the application of this test, no one, competent to speak instructively on the subject, has ventured to deduce the Japanese from a Chinese origin. The structure of the languages of the two people is essentially different. It is true that certain Chinese words, the names of objects, introduced by the Chinese, may be heard from the lips of a Japanese, modified however in the pronunciation; it is also true that the Chinese dialect of the Mandarins forms a species of universal language among the learned, a sort of latin in the extreme east that is understood by the highly *educated*, not only in China, but in Corea, at Tonquin, and other parts, and also in Japan; but so little is the affinity between the primitive language of Japan and that of China, that the common people of the two countries, neighbors as they are, cannot understand each other without the aid of an interpreter.

Probably those Europeans who too hastily adopted in former times the conclusion of a Chinese origin for the Japanese, may, in their ignorance of the languages, have been misled by observing among the Japanese the occasional use of the idiographic cypher of the Chinese in some of the Japanese *writings*. It was introduced into Japan A. D. 290, but the Japanese have an alphabet, or rather a syllabarium of their own, constructed on a principle entirely different from the Chinese idiograph. Each of these Chinese characters is in Japan pronounced in two distinct manners. The one, as among the Chinese, with a slight variation in the Japanese pronunciation. This idiom is called *Koye*, which means simply "*a Chinese sound or word;*" the other mode of pronouncing is Japanese, and is called *Yomi*, which signifies "*interpretation; the meaning of the Koye word.*" An example will illustrate. The words (according to Japanese pronunciation) *tin, chi, nin*, all Chinese, are *Koye*, and mean respectively *heaven, earth, man:* the words *ame, tsoutsi, fito*, are the *Yomi* (pure Japanese) of those *Koye* words, and have, in the proper language of Japan, the same meaning as the three Chinese words above named.

Hence, among the Japanese, there are three dialects; the first is pure *Yomi*, without any admixture of the *Koye*. This is the primitive language of the country, and is at this day used in poetry and works of light literature. The second is pure *Koye*, and is employed by the bonzes in their religious books.

The third is a mixture of the two, and constitutes the common language of the Empire.

But the construction of sentences in the Chinese and Japanese, as to the collocation of words, is entirely different, as is also the pronunciation by a Chinaman and a native of Japan. That of the last is neat, articulate, distinct, and rarely is there heard a syllable composed of more than two or three letters of our alphabet; while the speech of the former is little better than a confused sing-song monotone, unpleasant to the ear, in which constantly occurs a disagreeable crowding together of consonants. If an analysis of the sounds of our letters be made, a Chinese pronounces our aspirate H very plainly, while a Japanese never sounds it, but invariably substitutes for it F; while, on the other hand, our R and D, which are sounded by a Japanese with a distinctness equal to our own, always become L in the mouth of a Chinese. But without dwelling longer on this point, it is sufficient to say that an examination of grammatical structure conclusively settles, on the testimony of language, that the original inhabitants of Japan were not Chinese.

But the question still remains to be answered, "whence came the primitive occupants of Japan?" On this subject a diversity of opinion is to be found. Kaempfer brings them from the plains of Shinar, at the dispersion. He supposes them to have passed from Mesopotamia to the shores of the Caspian, thence through the valleys of the Yenisi, Silinga, and parallel rivers to the lake of Argueen; then following the river of that name, which arises from the lake, he thinks they reached the Amoor, following the valley of which they would find themselves in the then uninhabited peninsula of Corea, on the eastern shore of Asia. The passage thence to Japan, especially in the summer season, would not be difficult. He supposes that this migration occupied a long time; that they stopped when they found a pleasant region, and then resumed their march when they were pressed on their rear, or annoyed by other nomadic tribes. It was easy for them to make a home wherever they could find water and pasture for their flocks and herds. From the purity of the primitive language of Japan, (the intermixture of Chinese words is within the historic period and easily accounted for,) he supposes that the original stock could not, in its migration, have remained very long in any one inhabited place, or mingled much with any people then existing, of whose language we at this day have any knowledge; otherwise words from such language would have been found incorporated in the primitive Japanese tongue.

This, if not satisfactory, is at least ingenious. Modern ethnologists, however, turn to language as the best evidence of origin. Dr. Pickering, of the United States exploring expedition, seems disposed, from an observation of some Japanese whom he encountered at the Hawaiian islands, to assign to them a Malay origin. Others, judging from language, consider them of the Mongol stock. Very close affinities cannot probably be found between the Japanese and any other Asiatic language; but in its grammatical structure the Yomi of Japan is by some thought to be most analogous to the languages of the Tartar family. Siebold found, as he supposed, analogies between it and the idioms of the Coreans, and the Kurilians, who occupy the islands of Jesso and Tarakai or Karafto. He has described the coast of Tartary opposite to this last island, (called improperly by Europeans Sakhalian,) and thinks he finds a resemblance in customs; but Klaproth has shown that the language of the Tartary coast (Sandan) is a Tungusian dialect, and says that the language of Japan bears no decided marks of affinity either with it or with any other of the idioms named by Siebold. It is clearly not Tungusian. Klaproth's vocabularies of some of the idioms of Asia, particularly of the Mongolian, the Finnish, and some Indian dialects, show a very considerable number of simple and original words which belong also to the Japanese. In the present state of our information, the more commonly received opinion seems to be that the Japanese are of the Tartar family. But they certainly do not all have the Tartar complexion or physiognomy. The common people, according to Thunberg, are of a yellowish color all over, sometimes bordering on brown and sometimes on white. The laboring classes, who in summer expose the upper parts of their bodies, are always brown. Their eyes are not round, but oblong, small and sunk deep in the head. In color they are generally dark brown or rather black, and the eyelids form in the great angle of the eye a deep furrow, which gives them the appearance of being sharp or keen sighted. Their heads are large and their necks short, their hair black, thick, and from their use of oil, glossy. Their noses, although not flat, are yet rather thick and short.

The inhabitants of the coast of Kiu-siu, according to Siebold, differ in physical aspect, as well as in other respects, from those in the interior of the island. Their hair is most frequently black, in some cases crisped, the facial angle is strongly marked, the lips puffed, the nose small, slightly aquiline and depressed at the root. In the interior the people, mostly agriculturists, are a larger race, with broad and flattened countenances, prominent cheek bones, large space between the inner angles of the eyes, broad and very flat noses, with large mouths and a reddish brown skin.

But beside these, Thunberg also tells us that the descendants of the eldest and noblest families, of the princes and lords of the Empire, are somewhat majestic in their shape and countenance, being more like Europeans, and that ladies of distinction, who seldom go out into the open air without being covered, are perfectly white. Siebold also, speaking of the inhabitants of Kiu-siu, informs us that "the women who protect themselves from the influences of the atmosphere have generally a fine and white skin, and the cheeks of the young girls display a blooming carnation."

These facts, as Dr. Latham has said, do not necessarily involve the assumption of a double source of population, while, at the same time, such a second source is not an ethnological improbability. The darker race, he intimates, may have come from Formosa.

SECTION III.

GOVERNMENT.

Japan presents the singular feature of having *two* Emperors at the same time, the one secular, the other ecclesiastical; but it is a mistake to suppose that this duplicate sovereignty was established from the beginning, as one of the original elements of her civil polity; it has resulted from historical events that occurred long after Japan had a system of government. The Japanese, like many other people, claim for their nation an immense antiquity; but the authentic history of the Kingdom commences with Zin-mu-ten-woo, (whose name signifies "the divine conqueror,") about the year 660 B. C. Klaproth thinks he was a Chinese warrior and invader; be this however as it may, he conquered Nippon, and built a temple palace, dedicated to the sun-goddess, and properly called a *dairi;* his own appropriate title was *Mikado,* though the two terms are frequently confounded by European writers. He was the founder of the sovereignty of the *Mikados,* and from him, even to this day, the *Mikados* descend.

He was sole sovereign, both secular and spiritual, and claimed to rule by divine right. His successors, asserting the same right, added to it that of inheritance also, and their government was a despotism. By degrees these monarchs ceased to lead their own armies, and entrusted the military command to sons and kinsmen, though the supreme power still was theirs. This power, however, appears gradually to have been weakened by a custom which prevailed, of abdication by the *Mikados,* at so early an age, that the sovereignty descended upon their sons while they were yet children, the abdicating monarch frequently governing for the young king. The cause of these abdications was the desire to escape from the grievous burden of monotonous ceremonies, and complete isolation from intercourse without, which made the occupant of the throne little better than a royal prisoner.

At length it happened that the reigning *Mikado,* who had married the daughter of a powerful prince, abdicated in favor of his son, a child three years old, while the regency passed into the hands of the grandfather of the infant monarch. The regent placed the abdicated monarch in confinement, and this produced a civil war. *Yoritomo,* one of the most distinguished characters in Japanese history, espoused the cause of the imprisoned king, and after a war of several years was triumphant, when he released the captive and made him regent. But his regency conferred a nominal authority only; the real power resided in the hands of Yoritomo, who was created *Sio i dai Ziogoon,* or "generalissimo fighting against the barbarians." Upon the death of the *ex-Mikado,* Yoritomo, as lieutenant of the sovereign, virtually ruled for twenty years; and when he died, his title and authority devolved upon his son. This was the commencement of the power of the *Ziogoons,* or temporal sovereigns.

Time contributed to strengthen it under the successive reigns of infant *Mikados,* until it became recognized as hereditary. But, though a very important, and indeed dangerous power, was thus vested in the Ziogoons, yet the *Mikado* was looked on as possessing the royal authority, and to him it belonged to appoint the *Ziogoon,* who was, in truth, vice regent, but did not openly aspire to coequal rights of sovereignty.

This condition of things remained until the latter half of the sixteenth century. The Emperor (*Mikado*) was an autocrat who had a sovereign deputy, (*Ziogoon,*) the efficient and active ruler. During this long period, however, the power of the *Ziogoons* was silently and imperceptibly increasing; until, at last, that happened which it requires but little sagacity to perceive could not but be, in the end, the unavoidable result. Men invested with power are more apt to encourage its growth than to keep it stationary or diminish it; more especially when those whose interest it is to check their ambition are known to be imbecile.

It was about the middle of the sixteenth century that two brothers, descendants from Yoritomo, became rivals for the office of *Ziogoon*. The princes of the Empire took part with the one or the other, domestic strife raged, and the end of the contest was the death of both the rival brothers. The mightiest prince of that day was the prince of Owari, who, on the death of the brothers, immediately set up for himself as *Ziogoon*. One of the most sagacious as well as bravest of his adherents was an obscure man named Hide-yosi or Fide-yosi. His station was so lowly that, even in his own times, his parentage was matter of doubt; but his zeal and talents commended him to the notice of his master, and he became the trusted friend and confidential adviser of the prince of Owari, who, by his aid, succeeded in being appointed *Ziogoon*. Men's minds had been wrought to such excitement by the civil strife, that when the prince triumphed over his opponents, the reigning *Mikado* did not dare to breast popular opinion, and therefore conferred on him the office. The new *Ziogoon*, of course, rewarded his faithful ally, and conferred on Fide-yosi a high military appointment. Presently, the prince of Owari was murdered by one who usurped his office; he, in his turn, shared a like fate; and now the hour had come for Fide-yosi. When all was in confusion, he seized upon the office for himself; and so well known were his talents and power, that the frightened *Mikado*, at once, without hesitation, approved and confirmed him in the office, and he took the name of Tayko-sama, (the Lord Tayko.) With his title thus legitimated, in the confidence of his abilities, he trusted to himself for the rest, and has left behind him a name among the most celebrated in the history of Japan.

He was a statesman and a soldier, and displayed on the throne all the energy and ability which had contributed to place him there. He put an end at once to the civil commotions, by giving to the opposing princes of the Empire work to do in the invasion and conquest of Corea. He was about marching to subdue China, when death arrested him, in the year 1598, at the age of sixty-three. The Japanese, to this day, consider him as one of the ablest men their country has produced. During his reign he made large progress in the work of reducing the sovereignty of the *Mikado* almost to a shadow; and inthralling him by more and more burdensome ceremonials, and a most rigorous seclusion, all under the seemingly loyal pretext of profound deference and respect for his heaven-born authority, he quietly left him to "wield a barren sceptre."

Tayko-sama left an only son, six years old. To secure him in the succession, his father, on his death bed, caused him to marry the granddaughter of one of his own most particular friends and counsellors, Iyeyas, prince of Micava, from whom he obtained a most solemn promise that when the boy should have attained his fifteenth year he would have him recognized as *Ziogoon*.

Iyeyas proved unfaithful, became *Ziogoon* himself, and his descendants to this day hold the office, while a veil of mystery covers up the fate of the wronged son of Tayko. As to the *Mikado*, Iyeyas pursued the policy of his predecessor, and depriving him even of the little power which Tayko had left to him in temporals, he reduced the once absolute autocrasy which he represented to a mere ecclesiastical supremacy, and brought him down to the utter helplessness and dependence which at this day mark his condition. And this is, in brief, the history of events by which Japan has come to present that singular and unique feature in government of *one* empire simultaneously under *two* sovereigns.

INTRODUCTION.

The residence of the *Mikado* is at Miako; that of the *Ziogoon* is at Yeddo; each is surrounded with imperial splendor; the one is monarch *de jure*, the other is Emperor *de facto*. But however absolute may have been the usurped authority of the *Ziogoon* in the beginning, it has been subsequently very much modified; and certain it is that at this day the rule of the *Ziogoon* is by no means arbitrary. He cannot do just what he pleases. The laws of the Empire reach him as much as they do the meanest subject. These laws are unalterable, and are exceedingly minute in detail, controlling almost every action of life. The Emperors, both spiritual and secular, are just as much enthralled by them as the humblest man in the Kingdom. In times of usurpation or political trouble they may, in some few instances, have been set at naught, but these are exceptional cases.

There are two prominent features in the Japanese system of government: the one elemental, the other practical; and the two serving as the bases of almost everything else in their polity. The first is feudalism, or something very similar to it; and the second, exhibited in the practical administration of the government, is a system of checks and balances, founded on an all-pervading secret espionage, ramifying through all classes of society, from the highest to the lowest.

To explain this we must briefly advert to the several grades of society. We have already spoken of the two Emperors. The *Mikado* is supreme in rank and nominally recognized as such; but he has not a particle of political power; is not allowed to have troops, and is literally, from birth to death, shut up at Miako, in his little principality of Kioto, with the revenues of which, and the rich presents sent him by the *Ziogoon*, he must be content. Even in his own principality he is governed for, as an independent prince, by some grandee of his court, so that never lived there sovereign with less of sovereign attributes allowed him. But for the tenacity with which the Japanese cling to their ancient usages and laws, the *Mikados* would, doubtless, have long since ceased to form a part of the cumbrous and complicated machinery of government. Formerly it belonged to them to name or appoint the *Ziogoon*; they may, indeed, still nominally have this power; but it is without any real value, as the office of *Ziogoon* has for a long time been hereditary.

But politically insignificant as the *Mikado* is, he is venerated with a respect little, if at all, inferior to that rendered to the gods themselves. Living in mysterious, though, for the most part, indolent seclusion, he is venerated because he is inaccessible; and is, in truth, a prisoner who must find, if he find at all, solace for his confinement in the golden chains and ornamental prison-house of his captivity. No wonder that the abdication of a *Mikado* is common in Japanese history. As to the *Ziogoon*, he commands the revenues of the country, has at his disposal an army, and is anything but a prisoner. Once in seven years he makes a visit, surrounded with royal pomp, to the court of his brother sovereign, whom he takes care to keep, at all times, under the surveillance of unsuspected secret spies. He sends, too, in the intervals between his visits, embassies with rich presents to the shadow king of the holy court, and receives in turn what he probably deems a valueless bundle of blessings and prayers.

The hereditary classes in society are said to be eight in number; and, except under very peculiar circumstances, no one can leave, through life, the class in which he was born without a forfeiture of respectability.

Class I. These are the hereditary vassal princes of the Empire.

Class II. These are hereditary nobility, below the rank of *princes*. They hold their lands as fiefs, subject to knight service or the rendition of military service to some one of the hereditary princes. If they belong to one of the imperial cities, their military service is due directly to the *Ziogoon* himself. The number of armed vassals required of them is regulated by the extent of their respective domains. These hereditary nobles have generally sub-vassals on their lands, who are bound to furnish their several quotas of fighting men. Out of this class, governors of provinces, generals, and officers of State are selected.

Class III. This includes all the priests of the Kingdom—seemingly, those of the ancient religion of Japan, *Sintoo*, as well as of Buddhism.

Class IV. This is composed of the vassal soldiers, furnished by the nobility of *Class II.*

These four classes are the higher orders of Japanese society, and enjoy certain privileges of dress. They carry two swords, and wear a species of loose petticoat trowsers, which none of lower rank dare to put on.

Class V. These constitute the higher portion of the middle classes, such as medical men, government clerks, and other professional men and employés.

Class VI. Merchants and shopkeepers, who rank low in Japan, no matter what may be their wealth. Any one of the classes above this would be disgraced forever should he engage in any trade or traffic. The richest men in the Empire belong to this class; and yet they are not permitted to expend their money in a luxurious or ostentatious style of living. Sumptuary laws impose restraints which they dare not violate. They are not allowed to wear even the single sword, unless they purchase the privilege, by becoming the menial followers of some great lord, at the price of a considerable sum of money.

Class VII. This is composed of retail dealers, little shopkeepers, pedlars, mechanics, and artisans of all descriptions, save one, to be mentioned presently. Painters and other artists belong to this class.

Class VIII. This consists of sailors, fishermen, peasants, and agricultural and day laborers of all kinds. The peasants seem to be a species of serfs, attached to the soil, like the ancient villein of feudal times, and belong to the land-owner. Sometimes the land is hired, and worked "on shares," the agriculturist paying the proprietor a certain proportion of the crops.

The exception alluded to among mechanics, in *Class VII*, is one which is supposed to have originated in one of the superstitions of the *Sintoo* religion, which tabooed all who had defiled themselves by coming in contact with a dead body. Whether this be the origin of the exception, we know not; but the fact is well established, that the *tanners, curriers, leather dressers,* and, in short, every one in any way connected with the making or vending of leather is placed under ban or interdict. Those of this proscribed class cannot dwell in the towns or villages that are occupied by the other classes; they are not even numbered in the census of the population. They dare not enter an inn, tea-house, or any public place of entertainment. If they are travelling, and want food or drink, they must wait outside of the wall of the house, and there be served in their own bowl or platter; for no Japanese, not of their own class, would ever touch or use the vessel out of which they had taken food. Out of this class come the public executioners and gaolers throughout the Empire. In short, they are shunned like the leper of old.

Before we proceed to speak of the singular system by which these various classes are governed, it is proper to premise that originally the Kingdom was sub-divided into sixty-six or sixty-eight principalities. These had been previously independent kingdoms, and were continued, as principalities, under the rule of their respective princes, subject, however, to a forfeiture of the rights of the governing family, in case of rebellion or treason. This penalty of forfeiture was incurred by many of the reigning princes, and advantage was taken of the circumstance, as often as it occurred, to split the forfeited principalities into fragments; so that, instead of the original number, there are now no less than six hundred and four distinct administrations, including therein principalities, lordships, imperial provinces, and imperial towns, of which last the *Ziogoon* himself is the ruling head.

1. There is under the Emperor, (*Ziogoon*,) a grand council of state, consisting of thirteen, which governs in the Emperor's name. Of these thirteen, five councillors are taken from the first class we have named, the hereditary princes and vassals of the Empire; the remaining eight are taken from the second class, the old nobility, below the rank of princes. There seems to be among these a head councillor of state, whose powers and functions are not unlike those of a grand vizier in Turkey. He is called "Governor of the Empire," and all the other councillors are subordinate to him. He decides upon all affairs of moment; has the universal appointing power; receives returns from all the authorities of the Empire; may, on appeal, sanction or reverse every sentence of death passed; and, in short, acts for the lay Emperor in all these and some other exercises of sovereignty. To this grand council, too, belongs the very important power of dethroning the *Ziogoon*. Important resolutions of the council are always laid before the Emperor, who generally assents without delay or investigation. Should he, however, dissent, a mode of proceeding is pursued, which we will describe presently. It is doubtful whether all these high offices are not hereditary; and under these are—

2. Inferior state functionaries, in regular and interminable gradation, consisting of lords, guardians of the temples, commissioners of foreign affairs, governors, ministers of police, superintendents of agriculture, &c. No relative of the spiritual sovereign, however, is ever put into any of these offices.

3. The vassal princes still govern the principalities or such fragments of them as may be left to them, with an outward show of their former sovereignty; but it is show only. The princes themselves can do nothing without the consent of the *Ziogoon* and council. And here we find in full development that system of espionage of which we have spoken. The prince himself, beside being surrounded with a multitude of private spies, unknown to him, who watch his domestic as well as public business and doings, has also *two* official spies appointed by the chief of the grand council, and these, in truth, conduct the administration of the principality. These are known as secretaries, and both are never permitted to reside in the province at the same time. They alternate yearly. The families of both secretaries reside constantly in Yeddo. The secretary who is in the principality therefore leaves his family behind him in the capital as a hostage for his fidelity. When his year expires he may rejoin them, and his colleague then, bidding adieu to his household for a year, takes his place. Each secretary, therefore, is a check upon the doings of the other; it is the interest of each to report any misfeasance in the official conduct of the other; in short, they are spies on each other. But the jealous suspicion of the government is not satisfied with even these precautions. The family of the prince himself is made to reside at Yeddo, and he must spend each alternate year there near the *Ziogoon*.

And this feature of making officials serve in pairs, as spies upon each other, we may here remark, once for all, pervades the entire polity of Japan. Every body is watched. No man knows who are the secret spies around him, even though he may be, and is, acquainted with those that are official. The Emperors themselves are not exempt; vizier, grand councillors, vassal princes, provincial secretaries, all are under the eye of an everlasting unknown police. The wretched system is even extended to the humblest of the citizens. Every city or town is divided into collections of five families, and every member of such a division is personally responsible for the conduct of the others; everything, therefore, which occurs in one of these families, out of the usual course, is instantly reported to the authorities by the other four to save themselves from censure. It has well been said that the government of Japan is a "government of spies."

We have said that the Emperors are not exempt. The *Ziogoon* has his minions about the *Mikado*, and the grand council have theirs about the *Ziogoon*. And the cowardice engendered by such ceaseless distrust necessarily leads to cruelty in penalties. Take as an illustration the case of a measure submitted by the grand council to the *Ziogoon*; to which, contrary to his usual custom, he does not at once assent without examination. Suppose he should disapprove, the measure is referred immediately to the arbitration of the three princes of the blood who are the nearest kinsmen of the *Ziogoon*, and their decision is final. If they do not agree in opinion with the monarch, he must instantly relinquish the throne to his son or to some other heir. He is not allowed even the poor privilege of revising or retracting an opinion. Should the three princes concur in the Ziogoon's opinion, then the member of the council who proposed the obnoxious measure thus rejected must *die;* and those who voted with him are often required to die also. Sometimes the whole council, with the "Governor of the Empire" at their head, have in this way been obliged to atone for a mere mistake in national policy by putting themselves to death.

4. As to the government of lordships, which are only smaller principalities, the rule is the same; a duality of governors, an alternation in the discharge of official duties, and a separation every other year from all domestic enjoyment.

5. In the imperial provinces and imperial cities the *Ziogoon*, or rather the vizier and grand council for him, select two governors from the nobility, and surround them with the usual apparatus of secretaries and under secretaries, police officers, spies, and all other officials.

As to the spies themselves, they are of every rank in life below that of the hereditary princes. The highest nobility dare not shrink from the occupation, and even stoop to disguise themselves, the more effectually to perform the degrading office. The fact is, if directed to act as spies, they must either do it or adopt as the alternative, *death!* Doubtless many of those who perform this dishonorable work would gladly, were it possible, escape from the degradation; while there are some, ambitious of succeeding to those whom they denounce, to whom the occupation is congenial enough.

A story is told by the writers on Japan which illustrates this. Complaints were sent to the grand council of the governor of the town of Matsmai; the council resorted to its usual plan of employing a spy. In a little while the offending governor was removed. To the amazement of the people, they recognized in his successor a man whom they had known as a journeyman tobacco-cutter in the town, who, a short time before the displacement of the old governor, had suddenly disappeared from his master's shop. The journeyman was a disguised nobleman, who had acted the part of a spy by order of the court.

A very singular custom of self-punishment, even unto death, prevails among all the officials of Japan. When one has offended, or even when in his department there has been any violation of law, although beyond his power of prevention, so sure is he of the punishment of death that he anticipates it by ripping up his own body, disembowelling himself, rather than to be delivered over to the executioner. In fact, he is encouraged to do so, inasmuch as by his self-destruction he saves his property from forfeiture and his family from death with him. With many of the high officials it is a point of honor thus to kill themselves on any failure in their departments; it is construed into an acknowledgment that they deserve to be put to death by the Emperor, and their sons are often promoted to high positions, as a sort of reward for the father's ingenuous acknowledgment of guilt.

It is easy to see, from what has been said, why the laws and customs of Japan are so obstinately unalterable. Every man is afraid of proposing an innovation, however wise or necessary, because the penalty is so fearful should it not be approved. He who in the grand council offers a measure which is disapproved by the tribunal of final resort pays for his act with his life. A governor, or lord, or prince, knows that if he attempt any alteration, no matter how salutary, he will be instantly denounced by his colleague, or secretary, a spy upon his conduct, as a violator of the established usages of the Empire, and the certain consequence is *death*. So, too, with the common people; broken up into their little sections of five families, they dare not depart in the slightest degree from what is prescribed, for they are quite sure that the authorities will be informed of it, and the penalty inevitably follows. There cannot, under such a system, be anything like judicious legislation, founded on inquiry, and adapted to the ever varying circumstances of life. All must proceed exactly as it has done for centuries; progress is rendered impossible, and hence, in some degree, the difficulty, so long experienced in all Christendom, of bringing the Japanese into communication with other nations. As a remedy for an existing evil, they saw fit, centuries ago, to interdict entirely all such communication; and though the fact admits of proof that many of their wisest men would gladly have seen the interdict removed or modified, as being no longer necessary in their altered circumstances, yet no man dared to propose any alteration.

We may venture to hope that, even in the partial communication with strangers allowed to the Japanese by the late treaty with our country, the first step has been taken in breaking down their long prevalent system of unalterable laws and unchangeable customs. But among a people so sensitive and suspicious considerable time must elapse before much progress is made in a better direction. And in the first exercise of our rights under the treaty, it is to be hoped the greatest care will be taken by our countrymen to avoid everything which can alarm the sleepless Japanese jealousy of strangers; if there be not, there is danger lest in their apprehensions, or perchance in mere caprice, they may seek to undo all that they have thus far done. It is obvious that a great deal depends now on the fairness, good sense, and good temper of our consular representatives. One rash man may overturn all that has been accomplished.

The system of espionage to which we have alluded explains also what all the writers on Japan, and all the officers of our late expedition, represent as a prominent characteristic. We allude to the systematic falsehood and duplicity exhibited, and often without shame, by the high Japanese officials and public functionaries in their negotiations and intercourse with strangers. We do not mean to say that these bad traits belong to the people generally. On the contrary, almost every writer describes them as naturally frank in manner, communicative and open in speech on ordinary topics, and possessed of a very high sense of honor. They are a people of very ingenious and lively minds, possessed of shrewdness, of great personal bravery, as their history shows, and far superior (at least in our opinion) to any other civilized eastern nation. But the officials are placed in a false position by the wretched system of spies, and dare not act openly and frankly. As government functionaries they lie and practice artifice to save themselves from condemnation by the higher powers: it is their vocation; as private gentlemen, they are frank, truthful, and hospitable. MacFarlane, who speaks of this official deception, says he has observed precisely the same thing among the Turks. Nearly every Turk, unconnected with government, may be described as being in his private intercourse a frank, truth-loving, honorable man; while nearly every one holding a government office may be considered as exactly the reverse. These facts present a seeming anomaly, and yet we are not sure that something very like it, and differing in degree only, may not be found nearer to home than Japan.

The severity of the Japanese laws is excessive. The code is probably the bloodiest in the world. Death is the prescribed punishment for most offences. The Japanese seem to proceed on the principle that he who will violate one law will violate any other, and that the wilful violator is unworthy to live; he cannot be trusted in society. Their laws are very short and intelligible, and are duly made public in more modes than one, so that no man can truly plead ignorance; and the proceedings under them are as simple as the laws themselves. There are no professional lawyers in the kingdom; every man is deemed competent to be his own pleader. If a party is aggrieved, he immediately appeals to the magistrate, before whom the other party is soon made to appear. The case is stated by the complainant in his own way, and the accused is heard in reply. The magistrate examines the witnesses, and it is said that this officer generally displays great acuteness in detecting falsehood. He passes sentence, and it is carried into execution *instanter;* and so ends an ordinary lawsuit. If the matter in controversy be of great importance, the magistrate may refer it to the Emperor in council; but if he sees fit to decide it himself there is no appeal. Sometimes, in trifling cases, he orders the parties to go and settle the matter privately with the aid of friends, and it is well understood that it *must* be thus settled, or unpleasant consequences will result. Sometimes, when both plaintiff and defendant are in fault, he awards censure to both, as they may deserve it, and sends them about their business. We have said their code is bloody in principle, and very often it is sanguinary in practice. Still the relentings of humanity have forced the administrators of justice to some modification of the theory which prescribes indiscriminate severity.

The magistrate *may* sentence to death, but he is not obliged to do so, except in cases of murder. He *may*, therefore, exercise a large discretion. He may imprison in a *raya* or cage. In this case, the prisoner is allowed a fair proportion of wholesome food, and provision is made for cleanliness and ventilation. But there is another prison, commonly a dungeon in the governor's house, known by the significant name of *gokuya, hell*. Into this more are thrust than it will conveniently hold; the door is never opened except to admit or release a prisoner; the food is passed within through a hole in the wall, and there is neither light or ventilation except through a small grated hole or window at the top. Books, pipes, and every species of recreation are prohibited; no beds are allowed, and the prisoner is subjected to what he considers the deep degradation of being made to wear a rope of straw around his waist instead of the usual silk or linen girdle. The diet is limited and very poor; but if a rich man is confined, he may buy better food, on condition that he will share it equally with all his fellow prisoners. The Japanese doctrine is that, if a man of wealth or influence is a criminal, he has no right to fare any better than the poorest man in the Kingdom who commits a crime, therefore all shall be treated alike.

We have already alluded to the well known, yet remarkable feature of Japanese polity, which has for so long a time induced the government rigorously to interdict all communication between its subjects and foreigners, with the single exception of the Dutch and Chinese. This exclusive system did not always prevail. We shall have occasion, presently, to give the history of its origin, and to place before the reader a statement of the means whereby the Dutch succeeded in the establishment of their commercial factory at Dezima, in the port of Nagasaki. It is only necessary now to remark that, prior to the visit of the United States' expedition, no other port but Nagasaki was open to a European ship, and, except at that spot, no Japanese was permitted to buy from or sell to a western stranger. The Chinese had some few privileges of trade, but these were hedged around with jealous restrictions that hampered their commercial relations and intercourse quite as much as those of the Europeans. With this general, and necessarily brief view of the leading features of the Japanese government and policy, we pass on to another topic.

SECTION IV.

RELIGION.

SUCH are the contradictions among the several writers on Japan upon the subject of the religion of the country that it is not easy to discover what is the precise truth. Nor is this discrepancy much to be wondered at, for, since the extirpation of Christianity from the Kingdom, there is, probably, no topic on which a Christian would find it more difficult to obtain from a Japanese accurate information than on the subject of religion. There are, however, certain particulars in which all agree, and which are doubtless correct.

The original national religion of Japan is called *Sin-syu*, (from *sin*, the gods, and *syu*, faith,) and its followers are called *Sintoos*. Such, at least, is the statement made by some writers; but Siebold says the proper Japanese name is *Kami-no-mitsi*, which means "the way of the *Kami*," or gods; this the Chinese have translated into *Shin-tao;* and the Japanese have modified the Chinese into *Sintoo*.

It is said that the only object of *worship* among the Sintoos is the sun-goddess, Ten-sio-dai-zin, who is deemed the patron divinity of Japan. But there are thousands of inferior deities, called *Kami*, of whom the greater number are canonized or deified men. It is through these and the Mikado, as mediators, that prayers are made to the sun-goddess, who is too great and holy to allow of an independent approach to her in prayer. The Mikado is supposed to be her lineal descendant. But with all these divinities the Sintoos are not idolators. They have no idols in their temples; there are images indeed of their *Kami*, but, as it is alleged, not for purposes of worship. This statement, however, is very questionable. The only decorations of the old temples were a mirror, the emblem of purity of soul, and many strips of white paper formed into what is called a *gohei*, also an emblem of purity. Siebold thinks the image of the *Kami*, introduced into the temples, is a foreign innovation, and never existed before the introduction of Buddhism. The numerous *Kami* he considers as analogous to the saints of the Romanist. MacFarlane looks on the Sintoo worship at this day as thoroughly permeated with Buddhism. Meylan would make the original religion of Japan a pure theism. It is not easy to say what it was or is. As to the Sintoo creed, its leading features, according to Siebold, are some vague notion of the immortality of the soul, of a future state of existence, of rewards and punishments, a paradise and a hell. Its five great duties are: 1st. Preservation of pure fire as an emblem of purity and instrument of purification. 2d. Purity of soul, heart, and body to be cherished, the first by obeying the dictates of reason and the laws, the last by abstaining from whatever defiles. 3d. Observance of festival days, which are numerous. 4th. Pilgrimages, which at certain times in the year are imposing and costly; and 5th. The worship of the *Kami*, both in the temples and in private habitations. Impurity may be contracted in various ways: By associating with the impure, by hearing obscene or wicked language, by eating certain meats, and by coming in contact with blood, or with a dead body. For all these there are the prescribed modes of purification.

The festivals all begin with a visit to the temple. There the votary performs his ablutions at a reservoir provided for the purpose; he then kneels in the verandah, opposite to a grated window, through which he gazes at the mirror, and then offers up his prayers, with his sacrifice of rice, fruit, tea, or the like. This done, he drops his coin in the money-box, and retires. This is the usual form of Kami worship at the temples. The moneys contributed are applied to the support of the *Kaminusi*, as they are called. These are the priests of the temple, and their name or title means, literally, the landlords of the gods. These priests live in houses within the grounds of their respective temples, and are hospitable to strangers. Siebold says that they marry, and that their wives are priestesses, who have prescribed religious duties; though we have been told by an intelligent Japanese, in reply to our inquiries, that the Sintoo priests do not marry.

Pilgrimage, however, is the great religious duty of the Sintooites. There are two-and-twenty shrines in the Kingdom commanding such homage; but the great and most sacred one is that of the sun-goddess, Ten-sio-dai-sin, at Isye. To make at least one pilgrimage to this shrine is incumbent upon everybody of the Sintoo faith. The very pious go annually. Even the Buddhists (with the exception of the Bonzes or priests) perform this pilgrimage. The *Ziogoon* is permitted to perform this religious duty vicariously, and annually sends an embassy of pilgrims to Isye.

The *Kaminusi* are the regular clergy of the Sintoo religion in Japan; but the European writers on the subject mention two institutions or religious orders, if they may be so called, composed entirely of the blind, and constituting a *quasi* clergy. The Japanese tell romantic stories about their origin. One of the fraternities they say was founded many centuries ago by Semmimar, a prince of the Empire, and the younger son of the then reigning Mikado. The prince was one of the handsomest men in the Kingdom, and loved a princess whose beauty was a match for his own. She died, and such was his grief, that he wept himself blind. He then founded this order. The other association had a different, but not less remarkable origin. In the times of Yoritomo, of whom we have spoken in the last section, there was a general named Kakekigo, who commanded a part of the troops of Prince Feki. In battle with Yoritomo, Prince Feki was slain, and Kakekigo was taken prisoner. So great was the renown of the prisoner, throughout Japan, that Yoritomo strove most earnestly to gain his friendship; he loaded him with kindnesses and finally offered him his liberty. Kakekigo replied: "I can love none but my slain master. I owe you gratitude; but you caused Prince Feki's death, and never can I look upon you without wishing to kill you. My best way to avoid such ingratitude, and to reconcile my conflicting duties, is never to see you more; and thus do I insure it." With these words, he tore out his eyes, and presented them to Yoritomo on a salver. The prince, struck with admiration, released him, when Kakekigo withdrew into retirement and founded this second order of the blind, which is called, after Prince Feki, the *Fekisado*.

There are two sects among the Sin-syu: the *Yuitz* and the *Rioboo-Sintoo*. The first are the rigidly orthodox, who will allow of no innovation. They are few in number, and consist mostly of the *Kaminusi* or priests. The other sect, which comprises the great body of the Sintoos, is eclectic, and has introduced a great deal of Buddhism into the system.

Buddhism is the most widely diffused of all false creeds. Its followers amount to three hundred and twenty millions, while those of Mohammed fall short of this number by fifty millions. The founder of this religion was a man called *Sakya-Sinha*, (Syaka in Japan.) who, by his virtues and austerity, attained to divine honors, and after death was deified under the name of *Buddha*, or "the Sage." It is impossible to say when he was born. The earliest period named is 2,420 years before the Christian era; the latest is but 543 years prior to that event. Neither can it be said with certainty when Buddhism was introduced into Japan. Klaproth and Siebold, both of whom profess to follow Japanese writers, differ as to dates. The probability is that it was brought in from India or Corea near the close of the sixth century of our era.

The leading features of this system of religion are the metempsychosis, whence arises the dogma that prohibits the taking of animal life; the worship of a countless host of idols; that the grand Lama, or high-priest King, never dies; that their priests constitute a distinct order in the State, and that they are bound to celibacy. The chief commandments of Buddhism are five in number, and constitute a code which is called the *Gokaï*, or five laws. They are these: not to kill, not to steal, to live chastely, not to lie, and to abstain from strong drink. The *Sikaï*, or ten counsels, contain the division and application of these laws to particular cases. Buddhism made its way in Japan by degrees, although the government tolerated it from the beginning. Indeed, no feature is more striking among the institutions of the Empire than its enlarged spirit of religious toleration. It was extended to Christianity on its first promulgation by the Portuguese; and was not withdrawn until the Japanese supposed that intolerance and treason lurked under the new religion. Christianity was driven from Japan on *political*, not on religious grounds. Such is the liberality of the government on the subject of religion that, at this moment, may be found in Japan no less than thirty-four sects, all quite distinct from Buddhism, (which is the faith of a majority of the Kingdom,) perfectly unmolested. The truth is, that the Japanese government exhibits now, as it always has done, a very remarkable indifference to mere doctrinal points, so long as they interfere not with the public tranquility. When the priests of the Japanese sects joined, centuries ago, in a petition to the Emperor that he would banish the Jesuits and the Romish monks, annoyed by their importunities, he asked them how many different religions there were then in Japan? They answered "thirty-five." "Well," said the Emperor, "when thirty-five religions can be tolerated we can easily bear with thirty-six; leave the strangers in peace."

The Buddhism of Japan, at this day, has probably much of the old Sintoo mixed up with it; but there is reason to think that no creed in the Kingdom has a very strong hold on the popular mind. Christianity, however, is viewed with suspicion by all, and at present is not, in any degree, tolerated.

The idolatry of the common people, who are Buddhists, is exceedingly gross, while among the learned the religion assumes the character of a high mystic creed, not wanting in some features that are pure enough.

There is a third sect, called by some writers religious, though Kæmpfer more properly speaks of it as a school of philosophers. It is known by the name of *Sintoo*, which means "the way of philosophers." It inculcates no particular faith, and can accommodate itself to any, whether true or false. In some of its features it borders closely on Pantheism. It is supposed, and we presume correctly, to be an importation from China, compounded of most of the moral precepts of Confucius, and some high, mystic Buddhist notions. It has no religious rites or ceremonies of its own. There are five great points which characterize it. They call them *Dsin, Gi, Re, Tsi, Sin*. *Dsin* teaches them to live virtuously; *Gi* to do right and act justly with everybody; *Re* to be civil and polite; *Tsi* sets forth the rules for a good and prudent government; and *Sin* treats of a free conscience and upright heart. Nearly all the early European writers say that by far the larger number of the learned men of Japan belong to this school, which is remarkable for its scorn of the Buddhist idolatry. When Christianity was driven from Japan, the *Sintooists* were suspected of a tendency toward that faith, and thenceforth every Japanese was required to have in his house an idol of some kind.

Meylan, the Dutch official at Dezima, speaks of a fourth religion, which co-existed with these three prior to the introduction of Christianity. His story is, that about A. D. 50, a Brahminical sect was introduced into Japan, which taught as doctrines the redemption of the world by the son of a virgin, who died to expiate human sin, thus insuring to man a joyful resurrection. It also taught a trinity of immaterial persons constituting one eternal, omnipotent God, the maker of all things, who was to be adored as the source of all good.

Some have hence intimated what certainly is not impossible, that Christianity may have thus early reached Japan through India. But there is probably some mistake in this statement of the doctrines held. No writer but Meylan has mentioned the story, and both the Buddhist and Brahminical systems afford materials which an over zealous and uninformed spirit of Christianity may easily convert into seemingly Christian doctrines. Thus, the old Spanish ecclesiastics who first came to America were quite convinced that the gospel had been brought to our continent by St. Thomas, long before their arrival.

SECTION V.

GENERAL VIEW OF THE PAST RELATIONS OF THE EMPIRE WITH THE WESTERN CIVILIZED NATIONS.

THE PORTUGUESE.

FERDINAND MENDEZ PINTO has been immortalized by Cervantes, but unfortunately for his reputation it is, to use the phrase of Shakspeare, as a "measureless liar." Like Marco Polo, when he told strange things that had befallen him in his wanderings, the men of his generation refused to believe him. But like Polo, he related a great deal that has since been found to be true; and we are inclined to think that, when telling what he professed to have seen himself, he interspersed his narrative with as few lies as some of his more accredited successors of modern times.

Pinto was a good representative of the Portuguese discoverer of the sixteenth century. In his day Portugal was a power. In less than two centuries she had traversed the Atlantic, conquered Madeira, the Cape de Verds, the coast of Guinea and Congo; had planted herself on the shores of India, and obtained a foothold in China. She had founded in her wealthy metropolis of Goa what has been called "the Rome of India." She possessed Macao, and was among the first of European maritime powers in the east. Albuquerque had laid for her the foundations of a magnificent oriental empire, which it needed a man like Albuquerque to consolidate and retain. The man was wanting, and the empire never grew to maturity. But this her prosperous day produced for her many a hardy sailor, half hero, half adventurer; now exhibiting a touch of chivalry and now a touch of traffic; a soldier on land to-day and a corsair of the seas to-morrow; exceedingly devout or surpassingly profane, according to circumstances; but always ready to encounter fatigue, privation or peril, to promote the gain of himself and the grandeur of his country, which on most occasions he felicitously contrived to reconcile and blend into one common end. Of this class Pinto was a type.

He visited Japan, and has told us the story of his adventures; and the better authorities of this day believe that he was an eye-witness and actor in such scenes as he relates of personal incidents.

There is, however, some room for discussion on the subject of dates; for if we may credit the Japanese annals, it would seem that about the same time there must have been two visits of Europeans to Japan; but if there were, both were made by natives of Portugal, so that to them unquestionably belongs the honor of having first landed on the Japanese soil, and of having brought that country into communication with Europe. The discovery, indeed, was accidental in both cases, if two there were, but that does not alter the fact that it was made by the Portuguese.

We incline to think, however, that there was but one visit. The annals of Japan record the arrival of the first Europeans, and substantially they agree with Pinto's story. So remarkable was the event, and so strange the appearance of the new comers, that the Japanese preserved portraits of them. The date assigned in the annals would correspond with our October, in the year 1543. Pinto makes the date of his arrival in 1545. Still the details given by Pinto, and confirmed by the annals, force us to believe that both are telling the story of the same event. Whether it were in the one year or the other of those named above, the story is, that a Portuguese ship or Chinese corsair, (we know not which,) on board of which was Pinto, after great stress of weather, was driven to the shores of Japan, and anchored at last in the harbor of Bungo, on the island of Kiu-siu. The Japanese at that time, though vigilant, yet manifested no reluctance to admit the strangers and hold communication with them. They extended courtesy and kindness to them, and no obstacle was interposed to a free trade with the inhabitants. The names of those who first landed are said by various writers, from Maffeius up to Thunberg, to have been Antonio Mota, Francisco Zeimoto, and Antonio Peixoto. Fraissinet, however, thinks that the names have been disfigured or altered, and that the individuals meant were Fernan Mendez Pinto, Diego Zeimoto, and Christoval Borallo. The Japanese annals speak of two under the names of Moura Siouksia and Krista Mota, and Fraissinet suggests that Siouksia may be the Japanese pronunciation of Zeimoto, and Krista their nearest approach to Christoval. The natives and strangers were so well pleased with each other that, by an arrangement with the viceroy or prince of Bungo, (the rulers of the principalities were then probably more independent of the Emperor than they are now,) a Portuguese ship was to be sent annually to the island of Kiu-siu laden with woollen cloths, furs, manufactured silks, taffetas, and other commodities needed by the Japanese. This ship was to be dispatched probably from Macao, or, it may be, from Goa. The returns were to be made in gold, silver, and copper, of the last of which there is undoubted abundance in Japan, and probably no small quantity of the first.

But with this introduction of commercial relations, the Portuguese soon introduced also priests of the religion they professed. In 1549, seven years only after the discovery, Hansiro, a young Japanese of some rank, had found it necessary to fly from his country, on account of a homicide, and had gone to the Portuguese settlement of Goa, on the Malabar coast. Here he encountered ecclesiastics of the church of Rome, by whom he was converted to the Christian faith and baptized. He was enterprising and shrewd, and soon convinced the Portuguese merchants of Goa that they might establish a profitable trade with Japan, and assured the Jesuits that they also might find a rich harvest of souls in the Empire.

The Portuguese hastened to act on both his suggestions; a ship was loaded with goods and presents and sent to establish a permanent trade with Japan; while, for the accomplishment of the second object, some of the Jesuit priests were ready enough to embark. Among them was that remarkable man, Francis Xavier, who possessed in an eminent degree many of the most important qualifications of the Christian missionary. To talents of a very high order he added a zeal and enthusiasm rarely equalled, and a courage never surpassed. The thought of the perils attending the mission, so far from disheartening him, served only to strengthen his resolve to undertake it. On board the ship returned the young Japanese convert who had suggested the undertaking. On arriving at the province of Bungo all were received with open arms, and not the slightest opposition was made to the introduction of either trade or religion. No system of exclusion then existed, and such was the spirit of toleration that the government made no objection to the preaching of Christianity. Indeed the Portuguese were freely permitted to go where they pleased in the Empire, and to travel, by land or sea, from one end of it to the other. The people bought the goods of the merchants and listened to the teachings of the missionaries. The labors of the last were very successful, for it is but justice to Xavier and the first missionaries to say that they were most exemplary men—humble, virtuous, disinterested, and very benevolent. Possessed of some medical skill, they used it kindly and gratuitously among the sick, and were deservedly viewed by the people as friendly and superior men, whose lives were devoted to doing good. They meddled with no public affairs; unmolested by the government, they troubled not themselves about its administration; and imitating the example of the devoted Xavier, they modestly and unceasingly pursued the appropriate duties of their holy calling only. In fact, they loved the Japanese. With one voice the early missionaries speak in terms of strong affection when they describe the docile and good disposition of the Japanese. Xavier says: "I know not when to cease in speaking of the Japanese. They are truly the delight of my heart."

This eminent man went from Japan to China in 1551, and in 1552 died at Shan Shan, on the Canton river, not far from Macao. He left behind him, however, among his beloved islanders, some very able and excellent men, and churches were built and converts made by thousands.

Nor were the commercial relations of the new comers less prosperous. They could readily obtain the commodities they wished for the Japanese market from their establishments at Macao and Goa. The profits they made on their European merchandise were commonly one hundred per cent.; so that, as Kæmpfer has said, if their commercial prosperity had continued but twenty years longer, Macao would have been so enriched from Japan that it would have surpassed all that was accumulated in Jerusalem during the reign of Solomon. As one of the old writers expresses it, the Portuguese obtained "the golden marrow" of Japan. In fact they had but to proceed prudently and they would ere long have been the dominant race in Japan. Many of them had married the daughters of the wealthiest Christian Japanese, and no other nation of Europe could have driven them from their strong position.

It was about the year 1566 that the Portuguese first called the attention of the reigning prince of Omura to the superiority of the harbor of Nagasaki over the ports they were accustomed to frequent; and it was at their suggestion that a settlement was formed there. Bungo, Firando, (Firato,) and Nagasaki were the principal places of commercial business.

But all this prosperity was destined to have an end, and we are sorry to say it was occasioned by the ecclesiastics themselves. Had the work begun by Xavier and his companions been left in the hands of men like themselves, we very much doubt whether the severe Japanese laws prohibiting Christianity in the Empire would ever have existed. But these prudent, inoffensive, and laborious men were soon outnumbered by swarms of Dominican, Augustinian, and Franciscan friars from Goa and Macao, who were attracted by the flattering accounts of the remarkable success of the Jesuits. They had not labored in making the harvest, they were ready enough to go and reap it. The Franciscans and Dominicans quarrelled with each other, and all the orders quarrelled with the Jesuits. In vain did the latter implore them to profit by their experience, to be discreet and suppress their strife, to respect the laws and usages of the country. In vain did they represent that their conduct would prove fatal, not merely to their own hopes and purposes, but even to the progress, possibly to the continuance in Japan of Christianity itself. All was of no avail. To the Japanese convert was presented the strange spectacle of one ecclesiastic quarrelling with another, of one body of priests intriguing with heathens to defeat another; while even the poor native Christian labored to reconcile the feuds and rivalries of these consecrated belligerents.

The quarrels of these Roman monastic orders may, therefore, be accounted as one cause of the expulsion of Christianity from Japan.

But this was not all. The pride, avarice, and extortions of the Portuguese laity had become excessive about the close of the sixteenth century, and disgusted the Japanese. Very many of the clergy, forgetful of the spirit of their office, instead of rebuking these sins, rather gave their countenance to their wealthy countrymen, and often sustained their acts without inquiring into their propriety. Indeed, their own pride quite equalled that of the laity; and even the native Christians are said to have been both shocked and disgusted when they saw that their spiritual instructors were quite as diligent in the effort to acquire their property as in the endeavor to save their souls. The Japanese traditions, to this day, represent the downfall of Christianity in the Empire as having been, in part at least, produced by the avarice, sensuality, and pride of the ecclesiastics. They treated with open contempt the institutions and customs of the country, and insulted the highest officials of the government by studied indignities. A circumstance is related as having occurred in 1596, which is said to have been the immediate cause of the great persecution. A Portuguese bishop was met on the high road by one of the highest officers of the State on his way to court. Each was in his sedan. The usage of the country required that, in such case, the conveyance of the bishop should be stopped, and that he should alight and pay his respects to the nobleman. Instead of conforming to this established act of courtesy, the bishop took not the least notice of the Japanese dignitary, but, turning his head away from him, ordered his bearers to carry him on. The insult, evidently intended, was so gross that the grandee took mortal offence, and confounding the Portuguese generally with their haughty clergy, he conceived toward all an implacable resentment. He forthwith presented his grievance to the Emperor, and touched his sense of dignity and national pride by a strong picture of the vanity and insolence of the Portuguese. Taiko, of whom we have already spoken, was at that time Emperor, and he was the last man to permit the laws and customs of his Empire to be treated with contempt by a set of presumptuous foreigners, who had neither good feeling nor good sense enough to repay the kindness they had received with the decency of common civility. With the Emperor's kind sentiments thus alienated the end was certain; it involved a question of time only; and such was the infatuation of these inflated ecclesiastics that this stupid act of episcopal insolence was perpetrated at a time when the Portuguese, by their pride and avarice, had already lost the best part of the favor they had once possessed.

At length a Portuguese ship, on its way from the East to Lisbon, was captured by the Dutch, and among other matters found on board were certain treasonable letters, written by Moro, a native Japanese, to the King of Portugal. Moro was a zealous Romanist, a warm friend of the Jesuits, and one of the chief agents and friends of the Portuguese in Japan. From these letters it appeared that the Japanese Christians, in conjunction with the Portuguese, were plotting the overthrow of the throne; and all they wanted was a supply of ships and soldiers from Portugal. It may be difficult to ascertain, with certainty, all the details of the conspiracy; but of the conspiracy itself there can be no doubt.

The Dutch, who were the sworn foes of the Portuguese, lost no time in communicating the intercepted letters to the authorities of Japan, and the result was that in 1637 an imperial proclamation decreed that "the whole race of the Portuguese, with their mothers, nurses, and whatever belongs to them, shall be banished forever." The same proclamation forbade, under penalty of death to those concerned, any Japanese ship, or native of Japan, to depart from the country. It directed that any Japanese returning home from a foreign country should be put to death; that any person presuming to bring a letter from abroad should die; that no nobleman or soldier should purchase anything from a foreigner; that any person propagating Christian doctrines, or even bearing the title of Christian, should suffer; and a reward was offered for the discovery of every priest, as well as of every native Christian. Under these severe edicts some of the Portuguese were at once frightened out of the country. Others, however, lingered, cooped up in their factory at Dezima, hoping that the tempest would presently pass over, and that they might resume their traffic. But the Emperor was firmly resolved to root them out forever, and forbade them ever to import even the goods of their own country; and so ended the trade of the Portuguese with Japan, and the toleration of the Christian religion in the Empire.

The writers of the church of Rome assert that it was owing to the malice and misrepresentations of the heretical Dutch that the missionaries and early Japanese converts were exposed to the persecutions, which afterward resulted in the expulsion of Christianity. An examination of dates, however, will show that this statement is entirely erroneous. The Portuguese, clerical and lay, must blame themselves only for their final expulsion. Doubtless, the Dutch, as we shall see presently, were ready enough to give increased impetus, whenever they could, to the tide of calamity which ultimately overwhelmed their rivals, but that tide had commenced its flow, in the form of persecution of Christianity, fully three years before a Dutchman set foot in Japan. It began, as we have said, in the quarrels of the monastic orders themselves.

It would be wrong to leave this brief sketch of the Portuguese relations with Japan without bearing witness to the noble constancy of the thousands of native Christians who were put to death for their religion. The history of Christianity's persecutions contains no more touching chapter than that which records the cruel torments and heroic Christian courage of men, women, and even children, as they bore testimony to the sincerity of their Christian convictions.

THE DUTCH.

It is to an Englishman that the Hollanders are indebted for an introduction to Japan, and for the establishment of their earliest commercial relations. After the grant by the Pope of all the western and about half the eastern hemisphere to the Spaniards and Portuguese, these people, who were then not without naval strength, were unwilling to allow any share of trade to the other powers of Europe; and, whenever they could, they seized their unarmed vessels as contraband, if they found them within the imaginary limits of their Papal grant, confiscated their cargoes, and treated their crews as sea-thieves and smugglers.

The Dutch and English, who had no respect for the Pope's geography, and as little faith in his religion, denied his title to the ownership of the whole earth, and profanely likened him to Satan when he offered to our Lord whole kingdoms, in which he had not title in fee to a single square foot. But as Spain and Portugal were, in the assertion of their title, as much in the habit of relying on powder and ball as on men's conscientious submission to the decrees of the holy father, the Dutch and English rarely sent out their ships, and especially to the "south seas," without taking care to arm them; and commonly they dispatched them in squadrons. Thus, cruising in company, they went wherever they thought they could find a profitable trade; and deemed it a religious duty (which they scrupulously performed) to seize and plunder, whenever they could, any Spanish or Portuguese ship, and to make a descent on their coasts, and burn their colonial towns and villages. Whoever would read the story of their wild, exciting, and often romantic adventures, may find them in Esquemeling's or Burnet's histories of the buccaneers. The hatred between Spain and Portugal on the one side, and the Dutch and English on the other, was intense. Differing in religion, the first named had no gentler epithets to apply to their enemies than "vile Lutherans," "schismatics," "accursed heretics;" while the latter repaid them, by applying the equally mild terms of "lying Papists," "foul idolators," "worshippers of wood and rotten bones." This state of embittered feeling prevailed all through the reigns of Elizabeth, James I., and Charles I. of England, and ceased only in the time of William III., when the peace of Ryswick allowed, on the part of Spain and Portugal, a little freedom of commerce to other nations, who, by the way, were becoming more powerful than the Spaniards and Portuguese on the Pacific and the eastern waters.

It was during this period of national animosity, in the latter part of the reign of Elizabeth, that the Dutch made their way to Japan. A fleet of five sail of Dutch ships, under the command of Jaques Mahu, left the Texel on the 24th of June, 1598. It was sent out by the Indian Company of Holland; and on board of the admiral's ship was William Adams, as pilot. Adams has told his own story with captivating simplicity; and it has been preserved in the pages of that worthy compiler, honest old Purchas. He tells us as follows: "Your worships will understand that I am a *Kentish man*, born in a town called Gillingham, two English miles from Rochester, and one mile from Chatham, where the queen's ships do lie." After stating that he was regularly apprenticed and bred a seaman, he thus proceeds: "I have served in the place of master and pilot in her Majesty's ships, and about eleven or twelve years served the worshipful company of the Barbary merchants, until the Indian traffic from Holland began; in which Indian traffic I was desirous to make a little experience of the small knowledge which God has given me. So, in the year of our Lord God 1598, I hired myself for chief pilot of a fleet of five sail of Hollanders," &c.

But the "little experience" of our English pilot proved both long and sad. Sickness broke out in the ships, the admiral and a great many of the men died; after divers calamities they reached the Straits of Magellan in April, 1599; they were forced, not by any fault of Adams but by the folly of the commander, to winter in the Straits, remaining in them nearly six months, until provisions were exhausted and some of the men actually died of hunger. At length, after getting into the Pacific, storms dispersed the fleet; some were lost, some captured; the savages on the islands where they landed in search of food and water, in more than one instance, lay in ambush and murdered the men; and finally, after great suffering, it was resolved, on Adams' advice, to make for Japan. Of the five ships that had left Holland together there remained but the one of which Adams was pilot. But he kept a stout heart, and at last, on the 11th of April, 1600, he saw the high lands of Japan in the province of Bungo, and on the 12th came to anchor, when there were actually but five men of the whole ship's company able to go about and do duty. They were hospitably received, soldiers were placed on board to prevent a robbery of their goods, a house was provided for the sick, and their bodily wants were all supplied by the prince of Bungo, who sent word to the Emperor of their arrival.

The Portuguese, it will be remembered, were already established in Japan, and one of their commercial depots was at Nagasaki. Five or six days after the arrival of the Dutch, there came from that place a Portuguese Jesuit, with some of his countrymen and some Japanese Christians. The former of these immediately denounced the Hollanders as pirates, denying that they had come for any purposes of trade, as they alleged, though their ship had a full cargo of merchandize on board. This created a prejudice against them in the minds of the Japanese, and the poor Hollanders lived in daily expectation of being put to death. This was precisely what the Portuguese would have been glad to see, influenced by the double motive of hatred of heretics and the wish to monopolize trade. But the case having been submitted to the Emperor, who was then at Osaca, he ordered that Adams and one of the Dutch sailors should be sent to him. He was sent accordingly, and furnishes a long and interesting account of his interview with the monarch, (conducted through the medium of a Portuguese interpreter,) in the course of which Adams had an opportunity of showing the Emperor samples of the merchandize he had brought with him, and of begging that he and his companions might have liberty to trade, as the Portuguese had. An answer was returned in Japanese, but Adams did not understand it, and he was carried to prison, but his comforts seem to have been duly regarded. He remained in prison forty-one days, during all which time, as he subsequently discovered, the Jesuits and Portuguese residents spared no efforts to induce the Emperor to put all the Dutch ship's company to death as pirates. At last the Emperor answered their application with equal justice and good sense, by telling them that, as yet, the Dutch had done no hurt to him or any of his people, and that therefore he had no just cause to take their lives; nor could he find any sufficient reason for such severity as they desired in the fact that wars existed between Portugal and Holland, with which he had nothing to do.

At length he summoned Adams before him again, and asked of him a great many questions. Finally, he enquired of him whether he would like to go to his ship again to see his companions? Upon his answering affirmatively he bade him go, and this was the first intimation Adams had that the ship had been brought by the Emperor's order to Osaca, and that his companions were alive. Everything was now taken out of the vessel, which was ordered to a spot nearer to Jeddo, whither the Emperor had gone. The whole ship's company were liberally provided for at the expense of the government. Presently, they petitioned that they might be permitted to take their vessel and depart, but the Emperor would not consent. Finally, at the expiration of two years, during which time they had been at liberty and mingled freely with the Japanese, they were informed that they could not have their ship any more, and that they must make up their minds to live, for the rest of their days, happily and peacefully in Japan. Hereupon the Dutchmen dispersed themselves, going where they pleased, and living comfortably enough upon the daily allowance made them by the Emperor. Adams, however, remained about the court, and, by his ingenuity and good qualities, soon made friends, and gradually rose in the esteem of the Emperor until he attained to a high position of honor in the country. He taught his majesty some of the principles of mathematics, and built for him two vessels. These things gave to him such commanding influence, that even the Jesuits and Portuguese, who, for the reasons already mentioned, were gradually losing favor, were glad to secure his friendly interposition with the Emperor for their benefit.

At length, in 1609, two armed Dutch ships came to Japan. Their object was to intercept and make prize of the large Portuguese carrack which made the yearly voyage from Macao to Japan with merchandize for the established trade. They were, however, a few days too late for her capture, and so they put in at Firando, and the commanders went thence to the court of the Emperor. Here *William Adams, being the chief negotiator for them*, they were kindly received, and obtained the Emperor's free pass, and permission for their nation to send annually a ship or two for purposes of trade; and this was the beginning of the Dutch commerce with Japan.

Adams, as we have said, rose to high distinction. He thus describes his situation: "Now for my service which I have done and daily do, being employed in the Emperor's service, he hath given me a living like unto a lordship in England, with eighty or ninety husbandmen, who are as my servants and slaves. The precedent was never done before. Thus, God hath provided for me after my great misery; to his name be the praise forever. Amen."

But, with all this external prosperity, poor Adams had a heartsore that could not be healed in Japan. He had left a young wife and two children in England, whom he tenderly loved. Some of the most affecting passages he has written are those in which he alludes to his family, and expresses the dreadful apprehension that he should never see them again. There are such honest, natural outpourings of a true and faithful heart in these passages, that it is impossible to read them without the deepest sympathy. The Emperor was not willing he should go at all. Had he been willing, Adams could not have gone in the Portuguese ships, which were, at first, the only vessels that came annually for trade; but when he had successfully negotiated for the

Dutch, his hopes of once more seeing his family began to revive. He thought that in some of their vessels God might at last provide a way for his return to England. But, though thus saddened at heart, he never lost his self-possession and prudence. He thought that, should he never be able to go himself, he might at least let his beloved family know where he was, and assure them of his unabated affection. From the Dutch ship which came in 1611, he for the first time learned that his countrymen, the English, were carrying on considerable trade in the East Indies, and had made a humble beginning, in the way of factories, on the Malabar coast. He, of course, knew not who of his countrymen might be there, or elsewhere in the east, but whoever or wherever they might be, they were English, and through them he might tell the sad story of his thirteen long years of separation from home and wife and children. He accordingly wrote two long letters, the one addressed to his wife, the other endorsed as follows: "To my unknown friends and countrymen, desiring this letter, by your good means or the news or copy of this letter, may come to the hands of one or many of my acquaintance in Limehouse or elsewhere, or in Kent, in Gillingham by Rochester." The last sentence in this is in these words:

"Thus, in short, I am constrained to write, hoping that by one means or other, in process of time, I shall hear of my wife and children; and so with patience I wait the good will and pleasure of God Almighty, desiring all those to whom this my letter shall come to use the means to acquaint my good friends with it, that so my wife and children may hear of me; by which means there may be hope that I may hear of my wife and children before my death; the which the Lord grant to his glory and my comfort. Amen.

"Done in Japan, the two and twentieth of October, 1611, by your unworthy friend and servant to command in what I can,

"WILLIAM ADAMS."

In both these letters Adams related the principal occurrences that had befallen him since he left the Texel, and from these we have drawn the facts previously related. The letters did reach England, but whether they found his wife and children living, or whether he ever heard from them we cannot tell. As to himself, he might have sadly appropriated the words of the poet:

> "Nor wife nor children more shall he behold,
> Nor friends nor sacred home."

He died at Firando, in Japan, in 1619 or 1620, after having resided there from the year 1600; and we have dwelt the longer on his personal history, not merely on account of its melancholy interest, but because when we come to speak of the doings of his own countrymen in Japan, these letters will be necessary to elucidate our narrative.

Leaving now these letters, we proceed with the history of the Dutch commerce. The first factory of the Hollanders was at Firando, and was on an humble scale. That of the Portuguese was at Nagasaki, on the island Dezima, which is now occupied by the Dutch. The rivalry between the two establishments was, of course, very great, and each sought to injure the other as much as possible with the Japanese authorities. At length, before the close of 1639, the Portuguese were totally expelled the country; and then occurred an act on the part of the Dutch in Japan too clearly proved to admit of denial, and too wicked and infamous to allow of palliation. It was no better than cold blooded murder, prompted by no higher motive than the base love of commercial gain. The facts were these: Though no Portuguese Christian remained in Japan, yet the native Christians were not all extirpated. These poor creatures, deprived of their European teachers, persevered in their faith, though threatened with imprisonment, torture, and death. Oppression presently drove them into open rebellion, and they took refuge and made a stand against the imperial forces in Simabara. The Japanese authorities called on the Dutch to assist them in making war against these Christians, and *the Dutch did it*. Kockebecker was then director of the Dutch trade and nation in Japan. The native Christians had endeavored to fortify themselves in an old town, which the troops of the Emperor could not take. A Dutch ship was lying at Firando, and on board of this Kockebecker repaired to Simabara, and battered the old town with the ship's guns as well as from a battery he had erected on shore. After a fortnight of this work the Japanese were satisfied to discharge the Dutch director; for though the Christians had not surrendered, yet they had lost so many of their number and the place was so weakened that it was obvious it could not hold out much longer. Requiring, therefore, of the Dutch director that he should land six more guns for the use of the Emperor, they dismissed him. The place was finally taken, after a very large number of the besieged had perished by famine, and a total massacre of men, women and children followed; not one was spared.

We have spoken of this act as perpetrated by the Dutch *in Japan*, for we cannot deem it fair to involve every Hollander in an indiscriminate censure. There were other Dutch ships at Firando beside that which was employed in the bombardment; but the commanders of these, either suspecting, or having intimation that the Japanese would demand aid at their hands, quietly left their anchorage, and went to sea before the demand was made, and thus escaped participation in this atrocious wickedness. To us it seems that the infamy must rest chiefly on the Dutch director, and that M. Kockebecker deliberately preferred this most foul murder of the innocent to the loss or interruption of the Dutch trade. Be this as it may, the *fact* is distinctly admitted by all the Dutch writers on Japan from the middle of the seventeenth century up to Fischer's work, published in 1833. It is true, one says, that the Dutch were *compelled* to do it; another states, that the Dutch only supplied cannon, powder, and ball, taught the Japanese artillery practice, and sent ammunition, arms, and troops in their ships to the scene of action; but old Kæmpfer, who, though in the Dutch service as a physician, was by birth a German, affirms positively that the Dutch were active as belligerents. Fraissinet (a recent French writer) endeavors to give a different coloring to the fact, but, as we think, in vain. He represents the case as one of *political* rebellion, in which the native Christians took sides with the rebels; and is pleased to consider the Dutch as *allies* merely of the Emperor, carrying on a lawful war as allies; and he says that the archives of the Dutch factory at Dezima, as well as the relations of natives of respectability, acquit the Hollanders of all blame. What the archives of the Dezima factory may *now* state, we have not the means of knowing, and we are not furnished by the French apologist with their language; but it is certainly very remarkable, if they do contain exculpatory evidence, that the Dutch writers, all of whom were officials at Dezima, and many of whom lived much nearer to the time of the transaction than an author of this day, should have overlooked this evidence; particularly when some of them seek to palliate the act itself. Surely the Dezima records were open to Fischer, the last Dutch writer on the subject, (1833;) why, then, instead of producing them, does he admit the fact, and urge in extenuation *compulsion* of the Dutch by the Japanese? As to the relations of respectable natives, we can only say we have never seen, in any work on Japan, such relations as M. Fraissinet has named. But there is one fact which, as it seems to us, conclusively negatives the supposition that it was a mere *political* insurrection which the Dutch assisted in suppressing. Over the vast common grave in which these unhappy

Christians were buried at Simabara was set up, by imperial order, the following impious inscription: "So long as the sun shall warm the earth, let no Christian be so bold as to come to Japan; and let all know that the King of Spain himself, or the Christian's God, or the great God of all, if he violate this command, shall pay for it with his head."

And now, as to what respectable natives really did say about this sad transaction, let us hear one who was on the spot, honest old Kæmpfer. He was the physician in the Dutch service, and thus writes: "By this submissive readiness to assist the Emperor in the execution of his designs, with regard to *the final destruction of Christianity in his dominions*, it is true, indeed, that we stood our ground so far as to maintain ourselves in the country, and to be permitted to carry on our trade, although the court had then some thoughts of a total exclusion of all foreigners whatsoever. But many generous and noble persons at court, and in the country, judged unfavorably of our conduct. It seemed to them inconsistent with reason that the Dutch should ever be expected to be faithful to a foreign monarch, and one, too, whom they looked upon as a heathen, while they showed so much forwardness to assist him in the destruction of a people with whom they agreed in the most essential parts of their faith, (as the Japanese had been well informed by the Portuguese monks,) and to sacrifice to their own worldly interest those who followed Christ in the very same way, and hoped to enter the Kingdom of Heaven through the same gate. *These are expressions which I often heard from the natives when the conversation happened to turn upon this mournful subject.* In short, by our humble complaisance and connivance, we were so far from bringing this proud and jealous nation to any greater confidence, or more intimate friendship, that, on the contrary, their jealousy and mistrust seemed to increase from that time. They both hated and despised us for what we had done." This, then, is the testimony as to the opinion of the natives who knew something of the occurrences; and it is a sad reflection, that, in the work of excluding Christianity from Japan, Romanists and Protestants alike bore their part. Neither can, with justice, reproach the other. If the worldliness and pride of the Portuguese Christian prompted him to conspiracy, and drove him and his companions from the Empire, the avarice and cruelty of the Dutch professed believer finished the work, and extirpated the last remnant of the faith in the destruction of the native followers of Christ. True Christianity indignantly disowns both.

In 1641, the Dutch were ordered to remove their factory from Firando, where they were comfortable and unrestrained, and to confine themselves to the now forsaken station of the Portuguese at Dezima, a miserable little island in the port of Nagasaki, "more like a prison than a factory," says Kæmpfer. Here they were placed under a surveillance the most rigid, and subjected to many a humiliating degradation. "So great" (says our honest old German) "was the covetousness of the Dutch, and so strong the alluring power of the Japanese gold, that rather than quit the prospect of a trade, (indeed, most advantageous,) they willingly underwent an almost perpetual imprisonment, for such, in fact, is our residence at Dezima, and chose to suffer many hardships in a foreign and heathen country; to be remiss in performing divine service on Sundays and solemn festivals; to leave off praying and singing of psalms; entirely to avoid the sign of the cross, the calling upon the name of Christ in the presence of the natives, and all the outer signs of Christianity; and, lastly, patiently and submissively to bear the abusive and injurious behavior of these proud infidels towards us, than which nothing can be offered more shocking to a noble and generous mind." And to such humiliation have they submitted even to this day. Dezima is shaped like a fan; and the island is, for the most part, of artificial construction. Its greatest length is about 600 feet, and its greatest breadth about 240. A small stone bridge connects it with the town of Nagasaki; at the end of this bridge there is always stationed a strong Japanese guard, and no one passes either to or from the island without license. The whole island is surrounded with a high fence, on the top of which are placed iron spikes. Two water gates, on the north side of the island, are opened to let in the Dutch ships when they arrive, and are at all times kept shut save at the ingress and egress of these vessels. The Dutch are not permitted to build a house of stone on the island, and their miserable habitations are of fir wood and bamboo. The island has on it, at all times, Japanese spies, in the situations of interpreters, clerks, servants, &c., whom the Dutch are obliged to pay; and is beside subject at any moment to the intrusion of the police of Nagasaki. In short, a more annoying and thorough system of imprisonment and espionage was never devised.

When a ship arrives, the first act is to take out of her all her guns and ammunition. She is then searched in every part, and an exact list is made of the goods and everything else she has on board. The crew are then permitted to land on Dezima, where they are kept, as long as the ship remains, under the inspection of guards. Every Japanese official, whose business is with the Dutch at the factory, is bound twice or thrice in a year to take a solemn oath of renunciation and hatred of the Christian religion, and is made to trample under his feet crosses and crucifixes. It is not true, however, as has been stated, that the Dutch also are required to perform this act; but they dare not say openly that they are Christians. A story is told of one who, in the time of the great persecution at Nagasaki, being asked by the Japanese police "if he were a Christian," replied: "No! I am a Dutchman." With such an exhibition of Christianity, who wonders that the Japanese despise it.

Formerly the chief of the factory, with the physician and some other officials at Dezima, visited the Emperor at Jeddo annually, and made to him costly presents. The visit is now quadrennial. On these occasions the Europeans had an opportunity of seeing and knowing something of Japan; and almost all they have published to the world has been gathered in these periodical journeys to the capital. The story, however, is so uniform that we are constrained to believe there is a well defined class of objects and subjects with which alone the strangers are permitted to come into communication.

Kæmpfer says that in his time (1690-'92) the Dutch were allowed, while the ships were away, once or twice in the year, to walk into the country in the neighborhood of Nagasaki; but they were always objects of suspicion and surrounded by spies. At present, (as we learn from Siebold,) if a member of the factory wishes such recreation, he must petition the governor of Nagasaki twenty-four hours beforehand; leave is granted, but the Dutchman is accompanied by a swarm of interpreters, policemen, (*banyoos*, as they are called,) and other official spies to the number of some twenty-five or thirty persons. Each of these, too, may invite as many of his acquaintance as he pleases, and the unfortunate Dutchman must entertain them all. This heavy expense is doubtless designed by the Japanese to prevent the members of the factory from leaving Dezima. Nothing is more obvious than that the Japanese, as a people, have but little respect for the Dutch. Thus, when one of the factory goes out on leave, the boys follow him in a crowd, hooting and shouting, *Holanda! Holanda!* or, as they pronounce it, *Horanda! Horanda!* The gentleman, in pursuit of pleasure and the picturesque, is not allowed to enter any private residence during his ramble, and he must be back at Dezima by sunset. If a Dutchman, at any time, wishes to visit a private acquaintance, or is invited by an inhabitant of Nagasaki to partake of his hospitality, he must present a petition to the governor, and obtain special permission to go; while on the visit, he is surrounded by spies as usual. And to all this humiliation, the Dutch have submitted, for more than two hundred years, for the purpose of securing the monopoly of the Japanese trade!

THE ENGLISH.

We must now remind the reader of the letters written by William Adams, one of which was addressed to any of his countrymen in the east into whose hands Providence might cause it to fall. Adams was, in truth, the founder of the English as he had been of the Dutch trade. The letters he wrote reached Batavia, and were thence sent to London, where they were submitted to a corporation then known as the "Worshipful Fellowship of the Merchants of London, trading into the East Indies," but in later times by the far more celebrated name of the "Honorable East India Company." No time was lost by the corporation in dispatching a ship for Japan, and Purchas has preserved for us the history of the voyage. The vessel was called the Clove, and was commanded by Captain John Saris, who had already made several voyages to the east. Taking on board such a cargo as was deemed suitable, and furnished with a letter from King James I. to the Prince of Firando, and one also, with presents, to the Emperor, Saris left England on the 18th of April, 1611, and stopping and trading at various places on the way, reached Firando on the 11th of June, 1613, when the English met with a most friendly reception from the natives.

Saris found on his arrival that Adams was at Jeddo, nearly 900 miles distant, and immediately put himself in communication with him, desiring him to repair at once to Firando. Until he came he carried on his conferences with the Japanese, by means of a native of the country whom he had picked up at Bantam, and who spoke the Malay language, which Saris understood. Saris delivered the King's letter to the Prince of Firando, Foyne Sama, who received it with pride, but would not open it until Adams (whom they called *Ange*) should arrive to interpret it. The Prince also sent intelligence to the Emperor of the arrival of the Clove.

On the 29th of July Adams arrived, and Saris conferred with him on the subject of trade; and let us hope he had also something to tell him of his wife and children. Early in August Saris left Firando for Jeddo, having in his company Adams and ten other Englishmen. The purpose of the visit was to offer to the Emperor the presents of the English King, and to negotiate a treaty. The Prince of Firando furnished the party with one of his own galleys of fifty oars. Saris gives us the particulars of his journey, which are not without interest, especially as it respects the manners and customs of the people, which (as there were then no restrictions on the intercourse with foreigners, and as he had Adams for a companion) he had ample opportunity of seeing under the most favorable circumstances. At length he had an interview with the Emperor, by whom he was graciously received, and from whom, after some little negotiation between Saris and the Emperor's secretary, he obtained privileges of trade, as follows:

"1. We give free license to the subjects of the King of Great Britain, viz: Sir Thomas Smith, governor, and the company of the East Indian merchants and adventurers, forever safely to come into any of our ports of our Empire of Japan, with their ships and merchandise, without any hindrance to them or their goods; and to abide, buy, sell, and barter, according to their own manner with all nations; to tarry here as long as they think good, and to depart at their pleasure.

"2. We grant unto them freedom of custom for all such merchandises as either now they have brought, or hereafter shall bring into our Kingdoms, or shall from hence transport to any foreign part; and do authorize those ships that hereafter shall arrive and come from England to proceed to present sale of their commodities, without further coming or sending up to our court.

"3. If any of their ships shall happen to be in danger of shipwreck, we will our subjects not only to assist them, but that such part of ship and goods as shall be saved be returned to their captain or cape merchant, or their assigns. And that they shall or may build one house or more for themselves in any part of our Empire where they shall think fittest, and at their departure to make sale thereof at their pleasure.

"4. If any of the English merchants or others shall depart this life within our dominions, the goods of the deceased shall remain at the dispose of the cape merchant; and that all offences committed by them shall be punished by the said cape merchant, according to his discretion; and our laws to take no hold of their persons or goods.

"5. We will that ye our subjects trading with them for any of their commodities pay them for the same, according to agreement, without delay, or return of their wares again unto them.

"6. For such commodities as they have now brought, or shall hereafter bring, fitting for our service and proper use, we will that no arrest be made thereof; but that the price be made with the cape merchant, according as they may sell to others, and present payment upon the delivery of the goods.

"7. If in discovery of other countries for trade, and return of their ships they shall need men or victuals, we will that ye our subjects furnish them for their money as their need shall require.

"8. And that, without other passport, they shall and may set out upon the discovery of Jesso or any other part in or about our Empire."

These certainly were privileges of the most liberal kind, and conclusively show that the original policy of Japan was not at all one of exclusion; and that Europeans may thank themselves for the introduction of that rigorous system which has so long shut her ports against the commerce of nearly all the civilized world. The Japanese, when they discovered that foreigners were conspiring to take their country from them, did not choose to permit it; and, as the shortest mode of preventing it, sent out such foreigners as were in the country, and forbade any more to come in. Now, whatever doubts may be entertained as to the wisdom or expediency of *such* a remedy, no sane man will question the right, or find fault with the desire, of the Japanese to keep Japan for themselves. If, unfortunately, some of the conspirators were European ecclesiastics, they justly paid the penalty of expulsion from the kingdom for making their religion a part of their politics. The blunder was their own, not that of the Japanese.

The Emperor also sent by Captain Saris the following letter to the King of England:

"*To the King of Great Britain:*

"Your Majesty's kind letter sent me by your servant, Captain John Saris, (who is the first that I have known to arrive in any part of my dominions,) I heartily embrace, being not a little glad to understand of your great wisdom and power, as having three plentiful and mighty kingdoms under your powerful command. I acknowledge your Majesty's great bounty in sending me so undeserved a present of many rare things, such as my land affordeth not, neither have I ever before seen, which I receive not as from a stranger, but as from your

Majesty, whom I esteem as myself. Desiring the continuance of friendship with your highness—and that it may stand with your good liking to send your subjects to any part or port of my dominions, where they shall be most heartily welcome, applauding much their worthiness in the admirable knowledge of navigation, having with much facility discovered a country so remote, being no whit amazed with the distance of so mighty a gulf, nor greatness of such infinite clouds and storms, from prosecuting honorable enterprises of discoveries and merchandizing—wherein they shall find me to further them according to their desires. I return unto your Majesty a small token of my love, (by your said subject,) desiring you to accept thereof, as from him that much rejoiceth in your friendship. And whereas your Majesty's subjects have desired certain privileges for trade, and settling of a factory in my dominions, I have not only granted what they demanded, but have confirmed the same unto them under my broad seal for better establishing thereof.

"From my castle in Surunga, this fourth day of the ninth month, in the eighteenth year of our Dairi, according to our computation. Resting your Majesty's friend. The highest commander in this Kingdom of Japan.

"MINNA, MONTTONO. *Yei, ye, yeas.*"

[Iyeyas.]

Three years after this, in 1616, a slight modification was made in the grant of privileges, without, however, injuriously affecting the commercial interests of England. The ships were directed, upon arriving on the coast, to repair to Firando, and carry on all their trade at their factory there. They might, however, in case of opposing winds or bad weather, enter and stay in any harbor of the Kingdom without paying anchorage duties, and though they could not sell, they might freely buy any necessaries their ships required. When Saris returned to England, he left in charge of the factory he had established at Firando Mr. Richard Cockes, who had under his direction eight Englishmen, three Japanese interpreters, and two native servants. Among the Englishmen was Adams, whom the company were very glad to employ at a liberal salary. The Protestant factories—Dutch and English—were thus neighbors at Firando, while the Portuguese were at Dezima, in the harbor of Nagasaki, and bore them no good will.

The English, however, soon gained the friendship and confidence of the natives, and Cockes paid more than one visit to the Emperor at Jeddo. He remained in the country many years, and, as it would appear from his letters, (printed in Purchas,) had ultimately trouble with his Dutch neighbors, who seem to us, at least, to have systematically acted, from the first hour of obtaining foothold in Japan, upon the policy of driving away all European traders but themselves. It is a policy from which (notwithstanding their professions) we think they have never swerved.

The English company, it is probable, made an injudicious selection of merchandise for shipment to Japan; at any rate, from this or some other cause, certain it is that the business did not prove remunerative; and, discouraged by this and some other circumstances, the company, in 1623, after an expenditure of £40,000, voluntarily closed their factory at Firando, and withdrew from the country. But they left with an unstained reputation, and departed with the esteem of the higher classes and the regrets of the more humble. It is useless to indulge in conjecture as to what might have been the present condition of Japan had they remained. Possibly, long ere this, she might have had commercial relations established with the rest of the world. The departure of the English took place before the bloody persecution of the Christians reached its height. They left native Christians in Japan; we are not prepared to believe they would ever have deliberately assisted in their extermination. It was, perhaps, fortunate for them that they were out of the Kingdom before the bombardment of Simabara.

Thirteen years after the abandonment of their factory, the English were disposed to make a new attempt. Accordingly, four vessels were dispatched, but they were ungraciously received at Nagasaki, the only port then open to foreigners, and occupied by the Dutch, and they returned without accomplishing their object. The Dutch were now becoming all-powerful in the east; established on the ruins of the Portuguese dominion at Amboyna and Timor, fortified in Batavia, masters of the Moluccas, Ceylon, the coasts of Malabar and Coromandel, they were not likely to admit a rival among them, and to them the English, without doubt justly, attributed the failure of this attempt to re-establish themselves in Japan.

But they deemed it best, for a time, to keep still; dark days were coming upon England; the country had to pass through the civil wars that marked the reign of the first Charles. It was no time to undertake bold commercial enterprises. The East India Company consequently did but little more for many years than keep up an intercourse with Bantam. They wanted a time of peace and a firmly settled government before they made further efforts.

At length, in 1673, the company renewed its efforts to re-enter Japan. It had received a fresh and much enlarged grant of powers from the King, and was in fact made little less than a sovereign power in the east. The ship that was now sent was called the "Return." A journal, as yet unpublished, was kept of the voyage; and Fraissinet says it is now in the possession of the Southwell family at London. He has had access to it, and furnishes us with many interesting extracts; observing very justly that it strikingly illustrates three particulars—the remarkable circumspection of the Japanese, their extreme opposition to the introduction of any strangers among them, and, above all, their unappeasable hatred of the Portuguese.

Charles II, it will be remembered, had married a princess of Braganza, and was therefore allied to the royal family of Portugal; and the Dutch were by no means backward in communicating this fact to the Japanese. Accordingly, on the appearance of the English ship in the Japanese waters, she was, from this cause alone, viewed with unusual suspicion. We give from the journal alluded to above, or rather from the French version of it, some of the conversations between the English and the Japanese officials.

"Are you English?"

"Yes. We have come here with the permission of our sovereign, the King of England, to carry on trade for the East India Company, and re-establish the commerce which our countrymen commenced with you and left fifty years ago. We have letters from our King, and from the company, to his Majesty the Emperor of Japan;" and with this was handed to the Japanese commissioner a copy of the privileges of trade already set before the reader. This was written in the Japanese character.

The governor next charged the interpreter to ask "if England was at peace with Portugal and Spain; if our King had been long married to the daughter of the King of Portugal; whether there were any children of the marriage; what was our religion, and what sort of merchandize we had?"

We answered that just now we are at peace with all the world; that our King had been married eleven years; that the Queen had no children; that we were Christians as the Dutch were, but not papists. As to our merchandize, the cargo of the ship was a general one.

At the next interview, the governor said, "it is fifty years since the English were here; we should like to know the reason of your long absence." The civil wars of England, two wars with Holland, and the expense and danger of so long a voyage were assigned as reasons and seemed to be satisfactory. The questioning then proceeded:

"Have you none among you who have been in this country before?"

"Not one."

"How, then, were you able to find your way here?"

"By means of marine charts which guided us."

"What is the religion of the Portuguese? is it not called Roman Catholic? have they not the image of a woman whom they call *Santa Maria*, and of a man named *Santo Christo?* do not they worship these images? and how many other saints have they?"

"We cannot answer the last question, not knowing enough of the Roman religion to do so."

"What is your own worship? Have you also images like the Portuguese?"

"No. We are of the *reformed* religion, which is like that of the Dutch. We offer our prayers to none but to Almighty God, the creator of heaven and earth, who fills all things with his presence. We never make any image or figure to represent him."

"Can you tell me who is that *Santo Christo*, and who is that *Santa Maria?*"

"We call the first the son of God, and the last the Virgin Mary; but we never offer prayers to the Virgin."

"How do the Dutch worship God?"

"I have told you, as we do."

"What do they call him?"

"They call him GOD."

"And the Christ?"

"They call him CHRIST?"

"What name do you Dutch and English give to the religion of the Portuguese?"

"We give the name of the 'Roman Catholic religion.'"

"And what to those who profess it?"

"We call them papists, Romans, Roman Catholics."

"What do the Portuguese call you?"

"*Hereyes* in their language, in ours *heretics*."

Just at this moment the British flag was hoisted, when instantly the question was put:

"Why do you hoist your flag to-day, and why have you not done it every day since you came in?"

"To-day is our Sabbath, and it is our custom always to hoist our flag on the return of the seventh day."

"At what times in the day do you pray?"

"Every morning and evening."

"And the Dutch, do they the same?"

"Certainly."

But the St. George's cross in the flag troubled the Japanese, and they made it the subject of many inquiries, desiring to know why it was there.

"We do not carry the cross in our colors from superstition, nor does it have any religious meaning there. It is nothing more than our distinctive sign. Beside, our flag and cross and those of the Portuguese are very different."

"Have you ever been under the dominion of Portugal or Spain?"

"Never. Our sovereign is King of three great States. He is a prince much more powerful than the King of Portugal."

"Is it not then from either of these nations that you have received your cross?"

"We have had it from time immemorial; for six centuries at least."

Notwithstanding all these explanations, however, the Japanese officers, not by command, but privately and as friends, advised the English not to hoist the flag with the cross, as a great many of the people mistook it for the Portuguese standard. At length the answer came from the Emperor, to whom had been referred the English application for a renewal of trade.

"We have received letters from the Emperor. Your request, as well as the reasons by which you enforced it, have been duly considered. But you cannot be allowed to trade here, because your King has married the daughter of the King of Portugal. That is the only reason why your request is refused. The Emperor orders that you depart and come back no more. Such is his will, and we cannot change it in any particular. You will therefore make sail with the first favorable wind, and at the latest within twenty days."

"It is impossible for us to leave before the trade winds change."

"In that case, how much time do you wish us to grant you?"

"Forty-five days; for in that time I suppose we shall have a change."

The English asked permission at least to sell their cargo before going.

"The Emperor forbids it; we dare not disobey. It is your unfortunate alliance with Portugal which stands in your way."

And thus ended this attempt to revive the English trade. It may be that other causes beside the Portuguese marriage operated; and of these the Dutch, it cannot be doubted, would gladly avail themselves; but if there were no other, then it is quite certain that the Hollanders, by communicating this unpropitious fact to the Japanese, were the *sole* cause of the exclusion of the English. And such was the opinion of all on board the "Return."

More than a century elapsed, after this unsuccessful experiment, before the English made another attempt; but in 1791, the "Argonaut," which was employed in the fur trade, on the northwestern coast of America, made an effort to barter with the Japanese. On the arrival of the vessel, however, she was immediately surrounded, according to the usual custom, by lines of boats, and no communication was allowed between the ship and the shore. All that was obtained was wood and water, and with these the "Argonaut" took her departure.

In 1803 the "Frederick," an English merchantman, was sent from Calcutta with a cargo to Japan, but was refused admittance to the harbor, and was ordered to depart within twenty-four hours. This unceremonious treatment of the English was, undoubtedly, owing to the Dutch. England had made great conquests in India, and securely established her power in the east; some of these conquests, too, were made at the expense of the Dutch. Under Clive and Warren Hastings all the fond anticipations the Hollanders had formed of a foothold in India had been dissipated. They could not accomplish their wishes, but they could use the very triumphs of their rivals as an instrument in defeating the English efforts to increase their trade. This was to be effected by awakening the jealousy and alarming the apprehensions of the Japanese. These last were uncommonly well informed of the progress of events in India, from the time of Clive downward. Where could they have learned them but from the Dutch? The Hollanders told the story with such coloring as suited them; whitewashing their own disgraces and defeats, and covering with blackness the acts of their successful rivals. They thus taught the Japanese to form an idea of the English character and ambition perfectly fatal to the establishment of friendly relations. And, unfortunately, in many instances, (one of which, in Japan, we shall detail directly,) the English were furnishing them, from time to time, with abundant material. We do not mean to apologize for England's misdoings in the east; but we do mean to impute to the Dutch the seeming pursuit, from the very beginning, of a uniform system of policy, which, whether it be so or not, appears, at least, to have sought the exclusion of Portuguese, English, Americans, and every other commercial nation in Christendom, from any participation in the trade with Japan, of which, at the price of a servility utterly unworthy of the noble deeds of Holland's past history, she had procured the monopoly.

The next English visit we have to record is that of an armed ship-of-war, in 1808. In October of that year an European vessel, with Dutch colors, appeared off Nagasaki. It was the time when the usual Dutch trader was expected, and M. Doeff was then director of the factory at Dezima. Supposing it to be the expected annual trader from Batavia, two of the employés of the factory, one of whom was a book-keeper, named Gozeman, put off to the ship; according to Doeff's account, the native interpreters, who never went on board, reported on their return that the ship's boat put off on the approach of the boat containing the two Dutch clerks, as if to meet them; and that the crew of the ship's boat had weapons concealed on their persons. The Japanese boat, with the interpreters, was astern of that from the factory. As the boats approached that of the Dutchmen was boarded from the other and the two employés were forcibly carried, as prisoners, on board the ship. Be this as it may, certain it is that Gozeman and his companion did not return, and that they were detained on board of the strange vessel. The Japanese could not conceal their astonishment, nor understand how Hollanders, in that part of the Kingdom where they were permitted to be, and lawfully employed, too, could be thus treated by men sailing under the Dutch flag. Doeff, however, instantly suspected that the vessel was English, and he knew that war then existed between his own country and England.

The governor of Nagasaki, enraged beyond measure, had driven the Japanese interpreters from his presence, and bade them not dare appear before him again without Gozeman and his companion; and instantly set about making preparations for repelling a warlike attack. But, to his horror, he discovered that, at a strong point on the harbor, where there should have been a garrison of a thousand men, nearly all were absent without leave; the commander was away, and not more than sixty or seventy soldiers could be mustered. Though it was not the governor's duty to command this point in person, yet to him belonged its oversight; and from the moment he discovered its condition he considered himself as a dead man.

At eleven o'clock that night, Doeff received a note in the hand-writing of one of the detained Dutchmen, in these words: "The ship has come from Bengal. The captain's name is Pellew; he wants water and provisions." The vessel was H. M. S. Phæton, belonging to the squadron of Admiral Drury, cruising in the eastern seas. As we have said, England was at war with Holland, which at that time was a mere dependency of France. The admiral had ordered Captain Fleetwood Pellew to cruise off the Japanese islands, for the purpose of intercepting the Dutch traders to Nagasaki. Captain Pellew, after cruising for a month, supposed that the Dutch vessels might have reached the harbor of Nagasaki, and put in to that port in the hope of finding them there.

Doeff did not dare to send off water and provisions without the concurrence of the Japanese governor; and when the latter asked his advice about acceding to the request, he declined giving it, and said he could give no support to any request made by one whom he now knew to be the enemy of his country.

In the midst of the embarrassment and confusion of the poor governor, his first secretary made his appearance to submit a proposition, strikingly characteristic of some of the traits of Japanese character: "This," said he, "is my plan. The foreign ship has entrapped the Dutchmen by treachery; therefore, all means are lawful to punish the treachery. I will contrive, then, to go on board alone under the guise of friendly professions. I will demand of the captain the two Dutchmen; if he will not surrender them, I will strike him dead, and then immediately kill myself with a dagger which I will conceal in my bosom. I know that assassination is repugnant to our national character; but the English commander, who has thus dishonorably invaded our country to attack those whose flag he has usurped for his protection, is worthy of no better fate. In short, to punish him, I am quite willing to sacrifice my life."

M. Doeff, however, represented to him that the consequence of this plan would certainly be his own death, and probably that of the two Dutchmen on board the ship; and the governor concurring in this view, the secretary abandoned his desperate scheme.

The plan next considered, was to detain the ship on one pretext or another, until the forces of the neighboring princes could be collected for an attack. In the course of the day, however, Gozeman was sent on shore with a note, as follows: "I have ordered my own boat to set Gozeman on shore to procure me water and provisions. If he does not return before evening, I will enter the harbor early to-morrow morning, and burn the Japanese and Chinese vessels that may be there."

Gozeman's story was, that when he was taken on board, he demanded to see the commander, whereupon he was carried before a youth, seemingly some eighteen or nineteen years old, who, taking him into the cabin, asked him whether there were any Dutch ships in Japan, threatening him with the severest punishment if he should deceive him. Gozeman told him truly, that the Dutch ships had not arrived that year. The commander, however, pretended to know better; accused the Dutchman of having spoken untruly, and said he would enter the harbor, and see for himself, and, in case he found any, Gozeman might consider himself a dead man. Accordingly, he did enter in his boat, and made examination, and on his return, told Gozeman it was fortunate for him that his statement had been found true. He then sent him on shore with the note given above, instructing him to return, whether he obtained the supplies or not, and informing him that if he did not come back, his companion, who was kept on board, should be hanged.

The governor was transported with rage when he heard this story, but was finally induced by what Doeff said to him to send off water and provisions by Gozeman. Soon after the two Dutchmen were sent on shore in safety. And now the Japanese governor employed himself in taking measures to detain the ship (as was his duty) until the pleasure of the government could be known. But how to do this was a question not very easy of solution. Doeff was again consulted, when he did not conceal the difficulty, not to say the impossibility, of the capture by the Japanese of a British frigate, in a perfect state of warlike equipment. One plan was suggested by the prince of Omura, who promised to take the lead in its execution, and the Japanese by no means lacked the courage necessary to attempt it. They are a brave race. The plan was to man three hundred boats loaded with reeds and straw and other combustibles, to surround the frigate and burn her. The calculation was that if the English destroyed two hundred of the boats, enough would still be left to effect the object. The rowers were to save themselves by swimming.

But Doeff advised another course. He recommended to the governor to amuse the commander of the ship by promises of water the next day, so as to detain him as long as possible, and to improve the time by causing a number of native boats to go with stones and throw them into the narrow channel by which alone the ship could pass out to the open sea. This he hoped could be done, without discovery by the English, in the course of the next day and night; and the work was ordered; but before anything was accomplished, a favorable wind sprung up, and the Phæton stood out to sea.

MacFarlane thinks that, anywhere but in Japan, the whole affair, having terminated bloodlessly, would have been laughed at as a clever *ruse de guerre*; but it was no matter for mirth to the unfortunate Japanese officials. The law of the Kingdom had been broken, and the consequence was inevitable. In half an hour after the ship made sail, the governor of Nagasaki was dead by his own hand; he had followed the custom of the country and disembowelled himself. The officers of the neglected garrison did the same thing; the interpreters were ordered to Jeddo, and never were seen again in Nagasaki; nor could the Dutch ever learn their fate; and this "*laughable*" ruse cost no less than thirteen Japanese lives. The governor of the province (Fizen) was the officer who had supreme command of the troops that belonged to the garrison; and was, at the time of the Phæton's arrival, residing, compulsorily, in the distant capital, (Jeddo,) yet was he punished by an imprisonment of one hundred days for the delinquency of his subordinate officers. The visit of the British frigate therefore brought in its train very sad consequences, creating very strong prejudices against the English, and to this hour it is remembered in Japan with embittered feelings.

Five years had elapsed after the visit of the English frigate before another attempt was made. During that period the wars of Europe had cut off the Dutch at Dezima, not only from communication with Holland and her colonies, but with all the rest of the world. They were in profound ignorance of all that had passed in this interval outside of Japan.

In July, 1813, they heard with joy that two European ships under the Dutch flag were off the port. They showed also the private Dutch signal, so that M. Doeff had no doubt they were the long expected vessels that had come from Batavia for the annual trade. Letters also were sent on shore to the factory, from which he learned that M. Waardenar, formerly president of the factory, and under whose patronage and friendship M. Doeff had commenced his career as an employé at Dezima, was on board one of the ships in the capacity of commissary of the government, with his secretary and physician; and that on board the other was M. Cassa, accompanied by three assistants, and charged to replace M. Doeff.

Immediately the storekeeper, Blomhoff, with another of the Dezima officials, (they had but three left in the whole factory,) put off to meet the ships; and, on their return, Blomhoff told Doeff that M. Waardenar was indeed on board, and that the Dutch captain, Voorman, who had often been to Dezima before, commanded; "but," added he, "everything aboard wore a strange aspect; and the commissary, instead of confiding to me, as usual, the papers from the government, said he would deliver them to you in person." Presently the vessels came into harbor; and as all the crew spoke English, the Japanese, who had been accustomed to hear that language since 1795, concluded that the vessels were American, and that they had been hired at Batavia by the Dutch, who they knew had sometimes sought to carry on their commerce, without risk of capture, under the flag of the United States. To ascertain the truth, M. Doeff himself went on board, when M. Waardenar met him with evident embarrassment, and handed him a letter. The Dutch director saw that there was something not yet intelligible to him, and prudently declined opening the letter until he should reach the factory, whither he soon returned accompanied by Waardenar and his secretary.

When they reached Dezima, Doeff opened the letter in the presence of Blomhoff and of Waardenar and his secretary. It was signed "Raffles, Lieutenant Governor of Java and its Dependencies," and announced that M. Waardenar was appointed commissary in Japan, with supreme power over the factory. The poor director was utterly bewildered. In his long isolation great events, and among them the utter absorption of his own nation into that of France, and the subjugation of all the Dutch colonies, had occurred; and he asked in amazement, "Who is Raffles?" Then was opened to him the last five years of European history, and he learned that Holland no longer had an independent national existence, and that Java belonged to England; that Sir Stamford Raffles, who ruled there, had appointed Waardenar and Dr. Ainslie, an Englishman, as commissioners in Japan, and required of him a surrender of everything into their hands. It was an ingenious but most hazardous attempt on the part of Raffles to transfer the trade which the Dutch had so long monopolized to the hands of the English.

Doeff instantly refused compliance, on the ground that Japan was no dependency of Java, and could not be affected by any capitulation the Dutch might have made on the surrender of that island; and further, that if Java was now an English island, then the order to him came from an authority to which he, as a Dutchman, acknowledging no allegiance to England, certainly owed no obedience. Doeff, who was exceedingly shrewd, saw also in an instant that the ships and crews were completely at his mercy. He had but to tell the Japanese the facts he had just learned, and, exasperated as they were by the affair of the Phæton, the destruction of the ships and their crews would inevitably follow. He saw his advantage, and shaped his course accordingly. Fraissinet (who in his work on Japan is very much of an apologist for the Dutch in all cases) represents this conduct on the part of M. Doeff as an example of exalted humanity and patriotism; while MacFarlane intimates that, such was the hatred of Doeff to the English, he would probably have denounced the ships to the Japanese but for the fact that M. Waardenar was his countryman, his friend, and early benefactor. We cannot undertake to arbitrate between these conflicting views, our business is to record the fact that, in the exercise either of loyalty, or friendship, or humanity, as the case may be, he contrived to preserve, in all its purity, the high reputation of the Dutch for taking care of their commercial interests in Japan, at any expense, particularly when such expense could be made to fall upon others.

The Dutch factory had for five years been without its annual supplies from Batavia, and had consequently been obliged to contract a large debt to the Japanese for their support during this long period. M. Doeff, after working upon the fears of Waardenar and Ainslie by a threat of exposure to the Japanese, induced them to enter into an arrangement with him, and to bind themselves in writing to the fulfilment of the contract, which was in substance this: In the first place, the ships were to be passed off as being American, employed by the Dutch, for the sake of obtaining the protection of the neutral flag of the United States. Secondly, the presence of M. Waardenar, well known to the Japanese as a Dutchman, and formerly President of Dezima, was to give countenance to this view. Thirdly, M. Doeff demanded as the price of holding his tongue, that is, as the price of saving the lives of Waardenar and the English, that the cargoes of the two ships should be delivered to him, as Dutch factor, in the usual manner; that he should dispose of them, and out of the proceeds pay first all that Holland owed the Japanese for the supplies of the last five years. The surplus was to be applied to the purchase of copper, to load the ships as far as possible, though the copper was to be estimated at more than the usual price to the English purchasers. Finally, it was provided that when the ships reached Batavia and sold the copper, twenty-five thousand rix dollars were to be placed to the *personal credit* of M. Doeff. On these terms the Dutch director connived at the imposition of a deception upon the Japanese, and successfully managed to secure the silence of such of the interpreters as he could not help trusting with the secret. The ships were loaded and dispatched as soon as possible, and they certainly encountered no small risk while they remained at Dezima; for the son of that governor of Nagasaki who killed himself about the affair of the Phaeton was now a man of office and influence at Jeddo, and would undoubtedly have availed himself of the opportunity, had he known it existed, to avenge his father's death.

Sir Stamford Raffles is generally supposed by his best friends to have made a mistake in sending these ships. If Doeff had surrendered the factory, the probability is that as soon as the Japanese discovered it to be transferred, and that, too, without consulting them, they would have destroyed Dezima, and put all the English there to death.

In 1814, however, Raffles sent Cassa back in one of the ships, (Waardenar was probably too wise to put his neck into the halter again,) when the same stratagem was resorted to, the same commercial profit was secured by the wily Dutchman, and Cassa failed entirely in superseding M. Doeff as director of Dezima. The latter was more than a match for him in the game of cunning and trickery by which each sought to countermine the stratagems of the other. Doeff kept Dezima; and for a time the flag of Holland floated nowhere else in the world but on that distant spot, where it was unfurled by sufferance only. At last, after the restoration of the house of Orange, and the return of Java to the Dutch, the old trade was resumed, and Doeff was succeeded by a new director.

In 1818, another attempt was made in a little vessel of sixty-five tons, that was commanded by Captain Gordon, of the British navy. She entered the bay of Jeddo, and was immediately surrounded with the usual line of boats. Her rudder was unshipped, and all her arms and ammunition were taken ashore. The interpreters, one of whom spoke Dutch, and one Russian, and both some English, inquired if the Dutch and English were now friends, and if the vessel belonged to the East India Company? They were quite civil, but utterly refused all presents and trade. The last English visit, prior to the time of the United States expedition under Commodore Perry, was in May, 1849. This was made by H. M. S. "Mariner," under Commander Matheson. She went to Oragawa, about twenty-five miles from Jeddo, but nothing of importance resulted from the visit.

THE RUSSIANS.

The efforts of Russia to obtain foothold in Japan commenced in the latter part of the last century. Her possessions in Asia, her seizure and occupation of some of the Kurile islands which belonged to Japan, and her small portion of territory in America, in the colony at Sitka, have placed her on every side of the Japanese Empire but the south. She has pursued her policy noiselessly; possibly meaning at the proper time to make her communications as complete as circumstances will allow between her Asiatic and American possessions. With Corea, Japan, and the Aleutian islands, stretching over to the promontory of Alaska on our northwest coast, and with a strong point at Sitka, she might be in a situation to show the world that her plans of extension were by no means confined to the limits of the Eastern hemisphere. With harbors on the coasts of Eastern Asia and Western America, opening on a sea which must be the seat of an immense and lucrative commerce, she might aim to be a great maritime power, and to rule mistress of the Pacific. If she possessed Japan, she would have an abundance of harbors, unrivalled in the world for excellency, and with her resources would control the commerce of the Pacific. It is not, therefore, the interest of any part of the commercial world that Russia should ever own Japan: but Russia has, doubtless, long seen the importance to her of its acquisition. If she aims at being a commercial nation, the possession of Japan would make her eminently so.

Some seventy or eighty years ago, a Japanese vessel was wrecked on one of the Aleutian islands belonging to Russia. The crew was rescued, and was carried to the Russian port of Okotsk, or Irkutzk. But, instead of being sent hoem at once, they were detained in Russia ten years. The object undoubtedly was, that the Japanese and Russians might learn each others' languages. It seemed to be a small matter, but it had a specific end. At last, the discovery was made that it would be humane to attempt, at least, the return of these poor shipwrecked Japanese to their country. Russia, probably, was ignorant that they would be refused admission. Had they been sent ten years before, the consequences would have been the same; but Russia did not know this; and beside, her later effort deprives her of any apology for her tardy humanity.

The Empress Catharine, however, directed the governor of Siberia to send them back, and to endeavor, through their instrumentality, to establish such mutual relations as might tend to the benefit of both nations. He was ordered to dispatch an envoy, in his own name, with credentials and suitable presents; and was expressly forbidden to permit any Englishman or Dutchman to be employed in the work. A Russian lieutenant, named Laxman, was the agent employed, and in the autumn of 1792, he sailed from Okotsk, in a transport ship called the "Catharine." He soon made a harbor on the northern coast of the island of Jesso, and there wintered; in the succeeding summer he went round to the southern coast of the same island and entered the harbor of Hakodadi. The Japanese were polite, but refused to take back their countrymen, informing Laxman that it was against their laws. They also told him that he had subjected himself and his crew, as being foreigners, to perpetual imprisonment for landing anywhere in the Kingdom except at the appointed port of Nagasaki; yet, in consideration of the Russian ignorance of this law, and of their kindness to the shipwrecked Japanese, they would not enforce the law, provided Lieutenant Laxman would promise for himself and his countrymen to return immediately to his own country, and never again come to any part of Japan but Nagasaki.

Laxman left without landing the Japanese, and the Empress Catharine made no further attempt during her reign. In 1804, her grandson, the Emperor Alexander, renewed the effort. A government ship, commanded by Krusenstern, was sent to Nagasaki, having on board Resanoff, sent as special ambassador to Japan. He had hardly arrived, however, before he furnished abundant evidence of his unfitness for the delicate mission with which he was intrusted. He commenced his intercourse with the Japanese officials by a dispute on a ridiculous point of etiquette, viz: whether he should make a bow to the Emperor's representatives. Next he positively refused to surrender the arms of the ship, according to the usual custom, though it was perfectly useless to retain them, as he had given up all the ammunition to the Japanese. He then very foolishly contrived to convince the inmates of the Dutch factory at Dezima, to whom he brought letters, that he suspected them of secretly intriguing to defeat his purposes with the Japanese; while, in point of fact, the sagacious Dutchman, Doeff, who had charge of Dezima, was exercising all his ingenuity to pursue such a nicely balanced system of non-committal, that, let the mission terminate as it would, he might be able to exclaim, "thou canst not say, *I* did it," and to turn events to the advantage of himself and his countrymen. But, at last, the ship was brought into safe anchorage, within the harbor; and after a great deal of negotiation and delay, consent was given that the Russian ambassador might live on land until an answer to his message was received from the Emperor at Jeddo. An old fish warehouse was cleaned out and prepared for his reception, and surrounded with a high fence of bamboos. At last, when he was summoned to go to Nagasaki to hear the Emperor's answer to his application, curtains were hung before the houses on each side of the street through which he passed, and the inhabitants were all ordered to keep out of sight, so that he saw nothing of the place. Indeed, as we read the account of Resanoff's mission, it is hard to resist the belief, that the Japanese took pleasure in mortifying the ambassador, and in overwhelming him, at the same time, with an affectation of great personal politeness. They kept him waiting, too, until 1805 for his answer; when it came, it was peremptory enough. "Order from the Emperor of Japan to the Russian ambassador." "Formerly, our Empire had communication with several nations; but experience caused us to adopt, as safe, the opposite principle. It is not permitted to the Japanese to trade abroad; nor to foreigners to enter our country." * * * "As to Russia, we have never had any relations with her. Ten years ago, you sent certain shipwrecked Japanese to Matsmai, and you then made us propositions of alliance and commerce. At this time you have come back to Nagasaki, to renew these propositions. This proves that Russia has a strong inclination for Japan. It is long since we discontinued all relations with foreigners generally. Although we desire to live in peace with all neighboring States, the difference between them and us, in manners and character, forbids entirely treaties of alliance. Your voyages and your labors are, therefore, useless." * * * "All communications between you and us are impossible, and it is my imperial pleasure that, henceforth, you no more bring your ships into our waters."

Resanoff departed, the Japanese paying all the expenses of the embassy while it was in Japan. It is easy to understand how the indignant Russian envoy immediately resolved to be revenged for the treatment he had received. He gave way to his angry feelings, and proceeding to Kamtschatka, directed two Russian naval officers, Chwostoff and Davidoff, who happened to be there in the temporary command of two armed merchantmen that traded between Asia and the northwest coast of America, to make a hostile landing upon the most northern Japanese islands, or their dependencies. He, himself, started for St. Petersburg, and died on the way.

The Russian officers did make a descent upon one of the southern Kurile islands that belonged to Japan. That Empire had once owned the whole Kurile archipelago; but Russia had contrived, by some means, to possess herself of the northern islands; and it was doubtful to the Dutch whether this appropriation of territory was even known at Jeddo. It is said not to be unlikely that the prince of these islands, (thus taken by Russia,) and his spy secretaries, deemed it expedient to conceal from the Emperor this loss of a territory, of but little value, rather than make known an event which would be deemed disgraceful to Japan, and subject them to punishment. If this be so, they had, of course, to buy up the spies of government. The islands were of but little value except from *position*. It was precisely on account of their position that Russia desired them. On the southern Kuriles, however, their officers landed, and wreaked their vengeance on the unoffending inhabitants, by plundering their villages, killing some of the people, and carrying off others in their vessels. This was in 1807.

The news of these events filled the Japanese court with surprise and indignation; and they sought, through the medium of the Dutch, to find out whether they had been authorized by the Emperor of Russia. Some time after, in May, 1811, Captain Golownin, of the Russian navy, was sent in the sloop-of-war "Diana," ostensibly to make a survey of the Kurile group, though it was suspected (not proved) that he had ulterior objects, and was instructed once more to attempt the establishment of commercial relations. When he came to the island Eeterpoo (which Siebold calls Ietorop) he landed, supposing he would find Kuriles only: but he was met by a Japanese officer and soldiers, who asked him if the Russians meant to treat them as Chwostoff and Davidoff had treated another island some few years before? Golownin, on this, thought it best to get away as soon as he could. He then went to an island called Kunaschier, and here the Diana was fired upon. Golownin, however, strove to show them that his purposes were friendly, and was finally, by the cunning of the Japanese, tempted to land with only a midshipman, pilot, four Russian seamen, and a Kurile interpreter. All were made prisoners, and passed through various adventures, which Golownin has recorded. They were kept prisoners for a long time, avowedly in retaliation for the injuries that had been committed to gratify the angry feelings of Resanoff; nor would the Japanese release them until they were satisfied that these injuries had not been ordered by the Russian Emperor. When Golownin left he was furnished with a document warning the Russians no more to attempt the impossibility of establishing trade with Japan. It is but just to the Japanese to add that Golownin, notwithstanding all his sufferings, unavoidable in a state of imprisonment, gives to the people of Japan a high character for generosity and benevolence.

Thus ended the efforts of Russia, until within a very recent period, of which we shall speak presently.

THE UNITED STATES OF AMERICA.

The attempts of our own country are all recent, and need not detain us long. In the year 1831 a Japanese junk was blown off the coast, and, after drifting about for some time in the Pacific, at length went ashore on the western coast of America, near the mouth of the Columbia river. Kindness was shown to the shipwrecked Japanese, and finally they were carried to Macao, where they received the protection and care of the American and English residents. It was determined, after a time, to return the poor creatures to their home. Either their benevolent friends were ignorant of the Japanese law which prohibited the return of natives to Japan, or, if they knew it, they supposed that, at any rate, those who went to Japan on such an errand of mercy would not be molested for entering one of the harbors of the Empire. Accordingly the "Morrison," an American merchantman, was fitted out by the American house of King for the voyage to Japan; and the more effectually to manifest her purely pacific purposes, all her guns and armament were taken out. In 1837 she made the voyage, notes of which have been published by Mr. C. W. King, an American merchant of great respectability, who sailed in the "Morrison." The ship reached the bay of Jeddo, and the Japanese very soon found out that she was entirely unarmed and defenceless. The official visitors soon showed their contempt after making this discovery, and early the next day the vessel was fired at with shotted guns. She immediately weighed anchor and ran to Kagosima, the principal town of the island of Kiu-sin, where she again came to anchor. After a while preparations were made here, also, to fire upon the vessel, and before she could remove, a battery opened upon her. The ship then returned to Macao with the Japanese on board.

In 1846 an expedition was sent from the government of the United States to Japan; its business was, if possible, to open negotiations with the Empire. The ships consisted of the "Columbus," of ninety guns, and the corvette "Vincennes." Commodore Biddle commanded the expedition. In July the vessels reached the bay of Jeddo, and were, as usual, immediately surrounded by the lines of guard boats. On this occasion they numbered about four hundred. Some of the Japanese went on board the "Vincennes," and one of them placed a stick with some sort of a symbol carved on it at the head of the vessel and another of similar kind at the stern. The act was not perfectly understood by the Americans, but they construed it to mean taking possession of the ship, and ordered the sticks to be taken away. The Japanese complied immediately without making any objection. The ships remained ten days, but no one belonging to them landed, nor was anything accomplished. The answer of the Emperor to the application for license to trade was very short: "No trade can be allowed with any foreign nation except Holland."

In February of the year 1849 the United States ship Preble, under Commander Glynn, formed part of the American squadron in the China seas, when information was received, by way of Batavia, of the detention and imprisonment, in Japan, of sixteen American seamen, who had been shipwrecked on the coast of some of the Japanese islands. The Preble was immediately dispatched to demand their release. As the ship neared the coast of Japan, signal guns were fired from the prominent headlands to give warning of the approach of a strange vessel; and when she entered the harbor of Nagasaki, she was met by a number of large boats which ordered her off, and indeed attempted to oppose further ingress. But the ship steadily standing on with a firm breeze soon broke their ranks, and came to anchor in a desirable position.

Fleets of boats, crowded with soldiers, shortly afterward began to arrive, and from that time until the Preble's departure, they poured in, in one constant stream, day and night. The troops they brought were encamped on the elevated shores surrounding the anchorage of the Preble. From these heights also were unmasked, at intervals, batteries of heavy artillery, numbering in all sixty guns, which were trained upon the Preble's decks.

Commander Glynn forthwith commenced negotiations for the release of the American seamen, who had been imprisoned for nearly seventeen months, and been treated with great cruelty and inhumanity. When they were first confined, they were made to trample on the crucifix, and were told that it was the "devil of Japan," and that if they refused to trample on it their lives should be taken. When Commander Glynn first demanded the release of the prisoners, the Japanese officials treated the demand with a well affected, haughty indifference; finding, however, that this would not answer, they resorted to evasive diplomacy; when the captain of the Preble, with the rough bluntness of a sailor, peremptorily told them, in most unmistakeable language, that they must immediately give up the men, or means would be found to compel them to do so, as the government to which they belonged had both the power and the will to protect its citizens. This very soon changed their tone, and deprecating any angry feeling, a

INTRODUCTION.

promise was immediately made that the men should be sent on board in two days from that time. This promise having been fulfilled to the letter, the Preble returned to join the squadron on the coast of China. The next effort made by the government of the United States was that of which the story is told in the subsequent pages of this work.

We have thus laid before the reader the chief features of the principal attempts made by civilized nations to open commerce with Japan; and, in the following tabular view, these may be seen at a glance, and thus, by showing what efforts were simultaneous, we may facilitate, perhaps, the understanding of the subject as a whole.

YEAR.	PORTUGUESE.	DUTCH.	ENGLISH.	RUSSIAN.	UNITED STATES.
1543–'45	First landing				
1550	Christianity introduced				
1597	Persecution of Christianity begins				
1600		First arrival			
1609		License to trade			
1613			Saris reaches Firando		
			License to trade		
			Factory at Firando		
1623			Leave Japan		
1636			Futile attempt to renew trade		
1639	Expelled from Japan.	Assist in persecuting native Christians			
1641		Sent to Dezima			
1673			Attempt again to renew trade		
1791			"*Argonaut's*" futile attempt		
1792				Laxman's visit	
1803			"*Frederick's*" attempt		
1804				Resanoff's mission	
1807				Descent on Kuriles	
1808			"*Phætons*" visit under Pellew		
1811				Captivity of Captain Golownin	
1813		Defeat Raffles' attempt	Sir S. Raffles' attempt		
1814		Defeat Raffles' attempt	Attempt repeated		
1818			Gordon's attempt		
1837					"Morrison's" visit
1846					Com. Biddle's visit
1849			"*Mariner's*" visit		Glynn, in the Preble.
1852					Com. Perry's visit

SECTION VI.

PROGRESS IN INDUSTRIAL ARTS, AND EXTENT OF CIVILIZATION IN JAPAN.

The Japanese are an exceedingly industrious and ingenious people, and in certain manufactures are surpassed by no nation.

Metals.—They work well in iron, copper, gold, and silver, and, indeed, in all the metals they have. Of iron, it is supposed the supply afforded by their country is not large; still they have extracted the metal from such ores as they possess, and wrought it into shape. Copper is very abundant, and they understand perfectly well the mode of treating the ore, and preparing the metal for market or for manufactures. Gold also exists, and probably to an extent as yet undeveloped; the deposits are likely, we think, to prove large on further and scientific exploration. At any rate, there does not seem now to be any scarcity of it for the purposes to which they apply it. They have silver mines which they work. They know, too, how to make some combinations of metals which produce a beautiful effect. Thunberg tells us that they work with great skill in what they call *sowas*. This is a mixture of gold and copper, which they color with *tousche*, or ink, making it a fine blue or black, by an art unknown among Europeans. They make steel, and temper their sword blades admirably. Clocks and watches are also made by them, but in these they are not entitled to the merit of invention; they have copied from European models. The same may be said of their astronomical instruments; they make very well the metallic portion of telescopes, &c., and buy mirror glasses from the Dutch, which they grind into suitable lenses. They also manufacture excellent metallic mirrors; and Golownin says, he saw carpenters' and cabinet-makers' tools, particularly saws, made in Japan, quite equal to any English tools of a similar kind. They are exceedingly quick in observing any improvement brought in among them by foreigners, soon make themselves masters of it, and copy it with great skill and exactness. They are very expert in carving metal, and can cast metal statues. Their copper coinage is well stamped, for they are good die-sinkers; and several of their operations in metal are carried on in very large and well-ordered manufactories.

Wood.—No people work better than they can in wood and bamboo, and they possess one art in which they excell the world. This is in lacquering wood work. Other nations have attempted for years, but without success, to equal them in this department. In this operation they select the finest wood of fir or cedar to be covered with varnish. They get the gum from which they prepare the varnish from the *rhus vernix*—a tree that is abundant in many parts of their country. On puncturing the tree the gum oozes out, of a light color, and of the consistence of cream, but on exposure to the air grows thicker and blacker. It is so transparent, that when laid unmixed on wood, the grain and every mark on the wood may be seen through it. They obviate this, however, where it is desirable, by placing beneath the varnish a dark ground, one element in the composition of which is the fine sludge caught in the trough under a grindstone. They also use for the purpose minutely pulverized charcoal, and sometimes leaf gold ground very fine. They then ornament the varnish with figures and flowers of gold and silver. They make, and thus varnish, screens, desks, caskets, cabinets, and other articles, exceedingly beautiful, and of which specimens may from time to time be seen in Europe and in this country. It is, said, however, that the best samples never are sent out of the Kingdom.

Glass.—They know how to make this article, and can manufacture it now for any purpose, both colored and uncolored. Formerly they did not know how to make the flat pane for window glass; and probably what they make is an inferior article, as they still purchase thick mirror glass from the Dutch to grind into lenses.

Porcelain.—This they make, and some say in greater perfection than the Chinese can. At any rate, specimens we have seen of Japanese porcelain are very delicate and beautiful; though some writers tell us, that, owing to the exhaustion of the best clay, they cannot now manufacture such as they once could.

Paper.—Of this they make an abundance, as well for writing and printing, as for tapestry, handkerchiefs, packing cloths for goods, &c. It is of different qualities, and some of it is as soft and flexible as our cotton cloth. Indeed, that used for handkerchiefs might be mistaken for cloth, so far as toughness and flexibility are concerned. The material of which it is made is the bark of the mulberry, (*morus papyrifera*,) and the process is described as follows: In December, after the tree has shed its leaves, they cut off the branches about three feet in length, and tie them up in bundles. They are then boiled in a ley of ashes in a covered kettle till the bark is so shrunk that half an inch of the wood may be seen projecting at either end of the branch. When they have become cool, the bark is stripped off and soaked in water three or four hours until it becomes soft, when the fine black skin is scraped off with a knife. The coarse bark is then separated from the fine; the new branches make the finest paper. The bark is then boiled again in fresh ley, continually stirred with a stick, and fresh water from time to time is added. It is then put in a sieve and taken to a brook, and here the bark is incessantly stirred until it becomes a fine pulp. It is then thrown into water and separates in the form of meal. This is put into a small vessel with a decoction of rice and a species of *Hibiscus*, and stirred until it has attained a tolerable consistence. It is then poured into a larger vessel, from whence it is taken and put in the form of sheets on mats or layers of grass straw; these sheets are laid one upon another with straw between, and pressed to force the water out. After this they are spread upon boards in the sun, dried, cut, and gathered into bundles for sale. This paper will better endure folding, and last longer than ours.

Woven fabrics.—They make silk, the best of which is superior to that of China. The best silks are woven by criminals of high rank, who are confined upon a small, rocky, unproductive island, deprived of their property, and made to support themselves by their labor. The exportation of these silks, it is said, is prohibited.

They have but small skill in producing cotton fabrics, though such are made. For many purposes to which we apply cloth of cotton, they use the coarse spongy paper to which we have alluded. They require woollen cloths, for the winters are cold; but, we believe, they make none. Indeed, they have no sheep or goats, and therefore lack materials from which to make woollen cloths.

Leather.—They convert the skins of certain animals into this article; but, as we have stated on a previous page, all those who have anything to do with the making or vending of leather are outcasts from all the rest of the population and universally proscribed. They never apply the article, as we do, to making shoes, or other coverings for the feet. They hardly ever wear shoes or slippers that are not made of plaited straw. Thunberg says the shoes are always the shabbiest part of the dress of the Japanese. As they are of straw, they consequently last but a little time. But they are made in immense numbers, cost but a trifle, and may be bought in every town and village in the Empire. The pedestrian, therefore, throws away the old pair by the road side, and buys new ones as he goes along; while the more provident man takes two or three pairs with him on starting. Immense numbers of these discarded shoes may be found on the sides of all the roads. In wet weather they wear under the shoe a wooden clog, which is attached to the foot by ties of plaited straw. Dignitaries sometimes wear slippers made of fine rattan slips neatly plaited.

Agriculture.—Japan is very mountainous, as we have already stated; but with the exception of that portion of the ground covered by the roads, and by the woods left to supply timber and charcoal, nearly every foot of ground, to the very tops of the mountains, is cultivated. Of animals to assist in culture they have the horse, ox, and a large species of buffalo, which they train to draw carts and carry heavy goods on the back. They plough with both the ox and cow. Of milk and butter they make no use. When they cannot use cattle to plough, as on the steep sides of hills, men are substituted; and sometimes the plough is laid aside and all the labor in preparing the earth is done by hand. Generally, their soil is rather poor; but by means of the immense labor they bestow upon it, by irrigation, and, especially, by the use of manures, which they understand well, they make very large crops.

Their chief grain is rice, of which they are said to produce the best in all Asia. They also make barley and wheat. The first is used for feeding the cattle; the other is not much valued, and is chiefly used for cakes and soy. This last is made by fermenting, under ground, wheat with a peculiar kind of bean and salt.

Next to rice, in importance, is the tea plant. This was not cultivated in Japan before the beginning of the ninth century, when it was introduced from China. Immense quantities of it are now produced, for its use is universal. Beside the plantations devoted to it, the hedges on the farms are all of the tea plant. Siebold says the finer kinds require great care and skill in the cultivation. The plantations are situated, as far as they conveniently can be, from all other crops and from human habitations, lest the delicacy of the tea should be impaired by smoke or any other impurity. They manure the plants with dried anchovies, and with the juice pressed out of mustard seed. The harvesting is a process of great nicety. Dr. Siebold thinks that the green and black tea are from the same plant, and differ only in the mode of preparation; though others have said the plants themselves differ. Neither, however, is ever dried on copper, but both are dried in an iron pan.

Beans of various kinds are produced, and some other vegetables. Several edible roots are carefully cultivated. They grow the mulberry tree in large quantities for the sake of the silk worm, and also for making paper. In Loo-Choo they make a coarse sugar from the cane; in Nippon they manufacture it from the sap of a tree. Our farmers deem it a part of their business to rear such animals as we use for food; but the Japanese farmer is most frequently a Buddhist and cares nothing for animal food. The Dutch, a great while ago, introduced some sheep and goats, and some few may, possibly, still be found in the Kingdom. If attended to they would thrive very well; but the religion of the natives forbids them to eat the flesh, and they do not know how to manufacture the wool and hair; hence the animals are little valued. They have, also, a few hogs, which were originally brought from China. Some of the country people near the coast keep them, but not to eat. They sell them to the Chinese junks which are allowed to come over to trade. The Chinese sailor has a passion for pork. The hog thrives well and becomes very fat in Japan.

Horticulture.—In this department the Japanese are very skillful. They possess the art, in a wonderful degree, either of dwarfing, or of unnaturally enlarging all natural productions. As an evidence of the first, may be seen, in the miniature gardens of the towns, perfectly mature trees, of various kinds, not more than three feet high, and with heads about three feet in diameter. These dwarfed trees are often placed in flower pots. Fischer says that he saw in a box four inches long, one and a half wide, and six in height, a bamboo, a fir, and a plum tree, all thriving, and the latter in full blossom. As proofs of the last, Meylan tells us that he saw plum trees covered with blossoms, each of which was four times the size of the cabbage rose; it produced no fruit, however. He also saw radishes weighing from fifty to sixty pounds; and those of fifteen pounds were not at all uncommon. The fir trees are represented as being forced to an enormous size; we are told that the branches, at the height of seven or eight feet from the ground, are led out, sometimes over ponds, and supported upon props, so that they give a shade around the tree three hundred feet in diameter. The cedar, also, is a tree which reaches a great size.

Navigation.—Formerly the Japanese made voyages, in vessels of their own construction, to Corea, China, Java, Formosa, and other places at some distance from their own islands; but when the Portuguese were expelled a decree was made that the natives should not leave the country; hence navigation declined. Still, short coasting voyages are made within the boundaries of the Kingdom; and fishing-smacks go to sea, but not very far from the coast. This coasting trade, however, is large; and the Japanese use fish for food so extensively that the number is immense of these trading boats and fishing smacks. The Japanese have the compass; not divided, however, into as many points as ours. The construction of their vessels, as to model, is very clumsy; and, as they have seen and examined many European ships, it may seem strange that a people so skilful and ingenious should not, ere this, have improved in naval architecture. The fault is not theirs; the fact is that they have, in more than one instance, built very good vessels after European models; but the law has interposed, for a special reason, and retarded improvement among a people whose insular position would have made them sailors, and whose quick perceptions would have made them good ones if left to themselves. Their craft are, by law, made with the stern open, so that they cannot weather an open and heavy sea. The smaller ones never, if they can help it, go out of sight of land, and upon any threatening appearance of rough weather they instantly run in to make a harbor. The object of this law of construction is to keep the natives at home.

Internal trade by land and water.—This is large, resulting from the variety of produce afforded by the variety of climate, and from the immense population. In many places, town joins on to town, and village to village, for miles, so that the road looks like a continued street. Kaempfer thus speaks of the population: "The country is indeed populous beyond expression, and one would scarcely think it possible that, being no greater than it is, it should, nevertheless, maintain and support such a vast number of inhabitants. The highways are almost one continued line of villages and boroughs. You scarce come out of one, but you enter another; and you may travel many miles, as it were, in one street, without knowing it to be composed of many villages, save by the differing names that were formerly given them, and which they after retained, though joined to one another. It hath many towns, the chief whereof may, of a certainty, vie with the most considerable in the world for largeness, magnificence, and number of inhabitants." Kæmpfer says of Jeddo, that he was one whole day, riding at a moderate pace, "from Sinagawa, where the suburb begins, along the main street, which goes across, a little irregularly indeed, to the end of the city."

As to the variety of climate and produce, the southern part of the Kingdom, reaching down as low as the twenty-fourth degree of north latitude, produces the sugar cane and the tropical fruits; while the northern, extending as high up as fifty degrees, yields the products of the temperate zones. The mineral wealth of the country is very great, the manufactures numerous, and, under such circumstances, the internal trade among so many people is necessarily active. Of the facilities for carrying it on, we remark that goods are conveyed by land on pack-horses and pack-oxen, and that the roads are excellent, and kept in admirable order. In the rugged and mountainous parts of the country where the road must pass, they make it zigzag on the side of the mountain, and, where necessary, cut steps in the rocks. Indeed, the roads must be kept in order, otherwise they could not accomplish what they do by their postal arrangements. As among the ancient Mexicans and Peruvians, the post is pedestrian, and very expeditious. Every carrier is accompanied by a partner to take his place in case of accident. The men run at their utmost speed, and as they approach the end of their stage, find the relay waiting, to whom, as soon as they are near enough, they toss the package of letters, when the new runners set off before the coming ones have stopped. Nothing must be interposed to delay them a moment on the road. The highest prince of the Empire, with all his train, must make way for the postmen, if he meet them on the road. Where necessary and practicable on their roads, the Japanese make good bridges, often of stone; but they do not seem to have arrived at the art of tunnel-making. Some principles of civil engineering they understand and apply, but of military engineering they know nothing. But beside their roads, they use their rivers and inland lakes for internal trade wherever it is possible; and in those parts of the Kingdom nearest the sea, probably the greater part of the inland trade is carried on by the rivers, which, though short, are navigable for some miles into the interior. On the roads, in all parts of the Empire, stables, inns, tea-shops, and other resting places occur at intervals, and the distances are regularly marked.

Scientific knowledge and its applications.—We have just said that the Japanese possess some knowledge of the principles of civil engineering. They know something of mathematics, mechanics, and trigonometry. Thus, they have constructed very good maps of their country; they have measured the height of some of their mountains by the barometer; they have made some very good canals; they have constructed water-mills, and lathes moved by water power. They make clocks, and herein, by the way, they have shown remarkable ingenuity and skill. Meylan gives the following account of a clock which they made, and exhibited to the Dutch, while he was an inmate of Dezima. "The clock," says he, "is contained in a frame three feet high by five feet long, and presents a fair landscape at noon-tide. Plum and cherry trees in full blossom, with other plants, adorn the foreground. The back-ground consists of a hill, from which falls a cascade, skilfully imitated in glass, that forms a softly flowing river, first winding round rocks placed here and there, then running across the middle of the landscape till lost in a wood of fir trees. A golden sun hangs aloft in the sky, and, turning upon a pivot, indicates the striking of the hours. On the frame below, the twelve hours of day and night are marked, where a slowly creeping tortoise serves as a hand. A bird, perched upon the branch of a plum tree, by its song and the clapping of its wings, announces the moment when the hour expires; and as the song ceases, a bell is heard to strike the hour—during which operation, a mouse comes out of a grotto and runs over the hill. * * * * Every separate part was nicely executed; but the bird was too large for the tree, and the sun for the sky, while the mouse scaled the mountain in a moment of time." Whatever may have been the defects of taste, the ingenuity and skill in this piece of mechanism are very apparent.

Fischer also tells us a story of the ingenuity of a Japanese fisherman, of which, perhaps, the specimen may now be found among ourselves. The Japanese, like many other people of lively temperaments, have a passion for things that are strange and odd, and rather prefer sometimes to be gulled. This fisherman, availing himself of this passion, contrived to unite the upper half of a monkey to the lower half of a fish, so neatly as to defy ordinary inspection. He then announced that he had caught a strange animal alive in his net, but that the creature had soon died when taken out of the water, and invited his countrymen to come, and, for a consideration, to see the curiosity. After he had put money in his purse to some considerable extent by this bold reliance on human credulity, he improved on the original story, and said that during the few moments of its life the strange creature had *spoken* to him, (whether in the language of Japan or in that of the Fee-jee islands, he did not say,) and had predicted a certain number of years of great fertility, to be followed or accompanied by a most fatal epidemic; and that against this last the only remedy would be the *possession of a likeness of the marine nondescript*, half human half fish. Pictures of the mermaid were forthwith in demand, and the sale was immense. Presently, as the affair had well nigh had its run in Japan, this mermaid, or one made like it, was sold to the Dutch factory at Dezima, and was sent off in the next ship to Batavia. Here one of our speculating brethren of the "universal Yankee nation" contrived to get it, and forthwith repaired to Europe, where he very successfully played the part of proprietor and showman of a veritable mermaid, during the years 1822-'23, thus settling a disputed question in natural history and filling his pockets at the same time. We are inclined to think that this is the identical mermaid which graces the collection at the New York Museum; if it be not, then our Japan fisherman furnished the parent, (so ingeniously made as to elude detection,) from which was born the Fee-jee prodigy.

But another more remarkable and far more creditable instance of the ingenuity and talent of a Japanese fisherman is related in the Dutch annals of Dezima. It occurred during the presidency of M. Doeff. The Dutch at Batavia, during the war, feared the English cruisers too much to send one of their own ships on the annual voyage to Japan. They therefore more than once hired American vessels. One of these having taken in at Dezima the usual cargo of copper and camphor, as she set sail in the night, struck upon a rock in the harbor, filled and sunk. The crew reached the shore in boats, and the authorities of Nagasaki, the Dutch factory, and the American captain, were all alike concerned to devise means of raising the vessel. Japanese divers were sent down to fetch up the copper, but the camphor had dissolved, and the effluvia thus disengaged cost two of the divers their lives. The idea of unloading her was then abandoned. Efforts were then made to raise her as she was, but without success. A simple fisherman named Kiyemon, who now perhaps for the first time in his life saw an European built ship, for he did not live in Nagasaki, promised to raise the ship, provided his mere expenses in doing it were paid; if he did not succeed he asked nothing. He was laughed at by the people for his presumption, but, as the case was hopeless, those interested permitted him to make the attempt. At low tide he fastened on either side of the vessel fifteen or seventeen boats, such as those by which the Dutch ships are towed in, and connected them all together firmly by props and stays. He then waited for a spring tide, when he came in a Japanese coasting vessel, which he attached firmly to the stern of the sunken ship, and at the moment when the tide was highest, he set every sail of every boat. The sunken vessel was lifted, disengaged herself from the rock, and was towed by the fisherman to the strand, where she could be unloaded and repaired. Fraissinet says he was handsomely rewarded for this. The reader will be amused to learn that his reward consisted in being allowed to wear two sabres, (which is the badge of elevated rank,) and to bear as his coat of arms *a Dutch hat and two Dutch tobacco pipes*. We have never read in any narrative of the circumstance that he received any *money* with which to support his rank. The Dutchmen and the American captain should have furnished that. If the circumstances had been changed, and either Hollander or Yankee had raised the vessel for the Japanese, it would have been very soon intimated to the natives that two swords with a picture of a Dutch hat and two tobacco pipes afforded very inadequate compensation for such a valuable service. We think it would scarcely have satisfied the Japanese mermaid maker, had he been the fortunate fisherman instead of the modest Kiyemon.

Medicine.—All the writers on Japan agree in the statement that on the visit of the Dutch president to Jeddo, his European physician, who accompanies him, is always visited by the native physicians, and closely questioned on points purely professional. Their object is to gain information. But they already know something. They have not, however, availed themselves at all of *post mortem* examinations, either to investigate disease or to study anatomy. We cannot suppose they are without opportunities of thus acquiring knowledge, for we read that after a criminal is executed it is not uncommon for his body to be hacked in pieces by the young nobility, that they may try the temper and edge of their sword blades. But superstition is in the way. To come into contact with death is deemed pollution. Without such examinations, it is obvious that the knowledge of the physician and surgeon must be but imperfect at best.

There are, however, in Japan, original medical works constantly appearing, and translations are also made of all such as they can obtain in the Dutch language, which they best understand. The European medical gentlemen, who have come in contact with their professional brethren of Japan, report favorably of them; and Dr. Siebold speaks with high praise of the zeal with which the native physicians thronged around him, from all parts of the Empire, seeking to enlarge the stores of their knowledge. He bears testimony also to their intelligence, as evinced by the questions they asked. Acupuncture and *moxa* burning are both used in Japan and are native inventions. They have an original treatise on the first, and the proper cases for its use. Their drugs are mostly animal and vegetable; they are too little acquainted with chemistry to venture upon mineral remedies. They study medical botany, however, with great attention, and their remedies are said to be generally efficacious. Some of their medicinal preparations are very remarkable, producing most singular effects. Of these there is one spoken of by Titsingh, who saw its application and its consequences; and from some of the officers of our own expedition we have heard of this preparation, of which, we believe, they have brought home specimens. Titsingh thus writes: "Instead of enclosing the bodies of the dead in coffins of a length and breadth proportionate to the stature and bulk of the deceased, they place the body in a tub, three feet high, two feet and a half in diameter at the top, and two feet at bottom. It is difficult to conceive how the body of a grown person can be compressed into so small a space, when the limbs, rendered rigid by death, cannot be bent in any way. The Japanese to whom I made this observation told me that they produced the result by means of a particular powder called *Dosia*, which they introduce into the ears, nostrils, and mouth of the deceased, after which, the limbs, all at once, acquire astonishing flexibility. As they promised to perform the experiment in my presence, I could not do otherwise than suspend my judgment, lest I should condemn, as an absurd fiction, a fact which, indeed, surpasses our conceptions, but may yet be susceptible of a plausible explanation, especially by galvanism, the recently discovered effects of which also appeared at first to exceed the bounds of credulity. The experiment accordingly took place in the month of October, 1783, when the cold was pretty severe. A young Dutchman having died in our factory at Dezima, I directed the physician to cause the body to be washed and left all night exposed to the air, on a table placed near an open window, in order that it might become completely stiff. Next morning, several Japanese, some of the officers of our factory, and myself, went to examine the corpse, which was as hard as a piece of wood. One of the interpreters, named Zenby, drew from his bosom a *santock*, or pocket-book, and took out of it an oblong paper, filled with a coarse powder resembling sand. This was the famous *Dosia* powder. He put a pinch into the ears, another pinch into the nostrils, and a third into the mouth; and presently, whether from the effect of this drug, or of some trick which I could not detect, the arms, which had before been crossed over the breast, dropped of themselves, and in less than twenty minutes by the watch, the body recovered all its flexibility.

"I attributed this phenomenon to the action of some subtle poison, but was assured that the *Dosia* powder, so far from being poisonous, was a most excellent medicine in child-bearing, for diseases of the eyes, and for other maladies. An infusion of this powder, taken even in perfect health, is said to have virtues which cause it to be in great request among the Japanese of all classes. It cheers the spirits and refreshes the body. It is carefully tied up in a white cloth and dried, after being used, as it will serve a great number of times before losing its virtues.

"The same infusion is given to people of quality when at the point of death; if it does not prolong life, it prevents rigidity of the limbs; and the body is not exposed to the rude handling of professional persons, a circumstance of some consequence in a country where respect for the dead is carried to excess. I had the curiosity to procure some of this powder, for which I was obliged to send to Kidjo, or the nine provinces, to the temples of the Sintoos, which enjoy the exclusive sale of it, because they practice the doctrine of Kobou-Daysi, its inventor. The quantity obtained in consequence of my first application was very small, and even this was a special favor of the priests, who otherwise never part with more than a single pinch at a time."

Titsingh, however, obtained a considerable quantity afterward, which he carried home with him in 1784. It has the appearance of sand, and when it is fully perfected for use is as white as snow. It is obtained on the mountain of Kongosen or Kinbensen in the province of Yamatto, where there are many mines of gold and silver. The process by which it is prepared is the secret of the priests. Their knowledge is doubtless the result of accidental experience; for their acquaintance with chemistry is so slight that we may safely conclude they do not understand the rationale of its preparation.

Astronomy.—In this science they have made very considerable proficiency. They understand the use of European instruments, and have caused many of them to be very successfully imitated by native workmen. Meylan says he saw good telescopes, chronometers, thermometers, and barometers, made by Japanese mechanics. They calculate eclipses accurately, and yearly almanacs are prepared in the Jeddo and *Dairi* colleges. Lalande's treatises and other astronomical works have been translated from Dutch into Japanese, and are studied with great ardor. They have in their division of time a cycle of sixty years, calculated out of their zodiac, which, like ours, has twelve signs, differing from ours in their names only. But this is not the place to consider minutely their astronomical system. We cannot leave it, however, without the remark that, on a comparison of it with that of the Muiscas, an ancient, semi-civilized, and now extinct race, that once inhabited the plains of Bogota, in New Granada, the resemblances were so striking that they produced on our mind a conviction that the astronomical systems of the two people were substantially the same.

SECTION VII.

LITERATURE AND THE FINE ARTS.

PAPER was made by the Japanese as early as the beginning of the seventh century, and printing from blocks, after the Chinese fashion, was introduced in the year 1206 of our era. The city of the *Mikado* appears to be the great metropolis of literature in Japan. A great many books are there made, and a great many reside there whose occupation is that of letters. Seminaries of learning of different grades have existed in the country ever since Europeans knew anything about it. Xavier says that in his day there were four "academies" in or near Miako, each having between three and four thousand pupils; and he adds that much larger numbers were taught at an institution near the city of Bandone, and that such seminaries were universal throughout the Empire. Beside the colleges or higher institutions at the city of Miako, we know of similar ones at Jeddo, and of one at Nagasaki. How many there may be in the Kingdom we cannot say; but education, such as it is, is by no means neglected in Japan. There would seem to be something like a common school system, for Meylan states that children of both sexes and of all ranks are invariably sent to rudimentary schools; whether supported by the State or not he does not say. Here the pupils are all taught to read and write, and are initiated into some knowledge of the history of their own country. Thus much the meanest peasant child is expected to learn. There are immense numbers of cheap, easy books continually issuing from the Japanese press, which are designed for the instruction of children or poor people; so it will be seen they have their "cheap literature." Books innumerable of a higher order are provided for the rich, and all, of both kinds, are profusely illustrated with wood-cuts, engraved on the same block with the type. Some of these books, which we have examined, show also that an art but recently introduced in Europe and America is very old in Japan, viz: that of printing in colors. So that in our modern inventions of stereotyping and printing in colors, and in our manufacture of cheap literature for the people generally, Japan has anticipated us by centuries. Their books consist of works of science, history, biography, geography, travels, moral philosophy, natural history, poetry, the drama, and encyclopædias. Reading is a favorite occupation with both sexes; and it is said to be common in Japan to see, when the weather permits, a group of ladies and gentlemen seated by a cool running stream, or in a shady grove, each with a book.

Of the merits of the Japanese books it is impossible for us to speak with much confidence. Very few Europeans or Americans know anything of the language; it is not the easiest of acquisition; and yet, all we have of the Japanese books is in translation. We doubt if any western scholar has ever yet mastered it thoroughly, for opportunity has been wanting; and very sure we are that Klaproth accuses Titsingh of ignorance, and Siebold and Hoffman similarly accuse Klaproth, while a Japanese at our side informs us that *all* are mistaken. Now, without a thorough understanding of the language, no translation can convey a correct idea of the sentiments expressed, much less of the spirit embodied in the original. An ex cathedra critical opinion on the Japanese literature is, therefore, premature. Let us hope that, ere long, both Europeans and Americans will master the language completely; and then let them speak.

Music.—The Japanese music, of which, by the way, the natives are passionately fond, has nothing in it to recommend it to the ears of Europeans or Americans. The principal instrument is the *samsie* or guitar, and every young female of the upper classes is taught to play upon it. It is the invariable accompaniment of ladies when they go to parties; and on these occasions the female guests sing and play by turns. They have, besides, various other instruments, but little can be said in commendation of their music.

Arts of design, paintings, prints, &c.—In this department they have made some progress, and in certain branches have attained to no small skill. Of anatomy, as we have already said, they know nothing, and consequently are no sculptors; neither are they portrait painters. They are ignorant of perspective, and, therefore, cannot paint a landscape; but in the representation of a single object, their accuracy of detail and truthful adherence to nature cannot be surpassed. Their deficiency is in composition. Nothing is more beautiful than their delineations of a flower, or a fruit, and especially of birds. The drawing is accurate and the coloring perfect. They make, too, colors which European artists pronounce to be unrivalled; and some of which excel any we can produce. The Japanese are very fond of painting, and are eager collectors of pictures. They sketch boldly with charcoal or ink; and of an isolated object the drawing, as we have said, is apt to be good. They do not paint in oil at all; all their specimens are in water colors, the management of which they certainly understand very well.

They have prints in great abundance; all, however, are made from wood cuts, and very often are printed in colors. Engraving on copper has but recently been introduced among them, and as it has been adopted with great eagerness, it will probably be prosecuted with success.

We have already said that they make castings in metal of vases and images, and the sides of their bells are adorned with *bas-reliefs*.

They cannot be said to understand architecture as an art, though they cut stone and lay it skilfully enough; nor have they any skill in the work of the lapidary. The country produces precious stones, but they do not know how to cut or polish them. Hence there is very little jewelry worn by either sex. But they have a substitute for jewels, such as we cannot make. This is called *syakfilo*, in which various metals are so blended and combined that they produce an effect resembling, very much, fine enamel. This is used, instead of precious stones, for girdle clasps, sword hilts, boxes, and other ornamental work.

SECTION VIII.

NATURAL PRODUCTIONS.

Mineral wealth.—Kaempfer, whom we believe to be as accurate as any writer on Japan, remarks that, "the greatest riches of the Japanese soil, and those in which this Empire exceeds most known countries, consist in all sorts of minerals and metals, particularly in gold, silver, and copper." The gold is found in many parts of the Empire. Sometimes it is obtained from its own ore, sometimes from the washings of the earth or sand, and sometimes it is mixed with the copper. The quantity in the country is undoubtedly great. An old Spanish writer of the seventeenth century tells us that, in his day, the palace of the Emperor at Jeddo, as well as many houses of the nobility, were literally covered with plates of gold. In the beginning of the Dutch trade, the annual export was £840,000 sterling; and in the course of sixty years the amount sent out of the Kingdom, through the Dutch alone, was from twenty-five to fifty millions sterling.

Silver mines are quite as numerous as those of gold. In one year, the Portuguese, while they had the trade, exported in silver, £587,500 sterling.

Copper abounds through the whole Japanese group, and some of it is said to be not surpassed by any in the world. The natives refine it and cast it into cylinders about a foot long and an inch thick. The coarser kinds they cast into round lumps or cakes.

Quicksilver is said to be abundant, but this, so far as we know, has never been an article of export.

Lead, also, is found to be plentiful, but, like quicksilver, it has not been sent out of the Kingdom.

Tin has also been discovered in small quantities, and of a quality so fine and white that it almost equals silver; but of the extent of this mineral little is known, as the Japanese do not attach much value to it, and therefore have not sought for it.

Iron is found in three of the provinces, and probably exists in others. The Japanese know how to reduce the ore, and the metal they obtain is of superior quality, of which they make steel unsurpassed in excellency.

Coal.—"They have no want of coals in Japan," says Kaempfer, "they being dug up in great quantities in the province of Sikusen and in most of the northern provinces." Dr. Siebold also speaks of coal as being in common use throughout the country; and on visiting one of the mines he saw enough to convince him that it was skillfully worked. For domestic purposes they convert the coal into coke. Viewed in the light of commercial intercourse between the two hemispheres, this coal is worth more than all the metallic deposits we have enumerated.

Native sulphur.—In a region so volcanic, this is, as might be expected, an abundant mineral. In some places it lies in broad deep beds, and may be dug up and removed with as much ease as sand. A considerable revenue is derived by the government from sulphur.

Precious stones.—No diamonds have been found, but agates, carnelians, and jaspers are met with, some of them of great beauty. But the wealth of the kingdom in precious stones is imperfectly known, as the Japanese are not lapidaries.

Pearls.—These are fished up on nearly all parts of the coast, and are frequently large and beautiful. The Chinese taught the natives their value, by offering them very high prices for the finest qualities.

Mother of pearl, corals, ambergris and naptha are also to be enumerated among the articles of export.

Forest and fruit trees.—The most common forest trees are the fir and the cypress; and so sensible are the Japanese of the necessity of preserving their timber trees, that neither of those above named can be cut but by permission of the local magistrate; and the law requires that for every full grown tree that is felled a young one must be planted. The cedar grows to an immense size; sometimes more than eighteen feet in circumference. An English ship at Nagasaki, within a recent period, wanted some small spars; they were furnished; all were cedar, about ninety-six feet long. This tree would, no doubt, prove a very valuable article of export.

There are two varieties of oak, both good and both different from the oaks of Europe. The acorns of one kind are boiled and eaten for food, and are said to be both palatable and nutritious.

The mulberry grows wild in great abundance; but it is so useful that the people transplant and cultivate it. Of the varnish tree we have already spoken.

The camphor tree is valuable and lives to a great age. Siebold visited one which Charlevoix had described as having been seen by him one hundred and thirty-five years before. It was healthy and covered with foliage, with a circumference of fifty feet. The country people make the camphor by a decoction of the root and stems cut into small pieces.

The chestnut and walnut are both found, and the former yields excellent fruit. There is also the pepper tree, or a tree which bears a species of pepper.

Of fruit trees, there are the orange, the lemon, the fig, the plum, the cherry, and the apricot. The plum and cherry, however, are not cultivated as much for their fruit as for their flowers. The vine is very little cultivated; and of the tea plant we have already spoken.

Having thus endeavored to furnish the reader with a condensed view of the leading features that characterize the past progress and present condition of Japan, we would at once proceed to the narrative of the expedition; but there is a duty which we owe to our country and which we will now endeavor to perform.

Of certain events which have transpired since the successful expedition under Commodore Perry, or occurred during its progress, it is due to the claims of truth that something should be said. It had been more gratifying to us to be silent on the topics to which we are about to allude; but official publications by other nations, as well as by some individuals, have been put forth, the obvious purpose of which is to deprive our country and her officers of whatever merit may attach to the fact that the United States were the first, by peaceful negotiations, to cause an alter tion in the policy of excluding foreigners hitherto pursued by Japan.

On the 24th of November, 1852, Commodore Perry left our shores on his mission to Japan. That such a mission had been resolved on by our government was announced to the world some twelve months before the time of its leaving, and had formed the subject of comment in more than one country of Europe. The general opinion abroad was that the mission would, like the many others that had been attempted by various powers, prove fruitless. Dr. Von Siebold, in particular, whose long residence in Japan was supposed to give great importance to his opinions, thus wrote to a friend concerning it: "My mind accompanies the expedition. That it will be successful by peaceful means I doubt very much. If *I* could only inspire Commodore Perry, he would triumph," &c. The progress of the expedition was, of course, watched by foreign powers with great interest.

Commodore Perry cast anchor in the bay of Jeddo, the commercial capital of Japan, on the 8th of July, 1853. On the 22d of August, 1853, a Russian squadron, under the command of Admiral Pontiatine, anchored in the bay of Nagasaki. We know not precisely of what vessels this expedition was composed; but we believe that, beside the frigate *Pallas* and the steamer *Vostock*, the *Aurora*, of 48 guns, and the corvette *Navarino*, of 22, were sent, the one to the Pacific, and the other ostensibly to Kamtschatka, while it is quite certain that not long after a Russian squadron of several vessels-of-war was at Copenhagen, the officers of which said that they were destined to remain five years in the waters of the Japanese archipelago. An unusually large Russian naval force was therefore collected in the Pacific, and in the vicinity of Japan, to be there on the expected visit of Commodore Perry. There were not wanting those who suspected that Russia was silently pursuing her own system of policy. If Commodore Perry unfortunately should fail in his peaceful attempts, and be brought into forcible collision with the Japanese, Russia was on the spot, not to mediate, but to tender to Japan her aid as an ally in the conflict, and if successful, to avail herself of the moment of confidence quietly to get a foothold in some part of the Kingdom, with the intention, at the proper time, of absorbing all. There is no power in the other hemisphere to which the possession of Japan, or the control of its affairs, is as important as it is to Russia. She is on one side of the islands, the United States on the other. The Pacific ocean is destined to be the theatre of immense commercial undertakings. Russia is, in a great degree, shut out by local position from easy access to the Atlantic; but with such harbors on the Pacific as Japan would give her, she might hope to become the controlling maritime power of the world. Our friendly relations and influence with the Japanese, therefore, might interfere materially with the ulterior plans of Russia. Hence she was first in the field to watch all our movements. Thus, we say, some interpreted her conduct. We do not mean to say that they interpreted it correctly, or that such was the policy Russia had resolved on. But the *fact* is, as we have stated, that simultaneously with our expedition she did largely increase her naval armament in the waters of Japan. Commodore Perry was at some loss to understand precisely the policy of Russia. In a letter of November 12th, 1853, the Russian admiral made a distinct proposition of joining his forces to, and entering into full co-operation with, the American squadron. This may have been prompted by an expectation of our success and a doubt of his own. At any rate, the Commodore civilly, but decidedly, declined the proposal, and, in a letter to the Secretary of the Navy, assigned most satisfactory reasons for so doing. He stated that it was "inconsistent with our policy of abstaining from all alliances with foreign powers; and for the reason, also, that his co-operation cannot advance the interest of the United States, however it might benefit the objects of the Russian Emperor, of the nature of whose designs I (says the Commodore) am utterly ignorant." But whatever were her secret purposes to promote her own, or throw obstacles in the way of our success, if she had any, one thing is certain, *for that success we are not indebted in the slightest degree to Russia, by any direct act of hers to that end.* Indirectly, however, she may have furthered the object. We are in possession of very recent information from Japan tending to show that the imperial government seems to be distrustful of the purposes of Russia. The movements of that nation on the Amour river have been viewed with so much apprehension that the Emperor some time ago dispatched a special agent to discover, if possible, their ulterior purposes. The

Japanese have resolved that they will raise an efficient army, and equip a navy, not composed of junks, but of vessels built after the European model. The restrictions on ship-building have been removed, and already, since our treaty was signed, one vessel for commercial purposes has been built and rigged like ours. The Japanese have heard, too, of the war in which Russia is at present engaged. The information produced intense excitement, and it was resolved by the imperial council that treaties similar to that made with the United States should be made with all nations seeking them. *This opens Japan to the trade of the world.* They knew, too, that the British Admiral Stirling was seeking the Russian vessels in the neighborhood of Japan, and they were hence the more willing to make treaties with all, as the means of securing Japan from aggression by any, and of enabling her to preserve, as she wishes, a strict neutrality.

The visit of Russia, however, led to no treaty. The squadron left Nagasaki on the 23d of November, 1853, and returned to it early in 1854. It left again, after several fruitless interviews with the Japanese authorities, on the 5th of February, and was absent until the 20th of April, when it reappeared at Nagasaki, but remained until the 26th only, when it took its final departure.

But other foreign powers have contributed as little to the success of our negotiations as Russia has. On the 7th of September, 1854, Admiral Stirling, in command of the English squadron, arrived at Nagasaki, one purpose of his visit being to make a treaty, in which he succeeded. But the English never pretended that they facilitated our negotiations; they may possibly have indirectly derived some benefit from our success; but we will not undertake to assert that they did. We think that they are more indebted to the Japanese apprehension of Russia's designs, and to the fact of the war in which she is now engaged, than to anything else. We may, indeed, by having induced the first departure from the long established rule to exclude all foreigners but the Dutch and Chinese, have made it more easy to commence negotiation, but our aid goes not beyond this accidental assistance. Of the precise terms of the English treaty it is not here necessary to speak. One of the officers of Admiral Stirling thus speaks of it in a public communication through the English newspapers: "The treaty now made with Japan contains nothing *about commerce*, yet it opens the way and prepares for future negotiation on this important point." "It is highly probable that what has been done by Sir James Stirling at Nagasaki may exceed in durability and value the work done at Yeddo by the Americans, although that cost a special mission, and was heralded to the world with a very loud flourish of trumpets indeed."

To this pert outbreak of transparent envy, we have only to say we earnestly hope that when a treaty is made which *does* say something "*about commerce,*" it may prove both durable and valuable to England; and to add that we should be sorry to think such flippant impertinence as is here exhibited is a common characteristic of British naval officers. From the brave we look for "high thoughts seated in a heart of *courtesy.*"*

But the Dutch have claimed, and that by an official document, that they, in effect, did most of our work for us. It is strange that a nation of which all Christendom has, for more than two hundred years, supposed that it has sought uniformly to secure to itself a monopoly in the trade of Japan, should venture, when their monopoly is destroyed, to stand forth and say, in substance, that they always lamented its existence and labored for its demolition. Has Christendom been so long deceived? We fear the world will ask embarrassing questions. It will say: "Did not the Dutch do what they could to drive out the Portuguese? Did not they assist

---

*Since the above was written, intelligence has been received of a commercial treaty between England and Japan.

in the bombardment at Simabara, and contribute to the extirpation of the native Christians, who were supposed to sympathize with the Portuguese? Did they not manifest hostility toward their Protestant neighbors of the English factory at Firando, established by Saris and conducted by Cockes, until the English left? When, in the reign of Charles II, the English sought to renew the trade with Japan, was it not the Dutch who hastened to inform the imperial government that the wife of Charles was the daughter of the King of Portugal, thus arraying the deep-seated and ancient Japanese hatred of the Portuguese against the English? When the 'Phaeton,' under Pellew, visited Nagasaki, in 1808, was it not M. Doeff, the Dutch chief at Dezima, who devised and counselled the plan whereby the English were to have been murdered to a man? When Java was in possession of the English, and Holland, for a time, had been blotted from the list of nations, was it not the same M. Doeff, who, to the craft of the trader added the cunning of the diplomatist, and, by treachery to the Japanese in the bribery of their officials, contrived, at one and the same time, to pay the debts of Dezima and enrich himself personally, out of the two expeditions sent by Sir Stamford Raffles?"

And *now*, when the United States have, without seeing a Dutchman, or using a Dutch document, successfully negotiated a treaty, Holland stands forth, and by a formal official report from her minister of colonies, declares that she will now "perform the agreeable task of showing the persevering and disinterested efforts which the Dutch government has made" to cause Japan to open her ports to the commerce of the United States. A brief notice of this extraordinary document is called for by a regard to the truth of history.

The statement of the Dutch "minister of colonies," when condensed, is substantially this: That in the year 1844, about the time of Commodore Biddle's visit to Japan, the then King of Holland, William II, wrote a letter to the Emperor of Japan, in which attention was called to the introduction of steam in navigation, the consequent increased development of commerce in the Japanese seas, and the danger likely to result to Japan from her rigid system of excluding foreigners from the Kingdom. It recommended friendly and commercial relations as the surest means of avoiding collisions; and finally, from a grateful sense of the long continued favor shown to the Dutch by the Japanese, it tendered to the latter the "disinterested counsel to relax the laws against foreigners," and offered to send an envoy to give fuller explanations to Japan of what she should do, provided the Emperor desired it. This letter, the Dutch document states, contains the principles which have formed the basis of all Holland's subsequent action, so far as other powers are concerned.

In 1845, the Emperor caused an answer to be sent to the letter, in which it was politely, but very decidedly, announced that Japan had no wish to alter her ancient laws with respect to foreigners.

With this the Dutch remained content; and, so far from pressing the subject in any way, in 1846 they became the medium of announcing to the civilized world an edict of Japan forbidding foreigners to make charts and drawings of the Japanese waters and coasts, and forbidding shipwrecked Japanese sailors to return to their country in any ships *but those of the Netherlands and China*.

Presently, when, in 1852, it became certain that an expedition was to be sent from the United States, under Commodore Perry, the Dutch forthwith sent out orders to their governor general in the Indies to address the governor of Nagasaki, requesting that he would appoint a confidential agent to enter into negotiations with the Dutch chief at Dezima, "about the means that the latter should indicate in order to *preserve Japan against the dangers that threatened her.*" And at the end of the governor general's letter was an intimation to the Nagasaki authorities that the Dutch might be forced to abandon Japan entirely if hostile collisions with other nations should be the result of perseverance in her system of exclusion. This, it is claimed, was a renewal of the effort to open Japan on the principles set forth in the letter of William II, in 1844. From 1844 to 1852 the Dutch made no effort at all, on the ground, as the document alleges, that it was expedient to wait a more favorable opportunity.

In 1852, the Dezima chief was furnished, by the governor general, with instructions to urge upon the Japanese government a change in its policy of exclusion, *not particularly with reference to the Americans*, but in favor of *all nations* who hitherto had lived in peace with Japan. At the same time powers to negotiate with Japan were sent to the Dezima chief, and the *draft of a treaty* was furnished him by his government. He was also ordered to conform to the instructions of the governor general and the draft of the treaty, if he should be consulted "in the Japanese *American* affairs." The draft of the treaty was substantially this:

Article I. The relations now existing between Japan and the Netherlands to be confirmed.

Article II. The port of Nagasaki to be opened to other nations beside the Dutch for the following purposes, viz: to procure provisions and navy stores; to repair vessels; and to take care of sick seamen.

Article III. Other nations beside the Dutch may "even be admitted to trade;" *provided they conclude a treaty with Japan on the bases expressed in the next article.*

Article IV. (*a*) Trade to be limited to the port of Nagasaki.

(*b*) Every nation admitted to trade to have its own consul.

(*c*) Japanese government to indicate to foreign merchants a quarter in Nagasaki for their residence.

(*d*) Trade to be carried on with the privileged Japanese merchants of the five imperial cities, Yeddo, Miako, Ohosaka, Sahai, and Nagasaki, and placed under the care of the governor of Nagasaki.

(*e*) Agents of the Japanese princes allowed to buy foreign wares, and to pay for them with the products of their principalities.

(*f*) Japanese government to make regulations as to the *manner* of carrying on traffic; such regulations to be enforced by the police of Nagasaki.

(*g*) Japanese government to issue notes, payable at the imperial treasury, to facilitate trade with foreigners.

(*h*) Foreign traders allowed to pay out and receive the Japanese copper coin, in the matter of daily household expenses.

(*i*) Right reserved to the Japanese government of imposing a *moderate* tariff of duties on foreign importations.

(*j*) All differences arising in trade to be settled by the consul of the foreign trader and the governor of Nagasaki, or his proxy.

(*k*) Crimes committed by a foreigner to be tried and punished by the nation to which the criminal belongs.

(*l*) The Japanese government to indicate two places where the foreign nations, admitted to trade, may establish depots for coal. One shall be in the bay of "Good Hope," in Jesso, in the northern part of the Empire; and the other in the southern part, on one of the islands of the Linschop archipelago.

Article V. The stipulations above mentioned shall be submitted to every foreign power that desires to make a treaty with Japan, and shall form the bases of such treaty.

Article VI. In case treaties are made with foreign powers on the foregoing bases, the Dutch shall have all the privileges granted to the most favored nation.

This draft was accompanied by a document from his Majesty the King of the Netherlands, entitled "Explanatory note to the draft of the treaty to be concluded between his Majesty the King of the Netherlands and his Majesty the Emperor of Japan."

This commences with the declaration that "his Majesty appreciates the difficulties which exist in the Japanese institutions, in satisfying the demands of foreign powers for entering into commercial negotiations with that Empire, and foresees the dangers to which Japan is inevitably exposed, if the government of that Empire does not listen to reasonable demands of that kind." It then proceeds to state that "his Majesty, by the communications of his subjects, who have long navigated to Japan, and are well acquainted with the affairs of that Empire, esteems himself, indeed, better able than any other prince to make propositions to the sovereign of that Empire, in order to mitigate the severe laws against foreigners." "Therefore, the King has taken the resolution to cause to be drawn up and presented a treaty between their Majesties the King of the Netherlands and the Emperor of Japan, in which, in respecting the laws and the ancient customs of the Empire of Japan, is indicated the way, by means of which, for the future, may be maintained, not only friendly commercial relations with the subjects of his Majesty the King of the Netherlands, but also with those maritime nations who desire commerce with Japan, or who, having peaceful purposes, are thrown by accident on the coasts of the Empire." "For the elucidation of a treaty drawn up in that spirit, his Majesty causes the following lines to be written." Then follows a separate comment on each of the articles of the treaty, and particularly on each of the bases enumerated under *Art. IV*, recommending and enforcing them all.

These documents were all prepared and placed in the hands of the Dutch officials as soon as possible after the government of the Netherlands became certain that an expedition would sail from the United States, and some months *before* Commodore Perry left our shores.

In anticipation of the contemplated enterprize, the government of the United States, in July, 1852, (at which time the Dutch draft of a treaty had been sent out on its way to Dezima,) applied respectfully to the government of the Netherlands, announcing officially that the American squadron would be sent, that its visit was meant to be friendly, and that its object was, if possible, to obtain from Japan some mitigation of her system of exclusion; it asked, also, that instructions might be given to the Dezima chief to afford, if it should be desired by us, his official co-operation in furthering the accomplishment of our object. This request was answered by a promise that such instructions should be given; and, by request, copies were furnished to the United States of the letter of William II, of 1844, and of the Emperor's answer to it of 1845; but of the draft of a Dutch treaty then on its way to Japan, or of any accompanying instructions to the Dutch officials in the east, the United States, of course, heard and knew nothing.

Thus affairs stood when our squadron sailed on the 24th of November, 1852. Long before it arrived in the Japanese waters, the Dutch chief at Dezima had been endeavoring to carry out his instructions, *and negotiate with the Japanese the treaty of which the draft had been sent to him.* But the authorities of Japan persisted in their refusal to appoint a person of consideration as their confidential agent to negotiate any treaty at all. In this state of affairs, the Dezima chief, "rightly resolving not to sacrifice the business to a mere matter of form," as the Dutch document expresses it, at once addressed the governor of Nagasaki, and attempted to open a negotiation with *him*. He laid before him the several items in the draft of the treaty with which he had been furnished, accompanying them with explanations, and set forth what he deemed the principles which were for the Japanese interest, and which should predominate *in the negotiations which he thought might result from the anticipated propositions of the United States;* for both he and the Japanese knew that our squadron was on its way. He concluded his letter as follows: "His Majesty, the King of the Netherlands, expects that the peace of the Japanese Empire can be preserved, if the government of Japan will answer the propositions of the United States in the manner indicated;" that is, on the bases set forth in the Dutch draft of a treaty. But the Japanese treated this attempt as they had all the previous ones from the Dezima chief; and its only effect was to quicken their native shrewdness, and prompt to more numerous demands for explanation, and more thorough investigations into the subject.

At length, in June, 1853, the American squadron, purposely avoiding Nagasaki, made its appearance in the bay of Jeddo, and thus was in Japan before the Dutch were able to *anticipate the American commissioner* in making a treaty. The American squadron never was at Nagasaki, and our representative never had the least communication with the Dutch chief at Dezima.

The Russian squadron soon after entered the port of Nagasaki, and the result of that visit has already been stated. Russia made no treaty with Japan.

Commodore Perry signed the treaty with Japan on the last day of March, 1854; and the Dutch government dispatched their war steamer *Soembing* from Batavia for Japan on the 25th of July, 1854. This was deemed a measure of expediency, as the sight of the American and Russian steamers had excited the liveliest interest in the Japanese. The *Soembing*, during her stay, was visited by men of the highest rank, and, in fact, was made a school of instruction for a large number of Japanese. Finally, the English squadron, under Admiral Stirling, came in on the 7th of September, 1854, and deepened the impression which had been made in Japan by the spectacle of so many armed ships of different nations.

The document before us concludes by claiming great merit for the Dutch, in having opened Japan to the world. It thus speaks: "The Netherlands have understood their mission when, in consequence of the course of events, they placed themselves at the head to operate, in the interest of all, a mitigation of the system of exclusion that existed relative to foreign nations in Japan. The letter of his Majesty, the late William II, is thereof an irrefragable proof." "The United States of North America have obtained, by treaty, the opening to their flag of two ports in the Japanese Empire; and one other power seems to have succeeded in a similar manner. In the face of such results, we cannot deny or undervalue the impression and effect produced by the presence of powerful fleets, or the influence exerted by the simultaneous and serious attempts of different nations. But we wish to see acknowledged the part that the Netherlands had in it by their advice and persuasion. Indeed, these fleets realized the predictions of your Majesty's royal father, and served to procure a more ready acceptance of his disinterested advice. The draft of a treaty of 1852—the letter of the chief at Dezima of the 2d of November, 1852—the communication of the governor of Nagasaki of the 9th of November, 1853—finally, the comparing of the said draft of a treaty with the convention concluded by the United States—all this presents the undeniable fact, that the measures taken, in consequence of your Majesty's orders, have powerfully contributed to the results obtained by other nations."

"In fact, the Netherlands have always desired an opening of Japanese ports, in the general interest, and in favor of commerce. Attached disinterestedly to that policy, the Netherlands have sought no privileges for themselves in Japan; but they have, in equity, desired and obtained treatment similar to that of others, when to these favors were granted."

These are the facts as set forth by the Dutch, and this the extent of their claims; nor would we in the slightest degree detract from what may be justly their due. We confess, however, that, to us, the importance as well as effects of Dutch co-operation in our treaty seem to be somewhat exaggerated. It sometimes happens that men and nations cannot work to the production of their own particular ends without thereby contributing, whether they wish it or not, to the accomplishment of similar ends sought by others. The success, however, of others, which they never sought, and which is but an accident resulting from their efforts to another end, can scarcely be claimed as a ground of merit, or demand very loud acknowledgments from those who may have been thus casually benefitted. The basis of a claim, *quantum meruit*, is some benefit *purposely* done by one to another, or some loss *purposely* sustained for his advantage. We readily concede that the Dezima chief, with the draft of the Dutch treaty in his possession, strove faithfully and judiciously, as became him, to induce the Japanese authorities to accede to the terms of that treaty and sign it, *before* our ambassador could reach Japan. Of this we have no right to complain. We concede also that his proceedings brought to the knowledge of the Japanese what the nature of a commercial treaty was, and furnished them also with some valuable hints as to some of its provisions, which afforded them topics of reflection and investigation, and prepared them for the consideration of our treaty when it should be proposed; but it will scarcely be pretended that the Dutch action was prompted by the direct design of aiding the United States; and still less, that it induced the Japanese government to depart from its long established policy of exclusion. The Dutch were themselves endeavoring to negotiate a treaty; and such a departure must be pre-supposed before it was expedient to present the terms of a treaty at all.

But further, as to this point of departing from their settled policy, it is on the record, that the letter of the King of Holland himself on this very subject, written in 1844, was answered by the Japanese government in 1845, with a most explicit declaration that they *would not abandon* their ancient policy and usage. At this time then (1845) the Dutch seem to have accomplished nothing; and it is not on the record that they ever renewed their effort from this time forward until 1852, *when they knew the American expedition would certainly be sent;* and the mode of renewal was to offer to Japan a treaty which they had prepared *to suit themselves*, and which was *for their own benefit*. For it will be remembered that by that treaty no foreign nation was to be allowed by treaty to trade with Japan, but on certain bases, laid down in the 4th article of the Dutch draft. Now suppose Japan had signed the treaty proposed to her by Holland, what would have necessarily resulted? The following consequences, viz:

1. That the Dutch should alone dictate what kind of treaties all other foreign nations might make with Japan.

2. That Japan, an independent power, should preclude herself from the right of making any treaty but such as Holland should approve.

3. That as Holland was to be placed on the footing of the most favored nations in any treaty Japan might make, the Dutch, in addition to the privileges they already possessed in Japan, and in addition to any others they might obtain by future negotiation, should have also every privilege of every kind that any nation might chance to get by treaty.

Had the Dezima chief succeeded in negotiating his treaty before Commodore Perry's arrival, would it have benefitted the United States?

But this is not all. We are constrained, from public documents of the Dutch themselves, to believe that they never cordially furthered our efforts to effect a treaty which should open Japan. In a letter from the Dutch governor general of the Indies, written from Java on the 22d September, 1852, addressed to Commodore Perry, (then on his way to Japan,) the commodore is informed that a dispatch for the Dezima chief is enclosed, which the commodore may transmit to him, in case he wishes his co-operation. Now, at this very time, the governor general well knew that the Dezima chief had the draft of a treaty, and instructions to have it ratified if possible; and every effort was being made to have it thus ratified *before Commodore Perry could arrive.* Had it been thus ratified, we have seen above what sort of co-operation the Dezima chief would have rendered; it would have been to allow Japan to negotiate just such a treaty as Holland had seen fit to make for her and for us. But further still—the last clause of the governor general's letter to Commodore Perry is suggestive of a fact pregnant with evidence as to the cordiality with which Holland seconded our efforts. "I beg to remark, in view of the object at present contemplated by both our governments, that in case the Netherlands chief of the factory at Dezima should have succeeded in opening negotiations with the government of Japan, it is not unlikely that any proof of co-operation between America and Holland would prejudice these negotiations, *as you are aware that the American expedition to Japan has not always been represented to be of a wholly friendly and peaceful character.*" Of course, these latter words, to have any meaning, must imply that *the Japanese* had doubts of the friendly nature of our visit. *Now, who told the Japanese that it was unfriendly?* The Dutch were the only Europeans with whom they had any intercourse, or from whom they could hear anything about it. And from the Dutch they did hear it; for, in anticipation of the American movements, instructions were sent by the Netherlands to their governor general in Batavia to write to Japan and invite negotiation about the means that should be adopted "to preserve Japan from the *dangers* that threatened her." The Dutch, therefore, told the Japanese to look for *danger* from our visit.

Commodore Perry never invoked the aid of the Dutch, from the beginning to the end of his mission, but purposely avoided them; and the treaty which he made is essentially different from that which the Dutch had provided. The draft from the Hague made Nagasaki the only port open to foreign ships for obtaining supplies, repairing vessels, and recruiting the sick; and provided that foreigners might "even be admitted to trade," after they had made a treaty on the Dutch basis.

The two ports of Simoda and Hakodadi, with a considerable space around each, are, by the American treaty, thrown open for trade; and in case of distress, or when driven by stress of weather, all the ports in Japan are open to ships of the United States; and as, when Holland shall succeed in making a commercial treaty with Japan, we cannot but hope and believe she will be admitted to like favors with ourselves, we have been inclined to think that the Dutch are far more indebted to us for releasing them from their imprisonment of two centuries and a half at Dezima, than we are for any aid they have rendered us, directly or indirectly, in negotiating our treaty with Japan. That Holland should seek to advance her own interest is both natural and proper; when other nations succeed in promoting theirs, it is scarcely graceful or dignified to deny to them the modicum of merit which may attach to their success.

It only remains to say a word about the singular statements of Dr. Von Siebold. This individual was the physician employed by the Dutch at Dezima, and has published, more largely than all his predecessors combined, the result of his observations during his residence. Of the value of his publications we have already spoken. During his continuance in the Empire, however, a circumstance is said to have occurred involving a very melancholy catastrophe, in which Von Siebold was an unwilling actor. The story is thus related by a modern writer on Japan. Siebold had been with Colonel Van Sturler, the Dezima chief, to Jeddo; the Japanese astronomer, Takahasi Lakusaimon, had, in violation of the law, furnished him with a copy of a recently made map of Japan. The draughtsman who made the copy having become, from some cause, offended with the astronomer, denounced him to the authorities. An investigation followed, Siebold's correspondence with Takahasi was demanded, and the topographical and geographical information contained therein, added to the fact that Siebold was not by birth a Hollander, led to the suspicion that the physician of Dezima was a *Russian spy*. This caused the investigation to become more rigorous still, and severe measures were threatened. All who were known to be friends and correspondents of Siebold, with a single exception, were thrown into prison. The excepted individual was made a witness for the government. He broke his oath in the cause of friendship, and privately informed Siebold of what was designed against him. This warning enabled him to place his most valuable documents in security, and to prepare copies for the use of the government commissioners, before his papers were seized and his person arrested at Dezima. Siebold was repeatedly examined by the governor of Nagasaki, and steadily refused to name any of his Japanese accomplices; and requested to be permitted to pass the residue of his life in a Japanese prison, as a hostage, for the innocence of his friends, and as a penalty for the consequences of his transgressions. The investigation lasted nearly a year. *Siebold was banished from Japan;* and Takahasi and the draughtsman who accused him both committed suicide. Whether this story be true or not, in every particular, it was, at least, circulated on the continent of Europe, and in this form it had reached the United States before our expedition sailed.

After Commodore Perry had been designated as commander, Siebold applied for employment as a member of the expedition, and so anxious was he to go, that he caused great and unusual influence to be exerted for the accomplishment of his wishes. Commodore Perry, for several reasons, and particularly from a desire not to compromit himself, or hazard the success of his mission by taking back to Japan a man generally believed to have been banished, resisted all influences, even the highest, and persisted in his positive refusal to have Siebold in any vessel of the squadron.

At length, our treaty was made, and the fact was announced to the world. Within a few months, and since such announcement, has appeared a pamphlet, by Siebold, published at Bonn, and bearing the following title: "Authentic account of the efforts of the Netherlands and of Russia toward the opening of Japan to the navigation and commerce of all nations." We regret its publication for the author's sake. It subserves no scientific end, nor does it add a single fact concerning Japan to what the author has already communicated in his previous valuable writings. It is evidently the product of mortified and irritated vanity, and has two objects in view which are perfectly obvious. The one is to glorify the author, the other to disparage the United States and its Japan expedition. Appreciating, as we sincerely do, the voluminous writings of Dr. Von Siebold concerning Japan, we regret exceedingly the egotism, vanity, and self-importance exhibited in the pursuit of the one object; while we are not disposed to overlook, without rebuke, the misrepresentations and impertinence displayed in the accomplishment of the other. The text and spirit of the whole work may be found at the commencement, on the third page of the book, in the following statement: "*We have now to thank the Russians, and not the Americans, for the opening of Japan.*" When we remember that, up to a very late period, *the Russians had effected no treaty at all with Japan*, the reader may possibly incline to the belief, that the shrewd Japanese were not far from the truth, when they suspected Von Siebold to be a Russian spy, and banished him.

Of his intimate connexion with Russia there can be no doubt; the pamphlet itself shows it; and though in the revelations it makes, its purpose is to glorify the author and show his great political importance, yet his boasts of services rendered to Russia, his published extracts from the flattering letter of a Russian official of high rank, his acknowledgment of a summons and visit to St. Petersburgh, and his declaration that Japan knows Russia to be the most powerful nation in the world, are all *facts* indicative of the author's close and interested relation to the great northern power. Indeed, it has been said by some, that by his advice the Russian squadron was sent to checkmate us in our attempt to open Japan. If this be so, then, his extreme desire to go in our squadron may have been produced by his entire conviction, nay, assured knowledge, that his presence alone would have proved fatal to the success of our mission.

Of the inordinate conceit and self-importance of Von Siebold there is, unfortunately, abundant evidence. Thus, he informs us, that he it was who induced King William II. in 1844, to write to the Emperor of Japan; and states that the original of the King's letter was deposited with him and is still in his possession. He dwells, at length, upon the vast amount of valuable information he had acquired in Japan, upon the admirable opportunities he enjoyed for that purpose, and more than insinuating that all the rest of the world, compared with him, is in almost entire ignorance, he contrives to make the pamphlet an advertisement of his really valuable works, of which he retains, we believe, the sale in his own hands; at least we know that it was not to be obtained in the book stores of Europe, and that the copy procured for the Astor library was purchased by the accomplished superintendent from Von Siebold himself.

So, too, the services he has rendered to Russia lose nothing of their value and importance in his representations; and we are furnished with an extract of a letter from a distinguished Russian statesman, addressed to our author, the publication of which by Von Siebold proves that the noble correspondent of whom he boasts could not have enumerated *modesty* among the personal qualities for which he commends the learned physician.

We are also told of his intimacy with some of the Japanese nobility, though he dared not show his face in Japan, nor was he at liberty even to address to them a letter.

A letter from M. Von Siebold, addressed to one of the gentlemen of the expedition, whom he ostentatiously calls in his pamphlet, "my correspondent on board of the Mississippi," is now lying before us. A single extract will illustrate the weakness of which we have spoken:

"I see with much pleasure that Commodore Perry knows how to appreciate my profound knowledge and long experience of Japanese affairs. I was very sorry not to have been called upon to trace a programme for the American expedition to Japan. I would have produced a plan to open the Japanese Empire to the world, under the watchwords 'humanity and patience.' I do not transgress the bounds of modesty when I say that *I, only, am able to trace such a plan*. The Netherland government knows my views, and has undertaken to support the peaceful intentions of the President of the United States toward the Japanese government."

"Probably all overtures will be declined, or they will try to delay, as long as possible, giving a final answer. The Japanese government understands perfectly the art of protracting diplomatic negotiations, to exhaust patience; of spinning out endlessly the thread of objections against overtures for a commercial treaty. They will recall constantly the unalterable nature of their laws; will urge the danger of breaches of etiquette or courtesy, the want of articles for exportation, the great influx of foreigners. It will also be pretended that the Siogun is not allowed to enter into negotiations with foreign nations (other than the Hollanders) without the co-operation of the Mikado; and it is easy to understand that the Mikado will decide for or against a treaty according to the will of the Council of State. All these are only pretexts, and the sole reason why the Japanese object to more intimate relations with foreigners is the fear that Christianity may be introduced into the country, and so the Siogun dynasty, which consolidated itself by the extermination of Christianity, may be put in jeopardy. The fanatic Gutzlaff and Father Forcade, (now in Heaven, I hope,) the narrow-minded missionaries, have, by their conduct of late, contributed to excite afresh the fears of the Japanese government, who saw in these two missionaries the whole of Christendom marching against Japan.

"It shows a want of caution, in that the letter of the honorable President states that the messengers whom he has sent to the Emperor of Japan are not missionaries. Why insert this assurance, calculated to excite distrust? It is a matter of course that an ambassador is not a missionary; and what guarantee can be given to the Japanese government that there prevails no intention to propagate Christianity in Japan? No maritime power but Holland enjoys her confidence. Holland only can make a movement to open Japan to the commerce of the world. Holland has not listened to my advice, and will repent it."

"Please to pray Commodore Perry not to allow his patience to be exhausted, to receive quietly the objections of the Japanese government; but then he must declare decidedly that America will not trouble herself about the present religion and politics of Japan. America leaves these untouched, but insists on a commercial treaty to be effected by peaceful negotiation. Probably the proposals will not be listened to; but beg Commodore Perry not to make hostile demonstrations against the good, faithful, innocent people of Japan, but to intimate to the Japanese government that it is in his power to destroy their cities, ships, and men, but that to do so would give him pain; that he will therefore give them a year to consider his proposals, because he would not by force of arms seek to obtain conditions which might as well be secured by friendly measures."

"Then, if notice is given to *me* in proper time, I would still be willing to submit a plan by which the United States government may attain its purposes."

With reference to this letter, in the pamphlet before us M. Von Siebold states that by means of his "correspondent on board the Mississippi" he did not fail "to advise Commodore Perry to follow a peaceful plan, which counsel seems to have borne good fruit."

It is very remarkable how strikingly facts in the history of our negotiation have contradicted the confident predictions of this gentleman, who professed such "profound knowledge and long experience of Japanese affairs."

The Dutch, he states, were the only people who could establish a commercial treaty with Japan, and they had undertaken to sustain our effort. The *facts* are, that they were not able to make a treaty for themselves until long after ours was consummated; that their support of our efforts consisted, as we have shown, in the attempt to make a treaty for themselves before our arrival, committing the Japanese to agree to no treaty with any foreign power but such as they prescribed; and that from the arrival to the departure of our ships in no mode, either directly or indirectly, did they have any communication with the Dutch, nor was the aid of the latter either invoked or employed in the slightest degree in the negotiation of our treaty.

M. Von Siebold predicted that our overtures would be declined, or that a final answer would be delayed as long as possible. The *facts* are, that our overtures were not declined, and that, under the circumstances of the death of the Emperor and other events, the delay was not unreasonably long. The squadron returned to Yeddo bay on the 13th of February, and all the terms of the treaty were substantially agreed on by the 23d of March, and it was formally signed on the 31st of that month. So that about six weeks elapsed from the commencement of the negotiation to its close in a treaty.

M. Von Siebold predicted that various pretexts would be resorted to by the Japanese to protract the negotiation. Singularly enough, the *fact* is, that of the six anticipated objections specified by Von Siebold not one was urged in the negotiation as insurmountable, and five were not mentioned at all. The only one named was the unalterable nature of the Japanese laws.

And as to the complacency with which M. Von Siebold congratulates himself on the "good fruit" resulting from his counsel, we have only to remark that we are very sorry his good advice did not arrive in time to afford the Commodore any aid, inasmuch as his course had been fully decided on and in part followed without the slightest reference to it. *In fact, Commodore Perry never saw M. Von Siebold's letter at all.*

Of the disposition to disparage the United States and its expedition to Japan, the proofs are quite as unequivocal as those we have given above of self-conceit and arrogance. Our country is more than once brought into disadvantageous comparison with Russia; is accused of being influenced by the most selfish motives: of seeking her own advantage without the slightest regard to those of Japan or of the rest of the civilized world; and in this respect her conduct is contrasted with that of Holland, which is affirmed to have been always prompted by a most liberal desire to open Japan to the commerce of the world. Russia, also, is said to be benevolently pursuing the same end, and also to be seeking the free exercise of Christian worship for all Russian subjects in Japan. With Russia's zeal for the protection of Christians in Japan we have nothing to do; we may remark, however, it is a little curious that Russia should not be warned to avoid the subject of Christianity in Japan, while Commodore Perry is so decidedly advised, by M. Von Siebold, carefully to proclaim that he is no Christian missionary; and is informed that the dread of the introduction of Christianity is the only real obstacle to his success.

The chief magistrate of our country is also rebuked for a want of the usual diplomatic form, and of the dignified tone, so necessary to be used toward the sovereign of a country so much accustomed to etiquette.

Piqued at Commodore Perry's success in the bay of Yedo, when M. Von Siebold had predicted that he would be obliged to go to Nagasaki, and that his proposals would not be listened to anywhere else, if, indeed, they would be listened to at all, he sneeringly attributes his success to what he imputes as a *fault*, viz: that Commodore Perry informed the Japanese that the mere request to go to Nagasaki would, if repeated, be construed into an insult to the United States. And, finally, though we have succeeded, it is to be of but little value to us, inasmuch as Russia and the Netherlands can better supply Japan's wants than we can, and their political and commercial regulations are such as the Siogoon can sympathize with, while ours are not.

Of the selfishness of our motives we readily admit that we sought commercial intercourse with Japan, because we supposed it would be advantageous. Such, we suppose, is the motive of all intelligent nations in establishing friendly relations with others. We can only smile at the simplicity of those who expect to deceive the world by professions of pure, disinterested friendship from one nation toward another, irrespective of all considerations of national benefit. We think that every nation which has sought intercourse with Japan has supposed that such intercourse would prove advantageous to the seeker; nor are we aware that there is anything very criminal or selfish in the desire that advantage may result from the communication. But it is quite possible to believe that benefit to *both* nations may result from the intercourse we would establish, and such benefit may be honestly desired, even while we seek our own interest. This is not selfishness. But further, we beg distinctly to state the fact that Commodore Perry did express to the Japanese commissioners the desire that other nations might have the benefits of our treaty, or of one similar to it, and received for reply that there were many commercial nations on the globe; and that if they wished to have a treaty they should do as we had done, visit Japan and seek to make one.

That our late President (Mr. Fillmore) should have been wanting in the courtly proprieties of diplomatic etiquette, and prove himself ignorant of the dignified language in which it became him to address a sovereign, is certainly very lamentable. But we are comforted by the reflection that his Japanese majesty was not offended by the manly, yet respectful, frankness of our republican chief; that the Emperor seems perfectly to have understood what he said, (which is something unusual in diplomacy;) and that, through his commissioners, he responded in a very friendly and cordial manner to the propositions made by our President. At all events, *we made a treaty with Japan satisfactory to both governments.* Our rude ignorance of propriety was thus kindly overlooked; and we, therefore, hope that M. Von Siebold, the self-constituted court chamberlain of Japan, will henceforth generously forbear to speak of the shortcomings of such a semi-civilized people and government as ours. It may indicate our barbarism, but we would rather be clowns than calumniators.

We plead guilty, too, to the charge that Commodore Perry went to the bay of Yedo and refused to go to Nagasaki; and that he added to this enormity the very plain declaration that "the Americans will never submit to the restrictions which have been imposed upon the Dutch and Chinese, and any further allusion to such restraints will be considered offensive;" to which we will add that the Japanese commissioners put in writing, as one of the points *agreed* upon between them and Commodore Perry, that "the citizens of the United States will not submit to degradations like those imposed upon the Dutch and Chinese." And Commodore Perry's countrymen expected him to say precisely what he did say, and are quite satisfied with the result.

It only remains to be added that, until since the return of our expedition, neither the Dutch nor Russians were able to effect a treaty. England and the United States alone succeeded; and England readily admits that, in point of time, ours was the *first*. This is all we have ever said; and we conclude with the wish that all the powers of Europe, seeking commercial treaties with Japan, may succeed as well as England and ourselves, and that most interesting Empire thus be opened to, and enriched by, free communication with the civilized world.

CHAPTER I.

PROBABILITIES OF A SUCCESSFUL MISSION FROM THE UNITED STATES TO JAPAN.—SUCH A MISSION PROPOSED TO THE GOVERNMENT BY COMMODORE PERRY.—EXPEDITION RESOLVED ON.—VESSELS SELECTED FOR THE SQUADRON.—VEXATIOUS DELAY IN THEIR EQUIPMENT.—COMMODORE PERRY SENT IN THE MISSISSIPPI TO THE GULF OF ST. LAWRENCE.—APPLICATIONS OF SCIENTIFIC MEN TO JOIN THE EXPEDITION REFUSED.—CAUSES OF SUCH REFUSAL.—DR. VON SIEBOLD.—VISIT OF THE PRESIDENT AND SECRETARY OF THE NAVY TO ANNAPOLIS TO TAKE LEAVE OF THE EXPEDITION.—FAILURE OF THE MACHINERY OF THE STEAMSHIP PRINCETON ON THE PASSAGE DOWN CHESAPEAKE BAY.—SUBSTITUTION OF STEAMER POWHATAN IN PLACE OF THE PRINCETON.—FINAL DEPARTURE OF COMMODORE PERRY ON THE MISSION WITH THE MISSISSIPPI ALONE.

HE treaty which closed the war of the United States with Mexico transferred to the former the territory of California. Its position on the Pacific could not but suggest the thought of an extended field for commercial enterprise; and with our territory spreading from ocean to ocean, and placed midway between Europe and Asia, it seemed that we might with propriety apply to ourselves the name by which China had loved to designate herself, and deem that we were, in truth, "the Middle Kingdom." If the shortest route between Eastern Asia and Western Europe be (in this age of steam) across our continent, then was it obvious enough that our continent must, in some degree at least, become a highway for the world. And when, soon after our acquisition of California, it was discovered that the harvest there was *gold*, nothing was more natural than that such discovery should give additional interest to the obvious reflections suggested by our geographical position.

Direct trade from our western coast with Asia became, therefore, a familiar thought; the agency of steam was, of course, involved, and fuel for its production was indispensable. Hence arose inquiries for that great mineral agent of civilization, *coal*. Where was it to be obtained on the long route from California to Asia? Another inquiry presented itself: With what far-distant eastern nations should we trade? China was in some measure opened to us; but there was, beside, a *terra incognita* in Japan which, while it stimulated curiosity, held out also temptations which invited commercial enterprise. True, we knew not much about its internal regulations; we knew that it had, for centuries, isolated itself, as it were, from the world, and persisted in a system of excluding foreigners from intercourse; that but one European nation was allowed to approach for purposes of trade, and that repeated efforts made by others for a similar privilege had uniformly failed of success. But we knew, too, that it possessed valuable productions, and ought to be brought into communication with the rest of the world. By some, indeed, the proposition was boldly avowed that Japan had no right thus to cut herself off from the community of nations; and that what she would not yield to national comity should be wrested from her by force.

It was, perhaps, but natural that the minds of our naval officers should be drawn strongly to a consideration of the subject of intercourse with Japan. Not simply to the desirableness or probable advantages of such intercourse, for on those points all men's minds readily reached the same conclusion; but on the *means* by which the wished for end might be best attained. And this part of the subject required some study and calm reflection, aided by such experience and knowledge of men of all latitudes as a naval officer would be apt to acquire in many years of active service on shipboard.

Commodore Perry, in common with other members of his profession and with the rest of his countrymen, had his thoughts directed to the subject, with especial reference to the probabilities of accomplishing the end in view. He knew that there must be causes for a state of things so singular as was presented in the complete voluntary isolation of a whole people; and his first object was, therefore, to obtain a correct history of the past career of Japan. For this purpose he mastered all that he could derive from books, and found that the exclusive system of Japan was not the result of any national idiosyncracy, but was caused by peculiar circumstances, long since passed, and was, in fact, in direct opposition to what history proved to be the natural temperament and disposition of the Japanese people. He also found, in a careful examination of the repeated efforts of other nations to break down the barrier that shut them out, what he supposed to be the secret of their failures. Peculiar circumstances in the then political condition of the power seeking admission; the rivalry of different nations striving to thwart each other; the indiscretion, not to say arrogance, of some of those entrusted with the mission, who sought to bully a brave people into acquiescence with their wishes; a misconception of the true character of the Japanese, who readily distinguish between obsequious servility and a manly spirit of conciliation, founded on the principle of doing what is kind and just, but submitting, not for an instant, to what is insulting or wrong; all these seemed to him to be elements of failure clearly to be traced, in a greater or less degree, in the efforts that had been made. Beside, a disadvantage under which the European nations labored was that Japan had known something concerning all of them for many years, and, indeed, had been more or less brought into contact with them. Thus Portugal had given early and unpardonable offence in encouraging domestic treason; England (who once had toothold) had abandoned it; one of her kings had married a Portuguese princess; one of her officers (Pellew) had committed what they deemed an insolent outrage in her waters; Russia had taken possession of some of her islands, had excited suspicions of ulterior designs by fortifying on another "annexed" territory, at the mouth of the Amour, and, as the Japanese Emperor said, "had an inclination for Japan;" while Holland had so quietly submitted to degradation, imprisonment and insult for two hundred years, that the Japanese unquestionably formed their opinion of European foreigners, in some measure, from the Dutch.

MISSION TO JAPAN PROPOSED BY COMMODORE PERRY.

The United States occupied a different position from all the above named powers, for they had not been brought into such contact with Japan as awakened unpleasant associations. The only effort we had made toward opening friendly relations, (and it scarcely deserves the name,) was in sending two ships under Commodore Biddle, which remained at anchor some eight or ten days, accomplished nothing, and quietly left when the Japanese desired it.

Commodore Perry, after careful examination, believed that, under all the circumstances, there was a favorable opportunity for our country to establish commercial relations with Japan, and avowed his belief to several of his brother officers, as well as to some of the dignitaries of the government, and eminent citizens, long before the subject was publicly discussed, and the expedition resolved on. There were doubtless others (and among them probably some of high station in the government) whose minds had been led to a similar conclusion, and who, like Commodore Perry, anticipated popular opinion on the subject of an expedition. Indeed, instructions had been sent out to Commodore Aulick, then on the East India station, directing him to proceed to Japan; and the State Department, then under the charge of Mr. Webster, had sought information concerning Japan from the officer who commanded the Preble on her visit, Commander Glynn, who very strongly felt and urged the importance of establishing, if possible, a friendly communication between that Kingdom and our own country. We believe, however, we do no wrong to any one, when we say that the thought of making an *immediate* effort was urged by Commodore Perry; and, at all events, on the recal of Commodore Aulick, he formally proposed to the government of the United States the expedition, which was finally sent. The proposition was favorably received, and it was determined that a squadron should be dispatched, under his command, on the peaceful mission of endeavoring to open a friendly commercial intercourse with the Japanese.*

The expedition having been resolved on, the following vessels were selected to compose the squadron, viz: The Mississippi steamer, which had been the flag ship of Commodore Perry in the Gulf during the Mexican war, and was deservedly his favorite vessel; the Princeton and Alleghany steamers; the Vermont, 74; and the sloops-of-war Vandalia and Macedonian. The steamship Susquehanna, and sloops-of-war Saratoga and Plymouth were already on the East India station, and were to form part of the squadron. The armed storeships Supply, Lexington, and Southampton, were also attached to the expedition. The liveliest interest in the undertaking was manifested by the President, (Mr. Fillmore,) by Mr. Webster, and his successors in the State Department, (Messrs. Conrad and Everett,) by the Secretary of the Navy, (Mr. Kennedy,) and indeed by all the members of the Cabinet. The most liberal equipment was authorized, and the commander of the expedition was invested with extraordinary powers, diplomatic as well as naval, because much was necessarily confided to his prudence and discretion. The instructions from the department designated the East India and China seas and Japan as the field of service; but the great objects of the expedition were to procure friendly admission to Japan for purposes of trade, and to establish, at proper points, permanent depots of coal for our steamers crossing the Pacific.

Orders were given to fit the squadron for sea with as little delay as possible; yet such was the mismanagement in the equipment of the vessels, that more than once the public were led to

---

* The subject of establishing commercial relations with the East occupied the minds of so many of our countrymen, that it is, of course, impossible to say, with certainty, with whom its discussion originated. It is, however, due to one gentleman, (Aaron H. Palmer, esq., of New York,) to say that he was, at least, among the earliest to call attention to its importance.

suppose that the enterprise had been abandoned simply from the delay in its departure. More than nine months had passed beyond the time when the chief of the Bureau of Construction and Equipment had promised that the Princeton should be ready, before that vessel was reported as completed; and when thus reported, she was found, on trial, to be utterly inefficient for the intended service, owing to the imperfection of her boilers. Some new, and in this country untried, plan had been adopted in their construction or arrangement, and the experiment cost the expedition the loss of a year. The Princeton never formed part of the squadron, as the Powhatan was substituted for her.

Amid these vexatious delays, however, the Commodore was not idle. While he was waiting for the completion of the Princeton, the misunderstanding arose concerning the fisheries in the Gulf of St. Lawrence, and it became necessary to dispatch an armed vessel to that region. The Mississippi was ready for sea, and Commodore Perry was ordered to repair in her to the fishing grounds, and assist in amicably adjusting the respective rights of the English and American fishermen. Having performed this duty satisfactorily to the government, he returned to New York, earnestly hoping that he should find removed all obstacles to his speedy departure on his mission to the East.

As soon as it was publicly announced that the United States had resolved on sending an expedition to Japan, applications came from all quarters of the civilized world for permission to take part in the service. Literary and scientific men, European as well as native, and travellers by profession, eagerly sought to accompany the expedition; and extraordinary influences, in some instances, were brought to bear upon our government inducing it to second some of the applications thus made; but Commodore Perry resolutely persisted in an unqualified refusal to all such requests.

And here it may be well to explain the grounds of such refusal. The duties confided to the commander were of a peculiar nature, and required the most prudent and delicate management on his part. He had his own views of what he had to accomplish and of the best mode of doing it; and an essential element to success was the possession of absolute authority for the time being. It was indispensable that the most exact order and discipline should be maintained. To effect this, strict military control would be necessary; but civilians could not be expected to submit patiently to the restraints of naval discipline, to the confinement on ship board, and to the sanitary regulations necessary to preserve health in crowded ships.

But, further, after the accommodation of the proper officers of the vessels there would be but little room left for that of scientific men, who were accustomed to the comforts and conveniences of life on shore, with abundant space for their books and instruments; and beside, they would severely feel the disappointment of not being able to go and come at their pleasure, when curiosity and their scientific researches might make it desirable, to say nothing of the embarrassments they might cause to the commander when they did land, by collisions with the people, arising from inadvertence or experience.

But paramount as a ground of refusal was the fact that the object of the expedition was not scientific, but naval and diplomatic; to attempt both would probably be to succeed in neither. If one, the last named, were prosecuted to a favorable result, the door would then be opened for success in the other. At any rate, the commander thought it would be best to do one thing at a time, and that *the* one thing confided to him for performance, must take precedence of every thing else.

Another matter, of no little delicacy in its adjustment, was likely to arise from the presence of scientific gentlemen not subject to the strict discipline of the navy. The Commodore's instructions required of him to prohibit those under his command from making any communications to the newspapers and other public prints touching the movements of the squadron or the discipline and internal regulations of the vessels composing it; and even private letters to friends were to avoid these topics. All journals and private notes kept by members of the expedition were to be considered as belonging to the government until permission should be given from the Navy Department to publish them. The object of these regulations was to withhold information from other powers which, if communicated, might jeopard the success of our mission. It was known that other nations, particularly Russia, had ordered ships to Japan as soon as it was known that the United States had sent there a squadron. Now, the correspondence of scientific gentlemen with their friends and families was a delicate subject to be discussed between them and the commander. The latter would neither demand to see their letters nor prescribe the topics on which they might write. It was, therefore, best to avoid embarrassment by preventing the possibility of its occurrence.

Some professional feeling also influenced the determination of the Commodore. He supposed that it was desirable to cherish a taste for scientific observation and study among the officers of the navy, many of whom are already not without reputation in science. If an opportunity were afforded them, and facilities furnished for observation, it would make them students of science; and though they might not always, in their early efforts, be able to account philosophically for what they saw, yet they could record facts which others might explain; and, as they would never forget the facts or the explanations, they would thus be adding to their stores of scientific knowledge. Many of the officers of our army are scientific men; there is no reason why our naval officers should not be so also.

These were the general causes which led the Commodore to the determination we have mentioned, without reference to persons. It is proper, however, to add, that, with respect to one individual, who manifested extraordinary desire to be of the expedition, and who has published untruths concerning it since its return, (Dr. Von Siebold,) Commodore Perry refused on personal grounds. From information received from abroad, he suspected him of being a *Russian spy*, and he knew that he had been banished from Japan, where, by a violation of law, he had forfeited his life.

On the Commodore's return from the Gulf of St. Lawrence, he found that the vessels under his command were by no means ready for sea; and, leaving New York, he proceeded in the Mississippi to Annapolis. He was not long in making the discovery that, unless he sailed alone and trusted to the chances of being joined at uncertain periods by the vessels assigned to his command, and then under equipment, he might be detained in the United States several months longer. He therefore, with the approbation of the Navy Department, determined to proceed on his voyage in the Mississippi without further delay; with the understanding that he should be followed, as soon as possible, by the other vessels of the squadron.

Before leaving Annapolis, President Fillmore, with the Secretary of the Navy and many other persons of distinction, both ladies and gentlemen, visited the ship and bade farewell to the Commodore and his officers. As the Mississippi and Princeton steamed down the Chesapeake bay, the discovery was made of the entire unfitness of the last named vessel to make the contemplated voyage. Her machinery failed, and it was on the arrival at Norfolk that

80   EXPEDITION TO JAPAN.

the Powhatan (which had then just arrived from the West Indies) was substituted for the Princeton.

The Commodore, tired of delays, was not disposed to wait any longer for a consort, and, accordingly, on the 24th of November, 1852, the Mississippi *alone* took her departure from Norfolk, on the mission to Japan, with the intention of touching on the outward passage, for supplies of coal and refreshments, at Madeira, the Cape of Good Hope, Mauritius, and Singapore.

U.S. STEAM FRIGATE MISSISSIPPI CROSSING THE GULF STREAM

CHAPTER II.

VOYAGE FROM THE CAPES OF THE CHESAPEAKE TO MADEIRA.—VIEW OF THE ISLAND.—FUNCHAL.—HOSPITALITY OF THE INHABITANTS.—SALUBRITY OF THE CLIMATE.—EXPORTS OF THE ISLAND.—NOVEL MODE OF CONVEYANCE.—DEPARTURE FROM MADEIRA AND ARRIVAL AT THE CANARIES.—EARLY FAILURE OF NORTHEAST TRADES.—EXTRAORDINARY SWELL FROM THE NORTHWEST.—GENERAL ORDER AS TO PRIVATE JOURNALS AND COMMUNICATIONS TO PUBLIC PRINTS.—GENERAL ORDER AS TO SCIENTIFIC INVESTIGATIONS BY OFFICERS.—THE "HARMATTAN," CONSIDERATION OF HYPOTHESES AS TO ITS ORIGIN.—SOUTHEAST TRADES.—SHIP STEERED FOR ST. HELENA.—OBSERVATIONS ON THE CURRENTS.—CHAPLAIN'S OBSERVATIONS ON THE ZODIACAL LIGHTS.—ARRIVAL AT ST. HELENA.—DESCRIPTION OF THE ISLAND.—JAMESTOWN.—LONGWOOD.—TOMB OF NAPOLEON.—THE CALCULATING HOSPITALITY OF THE INHABITANTS OF THE ISLAND.—ADVENTURE OF LIEUTENANT ———.—FORTIFICATIONS OF THE ISLAND.—THEIR SUFFICIENCY AGAINST SAILING VESSELS.—PROBABLE INSUFFICIENCY AGAINST AN APPROACH FROM THE WEST BY STEAM.—DEPARTURE FROM ST. HELENA.

N leaving the capes of the Chesapeake, the wind for ten days was strong from the southward; it then changed to N.N.E., making a heavy "wallowing" sea; and then, hauling to the westward, blew with such violence as to render the ship uncomfortable. She, however, sustained the high opinion the Commodore entertained of her good qualities, behaving (as she always had done) most admirably, and averaging more than seven knots during the whole passage. Though unusually deep in the water, but eight of her twelve furnaces were put in requisition, and her daily consumption of Cumberland coal was about twenty-six tons.

After crossing the Gulf stream a southwestern current of about a knot per hour was experienced; and this continued until the ship was within a thousand miles of Madeira, when it ceased entirely. No other current was observed during the remainder of the passage to the island.

The land was made on the evening of December 11th, seventeen days after leaving Norfolk. On making the northern extremity of the island, "Point Atristow," the wind was blowing a gale from the W.S.W., which occasioned a heavy "rolling" sea. The ship was, therefore, run along the northern end of the island with the view of finding smoother water, the more conveniently to bend the cables.

In coasting the island, several very pretty villages were observed occupying sheltered nooks, usually at the bottom of some ravine, and near an indentation of the coast, which offered indifferent anchorage to the small vessels employed in transporting the produce of the island to the shipping port, "Funchal."

What added to the beauty of the scenery and roused the admiration and enthusiasm of the artists of the expedition was, that, as the rainy season had just passed, the torrents could be seen from the ship rushing down the sides of the mountains and forming in their descent many beautiful cascades.

View of Funchal, Madeira.

Knowing that the wind, for the last few days, must have thrown into the bay of Funchal a heavy swell, rendering anchorage there unsafe, it was determined to run under the lee of the "Deserters," and there wait a favorable moment for anchoring in the roads. But on rounding the southeastern point of the island it was found that the wind had considerably abated, and had hauled to the northward of west, making it safe to proceed immediately to the anchorage; and accordingly, just at dark, on the 12th, the ship came to anchor in thirty-three fathoms, the castle back of the town just open with the Loo rock.

The vice consul of the United States, Mr. Beyman, with several coal agents were soon alongside, and arrangements were promptly made to send on board all the coal and water that might be required, so that the vessel would be ready to sail on the next Wednesday night. Accordingly, at daylight the next morning, (Monday, the 13th,) lighters containing coal and water were seen coming off, and by Wednesday, at four o'clock, p. m., between four and five hundred tons of coal, and ten thousand gallons of water, with many other articles, had been received on board. It may here be remarked, that the coal agents were very desirous that the vessel should be anchored much nearer the town, in about ten fathoms, and in a position where she would be

sheltered from the westerly winds by the Loo rock; but upon an observation of the locality, the Commodore was satisfied that in blowing weather it would be difficult even for a steamer to get safely out from such an anchorage, and he therefore positively forbade the removal of the vessel to the spot indicated. The anchorage anywhere in Funchal bay is unsafe in the winter season, and vessels lying in the road, when expecting a gale from S.E. around to W.S.W. generally put to sea, and remain out until the return of fine weather. In fact, Funchal, which lies on the south side of the island, has only an open roadstead, with a very rocky and uneven anchorage. The whole island is a mass of basalt. From November to February gales prevail from the southeast and southwest, rendering the roadstead very dangerous.

Funchal Cathedral, Madeira.

Funchal still retains its character for hospitality, and by no one was this virtue more gracefully exercised towards the members of the expedition than by Mr. J. H. March, who for more than thirty years has filled the office of consul of the United States, and in the enjoyment of his large fortune takes delight in making welcome to his houses, both in town and country, such of his countrymen as are deserving of his attentions.

The town consists of a wide street along the sea shore, containing several good buildings. From this, numerous small streets extend back at right angles, for a considerable distance up the slope of the hill. The population amounts to some twenty thousand. The commerce of the island is considerable, and most of it is with England. Its exports have been said to amount to the value of £500,000 per annum. Wine is the principal commodity. When the island was first settled by the Portuguese, sugar was cultivated to a considerable extent, but this was discontinued after the West Indies were brought under culture, and wine became the staple.

The salubrity of the climate has made Funchal a resort for invalids, and hence it is not difficult to find in it agreeable and refined society. The greater number of those who visit the island are English, and the known love of Englishmen for exercise in the open air has led to the introduction of some novel modes of affording to invalids the benefit of locomotion.

Carriage on Sled.

As the streets of the city are paved in such manner as to forbid the use of wheel carriages, sedan chairs and hammocks were, until very recently, used not only for invalids, but by all persons making visits. The inconvenience of these vehicles has led to a substitute, which consists of nothing more than the ordinary sledge used for transporting casks of wine and other heavy articles through the streets, surmounted by a gaily decorated carriage body, and drawn by a yoke of oxen. This is now the fashionable conveyance, and in such an one did the Commodore, with his flag captain and aid, make all his official visits. There are stands in the streets, as for our cabs and carriages, where these vehicles may be found with the oxen yoked, and all things prepared for immediate transportation.

It must not, however, be supposed that there are no other modes of conveyance; horseback riding may be seen, and the fair equestrian makes her appearance without an attendant cavalier or groom, but with a footman, who keeps pace with the easy gait of the horse, and protects him from the annoyance of flies and other insects. Asses are common, and are probably the best beasts of burden on such roads as the island possesses.

While the ship was at Madeira, the Commodore, who had reflected much and anxiously on the important mission with which he had been entrusted, thought it best to bring distinctly before the department the views he entertained of the steps he ought to undertake, more particularly as so much was necessarily confided to his discretion. He accordingly addressed to the Secretary of the Navy an official communication, which is here presented, not only as affording a record of his matured opinions on the important work before him, but also as furnishing the reader with the means of ascertaining, as he proceeds in the narrative, how far the Commodore's anticipations were fulfilled, and how nearly he was enabled to follow out his original intentions.

Commodore Perry to the Secretary of the Navy.

UNITED STATES STEAM FRIGATE MISSISSIPPI,
Madeira, December 14, 1852.

SIR: Since leaving the United States I have had leisure to reflect more fully upon the probable result of my visit to Japan, and though there is still some doubt in my mind as to the chances of immediate success in bringing that strange government to any practicable negotiation, yet I feel confident that in the end the great object in view will be effected.

As a preliminary step, and one of easy accomplishment, one or more ports of refuge and supply to our whaling and other ships must at once be secured; and should the Japanese government object to the granting of such ports upon the main land, and if they cannot be occupied without resort to force and bloodshed, then it will be desirable in the beginning, and indeed, necessary, that the squadron should establish places of rendezvous at one or two of the islands south of Japan, having a good harbor, and possessing facilities for obtaining water and supplies, and seek by kindness and gentle treatment to conciliate the inhabitants so as to bring about their friendly intercourse.

The islands called the Lew Chew group are said to be dependencies of Japan, as conquered by that power centuries ago, but their actual sovereignty is disputed by the government of China.

These islands come within the jurisdiction of the prince of Satsuma, the most powerful of the princes of the Empire, and the same who caused the unarmed American ship Morrison, on a visit of mercy, to be decoyed into one of his ports and then fired upon from the batteries hastily erected. He exercises his rights more from the influence of the fear of the simple islanders than from any power to coerce their obedience; disarmed, as they long have been, from motives of policy, they have no means, even if they had the inclination, to rebel against the grinding oppression of their rulers.

Now, it strikes me, that the occupation of the principal ports of those islands for the accommodation of our ships of war, and for the safe resort of merchant vessels of whatever nation, would be a measure not only justified by the strictest rules of moral law, but what is also to be considered, by the laws of stern necessity; and the argument may be further strengthened by the certain consequences of the amelioration of the condition of the natives, although the vices attendant upon civilization may be entailed upon them.

In my former commands upon the coast of Africa and in the Gulf of Mexico, where it fell to my lot to subjugate many towns and communities, I found no difficulty in conciliating the good will and confidence of the conquered people, by administering the unrestricted power I held rather to their comfort and protection than to their annoyance; and when the naval forces left, they carried with them the gratitude and good wishes of their former enemies; and so I believe that the people of the islands spoken of, if treated with strict justice and gentle kindness, will render confidence for confidence, and after a while the Japanese will learn to consider us their friends.

In establishing those ports of refuge it will be desirable to provide the means of supply to the vessels that may resort to them, and hence the necessity of encouraging the natives in the cultivation of fruits, vegetables, &c.; and to carry out, in part, this object, garden seeds have been provided; but to pursue the purpose still further, I have thought that if a few of the more simple agricultural implements of our own country were sent to me for use, and for presents, they would contribute most essentially to the end in view; such, for instance, as the common cultivator, the plough and harrow, spades, hoes of various kinds, the threshing and winnowing machines, and especially those inventions for separating the cotton from its seed, and rice from its husks.

And with reference, also, to the subject of my letter to Mr. Folsome, chargé at the Hague, a copy of which has been enclosed to the Department of State, it would be good policy to counteract the discreditable machinations of the Dutch, by circulating printed publications representing the true condition of the various governments of the world, and especially to set forth the extraordinary prosperity of the United States under their genial laws.

To effect this object, I am already provided with works for presentation, descriptive of the civil and political condition of the United States, such as the census tables, post-office and railroad reports, reports of the Indian and Land offices, military and naval registers, also with the magnificent publications of the State of New York, &c.

And I have thought that a small printing press, with type and materials, would go far to facilitate our plans, by giving us the means of putting forth information calculated to disabuse the Japanese of the misrepresentations of the Dutch.

The government of Japan keeps in employment linguists in all modern languages; and such is their curiosity, that these publications, if admitted at all, will soon be translated.

Having thus, at least in anticipation, established harbors of resort, and organized certain rules of equity to govern our intercourse with the natives in the payment for labor, supplies, &c., and having depots of provisions and coal near at hand, we shall be able to act with more effect in bringing about some friendly understanding with the imperial government. At all events, steamers, or whatever vessels that may be passing to and from California and China, will find safe harbors in their way, and it may reasonably be expected that in the course of time the intercourse thus brought about will lead to a better understanding of our pacific intentions.

It may be said that my anticipations are too sanguine. Perhaps they are, but I feel a strong confidence of success. Indeed, success may be commanded by our government, and it should be, under whatever circumstances, accomplished. The honor of the nation calls for it, and the interest of commerce demands it. When we look at the possessions in the east of our great maritime rival, England, and of the constant and rapid increase of their fortified ports, we should be admonished of the necessity of prompt measures on our part.

By reference to the map of the world, it will be seen that Great Britain is already in possession of the most important points in the East India and China seas, and especially with reference to the China seas.

With Singapore commanding the southwestern, while Hong Kong covers the northeastern entrance, and with the island of Labuan on the eastern coast of Borneo, an intermediate point, she will have the power of shutting up at will and controlling the enormous trade of those seas, amounting, it is said, in value to 300,000 tons of shipping, carrying cargoes certainly not under £15,000,000 sterling.*

Fortunately the Japanese and many other islands of the Pacific are still left untouched by this "annexing" government; and, as some of them lay in the route of a commerce which is destined to become of great importance to the United States, no time should be lost in adopting

---

* See Governor Crawford's opinion, in "The Expedition to Borneo by Her Majesty's Ship Dido," chapter 24, published by Harper Brothers, New York, 1846.

active measures to secure a sufficient number of ports of refuge. And hence I shall look with much anxiety for the arrival of the Powhatan and the other vessels to be sent to me.

I have thus exhibited, in this crude and informal communication, my views upon a subject which is exciting extraordinary attention throughout the world, and I trust the department will approve the course I propose to pursue.

With great respect, I am, sir, your most obedient servant,

M. C. PERRY,
Commanding East India Squadron.

Hon. JOHN P. KENNEDY,
Secretary of the Navy, Washington.

The answer to this communication did not, of course, reach the Commodore for many months; but as it preserves the continuity of the transaction, as well as shows the spirit of the government, and its confidence in the Commodore, it is inserted in the note below.*

On the evening of Wednesday, December 15, the Mississippi weighed anchor and proceeded to sea, under steam, shaping her course to pass to the westward of Palma, one of the Canaries. This island was made at daylight on the morning of the 17th, and after reaching the lee of Hierro or Ferro, the southwesternmost of the group, the immersed floats or paddle boards on each side of the vessel were removed, the fires were extinguished and the ship left entirely dependent upon her sails.

This change was made from an expectation that the ship would soon be under the impulse of the northeast trade winds. At the time the floats were removed there was a moderate breeze from E.S.E., which it was supposed would gradually settle into the northeast trades; but, much to the surprise of the officers of the ship, it hauled more to the southward, and eventually came from the S.S.W. Such was the obscurity of the weather at the Canaries that Teneriffe was not seen at all, and but an indistinct view was obtained of Gomera. This was the more

---

* *Mr. Everett to Commodore Perry.*

DEPARTMENT OF STATE, *Washington, February 15, 1853.*

SIR: Your dispatch of the 14th of December has been referred by the Secretary of the Navy to this department, and by me submitted to the President.

The President concurs with you in the opinion that it is highly desirable, probably necessary for the safety of the expedition under your command, that you should secure one or more ports of refuge of easy access. If you find that these cannot be obtained in the Japanese islands without resort to force, it will be necessary that you should seek them elsewhere. The President agrees with you in thinking that you are most likely to succeed in this object in the Lew Chew islands. They are, from their position, well adapted to the purpose; and the friendly and peaceful character of the natives encourages the hope that your visit will be welcomed by them.

In establishing yourself at one or two convenient points in those islands, with the consent of the natives, you will yourself pursue the most friendly and conciliatory course, and enjoin the same conduct on all under your command. Take no supplies from them except by fair purchase, for a satisfactory consideration. Forbid, and at all hazards prevent plunder and acts of violence on the part of your men toward these simple and unwarlike people, for such they are described to be. Let them from the first see that your coming among them is a benefit, and not an evil to them. Make no use of force, except in the last resort for defence, if attacked, and self-preservation.

The President approves the idea suggested by you of encouraging the natives to turn their attention to agriculture, and has given orders to have the implements of husbandry mentioned by you sent out by the Vermont. He has also directed a small printing press, with type and materials for printing of all kinds, to be sent out by the Vermont.

The President is gratified to perceive that you are impressed with the importance of the enterprise confided to your direction, the success of which will mainly depend upon your prudence and address. It will attract a large share of the attention of the civilized world; and the President feels great confidence that the measures adopted by you will reflect credit on your own wisdom and discretion, and do honor to your country.

I am, sir, respectfully, your obedient servant,

EDWARD EVERETT.

Commodore M. C. PERRY,
Commanding the United States naval forces in the China seas.

remarkable, because, as Baron Humboldt has remarked, although the peak of Teneriffe is seldom seen at a great distance in the warm, dry months of July and August, yet in January and February, when the sky is slightly clouded, and immediately before or after a heavy rain, it is seen at very extraordinary distances. This arises from the fact that when a certain quantity of water is uniformly diffused through the atmosphere its transparency is thereby greatly increased.

There was a circumstance which the Commodore had observed ever since the ship left Norfolk, a month before, and which surprised him not a little. He found an extraordinary swell coming from the northwest, and which never intermitted for a moment until the ship was fairly within the trades; and even then its influence could be felt in the disturbance of the usually regular sea produced by the periodical winds, and by the production of a disagreeable cross movement of the waves. It was difficult to account for this swell so long continued; it was quite certain the ship had experienced no violence of wind sufficient to produce it in the region which she had traversed, and since the 18th the winds had been quite moderate. The conjecture of the Commodore was that there must have been in the higher latitudes a succession of northwesterly gales, which had prevailed long enough to set in motion an ocean wave which was never subdued until it came in contact with the steady, though more quiet, tropical swell.

This swell, too, possibly had an effect in throwing further south than usual the northern boundary of the trades. From the time of removing the floats up to the 20th the wind continued from the southward and westward; it then hauled to the northward and westward, and finally into the northeast; and it was not until about this period, about 8 p. m. of the 20th, in latitude 25° 44' north, longitude 20° 23' west, that the ship could be considered fairly to have entered the trades. This is a point unusually far south for the northern boundary of these winds at this season; for it is not to be forgotten that the northern and southern boundaries of the zone of the trade winds are variable. The southeast has its northern boundary furthest to the north during our summer; the northeast is then weakest. In our winter this state of things is exactly reversed. In our autumn the zone of the trades reaches its greatest northern declination; and in our spring it is at its utmost southern limit.

On the 22d of December, the Commodore issued a general order, promulgating the directions of the Secretary of the Navy forbidding communications to the public prints at home touching the movements of the squadron, and prohibiting also such infomation through the medium of private letters to friends. The Secretary also required that private notes and journals kept by any members of the expedition should be considered as belonging to the government until their publication should be expressly permitted by the Navy Department.

A second general order, issued the next day, was as follows:

"Entertaining the opinion that the talents and acquirements of the officers of the squadron, if properly directed and brought into action, will be found equal to a plain and practical examination and elucidation of the various objects pertaining to the arts and sciences that may come under their observation during the present cruise, and being aware of the limited accommodations of the vessels under my command, I have invariably objected to the employment of persons drawn from civil life to conduct those departments more immediately connected with science.

"Therefore I have to request and direct, that each officer of the respective ships will employ such portions of his time as can be spared from his regular duties and proper hours of relaxation, in contributing to the general mass of information which it is desirable to collect; and in order to simplify and methodise these researches, a paper is subjoined particularising the various departments in reference to which information is more especially wanted; so that each officer may select one or more of those departments most congenial to his tastes and inclinations.

"All captains and commanders are required to render every facility consistent with the proper duties of their respective vessels to those officers who may manifest a zealous co-operation in the pursuits herein specified; and it is to be plainly understood that I do not *officially* require the officers to perform any involuntary duty. I shall exact that only which may come within the legitimate sphere of my authority, leaving to the officers themselves to engage, as far as they may see fit only, in those investigations which, in an official point of view, may be considered as on their parts gratuitous.

"It will always give me the greatest pleasure to bring to notice the labors of each and every individual who may contribute to the general work." *

During the 21st, 22d, and 23d of December, the wind continued from the northward and eastward; about noon of the 23d it inclined to the southward of east, hauling around at night, however, more to the north; and on the 24th, when the ship was abreast of Brava and Fogo, it stood at E.N.E.

The haze, however, was such that nothing more than a glimpse could be obtained of Fogo; and the winds are thus particularly referred to above because of their possible connexion, at this time, with the haze. They are physical facts, and therefore ought to be recorded. This haze is common to these latitudes, and is by many supposed to be caused by what is called the "Harmattan." This is the name given to a wind which, passing over Africa, takes up in its sweep, as is supposed, an impalpable dust, and carries it far away to the westward. The Commodore himself had remarked the haze or dust, on former cruises, more than five hundred miles west of the Cape de Verd islands. When commanding a squadron, in 1844, on the western coast of Africa, he had carefully noted several facts connected with this wind, certainly the most remarkable on that coast. A thousand incredible stories are told of its singular effects. It is said, for instance, that its dry and subtle properties will check or cure various diseases, heal up the most inveterate ulcers, destroy cabinet work, break window glass, and stop the motion of timepieces. But apart from these strange stories, it must still be said that the effects of this wind are extraordinary. In some respects it resembles the Sirocco, and also the Levanter of the Grecian archipelago.

It commences about the middle of December, and continues until the latter end of March. Like the Sirocco, it has been supposed to take its rise in the deserts of Africa; but, unlike the Sirocco, instead of producing a burning and oppressive temperature, it is a chilling wind. Its direction is always from the land, and it sometimes increases to a strong breeze; it does not, however, blow steadily during its season, but frequently intermits, when land or sea breezes take its place.

At the Cape de Verds and the Gambia, the "Harmattan" appears to form a junction with the northeast trades prevailing there at a certain season, and to blow with little interruption from January until April.

---

* The subjects suggested by the Commodore, in his order, embraced hydrography, meteorology, naval architecture in its adaptation to war and commerce, military affairs, geology, geography, terrestrial magnetism, philology and ethnology, artistic matters, costumes, &c., religions, diseases and sanitary laws, agriculture, statistics of supplies, botany, entomology, ornithology, zoology, conchology, ichthiology, and the magnetic telegraph; and we trust the appendices to this narrative will show that the commander did not misjudge either as to the attainments or zeal of his officers.

The hypothesis of some is, that in passing over the deserts and lands of Africa the "Harmattan" takes up an immense quantity of sand and dust, sufficient to form a floating mass, producing an atmosphere so hazy as frequently to obscure the sun, and prevent a sight of the land at the distance of five miles only. There is no doubt of the wind, the dust, and the hazy atmosphere, and possibly the latter may be occasioned entirely by the dust. At the season of the "Harmattan" this peculiar atmosphere may always be seen at the Cape de Verd islands, four hundred miles from the continent, and is constantly falling in quantities sufficient to cover the sails, rigging, and deck of a ship. It is also said to have been met with seven hundred miles further westward.

Recent investigations, however, certainly create some doubt as to the source whence the dust is derived. It was natural enough, as it was found on the coast of Africa, to refer its origin to the nearest known desert land; but the microscope, in the hands of Ehrenberg, would seem to intimate the possibility of a more distant origin. This dust, from the Cape de Verds, is found, upon examination, to consist of infusoria and organisms, the *habitat* of which is not Africa, but *South America*, and in the southeast trade wind region of that country. It is, therefore, possible that the southeast trades may have brought the dust, great as is the distance, from South America. But if such be the fact, it must be confessed that there are agencies in the philosophy of the winds, producing atmospheric phenomena, which are not yet sufficiently understood by us to justify positive assertion. A greater accumulation of *facts* is wanted. That stated by Ehrenberg is very important, and quite sufficient to create doubt of the correctness of the ordinary hypothesis.

Until the 30th of December the northeast trades continued, the ship having then reached 6° 8' north latitude, and 16° 34' west longitude, when, in a squall from the eastward, the wind changed to the southward, and so continued, though somewhat variable, until January 2, 1853, in latitude 1° 44' north, and longitude 11° 37' west, when the southeast trade was met, bringing with it a swell, which retarded the ship's progress considerably. Before this, however, on the 29th of December, as the northeast trades had become light and unsteady, with occasional calms, the floats were replaced on the wheels, and the ship was put under steam, using the two after boilers only. With light winds and a smooth sea, these proved sufficient to make a progress of seven knots an hour; but when the southeast trades fairly set in, accompanied as they were by a head sea, the speed was diminished to four and a half or five knots. The use of two additional boilers, however, soon brought the ship up to seven, at a daily consumption of twenty-six tons of coal.

It had been the purpose of the Commodore, on leaving Madeira, to make the entire run to the Cape of Good Hope without stopping; as it was supposed that with a proper use of the sails, and the supply of coal on board, this might readily be done; but the northeast trades having ceased at a point much further north than usual at this season, and the southeast winds having also set in at a correspondingly early period, he ordered the ship so to be steered as that she might touch at St. Helena, should it be deemed desirable so to do, as a measure of prudence, to procure an additional supply of coal.

In the observations made upon the currents since leaving Norfolk, the Commodore was of opinion that such as he encountered were caused merely by the winds acting on the surface of the ocean; and as a general rule, though not perhaps universally true, it may be remarked that the current will be found setting in the direction of the prevailing winds; at least

such has been the opinion formed from the long observation and experience at sea of the Commodore. There may be, however, and probably are, currents other than those partial ones created on the surface by the winds. These are caused by a difference in the specific gravity of the sea water at different places and depths. This difference disturbs the equilibrium, and the effort of the water to regain it must cause a current.

There is, consequently, on and under the surface a system of currents and counter currents constantly operating in a greater or less degree. They are far from being yet perfectly known and understood, but the principle on which they must exist is the law of hydrostatics, that when two fluids on the same level differ in specific gravity, the one will not balance the other, both must move; that motion is a current.

Various interesting experiments have been made on the subject of submarine currents, counter to those on the surface, and their existence would seem to be conclusively proved; their direction, however, cannot always be ascertained. Practical seamen have also endeavored to find out the depth of surface currents; this depth is not always the same, but there is, if not impossibility, yet great difficulty, at times, in ascertaining the depth with accuracy.

On Monday, January 3, 1853, the ship crossed the equator in longitude 11° 01' west, and from that time up to the 7th had a moderately fresh breeze directly ahead. The effect of this wind, instead of affording refreshment by the motion of the vessel meeting it, (her course was due south,) was to render the officers' apartments, especially the cabin, and, indeed, all the after part of the ship, particularly uncomfortable, as the wind brought much of the heat and smoke directly aft. The *wind*, however, does not always retard the progress of the vessel, though it may be directly ahead; for it must be remembered that, in a steamer, motion is not so much retarded by adverse winds as by the head sea which the wind produces. Indeed, a steamer will sometimes go faster against a moderately fresh breeze, provided she be on a smooth sea, for the wind drawing from forward increases the draught of the furnaces.

After crossing the equator a current of about one and a half mile per hour was observed, setting in the direction of the wind, north 30° west.

The chaplain, the Rev. Mr. Jones, employed himself with great care and assiduity, while passing through the equatorial latitudes, in observing and noting the zodiacal lights. They were very brilliant, and so remarkable that they proved an object of great interest to all on board. He preserved with great care the result of all his observations, in the hope of their future usefulness to the cause of science.

On the 10th of January, at noon, the ship arrived at Jamestown, island of St. Helena.

Here, as a measure rather of prudence than necessity, she took on board an additional supply of coal. Water and fresh provisions for the crew were also procured.

St. Helena was discovered in 1502 by the Portuguese. It was afterwards taken possession of by the Dutch, who, in 1651, abandoned it for the Cape of Good Hope. The English East India Company then took possession of it, and it became a stopping place for their ships between England and India. The Dutch took it from the company in 1772, but it again fell into their hands in the following year. From that time up to 1833 it remained in the company's possession, when it was transferred to the crown. The base of the island is basalt, and lava and scoria are scattered about its surface. It is evidently volcanic, and seen from a distance it appears like a pile of barren rocks rising from the ocean in the form of a pyramid.

On a nearer approach the island is seen to be encompassed by rugged and almost perpendicular cliffs from six to twelve hundred feet high. These are broken in several places by chasms which open to the sea shore, and form narrow valleys winding up to the table land above. In the centre of the island is an elevation known as Diana's peak, 2,693 feet above the sea level. A calcareous ridge runs across the island from east to west, and divides it into two unequal parts, the larger and better of which is on the north side, containing, among other spots of interest, Jamestown, Longwood, the Briars and Plantation house, the governor's summer's residence. The whole circumference of the island is about twenty-eight miles. At the termination of James' valley on the sea stands Jamestown, the only town and port of the island, with a population of about twenty-five hundred. It is built on both sides of a well paved street which runs nearly a mile up the valley. A strong water battery commands the bay. Ascending James' valley, the traveller arrives on the plain or table land of Longwood, which consists of fifteen hundred acres of good land, elevated about 2,000 feet above the sea, and slopes gently toward the southeast. Though the island looks so barren from the sea, yet the interior is covered with a rich verdure, and is watered by numerous springs which irrigate a very fertile soil. The fruits and flowers of Europe and Asia are successfully cultivated, while horned cattle, sheep, and goats thrive on the rich pastures. Barley, oats, Indian corn, potatoes, and most of the common vegetables are easily produced. Fresh beef, mutton and poultry may at all times be procured, and fish are abundant.

The climate is one of the most salubrious under the tropics. At Plantation house the thermometer ranges from 61° to 73° within doors, and sometimes, between June and September, (the winter season,) falls to 52° in the open air. At Longwood the thermometer is generally a little lower, and at Jamestown a little higher, than it is at Plantation house. The summer rains fall in January or February, and the winter rains in July or August.

The East India Company, while in possession of the island, constructed excellent roads, which are kept in admirable order by the present government; they are inclined planes, adapted as well for wheel carriages and artillery as for horses and foot passengers; and as one rides through the country the appearance of the cultivated fields, kept constantly green by the rains which fall in light showers from the clouds, driven over the island by the southeast trades, forms a striking and agreeable contrast to the barren cliffs which shelter the valleys. During the winter months, indeed, the rains are commonly very copious, and sometimes fall in such torrents as seriously to injure the cultivated grounds, and make for a time the roads impassable.

It will thus be seen that, so far as physical comfort is involved, St. Helena is not the worst of prisons; and if it provoked indignant remonstrance from the illustrious captive who laid his bones there, his complaints were prompted not so much by the aspects of nature around, which never insulted him, as by the petty indignities offered him by little minds, and the irksomeness of restraint to a chafed spirit, which, in its isolation, felt deeply the contrast between its now enforced solitude and its former mingling and ruling in the crowd of men, wielding as if by magic the destinies of Europe. To him a hemisphere for his theatre and nations for his playthings had become in some sort a necessity. His own spirit forged his heaviest chains on St. Helena.

But it was the memory of that captive that gave to the officers of the ship the chief interest of the island, and every one accordingly made it his first object to visit Longwood and the spot where the ashes of Napoleon had once rested.

In viewing the miserable building where, for more than five years, this extraordinary man resided, and where he breathed his last, it is difficult to suppress a deep feeling of the instability of earthly glory. The palaces of France and the farm house of Longwood, Napoleon in his splendor and Napoleon on his death bed, are suggestive of reflections which will tempt the thoughtful silently to moralize. But, humble as was this residence of the dethroned Emperor, it had been the abode of fallen greatness, and that should have protected it from desecration. Longwood has been permitted to fall into decay, and the apartments which the Emperor once occupied are now but a common stable. The property has been rented by the crown to a farmer of the island, and he seems to have been permitted to make what use he pleased of the tenements upon it.

Old House, Longwood, St. Helena.

Without here questioning the necessity, as a measure of state policy, for confining the great and ambitious disturber of the peace of Europe in a place whence escape was impossible; admitting the force of all the arguments by which the act at the time was justified to the world, yet one cannot look on Longwood without feeling that there was more of annoyance and insult in executing the purposes of the English government than was necessary, or than the government probably intended. At this day there are many Englishmen who think that England was singularly unfortunate in the choice of her jailors.

A view of the grounds forcibly suggests this thought. Surrounded as the prescribed limits were by successive lines of sentinels, with a regiment encamped within musket shot of the dwelling, with every avenue to it closely guarded by pickets of soldiers, and with the cliffs which bound the ground toward the sea perfectly inaccessible, it is impossible not to see at a glance, that there was not the remotest chance of escape. Might there not then have been some relaxation of minute and indelicate personal supervision, at least in the day time, when the island was surrounded by British cruisers, and the numerous forts fully garrisoned? Was it necessary for security to make the captive *feel* incessantly that he was watched?

The British ministry had enjoined the safe custody of the prisoner; unfortunately they left it to the jailors to settle all the details of the mode of keeping him.

The tomb in which Napoleon was placed has lost some of its interest from the removal of his body to France. He died on the 1st of May, 1821. On the 4th of October, 1840, his remains were embarked on the French frigate Belle Poule, which had been sent, under the command of the Prince de Joinville, for the purpose of transporting them to France.

The inhabitants of St. Helena seem to be industrious, but the general opinion of the officers of the ship, founded on their experience, was, that in their rambles over the world, they had never met with more polite and unscrupulous extortioners. It is said to be the practice of householders to entertain unsuspecting strangers with great seeming kindness, and then to mulct them most unmercifully for the supposed hospitality. This may be slander, but an incident occurred while the ship was at Jamestown, which leaves no doubt that proffered favors are sometimes done with the expectation of receiving for them—a "consideration." One of the lieutenants of the ship was the victim of excessive civility. Contemplating a visit to Longwood, he had engaged a horse at the livery stable, which, on landing, he found saddled and waiting for him according to appointment. He was about mounting, when a citizen of Jamestown, whom he had casually met the day before, stepped up and told him that he had a horse, much superior to that he was about to mount, which was altogether at his service, and that he would send for it. Consequently the hired horse was dismissed, with a compensation to the disappointed attendant, and that of the polite friend was accepted, unfortunately, however, proving to be inferior to the one dismissed. However, he was used for a few hours, and returned with a douceur to the servant who received him.

The same evening the owner of the horse visited the ship, when the lieutenant was profuse of civility and thanks, and after entertaining him, pressed upon him the acceptance of some little presents, quite equal in value to the hire of the horse. These gifts were received in such manner as induced the officer to think there was still something more wanting, when he said, "Will you allow me to pay for the use of your horse?" and was answered: "Well, I am glad you were pleased with the animal, and you need only pay me the usual charge of three dollars." It was immediately handed to him, when he coolly offered his services at any future time, and said, with a peculiarly knowing look: "If, when you again visit the island, you will place yourself under my guidance, I will put you through all charges at half price." Then politely wishing a good voyage to all on board, he passed into the boat, with the neck of a wine bottle protruding from one pocket, and a liberal supply of Havanas filling the other, the offerings of his grateful friend, the lieutenant.

At the time of Bonaparte's residence, the island was strongly fortified and fully garrisoned, and indeed was deemed impregnable. But this was before the introduction of armed steamers into the navies of the world. The island is strongly fortified on the north side, while the south, exposed to the whole strength of the trade winds, is on that account almost inaccessible. But the batteries were constructed to prevent the approach of sailing vessels, and this they might probably accomplish, as they are on the high cliffs commanding the only ways by which sailing vessels can approach.

Sailing vessels approaching the Jamestown anchorage are obliged, by reason of the lee currents, to pass to the *eastward* of the island, and haul close around Sugar-loaf point; and as soon as they luff under the lee of this they become partially becalmed, and are at once exposed to the guns of a very heavy battery, called "Prince Rupert's Line;" and from thence all the way to the anchorage is a succession of forts, well provided with heavy artillery. On the *westward*, the fortifications are less strong, because, as the current is constantly setting in that direction, it is exceedingly difficult, and at times impossible, for a sailing vessel to beat up to the town; hence there are but two small batteries on that side, which it would not be difficult to silence. But it is easy to see how, with the aid of steam, a moderate land and naval force might now attack the island with strong probabilities of success. But the approach should be from the west. Just under the lee of "West Point," the western extremity of the island, the water is always smooth, and by the aid of steam, the forces might all be concentrated there.

A close line of battle ahead might be formed, securing the armed sailing vessels as closely as possible to the steamers, the armed ships in tow, and the troop ships lashed to the port quarters of the steamers. The land troops might be formed into two divisions, and supplied with light artillery, for forcing the gates of the town, and for covering the advance of the attacking columns up the steep roads which lead into the country and to the rear of the batteries on the cliffs. The boats should be lowered and secured to the port sides of the troop ships, ready for receiving and landing the soldiers, the two divisions of which should be destined for different points.

These arrangements having been made, and the ships cleared for action, with springs from both quarters, so as to spring to starboard or port, as might be necessary, the whole flotilla might be moved close to West Point, and thence trace the shore along at the distance of about a quarter of a mile, avoiding the shoal called "Long Ledge" on the charts, and keeping as close as possible under "Ladder Hill," on which there is a heavy battery, until it opened the town and anchored with springs in line of battle, and extending along the whole front of the road. On giving the starboard broadside, the ships might be sprung to port or starboard, as winds or currents made necessary, remembering, however, that vessels do not always swing to the wind in this road.

Meantime one division of the troops might keep to the eastward, and land at the quay, and thence marching along the causeway, force the gates with their artillery; while the other, avoiding the line of fire of the ships, might pass to the westward of it, and tracing the shore under "Ladder Hill," land at the west flank of the water battery which covers the town front. The town once gained, the troops might at once secure the summits of the roads leading into the country, as guns temporarily mounted on the adjoining hills would effectually command the town and harbor.

The only real obstacle to a force thus approaching from the *west*, by steam, would be the strong water battery, commanding the whole extent of the little bay which forms the harbor. This, of course, would have to be silenced before there would be any chance of capturing the place; but, then, it must be remembered that the fire of the whole attacking force could be concentrated on this spot, if it approached from the west by steam. In such an approach, it could keep close to the shore, which is bold; and such is the elevated position of the principal forts, that their guns could not be sufficiently depressed to bear upon steamers coming from the westward.

These remarks were made by the Commodore, simply as illustrating the great changes wrought by the introduction of steam into naval warfare. In the absence of a resisting naval force, the capture of the island, in the mode above indicated, would certainly not be very difficult. When the island was fortified, engineering skill accomplished all that was required in the existing condition of things. To a force approaching by sailing vessels, it probably would now prove impregnable, for wind and tide were valuable auxiliaries, which were taken into account in planning the works; but a new motive power makes its appearance, which is quite regardless of these natural auxiliaries, and new systems of defence are at once made necessary. This is but one of the changes wrought by this mighty agent, which seems destined to do so much in revolutionizing the condition of the world.

On Tuesday, January 11th, at 6 p. m., the Mississippi weighed anchor and took her departure from Jamestown.

The Briars, St. Helena.

CHAPTER III.

PASSAGE TO THE CAPE.—FUEL FOR STEAMERS.—TABLE ROCK AND CAPE TOWN.—DESCRIPTION OF CAPE TOWN.—CLIMATE.—ANNOYANCE FROM DUST.—VIOLENCE OF WINDS AND DIFFICULTY OF HOLDING TO ANCHORAGE.—SUPPLIES AT THE CAPE.—CAFFRE WAR AND ITS EFFECTS.—MODE OF TRANSPORTING PRODUCE ON LAND.—VINEYARDS OF CONSTANTIA.—EFFECTS OF EMANCIPATION OF SLAVES ON AGRICULTURAL LABOR.—MODE OF CULTIVATING THE VINE.—POPULATION OF CAPE COLONY.—BUSHMEN.—THE CAFFRES.—PHYSICAL CHARACTERISTICS.—FINGOES.—MILITARY ORGANIZATION OF CAFFRES.—CONDITION OF THE EMANCIPATED SLAVES.—DEPARTURE FROM TABLE BAY.—PASSAGE TO, AND ARRIVAL AT, MAURITIUS.—HARBOR OF PORT LOUIS.—DANGERS OF THE HARBOR.—SKILL OF PORT OFFICERS IN MOORING VESSELS.

AFTER leaving St. Helena the ship was put on her course for the Cape of Good Hope. Prudential considerations alone induced the Commodore to touch at St. Helena. His opinion was that the best and most expeditious route for a steamer, going from Madeira to the Cape, (provided she can carry a sufficiency of coal,) is to be found by steering from the Cape de Verd islands direct toward Cape Palmas on the coast of Africa, and thence tracing the shore down to Table Bay.

On leaving Jamestown the ship encountered the trade, deviating very little from the southeast, and blowing alternately moderate and fresh. It was observable, however, that it was always stronger at night than in the day time, and brought with it a short head sea, which greatly retarded the progress of the vessel. It would have been easy to increase the steam power; but experience had shown that about twenty-six tons of coal per diem enabled the ship to accomplish the greatest distance with the most economical expenditure; and considering the extreme difficulty of procuring fuel in that region, its enormous cost, and the labor and delay incident to its shipment, the Commodore deemed it most expedient rather to protract the passage than allow extravagance in the use of an article so essential to the movements of the vessel. A current of one and a quarter knots was found setting in the direction of the wind, and this, as a retarding cause, was to be added to the force of the trade.

As to the possibility of obtaining a supply of fuel in this part of the world, it may be remarked that at St. Paul de Loango the English maintain a depot of coal for the accommodation of the African steam cruisers, and this would be a convenient point to which to send a coal vessel from the United States. Within a few years a depot of coal has been established by an English company at Port Grand, Island of St. Vincent, of the Cape de Verde group, and it is said that a reasonable supply can always be obtained there by transient steamers.

Steamers from the United States might proceed direct to St. Vincent's, provided there be certainty of obtaining coal at that place, and thence proceed to the Cape by Cape Palmas, via Loango; but it is much better that cargoes of coal should be sent ahead of steamers leaving the United States, as the only security for a certain supply.

As to the route from England, that which is prescribed for her mail steamers bound round the Cape of Good Hope, is to touch at St. Vincent, and thence proceed to the Cape, via Ascension Island, replenishing their coal at all their stopping places. In pursuing this route, (which they are compelled to do to leave a mail at Ascension for the African squadron,) they are obliged to contend with the entire range of the southeast trades, which are directly ahead, blowing most of the time quite strongly, and always producing a lee current of from one to one and a quarter knots. By taking the route along the African coast a steamer has the advantage of the sea and land breezes, and the favorable current usually setting to the south.

On the 24th of January, at nine in the morning, the ship made the land in the vicinity of Saldanha bay, and at two p. m. Table Mountain was in sight. After passing outside of Dassen Island, and through the channel between the main land and Robben's Island, at half past eight p. m. the ship came to anchor in Table Bay in seven fathoms, and the following day moved further in toward the town.

This port is easy of access either by night or day, if the two lights can be distinctly seen, so that the distance from Green Point can be accurately estimated. This is important, as by bordering upon that point too closely there is danger of a ledge of rocks near the Cape shore, and by keeping too far to the northward, the Whale Rock, at the southern end of Robben's Island, may bring a vessel up. Particular instructions for entering Table Bay at night will be found in the Appendix.

The Cape of Good Hope was first discovered by Bartholomew Diaz, a Portuguese, in 1493. During an exploration of the Atlantic coast of Africa, this navigator was driven out to sea by a storm, and the first land he made, after the subsidence of the gale, was Algoa Bay; he having thus doubled the Cape without his knowledge. Diaz gave the name of Cabo Tormentoso (the Cape of Storms) to the Cape, which was afterwards changed to that of Good Hope by the king of Portugal, as he rightly thought the discovery auspicious of a favorable result to the great prospect entertained by the Portuguese navigators of reaching India. In 1497, Vasco de Gama, another Portuguese navigator, doubled the Cape on his voyage to the Indian seas.

The Cape of Good Hope forms the southern extremity of a narrow peninsula about thirty miles in length, with the Atlantic ocean on the west, False Bay on the east, and Table Bay on the north. Cape Town is situated on Table Bay, and was originally founded by the Dutch in 1650, but fell into the hands of the English in 1795; and, it having been restored to its original possessors after the peace of Amiens, was finally retaken by the British in 1806, in whose possession it now remains.

The town is well built with substantial houses of stone and brick, and wide, regular streets. The general aspect of the place, with its well constructed public buildings and private residences, and its park, in the neighborhood of the government house, shaded by oaks of magnificent growth, is exceedingly agreeable.

The heat, however, in consequence of the position of the town, which is faced by the noonday sun and walled in behind by naked mountains, is excessive. This, added to the dust, caused those who went on shore to keep much within doors, so that Cape Town was found by the officers of the expedition but a dull and stupid place. The streets are unpaved, and, consequently, when the southeast gales, which prevail in midsummer, blow, the dust is raised in clouds and deposited in drifts of sand along the sidewalks several inches in depth, which keeps the street sweepers in constant occupation, who may be seen continually at work collecting the dirt in heaps, to be carried away by the dirt carts. So general is the experience of this nuisance from the dust that the male, as well as the female inhabitants, of all classes, are in the practice of wearing veils attached to their hats. The northeastern winds, which prove in raising the dust of such discomfort to the residents of Cape Town, prevail during midsummer, and their approach is always indicated by the appearance of a dense white cloud, which settles upon the summit of Table Mountain, therefore called the Table Cloth, and remains there until the gale subsides. These winds blow with great violence, sweeping along the land east of Table Mountain. If it were not for the perfect smoothness of the water in Table Bay, vessels would not be able to hold to their anchors during these southeasterly gales, of which two were experienced in the course of seven days, while the Mississippi was lying at Cape Town. Such is the severity of these winds that all business in the harbor is suspended during their height.

The town seemed to be in a highly prosperous condition, business of every kind was flourishing, and there was a general appearance of affluence among the government officials, and the high rents, among other indications, show the prosperous condition of trade. Handsome equipages are constantly seen in the streets, and the prosperity is so universal that even the lowest classes are hardly known to suffer from want. The Cape of Good Hope is of great commercial importance to Great Britain as a convenient rendezvous for her cruisers stationed in the neighborhood, and as a stopping place for vessels bound to and from the Indian Ocean. Excellent water, fresh provisions, fruit and other necessaries can be obtained in any quantity and at reasonable prices. Wood is scarce, but almost every description of article usually needed by vessels may be procured from the numerous well stocked stores and warehouses at Cape Town. Live stock can be readily obtained, bullocks at £6 per head and sheep at 15 shillings. The Mississippi was supplied with twelve of the former and eighteen of the latter at these prices.

Since the abolition of slavery in the British colonies the agricultural interests of the Cape have suffered, and although the commerce of some few of the colonial ports continues thriving, as, for example, that of Cape Town, the interior of the country has declined in prosperity, there being at present but few examples of prosperous farming, in consequence of a want of laborers. The agricultural condition of the country has also suffered from the effects of the war carried on between the British colonists and the Caffres, which, although it has enriched the merchants and tradesmen by the large expenditure of public money, has impoverished the farmers by depriving them of the necessary laborers, and by unsettling the tranquillity of the country. The consequence has been that many of the farms have been allowed to run to waste, and though the soil is capable of producing Indian corn, wheat, barley, oats, and several other descriptions of grain, such has been the unfavorable influence of the cause alluded to that the home consumption of these products is not fully provided for. There are, however, some articles produced for exportation, among which may be enumerated wine, hides, tallow and wool. The farming is chiefly of a grazing character, and vast herds of cattle, sheep, horses and mules are raised. At Cape Town horses can be obtained at a price varying from thirty to one hundred and fifty dollars, and mules from thirty to seventy-five dollars. The cattle, which are indigenous to the country, somewhat resemble the buffalo in appearance, and the sheep are of the broad tailed species, which are highly esteemed for the excellence of their meat. The large teams of oxen passing to and from the city are characteristic objects at Cape Town. These teams are composed often of seven, eight, or even nine yoke, and are guided by two teamsters, one seated in front of a wagon, not unlike the wagons generally in use in Pennsylvania, where he urges the animals along by his voice and a long lash, while the other precedes the team, holding a halter fastened to the horns of the two leaders, with which he guides them. The arrangement of the team for an excursion of greater length is somewhat different, as then horsemen accompany it. The wagon, however, is the same. The ox of the Cape is a serviceable animal, which has a good deal of the general aspect of the buffalo, with long horns, a compact body and tapering rump.

Travellers in South Africa.

The Commodore, accompanied by some of his officers, took occasion to visit one of the celebrated vineyards of Constantia, having provided himself with a barouche drawn by four beautiful stallions, driven four-in-hand by a negro boy, who evinced much skill in handling the reins. The drive was through a picturesque country, with pretty villas scattered about, and approached by beautiful avenues formed of the oak and the fir, which trees are raised from the seed, and generally cultivated in the colony, not only for ornamental purposes, but for fuel. Substantial hedges were also observed, formed of the young oak, of only three year's growth from the acorn. The vineyard visited was of limited extent and the culture of a character that somewhat disappointed the expectations of the visitors.

The proprietor accounted for the inferior condition of his vineyard on the score of being unable to provide himself with the necessary supply of laborers, and remarked that he should be obliged to abandon the cultivation of the grape altogether had he not supplied himself with an American cultivator, which he had recently imported from the United States, and which simple plough, as he stated, drawn by a single horse, actually accomplished the labor of fifty men, according to the usual mode of working and cultivating the vine with a hoe. The grape is cultivated at Constantia, as in Sicily, by trimming the vine close to the ground, and not permitting it to grow higher than a gooseberry bush. The richness of the wine is dependent upon the condition of the grape when it goes to the press. Although the grape begins to ripen in the early part of February, it is not gathered until the middle of March, when the fruit has assumed almost the appearance of the dried raisin, in which condition it is pressed. The prices of these Constantia wines vary from two to six dollars a gallon, according to their quality.

The census of 1848 gives 200,546 as the population of Cape Colony. Of these 76,827 whites and 101,176 colored inhabitants make up the whole number of the inhabitants of the various parts of the colony, with the exception of Cape Town, which contains a population of 22,543. There are but few of the aboriginal Hottentots of pure race to be found, as their blood has been intermingled with that of the Dutch, the Negro, or the Malay. The first European discoverer of the southern promontory of Africa found it tolerably well peopled, and the natives, in some respects, in better condition than many of the more northern tribes. They were in possession of herds of cattle and sheep, and led a pastoral life. They were a comparatively happy people, divided into tribes under a patriarchal government, and wandered about with their flocks and herds, taking with them their moveable huts, constructed of boughs and poles, which were conveyed from pasture to pasture on the backs of oxen. Their tribes, however, have been mostly exterminated by the cruelty of the Europeans, although a wretched remnant have survived and live as miserable outcasts in the fastnesses of the desert and the forest, and are known as Bushmen. They are still savage in character, and disgusting in their persons and habits, having received but little benefit from the civilization of their white conquerors, who have always pursued them with a cruel wantonness, "though we, as Americans," remarks Commodore Perry, "have no right to rail at other nations for the wrong they have inflicted upon the aborigines of countries seized upon by them, for though hardly equal to the English in the disgusting hypocrisy with which they excuse their acts, we are not far behind them in the frauds and cruelties committed upon our native tribes."

The warlike Caffres still retain their characteristic wildness, and pursue their predatory life. They are in many respects inferior to the ordinary African, and have some of the peculiarities of the Egyptian races. They are of greater height and strength than the inferior negro; their color is browner, and though their hair is black and woolly they have fuller beards. Their noses are more prominent, but they have the thick negro lip, and with the prominent cheek bone of the Hottentots they possess the high European forehead. The Fingoes, though traced in origin to some scattered tribes of the Caffres, differ from them in some degree, and although spirited and brave in battle, are of a less savage nature, and have the character of being a comparatively good natured people. The Fingoes are pastoral like the Caffres, but more given to the culture of the land, in which the men engage as well as the women, although this kind of labor is confined among the Caffres to the females alone. On the return of the Commodore

Caffre Chief.　　　　　　　　　　　　　　　　Fingo woman.

from Constantia, he stopped to pay a visit to a captive chief and his wife, whom the fortune of war had thrown into the hands of the Europeans. The chief was confined in a sort of country jail, at no great distance from the town. The keeper of the prison very civilly allowed free communication with the prince, a remarkably fine looking negro, about twenty-five years of age, who had been accompanied to imprisonment by his favorite wife and confidential lieutenant, who also had a similar companion to cheer his captivity. These women were counterparts of the men in good looks. Subsequently, Mr. Brown, one of the artists of the expedition, visited the prison and secured excellent likenesses of the prince and his wife.

African Chief, Soyolo.　　　　　　　　　　　　　　　Wife of Soyolo.

The war carried on by the English with the Hottentots and Caffres, which has continued so long, costing an immense amount of blood and treasure, is still prolonged by the obstinacy of the blacks. The whole frontier has been already devastated, and although there is some hope of bringing about a peace, no one believes that any treaty that may be made will be respected longer by the negroes than may suit their convenience. In the last battle, at the date of the visit of the Mississippi, in which the English force, headed by General Cathcart himself, was victorious, it is said that the Caffre chief brought into action six thousand foot and two thousand horse. These numbers are probably exaggerated, but it is well known that the blacks have acquired a tolerable organization, and that they are well supplied with arms and ammunition. They have hitherto had an abundance of provision, obtained from their own herds or from those stolen from the whites, but report says that, owing to the carelessness and waste always attendant upon the military movements of savages, the supply of food is running short with them. The English declare that the Caffres have been instructed in the art of war by numerous deserters from the British army and by a French missionary settled among them, who passed his early life in the army. Allusion has already been made to the disastrous effects of the war upon the agricultural and other resources of the country.

The principal white inhabitants of Cape Town are the government officials, army officers, and merchants and tradesmen. The laboring class is composed of the mixed races, the Malays, Coolies, and the negroes. The emancipated negroes and their descendants are very much in character and condition like the free blacks in the United States, though by no means as intelligent and good looking. They are perfectly independent of all restraint, so long as they do not violate the laws. They work when it suits them, and at their own prices, and break off from their labor if spoken to in a manner which they deem offensive. Their ordinary charge for labor is $1 25 for a day of ten hours.

The Mississippi having taken on board from the ship Faneuil Hall a supply of coal, and a good supply of bullocks and sheep, and having filled the water tanks, left Table Bay at eleven o'clock, a. m., on the 3d February. On getting fairly out of the harbor, the wind was found to be blowing strong from the westward, with a heavy swell setting in from that quarter. In seven hours after leaving Table Bay the steamer was off the pitch of the Cape, whence, having Cape Hanglip full in sight, her course was directed southeast, in order to reach the parallel of thirty-seven degrees of latitude, to avoid the southeast gales which prevail near the Cape, and cause a strong current to the northward and westward, and to meet the variables which are found south of the border of the southeast trades.

For the first three days after leaving the Cape the wind blew from the northwest to the southwest until the steamer reached the latitude of 36° 16′ S., and the longitude of 23° 40′ E., when it changed to the northward and eastward, rather northwardly, and so remained to the latitude of 35° 06′, and longitude 44° 03′. At this latter point the wind gradually hauled to the southward, allowing the course of the ship to be inclined more to the northward, until the southeast trades were met. The Commodore, however, fearing that the wind might back again to the eastward, was careful not to make too much northing, lest he might fall to the leeward of Mauritius, thus losing the benefit of a fair wind, which not only increases the rate of going of a steamer, as of a sailing vessel, but also saves the fuel of the former. From the 11th to the 14th of February, inclusive, the wind continued from the southward and eastward, and at the latter date the ship reached latitude 29° 34′, and longitude 55° 22′, from which period to her arrival at Port Louis on the 18th the wind hung to the northward and eastward, the trades having entirely failed. The weather throughout the passage was fine, the barometer varying from 29° 80' to 29° 95', the thermometer from 74° to 84°, the currents setting with the wind, and running at about three-quarters of a knot per hour.

There is no reason to doubt the correctness of the opinion of Horsburgh, to the effect that the best route for a sailing ship bound from the Cape of Good Hope to Mauritius is that in which nearly the whole, if not all, the easting is made between the parallels of 35° and 38° of latitude, and the southeast trades are struck between the latitude of 27° and the longitude of 55° or 57°. This course brings vessels well to the windward, and enables them to fetch the island of Mauritius without difficulty, provided the trade winds do not haul north of E. by N. In the passage of the Mississippi the wind actually hauled as far as N.N.E., an occurrence not usual at the season, when northerly and northwesterly winds frequently prevail from Madagascar toward and beyond the island of Bourbon, (or, as it is now termed, Réunion,) and Mauritius.

The question has been agitated as to whether it is advisable for steamers to make this curve in their route to Mauritius, or to steam directly from the Cape to the island, passing close round Cape Aghilus. The Commodore is decidedly of the opinion that, unless the steamer be one of first-rate speed, it would be unwise to take the direct route, in which she would have to contend against a strong trade wind and its consequent current. The difference between the two routes is about 240 miles, which would hardly seem to compensate for the loss occasioned by head winds and currents, leaving out of consideration the advantage of the cooler and more agreeable weather of the southern passage. The mail, and indeed all the European steamers, have usually taken the latter route: and the Susquehanna, which attempted the direct course, although a faster steamer than the Mississippi, had a passage of seventeen days, while the Mississippi, of inferior powers and speed, made the run by the other course in fifteen days.

The Mississippi, in doubling the Cape of Good Hope in midsummer, escaped any very heavy blow, although hardly a week passes without a gale from some quarter. Horsburgh remarks, in regard to the weather, that "in the storms off the Cape Bank and to the eastward, the sea is turbulent, and then generally accompanied with a black overcast sky; when they are about to commence, and during their continuance, numbers of albatross, petrels, and other oceanic birds, are seen flying about, although in moderate weather few are perceived, for at this time they rest on the surface of the sea to fish, which they cannot do in a storm."

Nothing was observed of a remarkable character in a meteorological point of view. The temperature of the air and water gave similar indications to those in corresponding northern latitudes. The barometer gave due notice of all the various changes of weather, and proved of great utility. There is a peculiarity in the action of this instrument in the neighborhood of the Cape, and in that part of the route across the Indian Ocean as far as the Equator, of which Horsburgh thus remarks: "In the vicinity of the Cape Bank, and in most parts of the southern hemisphere, the mercury rises with northerly and falls with southerly winds; these latter proceeding from a warmer atmosphere are much rarefied, consequently the mercury falls in the barometer, whereas northerly winds coming from the frozen regions near the pole are more dense, and cause the mercury to rise. This ought to be kept in remembrance, for, when the wind is from southeast," continues Horsburgh, "I have several times observed the mercury to fall considerably before it changed to the north, and expected a gale, but the fall resulted only from the warmer air coming in contact with and repelling the former."

MAURITIUS FROM THE POUCE

In the course of the passage the Mississippi spoke her Britannic Majesty's steamer Styx, thirteen days from Simon's Bay, bound to Mauritius. She was under sail, her engine having been disconnected, and the wheels, with all their buckets, allowed to revolve by the movement of the vessel through the water. She made tolerable way, but drifted much to leeward. The English war steamers frequently, by a simple arrangement, disconnect their engines for the purpose of saving fuel. This process of connecting and disconnecting is accomplished in a few minutes. In American naval steamers it is almost impossible to disconnect the engines, and the only practicable mode of using the sails exclusively is by the removal of the immersed floats. This requires moderate weather for its accomplishment, and the time necessary for doing it is about two hours, and double that time is required for the readjustment of the floats or buckets.

It must be acknowledged with mortification that our navy is in many respects very backward in availing itself of some of those improvements in steam vessels which have been already adopted by other nations, and even by private enterprise. Since the construction of the Mississippi and the Missouri, the two first ocean war steamers introduced into our naval service, and for a time esteemed the finest in the world, there has been less progress in the building of such vessels than our position as a nation would seem to demand. Most of the maritime powers of Europe and many companies, and even private individuals, have put afloat such vessels as it must be acknowledged but few of our steamers could fairly compete with in excellence of construction and equipment. The San Jacinto, Saranac, Fulton, and the Princeton, may be pointed to in illustration of these remarks.

At half-past nine o'clock, on the morning of the 18th of February, the Mauritius was first seen from the deck, bearing N.N.E., and at noon the Mississippi was nearly abreast of Cape Bravant, having passed in sight of Grand Port, the scene of the memorable action in August, 1810, between an English squadron, under the command of Captains Pyne and Willoughby, and a French force, under Commodore Duperie. In this engagement the English were worsted, having lost nearly all their vessels. The battle was fought within the coral shoals which form the harbor of Grand Port, the batteries on the shore taking part in the action, which was prolonged several days.

Early in the evening, the pilot having boarded the Mississippi near the mouth of the harbor, anchored and secured the steamer for the night at the outer, which are termed the Admiral's moorings. Next morning the pilot returned to the ship, bringing with him several launches, manned by natives of Malabar, who, with the assistance of the crew of the Mississippi, completed her moorings, which was a process requiring much time and labor. All vessels entering the harbor of Port Louis are secured by frigates' chains attached to mooring anchors, and brought on board, one at each bow and one at each quarter. This operation is entirely under the direction of the pilots, who with their launches, warps, and numerous hands, are constantly occupied in mooring and unmooring the various vessels as they enter or leave the harbor. Vessels are moored head and stern, with their bows to the southeast, the direction from which the hurricanes usually come. As these generally blow directly out of the harbor, they are accompanied with very little sea; but such is often the violence of the wind, that the strong moorings give way, and the most destructive results ensue, the vessels being dashed against each other, and the shores strewn with wrecks. It is rarely that these gales blow into the harbor, but when they do, a tremendous sea is thrown into the little port, and the strongest moored and best found vessels can hardly escape disaster.

Every possible precaution has been taken by the government to provide against the destructive effects of these furious storms, and the authorities are vigorously seconded in their efforts by the intelligence and indefatigable attention of Lieutenant Edward Kelly, of the royal navy, the harbor master, who is ever on the alert to meet the wants of vessels, giving warning of the appearance of an approaching gale, and suggesting such measures as may the better guard them against accident. Such was the favorable impression made upon the Commodore by the perfect state of the port regulations, that he was induced to address a note to Lieutenant Kelly, expressing his satisfaction, and thanking him for the facilities which had been rendered to the Mississippi.

Our Light-house Board might gather from the example of these excellent regulations some useful hints; but it is feared that that branch of administration, like too many others, is so much exposed to ignorant legislation, that any disposition it may have toward reform and progress would be hindered by unwise interference.

Cape of Good Hope.

CHAPTER IV.

MAURITIUS, ITS DISCOVERY.—GEOLOGICAL FORMATION AND PHYSICAL ASPECT.—PRODUCTION OF SUGAR.—EFFECT ON AGRICULTURE OF THE ABOLITION OF SLAVERY.—COOLIES.—POPULATION OF THE ISLAND.—STATE OF FEELING BETWEEN ENGLISH AND FRENCH RESIDENTS.—HOSPITABLE TREATMENT OF THE EXPEDITION.—DESCRIPTION OF PORT LOUIS.—GRAND PORT—PAUL AND VIRGINIA.—FACTS ON WHICH ST. PIERRE FOUNDED HIS STORY.—TOMBS OF PAUL AND VIRGINIA.—BUILT BY AN ECCENTRIC FRENCHMAN.—CYCLONES.—THEIR PROBABLE CAUSES.—INTEREST FELT IN THEM AT MAURITIUS.—DEPARTURE OF THE MISSISSIPPI FROM PORT LOUIS.—HER COURSE THENCE TO POINT DE GALLE, ISLAND OF CEYLON.—REASONS FOR TAKING IT.—POINT DE GALLE, DESCRIPTION OF.—GREAT RENDEZVOUS OF STEAMERS.—DIFFICULTY OF PROCURING FUEL THERE.—AMERICAN CONSUL.—THOUGHTS ON CONSULAR SYSTEM.—EARLY KNOWLEDGE OF CEYLON.—ITS SEVERAL EUROPEAN POSSESSORS.—CLIMATE.—SALUBRITY.—CAUSES OF ITS DIMINISHED PROSPERITY.—PRODUCTIONS.—VALUE OF COCOA-NUT PALM.—PEARL FISHERY.—IMMENSE NUMBERS OF ELEPHANTS.—GREAT SLAUGHTER OF THEM.—BOA CONSTRICTOR.—POPULATION OF CEYLON.—PHYSIQUE OF CINGALESE, MALABARS, AND MAHOMMEDANS IN THE ISLAND.—RELIGIOUS CONDITION.—BUDDHISM.—PILGRIMAGE TO THE TEMPLES.—INTERCOURSE WITH A SIAMESE NAVAL OFFICER AT CEYLON.—COMMODORE'S LETTER TO THE SECOND KING OF SIAM.—DEPARTURE FROM CEYLON.—PASSAGE THROUGH THE STRAITS OF MALACCA.—ARRIVAL AT SINGAPORE.

ACARENHAS, a Portuguese commander, discovered Mauritius, with its neighboring island of Bourbon, in 1505, and the whole group was then named the Mascarenhas islands. The Portuguese took formal possession of Mauritius in 1545, but appear to have formed no settlement. In 1598, the Dutch surveyed it and gave to it its present name, in honor of Maurice, the Stadtholder of the Netherlands. They, however, did not settle the island until after they had formed an establishment at the Cape in 1640; and then they fixed themselves on the shore at Port Grand. In 1708, from causes not now known, they abandoned the island, and from this time up to 1715 its only inhabitants were a few negroes, who had been brought there by the Dutch as slaves, and who, having escaped from their masters, concealed themselves in the mountain forests. In the year last named (1715) the French took possession and formed a settlement at Port St. Louis, giving to the island the new name of the "Isle of France." They kept undisturbed possession until 1810, when it was taken from them by the British; and since the peace of 1814, these last have retained it.

The island is, without doubt, volcanic in its structure, and is surrounded by a coral reef, which generally runs parallel to the shores, at a short distance from them, and is mostly left dry at low water. There are, however, in this reef eleven breaks or openings, through most of which vessels of considerable burden may pass. The interior of the island consists of a great number of lofty hills, mostly isolated, though in one or two instances they form small chains. The Brabant mountains and the Bamboo ridge are the greatest elevations, and these are about three thousand feet above the sea level.

Port Louis, Mauritius.

The soil is generally shallow and not very productive. This is owing to its dryness. The mean annual heat is about 76° of Fahrenheit. It is true they have rains, and in June, July, and August showers are frequent, but of very short duration. The average fall of rain throughout the year would appear, from observation, to be about thirty-eight inches. The rainy season lasts from November to March or April, and then the water descends in torrents, accompanied with heavy gusts of wind, and not unfrequently with thunder and lightning. This region is subject also to hurricanes quite as violent as any encountered in the West Indies; there is, however, no regularity in these, though five years rarely elapse without their appearance. The island is traversed by numerous water courses, which diverge in all directions from the centre; these, however, are filled with water in the rainy season only, and then they form numerous cascades and cataracts. In the dry season the water rapidly evaporates.

The island was once well wooded, and a considerable part of the native forest still remains. The cocoa-nut palm, and sago, are common, as are also tamarind trees, mangroves, and bamboos.

Yams, cassava, Indian corn, plantains, bananas, and melons are all cultivated as articles of food, as well as some of our vegetables, as spinach, asparagus, artichokes, cabbage, and peas. Wheat and rice are also produced, but in small quantities. Of fruits there are mangoes, shaddocks, and pine apples; but oranges, grapes, peaches, and apples are inferior. The French introduced the spice trees of the Indian islands; none, however, succeeded but the clove. The chief article of cultivation, since the British obtained possession, is sugar; not more, however, than three-eighths of the island is cultivated at all. The sugar cane is planted in the usual manner, though the fields present one peculiarity. The surface of the ground, in its original state, was covered with loose rocks and stones. These have been formed into parallel ridges about three or four feet apart, and between these the cane is planted. The cultivators are of opinion that these ridges, instead of being injurious to the cane, are rather advantageous; they retard the growth of weeds, shade and protect the young cane from violent winds, and retain moisture which reaches the roots of the cane.

Before the introduction of guano as a fertilizer the product was from 2,000 to 2,500 French pounds of sugar to the arpent or French acre; but the increase since the application of the guano has been so extraordinary as to be scarcely credible. In ordinary seasons the product has been from six to seven thousand pounds, and, under peculiarly favorable circumstances, it has even reached eight thousand pounds to the acre. Official returns show a gradual increase in the amount of sugar exported from the year 1812 up to the present time. Thus, in that year, it was but 969,260 French pounds; in 1851 it amounted to 137,373,519 pounds, and the estimated crop of this year (1852) is 140,000,000 pounds. The land would produce cotton and tobacco, but the entire thoughts of the agriculturists of the island are directed to sugar. The proportion of guano used is about one-fourth of a pound to a cane, and the French arpent or acre is estimated to contain about two thousand plants.

The general abolition of slavery by the English government caused here, as it did in the other English slaveholding colonies, much agricultural distress; but after a time the introduction of laborers, chiefly from the Malabar coast, under certain prescribed regulations, enabled the planters not only to dispense with the services of the freed negroes, but to obtain labor on cheaper terms than before. The free blacks here, as elsewhere, seemed to think emancipation meant an exemption from all labor; they were consequently indisposed generally to work at all, even for fair wages, and capriciously left their labor just when they pleased. The imported laborers, known under the name of coolies, perform nearly all the agricultural work of the island, as well as load and unload all the ships. On the sugar estates large communities of them are to be found. Comfortable houses are provided for them and their families, and exclusive of house rent and provisions, which are furnished to them, they receive from two to three dollars a month as wages. This is cheaper to the planter than slave labor was. The municipal laws for the protection and government of the coolies are judicious and sufficently minute, yet these people pay but little regard to any bargain they may make with their employers; they go and come very much as they please, and are tolerated in the exercise of a much larger liberty than is accorded to laboring men in either England or the United States. Notwithstanding all these disadvantages, however, the planter makes large profits from their labor.

The population of the whole island is about 180,000. Of these nearly 100,000 are negroes from Madagascar and the eastern coast of Africa, who were once slaves. Beside these, are Malays, fishermen from Malabar, Lascars and Chinese. Some of these latter have been imported for agricultural labor. The white population is nine or ten thousand. Of these the larger part are creoles of French origin, and speak the French language. They also form the wealthier portion of the white population. The English in Mauritius having, for the most part, a connexion, direct or indirect, with the colonial government, are somewhat exclusive in

Costumes, Mauritius.

their social relations. The French are not less tenacious, and hence, though there are no open dissensions between them, yet to the impartial stranger, who mingles freely with both, it is quite apparent that there is little real harmony between them, and a feeling of nationality exists which would probably induce the majority to hail with pleasure a return to the dominion of France. As in most countries which, like Mauritius, have involuntarily changed their nationality, the females indulge, in a greater degree than the other sex, the prejudices of country; perhaps because they mix less with the new comers.

Both classes of the population, however, English and French, were exceedingly kind and hospitable to the members of the expedition. On arriving in an armed United States vessel at any of the English colonial settlements, great hospitality is usually extended to our officers, and visits of ceremony, with a constant interchange of dinner parties and other courtesies, commonly leave to the commander but little opportunity for quiet observation of that which may characterize the people generally. In fact, he is for a time unavoidably subjected to the bondage of official restraint, and is sometimes made a prisoner even by the friendly tyranny of kindness and hospitality.

During the brief stay of the ship at Mauritius the English officials and merchants exhibited the most profuse hospitality toward the Commodore and his officers, while the French population were no whit behind them in the unostentatious display of their kindness. These last evinced the most friendly feelings and no small share of intelligence, and while both classes were equally hospitable, the only difference was that the Englishman was, perhaps, a little the more stately, and the Frenchman a little the less ceremonious. Nothing could be kinder than the treatment of both.

Port Louis, the capital of the island, is situated near its northwestern extremity, on a small bay, which is but a narrow inlet of the sea, somewhat more than a mile long, and about five hundred yards broad. At the extreme southwestern corner the town is built. The streets are straight, but not paved. The principal street runs parallel to the shore of the bay. The houses are chiefly of wood, and of but a single story. The population is, perhaps, from twenty-five to thirty thousand, of which from four to five thousand are white. The residue are for the most part blacks. Grand Port, on the southeastern side of the island, is sufficiently capacious, and is more convenient for shipping the sugar, of which large quantities are grown in the neighborhood; but apart from the intricacies of its entrance, it is open to the southeast, from which quarter the hurricanes blow most furiously.

Public Square, Port Louis.

It is not to be supposed that among those who read at all there are many who are unacquainted with the beautiful story of Paul and Virginia, by Bernardin St. Pierre. The accomplished author was an officer of the garrison of Mauritius in 1744, and at that time a melancholy catastrophe which happened on one of the coral reefs surrounding the island furnished a basis of facts on which he reared his interesting fiction.

One is rather reluctant to destroy the illusion produced by the romantic narrative of St. Pierre; but, in sober truth, he was indebted to his imagination for the picture of the storm, and the brave and generous Paul is but a myth. The facts are these: On the night of the 18th of August, 1744, the French ship St. Gévan was wrecked on one of the reefs on the northeastern coast of the island. On board the ship were two young ladies, by name Mallet and Caillon, (who were returning as passengers from France, whither they had been sent for education,) both of whom were lost. The depositions taken at the time by the French officials, and from which these facts are gathered, state that Mademoiselle Caillon was last seen upon the top-gallant forecastle of the wrecked vessel, with a gentleman, Monsieur Longchamps de Montendre, who was at the time endeavoring to persuade her to trust herself to his efforts to save her. To enable him, however, to accomplish the object, it was necessary for her to disencumber herself of some portion of her clothing, and this, from a sense of modesty, she declined doing, and so perished with Monsieur Montendre and the larger part of the crew of the ill-fated vessel. It was conjectured that Monsieur Montendre was the lover of Mademoiselle Caillon, as, after lowering himself down the ship's side to throw himself into the sea, he returned and earnestly endeavored to prevail on the young lady to leave the vessel with him, and on her refusal would not again leave her.

Mademoiselle Mallet was on the quarter deck with Monsieur de Peramont, who never left her for a moment. On these facts as a basis St. Pierre framed his story. The celebrity given to it has always awakened the interest of strangers visiting the island, who have naturally desired to look upon scenes consecrated by the pen of genius, and associated in their minds with incidents which, if not literally true, have at least deeply touched their sensibilities. The officers of the ship were, therefore, glad to land, and among other objects visited, strange to say, they were conducted to what the islanders are pleased to call the graves of Paul and Virginia. The history of these resting places of the imaginary dead is this: An eccentric French gentleman having a country residence about eight miles from St. Louis, and possibly near the supposed graves of some of the lost, erected in his garden two monuments to the memory of the unfortunate fictitious Paul and Virginia, (Mademoiselle Caillon and Monsieur Montendre.) The object was simply to add the stimulus of curiosity to the other attractions of his residence, and thus draw around him a more numerous circle, to whom he might extend that hospitality for which he, in common with the French of his day, was famous, and thus enjoy the pleasures of society. This benevolent and eccentric being has been long dead, but the tombs are still standing, though in a state of dilapidation, and still attract strangers. Alas! no hospitable greeting now awaits the visitor. His money is demanded at the garden gate, all sentiment evaporates, and he walks in to *see the show*. This custom of demanding payment from visitors to places of public interest is almost peculiar to the English, and its existence is to many of the people of England themselves a source of mortification and annoyance. There are certain places in which payment is perfectly proper, but there are others in which, though regularly exacted, it should not be asked. The sight of Longwood and a glance at Napoleon's tomb were both paid for by the gentlemen of the expedition at St. Helena; but the custom alluded to is one which may be found throughout the extent of her Majesty's dominions.

So much was said at Mauritius of the hurricanes, or cyclones, common to this part of the

HINDOO COSTUMES, MAURITIUS.

Indian ocean, that the Commodore scarcely entertained a hope of escaping from this region without encountering one. These hurricanes, at the season of their occurrence, (from December to April,) form the great topic of interest and discussion to the Mauritians. In fact, they talk of little else at that period. Meteorological instruments of every kind are kept in use and under the most watchful observation. Nor is this great solicitude without reason, for these cyclones, when they do come, are but too apt to bring ruin and desolation to the merchant and planter.

The immediate cause of these atmospherical phenomena has been supposed to be a disturbance of the equilibrium in the air that takes place at the change of the monsoons. This period of strife lasts about a month, and then the hurricanes rage with terrific violence. Redfield and Reed, and others, have explained the laws by which they suppose them to be governed; and their hypothesis is perfectly well known and understood by the Mauritians. The islands of Mauritius, Bourbon, and Roderique, lie directly in their ordinary track, and if either of them happens to fall within the vortex of one of these hurricanes, the consequences to life and property are terrible indeed.

The natural interest felt in the subject, as well as its great practical importance, have given rise to many discussions as to the best means to be adopted, should a vessel unfortunately find herself within their sweeping influence or in their proximity; and though these discussions may, and doubtless will, result in a better understanding of the laws which govern these winds, yet it must be confessed that some of them have rather a tendency to confuse the simple minded and practical seaman, who, if caught in one of these storms, should undertake *then* to find rules for his guidance. He can spare no time from the handling of his vessel, and however plain abstract principles may be to him who is at leisure quietly to master them on shore, the cabin of a ship in a storm is a poor school of philosophy. This, however, only shows the necessity there is that the seaman who would understand his profession should study and master all that science has brought to light, when he can do so on shore, and before he is caught in a storm which demands its immediate application. However, the instructions given by the earlier writers on these hurricanes are now more generally understood than they were, by the well informed seaman, particularly since they have been further explained and simplified by the more recent publication of Piddington.

Of those residing at Mauritius who have earnestly studied and discussed the laws which govern these storms, may be mentioned Dr. Thom, whose writings are well known, Lieutenant Fryers, of the royal engineers, and Mr. Sedgewick, who has published a little work, which he calls "The True Principle," and which has been reviewed by Dr. Thom; and, lastly, a creole gentleman attached to the observatory at Mauritius, Mr. Bosquett.

This last named gentleman, who has translated into French Piddington's Horn book, with annotations of his own, claims to be able, by careful and constant meteorological observations, to foretell the existence of hurricanes in the Indian ocean, and to describe the course they will take. The day before the Mississippi left Mauritius, he informed the Commodore that a cyclone was then blowing in a direction E. by N. from the island, and that it would pass to the southward and eastward.

By reference to the chart in Piddington's Horn book it will be seen that these cyclones never extend to the northward of 10° or 12° south latitude, in the meridian of Mauritius. Therefore, vessels leaving the island in the hurricane season, for any part of India, should steer to the northward, passing well to the westward of the Cargados, a most dangerous group, thus keeping a clear sea open to the westward that there may be nothing in the way should it be desirable to run to the northward and westward, which would be the true course to take in case of encountering the southwestern or northwestern quadrants of a cyclone, (which, in the hurricane season, a vessel from Mauritius is in danger of,) and this course she should keep until she is sufficiently far north to be beyond its influence. Steamers, of course, have superior means of avoiding these storms, as they have the power of steering the most judicious course to escape from their greatest fury.

Following the advice of several experienced seamen, when the Mississippi left, she took the circuitous route (the distance from Mauritius to Ceylon being thereby made 150 miles greater) and passed to the westward of the Cargados and between the island Galega and Laya de Mahla Bank; thence, doubling the northern extremity of that bank the ship was steered to the eastward for Pona Moluque, the southernmost of the Maldives; after passing this the course was direct for Point de Galle in Ceylon.

Before leaving the United States, Messrs. Howland & Aspinwall, of New York, at the suggestion of the Commodore, had dispatched two ships laden with coal, one to the Cape of Good Hope, and the other to Mauritius. The prudence of this precaution was proved by the result; but for these two cargoes the Mississippi, as well as the other steamers of the squadron which were to follow her—the Powhatan and Alleghany—would have had the greatest difficulty in procuring fuel. In the case of both cargoes, they arrived at their respective places of destination a few days before the Mississippi, so that both at the Cape and Mauritius the ship was enabled at once to take in fresh fuel, and leave a supply for the steamers that were to come after.*

Having taken on board about five hundred tons of this coal, with such other supplies as were needed, the Mississippi left St. Louis on the morning of the 28th of February, intending to touch for a further supply of fuel either at Point de Galle or Singapore, if it should appear possible to reach the latter named place with the coal taken on board at Mauritius. The course was that already indicated above, and on the evening of the 10th of March the light was made on Point de Galle, island of Ceylon, after a passage of thirteen days.

The port of Point de Galle is the general rendezvous of the English India mail steamers, not only of those which ply to and from the Red sea, but of those which double the Cape of Good Hope, bound to India or the China seas. Large quantities of coal and patent fuel are brought from England and deposited there; and though the quantity would seem to be enormous, yet so great is the consumption of the numerous steamers, of which there are about ten each month touching at the port, that there is sometimes an apprehension felt of the supply of fuel falling short. The Oriental Steam Navigation Company have consequently given positive orders not to supply a single ton to any foreign vessel-of-war, and consequently the Mississippi could obtain only a limited supply from the Bengal government.

The town of Galle is situated upon a peninsula, the inner curve of which forms the harbor. Thick walls of considerable height enclose the town within a space of about fifteen acres. The

---

* "To the zealous and energetic services of Messrs. Howland & Aspinwall, in the faithful fulfilment of their engagements with the Navy Department, I am greatly indebted: had it not been for their prompt and effectual agency, I should have found myself seriously embarrassed in controlling the movements of the steamers of my command. The ample provision thus placed at my disposal not only relieved me from care upon the score of fuel, without which side-wheel steamers are worse than useless, but enabled me to exercise a most gratifying courtesy in furnishing to several foreign war steamers supplies of this essential article, which could not be obtained at the time from any other source."—*Extract from the Commodore's Journal.*

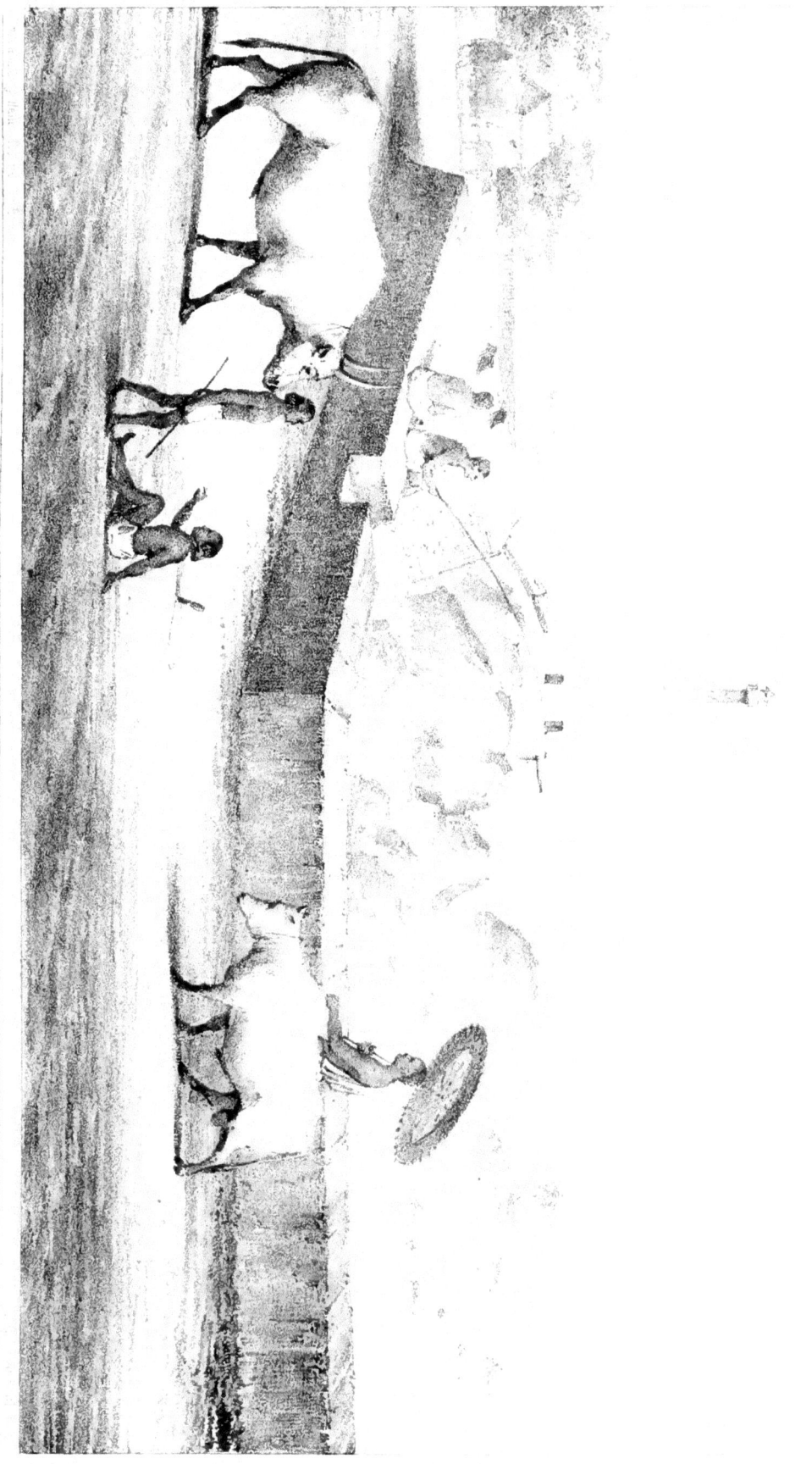

inhabitants are thus shut up within a close fortress, from which the sea breezes are almost entirely excluded, and must suffer very much from the heat, which cannot be otherwise than excessive, in a latitude almost under the equator. The heat, however, is not so intense as on the neighboring coast of India. During the stay of the Mississippi the highest range of the thermometer (Fahrenheit) was 85°, and the lowest was 82°. The ordinary range at Point de Galle, however, is set down at from 70° to 87°.

Point de Galle, Ceylon.

Fresh supplies of food of almost every description can be readily obtained at this port; bullocks, pigs, fruit, and vegetables, abound. The fish are abundant and good. Wood is plentiful and tolerably good. Water can be obtained in reasonable quantities, but it is bad.

The population of the town is composed of English officials and merchants, and a motley collection of tradesmen and laborers of all varieties of color, from negro black to dingy brown.

The Commodore and his officers were not a little mortified, as well as somewhat embarrassed, by finding, on their arrival at Point de Galle, the United States commercial agent, a native of Scotland, confined to his premises under an execution for debt. Various accounts of the circumstances connected with this unfortunate position of affairs were communicated to the Commodore, but he studiously avoided any interference with the matter. It was no part of his business or duty to interpose; and humiliating as was this state of things, he could not but feel that the fault was in the former consular system of the United States. Our country had no right to expect our consuls and commercial agents, many of whom were unfitted in every respect for their stations, either to represent or sustain the commercial interests of the nation so long as the system then existing was followed. The fees at many of the places where our consular agents were accredited, it was notorious would scarce suffice to clothe them, and, accordingly, to eke out a scanty living, they were often obliged to resort to some sort of business, often not of the most dignified character. Of course, there were always honorable exceptions to this unfavorable state of things. Many of our consuls have been and are men of high position, who have not failed to exercise a strong influence upon the local governments within which they may have resided. But for this they have been less indebted to the consular office than to their deservedly high commercial standing; at the same time it may be true, that possessing such high personal characters as they do, in their cases, the consular office, worthily bestowed, may add somewhat to their influence. The recent action of Congress has shown the sense entertained by that body of the correctness of these views and of the need of reform; and it is hoped the measures adopted will guarantee for the future a dignified representative of our commercial interests wherever we have a consul.

Ceylon has been long known to Europe. The first accounts were received from two of the commanders of the fleet dispatched by Alexander the Great from the Indus to the Persian Gulf. A description of the island may be found recorded by ancient authors; both Pliny and Ptolomeus have left accounts of its character and condition. It is supposed that the Persians had formed a Christian establishment on the coast before the sixth century; and in the thirteenth the celebrated traveller, Marco Polo, visited Ceylon, of which he has left a glowing description, having been so much struck with its beauty and richness that in his enthusiasm he has termed it the finest island in the world. Sir John Mandeville, the English traveller, also visited it some fifty years later.

The Portuguese, however, were the first among the Europeans to establish intimate relations with Ceylon. When they found their way to India, by the Cape of Good Hope, they were welcomed by the king, whose dominions at the time were a prey to intestine war. The Europeans taking advantage of the civil dissensions which prevailed, and offering themselves as mediators, succeeded in establishing a foothold in the country, which they took care to maintain. In 1520, the Portuguese strongly fortified themselves at Colombo, and held a controlling influence over the natives, until they were dispersed by the latter, aided by the Dutch, who, in their turn, changed their relation of friends to that of masters of the people. The war with the Portuguese lasted more than twenty years, and they were not finally expelled the island until 1656. The various fortified positions at Batticolo, Point de Galle, Negombo, and Colombo fell into the hands of the Dutch, who thus controlled the maritime provinces.

During the European wars at the end of the eighteenth century, the French got possession of Trincomalee, but they were ejected by the British, who in their turn were forced to yield it up to the former possessors, and it finally was restored to the Dutch, who continued to hold it, together with the sea coast, until they were wrested from them, in 1796, by the British, who were formally acknowledged as the possessors by the treaty of Amiens. English history records that the whole island, by the invitation of the natives, was taken possession of, in 1815, by the British crown, under the sovereignty of which Ceylon still remains. It is difficult to say who, of the successive masters of the poor Cingalese, have been the most cruel and oppressive, and, in fact, it is feared that but little can be said in palliation of the fraud and perfidy of either of them.

In olden time, before its occupation by the Europeans, Ceylon was one of the richest and most productive of the kingdoms of the east. The natives, at a very early period, showed great skill in the development of the resources of the island, and increased the fertility of the soil by ingenious modes of artificial irrigation; and numerous vestiges of imposing works, constructed for this purpose, remain to this day.

The climate of Ceylon is very much influenced by the monsoons. The northeast prevails from November to February, and the southwest from April to September; but there are certain local causes which influence these winds and modify their temperature. There is a great difference between the climate of the northern and southern portions of the island, and a curious effect results therefrom; for not seldom on one side of a mountain the rain is falling abundantly, while on the other it is so dry that the herbage is parched and withered; and thus while the inhabitants of the former are doing their utmost to protect their lands from the flood, those of the latter are striving to obviate the consequences of the drought by availing themselves of the scant reservoirs of water which may have been left from previous rains.

The island is comparatively healthy, as is indicated by the rate of mortality, which, being less than three per cent., shows a remarkable salubrity for an eastern country. As the clearing of the jungles and the draining of the marshes proceed, a still higher degree of health may be reasonably expected.

Ceylon did not appear as flourishing a colony as the Mauritius, though it possesses superior geographical advantages. Lying, as it does, as a sort of outpost to the principal possessions of the English in the east, and offering, in its port of Galle, a point for the distribution of intelligence throughout India and China, it is much resorted to.

With all its natural advantages, however, the island at present is far less flourishing than might have been expected. The exports are limited in comparison with the acknowledged fertility of the island, to the productive power of which there would hardly seem to be any limit. Labor may be obtained, too, for twelve cents a day, and yet the agricultural interests are not as promising as, under such favorable circumstances, they should be. The natives, too, are said not to be wanting in industry, but their needs are so few, living, as they do, upon fish, rice, and cocoa-nuts, that they are never forced by necessity to labor hard for their subsistence.

Of the productions of the island the cocoa-nut is probably the most valuable to the natives. Everywhere in Ceylon, as far as the eye can reach, extensive plantations of this tree are to be seen, and the numerous roads throughout the island are bordered with it. The weary and heated traveller finds not only protection from the sun in its shade, but refreshment from the milk of the fruit, which is both agreeable to the taste and wholesome. The cocoa-nut palm has a great variety of uses. The green fruit, with its delicate albuminous meat and its refreshing milk, is a favorite article of food. When ripe, the kernel of the nut is dried, forming what the natives term copperal, and an oil of great value is expressed from it, while the residuum forms an excellent oil-cake for the fattening of animals. Even the husk of the nut is useful; its fibres are wrought into the coir rope, of which large quantities are annually exported, and the shells are manufactured into various domestic utensils. From the sap of the tree a drink is obtained which is called "toddy," and made into arrack by distillation. The leaves afford a good material for the thatching of the native huts, and are moreover given as food to the elephants. The Palmyra palm, which also abounds in the island, shares with the cocoa-nut tree in many of its advantages.

The other staples of Ceylon are cinnamon, coffee, sugar, rice, arica nut, precious stones, plumbago, (probably the best in the world,) and other vegetable and mineral productions. The pearl fisheries, for which the island was once famous, have very much diminished in their yield. The natives account for the diminution by declaring that the pearl-oyster has the power of locomotion, and has shifted its former quarters to some new ground not yet discovered. The scarcity is probably owing to the fact that the pearls have been disturbed before they have reached their full development, which is said to require a period of seven years. At one time the fishery was a source of handsome revenue to the government; in 1797 the sum of £140,000 was derived from it. Since that period the proceeds have gradually fallen off, until at present they amount to almost nothing. Diving for the pearl-oyster is a favorite occupation among the natives of Ceylon, as a skilful diver can earn ten times the wages of a farm laborer, and the employment is not, as has been stated, unfavorable to health, but, on the contrary, conducive to strength and vigor of body.

Ceylon abounds in a rich vegetation and many trees of a vigorous growth, among which, in addition to the cocoa-nut and Palmyra palm, there is the kettal tree, from the sap of which is produced a coarse sugar, and from its fruit, when dried and reduced to powder, a substitute for rice flour. The talipot, with its immense foliage, is one of the wonders of the island; a single leaf of this tree is sufficient to cover beneath its shade several persons, and it supplies, when softened by boiling, a substitute for paper, upon which the natives are in the habit of writing, and find in it a most durable material. The cinnamon, with its beautiful white blossom and its red tipped leaves, and other odoriferous trees, are among the native products of Ceylon; but the stories of the fragrance of the aroma exhaled from these trees and the plants, and which voyagers have described as sensible at a distance from the land, are gross exaggerations. No fragrance was observed equal to that of the magnolia or of the delightful perfume of the newly-mown grass of our own country, or in any degree approaching the delicious odor of the heliotrope and geranium hedges of Madeira. The cultivated flowers that were seen at Ceylon and at Mauritius were, in fact, remarkable for their want of fragrance. Rich woods of various kinds, as the rose, the ebony, the satin, and lime, grow in abundance on the island, and are used for many purposes of utility and ornament.

Within the forests and in the jungles of Ceylon are found a great variety of wild animals—the elephant, the hyena, tiger-cat, the bear, the deer, and the monkey, are among the most abundant. The number of elephants is incredibly great, and, issuing in troops from their lairs, they come crushing down the cultivated fields and plantations and devouring the crops, with great loss to the proprietors. They are found in all the uncultivated parts of the island, but their favorite haunts are near to the farms, to which they prove so destructive that the colonial government pays a reward of 7s. 6d. (about $1 85) for every tail of the animal which is brought to the authorities. Mr. Talbot, the government agent at Galle, stated, surprising as it may seem, that he had paid during the preceding year two hundred pounds sterling for tails, which would give six hundred as the number of elephants destroyed.

An army officer, as was stated to the Commodore, actually killed, during his residence on the island, no less than six hundred of these gigantic animals. Within a few months of the arrival of the Mississippi, two officers of the garrison, one of whom (Lieutenant Lennox) became personally known to the Commodore, destroyed no less than forty elephants in the course of a sporting visit of six weeks to the jungle. They are ordinarily shot with a rifle;

the sportsman approaches his game in front, or perhaps, as the sailors would say, on the quarter, that he may aim at either of the only two vital parts upon which a rifle ball will have any effect, one being directly in the forehead, through which the brain is penetrated, and the other behind the ear. If the hunter chance to come up to his elephant in the rear, he raises a shout or makes a noise, by which the huge animal is attracted, and, throwing forward its ears, exposes the vital spot, at which his ruthless enemy aims the deadly ball and brings down his huge victim. The elephants of Ceylon are not so large as those of other parts of India, and but a small proportion of them have tusks.

Of serpents, there are but twenty species, four only of which are venomous, the cobra and tic prolango being the most deadly. The latter is said to be endowed with great cunning, and to lie in wait for the purpose of attacking the passing traveller. The stories which are told of the anaconda, boa constrictor or python, seizing upon cattle and horses, and even horsemen, must be received as fabulous. There is, however, a species of boa peculiar to the island, which is capable of swallowing a deer whole, and after they have indulged in venison to that degree, and become surfeited with so substantial a meal, they fall readily a prey to the captor. This is believed to be the extent of the powers of deglutition of the Ceylon boas; those enormous serpents, which are said to swallow an entire ox, horns and all, being unknown in that region. It may not be amiss to refer here to a remedy for venomous bites, for which popular opinion in the east claims considerable efficacy, this is a paste made by moistening the powder of ipecachuana with water, and applying it to the external injury. Some wonderful effects have been reported from the use of this simple means in various cases, of not only bites from venomous serpents, but of stings by the scorpion and various poisonous fish.

The population of Ceylon is estimated at about 1,442,062, of whom 8,275 are whites, 1,413,486 colored persons, and 20,431 aliens and resident strangers. The inhabitants are composed of the natives, termed Cingalese, of a small proportion of Europeans, principally government officials, military officers and merchants with their families, and of negroes, Malays, and Chinese. The Cingalese were less ugly in appearance than was expected, many of the men, in fact, (as for the women few were seen, and none of the better class,) have expressive and even handsome faces, and their forms are not without symmetry. They seem to be amiable in disposition and are remarkable for their effeminate habits. So similar is the costume of the two sexes that it is difficult often for the casual observer to distinguish the man from the woman. The males allow their hair to grow to a great length, which they foster with much care, and fasten to the tops of their heads with large tortoise shell combs, such as our ladies at home might not be ashamed to wear.

The common dress of the better class of the Cingalese is a jacket, worn next to the skin, and from the waist downward a colored petticoat, wrapped in graceful folds round the limbs and falling to the feet. The head, well protected as it is with the superabundant hair, is generally bare of any artificial covering. Some of the common people, however, wrap a cloth turban-wise around their brows, which they shift to their body when mingling with the crowds, and thus eke out their scanty drapery, which ordinarily consists only of a petticoat. Some of the aborigines, who live in a rude condition within the fastnesses of the great forests, confine themselves in dress to the simple wardrobe of nature.

In addition to the Cingalese, who are doubtless descendants of the aborigines of the island, there are the Malabars, whom tradition traces to the neighboring shores of India, and whose religion and social characteristics would seem to connect them with that country. They are Hindoos and preserve their religion and system of caste, together with the costumes of their original country, as well as their language, somewhat modified, however, by their relation with the Cingalese. The neighboring islands and continents supply a population of Mahommedans or Moors to Ceylon, and they abound in several parts of the country, where, in the various orders into which their law of caste divides them, they carry on a prosperous business as weavers, fishermen, merchants, and bakers. They are among the most enterprising and thriving of the population, and their well known skill and industry have secured them much of the commercial wealth and influence of the island.

The native language of the aborigines is peculiar to themselves, but their writings are in Sanscrit or Pali. A provincial dialect of Portuguese is, however, generally spoken by those natives who have passed their lives in the European portions of the island.

The Christian religion was introduced at a very early period into Ceylon. It has been supposed that the apostle Saint Thomas preached there; however this may be, there is but little doubt that the Nestorians accompanied the Persian merchants, many years ago, to the island and made converts there and established Christianity. On the arrival, however, of the Portuguese navigators there were no remnants of those churches which are said to have existed in Ceylon in the sixth century. The zealous Francis Xavier, the Roman Catholic missionary, however, was the first, by his earnest preaching and proselyting energies, to establish the Christian religion permanently on the island, and most of that faith are, accordingly, Romanists. The Church of England is, of course, sustained in accordance with the religious opinions of the British authorities; and the various other Protestant churches have their members among the European residents. There are missionaries of various sects engaged in efforts to evangelize the native heathen, but with what success did not appear. Among these there are no less than eleven Americans; and the different churches are represented in the proportion of thirty-four Romanist missionaries, twenty Wesleyan, fourteen of the English church, and thirteen Baptists. The predominant religion among the Cingalese is the Buddhist, which was at one time maintained by the British government, a heathen inheritance derived from the succession to the native kings. The tooth of Buddha, the relic so highly revered by his followers, was taken under the especial protection of English orthodoxy, and the ecclesiastical patronage of the Buddhist establishment was exercised by England, in accordance with the not very scrupulous views of political expediency. The guardianship of the tooth of Buddha, and the dispensation of Buddhist church patronage, have been, of late years, properly delegated by a Christian nation to a heathen priesthood.

There are numerous Buddhist temples in Ceylon, some of which present an impressive aspect; and there is one of great antiquity and so much venerated as to attract votaries from various parts of India. On the arrival of the Mississippi there was a Siamese sloop-of-war in the harbor, which had brought a number of Buddhist priests on a pilgrimage to this temple.

An interesting incident occurred in connexion with the presence of the Siamese man-of-war. For many reasons the Commodore was desirous of showing some marked attention to the commander of this vessel, who, on acquaintance, was found to be a young man of much intelligence and possessing some knowledge of the English language. The Commodore, therefore, dispatched his aid, Lieutenant Contee, to offer to him his services and to invite him on board the Mississippi. The Siamese commander seemed pleased with the compliment and came on

board the Mississippi the following day, where he was received with due honors. He was accompanied by two of the Buddhist priests who had come from Siam in his vessel on a pilgrimage to the famous temple. It was learned, on inquiry, that Prince Phar-Pen-Clow-Chow-Yon-Hon, who was so civil to Mr. Roberts and the officers of the Peacock on the occasion

Buddhist Temple, near Point de Galle, Ceylon.

of their visit to Siam, in 1836, was the second in rank in his kingdom, or second king, as it is termed. The Commodore, therefore, being desirous of renewing the good understanding which formerly subsisted between him and our officers, which, however, had been somewhat disturbed by the visit of Mr. Ballastier, sent him a beautiful pistol, of Colt's patent, and addressed to him the following letter:

United States Ship Mississippi,
Point de Galle, Island of Ceylon, March 14, 1853.

Most Exalted Prince: I have been most happy to meet at this port a vessel-of-war belonging to the kingdom of Siam, one of beautiful form and construction, and commanded by an officer of skill and merit.

In remembrance of the kindness you extended to the late Mr. Roberts and the officers of the United States ship Peacock, in 1836, I beg your acceptance of a curious pistol which has been entrusted to my charge, to be presented to some high functionary who has sufficient acquaintance with the arts to understand its mechanism and use.

The renown which your Highness has acquired in America, for your attainments in every branch of science, induces me to place at your disposal this trifling gift of Mr. Colt.

I hope that you will send one of your ships of Siam to America, where I can promise the officers a friendly and honorable welcome.

It will, at all times, give me the greatest pleasure to render to all vessels under the Siamese flag whatever aid or assistance it may be in my power to command.

With profound respect I have the honor to be your most obedient servant,

M. C. PERRY, *Commander-in-chief of all the U. S. naval forces in the East India, China, and Japan seas.*

To his Royal Highness PHAR-PEN-CLOW-CHOW-YON-HON.

The Commodore was induced thus to take the initiative in endeavoring to open communications with Siam, in the hope that he might possibly be able to revive the treaty between that kingdom and the United States, made on our part by Mr. Roberts. This had virtually become a dead letter and altogether inoperative, as had, indeed, also that made by England with the same people. Sir John Davis and Sir James Brooke, on behalf of England, and Mr. Ballastier, on the part of the United States, had made subsequent efforts and been politely repulsed; but the Commodore hoped that possibly another attempt might result more successfully; and as he had been entrusted by the government with several blank letters of credence, he was prepared to act on the authority of one of them should he find a favorable opening. Both the kings of Siam, and many of their officers, understand the English language, and one object of the Commodore was to induce the monarch to send one of his ships to the United States (they are all vessels, at once, both of war and commerce) to examine into our institutions, resources, &c., and thus lead to friendly commercial relations.

The Commodore subsequently received a courteous answer to his letter, and from that and private information which he had taken pains to get of his probable reception, he would have gone to Siam had not uncontrollable circumstances prevented.

The Commodore also presented to Mun-Clow-Sar-Coun, captain of the Siamese sloop-of-war, a service sword and a copy of "Bowditch's Navigator."

The Mississippi left Galle on the morning of the 15th of March, and after getting clear of the harbor, shaped her course for Great Nicobar Island, the southernmost of the group of that name, with the intention of passing between it and Paloway, a small island or rock lying off the northern extremity of Sumatra. On the 20th, Great Nicobar was made, and the proposed course having been taken, the steamer entered the straits of Malacca, steering for the Malay shore, on which side the weather is represented as being more settled and the sky less obscured.

Fortunately, the weather was favorable during the passage through the straits, and it was found necessary to anchor once only during the night, at the entrance between the North and South Sands, within sight of the Aroa islands. The navigation of the straits did not appear to the Commodore as dangerous as an examination of the chart had led him to expect; yet it is somewhat intricate and certainly not free from danger.

A vessel has, however, the advantage of being always able to anchor, though, in some parts of the channel, necessarily in rather deep water. The two most dangerous passages are those termed the East and West Channel; and the narrow one between Formosa bank and the Pyramids lying opposite, and the northern end of the middle bank. A light vessel recently anchored on "Two-and-a-half fathom bank" renders the former passage more safe; while the latter is made more secure by the high land of Cape Formosa, the bearings of and distance from which will, in clear weather, indicate the mid-channel.

Pilots may be procured for vessels, when bound toward the China seas, at Penang, and at Singapore when their course is in an opposite direction. The Mississippi took no pilot, as time could not be spared for communicating with Penang; and, in fact, with good charts and a careful look out, together with proper precautions in anchoring when necessary, a pilot is of little further service than to identify the names of headlands and islands, and to explain the tides and currents. Indeed, by trusting too much to the pilots, who are mostly irresponsible natives, ships may fall into dangers which the experience and prudence of their captains, if left to their own judgments, would avoid. In passing through the straits, the Mississippi met H. B. M. ship Cleopatra, towed by a small war steamer, bound in an opposite direction. The senior English ship, on coming near, honored the broad pendant of the Commodore with a salute; which compliment was promptly responded to by an equal number of guns.

Mississippi saluted by an English Frigate in the Straits of Malacca.

It is a fact worthy of remark, that the usual vertical rise and fall of the tides in the Straits of Malacca is from twelve to fourteen feet, while in other parts of the world, in the same latitude, there is scarcely any variation. The tides at Singapore correspond, in this respect, with those in the Straits.

On entering from the Straits of Malacca into what is called the Straits of Singapore, the islands became numerous and the passages consequently various and intricate; but the directions

124   EXPEDITION TO JAPAN.

given by Horsburgh are so full and explicit, that by a strict observance of them, together with proper vigilance and judgment, the lead being kept in constant use and the anchor always in readiness, there is no very great danger of touching.

With a judicious regard to these precautions, the Mississippi made her way securely through all the intricacies of the course, and finally, on the 25th of March, came to anchor in the port of Singapore.

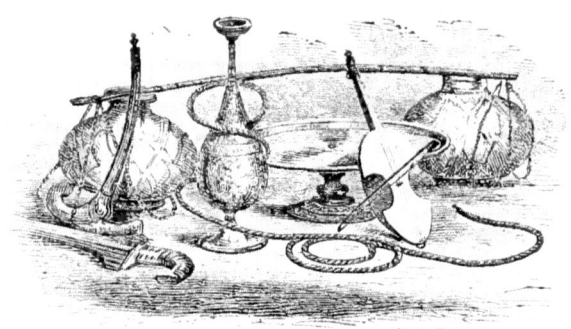

CHAPTER V.

SINGAPORE.—ITS GREAT COMMERCE.—POPULATION.—RAPID INCREASE.—HOSPITALITY OF A WEALTHY CHINESE MERCHANT.—IMPORTANCE OF SINGAPORE TO ENGLAND.—COAL DEPOT AT SINGAPORE.—PHYSICAL ASPECT OF THE COUNTRY.—AGRICULTURAL PRODUCTS.—ANIMALS.—FEROCITY OF THE TIGER—WATER BUFFALO.—PASSAGE FROM SINGAPORE TO HONG KONG.—CURRENTS, ROCKS, TIDES.—CHINESE FISHING BOATS.—ARRIVAL AT HONG KONG.—FINDING THERE SLOOPS-OF-WAR SARATOGA AND PLYMOUTH AND STORE SHIP SUPPLY.—SUSQUEHANNA GONE TO SHANGHAE.—DISAPPOINTMENT OF THE COMMODORE.—CONDITION AND PROSPERITY OF HONG KONG.—RUN TO MACAO, THENCE TO WHAMPOA ON CANTON RIVER.—NAVIGATION OF THE RIVER.—FIRST IMPRESSIONS MADE BY THE CITY.—DISAPPOINTED EXPECTATIONS.—HOSPITALITY OF AMERICAN CONSUL AT CANTON.—THE HONGS OR FACTORIES.—STREETS IN CANTON.—PROPER NAME OF THE CITY.—BOCCA TIGRIS.—CHINESE FORTS.—PIRATES ON THE RIVER.—ATTEMPT TO ROB ONE OF THE OFFICERS.—CANTON MARKET PLACE.—TRADE OF CANTON WITH EUROPE AND AMERICA.

HE port of Singapore is a great resort for ships of all nations. Vessels from China, Siam, Malaya, Sumatra, and the various commercial countries of Europe and America, are to be seen anchored together at the same time. The products of these different parts of the world are all to be found in Singapore, brought thither for reciprocal exchange. The policy which has made Singapore a free port has been fully justified by the prosperous result. Its commerce, being entirely unshackled, flourishes even beyond the most sanguine anticipations of those enlightened and enterprising men who but a few years ago established Singapore as a free port.

Notwithstanding the restricted productions of the place, which could do no more than supply business for the scant trade of a few vessels, Singapore has been, by the liberal policy pursued, elevated to the imposing position of a great commercial mart. Its trade embraces China, India and the archipelagos of the oriental seas, Australia, Europe, and America. Nearly the whole world of commerce seeks, in a greater or less degree, its ever crowded harbor.

The commerce with China is very considerable, and is carried on by means of Chinese vessels. The junks come down from the China seas with the northeast monsoon, and remain in port, retailing their cargoes of teas, silks, and other products, until the southwest monsoon is fairly set in, when they return to prepare for another voyage, and thus keep up a succession of periodical trading visits. They bring large numbers of enterprising Chinese emigrants, together with abundant supplies of dollars, teas, silks, chinaware, tobacco, cassia, nankeens, gold thread, and the thousand "nicknackeries" of cunning invention for which Chinese ingenuity is famous. They take back the pernicious opium, edible birds' nests, and various articles of European manufacture.

The town of Singapore is built upon an island, separated from the Malay peninsula by a narrow and scarcely navigable strait. The ancient capitol of the Malayan kingdom, or, as it was sometimes called, the kingdom of Malacca, formerly stood upon the site of the present town. This old city was built in the twelfth century, and conquered by a chief from Java, who transferred the royal residence to Malacca. From that period its population and wealth gradually declined, so that in 1819, when the English took possession, there were but few vestiges of the former city, which indeed had become but a haunt for pirates, where, as well as in the neighboring islands and passages, they found a secure retreat from the vessels of the English and the Dutch sent in pursuit of them. The natives still offer for sale models of the various descriptions of the Malay war, pirate, and sailing proas; and most of them present exceedingly beautiful specimens of graceful form. So much was the Commodore struck with the beauty of the model of the sailing proa that he purposed sending one home to the New York yacht club.

Malay Proa.

The town bears all the appearance of being in a most prosperous condition; its port, as we have said, is always crowded with shipping, and its traders are thriving and wealthy. Marine storehouses are seen throughout the place, but chiefly along the front of the harbor and upon the quay. The principal merchants occupy commodious and tasteful residences, built fronting the bay. There is a striking contrast in the dwellings of those who have settled in this thriving place, between the elegant and convenient town and country houses of the colonial officials and merchants and the ill ventilated and filthy domiciles of the Chinese, or the frail tenements of the Malays. The latter ordinarily select some marshy ground in the suburbs, near a road or pathway, and rear upon piles their wooden houses, the only entrance to which is by means of temporary bridges, often constructed of a single plank.

The prosperity of Singapore, so apparent even to the casual observer, is mainly to be attributed to the sagacious and energetic Sir Stamford Raffles, who pursued with untiring zeal, in spite of the opposition of many in higher authority, his determined purpose of carrying out his favorite projects of policy in the administration of the colony.

The population at the period of the Mississippi's visit was estimated at eighty thousand, a number which shows a very rapid increase since it fell into the possession of the British, at which time there were scarce two hundred on the whole island of Singapore. The inhabitants are made up of Jews, Chinese, Arabs, Malays, and natives of the neighboring countries. The Europeans count the least, and the Chinese the largest number: of these last it was stated that there are no less than sixty thousand, who are the artisans, fishermen, laborers, and small dealers of the place; an industrious class, to which the colony is indebted for much of its trading activity.

Mosque in Singapore.

These various people who inhabit Singapore retain their national habits and customs, and their peculiar modes of worship. The Chinese lets grow his tail, smokes his opium, and offers incense to Jos; the Arab sports his turban, invokes the name of the prophet, and prostrates himself within the mosque, while the European shaves his beard, drinks London porter, and takes his seat in the church pew. Most of the different nations have their places of worship; there are Chinese temples and Mahommedan mosques, as well as Christian churches. A curious confusion of religions seems to have resulted from the intermingling of sects, as may be inferred from what was seen by the Commodore on a visit to a Chinese temple. In one of the recesses of the place the devil was represented in human form, but of exceedingly hideous physiognomy, while in front of him was placed an image of the virgin and child. This was certainly a very strange assortment of company, and naturally set the Commodore to conjecturing as to what could possibly have brought together such very opposite characters; whether the intention was to represent the mother and child as at the mercy of the devil, or the reverse, was not very clear, although, from the decidedly uncomfortable expression of his satanic majesty's face, it might be inferred that he was less at his ease than any of the company, and quite out of his element. It was, however, concluded that the bringing of Christian personages into a Chinese temple was in some way connected with the early introduction of the Romish religion by the Portuguese missionaries.

The stay of the Mississippi at Singapore was so short that there was but little opportunity to see much of the European society. Visits and salutes were exchanged with the acting governor and with the commander of the military forces; these, together with some official business transacted with the United States consul, were the extent of the Commodore's intercourse with the European residents. With, however, a Chinese merchant, who seemed to be imbued with the true spirit of hospitality, many of the officers of the ship formed an agreeable acquaintance, and were hospitably entertained at his house. This gentleman's name is Whampoa, a man of courteous bearing and great intelligence, and who had made considerable progress in the English language, which he spoke with some fluency. His country residence was the most beautiful on the island. The house was large, commodious, and tastefully furnished, and its rooms were filled with objects of curiosity and vertu. Surrounding the dwelling were extensive pleasure grounds and plantations, on which the various productions of the island, the useful as well as ornamental, were cultivated to great perfection. There were collections of animals and rare birds, among which were the cassowary and crowned pigeon from New Guinea, and a singular breed of perfectly white pea-fowl. The residence of the hospitable Whampoa, where the Commodore dined and spent the night, was surrounded by all that could delight the eye, or add to the enjoyment of life. Among other luxurious appanages of the establishment, there was a beautiful white Arabian horse, kept by Whampoa for his own especial use under the saddle, and the Commodore was very much struck by its symmetry of form, purity of color, and excellence of temper, for it was as docile as a lamb.

In a military and geographical point of view, Singapore is of vast importance to England. By means of it, and with an effective naval force, this entrance to the China seas may be commanded. Its position is vastly advantageous in a commercial point of view, from which it has become an entrepot for the neighboring kingdoms of Sumatra, Borneo, Siam, Cambodia, and Cochin China.

To Sir Stamford Raffles, who proved himself a master spirit in every enterprise he undertook, the British government and the East India Company are indebted for this valuable acquisition, and there was, it must be confessed, some show of equity in his mode of proceeding. Raffles actually purchased from the Rajah of Jahore and Singapore the right of sovereignty over the island and its dependencies for a stipulated sum and an annual pension, and it is believed that

the payments have been regularly made. This is an example which has been very rare among the European governments, who have generally seized violently upon the finest countries without scruple, and subjected the inhabitants to political, if not to social, servitude. The Rajah had reason to pride himself upon his bargain with Raffles, when he reflected how much better he had been treated than his royal ancestors, who had been driven from their homes and despoiled of their possessions by the former European invaders.

The present Rajah, with his numerous wives and children, occupy a native village about a mile from the English town. The Commodore did not see him, but his son, a fine intelligent youth, came on board the ship to pay his respects. His father probably thought his dignity called for the first visit from the Commodore, which, however, was prevented by reason of engagements.

As a stopping place and depot for coal Singapore, is of great importance to the English mail-steamers. The wealthy and enterprising Oriental Steam Navigation Company have erected at New Harbor, about two and a half miles from the town, a magnificent depot, comprising wharves, coal-sheds, storehouses, workshops, and other buildings, such as would do credit to any English colonial establishment; and this is no slight praise. Singapore is in the course of the regular mail route between India, China, Australia, and Europe. There is a constant postal communication, by means of the English and one or more Dutch steamers, with Hong Kong, Penang, Batavia, Shanghai, Calcutta, Madras, Bengal, Bombay, Ceylon, the Mauritius, Cape of Good Hope, and, by the Red Sea, with Europe and America.

Supplies of most kinds required by vessels can be obtained at fair prices in the port of Singapore. The water is good, and is supplied from tanks, under the supervision of an official of the place, the master attendant. There was not a pound of coal, however, to be purchased at Singapore, and there was reason to fear that the Mississippi would be deprived of her necessary supplies. It was not practicable to make any arrangement with the Labuan Company, for the whole produce of the mines under their control was exhausted by the Oriental and Pacific Company, with which a contract existed for a supply of one thousand tons per month. Fortunately for the Mississippi, however, the stock of the last named company at Hong Kong was falling short, and, as it was difficult to procure vessels to transport an additional supply, the agent of the company at Singapore agreed to lend the Commodore two hundred and thirty tons, provided it would be returned at Hong Kong. By this arrangement both parties were accommodated, the Mississippi obtaining her necessary supply at Singapore, and the company securing what they wanted at their principal Chinese depot, without the expense of its conveyance.

The chief articles of export from Singapore are tin, nutmegs, sugar, drugs, tortoise shell, and some minor commodities, the product of the neighboring countries. The British settlement of Singapore embraces not only the island of that name, but a number of smaller ones scattered about in the neighboring seas. The main island, Singapore, is about twenty-five miles long, and fifteen in breadth, containing an estimated area of two hundred and seventy-five square miles. Inland, the surface of the country is diversified with low hills and shallow valleys, while the sea shore is low and overgrown with mangroves, and occasionally broken by the entrances of salt creeks, which, penetrating sometimes to the extent of six or seven miles, overflow their banks, and convert the neighboring soil into marsh. The artists of the expedition have supplied a view of the river Durong, which will give an idea of the characteristic scenery.

When the English first obtained possession of Singapore the island was covered with a forest, and entirely without cultivation. Now, in the neighborhood of the town, and extending more or less into the interior, there are considerable plantations, which have been chiefly cultivated by the industrious immigrants from China. Rice, coffee, sugar, and other agricultural productions of the warmer latitudes are obtained, but the supply is not sufficient for the consumption of the island. The tropical fruits grow readily, among which the mangusteen reaches great perfection, although its taste did not equal the anticipations formed from the boasted deliciousness of its flavor. The fruit, however, was not in full season during the ship's stay, and it may possibly not have reached the height of its excellence. The nutmeg is cultivated with considerable success, as well as the cocoa-nut, orange, and other tropical fruits.

Various European animals have been introduced into the island. The horse in use is a stumpy, fiery little creature, wonderfully strong for its size. It is generally harnessed to a light carriage which is in common use on the island, and may be hired in the streets of the town at a moderate price for the day. The driver seldom takes his seat upon the box, but runs at the head of his horse, and keeps up a speed in company with the animal of six and sometimes even seven or eight miles an hour. This plan suggests a good hint for the prevention of cruelty to animals, as it has the effect of securing a humane consideration for the beast, which is not likely to be over driven, when for every step it takes its driver takes two, and is thus forcibly reminded of a fellow feeling which cannot fail to make him "wondrous kind."

The native animals are generally the same as those of the adjacent peninsula, from which many of them migrate. The tigers especially entertain a great partiality for Singapore, and resort there in great numbers by swimming across the strait which separates the main land from the island. These are the genuine animals, which have no hesitation in pouncing upon a passing traveller, or snatching up and making a meal of any unfortunate Chinaman or native who may happen to be in the jungle, busy in cutting wood, clearing land for the rice plantations, or otherwise occupied. It was stated on the best authority that not a day passes without the destruction of one human being at least by these ferocious beasts. The Commodore was at first somewhat disposed to be incredulous of this statement, but as the acting governor and commander of the forces both confirmed it, he could no longer hesitate to accept it as truth. He was told by them that so much of an every day occurrence was this fatality, that many of the cases were not reported, in order to avoid the trouble and expense of a coroner's inquest, which the laws require. "Death by tiger," however, is a verdict that might be rendered daily were the legal formalities complied with.

It is said, and probably with truth, that the tiger, after he has once tasted of human flesh, becomes so fond of it that he prefers its flavor to that of his ordinary venison or wild boar, and will make every effort to obtain a supply of his favorite food. It is this intense longing for human flesh which makes the tiger so very dangerous to the inhabitants of Singapore, especially to the poor Malay or Chinese who may be obliged to expose himself in the jungle and the forest. It was said, too, that the animal showed decided preference for a Chinaman.

Nor do these stories of the tiger seem very wonderful, when the fact is well established that those savages who are addicted to cannibalism become passionately fond of their horribly unnatural food. There is a tribe of Malays, called Battas, who, like their fellow Malay tigers, are said by Sir Stamford Raffles to eat one another, and to prefer such food to any other. Nor are they to be classed entirely among barbarians, for these Battas can read and write, and have codes of laws of great antiquity; and yet, according to the authority just named, not less than from sixty to a hundred Battas are eaten annually, even during a time of peace.

In addition to the tigers there are deer and wild boars found upon the island, and several varieties of smaller animals, the monkey, the wild hog or peccary, the porcupine and the sloth. Birds abound, and among them are some of great beauty. Serpents are not very numerous, but among them is the venomous cobra. A singular animal, called the water buffalo, was more particularly observed at Singapore. It approaches in size to the ox of our country, and like it is used as an animal for draught, being harnessed to the shafts of a cart and guided by a driver, who holds a rope which is fastened to a ring or thong passed through the cartilage which divides the nostrils of the animal. The skin of this beast is rough and not unlike that of the rhinoceros, and though the water buffalo has somewhat the general appearance of the ox, its head is altogether different. Notwithstanding the seeming thickness and toughness of its hide, it suffers greatly from the flies, and to avoid them keeps, except during feeding time, in the water; hence, probably, its name.

Inquiries were made about two remarkable inhabitants of the waters about Malacca and Sumatra, described by Raffles: the sailing fish, called by the natives *ikan layer*, and the duyong, mentioned by *Valentin*, and so long talked of as the mermaid; but the Commodore was told by the inhabitants of Singapore that these fish had become very scarce, if not entirely extinct.

Malay Tombs, Near Singapore.

Shells collected upon the adjacent coasts and along the Straits of Malacca are brought in large quantities to Singapore for sale, and some excellent specimens were obtained.

The various people who inhabit Sumatra, the Malayan peninsula, and the numerous islands in the adjacent seas, are all of the Malay family. This race is widely distributed, not only over the Indian archipelago, but throughout the South Sea islands, as it is generally conceded that the natives of the latter are of the same origin as the former. Analogous physical characteristics, customs and languages would seem to prove this relationship.

The Mississippi having taken on board the necessary supplies of fuel, left Singapore on the 29th of March. The ship proceeded through the middle channel, passing near a light-house erected on the rock called "Pedra Branca." This course was taken with the view of running up on the Cochin China and Hainan shores. It is not necessary to say much in regard to the navigation of the China sea, since so much has already been published on the subject. It may, however, be stated in general terms, that nearly the whole expanse of sea from Borneo and Palawan across to Cochin China is rendered dangerous by numerous coral reefs, banks and islands. Many of these banks and reefs are below the surface of the sea, and although the hydrograpical surveys may have truthfully stated their depths when they were taken, and reported a sufficiency of water for vessels to pass, it must not be forgotten that such is the rapidity with which those little architects, the coral zoophites, build up these foundations of future islands, that the work of a few years may materially change the character and depth of the soundings. With such obstructions the China sea cannot be navigated without danger, and especially in stormy weather. Notwithstanding, thousands of vessels go annually through its various passages in safety, while a disaster occurs now and then only.

The surface currents are influenced by the prevailing winds, but the tides, as in other parts of the world, are governed by some mysterious laws which the wisdom of man has not yet entirely fathomed. The vertical rise and fall of the tide upon the coast of Cochin China varies from six to fourteen feet, and the periods and duration of the ebb and flood are by no means regular. In latitude 12°, on the same shore, there is but one tide in the course of twenty-four hours. It has been said that the tides in the tropics rise and fall very little. Although it is granted that in high latitudes the perpendicular flow and ebb is generally greater than in low, still there are many examples of considerable tides in the latter. At the head of the Gulf of Cambay, in latitude 22°, Horsburgh states that the perpendicular depth of the rise and fall of the tides is from thirty to thirty-six feet at the full and change of the moon. So also, according to the same authority, in Surat road, it is from twenty to twenty-one feet, and from fifteen to seventeen in Bombay harbor. Again, in the Gulf of Martaban, which is far within the tropics, the rise and fall of the tide, at the full and change of the moon is twenty-three and twenty-four feet, and off Rangoon bar about twenty or twenty-one feet. In Gaspar straits, within $2\frac{1}{2}°$ of the equator, there is occasionally, from local causes, a rise and fall of sixteen or seventeen feet on the spring tide, but this is rare in places so near the equator. These instances, all from Horsburgh, show that very considerable tides occur within the tropics.

The observation of the Commodore in regard to the single tide in twenty-four hours, on the shore of Cochin China, is paralleled by analogous instances, also reported by Horsburgh, who remarks: "Although in most places the tide ebbs and flows twice in every twenty-four hours, this is not universally the case within the tropics; for among several of the eastern islands the tide flows only once in twenty-four hours." In many places, far beyond the tropics, the tide likewise flows only once in twenty-four hours, particularly on the southern coast of Van Dieman's land; but at Port Dalrymple, on the north coast, the tide flows twice in twenty-four hours. The zodiacal lights glowed in brilliant radiations almost every morning and evening during the time the Mississippi was in the equatorial latitudes; and the chaplain, (Mr. Jones,)

who made this matter a subject of especial notice and study, had a good opportunity of continuing his observations upon the phenomena of this remarkable appearance.

On the morning of the 6th of April, as the ship was proceeding on her course, vast numbers of fishing boats were descried as far as the eye could reach. No less than two hundred and sixty-nine of these little craft were counted, at one time, from the poop. They were sailing in couples, about ninety fathoms apart, before the wind, with a net extended between each two. They were curiously rigged, having square sails set upon two or three masts, which had, at a distance, somewhat the appearance of courses and topsails, which they hoisted and lowered as they desired to graduate the rate of sailing, in order to keep way with their consorts. These vessels were engaged in taking a small fish similar to the sardine of the Mediterranean, and the same mode of netting them is pursued in both localities.

The appearance of these craft was a sure indication of the proximity of land, and accordingly, at half past ten in the morning, it was sighted. The ship continuing her course toward the roadstead of Macao, was anchored at dark under the Ladrones. On the following morning she proceeded to Macao roads, and after a communication with the shore, the course was continued on to Hong Kong, where she finally came to anchor about sunset of the same day.

Here were found the sloops-of-war Plymouth and Saratoga, and the store-ship Supply; the two former of which, as the Mississippi let go her anchor, fired the usual salute, which was duly returned from the guns of the Mississippi; the Susquehanna, however, was nowhere to be seen. This vessel had been designated by the government as the flag-ship of the Commodore, who, much to his surprise and disappointment, found that she had sailed a fortnight previously for Shanghai, having on board the United States commissioner to China, the Honorable Mr. Marshall, as well as Dr. Parker, the secretary of legation, and Mr. Forbes, the United States consul at Canton, all of whom the Commodore desired particularly to see, before sailing for Japan. No other course was left to him therefore, but to dispatch the Plymouth to the same port, with instructions to Commander Buchanan of the Susquehanna to await there the Commodore's arrival in the Mississippi, which he meant should follow the Susquehanna as soon as she could be prepared for the northern cruise; and fortunately Shanghai was at no great distance out of the route to Japan.

On the following day the customary interchange of salutes was made with the forts and the foreign vessels of war in port, and this was succeeded by an exchange of personal courtesies among the officers of the various nations represented. With Commodore Roquemausel, of the French navy, particularly, who had his pennant on board the frigate Capricieuse, the Commodore enjoyed a very agreeable intercourse, both official and personal. The English admiral, Sir F. Pellew, was absent. It is unnecessary to note, on every occasion, the courtesies that American officers invariably receive from the British authorities abroad, civil, naval, and military. "In no instance," remarks the Commodore, "during a long service in foreign countries, have I experienced any want of hospitable attention; and, in fact, the governments of all nations, with the exception of that of the United States, furnish the means for public entertainments by ample allowance of 'table money,' and it thus becomes a duty, as it is doubtless the pleasure, of these officials to expend it hospitably."

The stay of the Mississippi was but short at Hong Kong; long enough, however, to make apparent every sign of commercial prosperity, although the place is not very attractive to visitors. There is no picturesque beauty in the appearance of the town, albeit some travellers have described it in glowing colors. It is a picture of busy activity; the shore is lined with Chinese boats, the harbor is crowded with the shipping of all nations, and the toiling Chinese are kept at work in the roads, or in other labors required by this progressive place. When the English took possession of the island of Hong Kong, in 1841, there was but a bleak and barren hill-side where there now stands the city of Victoria. The population of the place now amounts to no less than 14,671, and while its commercial warehouses, its docks and piers, and its fleet of traders, give evidence of its material prosperity, its social, intellectual, and

Barber Boy, Hong Kong.

religious progress are proved by its club-houses, reading-rooms, schools, and churches. Heathenism has also its visible signs. The Chinese have three temples, and the Mahommedans a mosque at Hong Kong.

The island rises at the north in a range of mountains, the base of which terminates near the sea, leaving a narrow edge, along which the town of Victoria extends for two or three miles.

There is a large trade in opium between India and Hong Kong, it being imported into the latter place, and thence smuggled into China along the coast.

There is no very extensive agricultural culture at Hong Kong, as the land for the most part is rocky, and of little fertility. On the southern part of the island, however, the soil is somewhat more favorable than that on the northern, and it contains a single valley which is tolerably productive. There is an abundance of excellent water. The climate is hot, and as the alternations of rain and heat keep up an active decomposition in the marshy districts of the island, they render it quite unwholesome. The southern side of Hong Kong is the more healthful, as it is refreshed and purified by the southwestern monsoon, but being destitute of good harbors, the English were obliged to fix their settlement on the north.

The laboring class and the small traders are chiefly Chinese, who are ever on the alert for gain. Their bazaars invite the passing stranger on every street, and the itinerant artizans go busily tramping in their daily routine. There are many striking figures among them, with their peculiar costumes and novel implements of labor. Our artist caught a vivid impression of the Hong Kong barber boy.

On leaving Hong Kong the Mississippi went to Macao, and thence to Whampoa, on the Canton river, where she anchored. In this river there are certain bars, and it is necessary not only to take a pilot, but to employ small Chinese boats, which are stationed at the sides of the crooked channel, and on the bars alluded to, as guides. As the boats receive a dollar each for this service, they are called "dollar boats." Whampoa, which is the anchorage for all large vessels whose business is with Canton, is on the river, about twelve miles from that city. The pagoda here is a marked object, and however it may be venerated by the Chinese, on religious grounds, is no less regarded for its usefulness as a land mark by foreign vessels, for they steer and anchor by its bearings.

The passage to Canton is made in boats, and is by no means very agreeable. The Commodore was sadly disappointed in the appearance of the stream, which he describes as muddy and shallow, with scarcely a hut upon its banks until the city is nearly reached; and then swarms of floating habitations are seen moored to the banks, five or six tiers deep, and occupied by a wretched half clad people. Through these two lines of receptacles of poverty and filth which thus border the stream you pass to the mercantile factory, the residence of most of the foreign merchants, and the spot where the stranger lands. Hence he is conducted to the houses of those to whom he bears letters of introduction, where he is hospitably received and takes up his lodging, as there are no comfortable places of public entertainment in this quarter.

The first impression made by Canton was one of decided disappointment. Perhaps too much had been anticipated, but, from the glowing descriptions the Commodore had read of the place, he had imagined that it would be more striking to a stranger than in his case it proved to be. He expected to behold myriads of boats, decked with gay banners, and moving with cheerful activity in all directions. His fancy had sketched a pleasing picture of beautiful floating domiciles, moored under the banks of the river, and inhabited by a hundred thousand people in variegated costume; he recalled to memory the stories of the lofty pagodas lifting roof above roof, the delightful residences expanding their spacious quarters from terrace to terrace, and the snug cottages with the picturesque bridges and the comfortable Chinaman under the shade of a willow, with nothing to do but fish, of all which we have been accustomed to read, and pictures of which served to amuse us in our childhood.

But the sketches of imaginative boyhood were, in this as in so many other instances, dispelled by the sober realities of maturer years. There was nothing of all this beautiful picture of crowded and happy life. There were, indeed, boats and people, pagodas and cottages, bridges and trees; but there were also filth and noise, poverty and misery, lying and roguery, and, in short, anything but a picture of quiet content and Arcadian simplicity.

On the visit of the Commodore to Canton, he, together with several of his officers, was accommodated at the house of Mr. Forbes, the consul of the United States and head of the firm of Russell & Co. Mr. Forbes was absent at the time, but the hospitalities of his establishment were most freely dispensed by one of his partners, Mr. Spooner. So well known was this establishment, and so highly appreciated were its proprietors by the Chinese, that all that was necessary in making a purchase in the city was simply to direct the shopkeeper to send the article to the house of Mr. Forbes, and there never was any hesitation in assenting at once. The same may be said indeed of all the American houses, with respect both to hospitality and the confidence of the Chinese.

The comparatively small space occupied by the foreigners on the river side is, notwithstanding its limited extent, quite a pleasant spot. The whole quarter contains but about four acres. The foreign merchants occupy the large buildings in the rear as places of business and abode, while the front, which includes a half of the whole area, is beautifully laid out as a garden, with an English church in the centre, and the flags of different nations floating from tall poles planted in various spots. The grounds are arranged with walks and ornamented with shrubbery and flowering plants, presenting a delightful resort in the freshness of the morning or the cool of the evening. The stranger is struck with the peculiar aspect of the place, when on one side, in proximity to low, dingy, Chinese houses, buildings of European structure rise to the height of three or four stories, while on the other, the river is densely populous with the inhabited boats. The foreigners term their residences and places of business factories, but the natives designate them as *Hongs,* which is the usual Chinese word for a commercial establishment or warehouse.

Although there are but few of the larger or public buildings in the foreign quarter, which is but a suburb of the city, there are all the ordinary varieties of streets, houses, and bazaars. Foreigners generally confine their visits to that part adjacent to the garden before mentioned, through which Old and New China streets run.

The only hotel in the place frequented by Europeans and Americans is near the latter street, and is quite inferior. It is (as has been intimated) the hospitable practice of the foreign merchants to invite strangers to their princely establishments, where a generous profusion and a warm welcome are extended to the visitor. In addition to Old and New China streets, there is, hard by, a narrow, filthy alley, not inappropriately called Hog lane, and filled with the most abandoned portion of the people, who minister to the vicious appetites of the foreign sailors, supplying them with wretched grog and other dangerous stimulants.

There are no drives or walks leading directly into the country from the foreign quarter; the residents are, therefore, limited to the river, where, in the evening, they exercise themselves in rowing their swift little boats. On the opposite side of the river, however, on the island of Honan, there is a walk extending a mile or more to a Buddhist temple; but there is little that is attractive in the surrounding country, and nothing peculiar about the temple, which is similar to the other joss houses. On a visit which was made to this spot by one of the officers of the expedition, a drove of sacred pigs were seen in their sacred styes, and they seemed to flourish exceedingly, for they were so fat that they could not stand. It was something of a curiosity (though somewhat saddening in the reflections it occasioned) to behold this sanctified pork, and the reverence with which it was worshipped.

Canton is the capital of the province of Kuan-tong, from which the name given to the city by Europeans has been corrupted. It is falsely applied, for it is the name of the province only, as we have just said; that of the city is Kuang-chow-foo. The city is built on two rivers, the Choo-Keang, or Pearl, and the Pi-Keang, which is a branch of the former. The mouth of the Choo-Keang,

View of Old China Street, Canton.

Pearl, or Canton river, is called the Bocca Tigris. It derives this name from the supposed resemblance of the hill tops, on Great Tiger Island, to the outline of a tiger's head. Although the resemblance is not at first very striking, it becomes quite obvious after examination. The river is guarded at its mouth, and at several points on its banks, by Chinese forts, which, with their white-washed walls and general pacific aspect, do not appear very formidable. The view, however, is pleasing, particularly at the Bocca Tigris, where the forts could be seen stretching their long white walls from the base to the summits of the hills. On one side is seen the "Dragon's Cave," and on the other the "Girl's Shoe," and various other fortifications with fanciful names; and though some of them are admirably situated, they are all of a structure which prove them to be more remarkable for show than for solid utility.

The river swarms with pirates, the fishermen occasionally becoming their allies, and they carry on their depredations unchecked in the very teeth of the forts. When the pirates fail of falling in with strangers whom they dare venture to rob, they fall out with each other, and murder and plunder their friends with as little compunction as if they were strangers. In the passage of the Mississippi from Macao to Whampoa, the anchorage on the Canton river, one of the two Chinese boats in tow was swamped by bad steering, whereupon the other, in fear of a similar catastrophe, cast off and attempted to proceed up the river. The owner, who happened to be on board the steamer, expressed his fears that she would be overhauled by pirates before her arrival at Whampoa; nor were his fears groundless; she was boarded and robbed a few hours only after she had lost sight of the Mississippi. While the steamer was at Hong Kong several piracies were committed almost under the guns of the vessels-of-war. As for the land pirates, they are to the full as expert at picking and stealing as the most accomplished thieves and pickpockets of New York or London. One of the lieutenants of the Mississippi, at early twilight one evening, just as he was stepping into a hired boat to return to the ship, was seized amid a crowd of people, and an attempt was made to pull his watch from his fob; fortunately his Pickwickian rotundity of form saved the watch, but the chain was carried off in triumph.

From the mouth of the river to Canton the distance is about thirty-two miles, but the large vessels do not proceed further than the anchorage at Whampoa, ten miles below the foreign quarter of the city, with which communication is kept up by boats. The country adjacent to Canton is intersected with rivers and creeks, in which fish abound, and a plentiful market is daily open in the city.

The alluvial ground south of the city is highly cultivated with rice fields and gardens. The higher ground to the north and east is wooded with firs and other trees. A wall encloses a portion of the city, which is subdivided by another wall running from east to west. North of the latter is that part called the inner or old city, which is inhabited chiefly by the dominant Tartar families, while to the south we find the new or outer city, where the inhabitants are mostly composed of the descendants of the original Chinese population. The streets are narrow, tortuous, and winding, like a corkscrew, but thronged by an immense population, and so very contracted that there is often barely room for two sedan chairs, the only vehicles allowed, to pass each other.

The great importance of Canton results from its being the emporium of the great trade of Europe and America with China; the annual amount of which was, some years ago, estimated at eighty millions of dollars, the principal part of which is under the control of the merchants of England and the United States.

Custom-house, Mouth of Canton River.

HIGH MARKET DAY

CHAPTER VI.

HOSPITABLE TREATMENT AT MACAO.—USAGES OF THE FOREIGN MERCHANTS TOWARD VISITORS.—DEPRESSED CONDITION OF MACAO.—DESCRIPTION OF THE PLACE.—TANKA BOATS, AND GIRLS WHO MANAGE THEM.—CAVE OF CAMOENS.—DEPARTURE OF MISSISSIPPI FROM MACAO.—SARATOGA LEFT TO BRING MR. WILLIAMS, THE INTERPRETER.—DIFFICULTIES OF NAVIGATION FROM HONG KONG TO THE MOUTH OF YANG-TSE-KEANG.—ENTRANCE OF THE RIVER DANGEROUS.—SUSQUEHANNA, PLYMOUTH, AND SUPPLY ALL AGROUND.—MISSISSIPPI SAVED BY THE POWER OF HER ENGINES ONLY.—DESCRIPTION OF SHANGHAI.—ITS IMMENSE TRADE.—CULTIVATION OF THE COUNTRY.—POPULATION OF THE CITY.—VISIT OF THE COMMODORE TO THE GOVERNOR OF THE CITY.—CHINESE REBELLION.—ITS EFFECTS.—PLYMOUTH LEFT AT SHANGHAI TO PROTECT AMERICAN INTERESTS.—DEPARTURE FOR GREAT LEW CHEW.—ARRIVAL OF THE SQUADRON AT THE CAPITAL, NAPHA, THE SARATOGA HAVING JOINED AT THE ENTRANCE TO THE HARBOR.

N leaving Canton, Mr. Spooner, of the house of Russell & Co., offered the Commodore the use of the magnificent residence at Macao belonging to that firm; accordingly he, together with three of his officers, took up his quarters in their sumptuous dwelling. The Commodore and his company, thinking that they were to be their own providers, their caterer, one of the officers of the squadron, was very particular in ordering the head servant in charge of the establishment to procure this and that, and no sooner was a wish expressed than it was promptly attended to. Great, then, was the surprise, on the completion of the visit, to find that not a penny would be received beyond the ordinary gratuity by that prince of major-domos. He said that his employers were always happy to have their house occupied by their friends, and he expressed a hope that the Commodore and his companions would not think of going elsewhere on their next visit to Macao.

When a guest is once received into one of these hospitable mansions he finds himself quite at home, in the enjoyment of the most agreeable society; for it is a custom of the merchants of the East to extend to strangers of respectability a hospitality that is quite unreserved. Such, indeed, is the freedom of the guest that he has only to order whatever he may require and his demand is complied with at once. The master does not trouble himself about the matter, but he is, for the most part of the time, away about his business; and the whole concern of the household devolves upon the major-domo, whose duty it is to satisfy every want. There is a very convenient official of these establishments, termed a comprador, whose vocation it is to pay all the bills accruing from the purchases and incidental expenses of the guests, who, however, of course, refund what has been paid.

While enjoying the luxury of these oriental establishments, one, in fact, might fancy himself in a well-organized French hotel, as he has only to express a wish to have it gratified, were it not that he has nothing to pay in the former beyond the usual gratuities to servants, while in the latter he is mulcted roundly for every convenience.

There is not much at present to interest the visitor at Macao, as it is but a ghost of its former self. There is almost a complete absence of trade or commerce. The harbor is deserted, and the sumptuous dwellings and storehouses of the old merchants are comparatively empty, while the Portuguese who inhabit the place are but rarely seen, and seem listless and unoccupied. An occasional Parsee, in high crowned cap and snowy robe, a venerable merchant, and here and there a Jesuit priest, with his flock of youthful disciples, may be seen, but they are only as the decaying monuments of the past.

At one time, however, the town of Macao was one of the most flourishing marts of the East. When the Portuguese obtained possession, in the latter part of the sixteenth century, they soon established it as the centre of a wide commerce with China and other oriental countries. Its origin is attributed to a few Portuguese merchants belonging to Lampaçao, who were allowed to resort there and establish some temporary huts for shelter and the drying of damaged goods. Huc, the Chinese traveller, gives a different account; he states that the Portuguese were allowed to settle by the Emperor, in return for the signal service of capturing a famous pirate who had long ravaged the coasts. From an humble beginning, the settlement gradually arose to an imposing position as a commercial place, for which it was greatly indebted to the monopoly it enjoyed of eastern commerce. It has, however, declined, and is now a place of very inconsiderable importance and trade. The town is situated upon a peninsula at the southward of the island of Macao.

It is sufficiently picturesque in appearance, built as it is upon the acclivities of the rising ground about the harbor, with its gay looking white houses, which overhang the terraces that bound the shore and look out upon the sea. The houses of the old merchants, though they now bear some appearance of neglect, yet attest, by the spaciousness of the apartments, and the luxuriousness of their appointments, the former opulence of the Portuguese traders. The pleasant walks about the circuit of the neighboring hills and the Praya invite the visitor to strengthen himself in cheerful exercise. The dull look of the place is somewhat relieved in the summer time, when the foreign residents of Canton and Hong Kong resort there to bathe in the waters of Bishop's Bay, and to recreate in the enjoyment of the healthful sea air of the place.

The harbor is not suitable for large vessels, which anchor in Macao roads, several miles from the town. It is, however, though destitute of every appearance of commercial activity, always enlivened by the fleet of Tanka boats which pass, conveying passengers to and fro, between the land and the Canton and Hong Kong steamers. The Chinese damsels, in gay costume, as they scull their light craft upon the smooth and gently swelling surface of the bay, present a lively aspect, and as they are looked upon in the distance, from the verandahs above the Praya, which command a view of the bay, have a fairy-like appearance, which a nearer approach serves, however, to change into a more substantial and coarse reality.

Tanka Boat, Macao.

The Cave of Camoens, where the Portuguese poet is supposed to have written a portion of his Lusiad, is a place of universal interest and resort at Macao. It is picturesquely situated upon the summit of a small hill, on the margin of the inner harbor. Large granite rocks are here gathered in a confused cluster, which form a natural cave, from the entrance of which

Camoens' Cave, Macao.

there is a wide prospect of the surrounding country. The banians, the pagoda, and other oriental trees unite their foliage and form a grove in which the rocky cave is embowered. Surrounding it are grounds cultivated with trees, creeping vines, and flowering shrubs, charmingly arranged by the borders of winding paths, and upon the sides of the hills. Artificial terraces, ingeniously disposed, invite the visitor to the enjoyment of the view or to rest beneath the shade.

Above the cave rises a rotunda, from which there is an enchanting prospect, and a marble monument, with a bronze bust and an inscription, here record the features, the genius, and virtue of Camoens, the poet.

Camoens' visit to Macao was during his banishment from Portugal, in consequence of his pertinacious courtship of a lady of rank, whose parents did not affect an alliance with the poet, who, although of a respectable family, was poor, and looked upon as an uncertain adventurer. In 1551, he proceeded to Goa, in India, where he again involved himself in trouble by writing

Camoens' Cave, Macao—Rear View.

his "Absurdities of India," and was banished to the Moluccas, and in the course of his exile he resorted frequently to Macao, which was a favorite residence of the poet. The cave was his chosen spot of retirement, where, in its "sweet retired solitude," he meditated his great work, the Lusiad. Camoens returned to Portugal, but only to live in misery and die in an hospital.

The interior of the island of Macao, which is exclusively cultivated by the Chinese, yields a variety of vegetable productions, with which the town is supplied. The whole population is about 20,000, and of these 13,000 belong to the peninsula and town, whereof more than one-half the inhabitants are Chinese, and in the interior of the island this race compose the whole. The government of the town is in the hands of the Portuguese. The Portuguese have a college, churches and various educational, benevolent, and ecclesiastical institutions in the town, where the Chinese also have their peculiar establishments and a temple.

On the evening of April 28th, the Mississippi was again under weigh, leaving the Saratoga at Macao to await the arrival of Dr. S. W. Williams, of Canton, who had been appointed interpreter to the expedition. The course was now directed for Shanghai.

The navigation of the coast of China, from Hong Kong to the mouth of the Yang-tse-Keang, is, at most seasons, difficult and perplexing. The frequent fogs and irregular tides and currents make it very annoying to those who are strangers to the navigation, when close in with the coast. Fortunately, however, vessels are always, when near the land, on anchoring ground, and although they are sometimes obliged to bring to, in situations exposed to winds from the sea, it is better to resort to the anchor than to drift blindly among groups of islands and reefs. If the weather be moderately clear, vessels may run from island to island, and thus navigate the coast with perfect safety and convenience, but the fogs which prevail at certain seasons scarcely allow of this advantage. During the passages of the Susquehanna and Mississippi from Hong Kong to Shanghai neither had a meridian observation of the sun.

The entrance to the Yang-tse-Keang, which leads to the commercial city of Shanghai, is obstructed on either side by shoals, which make it dangerous for vessels not having pilots. On the north side is a shoal called the North Sand, extending some six leagues westward from the main land, and on the south side is a parallel shoal, called the South Sand, projecting nearly as far from the shore on that side. The outer extremities of these shoals are beyond sight of the main land. The channel between the two shoals may be estimated at about two miles in width, and there are no light-houses, boats, beacons, or buoys to indicate to strangers the entrance. A small islet called Gutzlaff island is the only indication, for the bearings of which, and other directions for entering the channel, the nautical reader is referred to the Appendix.

The rise and fall in the Yang-tse-Keang averages about ten feet, and vessels are obliged to find their way hap-hazard into the channel, or perchance run upon one of the sister sands. Numbers of vessels resorting to Shanghai are lost, and still nothing has been done to remedy the evil. The Commodore was convinced, on visiting this river with the Mississippi, that until proper landmarks and beacons are established to indicate the entrance, it must be an unfit resort for any but the smaller vessels of a squadron, and consequently, an unfit place for a naval depôt. The Susquehanna, the Plymouth, and the Supply, all grounded on going in, and the last remained thumping on the North Sand twenty-two hours, and was only saved from total loss by a providential change of wind. The Mississippi was carried, in the confusion of her pilot, out of the channel, but by good fortune did not stop, though she ran into nineteen feet water, one foot less than her draft, on the South Sand, but the power of the engines proved her salvation. The wealthy foreign merchants established at Shanghai, who are gathering a plentiful harvest from the increasing trade of the place, should contribute some of their thousands toward rendering the navigation less dangerous. It is but justice to say that a willingness has been expressed by some of these gentlemen to subscribe liberally toward the accomplishment of the desired object, and, in fact, a boat had been ordered to be built in the United States, for the purpose of towing vessels up and down the river.

Shanghai is built upon the left bank of the river Wampon, a branch of the Yang-tse-Kiang. Near the mouth of the Wampon is the village Woosung, the station where the foreign merchants

formerly established their receiving ships, and the trading vessels their anchorage. Nothing can be less picturesque than the scenery of the banks of the Wampon in the approach to Shanghai. Monotonous flats of alluvial grounds stretch their wide expanse on either side of the tortuous river. The fertile fields, rich with an abundant harvest of rice and grain, are encouraging prospects to the eye of the agriculturist, but the poetical observer is sadly disappointed in a view which presents a dead level of landscape, without a mountain, a hill-side, or even a tree to relieve the monotony.

In front of the city of Shanghai quays have been built out, and along them extend the storehouses and sumptuous residences of the foreign merchants, which have been constructed since the termination of the opium war with Great Britain. Here are to be found wide and well graded streets, beautiful gardens, and all the comforts and conveniences that are to be found in any part of the world. Two Gothic churches, one belonging to the English, and the other to the American Protestant Episcopal mission, show an encouraging success of missionary effort, and excite the hopes of the Christian, for the progress of his faith.

American Consulate, and Port of Shanghai.

The Commodore was a guest, while at Shanghai, of the American firm of Russell & Co., in whose splendid establishment, as at Macao, every want was satisfied. So complete are the conveniences of these residences, and so perfect every appointment, that the stranger finds himself surrounded with all the necessaries and luxuries of his own home. A trifling incident will illustrate the effectiveness with which the most insignificant demands of the guest are complied with. The Commodore was asked if he liked soda water, to which polite request he responded that the only mineral water he cared for was that from the Congress spring in Saratoga; the next morning the servant entered his room with a bottle of it. During the stay of the ships at Shanghai there was a constant succession of dinners and balls, and the officers were entertained everywhere with the most generous hospitality.

The native city is a great contrast to that part of the suburbs inhabited by the foreign residents, although the portion of the latter occupied by the natives is miserable enough. Shanghai, proper, is enclosed within a wall, and has the appearance of most of the Chinese cities. The place is quite large, and very populous. Its streets are narrow, like most of those of the native cities, not being much more than eight or ten feet in width, and are intersected by dirty alleys, which lead to the rear of the small and contracted dwellings of the Chinese, who live in the midst of foul air and all kinds of filth. The filthiness of Shanghai gives no favorable idea of the domestic habits of the people; a slight glance at the men and women usually met in the streets was quite convincing enough of their want of reverence for what the proverb says is "next to godliness." During the stay of the Commodore at Shanghai, the shops had been emptied of their contents and carried into places of safety, in expectation of an attack upon the city by the rebels, consequently, the bazaars had a dull look, and but few of the native fabrics could be seen.

The domestic trade of the city has been immense for a long time, being carried on in all directions with the vast interior of China. A multitudinous population swarms in that part of the country which stretches back of Shanghai, and the commercial intercourse with the large cities of Nankin and others, with their millions of inhabitants, and incessant trading activity, was constant, until interrupted by the Chinese rebellion. The trade of Shanghai has been stated to be as large as that of any part of the world, not excepting even London.

The immediate neighborhood of Shanghai is highly cultivated, and fertile fields stretch in all directions as far as the eye can reach, rich with their harvests of cotton, rice, wheat, barley, beans and potatoes. The markets of the town are well supplied, and at moderate prices, with beef, mutton, poultry, game, fish and vegetables of all varieties. Among the different kinds of game, the pheasant, woodcock, and snipe abound, and of the fish, the shad is common during its season, of good size and flavor; some, indeed, larger than are seen in the United States, though in taste inferior to those caught in our rivers. Fruit is scarce, and of inferior quality, as the Chinese pay but little attention to its cultivation; some cherries, however, were tasted, which proved to be tolerably good, and it was said that the peaches were also good. All the varieties of Chinese manufactured articles can ordinarily be obtained at Shanghai, and especially a silk of famous fabric, woven at Su-Chau, a neighboring city. But the intestine disturbances prevailing deprived the Commodore of any but a hearsay knowledge of many of these articles, which, however, are said to be obtained, in pacific times, more easily at Shanghai than at Canton.

The foreign commerce has greatly increased since the termination of the war with Great Britain, and the general belief is entertained that Shanghai, with its superior advantages, will monopolize most of the foreign trade with China.

The population of the place was estimated at two hundred and eighty thousand, and the Chinese who composed it seemed to be of a better class than those at Canton and Hong Kong. Like all their countrymen, they are indefatigable in labor and untiring in trading activity, for which they have, undoubtedly, a natural instinct.

The Commodore, while at Shanghai, made an interesting return visit to the Taou-tai or governor and commander of the city, who first called upon him at the American consulate, and afterward visited the ship. The Taou-tai has a lucrative, but by no means easy office. Among his other duties, he has to watch, especially, the interests and conduct of the foreign residents, and what with the caprices of strangers, the sometimes inordinate claims of their representatives, and the arbitrary requirements of his imperial master, he must have hard work to keep up a fair balance between his duties to his government on the one hand and the foreigners on the other. This high official has also to sustain the responsibility of a secure transport of the taxes of the province, and to fulfil the by no means sinecure duty of protecting the commerce of Shanghai against the pirates who swarm the coasts. His highness makes his official visits with a pomp and circumstance suitable to his dignified station. The ringing sounds of gongs herald his approach, and he comes seated grandly in his chair of state attended by his suite of subordinate mandarins. The office, in common with the general practice of China, is bestowed ordinarily upon him who has earned one of the topmost of the nine colored buttons, which, worn above the official cap, serve, by their vari-colored grades, to distinguish the mandarins. As literary eminence is the passport to office, the Taou-tai is ordinarily well up in Chinese literature, and can quote whole passages of Confucius or Mencius with the utmost volubility.

In the Commodore's visit to the Taou-tai he was accompanied by twenty of his officers and the American consul, who were all, with due regard to the importance of the occasion, dressed up in full uniform. The party, thus adorned, and duly seated in sedan chairs, were conveyed from the consular residence to the government house, situated in the centre of the city, within the walls. On arrival at the entrance, the Commodore and his suite were saluted with the usual salvo of three guns (the extent, with the Chinese, of honorable ammunition on such occasions) and the music of a band. The Taou-tai was at the threshold to meet his visitors, and as the Commodore alighted from his sedan chair his highness escorted him into the hall of audience, while the rest of the company followed in respectful sequence. The Commodore was placed, in accordance with Chinese ceremony, at the side of the Taou-tai, on a platform raised a little above the floor.

On entering and departing from the government house, the party passed through an open apartment, adorned with a bold representation of a gigantic Chinese deity on the wall, and furnished with large wooden chairs, stuffed with red cloth cushions, which were ranged along the sides. A table standing in the apartment, and holding the vessel containing the pieces of bamboo which are thrown by the hand of the Chinese judge to the executioner, to indicate the number of strokes to be applied to the convicted criminal, showed the ordinary purposes of the chamber, which was that of a hall of justice.

Refreshments, consisting of teas, liquors, (including champagne,) cake, and so forth, were handed round to the visitors in succession; and, after a stay of an hour, the commodore and his party returned in the same manner as they came. Entering again their sedan chairs, and traversing the narrow streets of Shanghai in long procession, and jostling every one who obstructed the way, they finally reached the American consulate.

While Commodore Perry was at Shanghai, the revolution, which is still in progress, had made great headway. Although new developments have taken place since, which have altered very much the position of affairs, it may not be amiss to give the results of the Commodore's observations of a civil commotion, which naturally excited his deepest interest. He writes on the spot, at the date of May, 1853: "The political condition of China at the present time is very unsettled; the whole empire seems to be in a state of agitation arguing some mighty revolution: one-half of the country is in occupation of an insurgent force, which claims to represent the old Chinese, who were dispossessed a long time since by the present ruling dynasty. At the head of the rebel force is a very sagacious man, who, from disappointment, or some imaginary wrong, growing out of his examination for literary honors, (so highly prized by the Chinese,) became disgusted, and at once showed his disaffection, and finally raised the flag of open rebellion. At first he had only a few followers, but in the course of time multitudes flocked to his standard; and now, after over-running a great many provinces, he is quietly in possession of the great city of Nanking.

"This man denounces the prevailing religion, and has caused to be destroyed numerous Buddhist temples. He professes a faith somewhat similar to that of the Mormons in America, and gives forth that he has constant communion with God, and has been acknowledged as his Son. His ignorant and lawless followers profess to believe in his pretended revelations, and with them he has acquired great power by his religious devices. He pretends to fraternize with Christians, and argues that all Christian nations, by reason of similar faith, should aid him in driving out of the empire the present usurping family, and putting upon the celestial throne a true son of heaven, a believer of the decalogue, and a scion of the old Chinese monarchs. He does not pretend to any claims himself to the imperial diadem; but it may be well imagined, from his professed dogmas of religion, that when the time comes he will turn out to be the proposed great Celestial on Earth."

In the state of agitation produced by these civil disturbances it was natural that the foreign merchants who had large interests at stake should be anxious about the security of their property; accordingly, the American commercial houses established at Shanghai addressed a letter to the Hon. Humphrey Marshall, minister of the United States to China, in which they stated that the amount of their property, at a fair valuation, then at risk in the port of Shanghai, was $1,200,000, and that they considered it fairly entitled to protection, which the rumored withdrawal of the naval force would seem to deprive them of. Commodore Perry, regarding the interests of American citizens in China, and at the same time not forgetting the great purpose of his expedition, resolved to leave the Plymouth to protect his countrymen and their property, but not otherwise to interfere with his own mission or the affairs of China. The request of the American commissioner to have a vessel of war to convey him to the mouth of the Peiho, in order to secure a recognition on the part of the Chinese government of his official presence, was not complied with by the Commodore, who declined not only on the score of policy, but from the necessity of concentrating all the naval force he could on the expedition to Japan.

The Mississippi had arrived at Shanghai on the 4th of May, and the interval between that date and the 17th of the same month, was chiefly employed in transferring the Commodore to the Susquehanna, which then became his flag-ship, and in taking in the usual supplies of coal and provisions for the voyage. No less than *five tons* of Chinese "cash,"* to be dispensed in the Lew-Chew islands, was rather an unusual addition to the ship's stores.

On Monday morning, May 16, 1853, the Mississippi moved down the river and was followed the next day by the Commodore in the Susquehanna, while the Plymouth was left behind, for

---

* The "cash" is but a small sum, about the twelve-hundreth part of a dollar

a short time, to await the course of events in the rebel camp, her commander having orders to follow as soon as he could do so consistently with the safety of American interests at Shanghai.

The day of departure was unusually clear, and the cultivated banks of the river, with their orchards and fields of grain, never appeared more beautifully green. With the fine day, which gave a bright, cheerful aspect to every object, the inspiriting music of the band, which struck up a succession of lively airs, the crowds of spectators on the shore, and the natural enthusiasm of all on the prospect of carrying out the enterprise which was the great object of the expedition, the departure from Shanghai was in a high degree animating.

The Mississippi had preceded, as we have seen, the Susquehanna, to which the Commodore had now transferred his flag, and joined the Supply, which, after having grounded on the North Sand, succeeded fortunately in getting off without damage. The squadron, which now prepared to sail for Lew Chew, was composed of the Susquehanna, the Mississippi, the Supply, and the Caprice, which was discovered standing in, as the other ships were standing out, and was ordered to follow. The Plymouth was, as has just been stated, left at Shanghai, as a guard of American property and interests, and the Saratoga remained at Macao, to await the arrival of Dr. Williams, the interpreter. These vessels were expected to follow, and join the rendezvous at Lew Chew.

The Susquehanna, on reaching the mouth of the Yang-tse-Kiang, came to anchor and remained there for three days. The Mississippi and Supply took up their positions on either side. The junk belonging to Russell & Co., the American merchants, which had been hired to carry a cargo of coal to the mouth of the river to be put on board the Mississippi, was, while under the charge of its own commander and officers, lost on the North Sand. From the anchorage of the Mississippi, Gutzlaff's island could be seen some six miles distant, and beyond it stretched the long uneven outline of Ruggles' islands. The weather was alternately clear and rainy, and when the sun did not shine the scene was particularly gloomy and oppressive to the spirits. The muddy waters of the Yang-tse-Kiang, looking more muddy still in the yellow light of a foggy atmosphere, and the dull constraint of a tedious anchorage, presented a sad prospect to the eye, and a wearisome sensation to the feelings, which made all anxious for departure.

The naturalists had an opportunity of gratifying their tastes in observing a flock of small birds from the land, which hovered in and about the ship. Mr. Heine, the artist, succeeded in obtaining several specimens, which had somewhat the appearance of the starling. He also caught a graceful dove, of a light brownish color. A beautiful king-fisher was brought on board, which had been caught by some of the sailors of the Mississippi. Its plumage was exceedingly rich and charmingly variegated; its long bill was of a bright red; its wings were black; its body was of a rich blue color, and its flossy neck was of a whitish cream tint.

The Susquehanna got under way at one o'clock on the 23d of May, followed by the Mississippi with the Supply in tow, all bound for Napha, the principal port of the Great Lew Chew island. In the course of the evening, about six o'clock, the low range of islands known as the Saddles, and inhabited by a sparse population of fishermen, was passed, the ships directing their course to the north of them, where there is an open channel free from shoals. The night was clear, with a full moon, and the weather was mild and agreeable. The Susquehanna moved on at a moderate rate, keeping about a mile in advance of the Mississippi, while the Caprice, gently fanned by the southwestern monsoon, managed to keep also in sight, though further in the distance, until she was lost in the darkness of the night.

It was found that the Mississippi, with the aid of topsails, although she had the Supply in tow, rapidly gained upon the Susquehanna; accordingly a foretopsail was set upon the latter, the good effect of which was soon shown, by her leaving her competitor so far astern that it was necessary to wait until the Mississippi could come up again. The Susquehanna's engines were only worked at half speed with the consumption, to which she was restricted, of one ton of coal per hour, but notwithstanding, with the aid of the regular breeze of the monsoon, she succeeded in making seven and a half knots an hour. As the course was southerly, the weather became every moment warmer, and the sea was as smooth as a lake. During the passage the crew were regularly called to quarters and exercised in all the usual manœuvres necessary for preparation for action, and on the morning of the 25th of May, after quarters, general orders 11 and 12 were read; the former related to the discipline to be observed on board ship during the visit to the Lew Chew Islands, and the latter enjoined the necessity of keeping up the most friendly relations with the Japanese inhabitants wherever found, and also stated that the expedition was ordered to use all possible friendly means, and not to resort to force but from the sternest necessity. In the evening the signal of land in sight was made by the Mississippi, and subsequently was reported by the man at the fore-topmast head of the Susquehanna. During the night the steamers were kept at slow speed, standing off and on; the Supply had been previously cast off from the Mississippi, and left to make her own way under sail. At half-past seven o'clock in the morning of May 26th the land was again made at a distance of nearly twenty miles, and as the steamers moved on, it was distinctly descried as a long island elevated gradually from the sea to a cliff at its northern extremity, and with a steep headland at the south. Beyond the island, which was passed, and its green foliage distinctly seen, was other land to which the Susquehanna was now headed, followed closely by the Mississippi, while the Supply was quite out of sight. Napha was reached in the evening, and entered in company with the Saratoga, from Macao, which ship the steamers had fallen in with off the harbor. It is due to Lieutenant Bent, an officer on board the Mississippi, to acknowledge that the Commodore availed himself of that gentleman's former experiences in a visit in the Preble to pilot the ships as they entered Napha.

GREAT LEW CHEW
and its dependencies

CHAPTER VII.

NUMBER AND POSITION OF ISLANDS OF LEW CHEW.—THEIR SUPPOSED POLITICAL RELATIONS TO JAPAN AND CHINA.—DESCRIPTION OF THE ISLAND OF GREAT LEW CHEW, AS SEEN ON THE FIRST APPROACH TO IT.—VISIT OF OFFICIALS TO THE SUSQUEHANNA.—VISIT OF DR. BETTELHEIM.—REFUSAL OF PRESENTS, AND CONSEQUENT MORTIFICATION OF THE LEW CHEWANS.—EXPLORATION OF THE ISLAND RESOLVED ON BY THE COMMODORE.—DAGUERREOTYPING ON SHORE.—CORAL INSECT AND ITS FORMATIONS.—SECOND VISIT OF THE AUTHORITIES OF LEW CHEW.—REGENT OF THE ISLAND RECEIVED BY THE COMMODORE.—FRIENDLY NATURE OF THE INTERVIEW.—SURPRISE OF THE LEW CHEWANS AT SIGHT OF THE STEAM ENGINE.—COMMODORE ANNOUNCES TO THEM HIS INTENTION OF RETURNING THE VISIT AT THE PALACE OF SHUI.—THEIR EVIDENT EMBARRASSMENT THEREAT.—LEAVE TO GO ON SHORE.—DESCRIPTION OF NAPHA AND ITS VICINITY, BY ONE OF THE OFFICERS.—EXPLORING PARTY SETS OUT, PLACED UNDER THE COMMAND OF THE CHAPLAIN, MR. JONES.—MR. BAYARD TAYLOR ATTACHED TO IT, WITH ORDERS TO TAKE NOTES AND FURNISH A DETAILED REPORT OF THE JOURNEY.—NEGOTIATIONS WITH THE LEW CHEW AUTHORITIES TO OBTAIN A HOUSE ON SHORE.—THEIR MANIFEST OPPOSITION.—COMMODORE PERSISTS AND SUCCEEDS.—OFFICERS, WHEN ON SHORE, CONTINUALLY WATCHED BY SPIES.—CAPTAIN BASIL HALL'S ACCOUNT OF THE LEW CHEWANS SOMEWHAT EXAGGERATED.—IMPRESSIONS MADE ON THE OFFICERS AS TO THE CHARACTER OF THE NATIVES.—HYDROGRAPHIC SURVEYS.—BOAT EXERCISE OF THE CREWS, AND DRILLING ON LAND OF THE MARINES.

ON Thursday, the 26th of May, the squadron found itself quietly anchored in the harbor of Napha, the principal port of the Great Lew Chew island, and the first point where the expedition touched on Japanese territory, if Lew Chew (or, as the natives call it, Doo Choo) be indeed a dependency of Japan. The group of islands known as the Lieou Kieou, or Lew Chew, is said to be in number thirty-six, at considerable distances from each other, and lying between the islands of Kioosioo and Formosa; they are between 24° 10' and 28° 40' north latitude and 127° and 129° east longitude from Greenwich.

It is a question yet discussed to what power Lew Chew belongs. By some it is said to be a dependency of the Prince of Satzuma, of Japan: others suppose it to belong to China. The probabilities, however, are all on the side of the dependence, more or less absolute, of Lew Chew on Japan, and probably, also, of some qualified subordination to China, as they undoubtedly send tribute to that country. Language, customs, laws, dress, virtues, vices, and commercial intercourse, all are corroborative of such an opinion. But of this more will be said hereafter.

The Great Lew Chew was seen from the ships, as they approached, at the distance of more than twenty miles, and, when near enough to render objects distinguishable, presented a very inviting appearance. It is thus graphically described by the pen of one of the officers of the expedition: *

"The shores of the island were green and beautiful from the water, diversified with groves and fields of the freshest verdure. The rain had brightened the colors of the landscape, which recalled to my mind the richest English scenery. The swelling hills, which rose immediately from the water's edge, increased in height towards the centre of the island, and were picturesquely broken by abrupt rocks and crags, which, rising here and there, gave evidence of volcanic action. Woods, apparently of cedar or pine, ran along the crests of the hills, while their slopes were covered with gardens and fields of grain. To the northward, the hills were higher, and the coast jutted out in two projecting headlands, showing that there were deep bays or indentations between." "By three o'clock we were so near that the town of Napha was distinctly visible, at the bottom of the bay. The cape, called Abbey Point, projected in front of it, covered with foliage, and the extremity crowned with an isolated group of crags, whose mossy turrets and buttresses evidently suggested the name of the point. The hills were dotted in various places with white specks, which I at first took to be dwellings, but which were tombs of limestone rock."†

As the ships entered, the British ensign was seen suddenly to rise on a flag-staff, placed near a house, which was perched on a curious overhanging point of rock, north of the town; this house was the residence of the missionary, Mr. Bettelheim, a convert from Judaism, who married in England, and had, for some five or six years, been resident on the island, under the auspices of an association of pious English gentlemen, officers of the British navy, very much, however, against the inclinations of the Lew Chewans. On passing Abbey Point, the mouth of the inner harbor became visible, and within it was a number of large Japanese junks, riding at

---

* The well known traveller, Bayard Taylor, who joined the Susquehanna in China. The circumstances under which this gentleman joined the expedition are thus detailed by the Commodore:

"On my arrival at Shanghai I found there Mr. Bayard Taylor, who had a letter of introduction to me from an esteemed friend in New York. He had been a long time, as I understood, exceedingly anxious to join the squadron, that he might visit Japan, which he could reach in no other way.

"On presenting the letter referred to, he at once made a request to accompany me, but to this application I strongly objected, intimating to him the determination I had made at the commencement of the cruise to admit no civilians, and explaining how the few who were in the squadron had, by signing the shipping articles, subjected themselves to all the restraints and penalties of naval law; that there were no suitable accommodations for him, and that, should he join the expedition, he would be obliged to suffer, with the other civilians, many discomforts and privations, and would moreover be restricted, under a general order of the Navy Department, from communicating any information to the public prints, or privately to his friends; that all the notes or general observations made by him during the cruise would belong to the government, and therefore must be deposited with me. Notwithstanding this, however, with a full knowledge of all the difficulties and inconveniences which would attend his joining the squadron, he still urged his application.

"Being thus importuned, and withal very favorably impressed with his gentlemanlike and unassuming manners, I at last reluctantly consented, and he joined the mess of Messrs. Heine and Brown, on board the Susquehanna. During the short time he remained in the squadron he gained the respect and esteem of all, and, by his habits of observation, aided by his ready pen, became quite useful in preparing notes descriptive of various incidents that transpired during our first brief visit to Japan and the islands. It was the only service he could render, and it was afforded cheerfully. These notes have been used in the preparation of my report, and due credit has, I trust, been given to him.

"Some of the incidents illustrative of the events mentioned in my official communications were, *with my consent*, written out by Mr. Taylor, and sent home by him for publication in the United States. These he has used in his late work. His original journals were honorably deposited in my hands. His *reports*, like those of every other individual detailed for the performance of a special duty, were, of course, delivered to me, and became part of the official records of the expedition."

† Extracted from the manuscript journal of Mr. Taylor, which, with those of other officers, pursuant to the orders of the Hon. Secretary, was placed in the hands of the Commodore.

anchor. Two persons were seen watching the movements of the squadron from the foot of the flagstaff; and, through a telescope, numbers could be seen leaving the town under white umbrellas.

The ships had not been at anchor two hours, before, notwithstanding the rain, a boat came off with two officials. On reaching the deck, they made many profound salutations, and presented a folded red card of Japanese paper, about a yard long. The principal personage wore a loose salmon-colored robe of very fine grass cloth, while the dress of the other was of similar fashion, but of a blue color. On their heads were oblong caps of bright yellow; they had blue sashes tied around their waists, and white sandals upon their feet. Their beards were long and black, though thin, and their ages were, seemingly, some thirty-five or forty years. They had the Japanese cast of countenance, and in complexion were a dusky olive. Who they were, or what the purpose of their visit, was not immediately known, as there happened to be no interpreter, at the time of their visit, on board the Susquehanna, to which ship they came; but one of the Commodore's Chinese servants was summoned, who understood the characters on their card sufficiently to explain that the visit was merely a *chin-chin*, or complimentary salutation on arrival. The Commodore, however, acting on his previously determined plan, declined seeing them, or receiving any other than one of the principal dignitaries of the island; and they accordingly returned to the shore. They had, no doubt, been sent to make observations, and, without committal, to ascertain what they could of the strangers, that the policy and treatment of the authorities of the island might be shaped according to circumstances.

Scarcely had they gone before Dr. Bettelheim came on board in a native boat; and such were the relations in which he stood to the islanders that he hailed the arrival of the squadron with delight, and manifested no little excitement of manner. He was conducted to the Commodore's cabin, where he remained for two or three hours; and in the course of the interview it appeared that he had never heard even of the intended American expedition; that a year and a half had elapsed since any foreign vessel had been at Napha, and that he was almost beside himself with joy. Grog and biscuit were given to his boatmen, and in their exhilaration, when they started for the shore, they contrived to carry the missionary some three miles up the coast.

The next day, the 27th, the shores looked, if possible, more brilliantly green and beautiful than ever, and all on board were struck with the loveliness of their appearance. About seven o'clock, four boats came off, bringing presents for the ship; in one of these were the two visitors of the day before, who brought another card, seemingly a list of the presents. He of the salmon-colored robe had given his name, on his first visit, as *Whang-cha-ching*; probably the Lew Chew pronunciation of *Whang-ta-zhin*, or "his excellency, *Whang*." The presents brought consisted of a bullock, several pigs, a white goat, some fowls, vegetables, and eggs. These were peremptorily refused, nor were those who brought them permitted to come on board. After waiting a short time, they returned to the town, with an evident expression of anxiety and uneasiness on their countenances. At this time it was observed in the squadron that several of the junks put out from the inner harbor and sailed to the northward, as it was conjectured, for Japan. Some of them passed quite near to the ships, to gratify their curiosity by a closer inspection of such large vessels. The junks were somewhat like those of the Chinese, and, like them, had two great eyes inserted in the bows, as if to see the way. Undoubtedly, the presence of the squadron had created great alarm among the junks; for no force, half as large, had ever been seen at Napha before, and probably some of the junks had been dispatched to Japan with the news of the squadron's appearance at Lew Chew.

A boat was sent off for Dr. Bettelheim, and he, with the Rev. Mr. Jones, chaplain of the Mississippi, and Mr. Wells Williams, the interpreter, breakfasted with the Commodore. An exploration of the island was resolved on by the chief. It was to consist of three parties, two by sea, and one into the interior. The former were to survey, respectively, the eastern and western coasts; the latter to make a thorough examination of the interior, and to collect specimens of its animals, minerals, and vegetables. The Commodore also resolved to procure a house on shore, and gave notice to Mr. Brown, the artist in charge of the daguerreotype apparatus, that he must prepare his materials, occupy the building, and commence the practice of his art.

On the 27th, the Commodore gave permission to the masters' mates to take the gig and pull about in the harbor, with a prohibition, however, of landing or communicating with the natives. Mr. Bayard Taylor was of the party, and we prefer to give our narrative in his own words, perfectly satisfied that we shall thus most gratify the reader.*

"The crew were Chinamen, wholly ignorant of the use of oars, and our trip would have been of little avail, had not the sea been perfectly calm. With a little trouble we succeeded in making them keep stroke, and made for the coral reef which separates the northern from the oar-channel. The tide was nearly out, and the water was very shoal on all the approaches to the reef. We found, however, a narrow channel, winding between the groves of mimic foliage, and landed on the spongy rock, which rose about a foot above the water. Here the little pools which seamed the surface were alive with crabs, snails, star-fish, sea-prickles, and numbers of small fish of the intensest blue color. We found several handsome shells clinging to the coral, but all our efforts to secure one of the fish failed. The tide was ebbing so fast that we were obliged to return for fear of grounding the boat. We hung for some time over the coral banks, enraptured with the beautiful forms and colors exhibited by this wonderful vegetation of the sea. The coral grew in rounded banks, with clear, deep spaces of water between, resembling, in miniature, ranges of hills covered with autumnal forests. The loveliest tints of blue, violet, pale green, yellow, and white gleamed through the waves, and all the varied forms of vegetable life were grouped together, along the edges of cliffs and precipices, hanging over the chasms worn by currents below. Through those paths, and between the stems of the coral groves, the blue fish shot hither and thither, like arrows of the purest lapis-lazuli; and others of a dazzling emerald color, with tails and fins tipped with gold, eluded our chase like the green bird in the Arabian story. Far down below, in the dusky depth of the waters, we saw, now and then, some large brown fish, hovering stealthily about the entrances to the coral groves, as if lying in wait for their bright little inhabitants. The water was so clear that the eye was deceived as to its depth, and we seemed, now to rest on the branching tops of some climbing forest, now to hang suspended as in mid-air, between the crests of two opposing ones. Of all the wonders of the sea which have furnished food for poetry and fable this was assuredly the most beautiful."

"We succeeded in obtaining a number of fine specimens of coral. The tips of the branches were soft and glutinous, and the odor exhaling from them was exceedingly offensive."

---

* It is due to Mr. Taylor here to state that we draw the principal part of the story of the first visit to Lew Chew from his journal, and are glad often to adopt his language, as we can frame none better. Commodore Perry has desired that we should do so. His own journal is less full in some particulars of this part of the voyage, because he relied on Mr. Taylor's, (which he knew would be accurate and careful,) to amplify topics on which he made but brief notes. The Commodore has particularly directed this statement to be made that justice may be done to Mr. Taylor for the services he rendered.

CHIEF MAGISTRATE OF NAHA

VISIT OF THE LEW CHEW DIGNITARIES ON BOARD.

On the 30th, it was rumored on board that some of the principal authorities on shore intended on that day to visit the Susquehannah. Mr. Williams, the interpreter, came on board and took up permanently his quarters in the ship, and a boat was dispatched for Dr. Bettelheim, to be present on the occasion.

On the preceding day, Lieutenant Contee and Mr. Williams went on shore to pay a visit to the then supposed governor of Napha, since ascertained to be the mayor. They were received in a very polite and friendly manner; though the mayor expressed his deep sense of mortification that his presents had been refused. Lieutenant Contee explained that it was the uniform practice of our government not to accept such presents for her ships, and that (in consequence of our custom) the offering of them not unfrequently subjected the commander and officers to mortification, as their refusal seemed like an ungrateful return for offered courtesy; and that in this case no disrespect was intended.

About one o'clock, a very ordinary native barge, containing the Lew Chew dignitaries, came alongside. The marines were in uniform, and every preparation had been made on board to show them respect and produce impressive effect. One of the inferior officers came first up the gangway with the card of his superior, which Mr. Williams, the interpreter, received and read; the officer then returned, and the regent of the kingdom of Lew Chew, a venerable old man, in a few minutes appeared, supported by two of his officers. Captains Buchanan and Adams received him at the gangway, and were saluted by the regent after the fashion of his country. His hands were joined upon his breast, while his body and knees were bent very profoundly, and his head was slightly turned away from the person he addressed. The prince, it was said, was a lad of eleven years old, and was represented to be ill. The old gentleman acted as regent for him. Six or eight other officers and some dozen subordinates followed the regent to the deck. A salute of three guns was then fired, which so startled some of the Lew Chew officers that they dropped upon their knees.

One of the most striking features in the visitors was their general imperturbable gravity. It was indeed plain that they had intense curiosity, not unmingled with considerable alarm; but they were careful to preserve the most dignified demeanor. They were conducted to the captain's cabin, and thence shown over the ship. They observed every thing with great gravity; but when they reached the ponderous engine, their assumed indifference was fairly overcome, and it was evident that they were conscious of having encountered in it something very far beyond their comprehension. They were much quicker of perception, however, than the Chinese, as well as more agreeable in features, and much more neat and tidy in apparel.

Up to this time they had not seen the Commodore. He had remained secluded in solitary dignity, in his own cabin. It was not meet that he should be made too common to the eyes of the vulgar. All this, of course, was mere matter of policy for the time being, as the Commodore was no very unusual sight to the officers and men of the squadron. The visitors were, however, informed that they were now to be conducted into his presence, and were accordingly taken to his cabin. Just as the regent reached the head of the steps the band struck up a lively air; but the dignified old man passed on without even casting an eye on the musicians. To him it was doubtless a solemn occasion. The Commodore received and entertained his guests most handsomely, and during the interview of an hour and a half between himself and the regent, assurances of amity and good will were exchanged between the parties. On the retirement of the regent he was escorted with great respect to the ship's side, and on his departure received honors similar to those that had been tendered on his arrival.

Among other matters that occurred at the meeting between the regent and the Commodore, the latter informed his guest that he should do himself the honor to return his visit, *at the palace*, in the city of Sheudi or Shui, on the following Monday week, (June 6th.) This information caused some consultation and discussion between the regent and his counsellors; but the Commodore put an end to it by stating that he had fully made a determination to go to the palace on that day, and should surely execute it. He further added that he should expect such a reception as became his rank and position as commander of the squadron and diplomatic representative of the United States in those regions; and with a distinct understanding, if not acquiescence, on the part of the regent, to this effect, he took his departure.

One result of the visit was very agreeable to the officers, for permission was immediately given them to go on shore, accompanied with a request that they would in no case intrude themselves where their presence might seem to be disagreeable to the natives. They very soon availed themselves of the privilege, and a party (of which Mr. Taylor was one) landed at the foot of the rock upon which Dr. Bettelheim had erected his flagstaff. They found the shore to be coral rock covered with a dense and luxurious vegetation; and about the distance of twenty yards from flood tide mark, the gardens of the natives commenced, divided from each other by coral walls and bristling hedges of yucca and cactus. Mr. Taylor thus describes this his first landing on Lew Chew: "Several groups of Lew Chewans watched our landing, but slowly retired as we approached them. The more respectable, distinguished by the silver pins in their hair, made to us profound salutations. The lower classes wore a single garment of brown cotton or grass-cloth, and the children were entirely naked. Even in the humblest dwellings there was an air of great neatness and order. Most of them were enclosed within high coral walls, in the midst of a small plot of garden land, some of which contained thriving patches of tobacco, maize, and sweet potatoes.

"Threading the winding lanes of the suburb for a short distance, we came into the broad paved road which leads from Napha to Sheudi. It is an admirable thoroughfare, almost equal to the macadamized roads of England. The walls on either hand of coral rock are jointed together with great precision. No mortar is used in their construction, but the stones are so well fitted, (very much in the manner of the cyclopean walls of Italy,) that the whole appears, at a little distance, to be one mass. We here came upon parties from the Mississippi and Saratoga. The natives collected in crowds to see us pass, falling back as we approached, and closing behind us. They were under the authority of several persons, who had evidently received a special appointment to watch us. Among them were many fine, venerable figures—old men with flowing beards and aspects of great dignity and serenity; but no sooner were any of these addressed than they retreated with great haste. The houses were all closed, and not a female was to be seen. The roofs were of red tiles, of excellent manufacture, and this, with the dark-green foliage of the trees which studded the city, the walls topped with cactus, and the occasional appearance of a palm or banana, reminded me of the towns in Sicily.

"As we entered the thickly inhabited portion of Napha, the road passed over the foot of a low hill, by regularly graded steps, and then descended to the inner harbor, where the Japanese junks lay at anchor. From this harbor a creek, or estuary, almost dry at low water, extends eastward into the island. The market-place is in this portion of the town. It was deserted, like the streets, except by the inhabitants of two or three large tents, which were closed, except a narrow aperture. On our asking (by signs) for water, the people went to these tents and

procured some in a square wooden ladle, exactly similar to those used by the Turcomans, in Asia Minor. I did not go down to look at the Japanese junks, but, with some others, followed the course of the creek. Two of the police officers—as we took them to be—stuck to us, and whenever we paused motioned to us to take the road which would have led us back to the beach.

Lew Chew Peasant.

For this very reason I was desirous of proceeding further. All of the town which we had seen was completely closed, the shops shut, and the stalls of vendors of small wares, in the streets, deserted with such haste, in some instances, that the articles remained exposed. We walked for about half a mile up the creek, and finally reached another road which appeared to be one of the principal thoroughfares. The appearance of the interior of the island was exceedingly beautiful. The land rose in bold hills, crowned with groves, of a variety of pine which was new to me, resembling the cedar of Lebanon in its physiognomy. The sides of the hills were covered with fields of brilliant green, spotted, here and there, by the white-washed sepulchres of former generations. In the vegetation there was a mixture of the growths of tropical and temperate climates, and in no part of the world have I seen a greater richness or variety. A stone bridge, of rough but substantial workmanship, crosses the creek near its head. I noticed several of the natives riding over it into the country, on the Lew Chew ponies—shaggy, little animals, probably descended from the Chinese stock.

"We strolled into a temple, from the walls of which several persons, probably females, had been watching us. They disappeared with great rapidity as we entered the door. The court-yard of the temple was shaded with fine trees, but we discovered nothing of interest except two long, narrow boats, of the kind called 'centipede' at Hong Kong, designed for public festivals. While we sat down upon them to rest, quite a crowd of natives gathered about us, and soon became familiar, though respectful in their demeanour. They were very neatly dressed in grass-cloth robes of a blue or salmon color, and (perhaps by contrast with the filthy Chinese) seemed to me the cleanest persons I had ever seen. The street vendors had not had time to get out of our way, and they sat beside their piles of coarse cheese-cakes. There were some women among them, but they were all old and hideously ugly. The costume of the female does not differ from that of the males, but they are distinguished by having a single instead of a double hair-pin."

On the 30th of May, the party ordered to explore the interior of the island, and its eastern coast, set out for the performance of that duty. It consisted of twelve persons—four officers, four of the crew, and four Chinese coolies. From the Susquehanna were sent Mr. Taylor and Mr. Heine; and from the Mississippi the Rev. Mr. Jones, chaplain, and Dr. Lynah, assistant surgeon. The command of the expedition was given to Mr. Jones, who was directed particularly to observe the geology of the island; as, if it contained coal, it was a most important characteristic. Mr. Taylor was ordered to take notes, and write out a detailed account of the journey. It was supposed the duty would occupy five or six days, and accordingly the expedition was furnished with provisions for that period, and with a tent. The men were armed with cutlasses and carbines, and ten rounds of ball cartridges each. It was not, however, supposed that there would be need of a resort to force on any occasion; still, it was deemed prudent to let the natives see the power of the party to defend itself; and beside, guns and ammunition were required for the purpose of procuring birds and animals.

On this day, also, the Commodore sent two of the officers of the squadron ashore, with the interpreter, to make arrangements with the authorities for procuring a house. On landing, they proceeded to a building which seemed to be what we should call, in the United States, a "town hall." It was the place, in the village of Tumai, where common strangers were received, and contained some thirty mats on the floor for sleeping; waiters were also in attendance with tea and pipes. The purposes to which the building is applied seemed, however, to be various. The literati meet there to converse and interchange opinions; and any one of them may spend the night there upon any unoccupied mat. Our officers, on reaching this building, sent for one of the principal men, who, after an hour's delay, made his appearance, and was most profound in his obeisance. Tea and pipes (the never failing preliminary) having been disposed of, the gentlemen made known their business to the Japanese official. He promptly declared that it would be utterly impossible for the Americans to occupy a house on shore. But, as Captain Hall, of the British navy, had, after much delay, at last obtained a house on shore, and our officers knew it, they reminded the Lew Chewans of the fact, and simply told him that they must have a house. He was very ingenious in arguments to show that the difficulties in the way were insurmountable.

He was then asked if some two or three of the Americans might not sleep in the house for that night, and replied that no American must sleep in a house on shore. Upon being pressed further he seemed to become somewhat impatient, and, rising from his seat, he crossed over to where the officers sat, and dispensing with the aid of the interpreter, (through whom all communications had thus far been made,) to the surprise of our gentlemen, said: "Gentlemen, Doo Choo man very small, American man not very small. I have read of America in books of Washington—very good man, very good. Doo Choo good friend American. Doo Choo man give America all provision he wants. American no can have house on shore." These were nearly his exact words; and the officers concluded that he had probably learned from Dr. Bettelheim what he knew of the English language.

When they insisted that two or three of their company should stay in the house, at least for the night, he begged permission to go and confer with the mayor of Napha. He was gone for some time, and probably went three miles beyond Napha, to the palace of Shui, to confer with the regent. "Well," (said one of the officers, on his return,) "we can sleep here to night?"—with a polite bow and marked emphasis, he replied "you cannot." But our officers had been ordered to procure a house, and resolved to obey; so they left one of their number with the interpreter to sleep there, unless they should be sent for by the Commodore, while they returned to the flag-ship to report what they had done. The officer and interpreter occupied two of the mats that night, and the islanders slept on the rest. There was no forcible taking possession of a building, as some have represented. Two men slept in the town-house for one night, surrounded by the natives, and this was all that was exacted or taken. The next day the Commodore sent a sick officer, with his servant, to the place, and those who slept there on the previous night came on board. *

---

* We have before us an original note from the regent of Lew Chew, addressed to the Commodore, with a translation of the same, made by Mr. Williams. We insert the latter as affording a specimen of the Lew Chew epistolary style, premising that to represent themselves as very poor and obscure, and indeed unworthy almost of notice, was the uniform practice of the officials of the island, in all their communications with our officers. It seems to be part of their settled policy; for we find the same humble and depreciatory representations of themselves pervading their letters to the British officers, on the visit of the Bishop of Victoria. The communication below relates to the two subjects of the Commodore's visit to the palace at Shui, and granting a house for the use of the squadron on shore; both of which events they strove hard, by various artifices, to prevent.

A prepared petition. Shäng Tá-mü, regent of Lew Chew, &c., &c., hereby urgently petitions upon important matters. On the 21st day of the present month (this, of course, is a translation of their mode of expressing time into ours) I received your excellency's verbal orders that on the 30th day of the present month, at 10 o'clock, you had concluded to come to the capital to return your respects. Also, on the 26th instant, Ching Changlieh, the mayor of Napha, received your excellency's communication saying, that on the 30th instant, at 10 o'clock, it was decided to go up to Shui, the capital, to return the visit of the regent at the palace, and wished this to be distinctly stated in the proper way.

Now, it is plain to all that the capital and towns of this little country are quite different from the provincial capitals of China; here there is only a palace for the king, and no halls, official residences, markets, or shops; and, up to this time, no envoy from a foreign country has ever entered into the palace. In February, of last year, an English general came here, bearing a public letter, and was strenuous to enter the palace, there to deliver it; the high officers repeatedly requested that it might be given them elsewhere, but he refused, and forced himself into the palace. At that time, from the young prince and queen dowager down to the lowest officers and people, all were alarmed and fearful, hardly keeping soul and body together; and the queen dowager has been dangerously sick even to this day, the physicians giving her broths and medicines for her alarming ailments which are not yet removed. All the officers in the country are really troubled and grieved on this account; and having heard that the ruler of your country is endued with great kindness and vast compassion, and highly prizes humanity and benevolence, they urgently beg of your excellency, that respectfully embodying the humanity and benevolence of your sovereign, and his great love for men, you will take the case of the queen dowager, and her severe indisposition, into your favorable consideration, and cease from going into the palace to return thanks. If you deem it necessary to make this compliment, please go to the residence of the prince, there to make your respects in person. Respecting the matter of renting a house for residing, it has been stated by the mayor of Napha that, on the 24th instant, he had clearly shown forth the circumstances; and, on the 26th, had received your excellency's reply, in which it was remarked—"that, whenever the officers and men from the ships were on shore, rambling about, they had no place of resort, and that, as there were no inns in the country, if they were overtaken by rain or bad weather,

There was evident opposition on the part of the authorities, at first, to visits on shore from the ships. This was expected, for the narratives of all who had visited the island had prepared the squadron for this. Notwithstanding, however, our officers did go on shore and wander over the town of Napha and its suburbs, objects of no little interest and curiosity to the natives, who followed them in crowds, and were very polite, bowing low to them as they passed. But, despite all this courtesy, our officers were quite sensible that the eyes of spies were upon them continually, and that every movement was watched. The women and children were taught by these officials to run away, as if affrighted, on the approach of the Americans, and, in short, a polite suspicion characterized the intercourse on the part of the Lew Chewans. The sick officer, however, on shore at Tumai, seemed to be on the best possible terms with the natives, and they certainly were kind. The inhabitants appear to be naturally not unamiable, but the experience of our officers does not altogether sustain the glowing accounts of the simplicity, friendliness and contentment of the people. Either Captain Basil Hall was mistaken, or the national traits have changed since the time of his visit. He represents them as without arms, ignorant even of money, docile, tractable and honest, scrupulously obedient to their rulers and their laws, and, in fact, as loving one another too well wilfully to harm or wrong each other. Many of the officers of the squadron went to the island, expecting to find these beautiful traits of character; but gradually and painfully undeceived in many particulars, they were constrained to acknowledge that human nature in Lew Chew was very much the same as it is elsewhere.

The system of government, of which secret espionage forms a distinguishing feature, must beget in the inferior classes cunning and falsehood, and these our officers certainly found. The Lew Chewans pretend ignorance of offensive weapons, and of such no open display is made by the people, but Dr. Bettelheim says that he has seen fire-arms in their possession, though they seek to conceal them from strangers; and they are doubtless, by nature, a pacific people. As to money, they know the value of gold and silver very well, and they traffic for the Chinese "cash," of which from twelve to fourteen hundred are equivalent to the Spanish dollar. They are an eminently shrewd people, and proved themselves to be somewhat "smart" in the matter of exchange, when the disbursing officers of the squadron came to settle with them the value of the "cash." They showed no reluctance to take our eagles and half-eagles, though Captain Hall says they would not, in his day, touch the British gold coins. They have, on the whole, many excellent natural traits, and their worst vices are probably the result, in a great measure, of the wretched system of government under which they live.

---

or were detained so that they were unable to return on board before night, there was no place to rest at, unless they abruptly entered the houses of the people; that, as the men on board ship were ignorant of the Lew Chewan language, if they wanted only a cup of water they could not get it; for these reasons, one or two houses were required, and if they were wanted for other purposes, these were all of a peaceable and friendly nature, but it was indispensible to have one. The mayor (of Napha) having intimated that the building already occupied by the sailors was a *kung-kwăn*, or public hall, if the officers would designate another building, they would remove to it according to their wishes." I find that the building now occupied is a public house, for the deliberations of officers and police, and meetings on public business; but having sought out a place which can be used, I find that the *Shing-hien-sz'*, or Holy Manifesting monastery, for preserving the anchorage of ships, can be obtained for a residence; and I beg that orders for removal to this place, as a temporary residence, may be given. Then will the prince and authorities, one and all, be greatly obliged by this great kindness. An important petition.

Hien fung, 3d year, 4th moon, 27th day, (June 3d, 1853.)

This building might readily have been granted on the first application. It was, we believe, the same used by the English, on Captain Hall's visit. As to the young prince, the reader will be surprised to learn that there were the strongest reasons in the minds of many for suspecting him to be an imaginary personage. No one believed a syllable of the story about the queen dowager's illness; indeed, there was no evidence to the Americans that there was a queen dowager.

The officers of the squadron were, during the period of the visit, most usefully and diligently employed in making hydrographic surveys, and the results are all embodied in the charts which form part of the records of the expedition. Boat exercise in the harbor formed also part of the

Lew Chew Merchant.

occupation of the several crews; while the marines were on shore, drilling under the charge of their officers. These things indicated that the Commodore was determined to have every department in the highest state of discipline, that he might be prepared for any event.

On Saturday, the 4th of June, the party that had been sent to explore the interior of the island returned in safety, and the result of their labors will be found in the following chapter.

Dr. Bettelheim's residence in Lew Chew.

CHAPTER VIII.

REPORT OF AN INLAND EXPLORATION OF GREAT LEW CHEW, BY A PARTY FROM THE SQUADRON, UNDER THE COMMAND OF COMMODORE PERRY.

ONDAY, the 30th of May, says the report, was the day fixed upon by Commodore Perry for our departure. We were ordered to cross the island to the eastern shore, follow the line of coast northward, and return through the interior, pushing our course as far as practicable, under our instructions to return within six days. All the stores having been procured, and packed in convenient parcels, together with portfolios and drawing materials, implements for preparing birds, &c., we landed about 10 o'clock, and proceeded to the house of the missionary, Dr. Bettelheim, which had been chosen as the rendezvous. The authorities had not been previously informed of our intention; and, as it was evident that we should not be allowed to advance far without an escort, or espionage of some kind, Dr. Bettelheim sent to request that a proper officer should accompany us as guide. After waiting about an hour, and no person appearing, we decided to set out, believing that our guide would be forthcoming before we left the city. In fact, we had no sooner reached the main street, communicating with the road to Sheudi, than a portly personage, with a long white beard, and two younger officers, with black beards and swarthy complexions, joined us. A crowd of curious natives had also collected, and followed us until we left the city.

"Each of the men carried a haversack, in addition to his arms, leaving about 120 pounds weight of baggage to be divided among the four coolies. The men, Terry and Mitchell, marched in advance, the former carrying the flag, while the other men, Smith and Davis, remained in the rear of the baggage; this order was preserved during the whole expedition. We had not proceeded half a mile before our coolies showed signs of breaking down under their loads, and, even though we might force them to keep up for some time longer, it was evident that we could not make much progress without further help; Mr. Jones, therefore, requested the portly old officer, who seemed to have special charge over us, to supply us with four more coolies, promising that they should be paid on our return. After waiting half an hour at the northern end of the city, four spare young natives came up with bamboo poles, and relieved the Chinamen of half their load. We now took the high road to Shendi, passing the salt creek which comes up from the village of Tumé, by a bridge of one arch; the crowd turned back at this point, leaving us about a dozen followers, who seemed to be attendants or subordinates of the principal officers.

Beyond the bridge we passed over a meadow, studded with singular broken rocks, of secondary limestone, covered with clumps of pine trees. The road then passed around the base of a hill, the front of which was occupied by a temple of massive stone masonry. It was shaded with large trees, resembling in foliage the Indian fig or sycamore. Paths, over which the hedges of bamboo formed complete arches, ran up the sides of the hill. On our right were meadows of bearded rice, a variety which Dr. Lynah declared to be unknown in the southern States. The country now became open and undulating, and covered with the richest vegetation; not only was all the low land planted with rice, but the hills were in many places terraced nearly to the top, and the water carefully conducted from field to field by artificial channels. The streams were lined with thick hedges of banana, and the knolls which dotted the landscape were crowned with groves of the Lew Chew pine, a beautiful tree, strongly resembling the cedar of Lebanon in its flat horizontal layers of foliage; it is probably a new species. There was something in the forms of the landscape which reminded me of the richest English scenery, mixed with the superb vegetation of the tropics. The views on each side increased in beauty as we approached Shendi, the capital city of the island, which is scattered along the southwest slope of a group of hills. The houses are half buried in foliage, and stretch over an extent of a mile, the citadel, or residence of the viceroy, occupying an elevated central position.

The day was dark and cloudy, threatening rain, and fresh wind blew in our faces as we climbed the heights. Near the summit we passed through a high wooden gate, upon which were inscribed two Chinese characters, signifying "the central hill," or "place of authority,") and entered the main street of the city, which is broad, handsomely-paved, and lined with high walls, behind which, and the foliage of their gardens, the principal dwellings are mostly concealed. As we reached the gate, the flag was unrolled, and fastened upon the end of a musket. A fine grove of old trees, with crooked trunks, gnarled boughs, and thick, dark-green foliage, attracted my attention on entering. We had not proceeded fifty paces before the officers attending us beckoned to us to enter a doorway on the right side of the street. We made a halt, and, leaving men and coolies outside, went in. It proved to be a *Cung-quá*, or resting place for travellers, or rather for officers of government, since in Lew Chew there are no other travellers. The *Cung-quá* corresponds very nearly to the Turkish khan, except that, being used only by persons of some consideration, it is far more neat and elegant in every respect. The house into which we were ushered resembled a private dwelling of the better class. The principal apartment was carpeted with very fine soft mats, and surrounded on three sides by an open verandah. Adjoining the building were kitchens and out-houses for servants, and in front a small yard planted with sago palms and a tree resembling the *Inocarpus*. We were politely received by a gentleman in a gray robe, who performed the *ko-tow* towards us in the most approved style. Seats were brought, and tea, prepared after the Chinese fashion, served in small cups. The attendant was directed, by signs, to wait first upon Mr. Jones, who was thenceforth recognized as the head of the party. The former served us on his knees, both when he offered and when he took away the cups. We remained but a few minutes, and took our leave, evidently to the surprise and perplexity of our conductors, who did not as yet comprehend our object.

On leaving Napha, we had noticed an expression of doubt and anxiety upon the faces of the natives, and this rather increased as we proceeded. No remonstrance whatever was made to us, but our movements were suspiciously scrutinized. When, therefore, we left the Cung-quà, and, instead of returning, took our course directly onward through the city, the faces of our convoy became clouded, and an expression of alarm communicated itself to those of the natives whose curiosity had attracted them around us. We soon reached the gate of the citadel, at the foot of the massive walls, which, rising through groves of trees, dominate over the city. The gate was closed, but had it been open, we should not have presumed to enter. The northern and eastern slope of the hill is covered with splendid old trees, divided by winding, shaded avenues, on the sides of which many natives were sitting, with fans in their hands. The sun, which shone out hot and clear for an instant, chequered this rich, park-like scenery with strong contrasts of light and shadow, and down through the depths of the trees illuminated the face of a pool of water, so completely covered with the floating leaves of a species of lily as to appear like a patch of green sward. We passed around the base of the citadel to its eastern side, and, after some deliberation, took a paved road which led through the suburbs of the city in an E.S.E. direction. Wherever we turned we could see scouts running in advance, and driving the inhabitants away from our path, so that a silence and desertion, like that which follows pestilence, took place wherever we moved. All with whom we accidentally came in contact saluted us politely, but with a settled air of melancholy, which I ascribed to the surveillance exercised over them by an unnatural government, rather than any ill-will towards us.

The northern side of Sheudi is a wilderness of rich vegetation. The appearance of a flourishing cocoa-palm, now and then, showed that the climate is entirely tropical. The eastern suburb of the capital is composed principally of bamboo huts, thatched with rice straw. The inhabitants were all hidden away out of sight, and blinds of split bamboo let down before the doors. We took a road which led along the hills towards the southeast, and after issuing from the capital, gained a ridge whence we could see a long line of the western coast, with the squadron riding at anchor in the harbor of Napha. From this point the interest of the journey properly commenced, as we were entering upon ground which no one before us had ever explored. The limit of the excursions made by others was Sheudi, and very few succeeded in entering that capital. We were, therefore, greatly enlivened by the prospect before us, and pursued our way with more alacrity than comported with the comfort of our disheartened conductors.

About a mile from Sheudi, the road turned more to the east, and after passing through a dense wood, came out upon a hill, whence we caught a glimpse of the sea on the eastern side. A temple, apparently erected during the past year, (for it was destitute of either altar or god,) stood in the shade of a clump of pines, and as it was now one o'clock we halted for refreshment. Some of the natives brought water, while the men picked up sufficient dead wood to boil our kettle, and in the course of time we were regaled with tea and ship's biscuit. We offered the former to the officers, but they did not appear to relish it. The Lew Chew coolies, however, ate heartily of the biscuit, which they had better earned than our vagabond Chinese. They gave

the name of the place as Piño. Mr. Heine took a sketch of it, and astonished the natives, some forty or fifty of whom had collected to look at us, by firing at a mark with his rifle. Immediately after leaving Piño, whence we started at 3 p. m., the paved road ceased, and the way became deep and miry. The soil was a lead-colored, stiff clay, the disintegration of shale rock, which here appeared for the first time. We had not proceeded more than half a mile before we reached the dividing ridge or crest of the island, and a magnificent panorama opened below us to the eastward. The sea-line of the Pacific formed the horizon, and a spacious sheet of water between two headlands which made out from the island led us to suppose that we were looking upon Barrow's Bay. Between us and the sea lay an amphitheatre of hills, cultivated to their very tops and clothed with the greenest verdure. Their sides were carefully terraced, and every advantage taken of the inclination of the soil, so as to collect the rains for irrigation. The cultivation was quite as patient and thorough as that of China. The picturesque formation of the hills gave a great variety of outline to the landscape, which embraced a compass of perhaps twenty miles. Towards the west we overlooked all the country we had passed, as far as a headland in the northwest, which I took to be Cape Broughton. Mr. Heine took a sketch of the view, looking eastward, while I attempted to take the western side.

Resuming our march, we descended the ridge, which was about 600 feet above the sea-level. The clayey path leading down was very wet and slippery, and the coolies fell and rolled over several times with the baggage. Passing through gaps between the lower hills, we reached a semi-circular plain, nearly two miles in breadth, extending around the head of the bay. On either side was a village of thatched huts, buried in trees. The scouts had already been before us, and the natives lay concealed in their habitations. The former supposed that we would take a road leading to a large village at the head of the bay, but as we turned abruptly to the northward, we soon saw them running across the fields to regain the road ahead of us. There were a number of villages at the base of the hills, on our left, but so thickly studded with trees that they were almost concealed from view. I collected a number of plants, one of them a species of althæa, with a splendid scarlet blossom. The road which we took led through the rice fields and was very deep and muddy. While stopping to rest on a bridge over one of the irrigating streams, our old conductor came up with his two assistants, and intimated to us by signs that it was time we should return to the ships. The sun would soon set, they said, and we should have no place to sleep. We replied, (also by signs,) that instead of returning we were going northward, and would not reach the ships again for five or six days. They appeared greatly surprised at this and a little troubled, since it was part of their duty not to lose sight of us. The old fellow, who, in his haste to keep up, had slipped down in the muddy road and soiled the hinder part of his robe, laughed heartily at the accident, and finally became resigned to the prospect of the long tramp before him. They then pointed to the west, saying that there was a Cung-quà in that direction, where we could spend the night. Our course, however, was nearly northeast, and about half past five, having reached a hill overlooking the bay, on the summit of which was an open space surrounded with young pines, we determined to encamp there. The people objected to our cutting down the trees, and we made tent poles by fastening together the bamboo staves used by the coolies. There was a village on the slope of the hill below us, and after some delay, caused by the difficulty of interpreting our wants to the native officials, we obtained four fowls, forty eggs, and two bundles of firewood. One of our Chinamen, "A-shing," professed to speak the Lew Chew language, but we soon found him as

166   EXPEDITION TO JAPAN.

miserably deficient in this as he was in all other useful qualities. His comrade, however, who spoke no English, could write Chinese, and the message having been thus communicated and written, was finally read by the old Pe-ching. The latter refused to accept either cash or dollars, saying that they were of no use to the people whatever, but that everything we needed would be furnished us. The Chinese suggested—probably on their own account—that we should pay the people in ship's biscuit, but we had scarcely enough for our own wants. It was at length decided that we should take what we required and settle for its value with the Pe-ching on our return.

The people were tardy in bringing our firewood, and we were obliged to eat our supper by the light of our camp fire. I succeeded in getting a sketch of the bay, while daylight remained. It is deep and spacious, and protected by reefs across the mouth, but, judging from the appearance of the water, too shallow to be made available for naval purposes. A large village lies at its head, and several fishing junks were at anchor before it. At night the plain sparkled with lights, some of them moving to and fro—probably lanterns carried by persons passing from one village to another. The officers determined to remain with us at all hazards, and at their

Explorers.—Lew Chew.—Night Camp.

command the people brought up bamboo poles and matting, out of which they erected a temporary structure beside our tent. They were perfectly good-humored in their demeanor, and submitted with great patience to what they could not avoid. Before going to sleep we arranged four watches of two hours each, from 9 p. m. until 5 a. m., and the subordinate native policemen kindled a fire and kept a counter-watch. We were all somewhat fatigued with our first march of ten miles, but the mosquitoes were so terribly annoying that few of us slept more than half an hour during the whole night.

We rose at dawn, and found the natives already stirring. The morning gave promise of fair weather. The Pe-ching and his associates came up and saluted us gravely as soon as we arose. It required about two hours to cook and eat breakfast, strike the tent, and pack the baggage for carrying. When we were all ready we found eight native coolies on hand, those whom we took from Napha having returned the evening previous. Leaving Camp Perry (as we named the spot) we took a path leading up a steep hill to the north. Winding around its brow, we descended into a valley, surrounded by abrupt, scarped hills. A stream flowing at the bottom of a deep gully, overhung with large banana trees, made its way out of this broad cul-de-sac towards the sea. We crossed the valley on the ridges of swampy grass, between the flooded rice-fields, and climbed a long and toilsome ridge, by wet, slippery paths, leading up through copses of young pine. We had now gained the spinal ridge of the island, and turned northwestward, over alternate hills and meadows, along its summit. The wood was principally pine, but I observed several new varieties of shrubs, not in flower. Now and then we passed the huts of the natives, generally in clusters of two and three, but even in this secluded region notice of our coming had reached them, and the inhabitants were hidden. I looked into some, and found the interiors to consist of a single room, smoke-blackened, and furnished with the rudest utensils. Two of them had a grating of bamboo, raised, like a floor, about six inches above the ground, and the thick mats which serve the Lew Chewans as beds were spread upon this.

Mr. Jones left the camp before us, and we had not yet found him. Coming to a deep, wooded gorge, with a stream flowing westward, we discovered that our true course lay further to the east, and retraced our steps through the pine woods, and over upland rice-meadows to an open, grassy height, whence we saw Mr. Jones, surrounded by a group of natives, about half a mile to the south of us. In a short time we again reached the summit ridge, overlooking the bay, and enjoyed the view of a superb landscape. The dividing ridge of the island, as we had already noticed, is nearest the eastern shore, to which the descent is much more abrupt than on the western. The cultivation on this side is also more thorough, and the crops more luxuriant. The knees of the mountains below us were feathered with beautiful groves of the Lew Chew pine, intermingled with terraced fields of grain and vegetables, while the plain below, through its whole sweep of fifteen miles, was brown with its harvest of rice. We counted a dozen villages, some of them of considerable size, dotting its expanse. To the northward extended a long headland, far beyond what we had supposed to be the extremity of the bay, and projecting from the island in a southeasterly direction. It was now plain that we had not yet reached Barrow's Bay, of which this headland formed the southern boundary. While halting to rest our coolies, in the shade of a clump of pines, Mr. Heine shot a raven, with a beak much broader than the European species. There was a very large tomb, of a shape nearly circular, on the northern side of the ridge. About two miles further, the road swerving a little to the west, we came upon a singular rock, rising high out of a forest of pines. The summit, which was very sharp and jagged, was seventy or eighty feet above the crest of the ridge, and being composed of secondary limestone, honeycombed by the weather, it was an exceedingly striking and picturesque object. While Mr. Heine stopped to sketch it, and Mr. Jones to examine its geology, I climbed to the summit, which was so sharp as to make it a most uneasy seat. Finding that it was the highest peak in that part of the island, commanding a view which embraced a considerable reach of both

168   EXPEDITION TO JAPAN.

shores, I ordered the flag to be brought, and unfurled it from the top of the rock, while the men fired a salute from the base and hailed it with three hearty cheers. We bestowed upon it the name of "Banner Rock." The natives looked on, unable how to understand our proceedings,

Banner Rock.

but not in the least troubled by them. A little to the north of where we were the island narrowed suddenly, between the head of the eastern bay and a deep bight, which makes in on the western side, between Cape Broughton and the headland bounding Port Melville on the west. I judged its breadth, at this point, to be about four miles, in a straight line. To the southwest I could see the position of Sheudi, eight or ten miles distant. The landscape was rich and varied, all the hills being coated with groves of pine. We found on the rock the "Wax plant" of our greenhouses, in full bloom, the splendid scarlet *Althæa*, and a variety of the *Malva*, with a large yellow blossom.

Continuing our march along the summit ridge, we came gradually upon a wilder and more broken region. Huge fragments of the same dark limestone rock overhung our path, or lay tumbled along the slopes below us, as if hurled there by some violent natural convulsion. As the hill curved eastward, we saw on its southern side a series of immense square masses, separated by deep fissures, reaching down the side nearly to its base. They were apparently fifty feet high, and at least a hundred feet square, and their tops were covered with a thick growth of trees and shrubbery. In the absence of any traces of volcanic action, it is difficult to conceive how these detached masses were distributed with such regularity, and carried to such a distance from their original place. The eastern front of the crags under which we passed was studded with tombs, some of them built against the rock and whitewashed, like the tombs of the present inhabitants, but others excavated within it, and evidently of great age. Looking

Tombs in Lew Chew.

down upon the bay it was easy to see that the greater part of it was shallow, and in some places the little fishing junks could not approach within half a mile of the shore. The rice-fields were brought square down to the water's edge, which was banked up to prevent the tide from overflowing them, and I noticed many triangular stone dykes, stretching some distance into the water, and no doubt intended as weirs for fish.

In less than an hour after leaving Banner Rock we were surprised by the discovery of an ancient fortress, occupying a commanding position upon the summit of one of the spurs of the central ridge. Its outline was irregular, but with a general direction from northeast to southwest; and while some parts of it were in perfect preservation, other portions were overgrown with vines and shrubbery, and hardly to be distinguished from the natural rock upon which it was based. Passing through an arched gateway, the road led to a terrace, overgrown with trees, upon which stood a structure of masonry resembling a cenotaph. A flight of stone steps conducted us to another gateway, after passing which, and a spacious vestibule, we entered the interior of the fortress. The space was occupied by a luxuriant grove of trees, and at the further end was a private dwelling of respectable appearance. Our Pe-ching was already there, and the master (whom our Chinese coolies designated the "Japanese Consul") respectfully invited us to enter. The day was oppressively hot, and we found two or three cups of Lew Chew tea an agreeable refreshment. Returning to the terrace, at the base of the outer wall, we halted in the shade to allow the men their mid-day rest and meal. A flight of steep steps, cut in the rock, led downward on the northern side to a grotto under the foundation of the castle, at the bottom of which was a pool of cold, sweet water. The place was completely overhung by dense foliage, and inaccessible to the beams of the sun.

While our meal was preparing, Mr. Jones traced out a rough plan of the fortress, and the men took measurements. The following are its dimensions, ascertained with tolerable accuracy:

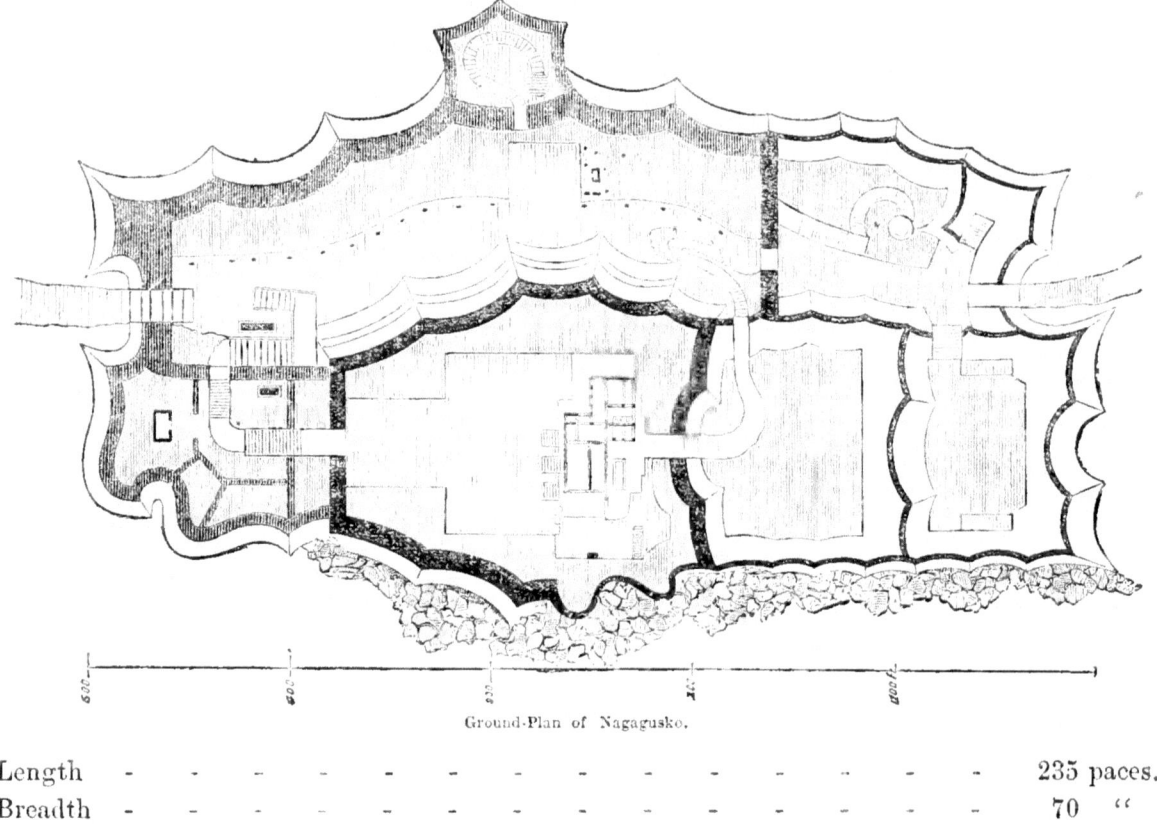

Ground-Plan of Nagagusko.

Length	235 paces.
Breadth	70 "
Thickness of walls at bottom	6 to 12 "
Thickness of walls at top	12 feet.
Greatest height of outer wall, measuring along the slope	66 "
Height of wall, from inside	12 "
Angle of outer wall	60°

The material was limestone, and the masonry of admirable construction. The stones, some of which were cubes of four feet square, were so carefully hewn and jointed that the absence of any mortar or cement did not seem to impair the durability of the work. There were two remarkable points about the work. The arches were double, the lower course being formed of

Nagagusko—Interior.

two stones hewn into almost a parabolic curve, and meeting in the centre, over which was the regular Egyptian arch, with its key-stone, as represented in the annexed outline, No. 1.

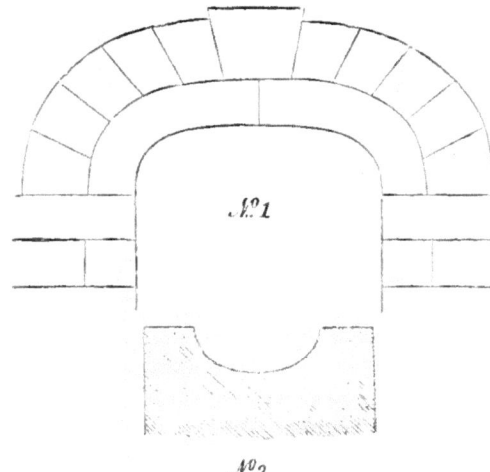

The other peculiarity was, that in place of bastions, there were square projections of masonry, presenting a concave front, (No. 2,) which would catch and concentrate the force of a cannon ball, rather than ward it off. But this fortress must have been erected many centuries before the use of fire-arms of any kind could have been known to the Lew Chewans. Our Chinese pretended to give the name of the place as Ching-King, which are Chinese words, signifying the chief or capital citadel.

We resumed our march at half past one o'clock. The old Pe-ching, "Chang-Yuen," who had become a little fatigued by this time, took a *ka-goo*, or Lew Chew chair, and followed in our rear, leaving the particular charge of us to his subordinates. The scouts were sent ahead, as usual, for our path descended again to the populous plain at the base of the hills. We already perceived indications of a fixed system in the espionage to which we were subjected.

Ruins of Nagagusko—North.

Chang-Yuen and his two secondary officers were deputed to accompany us during the whole journey, while their dozen or more attendants and helpers were changed as we passed from one district of the island into another. Nothing could exceed the vigilance with which they watched us. We might separate into as many divisions as there were men, and yet each of us would still retain his native convoy. We could neither tire them down, nor run away from them. When, by chance, we suddenly changed our course, we still found them before us. And though this was the result of a jealous and exclusive system, yet they managed to give it the appearance of being done through respect for us.

I was curious to obtain some information regarding the domestic life of the natives, and frequently entered their huts unawares, in the hope of finding them at their avocations within. In most cases I found the huts deserted, but in some others caught the merest glimpses of Lew Chew life, in its more humble aspects. Near the castle, while our convoy was passing around a village, I slipped into one of the alleys and entered a bamboo enclosure, within which were five neat dwellings. The mats were let down before the doors, but the people were all hidden behind screens and in lofts under the thatch, for on looking in I found no one but a child and an old

man, who immediately knelt down and knocked his forehead on the floor before me. In another hut, in a village on the plain, I found an old woman and a girl of about twelve years of age, both of whom fell on their knees, and held up their hands with an expression which was at once imploring and reverential. A few words of friendly greeting, though in English, encouraged them, and I should no doubt have been able to inspect the interior of the hut, had not one of the spies come up at that moment and driven them away.

In the rich rice plains to which we descended we found sugar-cane for the first time, *sorghum*, or millet, and three varieties of the grain known in the United States as "broom-corn." The road struck out into the swampy rice fields, and we made for a green headland covered with pines. A village, almost completely buried in bowers and arcades of bamboo, lay at its foot. As we were about entering, we came upon two curious stones planted in the earth. The largest was about four feet high, and from its peculiar form struck me at once as a *lingam*, or emblem of the Phallic worship. The same idea occurred to Mr. Heine, who made a sketch of it. It was a very hard, dark-colored stone, resembling porphyry, and the only thing we could learn from the natives respecting it was, that they called it "*ishee*." There is no trace of this feature of the Hindoo religion existing either in Japan, China, or Lew Chew. The discovery of this stone, if it should prove to be a Phallic emblem, is therefore exceedingly curious. In the course of the afternoon we found two more, one of which was prostrate and broken. In conjunction with these remains, the face of the hill behind, for a distance of two miles, is almost entirely covered with excavated tombs, resembling the simpler forms of the rock tombs of Egypt and Syria. Our native conductors, when interrogated respecting them, called them "the houses of the devil's men," and seemed amused at our taking notice of them. This fact, in a country where ancestral tombs are considered sacred, as among the Chinese, seems to point to the existence of another race on the island, in ancient times—a race who may have received the worship of the Lingam from Java, or other islands where memorials of it exist.

After an unavailing attempt to shoot a couple of herons in a rice field, we kept a course nearly due north, passing through several beautiful villages. The houses were surrounded with banana trees, and the alleys completely overarched with bamboo. In one of the houses I found a woman weaving grass-cloth, in a loom of primitive construction. She ceased from work as I approached the door, but commenced again, in obedience to my gestures. The shuttle was a little longer than the breadth of the stuff, and thrown by hand. At the foot of the hill Dr. Lynah found a piece of lignite, which resembles coal, but is unfortunately no indication of its presence. We had a long and toilsome ascent up a barren hill which brought us again upon a cultivated upland. There were three or four cattle grazing here, the first we had noticed since leaving Napha. We saw a horse now and then, but this animal appeared to be scarce. The dividing ridge between the bays was about three miles in advance, and though the afternoon was nigh spent, and the whole party was considerably fatigued, we determined to get sight of Barrow's Bay before encamping. At last we reached a large village on the western slope of the ridge. It was surrounded with plantations of banana, and a tall pine grove towered over it. Through a deep road gate, cut in the crest of the hill, a fine picture of Barrow's Bay and the mountains beyond presented itself to our view. The southern shore of the bay was about three miles distant, and a singular range of rocks, rising in detached square masses like the walls and towers of a ruined city, intervened. The landscape was more richly wooded than those on the southern bay, and the outlines of the hills were rounder and more gently undulating. We seemed to have reached a region of a different geological character. We were about to pitch our tent at this place, when the native officers gave us to understand that there was a *Cung-quà* a short distance further, and urged us so strongly to go on that we shouldered our muskets and haversacks and started again. But we had a rough tramp of nearly three miles further, and finally came, with bruised feet and aching shoulders, upon the last descent to Barrow's Bay. Picturesque crags studded the hillside, and a large village, completely covered with thickets of banana and bamboo, lay before us. Over it towered a tall crag, rent through the centre and surmounted with a square rock, like a ruined tower. We threaded the village by shaded alleys, and at the further end, on a spot commanding a fine view of the bay, found a handsome *Cung-quà*, in an enclosure planted with trees. A dignitary of some kind welcomed us, and we were at once served with small cups of excellent tea. The soft, thick mats, the shelter and comfort of the building, were well worth the fatigue of our forced march. Fresh water in earthen jars, with a square wooden ladle floating on the top, stood ready for us, and there was a kitchen in the rear where our men could cook conveniently. The Pe-ching came in after sunset and greeted us with much cordiality. Eggs and fowls were immediately furnished, and, as at our former camp, all payment was refused. The utmost curiosity appeared to prevail in the village respecting us, and, as it grew dark, the circle of heads peering over the wall enclosing the Cung-quà increased rapidly, till there could not have been less than two or three hundred. Fires were kindled all around us, and the ruddy glow thrown up by them and by the torches carried back and forth flickered brilliantly over the dusky foliage of the trees.

A watch was set as before, and the mosquitoes being less annoying we all enjoyed a tolerable rest. The Chinamen were, or feigned to be, completely spent, and for the greater part of the day the baggage had been carried by Lew Chew coolies. The patience, good humor, and endurance of the latter, quite put to shame the worthless and deceitful creatures whom we had been indiscreet enough to bring with us. The natives kept their counter-watch, and on rising before sunrise the next morning, we found that fifty or sixty of them had passed the night at their camp fires. The object of the officers in having a watch kept seemed to be both to prevent any of us from stealing a march upon them during the night, and to hinder any of the natives from annoying us.

Mr. Jones made application for a boat to carry us across the bay, but there was none to be had. The name of the village to which the Cung-quà belonged was "Missikya." We set our little file in motion and proceeded, by a pleasant path, over level land, a mile or two inland. The cultivation was thorough, but confined mostly to beans and sweet potatoes. The villages were so hidden away behind their alleys of tall, arched bamboo that the police scouts had little need to precede us. A native guide ran ahead; but as he constantly took the left-hand road, leading into the middle of the island, evidently with a view of conducting us back to Sheudi, we finally halted at the foot of an isolated hill, covered with wood, and held a consultation. The wild mountain-range north of Barrow's Bay now appeared on our right, and it was plain that our course was leading us away from the head of the bay, which we desired to reach. We, therefore, turned, in spite of the protestations of the guide and the native officers, and passed around the eastern brow of the hill, whereon we found two grottoes of soft limestone rock. The scenery here was a charming mixture of pine forest and cultivated field; and both in its features and its prevailing hue of dark-green resembled the landscapes of southern Germany.

In the bottom of the valley was a stream lined with bristling ranks of the *pandanus*, or false

pine apple. We were obliged to pull off our boots and wade. We here found a shrub with small white blossoms and bright-green milky leaves; another with yellow berries of a powerful aromatic taste; and a liliaceous plant, with a racine of flowers resembling those of the snap-dragon, but white in hue, with a fringed lip of the richest orange. At one of the villages on the plain I noticed the plum and the orange, and a new variety of the banyan, with very small glossy leaves. Beyond the stream we struck into fragrant pine woods, and finally into a dense forest, where the path was still wet and slippery from the rains, and the branches, meeting overhead, made a perpetual shade. There were few flowers, and still fewer birds, in this wilderness. In fact, the scarcity of birds all over the island, considering that they are not destroyed by the natives, is rather singular. The day was very clear and hot, and the trees, while they shaded us, quite shut off the sea breeze. The foliage was almost tropical, consisting of dense glossy-leaved shrubs and luxuriant ferns, overtopped by woods of pine. Smaller paths branched off here and there to the distant huts of the woodmen. After ascending for more than two miles, we crossed a ridge and the path became gradually more open, exposing a view to the west, over high hills, covered entirely with copsewood and patches of pine forest. The country resembled the wild lands of America. There were swamps in the hollows, and we began to look out for the wild boars which are said to exist in this part of the island. Catching another view to the eastward, we found ourselves near the head of Barrow's Bay, and after a half hour's halt, to rest the coolies, set out again. Our official escort came up during the halt, much fatigued, but as cordial and good humored as ever. Indeed, considering that all their trouble and fatigue were caused by ourselves, we had every reason to admire the unshaken patience with which they submitted to our apparently wayward course.

Crossing another hill, we passed down broad, well-trodden paths, shaded by magnificent arches of foliage, through a neat village. The houses were larger than usual, and there was an aspect of greater wealth. Among the trees was one fifteen feet high, covered with cream-colored blossoms, which exhaled the fragrance of nutmeg. An avenue of pines led down from this lovely spot to a narrow plain at the head of Barrow's Bay. The rice growing in these parts was very scanty and not yet in head. A large village, buried in trees, extended for half a mile inland from the sea shore. We took a path leading down to the beach; but Mr. Jones, who was in advance, entered the village, where he was very courteously received and twice presented with tea and pipes. The exhibition of his watch, and a pocket microscope, excited the unbounded wonder of the natives. The village was named "Isitza."

We forded a salt creek and pitched our noonday camp on a piny knoll, at the foot of the hills. As Mr. Jones had not arrived, we fastened our flag to the top of a tree and fired signals. I took a bath in the sea, with the men, while our kettle was boiling. The water was excessively saline, and the fine white particles of salt covered my face like dust as it became dry. At this point Mr. Jones found a stratum of gneiss, for the first time, at the water's edge. Our native friends drank three cups of our tea and asked for some biscuits, which they seemed to relish. Before starting again we had a talk with them about the route. We wished to reach a point on the coast north of Barrow's Bay, marked as "Kaneja" on our copy of the Japanese chart of Lew Chew. The officers did not seem to recognize any such place, though they spoke of "Kannâh," where there was a Cung-quà, 30 *li*, or ten miles distant, and we decided to reach it, if possible.

We left at half-past one, taking one of the natives as a guide. The path followed the line of the bay, and we walked, for two hours, in deep sand and crushed shells, around curve and headland. It was very toilsome work, especially as the glare of the sand struck directly in our faces. The beach was narrow and bordered with thick hedges of the pandanus, the fruit of which resembles that of the pine apple. The mountains on our left were wild and uncultivated. There were occasional paths striking up their sides; but, although the compass told us that the shore-path led us out of our true course, the guide refused to take any of them. At the end of two hours we reached a large village, where the guide, who had followed us from "Isitza," levied a substitute and turned back. A two-masted junk, of thirty or forty tons burden, lay at anchor in a cove near this place. We were now approaching the northern extremity of Barrow's Bay, and had a full view of the long headland south of it, and the four islands which lie, like a breakwater, across its mouth. The bay appeared to be extremely shallow, except near the entrance; and I doubt whether it would be of much value, as a harbor, for shipping of large size.

The path, finally, turned off to the north, up a steep hill, which brought us upon a rolling upland, covered with abundance of wood. The mountains we had passed exhibited an outline similar to the Catskills, and there was nothing in the scenery to remind us of the vicinity of the tropics. We presently entered a fine, broad avenue of pines, at the extremity of which appeared a handsome house, with a tiled roof. Our native conductors passed on into some bamboo arches, which denoted a village beyond; but I slipped suddenly into the open entrance and found a spacious house in the midst of a garden, with a small Buddhist temple beside it. Quick as my motions had been, the mats were already let down before all the doors, and nobody was to be seen. Before the house was a plant about ten feet high, with large scarlet panicles of flowers. I had barely time to break off a cluster when one of our officers came hurrying up and urged me, by signs and words, to leave, saying that the Bunyo, or Governor, as he designated Mr. Jones, had gone on. I, therefore, followed him through the village to a Cung-quà, which was larger and finer than any we had yet seen. It was like an elegant private residence; having a garden, enclosed by a square, clipped hedge of jessamine, and a separate establishment for servants and attendants. There were rows of chrysanthemums (a flower much esteemed by the Japanese) and two peach trees in the garden, besides a stout *camellia*, clipped into a fanciful shape. We installed ourselves in the chief apartment, on the soft matting, while the Pe-ching and his train took the other building. The only supplies we could procure were raw salt fish and sweet potatoes, with some roots of a native onion, pickled in salt. Neither fowls nor eggs could be found. The natives gave the name of the village as "Ching," which, being a Chinese word, is evidently incorrect; but we could get no other. The paper screens between the rooms were removed on our arrival, tea was brought in, and the natives busied themselves to make us comfortable; but the same unrelaxing espionage, as at "Missikya," was kept up through the whole night. Again camp-fires were kindled and guards posted around us, while crowds of curious natives peeped from behind the bushes and walls to gratify their desire of seeing us. Mr. Heine, who had the first watch, went out to the camp fire, showed the people his watch, and other curiosities, and soon had a large crowd of villagers gathered about him; but one of the officers making his appearance, a single word of command scattered them in all directions, and they did not return again. In the evening I offered a handful of cash to one of the boys who had accompanied us from Napha. He refused it very earnestly, as there were two other boys standing near; but, watching an opportunity, when he was alone, I offered it again, when he immediately accepted it, with gestures expressive of his thanks.

ENCAMPMENT OF THE EXPLORING PARTY IN LEW CHEW.

The Pe-ching, who had fallen in the rear, came up after dark, and immediately sought us, to make his salutations. We found that he and his associates had been keeping a journal of our proceedings, and had already filled a roll of paper several yards in length with their remarks. We had but few mosquitoes, and slept so well that I had some difficulty in rising for the mid-watch. After much search, two tough old hens were found for our breakfast, which we ate under the scrutiny of an hundred eyes, continually peering at us over walls, or popping out from behind bushes. Whenever we noticed any of them the heads disappeared, but they returned again as soon as our gaze was removed.

We were now commencing our fourth day, and it was time to think of turning back shortly. After some consultation, it was determined to follow the coast for a short distance further, then strike across the island in the direction of Port Melville, and reach in the evening a point on the western shore corresponding to the latitude of our present camp. On starting, the native officers were very urgent in requesting us to take a road leading westward. We kept, however, a course nearly due north, and soon reached a hill, whence there was an excellent view of the country on all sides. The northern headland of Barrow's Bay lay behind us. The general direction of the coast in advance was N.E., stretching away to a distant promontory. A spinal ridge of mountains, covered with a wilderness of forests, ran parallel with the coast, leaving a narrow strip of cultivated land next the sea. A column of smoke ascended from one of the northern peaks, which we judged (and rightly, as it afterwards proved) to be a fire in the woods.

Mr. Jones decided to make for a gorge between two peaks, about six miles distant, and rather to the east of north. We crossed a deep valley, with a salt creek at its bottom, and, after following the coast for some time, took a road which, after ascending a long barren ridge, plunged into the woods. The further we advanced, the more dense became the wilderness. The only persons we met were woodmen, whom we saw occasionally felling trees with their rude axes. The path was narrow, wet, and slippery, and for two or three miles a continual ascent. At length we reached a conical peak covered with trees. The ascent was very difficult, and I halted with the coolies at the base, while Mr. Jones, Dr. Lynah, and Mr. Heine, went up to obtain a view. By climbing the trees and cutting away some of the limbs, they opened space for a grand central panorama of the island, which Mr. Heine set about sketching from the tree-top. The path, which by this time had dwindled almost out of sight, passed directly over the summit. We found the ascent like a staircase, and were obliged to use hands and feet to reach the top. The Lew Chew coolies who carried our baggage made their way up with great difficulty. As we were all suffering from thirst, I started in advance, with the seaman Mitchell, the Chinamen, and the coolies. The path, which was now a faint woodman's trail, did not appear to have been travelled for months. It was shut in by a species of small bamboo, so dense as almost to exclude light, and a large, red, hairy spider had woven innumerable webs across it. Now ascending, now descending, we pushed ourselves or crept through the almost impervious copse wood, for nearly two miles, till the path became more open, and a partial look-out to the westward showed us the China sea. On the side of the nearest peak to the northward, we distinctly saw the woods on fire and a bare space of about ten acres studded with charred trunks. The descent was very slippery, but becoming more and more open, I at length recognized our position. We were approaching the head of the deep bight south of Port Melville, and separated from it by an arm of the island, which stretches out to the northwest,

178 EXPEDITION TO JAPAN.

at right angles to the main body. The curious peaked island called the "Sugar Loaf," off the point of this promontory, was in view before us. The western slope of the island at this point is covered almost entirely with forests, the cultivation being confined to the bottoms of valleys and ravines opening upon the sea.

The path led across the top of a narrow ledge about a yard wide, with chasms more than a hundred feet deep on each side, and then dropped to the bottom of the glen, where we found a stream of deliciously cool and sweet water. We all drank to excess, and then climbed a little ridge beyond, where the air blew fresh, and sat down to await the rest of the party. Mr. Jones found granite of fine quality in the ravine, and we afterwards met with another broad stratum in a rocky gateway further below. Our only path made for a village on the shore, whither we repaired for our mid-day halt. The houses were lined with luxuriant bananas, in blossom, and the lanes between them hedged with the glossy *inocarpus*, forming walls of foliage twenty feet in height, outside of which were neat wicker fences of split bamboo. Near the village were three structures raised upon timber frames, and covered with thatched roofs.

Valley and Rice Houses.

They appeared to be storehouses, elevated in this manner to preserve the grain from the moisture of the earth. Beneath them were wooden platforms, offering us shade and convenience for our halt. The people brought us sweet potatoes, a small pan of salt fish, and a pumpkin, which was all they could supply. Even these were refused us until the arrival of the Pe-ching, to whose authority all the others deferred. The rapidity of our march had left him in the rear, but he came up after an hour, and set himself to work with great good humor to supply our wants. In order to shield themselves from the heat of the sun, some of his attendants had tied banana leaves around their heads, and they all complained of fatigue.

We left Ny-komma, as the village was called, about half past two. At this, the most northern point we reached, we could not have been more than eight or nine miles distant from Port Melville. The intervening land was low, and another day would have enabled us to reach the head of that harbor. The native officials explained to us by signs, and by tracing lines on the sand, that the road to Sheudi lay along the beach, and that there was a Cung-quà about 20 *li* distant. We tramped along sandy beaches and over stony headlands, following the general course of the shore, and never diverging far from it. The bay, or bight, marked with numerous abrupt indentations, presented some fine bold outlines of shore. Off the many interior promontories lay rocky islets, covered with rich vegetation. The wooded mountains on our left were the same which we had skirted the day previous on the northern side of Barrow's Bay. The lower slopes on this side were partially cultivated, but the principal thoroughfare of the island, which we were following, kept near the sea, and often ran for half a mile through deep sand and shells. The scenery was extremely picturesque, reminding me of the coast of Sicily. Inside of the Sugar Loaf we espied two small boats, with lug-sails of white canvass, which the men declared were our ship's boats; but this has since proved to be a mistake.

Notwithstanding the sultry heat of the afternoon, the Lew Chew coolies kept pace with us, under their heavy loads, while our lazy and complaining Chinamen lagged behind. These coolies were mostly boys, from twelve to sixteen years of age. I noticed as a curious fact that, in spite of the heavy loads they carried, and the rough by-ways we frequently obliged them to take, they never perspired in the least, nor partook of a drop of water, even in the greatest heat. They were models of cheerfulness, alacrity, and endurance, always in readiness, and never, by look or word, evincing the least dissatisfaction. Our official conductors drank but two or three times of water during the whole journey. Tea appears to be the universal beverage of refreshment. It was always brought to us whenever we halted, and frequently offered to Mr. Jones, as the head of the party, in passing through villages. Once, at an humble fisherman's village, when we asked for *mizi*, which signifies cold water, they brought us a pot of hot water, which they call *yu*, and were much surprised when we refused to drink it.

After a march of ten miles along the picturesque shore, we reached one of the loveliest spots on the island. It was a village perched on a bold promontory, overgrown with the pine, banyan and sago palm, at the mouth of a charming valley which opened up between the hills to the base of the lofty peak behind Barrow's Bay. A stream of sweet water threaded the valley, which was covered with the freshest verdure, and overhung with beautiful groves of pine. It was a picture of pastoral loveliness, such as is rarely found in any country. Nothing struck me more during the journey than the great variety of scenery which the island encloses in its narrow compass. We passed through, at least, four different districts, which bore but the slightest resemblance to each other, either in features or character. We had both the groves of the tropics and the wild woods of the north; the valleys of Germany and the warm shores of the Mediterranean.

The village was large, thriving, and as neatly laid out and hedged in as an English garden. The scrupulous neatness and regularity of the Lew Chew villages was doubly refreshing to one familiar with the squalor and filth of China. The sight of the Cung-quà, which occupied the

180   EXPEDITION TO JAPAN.

place of honor at the top of the promontory, completed our raptures. Its roof of red tiles glittered in the sun; a row of feathery sago palms threw their brilliant leaves over the wall of the enclosure; the whitest and softest of mats covered the floor; the garden blazed with a profusion of scarlet flowers; and stone basins, seated on pedestals, contained fresh water for our use. Its aspect of comfort and repose was a balm to travellers as weary as ourselves, and I directed Terry at once to hoist the stars and stripes upon the roof. I hastened back to make a sketch of the beautiful valley before sunset, while Mr. Heine occupied himself with a view of the Cung-qua. A venerable old man, with a snowy beard reaching nearly to his knees, approached the bank where I sat, but upon noticing me, made a profound yet dignified reverence and retired. The village was named Uñ-ña. We had not yet reached the region of fowls, but the people sent us two small fresh fish, with a pumpkin and some cucumbers. Our own stores were quite low, both sugar and pork having been exhausted, so that we had nothing left but tea, coffee and ship biscuit.

Kung Kwa near On-na, Lew Chew.

The natives kindled a fire inside the grounds of the Cung-qua, and half a dozen of them sat around it all night. The morning was dull, and a cap of mist on the mountain threatened rain. A bath in the sea before sunrise refreshed us for the day's march. For our breakfast, there were sent two long, eel-like fish, resembling the gar, a few young egg-plants, two gourds and a basket of sweet potatoes. So much time was occupied in cooking and consuming these delicacies, that we did not get under way before 8 o'clock. Another consultation was held with our attendants, who declared that Shendi was 90 *li* distant, and that it would require three days for us to reach Napha; this did not correspond with our own ideas of our position, and we determined to attempt reaching Napha the next evening, as we had been ordered.

We passed through the village of Un-ña, and over the headland to a deep bay. The tide was running out, and instead of wading through the sand around its entire curve, we made a straight line for the opposite shore, tramping through water two or three inches deep over beds of decomposing coral. We had proceeded along the shore for an hour and a half, when A-shing, one of the Chinese coolies, fell sick in consequence, as it afterwards appeared, of drinking sackee, and eating green peaches. His load was given to the Lew Chew coolies, and he obtained a temporary relief by punching his throat, in three places, so violently as to produce an extravasation of blood. Counter irritation is the usual Chinese remedy for all ailments, and it is frequently very efficacious. We were near a fishing village, and Mr. Jones endeavored to obtain a canoe, in which to send both our Chinamen back to the vessel. The Pe-ching begged him to give up the idea, since one of the native officers would be obliged to accompany them, and they all feared to trust themselves in the frail craft. They brought a *kagoo*, or rude sedan, in which they offered to have the man conveyed to Napha, but he was better by this time and declared himself able to proceed on foot. The officers expressed the greatest satisfaction when they found that none of them would be required to return in the canoe.

In the meantime the rest of us had pushed forward with the baggage. The morning was very hot, the glare from the white beach-sand struck in our faces, and we began to tire of an endless tramp around cove after cove, and headland after headland. We were now, as we calculated, opposite the head of Barrow's Bay, and Sheudi was almost in a due southerly direction; yet the road still clung to the coast, as if intent on carrying us to the extreme point of Cape Broughton, thus greatly lengthening our journey, besides which, our orders were to return through the centre of the island. In answer to all our inquiries, the native officers and guides pointed along the shore, and were extremely anxious to prevent our taking any inland paths. This excited our suspicion, and we imagined their object to be to prevent our seeing the interior. Finally, coming to a well-trodden path, which struck off up the hills, we shut our ears to all remonstrance and took it. In a short time it brought us to a handsome village, shaded not only with bamboo, but with splendid banyan trees. Beyond it there was a deep ravine, with a faintly marked foot-path leading to some water at the bottom. Again the natives entreated us to take a path which plainly led to the shore. They pointed to the gorge, crying "*mizi*," intimating that the path went no further than the water. Nevertheless, seeing traces of a path on the opposite side, we descended, followed by the unwilling officers and coolies. The pool of water which supplied the village was shaded by the largest pines I saw on the island. They were 70 or 80 feet in height, whereas the average is not more than 40 feet.

Our suspicions did injustice to the natives, for we soon found that they had our convenience in view. Our path struck into a side-branch of the ravine, which, though not more than twenty feet wide, was a rice-swamp at the bottom. The sides were nearly perpendicular walls of earth and loose rocks, so that we were obliged to plunge up to the knees in mud. One of the men, Smith, sank so deep that it required the strength of three natives to extricate him. When, at last we reached the top of the hill, we found it covered with waste thickets, and no path to be seen except one on an opposite height, which we reached with some trouble. The path, an old and unused one, led us back to the beach, which it now seemed impossible to leave. The coolies, who had had a hard tug to get through the rice-swamp, took the whole matter very good humoredly, and the officers laughed, as I thought, with a sort of malicious pleasure at our discomfiture. The walk over the white sand was doubly fatiguing after this, and on the arrival of Mr. Jones we determined again to make for the interior, especially as we had reached the head of the last cove, whence the coast appeared to run almost due westwardly to Cape Broughton.

Mr. Jones and Dr. Lynah, with the men Davis and Smith, took a foot-path leading southward into the mountains, and after proceeding a little further along the coast I followed them with the seaman Mitchell. Mr. Heine, with Terry and the Lew Chew coolies, still kept the shore. We (Mitchell and I) reached with great difficulty the path taken by the first party. It ascended steeply through pine forests, alternating with dense copsewood, for about two miles, till we gained the summit of the ridge. The whole expanse of Barrow's Bay came full into view to the eastward, while to the south we looked beyond the promontory we had been doubling so tediously, and saw the same deep cove we had beheld three days before from the top of Banner Rock. But all the interior of the island was still a wilderness, and for ten miles in advance stretched an unbroken forest. Our path did not appear to have been much travelled—other small paths branched from it, but the party in advance had broken off boughs and left them as guides for us. I was much spent with the heat and the exertion of climbing so rapidly, and after drinking out of a muddy hole filled with leaves, felt an attack of mingled heat and cold, with an oppression of the heart, which took away all my strength. We saw the other party on the top of a high peak ahead of us. The path crossed a ledge as narrow as a wall, with deep gulfs on each side, and then ascended a rocky ladder, the steepness of which took away what little strength I had remaining—I was obliged to lie down for some time before I could proceed further. A raincloud coming up rapidly over Barrow's Bay admonished us to leave our lofty look-out. The path kept on southward through miles of wilderness, but the natives who had accompanied us pointed to another, which led back almost the way we came, and which they said would bring us to a Cung-quà. As there were no signs of the baggage, we were thus under the necessity of retracing our steps almost to the shore. On our way we passed through a singular gorge, which was closed up, in its narrowest part, by fragments hurled from above by some convulsion of nature. The stream flowing at the bottom disappeared for about fifty yards, when it again issued to the light through a cavernous opening.

A rain now came on, which continued for two or three hours, and made the road slippery and toilsome. We passed through a village, romantically situated in a wooded glen, and over uplands, covered with groves of pine, the path gradually swerving to the south, till it finally struck directly across the promontory. A great part of the way was a waste of wild thickets, with marshy hollows between the hills. We saw, several times, the tracks of wild boar, which the natives assured us were abundant; but we were not so fortunate as to get a sight of one. There were no traces of our baggage until we found the Pe-ching, and two other natives, crouching under a bush to keep out of the rain and smoking their pipes. Finally, about half-past two, we heard the report of fire-arms, and soon after reached the Cung-quà of "*Chanda-kosa*," where M. Heine and the coolies had already been waiting some time for us. We were uncertain whether the building was a *bona fide* Cung-quà or the residence of a *bunyo*, or officer, for it was occupied, when Mr. Heine arrived, by a personage of some kind with his attendants, but immediately given up for our use. There was a crowd of at least a hundred natives collected within the enclosure and looking on, with great astonishment, while Mr. Heine fired at a mark. What seemed most to interest them, next to the accuracy of his aim, was the fact of the piece exploding without the application of fire, (nothing but Japanese matchlocks ever being seen on the island,) and its being loaded at the breech. They appeared familiar with the nature of

gunpowder, and the use of our cutlasses; but during our journey we never saw a single weapon of any kind. There is said to be a small garrison of Japanese soldiers, both at Napha and Sheudi; but, if so, they were carefully kept out of the way.

The Pe-ching, who soon afterwards came up, informed us that we had come 30 *li*, and that Sheudi was still 60 *li* distant, and we could not reach it on the following day. Learning, however, that there was another Cung-quà 20 *li* further, we decided to rest an hour or two, and push on to it the same evening. The people brought two fowls, with abundance of eggs and cucumbers, and, hungry and tired as we were, we made a most palatable meal.

We left again at half-past four. The road was broad, well beaten, and shaded by a double road of pine trees. It ran in a southeastern direction, parallel with the coast, and about two miles inland. The country continued open, slightly undulating, and pleasantly diversified with groves of pine for four miles, when we came suddenly upon a deep glen, traversed by much the largest stream we had seen upon the island. The road crossed by a massive stone bridge, of three arches, remarkable for the size and rude strength of the piers, each of which had, on the inner side, in order to protect it from floods, a triangular abutment, projecting ten or twelve feet. The sides of the glen were nearly perpendicular, and covered with wild and luxuriant vegetation. Towards the sea, under a range of broken limestone crags that hung high over the stream, were several ancient excavated tombs. A spring of excellent water gushed out from the foot of one of these crags. Mr. Heine took a sketch of the place, which was remarkable for its seclusion and picturesque beauty. The natives called the stream the "*Fi-ija*."

On reaching a height overlooking the sea, we were agreeably surprised with the sight of the squadron, lying off the furthest point to the southwest, and between fifteen and twenty miles distant, in a straight line. This encouraged us to believe that we could reach Napha at the time appointed, and we pushed on rapidly and cheerily, for it was now growing dark, and no appearance of the Cung-quà. The road approached the shore, and became a raised causeway, passing through rich rice swamps. The natives whom we met in the dusk of the evening took to flight on seeing us. At last, at half-past seven, weary and spent with a tramp of twenty-seven miles, the native herald who ran before us turned into a gateway, over which towered a magnificent banyan tree. We followed, and discharged our pieces in a general *feu-de-joie*, on seeing a Cung-quà with the lamps lighted, attendants waiting with their trays of tea-cups, and a polite old gentleman standing in the verandah to receive us. The Lew Chew mats were never so soft, nor the cups of unsugared native tea so refreshing, as on that evening. Eggs, cucumbers, rice, and fowls were immediately forthcoming, and our men concocted a soup which, to our minds, could not have been improved. The old Pe-ching made his appearance at a late hour, nearly as fatigued as ourselves, but overflowing with cordiality and good humor. A company of native guards kindled a fire under the banyan tree, and prepared to spend the night there. Our men were so fatigued that, in anticipation of another hard journey on the morrow, we dispensed with the usual watch. It was the less important, as we had found the native guard exceedingly vigilant in keeping away all stragglers from our vicinity. The light of the ruddy camp-fire, playing over the spreading boughs of the banyan-tree, brought into strong relief the groups of swarthy faces clustered around it, and presented a picture so fantastic and peculiar that I sat looking at it long after I ought to have been asleep.

The sound of rain upon the tiles of our Cung-quà awoke us frequently during the night, and when we arose at daybreak the sky was overcast, the roads flooded, and a steady dismal storm had set in. The Pe-ching and his associates wished us to stay at "Pi-ko," as the Cung-quà was called, until the next day, slapping their legs to indicate how tired they were, and making signs of slipping up and falling down in the mud. But we were inexorable, and they sent for a new set of coolies to carry our baggage. We had another discussion about the distance, which ended in their declaring that Sheudi was 65 *li* and Napha 30 *li* distant. This was absurd, and probably ought to be attributed to the ignorance of the Chinese, through whom we communicated with them. The coolies prepared themselves for the rain by putting on shaggy jackets of grass, resembling the sheep-skin garments of the Roman herdsmen. Our men had their pea-jackets, and we were partially protected by ponchos of gutta-percha and oilcloth. We were delayed in getting breakfast, and did not break up our camp until half-past nine, when we set out, everybody stiff and sore from the previous day's travel. The rain was still falling, though not so heavily as at first, and the road was an alternation of water and stiff mud, through which we trudged with difficulty, and at the risk of leaving our boots behind us. After rounding the head of the bight, we struck off over the hills to the southwest, and in an hour and a half came upon another deep glen, in the bottom of which were two massive bridges over a stream so broad and deep that it was doubtless a frith of the sea. We stopped an hour to rest and enable Mr. Heine to take a sketch of the place. I noticed that the heavy triangular abutments to the piers were here placed on the side next the sea. The natives gave the glen, or river, the name of "Machinatoo."

The rain had ceased by this time, except an occasional sprinkle, and the road improved. After another hour the roads branched, that on the left striking off up the hills to Sheudi. We kept on over the hills towards Napha, the scenery gradually assuming a familiar appearance, till finally, from a height covered with pine trees, we looked down upon the harbor and the American squadron. After fording a broad salt creek, and crossing another ridge, we descended to the village of Tumé, opposite Napha. We reached our starting point, the house of Dr. Bettelheim, at 2 p. m., and there took leave of our worthy Pe-ching and his two assistants, after having appointed a time to meet them again, and endeavor to return some compensation for the provision furnished during the journey.

The distance we travelled during the six days was 108 miles, as nearly as we could calculate. Our trip embraced a little more than half the island, leaving the extremity south of Napha, (which is of limited extent,) and that part north of the head of Port Melville, and lying on both sides of that harbor, for future exploration."*

On the return of the party Mr. Jones submitted the following report to the Commodore of his observations:

"Before describing the ancient royal castle of Chun-Ching, which we discovered in our recent exploration of Lew Chew, it may be well to say a few words about the geology of the island, as the two are connected with each other.

Going northward from Napha we find the general surface-rock to be argillaceous, either compact or shaly, which is intersected, at frequent intervals, by dykes or ridges of secondary limestone, of a very remarkable character. When we get as high up as Barrow's Bay the argillaceous rock ceases, and is succeeded by talcose slate, in which, however, the same limestone dykes occur. At the most northern point reached by us, that is, at the village of Nacumma, on the west side of the island, say forty-two miles north of Napha, we reached granite, rising there

---

* This report is from the pen of Mr. Bayard Taylor, who, it will be remembered, was directed by Commodore Perry to keep a journal of the incidents of the exploration, and make the report.

into a hill of some elevation, but so soft as easily to be cut by a hatchet. This granite is of a grey color, sometimes almost white; and its mica, which is black, lies scattered about in the mass in beautiful six-sided crystals, giving it often a handsome appearance.

The talcose slate has a strike of S. 10° W., and a dip to the W. of 60°. It is mixed with quartz and other foreign ingredients of a hard character, and comes to the surface in sharp, jagged edges: very severe upon the feet.

The argillaceous rock gives some marked features to the island. The rounded hills south of Barrow's Bay are all of this. Being soft, it yields readily to foreign agencies, and is often broken into bare faces, with perpendicular sides; and thus, at the head of their valleys, sometimes presents us with beautiful cascades. It also forms the chief ingredient in the soil of the island—in wet weather a very adhesive clay.

But the limestone dykes are the distinguishing feature of, at least, this portion of Lew Chew. They cross the island in ranges of N. 50° E. and N. 60° E., rising up into peaks and castellated forms, often so much like ruins of ancient buildings as to make a near examination necessary in order to undeceive ourselves. The rock is highly granular, but still has in it, not unfrequent remains of marine animals. Sometimes it is sufficiently compact; but, though always hard, it is generally so vesicular as, when weather-stained, to have exactly the appearance of lava, for which, indeed, it is often mistaken. Its vesicular character opens it to the action of foreign agencies, and, in consequence, along the sea and bay shores it is often undermined by the waves, or, if harder pebbles find their way there, is by their friction worked into kettle-shaped holes, with ragged, knife-shaped edges between. Where the roads in Lew Chew are paved it is with this vesicular rock; and the pavement can be exceeded, in discomfort to the traveller, only by the sticky mud, from which it is intended to be a protection.

On the second day of our journey (Tuesday) we were, towards noon, travelling on the summit of one of these limestone ridges, with precipitous sides descending on either hand. I was ahead of the party and saw before me, by and by, a something, which I took, at first, to be the natural rock crossing my road; till, presently, I saw what looked like a window, or some such opening, at its top. A nearer approach showed it, to my great surprise, to be this old deserted castle of Chun-Ching.

The builders had taken advantage of a spot where the two perpendicular faces of the ridges approached each other sufficiently near; and here, on the edges of the natural rock, had erected their walls, giving to the sides of their castle a great additional height; one end, also, was in part protected by a similar bold face of the rock. The road by which I came was conducted along outside of the main castle, though it was still carried through the fortifications, which it entered and left through gateways in very thick walls. The walls themselves were in the style so common in Lew Chew, called in architecture the Cyclopean style, though the stones employed here are much smaller than their architypes in the old Cyclopean walls of Greece. The builders of Chun-Ching contrived also to give their walls that inward curve which seems to have been the fashion in Lew Chew castellated buildings, and which we see also in the royal castle in Sheudi.

Since our return I have learnt, through Dr. Bettelheim, that Chun-Ching was once a royal residence. There were, in early times, seven kingdoms in Lew Chew, each with its royal castle or capitol, and Chun-Ching was one of them. The number was afterwards reduced to three, then to one, as it at present remains.

What I have marked as places for burning incense (*a*, *a*, &c.) are little oven-like buildings, which are common, also, to their temples and *kung-kwas*, and which Dr. B. tells me are for burning paper. The Lew Chewans have a regard, somewhat like that of Mohomedans, for any paper with a sacred name upon it; and lest such may be trodden under foot, and so desecrated, they burn them in the little edifices alluded to.

Before dismissing the geology of Lew Chew, I ought to say that, just south of Nacumma, we crossed, along the shore, numerous patches of recently formed rocks. The rolled pebbles of the shore, together with fragments of coral, and anything else that may happen to come in, are agglutinized by carbonate of lime, (probably the washings of coral reefs,) and are formed into a firm compact rock. This rock is only about a foot thick, and lies in table-like fragments upon the sands, where it was formed. I saw a similar recently made rock, of fine sandstone, on the beach, just west of Point de Galle, in Ceylon.

The Lew Chew Islands.

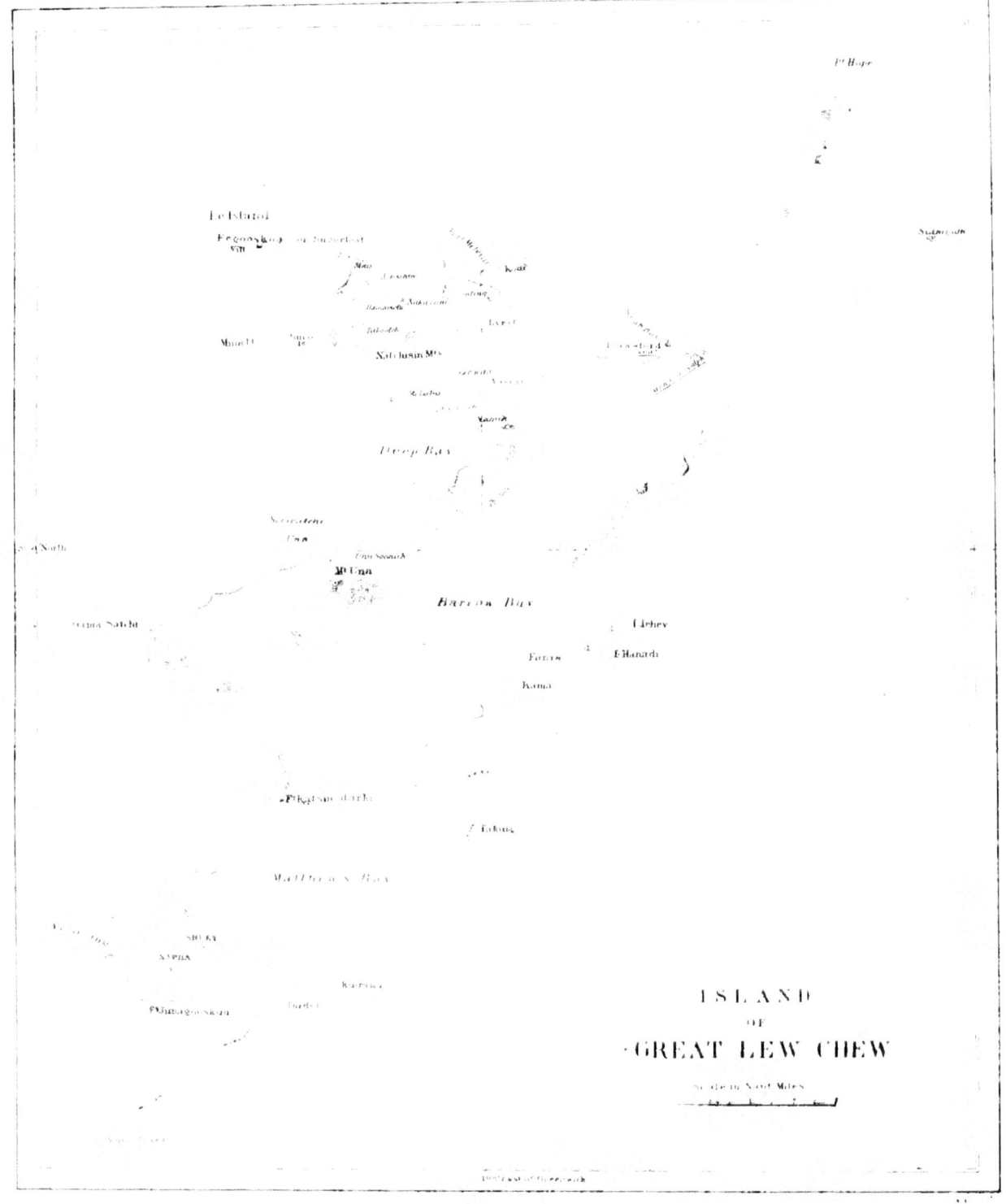

CHAPTER IX.

EFFORTS OF AUTHORITIES OF LEW CHEW TO PREVENT A VISIT TO THE PALACE.—ALL UNSUCCESSFUL.—LANDING FOR THE VISIT.—PROCESSION.—APPEARANCE OF THE COUNTRY.—RECEPTION AT THE PALACE.—EMBARRASSMENT OF THE REGENT.—ENTERTAINMENT AT THE REGENT'S HOUSE.—SAKI.—NEW DISHES.—COMMODORE INVITES AUTHORITIES TO A DINNER ON BOARD THE SUSQUEHANNA.—GENERAL IMPRESSIONS PRODUCED BY THE VISIT.—ESPIONAGE STILL KEPT UP.—DAILY EXERCISE OF SAILORS AND MARINES.—SETTLEMENT OF ACCOUNTS WITH LEW CHEW AUTHORITIES.—MISSISSIPPI AND SUPPLY REMAIN AT LEW CHEW.—SUSQUEHANNA AND SARATOGA LEAVE FOR THE BONIN ISLANDS.—DEATH OF AN OPIUM SMOKER ON THE PASSAGE.—INHUMANITY OF CHINESE.—SUNDAY ON BOARD.—ARRIVAL AT PORT LLOYD.

HE determination of the Commodore to return the visit of the regent, at the palace, and nowhere else, had been seemingly acquiesced in by the Lew Chew dignitary; but, in truth, he had but yielded to a necessity. The Commodore had power to carry out his determination, and the regent deemed it most prudent to concur, with the semblance of politeness, in that which he could not prevent.

This, however, did not induce that functionary and his subordinate officers to spare their efforts in the attempt to escape the much dreaded visit to the palace. Accordingly, they resorted to divers devices and stratagems, too clumsy, however, to be deemed either ingenious or cunning. In the first place, they begged that the Commodore would return the visit at Napha instead of Shui; then the effort was made to entrap the commander into a meeting with the regent, which would have been considered a return of the latter's visit. In pursuance of this scheme, the mayor of Napha made a great feast, some days before that named by the Commodore for his visit, and invited him to be present, with the intention of having the regent attend and preside. The invitation was politely declined, on the ground that the storeship, Caprice, was about to be dispatched on the appointed day to Shanghai, and the Commodore would necessarily be occupied. When the Lew Chewans found that the Commodore did not attend, they were determined that he should not, at any rate, lose the feast that had been prepared for him, and accordingly sent off to the ship numerous dishes of the intended banquet. These, as a matter of courtesy, were allowed to come on board, and very soon the quarter-deck exhibited various preparations of poultry, fish, vegetables, and fruits. The Commodore, however, from considerations of policy, thought it best to be invisible.

The next device was to appeal to the humanity of the Commodore, and the request was preferred that he would make his visit to the palace of the prince instead of at the royal residence,

The reason assigned was, that the queen dowager was sick, and had been for a year, in consequence of the shock received on the visit of a British naval officer, who persisted in entering the royal residence, to present a letter from Lord Palmerston to the Lew Chew government; and it was intimated that a repetition of such desecration of the palace would add to the malady of the queen, if, indeed, it did not produce a fatal termination.

The Commodore, who did not believe one word of the queen dowager's illness, and who was quite convinced also that all this manœuvring and trickery were designed merely to satisfy the spies kept about the Lew Chewans by the Japanese government, replied to this affecting appeal, that it was his duty to go where an officer of the Queen of England had been before him to have an audience; and that, if the queen dowager did not see fit to remove to the palace of her son during his intended visit, he thought that the pageantry, music, &c., attending it (purely peaceful) might divert her mind, and tend rather to amuse her; while, if she wished, his learned physicians, who would accompany him, would be most happy to exercise their skill for her benefit, and assist in restoring her to health.

At last, all devices having utterly failed to move the Commodore from his purpose, the day came which he had designated for his visit to the regent. It was matter of policy to make a show of it, and hence some extra pains were taken to offer an imposing spectacle. The day opened cloudily with a brisk wind stirring, and did not at first seem to promise a propitious season; but after a morning shower the sky came out bright and blue, and until evening the aspect of nature was as fresh and beautiful as could have been desired.

The hour of departure had been fixed at 9 o'clock. Presently the signal was made from the flag-ship, and all the boats of the other ships pushed off at the same time, and as they pulled to the land presented a very lively appearance. The point selected for landing was the little village of Tumai, about two miles from the palace of Shui. After all the other boats had gone, the Commodore set out in his barge, and on his arrival the marines were found, under arms, and in line, under a grove of trees by the road-side, near the landing. Groups of officers in uniform were gathered in little knots under the shade of the trees; the boats' crews rested on their oars, looking with interest on the proceedings, while the natives to the number of hundreds (many of them of the better class) stood around, evidently not a little moved and excited by the scene before them.

The Commodore, with the captain of the fleet and Commanders Buchanan, Lee, and Walker, then passed down the line of the marines and artillerymen, when the procession was immediately formed. First came two field-pieces, under the command of Lieutenant Bent, each having above it the American ensign, and immediately preceded by the master of the Susquehanna, (Mr. Bennett,) with Mr. Williams and Dr. Bettelheim, the interpreters. Next followed the band of the Mississippi with a company of marines, under command of Major Zeilin. The Commodore followed then in a sedan chair, which had been manufactured for the nonce, by the carpenter on board the ship. It was emphatically a dignified vehicle, as became the occasion, large and stately, deeply indebted to paint and putty, not quite as polished as a turnout from Newark or Longacre, but, on the whole, decidedly a feature in the procession, though its hangings of red and blue were not of the finest. At all events, it was the most imposing sedan the Lew Chewans ever saw. It was borne by eight Chinese coolies, four relieving each other alternately. On each side of it marched a marine as body guard, while a handsome boy had been selected as a page, who, with a Chinese steward, were the immediate personal attendants.

Captain Adams, Lieutenant Contee, and Mr. Perry, followed the sedan. Next appeared six coolies bearing the presents designed for the prince and queen dowager, and guarded by a file of marines. Then came the officers of the expedition, headed by Captains Buchanan, Lee, and Sinclair, followed by their servants. Next were the band of the Susquehanna, and a company of marines closed the procession, which in numbers amounted to some two hundred or more.

The whole procession was well arranged and picturesque in effect; while the beauty of the day, the verdure of the hills and fields, and the cheerful music of the bands gave life and spirit to the occasion. The natives clustered thickly on the sides of the road to gaze on the glittering novelty, while crowds of them hung in the rear of the cortege. They did not manifest the smallest apprehension, notwithstanding the presence of the marines under arms, and evidently were pleasantly excited by the spectacle before them. When the procession passed through any narrow lane the natives nearest to them knelt, the rank behind stooped down, and the rear remained erect, that all might have an opportunity of seeing. Very soon the procession emerged from the village, and came out upon the open undulating country south of Sheudi. The picture here was perfect. The fields of upland rice were gracefully bending like waves before the wind; the groves and hill sides were dark with the deep-green foliage, so suggestive of cool shady retreats, while, in the distance, the roof-tops of Sheudi, glittering in the sun, revealed, here and there, a spot of dazzling brightness amid the thick leafy covering of the trees in which the city was embosomed. Under clumps of the Lew Chew pine the pleased natives were gathered in groups, while others might be seen running along the ridges that divided the rice fields, that they might head the procession, and thus gain another view; while over all the music from the bands floated far around, and added to the pleasurable excitement of the march. As the procession ascended the hill of Shui the officers and men, who had been so long confined to the monotony of ship-board life, gazed around with delight, perfectly charmed with the rich cultivated landscape that stretched away to the southward and westward.

The officer designated to receive the Commodore at the landing, and conduct him to the capital, was the Pe-ching who had been, in the previous week, with the exploring party into the interior. When the procession arrived at the gate of Shui, it was met by a crowd of native dignitaries, with their attendants, all in their best robes of grass cloth, and with the red and yellow *hatchee-matchees*, or peculiar Lew Chew cap, on their heads. The old regent and his three venerable coadjutors here appeared, and after salutations, turned and accompanied the procession into the city. It passed on without halting, through the central arch, and marched up the principal street. A large train of attendants was in the retinue of the regent and chiefs; some carried umbrellas, others bore *chow-chow*, or refreshment boxes, cases for cups, and other articles. There was an inscription in Chinese characters over the central arch, which was translated by Mr. Williams to signify "The place of authority;" under this arch the common people were not allowed to pass.

The main street showed, on either side, high walls, with occasional alleys branching from it on both sides. The native officers kept the streets clear of spectators, except at one spot, where an alley branched off to the left. Here was a dense crowd, and here also was exhibited the final device to prevent the Commodore from going to the palace. The regent's own residence was not far from the entrance of the street thus crowded, and here that dignitary requested, through the interpreter, that the procession should at once go to his house and partake of the refreshments he had provided. Mr. Williams, who saw at once the object of the request, paid no attention to it, but marched straight on to the palace gate. It was obvious that the regent had anticipated that his stratagem would prove successful, for the gate of the palace was closed. A messenger, however, was dispatched, at full speed, to cause it to be opened, and make preparations for the Commodore's reception. On arriving at the entrance, the artillery and marines were drawn up in line, and the Commodore and his suite walked past them into the castle or palace; the troops presented arms, the ensigns were lowered, and the band played "Hail Columbia."

On entering the first gateway, a second wall and portal were seen above, (for the edifice stood on a cliff or elevation of rock, which formed, indeed, part of its foundation,) and this second gateway formed the entrance to the outer court of the palace, which crowned the height. This court was surrounded by houses, which seemed to be designed for servants and others belonging to the royal household. On the eastern side, however, was another gateway, resembling the Chinese portals of honor. This consisted of *two* arches, and the Commodore was conducted, as a mark of honor and respect due to his rank, through that on the right hand, into what appeared to be the central court of the palace. It was about eighty feet square, with very plain wooden buildings, of one story only, on its sides, and was paved with gravel and large tiles, arranged in alternate lozenges. The hall of reception was on the north side. All the other buildings, on the other sides, were protected by screens from the view of those in the court.

The Commodore was conducted into the hall of audience, and placed in a chair at the head of the room, on the right hand side; the officers followed, and were ranged in chairs on a single line, next to the Commodore, according to rank. These chairs were of some dark wood, lacquered, and were like our camp stools. There was also a double line of members of the Commodore's retinue across the bottom of the room. On the left side of the apartment sat the regent, with his three principal councillors, and a double rank of attendants stood behind them. The interpreters stood at the head of the room, near the Commodore, but between him and the regent. All having been thus accommodated, time was afforded for looking around. On the wall was a large red tablet, inscribed with Chinese characters, which signify, in English, "The elevated inclosure of fragrant festivities;" an inscription, by the way, which seems more appropriate to a place of feasting than to a hall of diplomacy or state receptions, where there is ordinarily little fragrance and less festivity.

The queen dowager, who had been so pathetically represented as being sick, did not, of course, make her appearance; nor did the boy prince, for whom the regent governed. After mutual salutations, tables were brought, and cups of very weak tea were presented to the guests. Smoking boxes were also distributed around the room, and twists of very tough gingerbread were placed on the table. In short, it was obvious that the visit at the palace was unexpected: it had been supposed, probably, that the stratagem of the regent to prevent it, by taking the Commodore to his own house, would succeed; and, consequently, no preparations had been made for the reception of the company at the palace. Presently the Commodore invited the regent and his three colleagues to visit him on board the Susquehanna. He stated that he intended leaving Napha in a day or two, but that, after ten days, he should return again, and would receive them at any time they might choose to appoint, either before his departure or after his return. They replied that they would leave the time of the visit to be named by the Commodore, and he stated that he would prefer it should be made after his return. To this they assented with seeming satisfaction. The next step in the ceremonies consisted in the regent's taking several large red cards, similar to those used on state occasions in China, when he

and his three companions rose, advanced a few steps, and bowed profoundly. The Commodore and all the officers rose and bowed in return, but without precisely understanding what the homage of the Lew Chewans particularly meant; they were determined, however, not to be outdone in the outward symbols of civility.

The Commodore then tendered to the regent such articles as he might need or desired to possess, provided he had them on board any of the ships, adding that it would give him pleasure to supply them. Hereupon, the four dignitaries rose again, advanced, and bowed as before. The interview was becoming rather uninteresting, and it was quite plain that the magnates of Lew Chew were, from some cause or other, not quite at their ease.

After about an hour the regent rose and proposed that the Commodore should visit him now, at his own house. This was alike intelligible and agreeable, and the procession was formed and marched to the street where it had been invited to enter on its way to the palace. The house of the regent was spacious, consisting of a central hall, with wings open to the court-yard, from which it was separated by a narrow verandah only. The floor was covered with fine matting. It was at once apparent that most hospitable preparations had here been made for the entertainment of the American visitors. Four tables were set in the central apartment, and three in each of the wings, and these were covered with a most bountiful collation. Immediately on entering the guests were desired to seat themselves, the Commodore, with Captains Buchanan and Adams, occupying the highest table on the right hand, and the regent and his associates the one opposite on the left. A pair of chop-sticks was placed at each corner of every table; in the centre was an earthen pot filled with *sakee*, (the intoxicating drink made by the Lew Chewans,) surrounded with four acorn cups, four large, coarse China cups, with clumsy spoons of the same material, and four teacups. On each table were dishes to the number of some twenty, of various sizes and shapes, and the exact basis of some of which no American knoweth to this day; *possibly* it was pig. Of the dishes, however, which were familiar to western apprehension there were sliced boiled eggs, which had been dyed crimson, fish made into rolls and boiled in fat, pieces of cold baked fish, slices of hog's liver, sugar candy, cucumbers, mustard, salted raddish tops, and fragments of lean pork, fried. Cups of tea were first handed round; these were followed by very small cups of sakee, which had the taste of French *liqueur*. Small bamboo sticks, sharpened at one end, and which some of the guests mistook for toothpicks, were furnished, to be used as forks in taking balls of meat and dough from the soup, which made the first course. Soup constituted also the next *seven* courses of the twelve, whereof the repast consisted. The other four were gingerbread, salad made of bean sprouts and young onion tops, a basket of what appeared to be some dark red fruit, but proved to be artificial balls composed of a thin dough rind covering a sugary pulp, and a delicious mixture compounded of beaten eggs and a slender white root with an aromatic taste.

Novel as was this bill of fare, the gentlemen of the expedition endeavored, with true courtesy, to do honor to the repast, and at the end of the twelfth course respectfully took leave, though they were assured there were twelve more to come. The number of the courses indicated the desire to do our countrymen a double share of honor, inasmuch as twelve is the prescribed number for a royal entertainment. The Lew Chewans, far removed as they are from the conventionalities of western civilization, seemed, notwithstanding, to understand very well the habit of drinking toasts and giving sentiments, and, indeed, were ready enough to drink on private account, without any stately formality, as the sakee circulated freely during the eight courses of soup.

When the Commodore supposed the solids were about to appear, he rose and proposed as a toast the health of the queen mother and the young viceroy, adding, "Prosperity to the Lew Chewans, and may they and the Americans always be friends." This, having been translated to the regent, appeared greatly to gratify him, and was drunk standing, with Lew Chew honors, which consist of draining the small cup of sakee, holding a teaspoon full, at one gulp, and turning the vessel bottom upward. The Commodore afterward proposed the health of the regent and his associates, which the latter returned by proposing the health of the Commodore and the officers of the squadron. By this time the embarrassment and anxious looks of the Japanese officials had entirely vanished; from what cause they had proceeded our officers could not learn, but most probably from the consciousness that they were under espionage, and that all they said or did would be reported to those above them. The entertainment, however, proceeded and terminated with the best possible feeling on both sides.

The interpreter of the regent was a young native, named *Ichirazichi*, who had been educated at Pekin, where he remained three years. He could speak a little English, but the Chinese was the language of communication. This youth had some knowledge both of the United States history and geography. He was not unacquainted with the character and conduct of Washington, and called him "a very great mandarin." Where is it that the honored name of the Father of our country, this man for all time, this man, whose peerless purity is the proud heritage of a common humanity the world over, has not reached? It is heard in the Arab tent, and in the Chinese village, under the shades of Lew Chew, and in the cities of Japan, in southern Asia, and on the shores of the Arctic: all western Christendom knows it, all honors it.

At length the feast was over, and the American guests took their departure, the procession forming in the same order as before. The subordinate Japanese officials escorted it to the gate, and the old Pe-ching again took his station in advance. On starting down the hill, four little ponies, which had gone up without finding riders, were now led by the grooms to the rear of the procession, and some of the younger officers determined to try their mettle in a ride down. They were very small animals, of bay color, but exceedingly spirited; and, kicking and plunging with untiring vivacity, and somewhat of temper, treated, at first, with sublime contempt all efforts to reduce them to a gravity befitting the occasion, and indignantly resisted every attempt to induce them, with the rational sobriety of discreet brutes, to take their places in the rear, and march understandingly, as became them. Like ill-bred ponies, as they were, they kicked up their heels, and endeavored to do much as they pleased. This, however, merely afforded more fun to the officers than if the wiry little creatures had behaved themselves discreetly as part of the American procession.

The descent of the hill was rather warm, as it was not far from noon, and the sun shone full in the faces of the procession; but, on reaching the wooded slopes, it was met by the grateful sea-breeze, and the boats were seen quietly resting on the waters of the bay, while their crews were scattered in groups under the trees, watching the coming on of the procession, and waiting to know whether due honor had been shown to the United States in the person of their "Old Commodore." Each boat had the American colors flying, and Jack was made happy by the assurance that all possible respect had been paid to his flag. By half-past two, the whole procession was again on board the ships, without any accident or untoward incident having occurred to mar either the pleasure or success of the trip; and thus ended the grand official visit to the palace. It was a judicious determination on the part of the Commodore to make it;

and, having announced such determination to the Lew Chewans, it was especially wise to carry it through to the letter. The moral influence produced by such a steadfast adherence to his avowed purposes very soon exhibited itself. It was part of the Commodore's deliberately formed plan, in all his intercourse with these orientals, to consider carefully before he announced his resolution to do any act; but, having announced it, he soon taught them to know that he would do precisely what he had said he would. To this single circumstance much of his success is to be attributed. He never deceived them by any falsehood, nor ever gave them reason to suppose that his purposes could be altered by their lies and stratagems. They, of course, saw at once that he was resolute, and that it was dangerous to trifle with him. His whole diplomatic policy was simply to stick to the truth in everything—to mean just what he said, and do just what he promised. Of course, it triumphed over a system which admitted of no truth, but for purposes of deception.

Several little circumstances connected with the excursion attracted the notice of the Commodore, and, as illustrative of manners and customs, deserve a passing notice. The first was the exceeding cleanliness of the Lew Chewans, and their striking contrast to the Chinese in this particular. The Commodore, speaking of Shui, says: "Never have I seen a city or town exhibiting a greater degree of cleanliness; not a particle of dirt, or even dust, could be seen, so different is it from the filthiness of all Chinese cities."

The road over which the procession passed was remarkably well constructed. It was elaborately paved with coral rock, very neatly fitted together, and the upper surface rendered smooth, either by artificial means or the constant attrition of travel.

The peasantry who hung upon the edges of the procession seemed to be of the lowest orders seen in Lew Chew, and exhibited a squalid and rather miserable appearance; many of them were naked, with the exception of a small piece of cloth about the loins; and among the thousands of these people attracted by the novelty of the spectacle, singular as it may appear, not a woman was to be seen. The great population of the island may, therefore, fairly be inferred from the large multitudes assembled, composed of but one half of the common people. These men who were seen probably compose the laboring class, receiving for their daily toil scanty food and harsh treatment. The idlers are the priests, and the hordes of spies and policemen who throng the highways, and who are watching everything by day and night.

On the whole, the Commodore was pleased with the suavity and politeness of the higher classes, and with the seeming cordiality of the hospitality which had been shown him; if the Lew Chewans were not sincere they were, at least, very good actors. As to the culinary skill that had been employed in preparing the regent's feast, there were certainly dishes of the composition of which the guests were ignorant, but still they were, in general, savory and very good; much more so than those presented by Chinese cookery. Whenever a fresh course was brought in at the regent's feast, the host and his brother dignitaries rose and emptied their small cups of sakee to the health of the guests; and the regent always gave a signal to the Commodore when to commence on a new course.

At the reception in the palace, though the queen did not appear, yet the Commodore was quite satisfied that the story he had been told about her desperate illness, by the regent, was all fiction; and, in fact, if she were not, as some suspected, a myth, he thought it not improbable that she and her attendant ladies were behind the screen looking through some crevice at the western strangers, possibly not a little amused at the novel show. At any rate, he was so certain that she would survive his visit that he caused to be sent to the palace a present for her of a handsome mirror, and a quantity of French perfumery; and left there also the gifts which he designed for the prince, the regent, the mayor of Napha, and other dignitaries.

The expected absence from the island, to which the Commodore had alluded on his visit to the palace, was to be occasioned by an intended examination of the Bonin Islands, a group lying to the eastward, in the neighborhood of 141° of longitude, and presenting some points of interest for investigation. Before our departure for these islands, however, the story of which will be told in its place, we must finish the narrative of events on this the first visit to Lew Chew. The old Pe-ching, who received the Commodore on his landing to go to Shui, was, as we have already mentioned, the same that with such exemplary patience and good nature accompanied (as chief spy, doubtless) the exploring party in their tedious excursion of a week over the island. Mr. Jones, the chaplain, accompanied by Mr. Taylor and Mr. Heine, having procured presents for the old man by the Commodore's order, and added thereto some pieces of Canton silk handkerchiefs of their own, went on shore and met the Pe-ching at Dr. Bettelheim's, when matters were satisfactorily adjusted. But on this visit, as on all previous ones, the system of incessant watching was kept up. Five individuals, in gray dresses, followed the American gentlemen, and sent forward a scout to warn the people to keep out of the way, and they accordingly fled in all directions on the approach of the strangers. There seemed to be special apprehension of their women being seen; but in the few instances when accidentally they became visible, they were found to be strikingly unhandsome.

During the period of stay at Lew Chew all military and naval drills and exercises were regularly performed daily, and the harbor of Napha was made lively, on two days, by a general boat inspection. Seventeen boats, fully manned and equipped, and five of them carrying twelve and twenty-four pounders, drew up off the Susquehanna, and were reviewed by the fleet officers. It was a fine spectacle, and was gazed on with lively interest by the Lew Chewans. They had never seen any thing of the kind before within their quiet harbor.

The pursers were sent on shore, before the squadron's departure, to settle accounts with the treasurers of the island, and pay for such supplies as had been furnished. By the Commodore's order Lieutenant Contee and Mr. Williams, the interpreter, accompanied them, carrying a number of presents, chiefly American cotton goods. According to their past usage the Lew Chewans demurred to receiving any compensation for supplies; but they were given to understand that this could not possibly be allowed; and that American ships of war always paid the people of all nations from whom they received supplies. After some persuasion they induced the native treasurers to take compensation for all that had been furnished to the ships, and also to receive the presents. The Commodore thought it was a point gained of some importance, that they had thus, for the first time, as it is believed, broke through their ancient custom of not receiving pay for provisions furnished to vessels. Henceforth visitors and their hosts will stand on terms of equality, and no superiority can be claimed, nor any exclusive policy practised on the ground of favors done to strangers.

The daguerreotypists, Messrs. Brown and Draper, were settled on shore in a house outside of the village of Tumai, and some of the embellishments of this volume are illustrative of the results of their very useful labors. Mr. Scott, of the Saratoga, (an invalid,) occupied another house, and enjoyed an agreeable intercourse with the natives, finding no difficulty in procuring from them abundant supplies. A tide-staff was planted, and Midshipman Boardman, with two

men, were encamped under a tent near it to make regular observations. The rise and fall of the tide during the stay of the vessels had averaged about six feet.

All arrangements having been finally made for a temporary absence, on the morning of the 9th of June the Susquehanna got under way for the Bonin Islands, having the Saratoga in tow.

The Mississippi and Supply were left at Napha, and the Commodore enjoined on Commander Lee, the senior officer, to cultivate the most friendly relations with the islanders, exercising all possible forbearance and kindness in his intercourse with the authorities and people, and to be careful to permit none but the most orderly persons to go on shore, lest some untoward event should mar the harmony then happily subsisting.

Passing through the southern channel the Susquehanna rounded Abbey Point, and took a southern course around the extremity of the island. This end of the island, though hilly and picturesque, did not appear to be either so fertile or so well cultivated as the eastern and western shores. In the course of the afternoon Lew Chew sank beneath the horizon, and the ship held on her course, east by north, at the rate of eight knots an hour. At first she had a light wind from the southwest, which soon died away; but presently she came within the influence of the monsoon, which filled her sails; the drawing sails of both ships were set, and though the steamer had the Saratoga in tow, and used but three of her boilers, she made nine and a half knots.

The southwest monsoon still continuing, good progress was made, notwithstanding a strong current from the eastward; and nothing occurred to interrupt the uniformity of sea life on board, save an event which interrupts the current of life itself alike on ship and shore. There was a death on board the Susquehanna. When Mr. Williams came from China to join the squadron, at Lew Chew, as interpreter, he brought with him an old Chinaman who had been his teacher, and who, it was supposed, might be useful in future operations; but it was very soon apparent that the old man's race was nearly run. He was a victim to the habit of opium smoking, which he was attempting to abandon. The consequences of this effort, and the effects of sea sickness on board the Saratoga, prostrated him so completely that no medicines had any effect, and he sank into a state of nervelessness and emaciation painful to look upon. For a week before his death his condition had been most pitiable: every joint in his skeleton frame seemed to be in perpetual motion; his face was a ghastly yellow: his cheeks sunken on the bones; the eyes wild and glassy; and his mind in a state of semi-madness. Death, when it came, was a relief to the poor old man, as well as to those who saw him die. On the day after his decease the ship presented that striking picture, a funeral at sea. The Commodore and other officers stood around, with a large part of the crew, while the chaplain committed his body to the deep until the day come when "the earth and the sea shall give up their dead."

A more frightful example of the terrible effects of the use of opium it would be difficult to find. It exceeded in horror all the loathsome and repulsive results of the use of intoxicating drinks. *Delirium tremens* is horrible enough, but the last scene of this old opium smoker was more horrible still. There was something revolting also in the conduct of the Chinese on board the ship. They manifested not the least sympathy with their dying countryman. For a day or two before he died, not one of them, with the exception of one of the Commodore's servants, would go near him: and on the last night of his life, when two of the deck coolies had been ordered by the captain to remain in the room, and were obliged to obey, they squatted down in the corner most remote from him, and never once approached him. Some of the quartermasters gave him what he needed, and were with him when he died.

During the run to the Bonin Islands, the crews were occasionally beat to quarters by way of exercise, and on one occasion after dark. Night signals were made to the Saratoga by means of lanterns and blue lights, and to those who were not "old salts" enough to have seen such sights before, the effect was alike novel and exciting. The blue lights illuminating the broad sails, at their full tension under the influence of the monsoon, the men at their several stations, all brought out in the glare of an artificial light, which, though bright as daylight, yet was of unearthly aspect, gave to the scene somewhat of a startling effect, and forcibly impressed the imagination with the peculiar features of a night engagement. The next morning after this exhibition (Sunday) was fresh and cool, and it was pleasant, as the vessels held on their prosperous way over a smooth sea, to see the crews all newly washed, clean, and dressed in their suits of snowy duck with broad blue collars, while everything about the vessel wore a trim, holiday air, and those not on duty were waiting for five bells to gather around the chaplain's temporary pulpit—the capstan—and join in the services of the day, so peculiarly appropriate from men "who go down to the sea in ships, and whose path is in the great waters." The favoring circumstances all continuing, on the 14th of June, at 10 a. m., the ships found themselves off the entrance of Port Lloyd, on Peel Island, one of the Bonins. The Saratoga had been previously cast off, and was now ordered to go ahead. Two vessels, apparently whalers, hove in sight, one on either quarter. The one to the northward showed American colors, and began to beat down toward the Susquehanna, anxious probably to know the meaning of such a strange event as the appearance of one of her country's large armed steamers in that remote spot. The three islands called Peel, Buckland, and Stapleton, constitute the principal part of that group, and lie close together. They are high, bold, and rocky, and, though not so beautiful and green as Lew Chew, are yet exceedingly picturesque. Pilots put off from the island to both ships, and soon both were safely anchored in the harbor of Port Lloyd.

Bamboo Village, Lew Chew.

CHART
OF THE
BONIN GROUP OF ISLANDS.

CHAPTER X.

SITUATION OF BONIN ISLANDS.—FIRST DISCOVERY OF THEM.—EUROPEANS HAVE NO CLAIM AS THE DISCOVERERS.—MIXED CHARACTER OF PRESENT SETTLERS.—EXTERNAL APPEARANCE OF PEEL ISLAND.—GEOLOGICAL FORMATION.—HARBOR OF PORT LLOYD.—PRODUCTIONS OF THE ISLAND, ANIMAL AND VEGETABLE.—RESORT OF WHALERS.—CONDITION OF PRESENT INHABITANTS.—COMMODORE CAUSES THE ISLAND TO BE EXPLORED.—REPORTS OF EXPLORING PARTIES.—KANAKAS.—EXAMINATION OF STAPLETON ISLAND, AND REPORT THEREON.—SURVEY OF HARBOR OF PORT LLOYD.—LAND PURCHASED FOR A COAL DEPOT.—DEPARTURE FROM BONIN ISLANDS ON THE RETURN TO LEW CHEW.—DISAPPOINTMENT ISLAND.—ITS TRUE POSITION.—BORODINOS.—ARRIVAL AT NAPHA.

HE Bonin Islands, lying in the Japanese sea, extend in a direction nearly north and south, between the latitudes of 26° 30' and 27° 45' north, the centre line of the group being in longitude about 142° 15' east. The islands were visited by Captain Beechey in 1827, and, with the proverbial modesty and justice of English surveyors, named by him, as if they had been then first observed. The northern cluster he called Parry's Group; the middle cluster, consisting of three larger islands, respectively Peel, Buckland, and Stapleton; and the southern cluster was named by him Bailey's, utterly regardless of the fact thus stated by himself: "The southern cluster is that on which a whale ship, commanded by a Mr. Coffin, anchored in 1823, who was first to communicate its position to this country, and who bestowed his name upon the port. As the cluster was, however, left without any distinguishing appellation, I named it after Francis Bailey, esq., late President of the Astronomical Society." * To the principal port of Peel Island he gave the name of Port Lloyd.

This was a pretty liberal distribution of honors by an accidental visitor in 1827, to a group of islands that had been known, and of which we have authentic accounts as early as the seventeenth century. According to Kæmpfer, these islands were known to the Japanese at a period as far back as 1675, and were described by them under the name of Buna Sima, signifying an island without people. According to the account of this traveller, whose words we quote, the Japanese accidentally, about the year 1675, discovered a very large island, one of their barques having been forced, in a storm, from the island Fatseyo, from which place they computed it to be three hundred Japanese miles distant, toward the east. They met with no inhabitants, but found it to be a very pleasant and fruitful country, well supplied with fresh water, and furnished with plenty of plants and trees, particularly the arrack tree, which, however, might give room to the conjecture that the island lay rather to the south of Japan than to the east, as these trees grow only in hot countries. The Japanese marked it as an uninhabited place, but they found upon its shores an incredible quantity of fish and crabs, "some of which were from four to six feet long." The description of Kæmpfer, as well as that of an original Japanese writer, given in the note below, was found by Commodore Perry to correspond exactly with the present appearance of the island. The arrack, or areca tree, alluded to in the extract, is found upon Peel Island.*

---

* Extract from Klaproth's translation of San Kokp Tsoir Ran To Sits.

"The original name of these islands is O-gasa-wara-sima, but they are commonly called Mon-nin-sima, (in Chinese, Wu-jin-ton,) or the islands without people, and this is the name which I have adopted in my work. That of O-gasa-wara-sima, or the O-gasa-wara islands, was given to them after the navigator who first visited them, and who prepared a map of them. In the same manner has the southern part of the New World been called Magalania, (Magellan,) who first discovered it some two hundred years since.

"The Bonin islands are found 270 ri to the southeasterly of the province of Idsu. From Simoda, in that principality, it is 13 ri to the island of Myake; from thence to Sin-sima or New island, seven ri; from Sin-sima to Mikoura, five ri; from thence to Fatsicio or Fatiho, (Fatsisio,) 41 ri; and, lastly, from this to the most northern of the uninhabited islands, it is reckoned to be 180 ri; and to the most southerly 200 ri.

"This archipelago lies in the 27th degree of north latitude. The climate is warm, and makes the valleys lying between the high mountains, watered by rivulets, to be very fertile, so that they produce beans, wheat, millet, grain of all kinds, and sugar cane. The tree called Nankin, faze or tallow tree (Stillingia sebifera) grows there, and likewise the wax tree. The fishery is good, and might be made very productive.

"Many plants and trees grow in these islands, but there are very few quadrupeds. There are trees so large that a man cannot embrace them with his arms, and which are frequently thirty Chinese fathoms in height, (or 240 feet.) Their wood is hard and beautiful. There are also some very high trees resembling the siou-ro-tsoung-liu, or chamarops excelsa, cocoa nuts, areca palms, that tree whose nuts are called pe-couan-tsy in Chinese, the katsirau, the red sandal wood, the tou-mou, the camphor, tub figs of the mountains, a high tree whose leaves resemble those of the ground ivy, the cinnamon tree, mulberry, and some others.

"Among the plants the smilax China, (or China root,) called san-ke-rei, the to-ke, a medicinal herb called assa-ghion-keva, and others are to be reckoned.

"Among birds there are different species of parokeets, cormorants, partridges, and some resembling white sea-mews, but more than three feet long. All these birds have so little wildness that they can be taken with the hand.

"The chief productions of the mineral kingdom in this archipelago are alum, green vitriol, stones of different colors, petrifactions, &c.

"Whales are found in the sea, also huge crawfish, enormous shells, and echini, which are called 'gall of the sea.' The ocean here is unusually rich in various products.

"In the third year of the reign Ghen-Fo, (1675,) Simaye Saghemon, Biso Saghemon, and Simaye Dairo Saghemon, three inhabitants of Nagasaki, took a sea voyage to the principality of Idsu. They were embarked in a large junk, built by a skillful Chinese carpenter. These three men were well acquainted with astronomy and geography, and accompanied by Fatobe, the chief ship-carpenter of the port of Yedo, who dwelt in the lane of nets. The vessel was managed by thirty sailors. Having obtained a passport from the imperial marine, they left the harbor of Simoda, the 5th day of the 4th moon, and steered for the island of Fatsio. From thence they sailed towards the southeast and discovered a group of eighty islands. They drew up a map and an exact account of them, in which are some curious details respecting the situation, climate, and productions of this archipelago. They returned the 20th day of the 6th moon, in the same year, to Simoda, where Simaye published an account of his voyage.

"It is singular that this writer makes no mention of the swift current, kuro-se-gaw, which is experienced between the islands of Mikura and Fatsio. Its breadth exceeds twenty matze, (about half a ri,) and it flows with great swiftness from east to west,(*a*) about one hundred ri. This omission would be inexplicable if this current was not much less rapid in summer and autumn than it is in winter and spring. Simaye, in his passage to the Bonin islands, passed it in the first part of the intercalary month, which succeeds the fourth moon; on his return, the latter part of the sixth moon, he should have found the currents less rapid, and thus his attention was not called to this dangerous passage."

"The largest of the eighty islands is fifteen ri in circuit, and thus is a little less than Iki island in size. Another is ten ri in circumference, and about the size of Amakusa island. Besides these two there are eight others which are from two to six and

---

(*a*) The writer in describing the direction of the current is mistaken.

The green turtles which abound in the island were probably mistaken for crabs, which may account for the gigantic size attributed by Kæmpfer to these animals. Other accounts give a much earlier date for the discovery by the Japanese than that of 1675, stated by the authority just quoted. At any rate, the English have not a particle of claim to priority of discovery. In illustration of the discovery of the Bonins by the accidental visit of a Japanese junk, it may be stated that the Commodore was informed by Mr. Savory, an American resident, that a Japanese vessel of about forty tons burden came into Port Lloyd thirteen years before, having been driven by stress of weather from the coast of Japan. After remaining during the winter she sailed on her return home in the spring, and, as she had brought with her nothing but a small supply of dried fish, was provided gratuitously by the settlers with provisions. On another occasion, some eight years subsequently, a French ship, cruizing off Stapleton island, discovered a fire ashore, and on sending a boat to the spot found the wreck of a Japanese junk and five of its crew, the only survivors, in a most helpless plight. They were then taken on board and carried to Port Lloyd, and thence subsequently removed by the humane Frenchmen with the intention of landing them on one of the Japanese islands. In confirmation of this statement we have the fact that a party of officers from the Susquehanna, on a visit to Stapleton Island, accidentally saw the wreck of this same vessel. The remains of the junk were found in a little bay where they landed, the wreck being still partially kept together by large nails of copper and portions of sheets of this metal. From these materials and other indications, it was inferred that it was a Japanese junk, and as the edges of the planks were but little rubbed or decayed, it was concluded that the wreck could not be very old.

Captain Coffin, whose nationality is not mentioned, but who, from his name, was probably an American, and if so, doubtless from Nantucket, visited and gave his name to that part of the group so singularly appropriated and modestly christened by Beechey as the Bailey Islands. They are spoken of by the inhabitants as the southern islands, and were always regarded by them as belonging to the Bonin group. They are about twenty miles to the south of Port Lloyd. It was not until 1827 that Captain Beechey, commanding the English surveying vessel, the Blossom, visited the islands, and taking formal possession in the name of the British king, gave English titles to them. The inhabitants practically disown the paternity of the English sovereign, and do not recognize the names given in his self-assumed sponsorship by the English captain. For example, the very dignified appellations of Buckland and Stapleton, with which Beechey has honored two islands of the northern group, are quite ignored by the inhabitants, who speak of these

---

seven ri around. These ten islands have flat plateaux which could be made habitable, and where grain would grow very well. The climate is warm and favorable to cultivation, as one might infer from their geographical position. They afford various valuable productions. The remaining seventy islets are only mere steep rocks, and produce nothing."

"A colony of condemned criminals has been sent to these islands, there to labor; they have tilled the earth and planted some patches. They are collected in villages, and have brought together the same things found in other provinces of the empire. One can visit these islands, and bring back its products in the same year. In this way a trade would easily spring up, and the benefit to be drawn from it would be considerable. This must be plain to all."

"In the reign An-Yei (from 1771 to 1780) I was sent on a commission into the province of Fisen, where I became acquainted with a Dutchman named Aarend Werle Veit, who showed me a geography, in which mention was made of some islands lying 200 ri to the southeast of Japan, called Woest eiland by the author. The word *Woest* means *desert*, and eiland (or yeirand, as the original reads) island. He remarks, that these islands are not inhabited, but that many sorts of herbs and trees are found there. The Japanese might establish a colony on one of these islands on which grain and other productions would thrive. In spite of the length of the voyage thither, the establishment would be useful to them for these purposes. The Dutch company would derive very little advantage from the possession of these islands, they being too small and too remote for their use."

"I have thought proper to repeat these words, which deserve to be borne in mind, and with them I bring to a conclusion all that I have to say respecting the Bonin Islands."

places respectively as Goat and Hog islands. When the English visited and took possession of the Bonins, the date of the visit and the act of appropriation were duly engraved upon a copper plate which was nailed to a tree, but the plate and the tree are no longer there, and the only evidence of British possession is the occasional hoisting of the English flag on one of the neighboring hills, a duty that was originally delegated to a wandering Englishman who chanced to be on the spot. It is now considered merely a signal to be hoisted on the arrival of a vessel. No government is recognized by the inhabitants, who declare that they have no need of any foreign control, as they can take good care of themselves.

In the year following the visit of Captain Beechey, a Captain Lutke of the Russian navy arrived and went through very much the same ceremony of taking possession and of otherwise appropriating as his English predecessor.

It is quite clear that the Japanese were the first discoverers of these islands. They probably settled and then subsequently abandoned them. It is possible that the early Spanish, Portuguese, and Dutch navigators may have been acquainted with the Bonins, and in later years they have been visited occasionally by the Americans, English, and Russians. The fact of a Spanish visit would seem to be proved by the name of Arzobispo or Archbishop, by which the islands are sometimes distinguished. One of the inhabitants reported that he recollected, on his arrival on the spot, that there was a board on a tree which recorded the first Russian visit. Neither of the European nations have as yet made any attempt at colonization.

In 1830, several Americans and Europeans came to the Bonins from the Sandwich Islands, accompanied by various natives—men and women—of that country.

The leaders of this adventure were five men, two originally from the United States—Nathaniel Savory and Aldin B. Chapin, of Massachusetts—one from England of the name of Richard Mildtchamp, one Charles Johnson, of Denmark, and the fifth a Genoese known as Mattheo Mazara. The only one of these remaining on the island during the visit of Commodore Perry was Nathaniel Savory, an American. Mildtchamp still survives, but has taken up his residence at Guam, one of the Ladrone islands. The Genoese, Mazara, is dead, and Savory has married his widow, a pretty and young native of Guam, by whom he has offspring. Savory occupies himself with the culture of a little farm, which is tolerably productive. He also carries on a trade in sweet potatoes of his own raising and in a rum of his own distillation from sugar cane, with the whaling ships which frequent the place; and he had prosecuted his business with such success as to accumulate, at one time, several thousands of dollars. These he deposited in the ground, when, some three or four years since, a schooner arrived under the American flag, bringing a few worthless scoundrels, who ingratiated themselves, under the pretence of great friendship, with the old man, who was thus induced to make them the confidants of his success, and of its proof which he had stored away. These villains, after living for several months on terms of great intimacy and confidence with Savory, left the island, having first robbed their benefactor of all his money, despoiled his household of a couple of young women, whom they took away with them, carried off his journal, and wantonly injured his property. Fortunately for justice, the guilty party were afterwards arrested at Honolulu, but the captive women expressed themselves quite contented with their lot, and declared that they had no desire to return. As for the money, it was not learned whether that was ever recovered or not.

The islands of Bonin are high, bold, and rocky, and are evidently of volcanic formation.

GEOLOGICAL FORMATION.

They are green with verdure and a full growth of tropical vegetation, which crowds up the acclivities of the hills, from the very borders of the shore, which is, here and there, edged with coral reefs. The headlands and detached rocks have been thrown by former convulsions of nature into various grotesque forms, which assume to the eye the shape of castle and tower, and strange animals, of monstrous size and hideous form. Numerous canal-like passages were observed opening in the sides of the rocky cliffs, which had almost the appearance of being hewn out with the chisel, but which were evidently formed in the course of volcanic changes, when the rock flowed in liquid lava, and found issue in these channels, which the torrents that come down the sides of the mountains in the rainy season toward the sea have worn smooth by constant attrition. Some of these dykes, or canal-like passages, less affected by time and the washing of the water, still retain their irregular formation, which has so much the appearance of steps that the observer, as he looks upon them, might fancy they had been cut by the hand of man in the solid rock, for the purpose of climbing the mountain. On the Southern Head, as it is called, within the harbor of Port Lloyd, there is a very curious natural cave or tunnel, which passes through the basaltic rock, from the Southern Head to the beach on the other side. The entrance has a width of about fifteen feet, and a height of thirty, but the roof within soon rises to forty or fifty feet, where it has so much the appearance of artificial structure, that it may be likened to a builder's arch, in which even the keystone is observable. There is sufficient

Natural Tunnel, Port Lloyd, Bonin Islands.

water for a boat to pass from one end to the other. There are several other caves or tunnels, one of which is at least fifty yards in length, and passes through a headland bounding the harbor. This is constantly traversed by the canoes of the inhabitants.

The geological formation of the island is trappean, with its various configurations and mineralogical peculiarities; columnar basalt appears, and hornblende and chalcedony are found. There are all the indications of past volcanic action, and the oldest resident of Peel Island stated that two or three tremblings of the earth, giving evidence of a liability to earthquake, are experienced annually even now.

The harbor of Port Lloyd (as Beechey named it) is on the western side, and nearly in the centre of Peel Island. It is easy of ingress and egress, and may be considered as safe and commodious, though of deep anchorage. Vessels usually anchor in from eighteen to twenty-two fathoms. The port is laid down on Beechey's chart as in latitude 27° 5′ 35″ north, and 142° 11′ 30″ east longitude. This position, however, is believed to be erroneous, for, according to two sets of observations, made by the master of the Susquehanna, the longitude was found to be 142° 16′ 30″ east; five miles more to the eastward than Beechey makes it. The safest anchorage is to be found as high up the harbor as a ship can conveniently go, having regard to depth and room for swinging and veering cable. Beechey's directions for entering the port are sufficiently correct, and these, together with the Commodore's own observations, will be found in the Appendix.

Wood and water can be procured in abundance, though the former must be cut by the crew, and taken on board the ship green. The water is obtained from running streams, and is of good quality. Timber for building purposes is rather scarce, and would soon be exhausted if any increase of population were to render the erection of many houses necessary. The best kinds of wood are the jamana and wild mulberry, the former of which is very like the red wood of Brazil and Mexico, and is very enduring.

The harbor of Port Lloyd and the neighboring waters abound with excellent fish, which may be taken by the hook or net, although the places for hauling the seine are few, owing to the coral which in many parts lines the shores. The best place for this purpose is upon the beach which borders "Ten Fathom Hole," a deep portion of the bay which is close to the coral reef that extends out from the shore. The varieties of fish are not numerous; among those taken in the seine belonging to the Susquehanna there were but five observed: the mullet, which seemed to be the most abundant, two varieties of perch, the gar, and the common ray. Sharks are very numerous, and, when quite small, frequent the shallow places among the coral rocks, and are there pursued by the dogs, seized upon and dragged on shore.

There is an abundance of excellent green turtle, of which the ships obtained large supplies; there are also plenty of cray fish. The varieties of the testacea are numerous, but none that was observed of any rarity, and none edible except the chama gigas, which, however, is very tough and indigestible. The family of the crustacea is very extensive, of which the land crab forms the chief part, and which exists in every variety of size, form, and color; one of the most abounding is that which is commonly known as the "pirate." This animal can be seen in every direction near the shore, travelling about with its odd-looking domicil upon its back, which it seems to have got possession of rather by chance than from choice. The "pirate" has no home of its own, but appropriates, whence its name, that which belongs to others. It has a decided preference for the shells of the buccina, murex, and bulla, which have the comfortable proportions of an inch and a half or so in length; but if such desirable quarters should, by any mischance, happen to be scarce, the "pirate" readily turns into the next most suitable dwelling of some neighbor at hand. It is necessary that the animal should have some snug corner wherein, if not to lay its head, at any rate to put its tail, for the latter is soft and requires constant protection. Thus, when the "pirate" moves about, his head and claws are always protruded, but his rear is covered with his borrowed shell. It is still an unsettled question whether this animal appropriates the domicils of others by first rudely ejecting their living occupants, or more considerately waits until a natural death or some fatality vacates the quarters, and then takes possession. The "pirate" is a voracious creature, and seizes with great avidity upon anything eatable that comes in its way.

The scarcity of birds, both of sea and land species, struck every one as singular. There were not more than four or five varieties of the latter, the largest of which were the crow and the pigeon, the others being of small size. There were but few gulls or other sea-birds; on approaching the islands, some petrel were observed, of unusually large size and of singularly brilliant plumage.

Among the quadrupeds there were found sheep, deer, hogs, and goats, with an infinite number of cats and dogs. The cats and dogs, having lost some of their quiet domestic virtues, had strayed into the jungle, and were dignified by the inhabitants with the title of wild animals, and were accordingly hunted with dogs. On Stapleton Island, the goats, which were placed there by some of the early settlers, have increased prodigiously, as have also these animals, together with the hogs, put upon the other islands. Commodore Perry left on shore on the north side of Peel Island, with a view to their increase, two bulls and two cows, and on North Island five Shanghai broad-tailed sheep, of which two were rams, and six goats.

Peel Island is the only one of the Bonin group inhabited, and it contained on the visit of the Commodore only thirty-one inhabitants, all told: of these, three or four were native Americans, about the same number Englishmen, one a Portuguese, and the remainder Sandwich islanders and children born on the island. The settlers have cultivated patches of land of some extent, and raise a considerable quantity of sweet potatoes, Indian corn, pumpkins, onions, taro, and several kinds of fruit, the most abundant of which are water-melons, bananas, and pine-apples. These productions, together with the few pigs and poultry that are raised, find a ready sale to the whale ships constantly touching at the port for water and other supplies. During the few days the Susquehanna was at anchor in the harbor, three whalers, two American and one English, communicated by means of their boats with the settlement and carried away a good stock of supplies. These are obtained ordinarily in exchange for other articles from on board the ships, of which ardent spirits is to some of the settlers the most acceptable. Were it not for the scarcity of labor a much greater extent of land would be cultivated. At present there cannot be more than a hundred and fifty acres throughout the whole island under cultivation, and this is in detached spots, generally at the seaward termination of the ravines through which the mountain streams flow and thus supply an abundance of fresh water, or upon plateaux of land near the harbor. The soil is of excellent quality and resembles very much that of Madeira and the Canary islands, which are in the same parallel of latitude. It is admirably adapted for the cultivation of the vine, and for the raising of wheat, tobacco, sugar-cane, and many other valuable plants. In fact, the settlers already produce enough sugar and tobacco for their own consumption.

The few people who live on Peel Island seem happy and contented. Those of European origin have succeeded in surrounding themselves with some of the comforts and appliances of civilization. In one of the cottages there was observed several compartments, and what with hangings from the walls of Chinese matting, a chair or two, a table, a plentiful distribution of blue paint, and some gaudily colored lithographs, there seemed not only on the part of the proprietor a desire for comfort, but even a taste for luxury.

The Sandwich islanders, or Kanakas, as they are now familiarly known to sailors and traders, live very much as they do in their native islands, and have grouped together their palm thatched huts which have very much the appearance of one of their native villages. The inhabitants, living a quiet and easy life in a climate which is genial and wholesome, and upon a land whose fertility supplies them, in return for but little labor, with all they want to eat and drink, do not care to change their condition. The Americans and Europeans have taken to themselves wives from among the good natured and substantial Kanaka women.

Commodore Perry being desirous of obtaining as full information as possible of Peel Island during his short visit, determined to send parties of exploration into the interior. He accordingly detailed certain officers and men for the purpose, who were divided into two companies, one of which was headed by Mr. Bayard Taylor, and the other by Dr. Fahs, assistant surgeon.

These gentlemen, having been duly armed and equipped, started early on the morning of the 15th of June, with the view of devoting the day to the proposed exploration. The party headed by Mr. Taylor, whose steps we shall first follow in the narrative, and whose report as submitted to the Commodore we shall freely use, was composed of eight: Mr. Bayard Taylor, Mr. Heine, the artist, Mr. Boardman, midshipman, Mr. Lawrence, assistant engineer, Mr. Hampton, purser's steward, Smith, a marine, Dennis Terry, seaman, and a Chinese coolie. As Peel Island is only six miles in length, it was thought that one day was quite sufficient time for two parties properly distributed to explore so small a space. The northern part of the island, which is that which stretches immediately around the harbor, was the field of operation appropriated to the doctor's party, while the southern half fell to the duty of the explorers whose steps we are now about to follow.

At early sunrise the party left the Susquehanna and were rowed ashore to the watering place at the head of the bay. On reaching this point the rations and ammunition were distributed to each, so that all might, as far as possible, be equally burdened. A Kanaka, who was met at the landing, was urged to accompany the party as a guide, but he was not disposed to comply, although he pointed out a small footpath, which he stated led over the hills to a Kanaka settlement about three miles distant. This direction was at once followed, which led them by a steep and slippery path through a wilderness of tropical growth. Palm trees, among which was the sago palm, that produces the sago of commerce, abounded; parasitic plants hung in festoons from branch to branch, and by their close net work, interwoven with the trees, hindered the progress at every step, while the dew which dripped in the early morning from the thick foliage of the overgrown thicket wetted each one to the skin. The soil was observed to be that which is common about Port Lloyd and other parts of the island, and seemed composed of the detritus of trap rock and the decomposed refuse of the plants and trees. Rock of trap formation protruded frequently in rough crags from the steep sides of the hills, and in the crevices grew a beautiful variety of the hibiscus, with its large flowers of a dull orange, whose petals were tipped with yellow of a lighter shade. A shower of white blossoms, which had fallen from a large tree of thirty feet in height, strewed here and there the ground.

The course was up the ridge of the hill, and as it continued to the summit the vegetation became more and more profuse, until the expanding tops of the palm, the crowding together of

KANAKA VILLAGE BONIN ISLANDS

the trunks of the trees, and the dense net work of the hanging vines, so shrouded the sun that the path was covered with a deep shade, through the darkness of which the eye could hardly penetrate to a greater distance, in any direction, than twenty or thirty feet. It was difficult at times to trace the path. When the party had reached the water-courses of the streams which flowed down the other side of the ridge they were ascending, multitudes of the land crabs pattered away in every direction, frightened out of their coverts by the approaching footsteps.

The ridge at its summit widened into an undulating surface of a mile and a half or so in breadth, and was furrowed with deep gullies. The declivity on the other side of the ridge, below which opened a deep ravine, was so steep that the men were obliged to let themselves down by swinging from tree to tree. This ravine between the steep mountains, which, with the exception of the bared rock here and there, were profusely covered with vegetation, presented a wild aspect, with a stream of water flowing over a rocky bed through thickets of undergrowth and masses of tropical vegetation spreading over the rocky cliffs and down the hills on all sides.

The party now crossed the stream, and coming upon a field of the taro plant, which was of remarkably luxuriant growth, struck directly through it and reached the forest beyond. Finding it impossible, however, to make their way in that direction, they turned back through the taro and regained the stream. The path was now recovered, which was found to lead through a valley which bore signs of habitation. Cultivated patches of ground showed themselves here and there with flourishing crops of sweet potatoes, taro, tobacco, sugar-cane, pumpkin, and the *sida* or Indian gooseberry, which seemed to grow with wonderful luxuriance. In the centre of the valley two palm thatched huts were observed, but the party, upon coming up to them and entering, found they were uninhabited, although there were signs of their having been occupied that morning. Guns were then fired to attract the attention of any inhabitants who might be within hearing, and a good result was soon apparent by the answering signal of a shout, which was immediately followed by the appearance of a South Sea islander, with a face tattooed of a light blue and clothed in coarse cotton shirt and trowsers. He introduced himself under the dignified title of "Judge," and professed to be a native of Nukahwa in the Marquesas islands. This Marquesite seemed to be in very flourishing condition. He had a hut to live in, a plantation to cultivate, and made a fair show of live stock with his dogs and four pigs. The "Judge" was very affable, and in a very friendly manner gave freely all the information at his command. He pointed out to his visitors how the valley turned round the spur of the mountain and opened westward to the sea. The stream was here only a creek in appearance, but was of sufficient depth to float canoes, in one of which the "Judge" had just arrived from a turtle hunt, and had brought with him a fine animal, which he busied himself with cutting up in the wishful company of his four dogs, who were licking their chops with a hopeful anticipation of their share of the feast.

The "Judge" was requested to guide the party to the southern end of the island, which he stated to be about three or four miles distant, without, however, any pathway to it. His companion, however, who knew the way, was sent for, and a copper colored Otaheitan, who hardly spoke English, soon presented himself. He acknowledged that he was acquainted with the route, and familiar with the wild boar haunts, but refused to go with the party unless joined by the "Judge," who, after some hesitation, consented, with the understanding that he should be allowed to stow away his turtle flesh before starting. This, of course, was readily conceded.

The valley in which the explorers found themselves was estimated to be about a mile in length, and its widest part was a quarter of a mile in breadth. The main branch of the valley was not that which had been entered, but took an easterly direction, through which a stream flowed; the southern part seemed to be impassable, from being walled up with rocks heaped one above the other. From the "Judge's" hut the sea was said to be about half a mile distant. The soil of the valley is of a rich loam, and, judging by the flourishing appearance of the vegetables and crops grown by the settlers, exceedingly fertile. The tobacco was particularly vigorous in growth, being five feet in height. The water of the stream is sweet and pure, and the supply constant. Some lemons, which the "Judge" had stored away in his hat, he said came from the north of the valley.

The party, now under the guidance of the "Judge" and his companion, took an E.S.E. course, following through the ravine the stream. The bed of the stream was in various places crowded with large boulders of trap rock, heaped confusedly one upon another. The vegetation presented the usual tropical profusion of trees, parasite plants, and under growth. From the denseness of the woods and the greasy, slippery nature of the soil, the progress of every step was toilsome and painful. Two of the party in the rear, while those in advance awaited upon a cliff their coming up, started a wild boar, and fired at him a passing shot, but without effect. The dogs which belonged to the settlers were not of much use, for they kept clinging to the heels of their masters, instead of ranging the forest and beating up the game from its cover.

On leaving the water-course the explorers climbed the southern side of the ravine, which they could only do by clinging to the roots or to the tough vines which hung from the trees. In the deep shadow and turnings of the wood, through which there was no path, the members of the party became scattered, and the leaders were again obliged to await at the summit of the ridge the coming of those who lagged behind. Among the various palms, which grow abundantly, some specimens of the *palma latina* were observed at this spot, with immensely broad leaves and stems nearly eight feet in length, the jagged edges of which wounded the travellers' hands as they struggled through the forest. The *pandanus* was also seen, with its shoots, sometimes twenty or thirty in number, sticking down and outwards from the lower part of its straight trunk, and rooting themselves in the ground, until they formed a pyramidal base, from which the tree rose in a slender column, covered with a graceful capital of foliage.

While some of the party were resting upon the ridge, waiting for their companions who had fallen behind, a great barking of dogs rose from a neighboring ravine, at which two of the party started off at once. Several shots from the company were soon heard, and Mr. Taylor, the leader, followed, making for the direction of the sound, and, after plunging through an almost impenetrable thicket, in the course of which he came upon the lair of a wild boar, arrived at the bed of a brook, where the hunters were grouped about a young boar. He was not over a year old, and, with his long snout and the dirty, dark grey color of his bristling hide, looked somewhat like the Chinese hog. Mr. Hampton, one of the party who had been left behind upon the ridge, was now sent for; but the "Judge," who had gone in search of him, soon returned, stating that he was sick, and unable to come up. Mr. Hampton, however, in a short time gathered strength enough to follow, and succeeded in reaching the party, although evidently much overcome with fatigue. As the Otaheitan guide, however, said that it was only two miles to the southern end of the island, Mr. Hampton resolved to continue with his companions, instead of returning, as had been proposed, with the "Judge" to the valley. The explorers having taken with them the liver and the kidneys of the wild boar, hung up his carcase upon a tree to remain until their return, and then continued their course.

In about a half hour afterward the ridge which divides the island was crossed and the top of the slope of the southern side reached. From this point the sea was seen and a view obtained of Bailly's Island, rising from the surface in the distance, a little west of south. It was now found necessary to alter the course of the route, for the guide had taken the party too far to the right and led them to the brink of a steep precipice which it was impracticable to descend. There was some difficulty now in retracing their steps, for they had got so near to the precipice that they were forced to creep along with great caution, clinging to the strong grass and shrubs which grew upon the brink. By this mode of procedure, for the extent of two hundred yards or so, they succeeded in reaching a place where the precipice terminated; but where the descent was still so steep that it was found necessary for each man, as he descended, to place himself upon his back and thus slide down the declivity, taking care to check his speed by occasionally clenching the earth or some projecting bush. Finally, the ravine below was reached, but there was considerable disappointment on finding that the worst was not yet over; for, instead of

Valley near South East Bay, Peel Island, Bonin Group.

coming upon a water-course, as was expected, which might lead gently to the sea side, it was discovered that there was a succession of rocky steps, varying from ten to fifty feet, down which it was necessary to clamber. At last the beach was reached; and as those in advance looked up to their remaining companions, some standing upon the edge of the cliffs, and others letting themselves down their precipitous sides, the undertaking just accomplished seemed a marvellous feat of labor, difficulty, and danger.

The party now found themselves in what the guide called the South East Bay, which was said to be frequently visited by the whalers; some of whom had left evidence of their visits in the stump of a tree, which showed marks of having been smoothly cut with a large axe. There was also a neglected bed of tomatoes, overgrown with weeds, seen stretched along the banks of the stream, which had certainly been planted there by the hand of man. On the gathering of all the company, who were almost worn out, and suffered much from the excessive heat, a fire was lighted, and the boar's liver and kidneys being duly cooked, a very excellent extemporaneous feast, with the addition of the pork and other rations brought with them, was prepared and voraciously discussed. The party being refreshed by their banquet and the rest they had enjoyed, and it being as late as two o'clock, determined to return. When the guides announced that it was necessary to go back the way they came, the resumption of the labors, and the exposure to the dangers which had just been undergone, seemed quite appalling. There was, however, no alternative, and the party was forced to retrace their steps, but succeeded, finally, with a renewed experience of their former troubles, and after excessive fatigue, in reaching the valley whence they had set out with the "Judge" and his Otaheitan companion.

South East Bay, Peel Island.

It was six o'clock in the evening when they arrived at the "Judge's" quarters, so they spared themselves but little time for repose, but soon continued their journeying. One of the party was so wearied with fatigue as to be obliged to proceed to the Kanaka settlement, at the south end of Port Lloyd, by the way of the sea, in a canoe, piloted by the Otaheitan. The rest went by land, attempting to return by the same route as that they had come. The path was not easily found, however, and the explorers suffered another hard experience in the forest and over the rough crags, where they were nearly lost among the entangled undergrowth and much battered by the irregularity of the ground. Another member of the party gave out, but was brought along by main force, and having been deposited in a safe place on the summit of the ridge, under the care of one of the men, the rest pushed on; and having reached the Kanaka settlement, at the south end of Port Lloyd, took their station on a cliff which overlooked the bay, and whence the great hull of the Susquehanna could be barely discovered in the surrounding darkness. Firing a volley with their guns, as a signal, they were soon answered by the arrival of the ship's cutter, and having sent back for the tired member of the party, they all pulled off for the steamer, where they arrived at ten o'clock at night, sorely bruised and fatigued by the hard day's work. The other party, under the command of the assistant surgeon, returned about the same time, and the result of the observations, as reported by Dr. Fahs, is now recorded.

The volcanic origin of the island was clearly manifest from the existence of ancient craters. Trap rock, intermingled with amygdaloid and green stone, formed the basis of the island, as it did the loftiest peaks of the hills; basaltic dykes were observed to pass through beds of sand, scoria, and cinders, and strata of old lava were traced along the seacoast and in other parts where deep sections of rock were exposed. A sulphur spring, characterized by the usual strong odor and taste of sulphuretted hydrogen gas, was discovered issuing from one of the ravines, and iron pyrites abounded in many places. The vegetation, too, was not such as is generally found in volcanic countries of the same latitude as the Bonin Islands. It would appear that Port Lloyd was at one time the crater of an active volcano, from which the surrounding hills had been thrown up, while the present entrance to the harbor was formed by a deep fissure in the side of the cone, through which a torrent of lava had poured into the sea, leaving, after its subsidence, a space into which the waters subsequently were emptied, bringing with them their usual deposits, which, together with the coral formation, now forms the bottom and sides of the harbor.

The surface of the island is varied. Plains extend from the basis of the hills toward the seashore, and are composed of a dark vegetable mould, sometimes five or six feet deep, intermixed with the shells of marine animals and the detritus of trap rock, and spread upon a foundation of coral. These plains are highly fertile, and those now cultivated produce a rich harvest of sweet potatoes of immense size, Indian corn, sugar-cane of wonderfully vigorous growth and excellent quality, yams, taro, melons, and the ordinary products of a kitchen garden. The Irish potato has been tried, but not sufficiently long to form an estimate of its probable success. The plains on the bay only have been cultivated as yet, but there is every reason to believe that the others are equally fertile, and might be made to yield sufficiently to support a large population.

The hills rise in some places by a gentle slope from the plains, and in others abruptly by steep ascents, which give them the appearance of terraces rising one above the other. At the head of the bay two prominent peaks rise, which are known by the name of the Paps, one of which reaches the elevation of a thousand feet, and the other eleven hundred. They are clearly seen on entering the harbor, and are important guides to the navigator. The springs in the northern half of the island, which was the field of survey now reviewed, are few, two only of which run constantly with a supply of pure drinking water. In the valleys there are several others, but they are so brackish or so frequently dry that they cannot be relied upon as sources of supply. Through the ravines which intersect the valleys streams pour down into the sea during the rainy season, but their beds, crowded here and there with large boulders of trap rock, are hardly moist during the dry weather.

The flora of the island is tropical, and was observed to be as beautiful as can be found in any similar latitude. In the valleys and along the sea beach a tree of large size, called by the people living on the island the *Crumeno*, was seen in abundance. It had a thick and short trunk, with a gray bark, a very dense foliage, with large oval leaves of smooth surface and bright green color, arrayed in clusters around the branches, from the ends of which grew tufts of beautiful white flowers.

Dense forests of palm crowded up the hill-sides and into the ravines, and were of such close growth that their full development was hindered and other vegetation prevented. The fan-palm was the most abundant of the six species observed. Among the various trees was noticed a variety of the beech of considerable size, a large tree growing in abundance on the mountains, which somewhat resembled the dog-wood, and an immense mulberry with an occasional girth of thirteen or fourteen feet. Of smaller trees and plants, there were the laurel, the juniper, the box-wood tree, fern, banana, orange, pine-apple, and whortleberry. Lichens, mosses, and

Stapleton Island.

various parasitic plants were abundant. There were but few kinds of grasses, and most of them unfit for pasturage. The jungle weed, in the uncultivated tracts, is so dense that it crowds out almost everything else of its kind.

The animals on the island were mostly imported but had become wild in their habits from straying in the woods. Pigeons, finches, crows, and sandpipers, were found among the native birds, and the tortoise, the iguana, and a small lizard were the principal indigenous animals seen.

In addition to the two surveys of Peel Island, the interesting results of which have been just recorded, the Commodore dispatched an officer to report on the general aspect and character of the island of Stapleton, from whose statement some valuable facts are derived. Stapleton Island, like the rest of the Bonin group, is of volcanic origin, and has a varied surface of plain, hill, and valley, with large tracts of fertile land. A small bay was found on the western side with apparently deep water, and surrounded by rocks and mountains varying from 800 to 1,500 feet in height, which protect it from the S.E. typhoons.

A small promontory and coral reef were observed to divide this bay, and on the land bordering the northern section was a spring of cool, well-tasting water, coming out of a rock and giving a supply of nearly three gallons per minute. The indigenous productions of Stapleton were the same as those on the other islands, but the goats which had been introduced there had increased marvellously, to the extent, it was supposed, of several thousands, and had become very wild in the course of their undisturbed wanderings through the secluded ravines and over the savage rocks of the island.

The Commodore, having been long satisfied of the importance of these islands to commerce, was induced to visit them, chiefly by a desire of examining them himself and recommending Peel Island as a stopping place for the line of steamers which, sooner or later, must be established between California and China. To this end he caused the island to be explored, the harbor to be surveyed, and a few animals to be placed upon two of the groups of islands, as the commencement of a provision for future wants. Garden seeds of every description were also distributed among the present settlers, and hopes were held out to them by the Commodore of a future supply of implements of husbandry and a greater number of animals. A suitable spot too was selected for the erection of offices, wharves, coal-sheds, and other buildings necessary for a depot for steamers. A title was obtained to a piece of land which is admirably adapted to the desired purpose. It is situated on the northern side of the bay, near its head, with a front on the water of 1,000 yards and a good depth near the shore for the length of 500 yards, it might, by the building of a pier extending out fifty feet, be conveniently approached by the largest vessel afloat.

In a letter addressed to the Navy Department Commodore Perry has given at length his views of the conveniences of Peel Island for the establishment of a depot for steamers. In this communication he says:

"As my instructions direct me to seek out and establish ports of refuge and refreshment for vessels traversing these distant seas, I have, from the commencement of the cruise, kept constantly in view the port in which we are now at anchor,* and the principal harbor of the Bonin Islands, as well for general convenience of resort as to furnish connecting links, or suitable stopping places, for a line of mail steamers, which I trust may soon be established between some one of our Pacific ports and China, an event so much to be desired, and, if accomplished, one that will be distinguished, even in the history of these remarkable times, as of the highest importance to the commerce of the United States and of the world.

---

* The Commodore is writing from Napha, in Lew Chew.

"The mails from the United States and Europe, by the way of Egypt, the Red sea, and Indian ocean, arrive regularly at Hong Kong, almost to a day, twice a week in each month. From Hong Kong to Shanghai, five days may be allowed for the passage. To this point the British government would doubtless extend its mail if it were taken up by us and continued on to California.

"Its transportation, by steam, from Shanghai to San Francisco, via the Bonin and Sandwich Islands, would occupy thirty days, allowing three days for stopping for coal, etc. Thus, the distance from San Francisco to Honolulu, in the Sandwich Islands, is roughly estimated at 2,093 miles; from Honolulu to Peel Island, 3,301 miles; and from Peel Island to the mouth of the Yang-tzse-Keang, or Shanghai river, 1,081 miles; in all, 6,475 miles; and allowing 240 miles per day, the time at sea would be twenty-seven, and the time in port three days: from San Francisco to New York twenty-two days would be required, making from Shanghai to New York fifty-two days.

"The usual time occupied in transporting the mail from England to Hong Kong, via Marseilles, (the shortest route,) is from forty-five to forty-eight days; add to that two days' detention at Hong Kong, and five more to Shanghai, would make the time required to reach the latter place from fifty-two to fifty-five days.

"Shanghai might be considered the terminus of the English and the commencement of the American mail; and thus an original letter could be sent west by way of Europe, and its duplicate east by way of California, the first arriving at Liverpool about the time its duplicate reaches New York.

"But apart from the advantages, and, I may add, the glory of perfecting a scheme so magnificent, this line of steamers would contribute largely to the benefit of commerce. Already many thousands of Chinamen are annually embarking for California, paying for their passages each $50, and finding themselves in everything, excepting water and fuel for cooking their food.

"These provident people are the most patient and enduring laborers, and must, by their orderly habits, add greatly to the agricultural interests of California.

"But Shanghai is now becoming the great commercial mart of China; already does it outrival Canton in its trade with the United States, and when it shall be considered that the fine teas and silks, and other rare and valuable commodities of that part of China, can be conveyed by means of steam to California in five, and to New York in eight weeks, it is impossible to estimate in anticipation the advantages that may grow out of an intercourse so rapid and so certain."*

---

* The importance of the Bonin Islands to the advancement of commercial interests in the east is so great that the subject has more or less occupied the mind of the Commodore since his return; and this importance is best shown by the following document which has been placed in the hands of the compiler by Commodore Perry since this chapter was written:

Notes with respect to the Bonin Islands.

My visit to the Bonin Islands forcibly impressed me with the idea of their importance as a point of rendezvous for vessels navigating that part of the Pacific ocean in which they lie, and especially as offering a port of refuge and supply for whaling ships resorting to those regions, as well as a depôt for coal for a line of steamers which, ere long, must unquestionably be established between California and China, via Japan.

Whales of several varieties abound in those parts of the ocean lying between the Bonins and the coast of Asia, and are in greater numbers in the neighborhood of Japan. Until the establishment of a treaty with that singular empire the masters of whaling vessels were cautious not to approach near to its shores, under a well-founded apprehension of falling into the hands of the Japanese, and suffering, as a consequence, imprisonment and cruel treatment. These fears should no longer exist, as the stipulations of the treaty make provision and offer guaranties not only for kind treatment to those Americans who may approach the coast, or be thrown by accident upon its hitherto inhospitable shores, but allow all American vessels under press of weather to enter any of its ports for temporary refitment; and the ports of Hakodadi and Simoda are open for all purposes of repair or supplies.

After a stay of four days at the Bonin Islands, the Susquehanna weighed anchor, and taking the Saratoga in tow sailed on the morning of Saturday the 18th of June, on the return voyage to Lew Chew. After clearing the harbor of Port Lloyd, the course was steered toward Disappointment Island. On the passage from Lew Chew to the Bonin Islands the Commodore had desired to sight and determine the position of this island, but, although it had been made by the Susquehanna which stood directly for it on the day previous to her arrival at Port Lloyd, there was no opportunity, in consequence of the approaching darkness, to make any observation but an approximation by means of computation. The Commodore, therefore, on his return voyage, was particularly desirous of seeing the island of Disappointment and determining with precision its position, about which so much has been said and written. Accordingly, as the island was made directly ahead a short period after noon, and passed at a distance of only three or four miles, its exact position was accurately determined by data derived from the noon-day observation.

It is a low island, with two detached rocks extending a cable or two in length from its extreme point, and lies in latitude 27° 15′ north, and in longitude 140° 56′ 30″ east from Greenwich.

It is presumed that Disappointment and Rosario are one and the same island. In addition to the nautical observation of the officers of the ship, the artist made a drawing of the appearance of the island, which will be found in the Appendix.

As, therefore, the obstacles to a free navigation of the Japan seas no longer present themselves, our whaling ships may cruise in safety and without interruption as near to the shores as may be convenient, or in the seas lying more to the eastward. But to render this part of the ocean in all respects convenient to our whaling ships something more is wanted, and that is a port of resort, which shall be in all respects free for them to enter and depart without the restraints of exclusive laws and national prejudices; for though, as before remarked, the ports of Hakodadi and Simoda, in Japan, to which we may add Napha, in great Lew Chew, are by treaty open to American vessels, a long time may elapse before the people of those ports will probably divest themselves of the jealousies which they have hitherto entertained against strangers, and it is well known that the crews of whaling vessels visiting the ports of the Pacific are not remarkable for their orderly behavior or conciliatory deportment, hence my argument in favor of an establishment at the Bonin Islands is strengthened. My plan is to establish a colony at Port Lloyd, Peel Island, the principal of the Bonin group, leaving the question of sovereignty to be discussed hereafter. I have already in the narrative described these islands, and shall now proceed to set forth my plan for building up a thrifty settlement which shall extend over the entire group of islands.

First, then, a company of merchants, in connexion with a few artisans, should form a joint stock company for the purpose of establishing a colony on Peel Island. The experiment need not involve any very great outlay. Two vessels, each of three or four hundred tons, suitably equipped for whaling, should be employed first in transporting to the island materials for the construction of a storehouse and a few small dwellings, and the necessary supplies for furnishing a store with chandlery, naval stores groceries, and all such articles as are usually needed by whaling and other ships. After landing the passengers and cargo, these vessels might proceed to cruise in the neighborhood and in the Japan seas in pursuit of whales—returning occasionally to the settlement for refreshment, &c.; when these two vessels shall have jointly secured enough of oil to load one of them, that one should be sent home to be again refitted and freighted with additional colonists and fresh supplies for the storehouse and for the settlers; and so the two vessels might alternate in their voyages to the United States. Thus in a short time a colony could be built up, and the results prove profitable to all parties concerned. Whaling vessels, American, English, and French, would resort in greater numbers to the port for refreshment and supplies, becoming customers in the purchase of needful articles for their vessels, and giving employment to the artisans and farmers of the colony. If money should be wanted by the whalemen visiting the port, to make payment for labor or supplies, oil at just prices would be taken in lieu thereof. There should be sent out by the company none but young married people, quarters for whom could be obtained in the houses of the present settlers till dwellings could be erected for their exclusive occupation. Thus the settlement would, in all probability, form the nucleus of a religious and happy community, and here a missionary station might be formed without obstacle, from whence missionaries at a proper season might be sent to Japan, Formosa, and other benighted countries in that quarter of the globe. At the present time whaling vessels cruising in the seas lying between the Sandwich Islands and Japan are frequently obliged to resort either to those islands or to Hong Kong for refitment and supplies, a distance from some of their whaling grounds of several thousands of miles; in such a voyage, and in the unavoidable delay in port, much time is occupied; and apart from the enormous charges made at those ports, which make it necessary to draw heavily upon the owners at home, the crews become sickly and demoralized by their indulgence in dissipation. Now, a depôt established at Peel Island would be central, and would probably be wanting, for a length of years, at least, in the means for improper indulgence, for which the ports before mentioned are notorious. The right of sovereignty undoubtedly belongs to Japan, as the earliest known occupant of the islands; beyond this claim the present settlers have unquestionably priority of right of jurisdiction.

From Disappointment Island the course of the ship was steered directly for the Borodinos as laid down in the ordinary charts. They were made on the 22d of June directly ahead, and were found to be two in number, situated five miles apart, and lying in a N.N.E. and S.S.W. direction. They appeared to be of coral formation but of great antiquity, as trees of considerable size crowned the uplands, the most elevated part of which may have been forty feet above the level of the sea. The navigation in the immediate neighborhood seemed free of danger, but no indentations were seen in the surrounding shore which might afford safe anchoring places. No signs of people were discovered, and it is presumed that the islands are uninhabited. The position of the extremity at the south of the southern island was estimated to be in latitude 25° 47′, and in longitude 131° 19′ east.

As during the return voyage moderate breezes from S.S.W. to S.W. prevailed with warm weather, and as, in fact, the wind ever since the first departure from Napha had continued from the southward and westward, it may be inferred that the southwest monsoon extends as far north as the parallels of latitude in which the course of the ships laid. The Susquehanna and Saratoga reached, in the evening of June 23d, their anchorage in the bay of Napha, where they found the Mississippi, the Plymouth, and the Supply.

Port Lloyd and Bonin Islands.

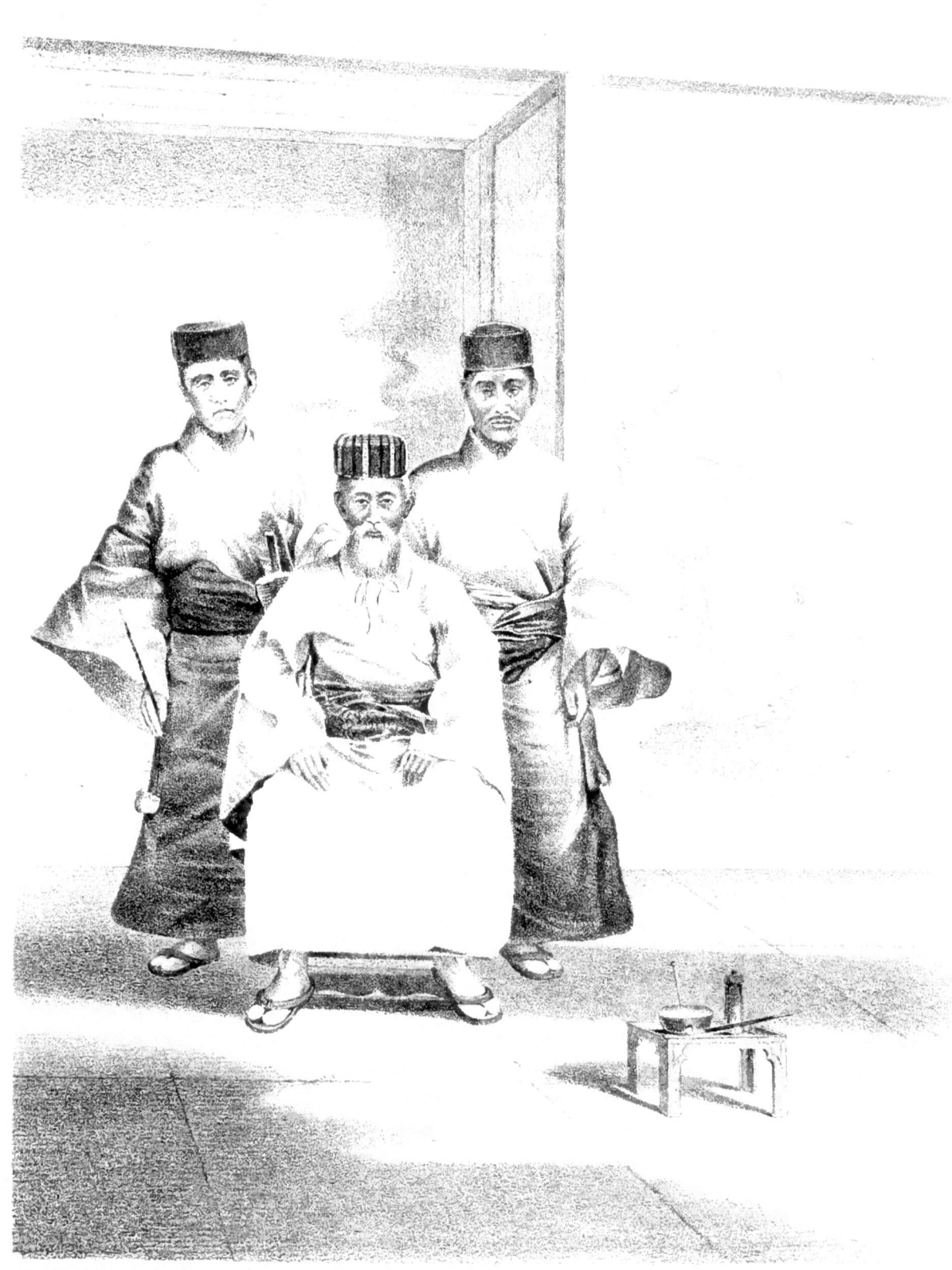

CHAPTER XI.

CHANGES AT NAPHA, NEW REGENT.—BANQUET ON BOARD OF THE SUSQUEHANNA.—EXCESSIVE DIGNITY OF THE NEW REGENT.—STATELINESS OF LEW CHEWANS THAWED OUT BY THE DINNER.—GUESTS SENT HOME.—BAMBOO VILLAGE.—INTERIOR OF LEW CHEW HOUSES.—MEN INDOLENT.—GOSSIPPING AT LEW CHEW.—LEW CHEW LOOM.—DIFFERENT CLASSES OF THE PEOPLE.—THEIR FEAR OF SPIES.—SLAVERY OF PEASANTS.—CAUSES OF DEGRADATION.—EXCELLENCE OF AGRICULTURAL CULTIVATION.—ORIGIN OF POPULATION OF LEW CHEW.—FORMER KINGDOMS ON THE ISLAND.—RELATION OF LEW CHEW TO CHINA AND JAPAN, RESPECTIVELY.—EDUCATION IN LEW CHEW.—RELIGION OF THE INHABITANTS.—CHRISTIAN MISSION IN LEW CHEW.—DISTINCTIONS OF DRESS.—PEOPLE SELL THEMSELVES AS SLAVES.—CLANSHIP.—COIN IN LEW CHEW.—SUGAR MAKING.—NATURAL PRODUCTS OF THE ISLAND.

WHEN the squadron returned to Napha, on the 23d of June, it was found that a new regent had been installed. The old occupant, who had so pertinaciously striven to prevent the Commodore's visit to Shui, and who had also so bountifully entertained our countrymen at his own habitation, had, it was said, been deposed. It was difficult to ascertain with certainty the causes of this degradation, but it was not to be doubted that, if true, it was in some mode connected with the presence of our ships at Napha, and probably resulted from the admission of the Commodore and his suite into the royal residence at Shui. It was not a pleasant reflection to the officers that they should have been, however innocently, the cause of the poor old man's degradation; and it seemed hard to understand why their visit should have led to more serious consequences than those produced by that of the officers of H. B. M. ship Sphynx to the same place. At first, it was rumored that the old regent had been obliged to perform the *hara-kiri*, or disembowelling operation; but the painful feelings produced by this intelligence were happily relieved by the sight of the old man in his house at Shui, by two of the officers of the Susquehanna. Dr. Bettelheim (who did not seem to feel any pity for the degraded dignitary) stated that he would probably be banished, with his family, to one of the smaller islands.

The Commodore, who was quite satisfied with the conciliatory measures that had been pursued during his absence, now renewed his invitation to the regent and treasurer to dine on board the Susquehanna, on Tuesday, the 28th of June, offering to send boats for them. This invitation was accepted; and the Commodore had reason to doubt the whole story of the old regent's degradation, from the fact that the new regent, *Shang Hung Hiun*, a member of the family of his predecessor, and a much younger man, did not hesitate to accept an invitation to the dinner, but went even further in his courtesies and attentions than the old regent had ever done. As far as he could ascertain the facts, the Commodore believed that the old man had voluntarily resigned in favor of the young one.

On the appointed day of the feast, three of the ship's boats were sent off to the creek at Tumai to bring on board the invited guests. On their arrival, and after the usual presentation of crimson cards, they came on board in robes of the finest and cleanest grass-cloth, and with *hatchee matchees* of showy color on their heads. Captain Buchanan received them at the gangway, and conducted them through the various parts of the ship. The day was oppressively warm, and the visitors found it so sultry between decks, and especially in the engine room, that they were glad once more to stand upon the upper deck. The marines were under arms, and the band played to give honor to their reception. When dinner was announced they were ushered into the Commodore's cabin, and immediately sat down to the table. The entertainment was, of course, entirely in accordance with European and American customs. The Commodore took the centre of the table, with the regent on his right hand and the chief treasurer on his left, while the mayor of Napha and one of the other treasurers were seated near the ends of the table, where they were taken in charge by the commanders of the different vessels of the squadron. Mr. Williams and Dr. Bettelheim were present as guests and interpreters; while at a smaller

Dinner to the Regent on board of the Susquehanna.

table were Messrs. O. H. Perry, Portman, Taylor, and Heine. None of the regent's suite were allowed to sit at table with him, but remained in attendance. His interpreter, Ichirazichi, the same whom we have already presented to our readers, stood behind him.

The new-regent was a small man, apparently about forty-five years old, of more swarthy complexion than any of his suite, and with a slight cast in his left eye. He was remarkably grave and taciturn, seemed to be perpetually awake to the novelty of his position, having at times a restless and uneasy expression of countenance, and never spoke except when he was particularly addressed. It was very evident that he was less at his ease than any person present. This, perhaps, arose from his newly acquired rank, to which he had not yet become accustomed, and possibly some embarrasment may have been caused by the apprehension that he should be wanting in some of the proprieties of etiquette at an American dinner table. Perhaps, too, he was not without his fears that, surrounded as he knew himself to be by spies, his visit might bring in its train some unpleasant political consequences. His dress consisted of a dark purple or violet-colored robe and a cap of crimson. The treasurers, both old men with wrinkled faces and scanty grey beards, wore similar caps, while their robes were yellow. The mayor was attired in a robe of pearl-white grass cloth, and had on his head a crimson cap. The hair of all was put up with massive gold pins, and their girdles were of rich Chinese silk. These various dresses were presumed to be official, and in their diversity of color indicative of difference of rank. The inferior attendants who stood behind these dignitaries were dressed in blue and yellow with scarlet caps.

Knives and forks were placed, in our usual fashion, for each guest. The first seemed to be very much in the way of the Lew Chewans; with the last they did better, and showed some dexterity in making them answer the purpose of chop sticks. This, however, was a matter of but little moment, as, be the implements used what they may, hungry men will contrive in some mode to convey food to their mouths, and the Lew Chewans, like sensible men, manifested no intention of avoiding awkwardness at such a heavy price as the loss of a good dinner; and the dinner was very good. Turtle soup, goose, kid curry, and various other delicacies formed part of the feast which was spread with bountiful profusion. To the soup the mayor and treasurer did ample justice, and in their appreciation of its excellence were not unworthy rivals of a London Alderman. The cabin was sultry, and as the feast proceeded the guests grew warmer, (for they were very much in earnest,) until finally they asked permission to remove their caps, and this having been done, the attendant of each, standing behind, vigorously fanned the uncovered head of his master. Punch followed the soup and furnished them with a new gustatory enjoyment. They had given the Commodore some of their *saki*, and he was now resolved to give them a taste of the *saki* made in all other parts of the world. So there were French and German wines, Scotch and American whiskey, madeira and sherry, and the gin of Holland, winding up with the sweet, smooth, strong maraschino, which decidedly, in their estimation, bore away the palm. They smacked their lips and shut their eyes at each sip of the limpid delicacy, and, in short, showed but a very sorry appreciation of the virtue of temperance. And while they were thus almost equalling Christendom in genteel dissipation, Mr. Heine, at the small table, was making a sketch of the group, and Mr. Portman was taking a portrait of the regent.

After feeding heartily on the substantials, they asked leave to smoke their pipes; it was of course accorded, and the chief treasurer, after a few whiffs, presented his, with the embroidered tobacco pouch attached, to the Commodore. The mayor and other treasurers followed his example by handing theirs to Captains Buchanan and Adams. There seemed to be no end to the capacity of stomach in some of these officials. Preserved oysters and other articles of food sealed up in America, excited an admiration as boundless as their appetites. Part of the dessert consisted of melons and bananas brought from the Bonin Islands. These took them completely captive and they begged that they might carry some home to their wives. They were, of course, told to do so, and forthwith the loose folds of each one's robe above his girdle was converted into a pocket and loaded with what it would hold.

When things had reached this stage, there was but too much reason to fear that "the tide of wine and wassail was fast gaining on the dry land of sober judgment." All reserve was now fully thawed out. The quiet repose of a calm contentment sat enthroned on the shining face of the jolly old mayor of Napha. The wrinkled visages of the two withered old treasurers flushed and expanded into rubicund fullness. The regent alone preserved his silent, anxious demeanor, and all he drank was neutralized in its effects by his excessive dignity. He appeared cordial and friendly but once, and that was when the Commodore offered him an assortment of American garden seed and vegetables. These he promised to plant and carefully cultivate. The Commodore had previously landed, as a present, cattle and buffaloes; these he also promised should be carefully looked to and their offspring preserved.

The band had been playing on the deck while the guests were feasting, and when the weightier part of the festival was over the Commodore ordered down some of the more expert performers, to play solos on the flageolet, hautboy, clarionet, and cornet-a-piston. The regent listened attentively, but the mayor and treasurers were too busy in stowing away the epular fragments to be moved by any "concord of sweet sounds." Coffee was offered them, under the name of "American tea." They did not relish it, and resorted once more to their pipes. The attendants had not been forgotten. They had enjoyed an abundance of meat and drink in the steward's pantry, and relished it quite as much as their masters. But all earthly enjoyment must have an end, and the feast at last was over. The guests were put on shore at Tumai, leaving the ship under a salute of three guns; and so ended the dinner given to the regent on on board the Susquehanna.

The return to Lew Chew afforded to some of the officers an opportunity of making further examinations as to the external aspect of the island, and of catching further glimpses of the habits and pursuits of the inhabitants. One of the gentlemen attached to the Saratoga thus describes the result of one of his explorations:

"Rambled over the hill this afternoon to a most remarkable village. Approaching toward the spot, it appeared to be a thick swamp of green brushwood. Not a house nor anything of the kind was to be seen. It looked like one of those long, low, marshy thickets, in which I hunted for blackbirds' eggs, in my boyhood. But on reaching it, after crossing a wide, clear field of grass, we passed into and through one of the sweetest little villages I ever entered, completely embowered with thickly matted tops of the tall and swaying bamboo, artistically laid off in squares, with level streets of red sandy soil, overarched with the branches of the bamboo, that formed hedges on either side, through which, at regular distances, were openings into the gardens surrounding the dwellings of the inhabitants, highly cultivated with a variety of vegetables. I had neither read of nor seen a town like this."

In the course of his ramble, the officer from whose journal this extract is made entered several of the dwellings, for the purpose of gratifying his curiosity concerning the domestic arrangements. He found the floors invariably covered with thick mats, of regular width and length, laid side by side, as a carpet. These he found constituted the sleeping place at night, and to preserve them from dirt, the inhabitants always step on them with the feet bare, or

AFTERNOON GOSSIP AT HA CHAU.

covered with stockings only; when they enter from without, they slip off their loose straw sandals at the door. In every instance where he entered, our informant found that the men were the drones of the hive, and the women the workers. From three to half a dozen of the former were invariably to be seen, seated upon their crossed ankles, in a circle, with a cup of live coals, a little box of fine cut tobacco, and a spittoon, in the centre. Thus seated, in dreamy indolence, they would draw forth their little pipes from their belts, unsheath them, take a mere pinch of the tobacco from the box, and place it in the little metallic bowl of the pipe, which was not more than half the size of a young girl's thimble, light it, and after two or three long whiffs, they would retain the smoke for a minute or more, and then, with a strong impulse, send it through the nostrils, as the opium smoker does. This ended the enjoyment for that occasion. The pipes were then returned to their sheaths, when a little tea-pot, holding less than half a pint, with half a dozen cups, each of about the capacity of three teaspoons, was brought by a servant, and a general sipping took the place of smoking. The tea disposed of, the pipes were again resorted to, and thus did they alternate between tobacco and tea. Before rising to separate, the *saki* was introduced and circulated, sometimes beyond the limits of prudence and discretion. These were the occupations of the "lords of creation;" the poor women, meanwhile, might be seen, half naked, delving with the hoe or the spade, in the adjacent gardens, under a scorching sun. Sometimes this idle gossiping over tea and the pipe is carried on in the open air, under the shade of some spreading tree.

When the poor females are not thus employed in the cultivation of the earth, there is still found work enough for them of some other kind, for their destiny is labor. In every house may be seen the loom for weaving grass cloth, and it is quite a curiosity in its way. It is small, not more than two feet high, and generally is placed in the corner of the room. The shuttle is two or three feet long, so that before it leaves one hand of the weaver it may be grasped by the other. It is but a rude implement, and yet the fine, glossy fabric wrought by its agency is exceedingly beautiful.

What has here been said must be understood as applying to the men who are not of the very lowest class. According to the best observations the Commodore could make, he classified the inhabitants into four grades: these were, first, the high officers of state; secondly, the priesthood and literary men; thirdly, the under officers and spies; and lastly the laboring class, (including particularly the fishermen,) by the toil of which last all the rest live; for it was never seen that any of the classes above named, except the last, ever appeared to have any thing to do, save the spies, and they might be met at every step. These infest every corner and every threshold. If the officers walked the streets, these fellows might be seen preceding or following them, directing all doors to be closed, and the women to keep out of sight. The people, indeed, whenever they were sure of not being seen by some of these vermin, manifested no indisposition to communication and intercourse, and gladly received from the strangers little gratuities and presents, which were taken with a trembling hand and instantly concealed, while their eyes glanced rapidly and furtively from side to side to see that they were unobserved. The Commodore was deeply moved, as indeed were all the gentlemen of the expedition, by the tyranny exercised toward the mass of the people. "God pity these poor creatures!" says the former in his journal: "I have seen much of the world, have observed savage life in many of its conditions; but *never*, unless I may except the miserable peons in Mexico, have I looked upon such an amount of apparent wretchedness as these squalid slaves would seem to suffer." "The poor, naked creatures, who toil from morning till night, know not the relaxation of a Sabbath, nor the rest of an occasional holiday, generally granted by even the most cruel taskmasters. The wages of a field laborer is from three to eight cents per diem; the mechanic may receive ten. Out of this, he has to provide food, clothing, and shelter for a family, with which most of the common people are burdened, and it is surprising to see how soon the boys, for we see but little of the girls, are made to labor. In looking into a blacksmith's shop at Napha, I observed a father and two sons making nails: the elder son, probably ten years old, was using the hammer, while the younger, not more than five, was blowing the bellows, or rather moving the piston of a sort of air pump, which required some amount of physical exertion. When we entered the shop, neither of the three took the slightest notice of us, but went on with their labor; even the little boy scarcely lifted his eyes; and this seeming indifference, it may be remarked, was the case with laborers and all others whom we met, when they supposed that the eye of a spy was upon them." "Whatever progress we may make in conciliating the higher classes, and we have made considerable, the lower orders of the people dare not, even by a look, evince the slightest emotion; their stolid and impassive features express nothing but toil and care, and are a sufficient index of their abject condition." "I can conceive of no greater act of humanity than it would be to rescue, if possible, these miserable beings from the oppression of their tyrannical rulers." "These poor creatures are the people who have been represented by Captain Basil Hall as so innocent and so happy!" Well disposed, peaceful, and naturally amiable, our gentlemen generally believed them to be; but they were ignorant, and had been long obliged to resort to the weapons of the weak; they were, therefore, cunning and insincere. Under proper treatment, something might be made of them, but at present, they want the essential element of self-respect. Another obstacle in the way of their improvement is the impossibility of their ever procuring a vested right of ownership in the land. As far as the Commodore could gather information on the subject, it would appear that the soil is held by the government, and its agents are employed to collect and consume its produce. According to the best accounts that could be obtained, the actual cultivator receives not more than two-tenths of the produce. Of the remainder, six-tenths go to the lord of the soil, or ruler, and two-tenths for the expense of supervision of the land, costs of collection, &c. The peasant has thus no stimulus to exertion. Wretched, however, as this system is, and degraded as is the condition of the operative, it is astonishing to see the large returns from agricultural labor. Nowhere do the people better understand the art of producing the largest crops of which the land cultivated is capable; no matter what may be the character and condition of the soil, or the relative position of the field cultivated. The same is said to be true of all the cultivated portions of the neighboring groups of islands. Every advantage is taken of circumstances, and irrigation is both understood and practised with skill and success. With such a soil and climate as Lew Chew possesses, if all parts of it that might be cultivated were made fields of agricultural labor, it would support a very large population.

One of the subjects to which the attention of the Commodore was drawn, was the origin of the population of Lew Chew. Want of sufficient material has not enabled ethnology as yet conclusively to settle this question; and, of course, the gentlemen of the expedition who attended to this particular had to find their way as best they might. Many speculations have been hazarded on the subject, founded on the very limited observations of the few Europeans who have visited the islands. Of Captain Hall we have already spoken. "The description of Captain Basil Hall," says the Commodore, "is a mere romance; the production of the inventive brain of a writer not very scrupulous of historical truth; and the account of Doctor McLeod, of the Alceste, is not much nearer to accuracy. Captains Beechey and Belcher, surveying officers of the British navy, have visited Great Lew Chew since those just named, and their statements may be considered as much more worthy of confidence; but, after all, such are the difficulties in the way, that they had not much, if any, better means of acquiring a knowledge of the history, laws, and civil institutions of this singular people, than had those who preceded them. Difficulties have also beset us in our investigations, and all the facts we may learn are but contributions on a subject yet open to, and demanding more thorough investigation. We throw what we can gather into the common heap."

As far as the Lew Chewans themselves bear testimony to their origin, they claim, like the Chinese, to have their descent from a divine source. According to Chow-Hwang, a Chinese writer, who was sent to Lew Chew in 1757, as an envoy from China, and who on his return published an account of the island, "the islanders declare that the original progenitors of the Lew Chewans were two, a man and a woman. They had five children; the oldest was a son, named Téén-Sun, (Offspring of Heaven.) who was the first master or ruler of the nation; the second son acted the part of his minister, and the third constituted the people. The older daughter, for the protection of the country, took the place of the God of Heaven, and the younger personified the God of the Sea. Téén-Sun and his descendants having maintained the government for 17,802 years, were at length succeeded by Shunteen, a branch of the then ruling family of Japan. This occurred about A. D. 1200, when the Ming dynasty arose in China. Three kings ruled in Lew Chew; one was styled 'King of the Central Hills;' the second 'King of the Southern Hills;' and the third 'King of the Northern Hills.' All were tributary, and reigned by permission of 'the Son of Heaven.' At length the first became master of the whole country, which has ever since remained under one king, always acknowledging himself a tributary of the Chinese empire."*

Klaproth, professing to follow Chinese and Japanese annals, gives an account agreeing pretty well with the foregoing by Chow-Hwang, and says further, that the race of kings reigning in Lew Chew is related to the imperial family of Japan; that both China and Japan claim the sovereignty, and that the Lew Chewans pay tribute to both.

As to the three kings of the "central," "northern," and "southern" hills, respectively, there is something in the discoveries of our exploring parties that may seem to give countenance to the truth of that portion of the story. It will be remembered by the reader that the explorers reported the discovery of the ruins of a castle or palace at Nagagusko; the ruins of another were afterwards found, of which an account will be given on a future page, and these were no doubt the residences of the northern and southern kings, while the third at Shui, perfect, and still used as the royal residence, was the palace of the "King of the Central Hills." The traditions of Lew Chew even to this day (as our officers found) preserve the memory of the former existence of distinct sovereignties on the island.

Chow-Hwang claims, as we have seen, sovereignty over the island at this day for the Chinese Emperor; and one of the points which appeared difficult to determine was the precise relation which Lew Chew bore to China and Japan respectively. That a tribute was sent in Chinese junks to China annually from Lew Chew seemed to be an established fact, yet the officials of

---

* Chinese Repository for July, 1837, vol. VI.

Lew Chew did not appear to be Chinese, and the common language of the country is not that of the celestial empire, though Chinese is understood and spoken by some of the Lew Chewans who are educated. As to any rights Japan may have, all we can say is, that the Japanese commissioners informed Commodore Perry at a subsequent period, when he met them in conference on the proposed points of a treaty, "that Lew Chew was a distant dependency, over which the crown [of Japan] had limited control." It is also certain that most of the trade to Lew Chew is carried on by Japanese junks. The testimony of the Lew Chewans themselves is contained in the following extract of a letter addressed to Commodore Perry by the officials of Napha: "Since the days of the Ming dynasty it has been our great pride to be ranked as one of the outer dependencies of China, and she has for ages given our king his investiture, and we have returned whatever we could prepare for tribute; nothing of great importance to our nation has transpired but it has been made known to the Emperor. Whenever the time came for us to send up the tribute, we there [in China] purchased silk and pongee to make suitable official robes and caps for ourselves, and selected medicines and other things for the use of the state; and if they were not enough for our own use, then through the island of Tuchara we have intercourse with a friendly and near nation, and exchange for our productions, as black sugar, saki, grasscloth, and other articles, things which we send to China as tribute." The friendly and near nation alluded to is Japan.

Dr. Bettelheim, who lived some years in Lew Chew, believed, for several good reasons, that "the country, though independent to a certain extent, (its ruler being permitted, for a good contribution to Pekin, to assume the high-sounding title of king,) yet is, to all ends and purposes, an integral part of Japan." His reasons were briefly these:

1. "There is a Japanese garrison quartered in Napha." It must not, however, be understood that they show themselves openly, for the Lew Chewans pretend that they are an unwarlike people, without military arms or accoutrements; but Dr. Bettelheim accidentally came upon a part of the garrison employed in cleaning their arms.

2. The trade of Lew Chew is entirely with Japan. If the island were a Chinese dependency this would not be so. Japan sends annually thirty or forty junks to Lew Chew, of about four hundred and fifty tons each; only one Lew Chewan junk goes annually to China, and every alternate year one more, said to carry tribute, but not a single Chinese junk is ever allowed to enter Napha.

3. The Japanese are to be found in numbers in Lew Chew, and stroll about as uninterruptedly as the natives; they intermarry with the Lew Chewans, cultivate lands, build houses in Napha, and, in short, seem to be perfectly at home. But a Chinaman is as much hunted and spied after, and pelted, and insulted as any other foreigner. This is strikingly confirmed by the journal of one of our officers, who remarks, from facts that he was witness to: "They [the Lew Chewans] are evidently quite as much opposed to intercourse with China as with all other nations, notwithstanding the similarity, if not the *identity*, of their religion, literature, and many of their manners and customs. Indeed, they are *de facto* and *de jure* a part of Japan, and their motto is, 'uncompromising non-intercourse with all the world.'"

4. In all Dr. Bettelheim's intercourse with the Lew Chew authorities there were always present, at least, two individuals, who, it was obvious, had the management of the meeting and controlled the Lew Chew officials. These he conjectured to be Japanese inspectors.

5. The language, dress, customs, virtues, and vices of Lew Chew correspond to those of Japan,

thus establishing a *prima facie* relationship. Of these the language is to the ethnologist the most satisfactory proof, and of the researches of some of our gentlemen, on this point, we shall speak more particularly in its appropriate place, on a future page.

The English Bishop of Victoria, who, in the discharge of his official duties, visited Lew Chew in 1850, thus speaks on this subject: "On the whole, it seems far the most probable opinion that Lew Chew was peopled by a colony from Japan, to which people their physiognomy, language, and customs have a close affinity; and that to China they owe the far more important debt of their partial civilization and literature. The government of the country appears to consist in a grievous oligarchy of literati immediately dependent upon Japan. They stand in great fear of the latter country, and look to it, and not to China, for protection in time of need. They have an historical tradition that a few hundred years ago, during the Ming dynasty, a war broke out between China and Japan, during which the former, wanting to detach Lew Chew from the latter, raised it to the dignity of a separate kingdom. In token of vassalage, every new king receives a formal investiture from a Chinese officer, specially deputed and sent for that purpose from Foo Chow; to which city, also, a biennial tribute-junk is sent from Lew Chew. At the Tartar invasion of China, and the commencement of the present foreign dynasty, above two hundred years ago, about thirty-six Chinese families, unwilling to conform to the Tartar changes of costume and rule, emigrated to Lew Chew, the descendants of whom have become, generally, the schoolmasters of the country, and amalgamated with the people." The Commodore, from such observation as he could make, thought that the Lew Chewans were a mixture, made up possibly of Japanese, (who preponderated,) Chinese, Formosans, and, perhaps, Malays; and that the island, commencing its population at a very early period, from some accident, such as shipwreck, had, from time to time, added to its inhabitants from the adjacent regions, until the whole was fused into the present stock. In personal appearance the Lew Chewans did not seem to him to be unequivocally either Chinese or Japanese in aspect. They are not a handsome people, nor yet can they be called decidedly ugly. Their complexion is rather Chinese, and they have black eyes and hair; the latter of which, by the way, they do not dress after the Chinese fashion; for, instead, of long plaited tails hanging down behind, it is gathered, with great care and neatness, into a knot on the top of the head, and there fastened with a pin of silver or other metal—the nature of the metal used indicating the rank of the wearer.

As to education, the opportunity afforded of acquiring information was necessarily limited, and the best account the Commodore could obtain on that subject was from Dr. Bettelheim, who had been for some years resident on the island. "In Shui," says he, "I have seen a building with an inscription, perhaps well rendered, '*University*,' on the door. In Napha is a school for proficients in Confucian lore. But in general, learning—as far as it goes, *i. e.* a mere knowledge of Chinese characters and of some of their classical books—is diffused by the elder instructing the younger; a kind of Lancasterian system, carried on in the whole country, in almost every house. Still, there are schools beside, and likewise the Kung-Kwas, government houses in Napha, as well as Tumai, serve as schools. In the Kung-Kwas, however, no teacher is appointed; but in the out-buildings usually added to every Confucian temple, I found often children assembled under the superintendance of a master, who seems to have the benefit of free residence and the adjoining grounds for salary." "Aping China in everything, Lew Chew has also its three yearly examinations, which, for the time being, make quite a stir in the learned world, but hold out no prospect for high station, as in China. At most, the fortunate candidate gets, beside a good fill of honor, a rice pension or a schoolmastership. The Samnus are also delegated, by turns, to teach in the country schools. By all these means the knowledge of the Chinese character is pretty widely diffused among the people, the women, only, being entirely without any literary culture."

As to what is taught, all the books, as well as learning, in Lew Chew come from China, whither, yearly, some of the native youths of the higher class are sent for education. The Chinese character is in general use in Lew Chew; but the inhabitants have also (says Dr. Bettelheim) a running hand of their own, which, he thinks, is the real ancient Chinese hieroglyphic, "awfully crippled." In some manuscripts which he saw in this writing, every Lew Chew character had opposite to it the modern legible Chinese sign; and many Lew Chewans do not understand the character at all. They are, however, very proud of it, and say it is a "language" of their own; though, as far as could be ascertained, the signs used do not at all express the sounds of the spoken Lew Chew language, which is, undoubtedly, a dialect of Japanese. Neither is this writing, as has been said, identical with the Japanese *hirakana*. Most of the books seen in Lew Chew were in the ordinary Chinese character. The Japanese character, however, is understood; for writings were seen, made by Lew Chewans, in the *Katakana*. With such apparatus for learning it may well be supposed that the attainments of the masses, except in those matters which are communicated orally, must be limited. The Lew Chewans have no literature of their own, nor has any author, so far as we know, ever appeared among them. The Confucian classics of China are the text books, and these, says the Bishop of Victoria, "consist more in an apparently mechanical repetition of sounds than in any mental recreation from the sentiments contained in those literary monuments of a venerable antiquity."

The reader will probably be somewhat interested to know something of the religious opinions of these distant islanders, and of the circumstances under which Dr. Bettelheim became a resident among them. As to the first, it may be said, in general terms, that the religion of the natives seems to be a mixture of Confucianism and Buddhism. But it is best to let them on this head speak for themselves. When the Bishop of Victoria was at the island, in 1850, the captain of H. B. M. steamer, the Reynard, received two communications from the native authorities, written in Chinese, in the latter of which they thus speak: "Now, as to the religion of the Lord of Heaven," [this is the phrase by which they designate Christianity,] "we have, from ancient times, attended to the doctrines of Confucius, and found therein principles wherewith to cultivate personal morality, and to regulate our families, each according to our circumstances and condition in life. We endeavor, also, to carry out the government of the country according to the rules and maxims which have been handed down to us by the sages, and are calculated to secure lasting peace and tranquility. Besides, our gentry, as well as the common people, are without natural capacity; and, although they have attended exclusively to Confucianism, they have as yet been unable to arrive at perfection in it. If they should now, also, have to study, in addition, the religion of the Lord of Heaven, such an attempt would surpass our ability, and the heart does not incline to it."

On the compound of Confucianism and Buddhism many superstitions have been grafted. Filial reverence here, as in China, is the chief of virtues, and, theoretically, at least, underlies as a basis the system of government, which is professedly patriarchal. This, as the Bishop of Victoria has well remarked, is the great source of slavery, and opens a wide door for the grossest tyranny on the part of the so-called paternal rulers. How far these poor and oppressed beings are in a condition to be impressed by the truths of Christianity it would be difficult to say; but, from the early experience of Dr. Bettelheim, there is reason to think that the common people, if left to themselves, would be willing listeners to the Christian teacher; and the benevolence of gospel principles would probably contrast so strongly and advantageously with the cruelty and oppression under which they groan, that we cannot but believe there are few spots of paganism where, under God's blessing, efforts to Christianize would probably be more successful than in Lew Chew, were the people left to freedom of thought and action.

As to the establishment of Dr. Bettelheim as a missionary in the island, its history, as we gather from the Bishop of Victoria, is briefly this: Not many years ago, certain pious officers of the British navy, (among whom was prominent Lieutenant Clifford, who, we believe, visited the island with Captain Basil Hall,) formed an association among themselves, under the name of the "Lew Chew Naval Mission," for the purpose of sending Christian missionaries to the island. The missionary whom they first sent was Dr. Bettelheim, a converted Jew, and by birth a Hungarian, not, however, in holy orders, but a christian layman. He had become a British subject by naturalization, and the husband of an English woman. He possessed many qualifications for his work. He was a physician, a good linguist, with great energy of mind and activity of body, and most indefatigable perseverance. He possessed, also, a boldness of nature, which caused him fearlessly to assert his rights as a British subject, and, perhaps, not always with discretion. Two missionaries of the Roman church were, at first, in Lew Chew with him, one of whom was made titular bishop of Samos and vicar general of Japan; but these, in utter despair of success, abandoned their mission, and left the island, while Dr. Bettelheim still abode at his post, and never relaxed his labors. Commodore Perry found him at Napha, as we have already related, and he had been there since May, 1846. The opposition to Dr. Bettelheim's labors did not come from the common people. At first his communications with them were freely allowed, and they seemed well disposed to be taught. But the authorities soon took the alarm, and, as there is reason to think, on political grounds merely. They were afraid of their Japanese masters, who, as they well knew, would tolerate no show of Christianity in the kingdom, and would look upon its introduction into Lew Chew as the first step toward breaking down the exclusive system of Japan. At first, therefore, the authorities at Napha used mild persuasion with Dr. Bettelheim to prevail upon him to leave the island; then followed less equivocal marks of opposition—the people were forbidden to go near him or to remain with him if he came among them; and, finally, a system of insult, annoyance, ceaseless espionage, and intimidation, was adopted, in the hope of driving him away. But all these means were in vain. The missionary stayed in Lew Chew, and at the time of the Commodore's arrival, he and the inhabitants were living in a condition of undisguised hostility toward each other. It was soon but too apparent that the presence of the missionary, however meritorious he might be, seemed to promise but little for the extension of Christianity in the island at that period.

A renewed opportunity of observation on this second visit enabled the gentlemen of the expedition to catch some additional features of social life, as well as to obtain further insight into manners and customs. There is a gradation in the rank of officers analogous to that existing in China, and here, as there, manifested by some peculiarity of dress. The great distinctive mark, however, between the higher classes and the general population consists in the hair-pin. The crown of the head, to the extent of two or three inches, is shaved, and into the vacant space the residue of the hair is all drawn, and plaited somewhat into the form of a circular comb. A free use is made of oil and lamp-black in arranging it. Two large hair-pins are then passed through the mass, to keep it in place, and the front end of the lower pin is finished with a head in the form of a star. The different metals of which the pins are made indicate the rank of the wearer. They are of gold, silver, brass, lead, and pewter. The lower class generally wear brass, though the very poorest use sometimes the metals last named. The literati or dignitaries use gold and silver. The pin, therefore, tells the rank at once. The lowest order of the people consists of the public slaves, (*oo-bang*,) who have no civil rights nor personal freedom, and must obey the slightest beck of the literati. Their condition is one of utter degradation. The intermediate class next above these is composed of the peasants or field laborers, (*Hat-koo-shoo*.) These farm the country, paying to the government one-half of the products in lieu of taxes, and paying also an exorbitant rent. We have already stated that two-tenths is all the laborer gets of the results of his toil. By this toil the literary class, which never works at all, is supported. The highest grade in the lower class is made up of the messengers, spies, menial officers, &c., in the service of government, and includes also the small traders and mechanics. This caste is known by the name of *We-dae-o-gang*. When doing duty for the government these receive no wages, nothing but their food, and the distant hope of promotion to the honor of substituting for the brass pin one of silver. The rich some-

Tombs in Lew Chew.

times purchase from a poor man his services for life, (a system of slavery,) but more generally for a term of years. The price of a common slave of this kind is from two to ten dollars.

Great respect is shown for the dead, and tombs elaborate and costly attest this feeling. They are constructed of stone, and often form a conspicuous feature in the landscape. Indeed, upon

the first approach of the squadron, their size, color, and position on the hill-sides caused them, at a distance, to be mistaken for dwellings.

A sort of clanship seems to obtain in each district, and the people of one village seldom marry with the inhabitants of another. The agriculturists, and indeed the common people generally, appear to know but few physical wants. They have sweet potatoes in abundance, and these, with a miserable hut to sleep in, seem to bound their very limited desires. Many of the poor are fishermen, but the larger number is composed of mechanics, employed chiefly in turning wooden implements and covering them with lacquer. The women commonly perform this latter branch, except as to the painting; this is done by men. The shops are few, and the articles sold are chiefly paper, rice, tea, sweetmeats, and clothing. The Lew Chewans always insisted that they had no current coin, and that their trade was always in a barter of specific objects. This may be in the main correct, as they appear to have but little metallic currency, and the Commodore endeavored in vain to procure from the authorities some of their coin in exchange for ours. They solemnly assured him they had no national currency; and, though they are very much in the habit, from motives of supposed policy, of exaggerating their poverty, this statement is probably true. They know, however, very well the value of the Chinese coin, and received it from our pursers in the settlement of accounts.

The vegetable and animal productions of Lew Chew are abundant enough. The sugar-cane thrives, and they have a rude mode of making sugar.

They export of this, as well as of saki, an intoxicating liquor distilled from rice, and very strong; they make also tobacco in considerable quantities, and smoking is a universal habit. Some cotton is also grown, and indigo is raised in the island. They also make salt by evaporation; and, were the island in other hands, its agricultural productions would support a large population, and furnish a surplus for exportation. Fowls, ducks, geese, pigs, goats, and a small species of black ox, are all very abundant. There is a small but active and tough breed of horses, and the wild boar is found in the forests. The general impression left on the minds of the gentlemen of the expedition was, that Lew Chew was a beautiful island, abundantly supplied, and needed but a good government to form, so far as bodily comfort is concerned, as pleasant a residence as could be desired.

Tombs in Lew Chew.

CHAPTER XII.

DEPARTURE FROM NAPHA FOR JAPAN.—COURSE OF THE SHIPS.—OHO-SIMA.—ISLAND SEEN BY COMMANDER GLYNN, PROBABLY OHO-SIMA.—CLEOPATRA ISLANDS.—CURRENTS.—FOURTH OF JULY ON BOARD.—APPROACH TO CAPE IDZU.—SQUADRON, LED BY THE SUSQUEHANNA, ENTERS THE BAY OF YEDO.—ROCK ISLAND.—HAZY ATMOSPHERE OF JAPAN.—SURPRISE OF THE JAPANESE AT SIGHT OF THE STEAMERS MOVING AGAINST WIND AND TIDE.—BAY OF SAGAMI.—APPEARANCE OF THE COAST AND COUNTRY INLAND.—FUSI-JAMA.—SHIPS MADE READY FOR ACTION.—FLEET OF JAPANESE BOATS PUT OFF FROM THE SHORE.—LEFT BEHIND BY SQUADRON.—BAY OF URAGA.—OPPOSITE COAST OF AWA.—JAPANESE FORTS.—SQUADRON COMES TO ANCHOR IN THE BAY OF URAGA.—SOUNDINGS ON APPROACHING THE ANCHORAGE.—JAPANESE GUARD-BOATS PUT OFF.—NO ONE PERMITTED TO COME ON BOARD THE SHIPS.—APPEARANCE OF GUARD-BOATS AND CREWS.—SKILL OF THE JAPANESE IN MANAGING THEIR BOATS.—GUARD-BOAT COMES ALONGSIDE OF THE MISSISSIPPI, AND JAPANESE FUNCTIONARY DEMANDS TO COME ON BOARD.—NOT PERMITTED.—NOTICE IN THE FRENCH LANGUAGE, ORDERING THE SHIPS AWAY, HELD UP TO BE READ.—INTERPRETERS DIRECTED TO INFORM THE JAPANESE THAT THE COMMODORE WOULD CONFER WITH NO ONE BUT THE HIGHEST OFFICIAL IN URAGA.—JAPANESE REPLIED THAT THEY HAD THE VICE GOVERNOR ON BOARD.—THIS OFFICER AND HIS INTERPRETER ALLOWED TO COME ON BOARD THE SUSQUEHANNA.—NOT PERMITTED TO SEE THE COMMODORE.—CONFERENCE WITH LIEUTENANT CONTEE, WHO EXPLAINS THAT THE AMERICANS HAVE COME ON A FRIENDLY MISSION AND THAT THE COMMODORE BEARS A LETTER FROM THE PRESIDENT OF THE UNITED STATES TO THE EMPEROR.—DESIRES THE APPOINTMENT OF AN OFFICER OF SUITABLE RANK TO RECEIVE IT FROM THE COMMODORE.—COMMODORE REFUSES TO GO TO NAGASAKI.—INFORMS THE JAPANESE OFFICIALS THAT IF THE GUARD-BOATS ARE NOT IMMEDIATELY REMOVED HE WILL DISPERSE THEM BY FORCE.—THE BOATS ARE WITHDRAWN.—VICE GOVERNOR RETURNS TO THE SHORE, PROMISING FURTHER COMMUNICATION ON THE MORROW.—POLICY RESOLVED ON BY THE COMMODORE.—METEOROLOGICAL PHENOMENON.—VISIT ON THE NEXT DAY FROM THE GOVERNOR OF URAGA.—CONFERENCE BETWEEN HIM AND COMMANDERS BUCHANAN AND ADAMS.—SECOND REFUSAL OF THE COMMODORE TO GO TO NAGASAKI.—DETERMINATION EXPRESSED TO DELIVER THE LETTER THERE, AND, IF NECESSARY, IN THE CITY OF YEDO ITSELF.—GOVERNOR PROPOSES TO REFER THE MATTER TO YEDO.—COMMODORE ASSENTS AND ALLOWS THREE DAYS FOR AN ANSWER.—SURVEY BY THE SQUADRON'S BOATS OF THE BAY OF URAGA, AND ULTIMATELY OF THE BAY OF YEDO.

EARLY on the morning of the 2d of July, 1853, after many unforeseen delays, the Commodore departed from Napha with four vessels only, the two steamers, the Susquehanna, his flag-ship, and the Mississippi, the Saratoga, and the Plymouth sloops-of-war. The Supply was left behind, and the Caprice dispatched to Shanghai. This was but a poor show of ships, in comparison with the more imposing squadron of twelve vessels which had been so repeatedly promised. But as none of these additional vessels had arrived, and as no calculation could be made as to when they might be looked for, the Commodore resolved to sail with the inferior force, which he trusted would so far answer his necessities as not to interfere seriously with the great object of the expedition, now fairly set out for Japan. The advantages of steam were fully appreciated in the opportunity it gave of making a uniformly steady and direct course of ascertained speed—advantages in which the sailing vessels were made to participate; for the Saratoga was taken in tow by the Susquehanna, as the Plymouth was by the Mississippi. The Commodore's ship led the van out of Napha and awaited, some five miles away, between the group of islands situated off the harbor and the southwestern extremity of the island, the coming up of her consort, as did the Mississippi for hers. Hawsers then being passed from the steamers to the two sloops-of-war, they were respectively taken in tow, the squadron fairly started and began the voyage to Yedo.

All seemed very well satisfied to get away from Lew Chew. The picturesque interests of the island were, for the time being, thoroughly exhausted, and the dull realities of life began to weigh rather heavily upon the visitors. Beside, the great object of the expedition was still before them, and anticipation naturally begat impatience. The weather, too, had become sultry and excessively oppressive, for the heat had reached the high degree of 88° Fahrenheit in the coolest part of the Susquehanna while she lay at anchor in the harbor. The people of Lew Chew, moreover, had not apparently been very much won over by the blandishments of their courteous visitors. The supplies with which they at first furnished the squadron had been gradually falling off, and their consent to receive payment for them seemed to be the principal change in their policy effected by the long sojourn of six weeks. Still some progress had been made. Their system of espionage had become less public and intrusive, although some suspected that it was as alert as ever though more concealed.

On getting clear of the harbor and stretching beyond the shelter of the southeastern extremity of the island, a strong wind was encountered from the east, and as the steamers were deep, it was thought advisable to stand off on the port tack in order to get well clear of the land, for the vessels in tow were dragging them to leeward notwithstanding the power of the engines. In the course of the day, as there was every prospect of weathering the eastern part of the island, the ships were put on the other tack, and their course directed for Japan.

The track taken by the squadron east of the chain of islands which stretch from Formosa to Lew Chew, and thence to Japan, (very properly called by Blunt the "Southern," "Middle," and "Northern" groups,) has been very rarely traversed by the ships of modern nations; while the islands on the eastern side of the chain are unknown to our present navigators.

The French admiral, Cecille, in 1846, employed one or more of his squadron in the exploration of the islands about Lew Chew, and along the western side of the northern group; but according to the best authorities, to which Von Siebold, among others, adds his testimony, the eastern side of the latter islands has never been visited by any modern navigator. The principal island of the northern group is called by the Japanese Oho-sima, and by the Chinese Tatao; these words meaning in their respective languages, "great island." It is about the size, including one or two adjoining islands in the estimate, of Great Lew Chew, and is probably governed by similar laws. It has one chief city and several towns, and the country is supposed to be highly cultivated. Von Siebold states that the island contains several good harbors, and it is undoubtedly, in every respect, of sufficient interest to claim an investigation. The Commodore resolved, at some subsequent period, to send some vessel of the squadron to make a proper survey.

The Susquehanna and the accompanying ships were probably the first either of European or American vessels that ever passed along the entire extent of the northern group. Von Siebold asserts that Broughton saw the northeast point, and that Captain Guerin, of the French corvette Sabine, traced the western shore in 1848. It was probably Oho-sima, the principal island of the group, that was seen by Commander Glynn in 1848, and which he supposed to be a new discovery. The islets which he speaks of having seen, bearing N.N.W., were the Cleopatra islands, examined two years before by one of the vessels of Admiral Cecille's squadron.

Von Siebold's charts, appended to his great work on Japan, and compiled by him, show these islands pretty accurately laid down, and it was found that the observations made on board the Susquehanna gave such bearings of the principal headlands of Oho-sima as correspond tolerably well with the position as given by Von Siebold. A current is said to be continually setting from these islands to the northward and eastward; or, as the islanders say, it always goes to Japan and never comes back. This was, however, found to be of no great strength during the passage of the Susquehanna, although it must be acknowledged to be a matter of difficulty to estimate in a steamer the rapidity and direction of currents, as they are generally over-logged, or in other words, surpassed in speed by the rate of going of the vessel. There is, moreover, another difficulty in consequence of the backward movement given to the water by the evolution of the paddle-wheels of a steamship.

The third day of the voyage, being the fourth day of July, 1853, brought with it a lively remembrance of home, as it was the seventy-seventh anniversary of our national holiday. The day opened fresh and pleasant, and the men were prepared to get up some amateur theatricals, and otherwise to celebrate the occasion; but the weather becoming unfavorable, and other circumstances interfering, it was deemed advisable, much to the disappointment of the sailors, to dispense with the show by which they had intended to give exhibition to their patriotism. The occasion, however, was duly honored by the firing of a salute of seventeen guns from each vessel of the squadron, and by the serving of an additional ration of grog to Jack, while the officers brought to bear also the resources of their various messes, to give due enjoyment and impressiveness to the day. All on board were allowed to feel that it was a holiday, in a respite from the usual muster at general quarters and exercises at the great guns and small arms, which had been kept up during the passage with great strictness and regularity, in order that the squadron might be prepared for any event on its arrival at Japan.

The weather, although generally warm, varied, and thus, while some days were excessively hot and oppressive, others were tolerably cool and pleasant. The winds occasionally blew with considerable freshness, and mostly from the east, but frequently there was hardly a breath of air to be felt, and, consequently, with a temperature which reached 88° in the coolest place on deck, all on board suffered greatly from the intense heat. And, indeed, the still heat and clear atmosphere which were experienced, even on a close approach to the shores of Japan, did not seem to confirm what has been said, and what was expected, of the cool and foggy climate of that country.

At sunset on Thursday, the 7th of July, the squadron was, according to observation, about forty miles from Cape Negatsuo, or Idsu, as it is otherwise called. In consequence of this proximity, the heads of the ships were put off shore from midnight until four o'clock next morning, when, not only the cape was seen from the masthead, but several of the islands to the eastward, called by Von Siebold *Goebroken Eilander*, (the Broken islands,) as well as the larger two of the group, bearing the Japanese names of Tosi-sima and Likinè-sima. The morning was fine, though the atmosphere was so hazy that there was but an indistinct view of the outline of the precipitous coast. Through the mist, however, the bold promontory of Idsu could be seen rising loftily out of the sea, and stretching back to the interior of Nippon in a crowd of mountainous elevations. The Susquehanna's course, as the leading ship, was laid directly for the entrance to the bay of Yedo, and as she passed the precipitous land of Cape Idsu she came up with a low, barren, and apparently uninhabited islet of about three-fourths of a mile in length, known as Rock island. There is a passage between this and the promontory which bounds the main land, and, although broken with several rocky islets, it is navigable. The United States ship-of-the-line Columbus took that course, although the other, on the outer side of Rock island, the one pursued by the Morrison, was preferred, and was accordingly taken by the Commodore, who passed within a mile and a half of the island. As the squadron sailed up the coast some eight or ten junks hove in sight, and two or three of them were observed soon to change their course and to turn back toward the shore, as if to announce the arrival of strangers.

The morning seemed to confirm the reputed character of the Japanese climate, for the atmosphere was so thick and hazy that the extent of view was unfortunately very much restricted, and it was not possible to get a distinct outline of the shore until the squadron came to anchor off the city of Uraga. The steamer, in spite of a wind, moved on with all sails furled, at the rate of eight or nine knots, much to the astonishment of the crews of the Japanese fishing junks gathered along the shore or scattered over the surface of the mouth of the bay, who stood up in their boats, and were evidently expressing the liveliest surprise at the sight of the first steamer ever beheld in Japanese waters.

As the day advanced the sun came out with a brighter lustre, glistening upon the broad sails of the junks within view, and dispelling the mist, through the openings of which the lofty summits and steep lava-scarred sides of the promontory of Idzu and its mountain chains, now left rapidly behind, could occasionally be discovered. Crossing the mouth of the bay of Sagami, with Vries' island, or Oo-sima, as it is called, on the starboard, the ships moved in toward Cape Sagami. The Great Fusi, now, as the fog occasionally lifted, rose to view behind the head of the bay of Sagami, and its cone-like summit was disclosed, rising to an enormous height, far inland, and covered with a white cap, but whether of snow or of fleecy clouds it was impossible to distinguish. The boats showed themselves more cautiously as the vessels entered the bay; but one was overtaken by the steamers, and those on board seemed in a terrible state of excitement, letting drop its broad sails, and taking to their oars, which they used with all their might, as they were evidently anxious to give a wide berth to the squadron.

As the ships neared the bay, signals were made from the Commodore, and instantly the decks were cleared for action, the guns placed in position and shotted, the ammunition arranged, the small arms made ready, sentinels and men at their posts, and, in short, all the preparations made, usual before meeting an enemy. About noon Cape Sagami was reached, when the squadron came too, for about ten minutes, and a signal was made for all captains to go on board the flag-ship and receive their orders from the Commodore. This done, the vessels now continued their course and soon came up with the peninsula of Sagami, at the south end of which a town was observed. When the squadron had approached within two miles of the land a fleet of large boats, amounting to more than a dozen, pushed off in the direction of the ships, with the seeming intention of visiting them. They were, however, not waited for, and were soon left behind, much puzzled, doubtless, by the rapid progress of the steamers against the wind. The boats appeared to be fully manned, but did not seem to be armed, although each of them bore a large banner with certain characters inscribed on it, which led to the conjecture that they were government vessels of some kind. The coasting vessels increased in numbers within the bay, and were sometimes so near that their construction and rig could be plainly made out. Their hulls rose forward in a high beaked prow, and aft, in a lofty poop, while a single mast, secured by fore and back stays, rose from the centre of the vessel and was rigged with a large square sail made of canvas; there were three other smaller sails, two at the bow and one at the stern.

On passing Cape Sagami, at the entrance of the bay, the shores were observed to rise in precipitous cliffs, which connected landward with undulating hills. Deep ravines, green with rich verdure, divided the steep slopes and opened into small expanses of alluvial land, washed by the waters of the bay into the form of inlets, about the borders of which were grouped various Japanese villages. The uplands were beautifully varied with cultivated fields and tufted woods, while far behind rose the mountains, height upon height, in the inland distance. The entrance to the bay seemed well fortified, and the hills and projecting headlands of Sagami were formidable with forts, the guns of which, however, were silent, notwithstanding the threatening entrance of the strange ships. The distant shores of the province of Awa, on the east, rising opposite to Sagami in a lofty peak, and stretching beyond in picturesque summits, was still more mountainous and bore fewer marks of cultivation and a less formidable appearance, being apparently destitute of fortifications. As the squadron passed through the straits into the inner bay of Uraga the numerous fishing boats hurried out of the way, and their crews, when they fancied themselves at a sufficiently safe distance, rested upon their oars and gazed with an anxious look at the strangers.

At about five o'clock in the afternoon the squadron came to anchor off the city of Uraga, on the western side of the bay of Yedo, the sloops-of-war (the wind being favorable) having been cast loose a little while previous, and the four vessels took up their positions, as had been directed, opposite the shore. Just before letting go the anchors the weather cleared up, and the lofty cone of Fusi was more distinctly visible, showing high above the accompanying range of mountains which extend inland. It was estimated to be eight or ten thousand feet in height, and its position W. $\frac{1}{2}$ N. from Uraga, at a distance of fifty or sixty miles. As the ships proceeded to their anchorage the lead was kept going every moment, and as a constant depth of twenty-five fathoms was found the vessels kept on their headway, rounding, at moderate speed, the elevation or cliff, within which is situated the bight of Uraga. They continued sounding and moving on slowly and cautiously until the squadron had nearly reached within a mile and a half of the promontory guarding the inner entrance of the bay of Yedo, at a distance of a mile further than any foreign vessel had ever advanced, when two guns were fired from a neighboring fort, and a ball of smoke in the air showed that a rocket had been discharged. The order was at once given to let go the anchor; but as the depth of twenty-five fathoms was still found, the steamers first closed in a little more with the shore and then anchored.

Previous to anchoring, a number of Japanese guard-boats had been observed coming off from the land in pursuit, but the Commodore had given express orders, both by word and signal, forbidding the admission of any one on board either of the ships but his own; and even as to

the flag-ship, he had commanded that not more than three persons, at one time, and those having business, should be allowed to come on board. It had heretofore been the practice of ships-of-war to admit these people indiscriminately to their decks. When the Columbus was in the bay of Yedo, there were many hundred Japanese on board of her at one time, who partook of the hospitalities of the officers without hesitation, and made themselves quite at home; but when they were spoken to about going on shore, answered by signs that it was impossible. The Commodore had, therefore, pre-determined to exercise an equal degree of exclusiveness with themselves, and to permit the Japanese functionaries to communicate only and directly with the Susquehanna. Several of the commanders in the Japanese boats signified by signs some dissatisfaction at not being permitted to come on board the ships; but the Commodore's orders were strictly obeyed.

On dropping the anchor, another gun was heard from one of the forts on shore, and when the squadron had assumed its line of anchorage, commanding with its guns the entire ranges of batteries and two considerable towns, a large number of the guard-boats came from all directions, evidently prepared to take their stations around the ships, as the Japanese crews had a supply of provisions, water, clothing, sleeping mats, and other requisites for a long stay. The Commodore, however, had fully determined beforehand that they should not thus surround the ships. They made several attempts to get alongside and on board of the Saratoga; their tow-lines, with which they made fast to any part of the ship, were unceremoniously cast off. They attempted to climb up by the chains, but the crew was ordered to prevent them, and the sight of pikes, cutlasses, and pistols, checked them, and when they found that our officers and men were very much in earnest, they desisted from their attempts to board.

These guard-boats struck every one with admiration of the beauty of their models, which, by the way, resembled in a remarkable degree that of the yacht America. They were constructed of unpainted wood, with very sharp bows, a broad beam, a slightly tapering stern, and a clean run. They were propelled with great swiftness through, or rather over, the water, for they seemed to skim upon its surface rather than to divide it. The crews, numbering in some of the larger boats thirty or more, were tall and muscular men, whose tawny frames were naked, with the exception of a cloth about their waists. Toward night, however, the men clothed themselves with loose gowns, some of red and others of blue, with hanging sleeves, upon which were white stripes meeting in an angle at the shoulders. On their backs were emblazoned coats of arms, or some insignia, in black and other colors. Most of them were bareheaded and showed the hair to have been shaved on the crown, while that on the sides had been allowed to grow long and was worn plastered with some species of ointment and fastened up into a knot on the bald spot upon the top of the head. A few, however, wore caps of bamboo, in shape like a shallow basin inverted, and reminding one of Mambrino's helmet. In some of the boats the men bore tall poles, surmounted by a cruciform ornament, which seemed to indicate some military office. The men in authority, wore light lacquered hats, with a coat of arms in front, probably signifying their official rank and position. The rowers stood to their oars, which worked on pivots upon the sides of the boat near the stern, and they handled them with such skill and effect that they approached the ships very rapidly, shouting loudly as they came. At the stern of each boat was a small flag, with three horizontal stripes in it, a white one on either side, and a black one in the middle, while in many of the boats there was, beside, an additional flag, with symbols upon it. One or two persons, armed each with two swords at their sides, stood in the boats, and were evidently men of rank and authority.

One of the boats came alongside of the flag-ship, and it was observed that a person on board had a scroll of paper in his hand, which the officer of the Susquehanna refused to receive, but which was held up to be read alongside of the Mississippi, when it was found to be a document in the French language, which conveyed an order to the effect that the ships should go away, and not anchor at their peril. The chief functionary, as his boat reached the side of the Susquehanna, made signs for the gangway ladder to be let down. This was refused, but Mr. Williams, the Chinese interpreter, and Mr. Portman, the Dutch, were directed to state to him that the Commodore would not receive any one but a functionary of the highest rank, and that he might return on shore. As there seemed to be some difficulty in making progress in the Japanese language, one on board the boat alongside said, in very good English, "I can speak Dutch." Mr. Portman then commenced a conversation with him in that language, as his English seemed to have been exhausted in the first sentence. He appeared to be perfectly familiar with the Dutch, however, and commenced a very brisk volley of questions, many of which were not responded to. He asked if the ships came from America, and seemed to have expected them. He was very pertinacious in urging to be allowed to come on board, but was constantly refused permission, and was told that the commander of the squadron was of the highest rank, in the service to which he belonged, in the United States, and could confer only with the highest in rank at Uraga. He then stated that the vice-governor of Uraga was in the boat, and pointed to one of those in authority at his side, who, he said, held the highest position in the city, and was the proper person to be received. He was now asked why the governor himself did not come off, to which he replied that he was prevented by the laws from going on board ships in the roads; and proposed that the Commodore should appoint an officer of corresponding rank with the vice-governor to confer with him, as he was desirous of communicating to the government the object of the squadron's visit. The Commodore, after some intentional delay, consented to this request, and appointed his aid, Lieutenant Contee, to receive him. The gangway-ladder was accordingly lowered, and the vice-governor, *Nagazima Saboroske*, accompanied by his interpreter, *Hori Tatsnoske*, who spoke Dutch, came on board, and was received in the captain's cabin, where a conference was held, in fact, with the Commodore, who, however, studiously kept himself secluded in his own cabin, and communicated with the Japanese through his aid only.

It was directed that the dignitary should be informed that the Commodore, who had been sent by his country on a friendly mission to Japan, had brought a letter from the President of the United States, addressed to the Emperor, and that he wished a suitable officer might be sent on board his ship to receive a copy of the same, in order that a day might be appointed for the Commodore formally to deliver the original. To this he replied that Nagasaki was the only place, according to the laws of Japan, for negotiating foreign business, and it would be necessary for the squadron to go there. In answer to this he was told that the Commodore had come purposely to Uraga because it was near to Yedo, and that he *should not go to Nagasaki;* that he expected the letter to be duly and properly received where he then was; that his intentions were perfectly friendly, but that he would allow of no indignity; and would not permit the guard-boats which were collecting around the ships to remain where they were, and if they were not immediately removed, the Commodore declared that he would disperse them by force. When this was interpreted to him, the functionary suddenly left his seat, went to the gangway, and gave an order which caused most of the boats to return to the shore; but a few of them still remaining in clusters, an armed boat was sent from the ship to warn them away by gestures, and at the same time to show their arms; this had the desired effect, as all of them disappeared, and nothing more was seen of them near the ships during the stay of the squadron. This, as says the Commodore, was the first important point gained. The vice-governor shortly afterward took his leave, saying, as he departed, that he had no authority to promise any thing respecting the reception of the President's letter, but in the morning an officer of higher rank would come from the city, who might probably furnish some further information.

The policy of the Commodore, it will be seen, was to assume a resolute attitude toward the Japanese government. He had determined, before reaching the coast, to carry out strictly this course in all his official relations, as he believed it the best to ensure a successful issue to the delicate mission with which he had been charged. He was resolved to adopt a course entirely contrary to that of all others who had hitherto visited Japan on a similar errand—to demand as a right, and not to solicit as a favor, those acts of courtesy which are due from one civilized nation to another: to allow of none of those petty annoyances which had been unsparingly visited upon those who had preceded him, and to disregard the acts as well as the threats of the authorities, if they in the least conflicted with his own sense of what was due to the dignity of the American flag.

The question of landing by force was left to be decided by the development of succeeding events; it was, of course, the very last measure to be resorted to, and the last that was desired; but in order to be prepared for the worst, the Commodore caused the ships constantly to be kept in perfect readiness, and the crews to be drilled as thoroughly as they are in time of active war. He was prepared, also, to meet the Japanese on their own ground, and exhibit toward them a little of their own exclusive policy; if they stood on their dignity and assumed superiority, that was a game at which he could play as well as they. It was well to let them know that other people had dignity also, which they knew how to protect, and that they did not acknowledge the Japanese to be their superiors. Hence he forbade the admission of a single Japanese on board any of the ships, except those officers who might have business with him; and the visits even of such were to be confined to the flag-ship, to which they were admitted only on the declaration of their rank and business. The Commodore, also, was well aware that the more exclusive he should make himself, and the more unyielding he might be in adhering to his declared intentions, the more respect these people of forms and ceremonies would be disposed to award him; therefore it was that he deliberately resolved to confer personally with no one but a functionary of the highest rank in the empire. He would have been ashamed, in the indulgence of a contemptible pride founded on mere official rank, to assume a superiority, and affect a dignity, too lofty to stoop to the level of men below him in station. As a man, he did not deem himself too elevated to hold communication with any of his brethren in the common heritage of humanity; but in Japan, as the representative of his country, and the accredited guardian of the honor of that flag which floated over him, he felt that it was well to teach the Japanese, in the mode most intelligible to them, by stately and dignified reserve, joined to perfect equity in all he asked or did, to respect the country from which he came, and to suspend for a time their accustomed arrogance and incivility toward strangers. The Japanese so well understood him that they learned the lesson at once. It was this feeling, and this only, which prompted him to refuse to see the vice-governor of Uraga, and to refer him to his aid for conference. He saw him often enough afterward, when matters had been arranged between the governments, on terms of friendship and equality. And we have been thus particular, not for the information of our countrymen, who know Commodore Perry, but for strangers who may read our story and, without this word of explanation, misapprehend the character of the man. No man is more easily approached by his fellow-men, or assumes less on account of the honorable position he fills in the service of his country.

The best proof that he judged wisely in determining on his course is in the results. The squadron was left free of all annoyance or interference on the part of the authorities during the whole period of its stay; an event unprecedented in the intercourse of Japan with foreign ships for more than two centuries. We have said there was no annoyance to the ships, but the Japanese were as yet too suspicious of foreigners not to resort to their favorite system of espionage: and, therefore, though the guard-vessels were withdrawn, as we have seen, there might still be observed floating here and there a boat in the distance, seemingly with the object of quietly watching the movements of the strangers; but they never came near the squadron, and were not by any act of the authorities forced upon the recognition of them, by the Americans, as guard-boats. That a watchful eye was kept upon the squadron was probable. Three or four rockets were shot up from the opposite land during the afternoon, which were supposed to be signals of some purpose or other. When night came on, the presence of the ships in their waters was evidently keeping up a very lively apprehension on the part of the Japanese on shore. Beacon fires were lighted upon every hill-top, and along the shores on either side as far as the eye could reach, and during the whole night the watchers on deck could hear the tolling of a great bell which was at first supposed to be that of a temple, but was probably an alarum or signal of some kind. The bay was otherwise as quiet as an inland lake, and nothing occurred to disturb the tranquillity of the night. When, however, the nine o'clock gun of the flag-ship, a sixty-four-pounder, was fired, the report reverberated loudly through the hills on the western side of the bay, and apparently created something of a commotion on shore, for here and there the fires were observed to be immediately extinguished. There seemed, however, no reason to expect any interference, although every precaution had been taken; the ships had quite a warlike aspect, with sentinels stationed fore and aft and upon the gangways at the sides, with a pile of round shot and four stands of grape at each gun, muskets stacked on the quarter-deck, and boats provided with carbines, pistols, cutlasses and other necessaries for service.

An interesting meteorological phenomenon was observed in the course of the night by Lieutenant Duer, in command of the watch, who describes it as a remarkable meteor seen from midnight until four o'clock in the morning. It made its appearance in the southward and westward and illuminated the whole atmosphere. The spars, sails, and hulls of the ships reflected its glare as distinctly as though a blue light were burning from each vessel at the same time. From the southward and westward, and about fifteen degrees above the horizon, it pursued a northeastwardly course in a direct line for a long distance, when it fell gradually toward the sea and disappeared. Its form was that of a large blue sphere with a red, wedge-shaped tail, which it could easily be observed was formed of ignited particles which resembled the sparks of a rocket as they appear upon its explosion. "The ancients" remarks the Commodore "would have construed this remarkable appearance of the heavens as a favorable omen for any enterprize they had undertaken," and adds "it may be so construed by us, as we pray God that our present attempt to bring a singular and isolated people into the family of civilized nations may succeed without resort to bloodshed."

As the sun rose next morning, gradually lifting the mist which had been spread during the night upon the surface of the bay, and still curtained, here and there, the land with its fleecy festoons, a beautiful view was disclosed. A bold shore, occasionally broken by steep escarpments of bare gray rock, extended along the western or Sagami side of the bay, with an undulating surface brightly green with verdure, tufts of undergrowth, and scattered groups of trees. Further inland the earth rose in a range of gently swelling hills, the sides of which were covered with vegetation. Two miles below the anchorage, the shore was less abrupt, and seemed more cultivated. From Uraga to the entrance of the inner bay of Yedo, marked by a promontory a mile and a half distant, innumerable towns and villages were grouped along the shores on either side. Uraga embraces two of these towns, separated from each other by a cliff; through the larger one of which a river passes and empties into the harbor, where floated a great number of small boats and several junks. As most of the vessels bound up the bay were seen to stop in their course at Uraga, that place was supposed to be an entrepot where certain custom dues had to be paid. Forts could be seen on the headlands here and there commanding the harbor, and as they were examined through the glass, some of them were found to be in an unfinished state, and in progress of construction or alteration. Some were mounted with cannon, though apparently of no great calibre, while others were without a gun. A length of screens had been stretched for a distance of several rods upon posts in front of the breastworks, as well as inside the forts behind the embrasures, and along parts of the shore. In the distance these screens seemed to be composed of cloth, and were marked with white and black stripes. Their purpose was not very obvious, although it was surmised that they were got up with the intention of making a false show of concealed force. The Japanese probably had not calculated upon the exactness of view afforded by a Dolland's telescope or a French opera glass. Companies of soldiers, in glaring scarlet uniforms, were seen to pass from garrison to garrison, some bearing flags with various insignia, and others large lanterns upon tall poles. The shore was lined with a formidable show of the same sort of government boats as had surrounded the ships on their arrival. They seemed to be picketed off from the town by two red flags which had been planted on the shore between them and the houses on the land.

The first approach to the Susquehanna from the shore was that of a boat at early sunrise next morning, (July 9th,) apparently containing a corps of artists, who came close to the ship's side, but making no attempt to come on board, busied themselves in taking sketches of the strange vessels. The important visit of the day, however, came off at seven o'clock, when two large boats rowed alongside, one of which contained a half dozen officials, whose presence was indicated by the three-striped flag at the stern. The interpreter who spoke Dutch was with them, and announced that the personage of highest authority in the city was present, and desired to come on board. The arrival of Kayamon Yezaimen, (for such was his name,) who presented himself as the governor and greatest functionary of Uraga, thus plainly contradicting the declaration of the vice-governor of the day before, was then duly announced to the Commodore, who ordered that his highness should be received by Commanders Buchanan and Adams and Lieutenant Contee, the Commodore himself still refusing, in accordance with his policy, to receive any one but a counsellor of the Empire. The governor was attired, in character with his high position, as a noble of the third rank. He wore a rich silk robe of an embroidered pattern resembling the feathers of a peacock, with borders of gold and silver. He was duly received by the officers we have named, and immediately commenced with them a conference, which, however, was in reality with the Commodore, though he still preserved his seclusion. The governor, after a long discussion, in which he more than once declared that the Japanese laws made it impossible that the President's letter should be received at Uraga, and that, even if it were, the answer would be sent to Nagasaki, added also that the squadron must proceed thither. In answer to this he was most distinctly told that the Commodore would never consent to such an arrangement, and would persist in delivering the letter where he was; and, moreover, that if the Japanese government did not see fit to appoint a suitable person to receive the documents in his possession addressed to the Emperor that he, the Commodore, whose duty it was to deliver them, would go on shore with a sufficient force and deliver them in person, be the consequences what they might.

In answer to this, the governor said that he would return to the city and send a communication to Yedo, asking for further instructions, and he added that it would take *four days* to obtain a reply. One hour's steaming would have taken the ships in sight of Yedo, and so the governor was informed that the Commodore would wait *three* days only, (until Tuesday, the 12th,) when a definite answer would be expected.

A boat had been sent at daylight from each ship of the squadron to survey the bay and harbor of Uraga. The governor, on observing these boats, inquired what they were doing, and when he was told that they were surveying the harbor, he said it was against the Japanese laws to allow of such examinations; to which he received for reply, that the American laws command them, and that Americans were as much bound to obey the American as he was the Japanese laws. "This," remarks the Commodore, "was a second and most important point gained." During all the questions and answers the interpreter had out his tablets, and was busy taking notes, and if all the importunate inquiries of the governor had been responded to, his reporter would have enjoyed no sinecure.

At the interview, the original letter of the President, together with the Commodore's letter of credence, encased in the magnificent boxes which had been prepared in Washington, were shown to his excellency, who was evidently greatly impressed with their exquisite workmanship and costliness; and he made an offer for the first time of water and refreshments, but was told that the squadron was in no need of anything. The governor was made to understand perfectly that there would be no necessity for any further discussion until the time appointed for the delivery of the answer from the Japanese government should arrive; and he left the ship fully impressed with this understanding.

During the conference, the governor and his interpreter were requested to use the same designation in speaking of the President of the United States as that by which they distinguished the Emperor. They complied with this request, although, previous to it, they had used different terms for the two dignitaries. In a country like Japan, so governed by ceremonials of all kinds, it was necessary to guard with the strictest etiquette even the forms of speech; and it was found that by a diligent attention to the minutest and apparently most insignificant details of word and action, the desired impression was made upon Japanese diplomacy; which, as a smooth surface requires one equally smooth to touch it at every point, can only be fully reached and met by the nicest adjustment of the most polished formality.

The surveying boats, which seemed to give so much uneasiness to the governor, had been well manned and armed, and Lieutenant Bent, of the Mississippi, who was in command, was instructed not to go beyond the range of the ships' guns, while a good look-out was kept upon the surveying party, in order that assistance might be sent to them should they be attacked. In addition to the usual boat ensigns at the stern, white flags, indicative of their peaceful intentions, were borne on the bows. They spread themselves out toward the opposite shore as they pulled away, sounding at every boat's length, and had reached about two miles further up the bay than the anchorage of the squadron, when they were recalled by a signal gun. On their return they were sent out again, with orders to keep nearer to the western shore. In the afternoon all the boats returned, coming alongside at about three o'clock p. m.

The hydrographic reports were of the most favorable character, as deep water was found as far up as four miles toward the head of the bay, which was the extent of the first survey. The soundings varied from twenty-nine to forty-three fathoms, and at the height of the ebb tide a current was observed running at the rate of two or three knots. The examination of the harbor of Uraga, which was carried to within a few feet of the shore, gave five fathoms at about a cable's length distance, while within that space from the land several reefs were found to extend out. As the boats approached the shores there was a good view of the fortifications, which did not seem to be of a very formidable character. Their construction did not exhibit much strength or art. Their position and armament were such as to expose them to an easy assault; their parapets were in earthwork, while many of the buildings, the barracks and magazines, appeared to be of wood. They mounted but few guns, and those of small calibre, while their embrasures were so wide that the cannon were greatly exposed.

On the first approach of the survey boats the soldiers showed themselves in considerable force, and were observed to be fully armed. They presented quite a bristling front with their spears and match-locks, while their lacquered caps and shields flashed brightly in the sun. They did not seem disposed, however, to make any very decided stand, for they retreated within the walls of the fortification as soon as the boats made in closer with the land. One of the officers in command of a ship's boat approached to within a hundred yards of the shore, and observing three persons, seemingly of authority, standing out upon an embankment, levelled his glass at them, whereat they disappeared on the instant, evidently much discomposed at being sighted with an instrument which they (though not unfamiliar with the telescope) might have supposed to be a weapon unknown to them, and capable of projecting something more deadly than the glance of an eye. The Japanese soldiers in the boats along shore beckoned to our officer to keep off, while he, in response, made a sign to show the direction in which he was going. The Japanese then put off and approached so rapidly that it appeared as if their intention was to intercept the ship's boat, and the officer in command accordingly gave orders to his men to rest upon their oars and adjust the caps to their carbines. There was, however, no attempt directly to interfere with this or any other of the ship's cutters, although they were followed by numbers of Japanese boats, which, however, on seeing our men well armed, did not venture to molest them. The artist who accompanied the surveying party had an excellent opportunity, which was well improved, of making sketches of the land, the forts, and various other objects on shore.

Everything seemed propitious, as the action of the Commodore had so far been crowned with success. He had gained his purpose in clearing the squadron of the presence of the guard-boats; he had compelled the visit of the first in authority at Uraga; he had surveyed the harbor; he had refused to go to Nagasaki, and kept his position in the bay of Yedo; and this last he determined to retain until he had some definite answer as to the reception of the President's letter by a person of proper rank and authority.

The weather added its smiles to the occasion, for nothing could be more propitious. The heat, which was not excessive, for the thermometer hardly ranged above 78°, was tempered by cool sea breezes, and the atmosphere was so clear that every object appeared with great distinctness, and there was a picturesque view disclosed to the eye on all sides. The peaked summit of Fusi rose, with great distinctness, above the high land on the western coast, and ten miles ahead the bold cliff, which guards both sides of the entrance to the inner harbor leading to Yedo, were readily discernible. Nearer, the houses of Uraga could be so plainly seen that their peculiar forms and construction could be made out, and they were perceived to be built of wood, with roofs of various forms—pointed, square, and pyramidal. Most of the buildings were of the natural color of the wood, somewhat discolored, however, by time, while some few were painted white. The Japanese boats and junks, to the number of several hundreds, extending from the headland, off which the Susquehanna was anchored, to the harbor, were so distinctly visible as to be readily counted. Nearer still, the eye could minutely distinguish the parts of the unfinished forts that were in the process of construction on the heights opposite to the ship.

The next day was Sunday, (July 10th,) and, as usual, divine service was held on board the ships and, in accordance with proper reverence for the day, no communication was held with the Japanese authorities. During the day, however, a boat came off with a striped flag, which indicated the high rank of the three or four Japanese sitting beneath its awning and languidly using their fans. They were evidently persons of distinction, and had the same intelligent expression and the remarkably courtly manners which were uniformly observed in all those of the better class. On coming alongside they, through their interpreter whom they had brought, requested permission to come on board. They were asked if they had any business with the Commodore, and answering that they had none, but merely wished to have a talk, were politely informed that, by his orders, they could not be received. Through the day, preparations were observed to be still proceeding on the land; the soldiers moved busily, with their glistening shields and long spears, about the batteries in sight, and some seemed to be engaged in removing the sham forts of striped canvas, and in training more guns upon the squadron. The reverberations of the report of a cannon, fired off apparently some distance up the bay, echoed through the hills, and were distinctly heard on board the ships. At night, the beacon-fires, though fewer in number than on the previous evening, again blazed, while the deep-toned bell tolled as usual until morning. Everything, however, remained on board the ships tranquil and without interruption, as befitted the Christian day of rest.

On the next morning early (Monday) the surveying boats were dispatched higher up the bay, and Commander Lee, of the steamer Mississippi, was directed to get his ship under way to protect them, if necessary. The governor of Uraga, on seeing the Mississippi going higher up, came on board, although he had been told that there would be no necessity for further communication or discussion until the reply from Yedo was received.

The Commodore had sent the Mississippi and the boats on the service, in part for effect, being satisfied that the very circumstance of approaching nearer to Yedo with a powerful ship would alarm the authorities, and induce them to give a more favorable answer to his demands. It happened as was expected. The governor pretended that his visit to the ship was simply for the purpose of bringing the information that it was very probable the letters (meaning, as was then supposed, the translations of the originals) would be received on the following day, and forwarded to Yedo. His evident object in coming on board, however, was to ascertain for what purpose the Mississippi and the surveying boats had ascended the bay, and he accordingly put the question.

The Commodore, anticipating the inquiry, directed that the governor should be informed that, unless the business which had brought the squadron to the bay of Yedo was arranged during the present visit, he, the Commodore, would be obliged to return in the ensuing spring with a larger force; and, as the anchorage in front of Uraga was not convenient or safe, he was desirous of seeking a more favorable situation nearer to Yedo, which would facilitate his communication with that city.

The surveying party, as on the previous occasion, was composed of boats from each ship of the squadron, under the command of Lieutenant Bent. They were sent out with general directions from the Commodore to go as far up the bay toward Yedo as possible, without getting out of signal distance from the squadron, and to avoid giving any occasion of conflict with the people of the country. Their departure was watched with considerable anxiety by those on board the Susquehanna. Thirty fathoms of her cable had been taken in, and the remainder was all ready to slip, while steam was got up, to be in readiness for any emergency. The movements on shore were quite lively: in the distance, on the eastern shore, large numbers of soldiers—as many apparently as a thousand—were seen to march down from the higher ground to the beach, and there embark in boats, which put off immediately in the direction of the surveying party. And, during the whole time, the various batteries were busy with the movements of the troops, who seemed to be either preparing for hostilities, or attempting to make a formidable show of force.

The boats proceeded from ten to twelve miles further toward Yedo than the anchorage of the squadron. In proceeding up the bay, numbers of government vessels appeared, waving off the intruders, and some thirty-five put off in a direction fronting the course of the surveying boats, as if intending to intercept them. Lieutenant Bent, who was in advance, ordered his men to rest on their oars, and to affix their bayonets to their muskets, but this proceeding did not seem to have the effect he had hoped for, of stopping the Japanese boats. They still came on. The lieutenant, anxious to avoid a rupture, then changed his course somewhat, to prevent an immediate collision, and dispatched a boat for the Mississippi, which was about two miles astern. The desired effect was soon produced by the approach of the steamer, and there was no apparent disposition shown afterward to interfere with the party, which continued the exploration. Deep soundings were found the whole distance, with a soft bottom of mud. A channel seemed to exist at the furthest point reached; in the centre the lead gave a depth of twenty fathoms, while on the sides it struck upon banks of mud at not more than five fathoms. It was inferred that there were deep soundings still further, and that the squadron might readily push on with safety to within a few miles of Yedo itself. At the extreme distance of the boats' passage there was a smaller bay, cut out, as it were, from the larger, which, it was supposed, would probably afford an excellent anchorage. On either side the shores were abrupt, and extended back into lofty hills, and from the position of the boats at this point a town was observed on the right side of the bay of Yedo. The Mississippi had disappeared for some time from the view of those on board the other ships; but, just as the signal gun was about to be fired for her recall, she shot round the promontory, some two or three miles up the bay, which had concealed her from sight, came steaming down, with the boats in tow, and was soon quietly settled at her old anchorage, passing on her way between the Susquehanna and the Uraga shore, and attracting the attention of numbers of soldiers on the latter, who came out to see her pass.

The bay was covered all day, as usual, with the Japanese junks, sailing up or down, apparently carrying on a brisk commerce, and not at all disturbed by the presence of the squadron. Some of the fishing smacks and other boats would, indeed, at times approach pretty near to the ships, but obviously merely to gratify curiosity, as their crews would stand up and gaze intently, but gave no sign either of alarm or hostility. The trading vessels were observed to stop at a town on the opposite side in coming down, and at Uraga in going up, in accordance, probably, as has already been intimated, with some regulation of the customs. Everything passed tranquilly, and the next day, which was to bring some reply or other to the Commodore's demands, was looked forward to with deep solicitude and interest by every man on board the ships.

In the Bay of Yedo.

CHAPTER XIII.

REPLY FROM THE COURT AT YEDO.—EFFORTS OF THE JAPANESE TO GET THE SQUADRON OUT OF THE BAY OF YEDO.—COMMODORE'S FIRM REFUSAL TO LEAVE URAGA.—AGREEMENT OF THE EMPEROR TO RECEIVE, THROUGH A COMMISSIONER, THE PRESIDENT'S LETTER.—HIGH BREEDING OF THE JAPANESE GENTLEMEN: NOT ILL INFORMED.—SURVEY OF THE BAY OF YEDO.—FOGS OF JAPAN.—SECOND VISIT FROM THE GOVERNOR OF URAGA.—HE BRINGS A LETTER FROM THE EMPEROR, AUTHORIZING A PRINCE OF THE EMPIRE TO RECEIVE, IN HIS NAME, THE PRESIDENT'S LETTER.—ARRANGEMENTS MADE FOR THE COMMODORE'S RECEPTION ON SHORE TO DELIVER THE LETTER.—MINUTE ATTENTION OF THE JAPANESE TO ETIQUETTE AND CEREMONIALS.—PREPARATIONS IN THE SQUADRON FOR THE VISIT ON SHORE AT THE RECEPTION.—SHIPS BROUGHT NEAR THE LAND, SO AS TO COMMAND THE PLACE OF MEETING.—LANDING AND RECEPTION, AND DELIVERY OF THE LETTER AND OTHER DOCUMENTS.—PRINCES OF IDSU AND IWAMA.—CONTENTS OF PRESIDENT'S LETTER.—COMMODORE'S LETTER OF CREDENCE, AND HIS LETTERS TO THE EMPEROR.—RECEIPT GIVEN BY THE JAPANESE FOR THE PAPERS.—RETURN TO THE SHIPS.

HE day appointed for the reception of a reply from Yedo (Tuesday, July 12) had now arrived. Accordingly, at about half past nine o'clock in the morning, three boats were seen to approach the steamer Susquehanna from the shores of Uraga. These were different from the usual government craft, and seemed, unlike the others, to be built after an European model; the rowers sat to their oars, and moved them as our boatmen do, though somewhat awkwardly, instead of standing and sculling at the sides, in accordance with the usual Japanese practice. The construction of the boats was evidently very strong, and their models fair. Their masts, sails, and rigging were of the ordinary Japanese fashion. The crews were numerous, there being thirty in the largest boat, and thirteen in each of the others, and their great swarthy frames were clothed in the usual uniform of loose blue dresses slashed with white stripes.

The boat in advance was distinguished, in addition to the government mark of a horizontal black stripe across her broad sail, by the black and white flag, which indicated the presence of some officers of distinction, and such in fact were now on board of her. As she approached nearer to the ship, the governor, Kayama Yezaiman, in his rich silken robes, was recognised, seated on mats spread in the centre of the deck of the vessel, and surrounded by his interpreters and suite.

The advance boat now came alongside, leaving the other two floating at some distance from the Susquehanna. His highness, Kayama Yezaiman, with his two interpreters, Hori Tatsnoske, the principal, and Fateisko Tokushumo, his second, were admitted at once on board, and having been received with due formality, were ushered into the presence of Captains Buchanan and Adams, who were prepared to communicate with them.

The Commodore had, previously to the arrival of the governor, written the following letter to the Emperor:

"UNITED STATES STEAM FRIGATE SUSQUEHANNA,
Uraga, July 12, 1853.

"The Commander-in-chief of the United States naval forces in these seas, being invested with full powers to negotiate treaties, is desirous of conferring with one of the highest officers of the Empire of Japan, in view of making arrangements for the presentation of the original of his letter of credence, as also the original of a letter with which he is charged, addressed to his Imperial Majesty by the President of the United States.

"It is hoped that an early day will be appointed for the proposed interview.

"To his Imperial Majesty the EMPEROR OF JAPAN."

The governor's first statement was to the effect that there had been a misapprehension as to the delivery of the translations of the papers before the originals had been received. Although the Commodore was certain that there had been no such misunderstanding, nevertheless he, on the second interview in the course of the afternoon, consented, after much discussion, to deliver the translations and originals, as also a letter from himself to the Emperor, at the same time, provided the latter should appoint a suitable officer to receive them directly from the hands of the Commodore, who repeated that he would consent to present them to no other than a Japanese dignitary of the highest rank. The governor then said that a building would be erected on shore for the reception of the Commodore and his suite, and that a high official personage, specially appointed by the Emperor, would be in attendance to receive the letters. He, however, added that no answer would be given in the bay of Yedo, but that it would be transmitted to Nagasaki, through the Dutch or Chinese superintendents. This being reported to the Commodore, he wrote the following memorandum and directed it to be translated into Dutch, and fully explained to the governer.

"The Commander-in-chief will not go to Nagasaki, and will receive no communication through the Dutch or Chinese.

"He has a letter from the President of the United States to deliver to the Emperor of Japan, or to his secretary of foreign affairs, and he will deliver the original to none other:—if this friendly letter of the President to the Emperor is not received and duly replied to, he will consider his country insulted, and will not hold himself accountable for the consequences.

"He expects a reply of some sort in a few days, and he will receive such reply nowhere but in this neighborhood." [Bay of Uraga.]

When this was communicated to the governor, he took his departure, probably to consult some higher authority, as doubtless there was more than one high officer of the court at Uraga, secretly directing the negotiations. The interview had lasted three hours, and it was fully one o'clock before the governor left the ship. All passed in the most quiet way without any interruption to the usual courtesies of friendly negotiation. The shore showed every indication of tranquillity, and no movement was observed on the part of the fortresses, or the many government boats along the shore.

The governor, in accordance with his promise on leaving in the morning, returned in the afternoon accompanied, as usual, by his interpreters and suite. He came off, however, in one of the ordinary Japanese boats, and not, as earlier in the day, in the vessel built after the European model. Captains Buchanan and Adams were in readiness to receive the party, and resumed the renewed conference with the same form and ceremony as before; the Commodore still preserving his seclusion and communicating with the Japanese only through others. The conversation is here given verbatim as reported.

CONVERSATION.

Present Captains Buchanan and Adams, Lieutenant Contee, Flag Lieutenant, and Yezaiman, governor of Uraga, and interpreters.

Yezaiman. As it will take a great deal of time to send up the copies of the letters first, and the originals afterward, I propose that the originals and the copies be delivered together, when the high officer comes. The governor and the high officer will do their best to entertain the Admiral and give him a suitable reception.

Capt. Buchanan. That is not the object of the Commodore: he wishes these communications to go because there is among them a letter to the Emperor from himself, which he desires to send to Yedo with the copies. The reply to the President's letter is not of so much consequence just now. We want a reply to the Commodore's letter which is in the package.

Yezaiman. If you send the original letter we will reply to it as soon as possible. We are here for the purpose of receiving the letter from the President to the Emperor, but now you speak of a letter from the Admiral to the Emperor.

Capt. B. The letter from the Admiral is in the package containing the copies of the President's letter. It states that he has in his possession the original letter of the President, and is empowered by the President to deliver it in person to the Emperor, or to a high officer of equal rank with himself, appointed by the Emperor.

Yezaiman. We are very sorry that you separate the two; it would be better to send the originals at once with the copies.

Capt. B. That is impossible. The letter of the Admiral states that he has the original letter of the President, and is empowered to deliver it, either in person or to an officer of his own rank; when the Emperor is aware of the fact that the Admiral has the letter, then he will appoint an officer of the same rank to receive the original, and the Admiral will return at some future day to receive the answer.

Yezaiman. Can you not contrive to manage it in such a way that the original letter may be sent with the copies?

Capt. B. It cannot be done.

Yezaiman. When the ships first came it was not mentioned that the copies must be sent first, and not the original letters; and now you mention it.

Capt. B. During the first visit you made here, you were shown the original letters, and also the copies, and the same statement was then made by us as now.—(*After a pause Captain B. resumed.*)—Will the high officer who will come here be accredited by the Emperor to receive the letters from the Admiral?

Yezaiman. He has the authorization of the Emperor.

Capt. B. Will he have any proof to show that he is thus authorized?

Yezaiman. Yes, he can prove it.

Capt. B. One of the letters is from the President, informing the Emperor of Japan that Commodore Perry is sent as a high officer appointed by himself, and Commodore Perry will expect similar credentials on the part of the officer appointed to speak with him.

Yezaiman. He will receive the letter, but cannot enter into any negotiations.

Capt. B. What is the rank and official title of the officer who is appointed?—(*While the interpreter is writing the title of the officer in question, in Chinese characters, Captains Buchanan and Adams retire to consult with the Commodore.*)

Lieutenant Contee. When will the high officers be ready to receive the letter?

Interpreter. To-morrow or the day after.

Lieut. C. Where is the house?

Interpreter. On the shore.

Lieut. C. Can you point it out from here?

Interpreter. It cannot be seen.

Lieut. C., (*repeating his last question.*) Can you point it out from here?

Interpreter. It is on the other side of the hills—you can see it from another position.

Lieut. C. What was the name of the officer who came on board on the day of our arrival?

Interpreter. Nagazhima Saberoske.

(*Captains Buchanan and Adams now returned.*)

Captain Buchanan. Captain Adams and I have just had a conversation with the Admiral.* He says that, since you appear to have wholly misunderstood the matter about the letter, if you can show proof that an officer of the proper rank is appointed to receive them, he will waive the matter in dispute, and deliver the original at the same time with the copies. But he requires strict evidence that the officer who shall meet him shall be of the necessary rank, and that he has been specially appointed for the purpose by the Emperor.

Yezaiman. Nagasaki is the proper place to receive letters from foreign nations, and because Uraga is not an appropriate place, the officer will not be allowed to converse, but only to receive the letters.

Capt. B. He is only desired to receive the letters. Will he come on board, or will the letters be delivered on shore?

Yezaiman. He will not come on board, but will receive them on shore.

Capt. B. Before the letters are delivered, the credentials of the officer must be translated into Dutch, signed with the proper signatures, and sent on board the Admiral.

Yezaiman. He will be accredited to receive the letter, but cannot speak.

Capt. B. He will not be desired to speak, but he must have a paper signed by the Emperor, stating that he is empowered to receive the letters.

Yezaiman. He will have a document properly signed.

[*Captain Buchanan now directed Mr. Portman to write in Dutch the declaration he had made, and to give it to the interpreter. The following is the English version:* "There has been a

---

* "It is proper to remark that the title of Admiral was necessarily used at these interviews, to designate your rank, as we found Yezaiman's interpreters were familiar with it, and were entirely unacquainted with that of Commodore."—*Extract from Captain Adams' official report to Commodore Perry.*

great deal of misunderstanding about receiving the original letter and the translated copies, whether to be received together or separately. The Admiral now is willing to meet with a high officer of Yedo, holding rank in Japan corresponding to the rank of Admiral in the United States. This officer shall be accredited, viz: possess a writing properly signed by the Emperor, authorizing him to receive the said letters. Of this writing or letter of credence shall be made a copy, translated into Dutch, and the same copy be transmitted to the Admiral before the interview takes place.

"At this interview there shall be no discussions whatever; no more than an exchange of civilities and compliments.

"The Admiral does not insist upon receiving an answer to the original letter of the President immediately, but will come back for that purpose after some months."]

Yezaiman. The high officer will not be allowed to speak on the matter; only to make and return compliments.

Capt. B. That is all that is necessary.

Yezaiman. The high officer will be here the day after to-morrow, to receive the letter on shore.

Capt. B. At what hour?

Yezaiman. At eight o'clock in the morning. As soon as we see the flag hoisted we will come on board the ship.

Capt. B. Will the high officer bring the copy of the letter empowering him to act, properly certified?

Yezaiman. He will bring it.

Interpreter. The governor is very grateful for his kind reception on board.

Capt. B. We are very happy to see him. Where is the place of reception?

Interpreter. I can point out the place, but the house cannot be seen.

Yezaiman. Will the Admiral await the Emperor's answer to the President's letter?

Capt. B. No; the Admiral will not now wait for it.

Yezaiman. When will he come for a reply?

Capt. B. He will return in a few months to receive the Emperor's reply.

Yezaiman. I would desire a statement in writing to that effect. [There being no satisfactory answer to this, Yezaiman continued.] The high officer who receives the letter of the President will give a receipt for it, as an assurance that it has been received.

Capt. B. Can you not appoint a place nearer the ship? The distance is very great for the men to pull in a boat. The Admiral will be satisfied to meet the high officer in a tent, or in one of the forts nearer the ships. The interview will not be long.

Interpreter. The house is not far off; it is less than a Japanese mile.

Capt. B. Can you not arrange to have it nearer the ships?

Interpreter. The governor says he will endeavor to arrange it.

Capt. B. Can you let us know to-morrow morning?

Interpreter. Yes.

The conference here ended.

Kayama Yezaiman and his companions seemed to be in the highest good humor, and readily availed themselves of the proffered courtesies of the officers of the Susquehanna, which were accepted and responded to in a manner indicating the most polished good breeding. In receiving the hospitalities of their hosts, it may be remarked that they partook freely, and seemed to relish particularly the whiskey and brandy which formed part of the entertainment. The governor especially appeared to appreciate the foreign liquors, particularly when mixed with sugar, and smacked his lips with great gusto, as he drained his glass to its last sweetened dregs. His interpreters, in the growing freedom of convivial enjoyment, made merry over his highness' bacchanalian proclivity, and laughingly expressing their alarm lest Yezaiman should take a drop too much, remarked, "his face is already growing red."

Though always preserving a certain gentlemanly aplomb and that self-cultivated manner which bespeaks high breeding, these Japanese dignitaries were disposed to be quite social, and shared freely and gaily in conversation. Nor did their knowledge and general information fall short of their elegance of manners and amiability of disposition. They were not only well-bred, but not ill-educated, as they were proficients in the Dutch, Chinese, and Japanese languages, and not unacquainted with the general principles of science and of the facts of the geography of the world. When a terrestrial globe was placed before them, and their attention was called to the delineation on it of the United States, they immediately placed their fingers on Washington and New York, as if perfectly familiar with the fact that one was the capital, and the other the commercial metropolis of our country. They also, with equal promptitude, pointed out England, France, Denmark, and other kingdoms of Europe. Their inquiries in reference to the United States showed them not to be entirely ignorant of the facts connected with the material progress of our country; thus, when they asked if roads were not cut through our mountains, they were referring (as was supposed) to tunnels on our railroads. And this supposition was confirmed on the interpreter's asking, as they examined the ship's engine, whether it was not a similar machine, although smaller, which was used for travelling on the American roads. They also inquired whether the canal across the isthmus was yet finished, alluding probably to the Panama railroad which was then in progress of construction. They knew, at any rate, that labor was being performed to connect the two oceans, and called it by the name of something they had seen, a canal.

After refreshments and conversation in the cabin, Yezaiman and his interpreters were invited to inspect the ship, an offer which they accepted with great politeness, and as they came upon deck, notwithstanding there were crowds of officers and men around who could scarce repress the manifestation of their curiosity, the Japanese never for a moment lost their self-possession, but showed the utmost composure and quiet dignity of manner. They evinced an intelligent interest in all the various arrangements of the vessel, observed the big gun and rightly styled it a "Paixhan," exhibited none of that surprise which would naturally be expected from those who were beholding for the first time the wonderful art and mechanism of a perfected steamship. The engine evidently was an object of great interest to them, but the interpreters showed that they were not entirely unacquainted with its principles. Much of this cool but not unobservant composure may have been affected, in accordance with a studied policy, but yet, there can be no doubt, that however backward the Japanese themselves may be in practical science, the best educated among them are tolerably well informed of its progress among more civilized or rather cultivated nations.

On leaving the cabin, the Japanese dignitaries had left their swords behind, two of which are always worn by those of certain rank in the empire. This gave an opportunity for inspection, on the part of the curious, of these badges of authority, which seemed to be, in accordance with their purpose, more suited for show than service. The blades, however, were apparently of good steel and temper, and highly polished, although their shape as well as that of their hilts, without a guard, was awkwardly constructed for use. The mountings were of pure gold, and the scabbards of shark's skin, remarkably well manufactured. The visit of the governor was prolonged into the evening, and it was seven o'clock before he took his departure, when he and his interpreters left the ship with their usual graceful courtesies, bowing at every step, and smiling in an amiable yet dignified manner. They were evidently favorably impressed with their reception and all they had seen. The studied politeness which marked their intercourse with our officers was evidently not assumed for the occasion, for it is so habitual with them that in their ordinary relations with each other they preserve the same stately courtesy; and it was observed, that no sooner had Yezaiman and his interpreters entered their boat alongside the Susquehanna, that they commenced saluting each other as formally as if they had met for the first time and were passing through the ceremonials of a personal introduction. While these scenes were in transaction on board, the boats of the squadron sent out by the Commodore were kept busy all day sounding and observing as on previous occasions.

The next day was Wednesday, (July 13th,) and the visit of the governor was naturally expected at an early hour, in fulfilment of his promise. There was, however, no indication through the morning of his coming, and every thing remained in a state of tranquil expectation. There seemed to be some little movement on the part of the authorities, as far as could be gathered from an observation of the neighboring land. From the opposite shores numerous vessels, loaded with soldiers, crossed to the Uraga side, and a large junk with the usual government flag and insignia put into the harbor. The brisk trade of the bay was carried on as usual, and Japanese boats, both large and small, were moving up and down in constant circulation. The various towns and villages grouped about the bay were thus interchanging their elements of life and, stimulated into commercial activity by the throb from the busy heart of the great city, poured into Yedo their overflowing abundance. There were no less than sixty-seven junks counted as passing up the bay during the single day.

The weather continued warm, with the thermometer indicating as high a point as 87°, but the heat was tempered by an agreeable sea breeze. The view of the shores was much obscured at times by the haze which is said to be so prevalent on the Japanese coast; but in the experience of the squadron the weather hitherto had been remarkably clear, and this day was the foggiest that had been seen since the ships arrived in the bay. Nothing could be seen of the great land-mark—the lofty peak of Fusi—which, by the way, was generally more plainly visible toward the evening than during the day, and was often observed beautifully distinct at sunset, when its summits would glow with a rich halo of crimson light.

The expected visit of the governor occurred at last, at about four o'clock in the afternoon. His highness Kayama Yezaiman, accompanied, as usual, by his first and second interpreters, presented himself, with a thousand apologies for not having come earlier, as the high officer from Yedo had but just arrived. The apologies having been made, the governor exhibited the original order of the Emperor, addressed to the functionary who had been appointed to receive the Commodore. The Emperor's letter was short, and was certified by a large seal attached to it. This imperial epistle, which was wrapped in velvet, and enclosed in a box made of sandal-wood, was treated by the governor with such reverence that he would allow no one to touch it. A copy of it in Dutch, and a certificate verifying the authenticity of the document, and of the Emperor's seal attached thereto, given under the hand of Kayama Yezaiman, the governor, were also presented. The translations were as follows:

Translation of letter of credence given by the Emperor of Japan to his highness, Toda, Prince of Idzu.

"I send you to Uraga to receive the letter of the President of the United States to me, which letter has recently been brought to Uraga by the Admiral, upon receiving which you will proceed to Yedo, and take the same to me.

[Here is the Emperor's seal.]

"SIXTH MONTH IN 1853."

Translation of certificate of Kayama Yezaiman, governor of Uraga, verifying the authenticity of the Emperor's letter and seal.

"You can rest assured that the high officer who has been accredited by the Emperor of Japan himself, and who consequently comes here to Uraga from Yedo for the purpose of receiving the original and translated letters, is of very high rank, equal to that of the Lord Admiral. I do assure that.

"KAYAMA YEZAIMAN."

The governor, in the course of the conference, took care to state that the person appointed by the Emperor had no authority to enter into discussions with the Commodore, but was merely empowered to receive the papers and convey them to his sovereign. He also stated that he had made inquiry as to the practicability of changing the place of meeting, and said that, as a suitable building had already been erected, it would be inconvenient to change. The Commodore was prepared for this reply, and as he could not know whether any treachery was intended or not, he had determined to provide, as far as he could, against every contingency, and had therefore ordered the surveying party to examine the little bay at the head of which the building had been erected for his reception. The officer sent upon this service promptly performed the duty, and reported that the ships could be brought within gun-shot of the place, where great numbers of the people had been observed employed in the completion of the building, in transporting furniture, and in otherwise preparing for the occasion.

The governor offered to accompany a boat to the place appointed for the reception, but this was declined, and he was informed that, as it did not befit the dignity of the Commodore to proceed a long distance in a small boat, the squadron would be removed to a position nearer the building designed for the reception. It was then agreed that the Commodore and his party should leave the ships between eight and nine o'clock the next day, (Thursday,) although the Japanese seemed particularly anxious that the interview should take place at an earlier hour, assigning as a reason that the heat of the day might thus be avoided.

The question was now asked as to how many officers would accompany the Commodore on the occasion, to which they received the answer that he would be followed by a large retinue, since it was the custom of the United States that when an officer of high rank bears a communication from the President to the sovereign of another country, for him to go with such an attendance as will be respectful to the power to which he is sent. Accordingly, the governor was informed that all the officers who could be spared from the squadron would accompany the Commodore, as the greater number would imply the greater compliment.

In the course of the conference, the Japanese dignitaries showed their great regard for ceremony by adverting to various minute points of etiquette in reference to the approaching reception. They announced that all the Japanese officers would be clothed in full official costume, and not in the dresses worn on ordinary occasions. They seemed to be considerably troubled because they would not be able to seat their visitors, on the morrow, in the same kind of arm chair as that then occupied by themselves in the cabin, and apologized for not having any such. They were no less anxious on the score of the wines and brandies, and begged that they might be excused for not offering the same as they had been regaled with, since the country did not possess them. They were told to dismiss their solicitude on these points; that, as the practice of hospitality, and manners and customs, necessarily differed in different countries, it was not reasonable to expect to find American habits prevailing in Japan; and that the Commodore would be satisfied to be seated in the same manner as the dignitary appointed to meet him, while the other American officers would content themselves with such seats as were provided for their equals in rank among the Japanese.

They then made some inquiries in regard to the minute details of the approaching ceremony, as to whether the Commodore would present the President's letter directly from his own hand into that of the Japanese commissioner, whose name and title, by the way, were now announced as Toda-Idzu-no-Kami, First Counsellor of the Empire.

It was asked whether the Commodore would immediately return to his ship after delivering the letter, and also when he would come back to Japan to receive an answer. The Chinese interpreter, Mr. Williams, showed them a map or plan of Yedo, which they said must have been drawn some seventy years ago, as the capital had changed much since the plan was made, having greatly increased in size, and much improved. They, however, recognized on the plan various conspicuous places, and pointed them out very readily, as if politely willing to gratify the natural curiosity of their company.

The whole conference had lasted about two hours and a half, and when the Japanese functionaries rose to depart it was already evening. They left the ship with the usual polite courtesies, bowing, as usual, at every step; and the chief interpreter, Hori Tatznoske, who had evidently a great aptitude for the acquisition of foreign languages, mustered English enough to say very distinctly as he departed, "Want to go home."

The Commodore, in preparation for the coming event of the next morning, summoned his captains, from the several vessels of the squadron, on board the flag-ship. Orders were then given that the vessels should be removed, early in the morning, to an anchorage in line, covering the whole bay, in front of the place of reception,* as the Commodore was resolved to be prepared against any possible treachery or duplicity on the part of the people with whom he had to deal, and as the object of the Japanese in the selection of this place of meeting was not very apparent to his mind. It was also ordered that all the officers who could possibly leave the ships should appear in full uniform, and accompany the Commodore to the reception, in order that he might present as imposing a retinue as practicable. The surveying boats had been kept busy during the day, completing their observations, and were allowed to proceed with their work without any molestation from the native authorities.

The Japanese seemed no less busy in active preparation for the morning's ceremony than the

---

* Marked on the chart as "Reception Bay."

Americans. Various government vessels sailed down the bay, and a large fleet of small boats arrived on the Uraga shore from the opposite coast, evidently preparatory to the approaching occasion. A constant sound of hammers, intermingled with the noisy voices of Japanese laborers, arising as was supposed from the quarter where the building was in progress, disturbed the quiet of the night and was prolonged into the morning watches. All was busy preparation for the coming day.

Thursday, (July 14) opened with a sun that was somewhat obscured at early dawn, but which soon came out brightly and dispelled the fogs and clouds which overhung the land and seemed to give an inauspicious aspect to the occasion. As the atmosphere cleared and the shores were disclosed to view, the steady labors of the Japanese during the night were revealed in the showy effect on the Uraga shore. Ornamental screens of cloth had been so arranged as to give a more distinct prominence, as well as the appearance of greater size to the bastions and forts; and two tents had been spread among the trees. The screens were stretched tightly in the usual way upon posts of wood, and each interval between the posts was thus distinctly marked, and had, in the distance, the appearance of panelling. Upon these seeming panels were emblazoned the imperial arms, alternating with the device of a scarlet flower bearing large heart-shaped leaves. Flags and streamers, upon which were various designs represented in gay colors, hung from the several angles of the screens, while behind them thronged crowds of soldiers, arrayed in a costume which had not been before observed, and which was supposed to belong to high occasions only. The main portion of the dress was a species of frock of a dark color, with short skirts, the waists of which were gathered in with a sash, and which was without sleeves, the arms of the wearers being bare.

All on board the ships were alert from the earliest hour, making the necessary preparations. Steam was got up and the anchors were weighed that the ships might be moved to a position where their guns would command the place of reception. The sailing vessels, however, because of a calm, were unable to get into position. The officers, seamen, and marines who were to accompany the Commodore were selected, and as large a number of them mustered as could possibly be spared from the whole squadron. All, of course, were eager to bear a part in the ceremonies of the day, but all could not possibly go, as a sufficient number must be left to do ships' duty. Many of the officers and men were selected by lot, and when the full complement, which amounted to nearly three hundred, was filled up, each one busied himself in getting his person ready for the occasion. The officers, as had been ordered, were in full official dress, while the sailors and marines were in their naval and military uniforms of blue and white.

Before eight bells in the morning watch had struck, the Susquehanna and Mississippi moved slowly down the bay. Simultaneously with this movement of our ships, six Japanese boats were observed to sail in the same direction, but more within the land. The government striped flag distinguished two of them, showing the presence of some high officials, while the others carried red banners, and were supposed to have on board a retinue or guard of soldiers. On doubling the head-land which separated the former anchorage from the bay below, the preparations of the Japanese on the shore came suddenly into view. The land bordering the head of the bay was gay with a long stretch of painted screens of cloth, upon which was emblazoned the arms of the Emperor. Nine tall standards stood in the centre of an immense number of banners of divers lively colors, which were arranged on either side, until the whole formed a crescent of variously tinted flags, which fluttered brightly in the rays of the morning sun. From the tall standards were suspended broad pennons of rich scarlet which swept the ground with their flowing length. On the beach in front of this display were ranged regiments of soldiers, who stood in fixed order, evidently arrayed to give an appearance of martial force, that the Americans might be duly impressed with the military power of the Japanese.

As the beholder faced the bay, he saw on the left of the village of Gori-Hama a straggling group of peaked-roofed houses, built between the beach and the base of the high ground which ran in green acclivities behind, and ascended from height to height to the distant mountains. A luxuriant valley or gorge, walled in with richly wooded hills, opened at the head of the bay, and breaking the uniformity of the curve of the shore gave a beautiful variety to the landscape. On the right some hundred Japanese boats, or more, were arranged in parallel lines along the margin of the shore, with a red flag flying at the stern of each. The whole effect, though not startling, was novel and cheerful, and every thing combined to give a pleasing aspect to the picture. The day was bright, with a clear sunlight which seemed to give fresh vitality alike to the verdant hill-sides, and the gay banners, and the glittering soldiery. Back from the beach, opposite the centre of the curved shore of the bay, the building, just constructed for the reception, rose in three pyramidal shaped roofs, high above the surrounding houses. It was covered in front by striped cloth, which was extended in screens to either side. It had a new, fresh look, indicative of its recent erection, and with its peaked summits was not unlike, in the distance, a group of very large ricks of grain.

Two boats approached as the steamers neared the opening of the bay, and when the anchors were dropped they came alongside the Susquehanna. Kayama Yezaiman, with his two interpreters, came on board, followed immediately by Nagazima Saboroske and an officer in attendance, who had come in the second boat. They were duly received at the gangway and conducted to seats on the quarter deck. All were dressed in full official costume, somewhat different from their ordinary garments. Their gowns, though of the usual shape, were much more elaborately adorned. The material was of very rich silk brocade of gay colors, turned up with yellow velvet, and the whole dress was highly embroidered with gold lace in various figures, among which was conspicuously displayed on the back, sleeves, and breast the arms of the wearer. Saboroske, the sub-governor of Uraga, wore a pair of very broad but very short trowsers, which, when his legs (which was not often the case) stood still and together, looked very much like a slit petticoat, while below, his nether limbs were partly naked and partly covered by black woollen socks. Saboroske, in spite of his elaborate toilette and his finery, all bedizened with gold thread, glossy silk, and gay colors, did not produce a very impressive effect; but by his comical appearance provoked mirth rather than admiration. He had, in fact, very much the appearance of an unusually brilliant knave of trumps.

A signal was now hoisted from the Susquehanna as a summons for the boats from the other ships, and in the course of half an hour they had all pulled alongside with their various officers, sailors, and marines, detailed for the day's ceremonies. The launches and cutters numbered no less than fifteen, and presented quite an imposing array; and with all on board them, in proper uniform, a picturesque effect was not wanting. Captain Buchanan, having taken his place in his barge, led the way, flanked on either side by the two Japanese boats containing the governor and vice-governor of Uraga with their respective suites; and these dignitaries acted as masters of ceremony and pointed out the course to the American flotilla. The rest of the ships' boats followed after in order, with the cutters containing the two bands of the steamers, who enlivened the occasion with their cheerful music.

The boats skimmed briskly over the smooth waters; for such was the skill and consequent rapidity of the Japanese scullers that our sturdy oarsmen were put to their mettle to keep up with their guides. When the boats had reached half way to the shore the thirteen guns of the Susquehanna began to boom away and re-echo among the hills. This announced the departure of the Commodore who, stepping into his barge, was rowed off to the land.

The guides in the Japanese boats pointed to the landing place toward the centre of the curved shore, where a temporary wharf had been built out from the beach by means of bags of sand and straw. The advance boat soon touched the spot, and Captain Buchanan, who commanded the party, sprang ashore, being the first of the Americans who landed in the Kingdom of Japan. He was immediately followed by Major Zeilin, of the marines. The rest of the boats now pulled in and disembarked their respective loads. The marines (one hundred) marched up the wharf and formed into line on either side, facing the sea: then came the hundred sailors, who were also ranged in rank and file as they advanced, while the two bands brought up the rear. The whole number of Americans, including sailors, marines, musicians, and officers, amounted to nearly three hundred: no very formidable array, but still quite enough for a peaceful occasion, and composed of very vigorous, able-bodied men, who contrasted strongly with the smaller and more effeminate looking Japanese. These latter had mustered in great force, the amount of which the governor of Uraga stated to be five thousand; but, seemingly, they far outnumbered that. Their line extended around the whole circuit of the beach, from the further extremity of the village to the abrupt acclivity of the hill which bounded the bay on the northern side; while an immense number of the soldiers thronged in, behind and under cover of the cloth screens which stretched along the rear. The loose order of this Japanese army did not betoken any very great degree of discipline. The soldiers were tolerably well armed and equipped. Their uniform was very much like the ordinary Japanese dress. Their arms were swords, spears, and match-locks. Those in front were all infantry, archers and lancers; but large bodies of cavalry were seen behind, somewhat in the distance, as if held in reserve. The horses of these seemed of a fine breed, hardy, of good bottom, and brisk in action; and these troopers, with their rich caparisons, presented at least a showy cavalcade. Along the base of the rising ground which ascended behind the village, and entirely in the rear of the soldiers, was a large number of the inhabitants, among whom there was quite an assemblage of women, who gazed with intense curiosity, through the openings in the line of the military, upon the stranger visitors from another hemisphere.

On the arrival of the Commodore, his suite of officers formed a double line along the landing place, and as he passed up between, they fell into order behind him. The procession was then formed and took up its march toward the house of reception, the route to which was pointed out by Kayama Yezaiman and his interpreter, who preceded the party. The marines led the way, and the sailors following, the Commodore was duly escorted up the beach. The United States flag and the broad pennant were borne by two athletic seamen, who had been selected from the crews of the squadron on account of their stalwart proportions. Two boys, dressed for the ceremony, preceded the Commodore, bearing in an envelope of scarlet cloth the boxes which contained his credentials and the President's letter. These documents, of folio size, were beautifully written on vellum, and not folded, but bound in blue silk velvet. Each seal, attached by cords of interwoven gold and silk with pendant gold tassels, was encased in a circular box six inches in diameter and three in depth, wrought of pure gold. Each of the

MEETING WITH THE JAPANESE COMMISSIONERS.

documents together with its seal, was placed in a box of rosewood about a foot long, with lock, hinges, and mountings, all of gold. On either side of the Commodore marched a tall, well-formed negro, who, armed to the teeth, acted as his personal guard. These blacks, selected for the occasion, were two of the best looking fellows of their color that the squadron could furnish. All this, of course, was but for effect.

The procession was obliged to make a somewhat circular movement to reach the entrance of the house of reception. This gave a good opportunity for the display of the escort. The building, which was but a short distance from the landing, was soon reached. In front of the entrance were two small brass cannon which were old and apparently of European manufacture; on either side were grouped a rather straggling company of Japanese guards, whose costume was different from that of the other soldiers. Those on the right were dressed in tunics, gathered in at the waist with broad sashes, and in full trowsers of a grey color, the capacious width of which was drawn in at the knees, while their heads were bound with a white cloth in the form of a turban. They were armed with muskets upon which bayonets and flint-locks were observed. The guards on the left were dressed in a rather dingy, brown-colored uniform turned up with yellow, and carried old-fashioned match-locks.

The Commodore having been escorted to the door of the house of reception, entered with his suite. The building showed marks of hasty erection, and the timbers and boards of pine wood were numbered, as if they had been fashioned previously and brought to the spot all ready to be put together. The first portion of the structure entered was a kind of tent, principally constructed of painted canvas, upon which in various places the imperial arms were painted. Its area enclosed a space of nearly forty feet square. Beyond this entrance hall was an inner apartment to which a carpeted path led. The floor of the outer room was generally covered with white cloth, but through its centre passed a slip of red-colored carpet, which showed the direction to the interior chamber. This latter was entirely carpeted with red cloth, and was the state apartment of the building where the reception was to take place. Its floor was somewhat raised, like a dais, above the general level, and was handsomely adorned for the occasion. Violet-colored hangings of silk and fine cotton, with the imperial coat of arms embroidered in white, hung from the walls which enclosed the inner room, on three sides, while the front was left open to the antechamber or outer room.

As the Commodore and his suite ascended to the reception room, the two dignitaries who were seated on the left arose and bowed, and the Commodore and suite were conducted to the arm chairs which had been provided for them on the right. The interpreters announced the names and titles of the high Japanese functionaries as *Toda-Idzu-no-kami*, Toda, prince of Idzu, and *Ido-Iwami-no-kami*, Ido, prince of Iwami. They were both men of advanced years, the former apparently about fifty, and the latter some ten or fifteen years older. Prince Toda was the better looking man of the two, and the intellectual expression of his large forehead and amiable look of his regular features contrasted very favorably with the more wrinkled and contracted, and less intelligent face of his associate, the prince of Iwami. They were both very richly dressed, their garments being of heavy silk brocade interwoven with elaborately wrought figures in gold and silver.

From the beginning, the two princes had assumed an air of statuesque formality which they preserved during the whole interview, as they never spoke a word, and rose from their seats only at the entrance and exit of the Commodore, when they made a grave and formal bow. Yezaiman and his interpreters acted as masters of ceremony during the occasion. On entering, they took their positions at the upper end of the room, kneeling down beside a large lacquered box of scarlet color, supported by feet, gilt or of brass.

For some time after the Commodore and his suite had taken their seats there was a pause of some minutes, not a word being uttered on either side. Tatznoske, the principal interpreter, was the first to break silence, which he did by asking Mr. Portman, the Dutch interpreter, whether the letters were ready for delivery, and stating that the prince Toda was prepared to receive them; and that the scarlet box at the upper end of the room was prepared as the receptacle for them. The Commodore, upon this being communicated to him, beckoned to the boys who stood in the lower hall to advance, when they immediately obeyed his summons and came forward, bearing the handsome boxes which contained the President's letter and other documents. The two stalwart negroes followed immediately in rear of the boys, and marching up to the scarlet receptacle, received the boxes from the hands of the bearers, opened them, took out the letters and, displaying the writing and seals, laid them upon the lid of the Japanese box—all in perfect silence. The President's letter, the Commodore's letter of credence, and two communications from the Commodore to the Emperor, are here given. A third letter from him has already been presented on a previous page. All these, however, accompanied the letter from the President and were delivered at the same time with it.

MILLARD FILLMORE, PRESIDENT OF THE UNITED STATES OF AMERICA, TO HIS IMPERIAL MAJESTY, THE EMPEROR OF JAPAN.

GREAT AND GOOD FRIEND: I send you this public letter by Commodore Matthew C. Perry, an officer of the highest rank in the navy of the United States, and commander of the squadron now visiting your imperial majesty's dominions.

I have directed Commodore Perry to assure your imperial majesty that I entertain the kindest feelings toward your majesty's person and government, and that I have no other object in sending him to Japan but to propose to your imperial majesty that the United States and Japan should live in friendship and have commercial intercourse with each other.

The Constitution and laws of the United States forbid all interference with the religious or political concerns of other nations. I have particularly charged Commodore Perry to abstain from every act which could possibly disturb the tranquility of your imperial majesty's dominions.

The United States of America reach from ocean to ocean, and our Territory of Oregon and State of California lie directly opposite to the dominions of your imperial majesty. Our steamships can go from California to Japan in eighteen days.

Our great State of California produces about sixty millions of dollars in gold every year, besides silver, quicksilver, precious stones, and many other valuable articles. Japan is also a rich and fertile country, and produces many very valuable articles. Your imperial majesty's subjects are skilled in many of the arts. I am desirous that our two countries should trade with each other, for the benefit both of Japan and the United States.

We know that the ancient laws of your imperial majesty's government do not allow of foreign trade, except with the Chinese and the Dutch; but as the state of the world changes and new governments are formed, it seems to be wise, from time to time, to make new laws. There was a time when the ancient laws of your imperial majesty's government were first made.

About the same time America, which is sometimes called the New World, was first discovered and settled by the Europeans. For a long time there were but a few people, and they were poor. They have now become quite numerous; their commerce is very extensive; and they think that if your imperial majesty were so far to change the ancient laws as to allow a free trade between the two countries it would be extremely beneficial to both.

If your imperial majesty is not satisfied that it would be safe altogether to abrogate the ancient laws which forbid foreign trade, they might be suspended for five or ten years, so as to try the experiment. If it does not prove as beneficial as was hoped, the ancient laws can be restored. The United States often limit their treaties with foreign States to a few years, and then renew them or not, as they please.

I have directed Commodore Perry to mention another thing to your imperial majesty. Many of our ships pass every year from California to China; and great numbers of our people pursue the whale fishery near the shores of Japan. It sometimes happens, in stormy weather, that one of our ships is wrecked on your imperial majesty's shores. In all such cases we ask, and expect, that our unfortunate people should be treated with kindness, and that their property should be protected, till we can send a vessel and bring them away. We are very much in earnest in this.

Commodore Perry is also directed by me to represent to your imperial majesty that we understand there is a great abundance of coal and provisions in the Empire of Japan. Our steamships, in crossing the great ocean, burn a great deal of coal, and it is not convenient to bring it all the way from America. We wish that our steamships and other vessels should be allowed to stop in Japan and supply themselves with coal, provisions, and water. They will pay for them in money, or anything else your imperial majesty's subjects may prefer; and we request your imperial majesty to appoint a convenient port, in the southern part of the Empire, where our vessels may stop for this purpose. We are very desirous of this.

These are the only objects for which I have sent Commodore Perry, with a powerful squadron, to pay a visit to your imperial majesty's renowned city of Yedo: friendship, commerce, a supply of coal and provisions, and protection for our shipwrecked people.

We have directed Commodore Perry to beg your imperial majesty's acceptance of a few presents. They are of no great value in themselves; but some of them may serve as specimens of the articles manufactured in the United States, and they are intended as tokens of our sincere and respectful friendship.

May the Almighty have your imperial majesty in His great and holy keeping!

In witness whereof, I have caused the great seal of the United States to be hereunto affixed, and have subscribed the same with my name, at the city of Washington, in America, the seat of my government, on the thirteenth day of the month of November, in the year one thousand eight hundred and fifty-two.

[Seal attached.]

Your good friend,

MILLARD FILLMORE.

By the President:

EDWARD EVERETT.
Secretary of State.

Commodore Perry to the Emperor.

UNITED STATES STEAM FRIGATE SUSQUEHANNA,
Off the coast of Japan, July 7, 1853.

The undersigned, commander-in-chief of all the naval forces of the United States of America stationed in the East India, China and Japan seas, has been sent by his government to this country, on a friendly mission, with ample powers to negotiate with the government of Japan, touching certain matters which have been fully set forth in the letter of the President of the United States, copies of which, together with copies of the letter of credence of the undersigned, in the English, Dutch, and Chinese languages, are herewith transmitted.

The original of the President's letter, and of the letter of credence, prepared in a manner suited to the exalted station of your imperial majesty, will be presented by the undersigned in person, when it may please your majesty to appoint a day for his reception.

The undersigned has been commanded to state that the President entertains the most friendly feelings toward Japan, but has been surprised and grieved to learn that when any of the people of the United States go, of their own accord, or are thrown by the perils of the sea, within the dominions of your imperial majesty, they are treated as if they were your worst enemies.

The undersigned refers to the cases of the American ships Morrison, Lagoda, and Lawrence.

With the Americans, as indeed with all Christian people, it is considered a sacred duty to receive with kindness, and to succor and protect all, of whatever nation, who may be cast upon their shores, and such has been the course of the Americans with respect to all Japanese subjects who have fallen under their protection.

The government of the United States desires to obtain from that of Japan some positive assurance that persons who may hereafter be shipwrecked on the coast of Japan, or driven by stress of weather into her ports, shall be treated with humanity.

The undersigned is commanded to explain to the Japanese that the United States are connected with no government in Europe, and that their laws do not interfere with the religion of their own citizens, much less with that of other nations.

That they inhabit a great country which lies directly between Japan and Europe, and which was discovered by the nations of Europe about the same time that Japan herself was first visited by Europeans; that the portion of the American continent lying nearest to Europe was first settled by emigrants from that part of the world; that its population has rapidly spread through the country, until it has reached the shores of the Pacific ocean; that we have now large cities, from which, with the aid of steam-vessels, we can reach Japan in eighteen or twenty days; that our commerce with all this region of the globe is rapidly increasing, and the Japan seas will soon be covered with our vessels.

Therefore, as the United States and Japan are becoming every day nearer and nearer to each other, the President desires to live in peace and friendship with your imperial majesty, but no friendship can long exist, unless Japan ceases to act toward Americans as if they were her enemies.

However wise this policy may originally have been, it is unwise and impracticable now that the intercourse between the two countries is so much more easy and rapid than it formerly was.

The undersigned holds out all these arguments in the hope that the Japanese government will see the necessity of averting unfriendly collision between the two nations, by responding favorably to the propositions of amity, which are now made in all sincerity.

Many of the large ships-of-war destined to visit Japan have not yet arrived in these seas, though they are hourly expected; and the undersigned, as an evidence of his friendly intentions, has brought but four of the smaller ones, designing, should it become necessary, to return to Yedo in the ensuing spring with a much larger force.

But it is expected that the government of your imperial majesty will render such return unnecessary, by acceding at once to the very reasonable and pacific overtures contained in the President's letter, and which will be further explained by the undersigned on the first fitting occasion.

With the most profound respect for your imperial majesty, and entertaining a sincere hope that you may long live to enjoy health and happiness, the undersigned subscribes himself,

M. C. PERRY,
Commander-in-chief of the United States Naval Forces
in the East India, China, and Japan seas.*

To His Imperial Majesty,
the Emperor of Japan.

Commodore Perry to the Emperor.

"UNITED STATES STEAM FRIGATE SUSQUEHANNA,
"*Uraga, Yedo Bay, July* 14, 1853.

"It having been represented to the undersigned that the propositions submitted through him to the government of Japan are of so much importance, and involve so many momentous questions, that much time will be required to deliberate and decide upon their several bearings:

"The undersigned, in consideration thereof, declares himself willing to await a reply to these propositions until his return to Yedo Bay in the ensuing spring, when he confidently hopes that all matters will be amicably arranged, and to the satisfaction of the two nations.

"With profound respect,

"M. C. PERRY,
"*Commander-in-chief of the United States Naval Forces*
"*in the East India, China, and Japan seas.*

"To His Imperial Majesty,
"*the Emperor of Japan.*"

Letter of credence to Commodore Perry.

MILLARD FILLMORE, PRESIDENT OF THE UNITED STATES OF AMERICA, TO HIS IMPERIAL MAJESTY THE EMPEROR OF JAPAN.

Reposing special trust and confidence in the integrity, prudence, and ability of Matthew C. Perry, a captain in the navy of the United States, I have invested him with full power, for and in the name of the said United States, to meet and confer with any person or persons furnished with like powers on the part of your imperial majesty, and with him or them to negotiate,

---

* It should be remarked that the Commodore framed this letter on his letter of instructions from the authorities of the United States.

conclude, and sign a convention or conventions, treaty or treaties, of and concerning the friendship, commerce, and navigation of the two countries; and all matters and subjects connected therewith which may be interesting to the two nations, submitting the same to the President of the United States for his final ratification, by and with the advice and consent of the Senate of the United States.

In testimony whereof, I have caused the seal of the United States to be hereunto affixed.

Given under my hand, at the city of Washington, the thirteenth day of November, in the year one thousand eight hundred and fifty-two, and of the independence of the United States of America the seventy-seventh.

MILLARD FILLMORE.

By the President:

EDWARD EVERETT.

[Seal attached.]

Secretary of State.

Accompanying the letters were translations of the same into the Chinese and Dutch languages. After the documents had been laid upon the lid of the imperial box, made as their receptacle, Mr. Portman, Dutch interpreter, by the Commodore's direction, indicated to Tatznoske, the Japanese interpreter, the characters of the various documents, upon which Tatznoske and Keyama Yezaimen, still kneeling, both bowed their heads. The latter, now rising, approached the Prince of Iwami, and prostrating himself on his knees before him, received from his hands a roll of papers, with which he crossed over to the Commodore, and again falling upon his knees, delivered it to him. The Dutch interpreter now asked "what those papers were?" to which it was answered, "they are the imperial receipt." The translation of it is as follows:

[Translation of receipt given by the Princes of Idzu and Iwami to Commodore Perry.]

"The letter of the President of the United States of North America, and copy, are hereby received and delivered to the Emperor. Many times it has been communicated that business relating to foreign countries cannot be transacted here in Uraga, but in Nagasaki. Now it has been observed that the Admiral, in his quality of ambassador of the President, would be insulted by it; the justice of this has been acknowledged; consequently, the above mentioned letter is hereby received, in opposition to the Japanese law.

"Because the place is not designed to treat of anything from foreigners, so neither can conference nor entertainment take place. The letter being received you will leave here."

[Here follow fac similes of signatures in Japanese.]

"THE NINTH OF THE SIXTH MONTH."

The above is a literal translation from the Dutch, in which language the conferences were held, and into which the receipt of the chief counsellors, the princes of Idzu and Iwami, was, doubtless, badly translated from the Japanese by their interpreter.

The following would probably be the correct translation from the Japanese:

"The letter of the President of the United States of North America, and copy, are hereby eceived, and will be delivered to the Emperor.

"It has been many times intimated that business relating to foreign countries cannot be transacted here in Uraga, but at Nagasaki; nevertheless, as it has been observed that the Admiral, in his quality of ambassador of the President, would feel himself insulted by a refusal to receive the letter at this place, the justice of which has been acknowledged, the above mentioned letter is hereby received, in opposition to the Japanese law.

TERMINATION OF THE CONFERENCE.

"As this is not a place wherein to negotiate with foreigners, so neither can conferences nor entertainment be held. Therefore, as the letter has been received you can depart."

After a silence of some few minutes, the Commodore directed his interpreters to inform the Japanese that he would leave, with the squadron, for Lew Chew and Canton in two or three days, and to offer to the government his services, if it wished to send any dispatches or messages to those places. The Commodore also stated that it was his intention to return to Japan in the approaching spring, perhaps in April or May. Tatznoske then asked the Dutch interpreter to repeat what he had said about the Commodore's leaving and returning, which he did, using the same words as before. Then the question was asked "whether the Commodore would return with all four vessels?" "All of them," answered the Commodore, "and probably more, as these are only a portion of the squadron." Allusion had been made to the revolution in China, and the interpreter asked its cause, without however translating to the Japanese princes, to which the Commodore dictated the reply, that "it was on account of the government."

Yezaimen and Tatznoske now bowed, and, rising from their knees, drew the fastenings around the scarlet box, and informing the Commodore's interpreter that there was nothing more to be done, passed out of the apartment, bowing to those on either side as they went. The Commodore now rose to take leave, and, as he departed, the two princes, still preserving absolute silence, also arose and stood until the strangers had passed from their presence.

The Commodore and his suite were detained a short time at the entrance of the building waiting for their barge, whereupon Yezaimen and his interpreter returned and asked some of the party what they were waiting for; to which they received the reply, "For the Commodore's boat." Nothing further was said. The whole interview had not occupied more than from twenty to thirty minutes, and had been conducted with the greatest formality, though with the most perfect courtesy in every respect.

The procession re-formed as before, and the Commodore was escorted to his barge, and, embarking, was rowed off toward his ship, followed by the other American and the two Japanese boats which contained the governor of Uraga and his attendants, the bands meanwhile playing our national airs with great spirit as the boats pulled off to the ships. While there was some little delay in embarking all the party, in consequence of the smallness of the landing place, which was now flanked by some sixty or seventy Japanese government boats, the soldiers took occasion to crowd in from various parts of the shore, either to satisfy their curiosity, or to show a more formidable front; and it must be confessed that, had such been the disposition of the Japanese, there would have been no difficulty, with their large force, in completely hemming in the Americans.

CHAPTER XIV.

CONCESSIONS OF THE JAPANESE.—RELAXATION OF THEIR RESTRICTIVE LAWS.—SATISFACTION OF BOTH JAPANESE AND AMERICANS AT THE RESULT OF THE VISIT ON SHORE AND DELIVERY OF THE PRESIDENT'S LETTER.—VISIT OF KEYAMA YEZAIMEN TO THE SHIPS.—IMPUDENCE OF THE INTERPRETER SABOROSKE.—THE SQUADRON GOES FURTHER UP THE BAY TOWARD THE CAPITAL.—POLICY OF THIS MOVEMENT.—ALARM OF THE JAPANESE GRADUALLY QUIETED.—BEAUTIFUL SCENERY UP THE BAY.—SURVEY OF THE BAY CONTINUED.—CONVIVIALITY ON BOARD.—SURVEYING BOATS ENTER A SMALL RIVER.—CORDIAL GREETING OF THE INHABITANTS.—CROWD DISPERSED BY A JAPANESE OFFICIAL.—COMMODORE TRANSFERS HIS PENNANT FROM THE SUSQUEHANNA TO THE MISSISSIPPI.—THE LAST-NAMED VESSEL GOES UP IN SIGHT OF THE SHIPPING PLACE OF YEDO.—SINAGAWA.—YEDO ABOUT TEN MILES DISTANT FROM THE POINT WHERE THE SHIPS TURNED ABOUT.—GOOD DEPTH OF WATER IN YEDO BAY, PROBABLY ALMOST UP TO THE CITY.—THE BAY PRETTY THOROUGHLY EXPLORED AND SOUNDED BY THE SURVEYING PARTIES.—INTERCHANGE OF PRESENTS WITH THE JAPANESE OFFICERS.—AVOWED SORROW OF JAPANESE OFFICIALS ON BIDDING FAREWELL TO THE AMERICANS.—COMMODORE'S REASONS FOR NOT WAITING FOR A REPLY TO THE PRESIDENT'S LETTER.—LEAVES YEDO BAY DECLARING HIS INTENTION TO RETURN IN THE ENSUING SPRING.—THE SARATOGA SENT TO SHANGHAI TO LOOK AFTER AMERICAN INTERESTS.—THE PLYMOUTH ORDERED TO LEW CHEW.—OHO-SIMA.—SHIPS ENCOUNTER A STORM.—GENERAL RESULTS OF THE FIRST VISIT OF THE SQUADRON TO THE BAY OF YEDO.

HE Commodore had, previous to setting out on the expedition ashore, placed his two steamers in such a position as to command the little bay, and had given orders that the decks should be cleared and everything got ready for action. Howitzers were placed in boats alongside, in readiness to be dispatched at a moment's notice, in case any trouble should occur on land, and the ship's guns were prepared to send their balls and shells in showers upon all the line of Japanese troops which thronged the shore, had they commenced hostilities. There was, however, no serious apprehension felt of any warlike termination to the ceremonies of the day, although every precaution was properly taken to provide against the least untoward occurrence. When the reception was over, there was a general feeling of satisfaction on the part of every man in the squadron at the successful result. Judged by the ordinary relations of civilized nations, there was not much ground for congratulation, but when considered in reference to the exclusive policy of Japan, there was every reason for a proud self-satisfaction on the part of each American who had shared in the event of the day.

The justice of the Commodore's demand to be received as befitted the envoy of a great nation, was acknowledged in the remarkable document received from the imperial government, and confirmed in the most impressive manner by the proceedings of the day, when two of the chief princes of the Empire, acting as the immediate representatives of the highest authority, had so far raised the iron-like mask of Japanese reserve as to show themselves face to face to the Americans, and receive from the hands of an American ambassador an urgent invitation to share in the comity of nations. "As it has been observed that the Admiral, in his quality of ambassador of the President, would feel himself insulted by a refusal to receive the letter at this place, the justice of which has been acknowledged, the above mentioned letter is hereby received in opposition to the Japanese laws." Such are the remarkable words of the Japanese document, and thus, in this striking phrase, "*in opposition to the Japanese laws*," has Japan herself emphatically recorded the American triumph, as she has, perhaps, foretold her own regeneration. The vigorous grasp of the hand of America which was proffered in a friendly spirit, but thrust forward with an energy that proved the power to strike, as well as the disposition to embrace, had stirred Japanese isolation into a sensibility of its relationship to the rest of the world. Japan had broken its own code of selfish exclusiveness to obey the universal law of hospitality.

The concession to the demands of the Commodore, though great for the Japanese, was yet very far from all that was to be reasonably demanded on the score of the usual comity of nations. The communication from the government of Japan, remarkable as it was for its breaking through the Japanese law of exclusion, was still marked with traces of their restrictive policy, and contained these words: "Therefore, as the letter has been received, you can depart." The Commodore, to show how little he regarded the order of the princes to depart, had no sooner reached his ship, after the interview on shore, than he ordered the whole squadron to get under way. This was not to leave the bay, as the princes doubtless expected, but to go higher up. The Commodore determined to examine the channel toward Yedo, being satisfied that the employment of so large a force in surveying service, and in so near a neighborhood to the capital, would produce a decided influence upon the pride and conceit of the government, and cause a more favorable consideration of the President's letter.

The Governor of Uraga, Yezaimen, and Saboroske, with the interpreters, had accompanied the party on the return to the ships, and, on going on board of the Susquehanna, were received by the captains and the Commodore's aid in the upper cabin, where the following conversation ensued:

Yezaimen. We are happy to state that everything has passed off well and favorably.

Captain Buchanan. We hope that Japan and the United States will always be friends.

Yezaimen. When do you intend to go away?

Capt. B. In the course of two or three days. The Commodore is going to take a sail up the bay to see the anchorage. He does not like his first place of anchorage.

Yezaimen. Will you anchor there?

Capt. B. Only for two or three days, until we get ready to go to sea.

Yezaimen. We desire to take leave officially to-day, that it may not be necessary for us to return before you go.

Capt. B. We hope to have the pleasure of seeing you again before many months. Commodore Perry did not bring this time with him the presents intended for the Emperor of Japan, but when he comes again he will bring them. Among them is a steam engine or locomotive, for railroads.

Lieut. Contee. There is also among them a telegraph long enough to reach from Uraga to Yedo, by means of which you can speak from one place to another in a single second.

Yezaimen. How many miles can you make in an hour with your steam engine?

Lieut. C. Eight Japanese or thirteen American miles, with steam only and without wind. In the United States, there are some very light steamers on the river which can go eighteen miles an hour.

Yezaimen. Where were steamers first invented?

Lieut. C. In America: an American named Fulton first invented them in New York.

Yezaimen having been urged to remain and observe the engine in motion, his curiosity prompted him to do so, and his boat and that of Saboroske being taken in tow, these two officials and their interpreters, while the anchors were weighing and the steamers were proceeding to their old anchorage, partook freely of the hospitalities of the officers, and busied themselves in gratifying their natural desire of seeing all that was to be seen on board the ship.

These Japanese officials, evincing as they always did a certain reserved curiosity, yet showed an intelligent interest in the structure of the steamer and all that pertained to its appointments. While the engines were in motion they minutely inspected every part, but exhibited no fear, nor any of that startled surprise that would be expected of those who were entirely ignorant of its mechanism. They seemed to acquire rapidly some insight into the nature of steam, and into the mode with which it was applied to put into action the great engine and move by its power the wheels of the steamers. Their questions were of the most intelligent character, and they asked again by whom steamers were first discovered, and to what speed they could be propelled through the water. They examined with marked interest various engravings which were shown them of American river and sea steam vessels, and also some views of New York, New Orleans, and San Francisco, which happened to be on board. Yezaimen having observed the revolvers in the belts of some of the American officers, expressed a desire to examine the construction and see one let off. His curiosity was accordingly gratified by one of the captains, who fired off a revolver from the quarter deck, and he watched the repeated discharges of the six barrels with very evident astonishment but no alarm.

There was a marked contrast observed between the bearing of the two officials. While Yezaimen always exhibited a modest reserve of manner, Saboroske was bold and pushing. The former evinced an intelligent curiosity, but the latter showed an importunate inquisitiveness. Yezaimen was always the quiet, courteous, and reserved gentleman, but Saboroske was perpetually bustling, rude, and intrusive. The latter was continually peering his bold and impudent face into every nook and corner, whether invited or not, and appeared more desirous of acting the spy than of gratifying the interest of a liberal curiosity.

A shrill blast of the steam whistle now announced the arrival of the steamers off Uraga, and startled the Japanese to their feet, as the time of their departure had arrived. The engines were stopped for a few minutes while the Japanese boats were brought alongside from the stern, where they had been in tow. Yezaimen and his party were evidently disappointed that their visit was brought so soon to a close, and expressed some reluctance at leaving before they had fully gratified their curiosity.

The whole squadron now got in position, the steamers having been joined by the two sloops-of-war, the Plymouth and Saratoga, and all four ships presented a formidable array as they stood off in a line abreast of each other and advanced with running lines of soundings up the bay. The course was now directed toward the eastern shore, leaving on the west the promontory of Uraga and a beautiful bay beyond, which disclosed to the view its surrounding hills of the richest verdure with numerous villages at their base, as the squadron moved along in a diagonal line.

As the land on the west was approached to within three miles, it was seen to rise gradually from the undulating slopes, near the waters of the bay, to steep mountains in the distance. Fertile fields, expanding parks, bounded with plantations, and varied here and there with carefully arranged clumps of trees of advanced but vigorous growth, terraces lifting their smooth surfaces one above the other, in the richest and greenest of verdure, and retired groves of deep shade, showed upon the acclivities of the nearer range of hills all the marks of a long and most perfect cultivation, and presented a beauty of landscape unrivalled even by the garden-like scenery of England when clothed in the fresh charms of a verdant spring. The distant hills were rugged and bare, and apparently without cultivation, but gave, by their contrasting barrenness and rudeness of aspect, a heightened beauty to the rich culture of the land which gradually undulated from their base to the waters of the bay. As the squadron advanced toward the north the shore became more level, and a stretch of sand was observed to extend for three or four miles into the bay, and to arise near its termination into two considerable elevations, upon which forts with ten guns each were erected, and there the Japanese troops had been seen to gather.

The ships now directed their course toward the proposed place for anchoring, which had been surveyed by Lieutenant Bent on the previous surveying expedition. Keeping in view a bold headland, which bounded the upper part of the bay, to which the squadron was tending, the ships steered toward the western shore, and finally dropped their anchors in the afternoon in a place which the Commodore then named the *American Anchorage*. This was about ten miles distant from the first anchorage off Uraga, and a mile and a half from the shore, in a depth of water which gave full thirteen fathoms. Within the bay in which the ships were anchored were two beautiful islands, covered with a green growth of herbage and scattered groves. The coast which bounded the anchorage was composed of a succession of steep cliffs of white rock, the summits of which were covered with a fertile soil, which produced a rich vegetation that hung over from above in heavy festoons of green shrubbery and trailing vines and plants, while the sea had washed the base of the cliffs here and there into caverns where the water flowed in and out. The headland at the north was about six miles distant and descended in green slopes to the bay, and from the thick growth of trees which covered them a white smoke was observed to wind through the close foliage, and was supposed to indicate the presence of some encampment. A great number of the usual government boats, distinguished by red banners, lined a long stretch of the shore of nearly a mile in length, and the fortresses had extended their usual cotton cloth batteries or screens, which were now, on longer experience, supposed to be rather military emblems, like the flag and banners, than sham exhibitions of force and intended evidences of hostility.

Immediately on anchoring the Commodore ordered the boats out upon a surveying expedition, and although this seemed to bring out the soldiers in numbers about the battery which lay opposite to the ships, as well as some of the government boats which were moored along the shore, there was no direct interference with the surveying party. The Japanese boats, however, moved backward and forward, as if watching the movement of the ship's cutters, but seemed indisposed to do more than show themselves in force and on the alert. Soon, however, Yezaimen, with his interpreters, were seen to approach the Susquehanna, in their usual boat, which the Japanese oarsmen were sculling with all their might, and at once dashed up alongside the steamer. Yezaimen and his companions hurried up the companion way, and were evidently much ruffled, and in a state of great anxiety. They were at once ushered into the cabin, where they were received as usual by the captains, who were coolly prepared to listen to what they had to say. Tatznoske at once burst out with the question, "Why do your ships anchor here?" He was answered that as they had been already informed by the Commodore, the ships had advanced up the bay in order to obtain a more secure anchorage. The interpreter then stated that that part of the Japanese waters had always been hitherto respected by strangers, and that the squadron must not go any further. He then asked whether the Commodore intended to go beyond, and if not, how long he intended to remain where he then was? He was told that the Commodore intended to remain three or four days longer for the purpose of finding out a good anchorage, as he was to return in the ensuing spring with many more ships and men, and that it was desirable that the most secure place should be found for mooring his vessels, and that for this purpose it was necessary to survey the bay. Uraga had been tried, but it was found insecure, as the water was rough, and the winds occasionally blew there with great force. Upon the interpreter Tatznoske asserting that the Commodore had promised to leave the bay immediately on the reception of the President's letter by the princes, he was reminded that the Commodore had only promised to leave the shore, but had distinctly stated that it was his intention to advance further up the bay with his ships. The interpreter continued by declaring that if the surveying boats should approach any nearer to the land that there would be trouble, as the people were already under considerable excitement from observing the close neighborhood of the strangers. He was then told that there was no need for any anxiety, as the boats should not land, and the Americans would not interfere with the Japanese unless they were first disturbed by them. Yezaimen still persisted through his interpreters upon the squadron leaving, and courteously expressed his assurance that the Japanese government was favorably disposed toward the Americans, and that as the President's letter had been received it would undoubtedly be considered with a favorable disposition. He concluded by expressing the hope that on the next visit of the Commodore he would not advance any further up the bay than Uraga, as that place offered every convenience for the proposed negotiation. Yezaimen was now assured that the Americans came as friends, and that therefore it was quite unreasonable that any opposition should be made to their ships seeking a suitable anchorage. They were moreover told that it was the custom in the United States to afford every facility to foreigners in that respect, and that if the Japanese came to the United States they would find the navigable waters of the country free to them, and that they would not be debarred even from the rich gold fields of California.

Yezaimen had nothing more to say, and, whether persuaded or not, had the courtesy to refrain from pushing his demands any further. He and his companions, upon being invited to partake of some refreshments, readily complied, and were soon engaged in discussing with a vigorous appetite the collation that was spread before them. Another government boat was at this juncture announced as being alongside, when immediately the Japanese officials who were on board of it were invited to share in the hospitalities of the cabin. Quite a convivial scene ensued, in the course of which abundant supplies of ham, ship's biscuit, and other stores, washed down by plentiful draughts of whiskey, quickly disappeared. The cheer seemed to be much relished, and the interpreters were so exceedingly delighted that they desired to bear away some substantial mementos of the pleasant feast, and, accordingly, not satisfied with well-filled paunches, they carried off in their capacious sleeves pieces of the bread and ham, wherewith to refresh their memories and their future appetites. As the night approached, the Japanese took their departure, full of courteous expressions of satisfaction at the hospitality of the ships.

The following morning (July 15th) a surveying party was again, at a very early hour, dispatched by the Commodore to sound further up the bay. Three of the boats pulled round to the other side of the battery which shut out a part of the country inland from the view of those on board ship. Here they found an inlet and a beautiful surrounding country watered by a stream, upon the fertile borders of which were grouped a great number of picturesque Japanese villages, while fertile fields and highly cultivated gardens stretched out beyond them. The officers ordered their boats up the river and were met as they advanced by crowds of the inhabitants, gathering upon the shores to satisfy their curiosity in a look at the strangers. Some of the people greeted the boats with every indication of welcome, and readily supplied those on board with water and some excellent peaches. There were a few government boats lying near, and the officers on board gladly welcomed our people to a visit, in the course of which such a mutual friendliness sprung up that the Americans joined the Japanese in a social pipe or two of tobacco. Our officers, in return for their hospitable entertainment, amused their newly-found hosts with an exhibition of their revolvers and fired them off, to the intense surprise and delight of the Japanese. In the midst of this enjoyment of social intercourse, where the greatest harmony prevailed, and in which the Japanese seemed remarkably genial in manner and expansive in hospitality, down came some severe official and beckoned off his countrymen, who rapidly scattered away, like so many children caught in the very act of some awful disobedience.

On the return of the ships' boats from sounding, all the officers and men were in raptures with the kindly disposition of the Japanese and the beauty of their country. In fact, nothing could be more picturesque than the landscapes wherever the eye was directed, and even those on board ship never tired of looking at the surrounding shores. The high cultivation of the land everywhere, the deep, rich green of all the vegetation, the innumerable thrifty villages embowered in groves of trees at the heads of the inlets which broke the uniformity of the bay, and the rivulets flowing down the green slopes of the hills and calmly winding through the meadows, combined to present a scene of beauty, abundance, and happiness, which every one delighted to contemplate.

In the course of the afternoon the Commodore transferred his pennant from the Susquehanna to the Mississippi. He then proceeded some ten miles further up the bay toward Yedo, and reached a point estimated to be distant twenty miles from the anchorage at Uraga. The port or shipping place of Yedo was distinctly seen on the southern side of the capital, but not the capital itself, which, being composed of low houses, like those of China, was completely hidden behind a projecting point, beyond which the bay took an easterly direction, and was bounded by a shore of low alluvial land. The town observed was probably Sinagawa, a suburb of Yedo. On the western side of the bay a view was obtained of Kanagawa and Konazaki, two populous places. Some four miles beyond the extreme point reached by the Mississippi there was a cape formed by a projecting point of land, and marked by a white tower, which resembled in appearance a light-house; it was some three or four miles still further where the shipping and supposed port of Yedo appeared to the view. The Commodore thus supposed that he had taken his ship within ten miles of Yedo, and as the lead gave twenty fathoms where he put about, he concluded that he could readily have gone still higher up. He was apprehensive, however, of causing too much alarm, and thus throwing some obstacle in the way of a favorable reception at court of the President's letter, that had only been delivered the day before, and which was probably then under consideration. The Commodore thus thinking that he had done enough, without going further, caused the ship to rejoin the squadron at the "American Anchorage."

During the passage of the Mississippi, there was no show of opposition to her movements, although there was a considerable display of troops about the batteries, loosely grouped, as if gathered for curiosity and not for martial manifestation, and an occasional government boat put out from the shore with the apparent design of watching the steamer. While the Commodore was absent on his expedition up the bay, Yezaimen and his interpreters came alongside the Susquehanna, bringing some boxes containing presents, but neither they nor their presents were received, as the Commodore had given orders that no one from the shore should be admitted on board the ship without his special permission. Upon being told this, the Japanese first expressed a wish to wait, but finally pushed off, saying that they would return another time. All the boats which could be spared from the several ships, amounting to twelve, were busily engaged during the whole day in surveying the western shore of the bay above Uraga.

At daylight next morning (Saturday, 16th July,) the ships were moved to a bay about five miles from Uraga, which the Commodore named "Susquehanna Bay," and in the survey of which the boats were kept diligently occupied, and without interference or, in fact, any expressed objection. The squadron was now anchored much closer to the shore than before, at a distance of less than a mile, and from the ship's deck a distant view was had of the land on the west, which was singularly green with vegetation and beautiful in aspect. The present anchorage was completely land-locked. On one side was the charming little island named "Perry Island," by Lieutenant Bent, who was in command of the surveying party which first examined its neighboring waters. Out of the trees which grew to the summit of the rising land peered, with a suspicious look, a Japanese battery. Below, some miles to the south, the promontory which extends out into the bay beyond Uraga closed in the ships which were moored so far under the cover of its lofty flank, that the view of the eastern shore for a considerable extent was entirely blotted out. Two villages, of the name of Orsa and Togirasaki, nestled among the trees within the curve of the bay, and presented to the eye a charming aspect of repose and rural delight.

Yezaimen, the governor of Uraga, was again alongside the Susquehanna before she had anchored. He came to renew his assurance of the favorable reception of the President's letter, and as nothing was said now of sending the answer to Nagasaki, it seemed that the nearer the Commodore approached the imperial city of the Japanese the more conciliating and friendly they became. The governor had brought with him some presents, consisting of some pieces of silk, some fans, lacquered tea-cups and tobacco pipes. These objects were interesting as specimens of Japanese manufacture, and though not very valuable, were creditable evidences of mechanical skill. The cups were made of a very light wood, neatly executed and beautifully polished in surface with the famous Japanese lacquer. The silks were of fine texture, richly interwoven with braids of gold and silver, elaborately wrought into various ornamental figures. The fans were covered with those "dragons and chimeras dire" in which the grotesque fancy of Japanese art seems especially to delight, and the pipes were small and like what had been previously observed in use among the Lew Chewans.

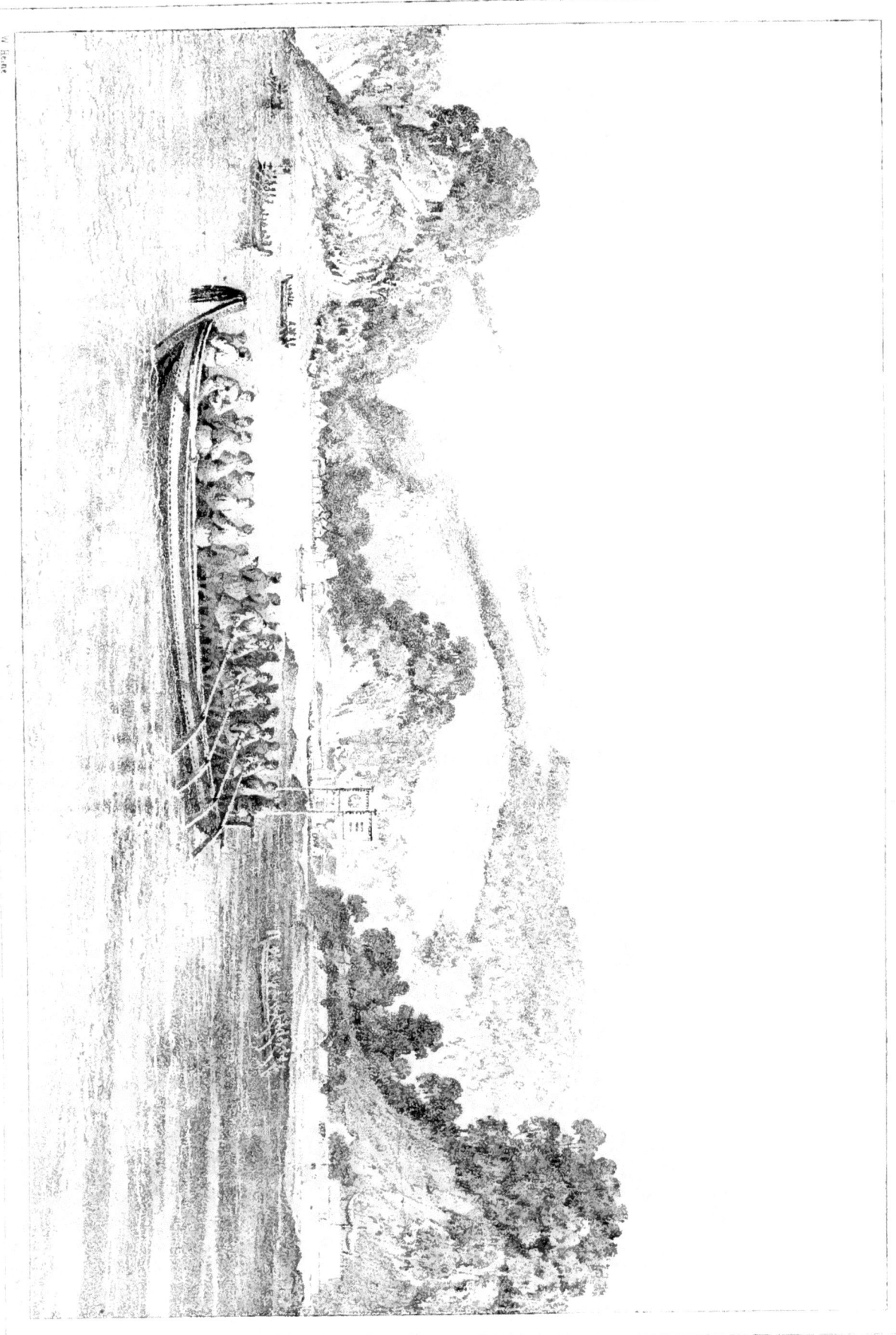

Yezaimen was informed, by the orders of the Commodore, that the presents which he had brought could not be received unless others from the Commodore were accepted in return. To this Yezaimen at first demurred by interposing the invariable plea that the Japanese law forbade it. He was now answered that American laws enjoined a reciprocity, and that his presents could not be otherwise received. Finding the Commodore resolute upon this, as upon all other points of ceremony, Yezaimen consented at last to receive in return whatever, with the exception of arms, there was a disposition to give him. Accordingly, some few articles of more value than those brought by the Japanese were sent on deck; but when Yezaimen saw them he declared that they were of too much value, and that he dared not take on shore anything but what he and his interpreter could conceal about their persons. He was then informed that if he could not receive the articles openly, and without concealment, that those which he had brought with him would be put back into his boat. He then departed, carrying with him all the Commodore's presents, with the exception of three swords, which he was permitted to leave.

In the afternoon, Yezaimen and his interpreters came on board again, with a trifling present of some fowls in wicker cages and several boxes of eggs. They seemed in very good humor, as there had been no objection urged on shore to their retaining the presents they had received from the Commodore in the morning. The Commodore, on receiving the fowls and eggs, sent presents to the wives of the Japanese officials, as he was determined to be under no obligation to them. Another important point had been gained in persuading the Japanese to consent to an exchange of presents, a concession which had hitherto been unprecedented in all their previous relations with foreign nations.

Among the articles given to Yezaimen was a large box containing a variety of American seeds and some, if not equally useful, not less acceptable, cases of wine. The governor had showed his appreciation of the latter article by the gusto with which he shared in the conviviality on board which marked his last visit. Yezaimen and his interpreters, Tatznoske and Toksaro, evidently lingered with pleasure on board the ship and were loth to say the final good-bye. Over the board which was spread to refresh and to do honor to them they became remarkably jovial and communicative. Yezaimen's disposition was naturally genial, and it became still more expansive in its bonhommie under the by no means restricted draughts of champagne. His affection towards his American friends was liberally acknowledged, and he confessed such a yearning for them that he declared he would not be able to restrain his tears on their departure. The interpreters, though less bibulous and more reserved than their superior, were evidently in a very joyous mood and disposed to be confidential. Tatznoske, with a knowing look, hinted in a low, whispering tone of voice, that the President's letter had a very fair chance of a satisfactory answer, and that Yezaimen had a good prospect of promotion from the governorship of Uraga to some higher grade of official distinction.

The Japanese, however, were always on the alert to gain a point in diplomacy, and despite their convivial freedom did not forget their official duties. Captain Buchanan had informed Tatznoske of the intention of the Commodore to leave Yedo Bay next day, whereupon that shrewd gentleman put down his glass of champagne, and showing his usual eager attention to business, even in the midst of pleasure, asked the captain for a declaration in writing of what he had said in words about the squadron's departure. This was refused with an expression of cold reserve on the part of Captain Buchanan, as it would seem to imply a doubt of his word.

The Japanese officials now prepared to depart, and finally, after expressing in the most courteous terms their thanks for the treatment they had received, and their regret on leaving their American friends, shook all the officers warmly by the hand, and went bowing and smiling over the side of the ship into their boat. No sooner were they seated on their mats, than Yezaimen showed his appreciation of the present of wine by ordering one of the cases to be immediately opened, and taking the first bottle that came, impatiently knocked off its neck, and without more ado commenced imbibing its contents, probably desiring, with his usual courtesy, to drink a parting health to his American friends. His boat soon pulled out of sight behind the projecting promontory of Uraga, and nothing more was seen of the courteous Yezaimen and his worthy and learned associates Tatznoske and Toksaro.

The survey of the west side of the magnificent bay having been completed from Uraga to a point about fourteen miles below Yedo, and the steamer Mississippi having ascended with the boats and sounded six miles nearer to that capital, the Commodore believed that a sufficient knowledge was obtained of the navigation of the bay to conduct the man-of-war, the Vermont, which was to join his squadron on his next visit, to the American anchorage, or even higher if necessary.

The governor of Uraga, as will have been observed, had evinced a great anxiety, during the several conferences on board the Susquehanna, to learn how long the Commodore intended to remain on the coast. On these occasions Yezaimen always took care to remark that it was the custom of the Japanese government to be very slow in deciding upon matters having reference to foreign countries. In consequence of these representations, and knowing that the propositions contained in the President's letter were of such importance as to require time for deliberation, overturning, as they would, if acceded to, many of the fundamental laws of the Empire, the Commodore deemed it advisable not to wait for a reply. To these were added other reasons of importance. The Commodore had not provisions or water sufficient to allow of his remaining on the coast more than a month longer, and he well knew that the Japanese authorities could easily, and with every apparent show of reason, defer any satisfactory reply to a period beyond the time when it would be absolutely necessary for him to leave. They would be prepared, as an excuse for delay, to allege the necessity of calling together and conferring with the princes of the Empire, as also of consulting the Dairi or Ecclesiastical Emperor, and thus the Commodore might be put off from day to day, and ultimately be obliged to sail without any satisfaction whatever. Such a result would have been construed into a triumph by the Japanese, and would have caused, as the Commodore believed, a serious injury to the success of his mission.

The Commodore, moreover, was glad to have a good excuse for waiting until the ensuing spring for the final answer from the Japanese government, because he knew that some of his ships were required to protect American interests on the coast of China, then somewhat endangered in consequence of the disturbed state of that country. He could not spare any of the squadron while he remained in Japan, for the vessels promised by the Navy Department had not yet followed him as he had expected. He was also unprepared to respond with becoming courtesy to any concession or act of friendliness on the part of the Japanese government, in consequence of not having received the presents from the United States that were expected in the Vermont, and which it was essential to have ready upon the reception of a favorable answer to the President's letter.

The Commodore preferred, then, to wait until the ensuing spring, when he would be able to concentrate his whole force, and be prepared with store and coal vessels, and all other conveniences for remaining an indefinite time to secure whatever concessions the Japanese should be disposed to make. His policy, though in conformity with the exigencies of his position, was at the same time a courteous concession to the deliberate ceremoniousness of Japanese diplomacy, and was crowned by the happiest result. A letter signifying his intention to leave immediately and return the ensuing spring for an answer to the President's letter, had been, it will be recollected, delivered with that letter on the occasion of the Commodore's reception on shore.

The squadron left the anchorage in Susquehanna Bay on Sunday morning, (July 17.) With the steamer Susquehanna towing the Saratoga, and the Mississippi the Plymouth, the four vessels began their voyage and started away rapidly without a yard of canvas set. The morning was fine, and as the departure of the Americans was a great event, and the appearance of the four ships moving off in stately procession, succeeding each other in regular line, was imposing and novel to the Japanese unfamiliar with the power of steam, crowds of people gathered upon the land to behold the sight. As the promontory of Uraga was doubled the soldiers thronged out of the batteries, and hurrying to the loftiest summits eagerly looked at the passing ships. The course of the squadron was down the centre of the bay, and the inhabitants on both shores could, in the clearness of the day, equally gratify their curiosity. Many were not content with the distant view, and crowding into boats had pushed off in the stream in such multitudes that the waters were covered with many hundreds of them.

As the squadron steamed out of the bay a parting look was obtained of the lofty summit of Mount Fusi, both behind and in advance; as the ships took an easterly course, the mountainous coast of the province of Awa, at the northern entrance to the lower bay of Yedo, rose to the view. Vries' Island, or, as it is otherwise called, Oo-Sima, was left to the south; and, though partly obscured with clouds, the convex outline of the lower part of its mountainous elevation could be distinctly traced. The course of the ships was now directed toward the south, when the various islands which extend in a line from the mouth of the bay of Yedo were gradually approached and observed. They mostly were marked with the usual features of volcanic origin, having a rounded contour, with their summits rising into cones, their steep sides scarred with the burning currents of lava, and their bases surrounded with irregular shaped detached rocks. A rich vegetation, as is common in such latitudes, had thrown its green mantle over the sides of some of the islands, which presented a striking contrast of verdant beauty with the bared ribs and fire-blasted surface of others. Vulcan Island was conspicuous among the rest with its volcanic summit and its acclivities of cooled lava. Fatsicio, the penal island of Japan, was in the distance at the south; but as the shades of evening gathered as the ships approached, it was not come up with before it was too dark to obtain a good view. As several of the islands were not laid down in any of the charts in possession of the Commodore, he took the usual privilege of American and European discoverers and gave names to some of the chain. One was called, after the steamer, the Mississippi Island; a cluster of rocks, described as resembling somewhat the basaltic formation of the Giant's Causeway, was called after the Susquehanna; and the other ships, the Plymouth and Saratoga, each came in for the honor of giving her name to a rock or an island. The whole chain was composed of a great number of islands or islets, as many as eight being in view at one time. They showed no marks of habitation; but from their proximity to the Japanese coast they were probably utilised for some purpose and peopled more or less. Fatsicio, it is known, is used as a penal settlement, and it is probable some of the other islands may be also forced into some service by the Japanese people, who seem ever on the alert to make any available use of their territory.

On the next day, after the departure of the squadron from Yedo bay, the wind, which had been steadily blowing from east to E.S.E., began to increase with such force as made it necessary to cast off the two sloops-of-war, the commanders of which, having been ordered by signal to proceed to the duty previously assigned them, then parted company. Commander Walker, in the Saratoga, had received written instructions from the Commodore to make the best of his way to Shanghai to protect American life and property and to look after the general interests of the United States in that vicinity. Commander Kelly, in the Plymouth, was instructed to proceed to Lew Chew, and on his way to examine the western shores of Oho-Sima. It was the intention of the Commodore to have surveyed the eastern shores of this island, but he was prevented by the weather.

After the Plymouth and Saratoga had been cast off, the wind gradually increased to a strong gale. The two steamers were now hove to on the port tack. The wind being at east by south, beating up an ugly sea, the Susquehanna rolled very deeply, but otherwise made tolerable weather. The Mississippi apparently was doing better, but nevertheless lost two of her boats during the gale. The storm did not begin to abate until the third day, when the Commodore continued his course, without delay, for Napha. During the passage to and from Yedo bay, the current set invariably with more or less strength, according to the wind, to the north and east, while in the bay of Yedo itself, the tides were regular and set up and down the channel opposite Uraga at the rate of two and a half knots.

At the close of a chapter which completes the account of the first visit of Commodore Perry to Japan, it seems appropriate to sum up briefly the results of that visit. Short as was the stay of the squadron in the waters of the bay of Yedo, the ships having first anchored on the eighth of July and taken their departure on the seventeenth of the same month, no unimportant results had been effected. These, to be fully appreciated, must be considered not absolutely in regard to their own intrinsic value, but relatively to the former policy of Japan, in its restricted intercourse with foreign nations.

During the eight days, which was the full extent of his first visit, Commodore Perry had gained in behalf of his country several advantages hitherto denied to all other nations. It is true certain concessions had been made, but in a very limited degree, to the Dutch and Chinese; and these, small as they were, were awarded to them at the expense, on their part, of the most degrading conditions. The first point conceded was the release of the American squadron from the perpetual presence of the Japanese guard-boats, which had always hitherto surrounded foreign ships, and placed them, as it were, under arrest during their visit. A resolute resistance was at once opposed by Commodore Perry to this degrading imposition of force upon a peaceful visitor, and, in spite of all the Japanese authorities could urge on the score of their own exclusive laws and inhospitable practice, a new precedent was established in conformity with the comity of civilized nations.

The second point gained was the accomplishment of the Commodore's predetermined intention to confer with no one but a dignitary of the highest rank in the Empire, and to obtain a reception in every respect honorable to himself and the country which he represented. This was effected without the slightest deviation on the part of the Commodore from those simple rules of diplomatic courtesy recognised by our institutions. For example, during the reception on shore, while the governor of Uraga prostrated himself on every occasion when he addressed the

FIRST LANDING AT MELBOURNE

Prince of Idzu and his associate, the Prince of Iwami, the Commodore and his staff remained quietly seated, and used no more ceremony toward the Japanese princes than would have been proper in a similar conference with the commissioners of any country duly credited.

The survey of the bay of Yedo, in spite of the protests of the authorities, and under the very guns of their batteries, was an important advantage. It not only taught the Japanese the folly of attempting to frighten away the Americans by bravado and sham exhibitions of force, but has proved to the world, for the first time, the practicability of sailing even to the capital of Japan, and secured every facility for approaching it in the charts which have been the results of the observations of the hydrographical department of the expedition.

The Commodore, conscious that he was dealing with a ceremonious people, never lost an opportunity of symbolising, even by form and etiquette, his resolute determination to uphold the dignity of his mission. Thus, in the matter of giving and receiving presents, it was taken care that the invariable eastern custom should be strictly followed, and that the advantage, on the score of the value of gifts, should never be on the side of the Japanese. Heretofore it had been the policy of China and Japan to consider and receive all presents as so many tributes to their superior power. In the equal exchange carefully regarded by the Commodore he determined that presents should be considered merely as a mutual interchange of friendly courtesy, and he accordingly never received anything without returning at least its equivalent.

While the Commodore strove to impress the Japanese with a just idea of the power and superiority of his country, he was ever studious of exhibiting the most friendly disposition in all his relations with the authorities of Japan, that they might understand that it was the desire of the United States to cultivate a kindly intercourse. Thus, on the one hand, a resolute determination was shown to demand a respectful hearing, and to secure at all hazards a protection for American citizens who might be at the mercy of Japan, and on the other, a courteous desire was expressed of cultivating a mutual trade and commerce, by which international good feeling and reciprocal interests are most securely created and safely guaranteed. The Japanese were reminded how closely the geographical position of their Empire had been brought to the United States by the new possessions on the Pacific, and the development of the mighty power of steam, the effective operation of which had been so strikingly revealed to the people of Japan by the appearance of the American naval steamers almost within gun-shot of their capital. How far this policy, which proved the power to compel, while it exhibited the disposition to conciliate, was successful, will be developed in the future pages of the narrative.

CHAPTER XV.

AMAKIRIMA ISLANDS.—STATE OF FEELING IN LEW CHEW.—COMMODORE'S MEASURES FOR PERMANENT ARRANGEMENTS WITH THE AUTHORITIES.—COAL DEPOT.—PROTEST AGAINST ESPIONAGE.—TRADE IN OPEN MARKET.—LETTER TO THE REGENT.—INTERVIEW WITH THE REGENT.—ENTERTAINMENTS OF THE COMMODORE.—DURING DINNER THE REGENT'S ANSWER IS BROUGHT.—UNSATISFACTORY TO THE COMMODORE.—LETTER HANDED BACK TO THE REGENT, AND THE COMMODORE PREPARES TO LEAVE THE HOUSE.—INFORMS THE REGENT THAT HE MUST HAVE A SATISFACTORY ANSWER ON THE NEXT DAY, OTHERWISE HE WILL LAND AND TAKE POSSESSION OF THE PALACE AT SHUI AND RETAIN IT UNTIL MATTERS ARE ADJUSTED.—PROBABLE EFFECTS OF HUNTING UP THE OLD SEDAN CHAIR ON SHORE.—COMMODORE'S PROPOSITIONS ALL ACCEPTED.—COAL DEPOT BUILT.—VISIT TO THE CASTLE OF TIMA-GUSKO.—PURCHASES IN THE BAZAAR.—DEPARTURE FROM NAPHA FOR CHINA.—PLYMOUTH LEFT BEHIND WITH ORDERS TO VISIT BONIN ISLANDS AND MAKE FURTHER SURVEYS.—CAPTAIN KELLY'S REPORT OF THE VISIT AND SURVEYS.—FORM OF GOVERNMENT AND CONSTITUTION OF THE SETTLERS ON PEEL ISLAND.—GENERAL EFFECT OF THIS LAST VISIT TO LEW CHEW.—ARRIVAL OF THE VANDALIA; OF THE POWHATAN.—OVERHAULING OF THE VESSELS OF THE SQUADRON AT HONG KONG.

HE storm which began to blow soon after the departure from the bay of Yedo continued for three days, and the two steamers rolled heavily and were much tossed by its violence, making it necessary to send down the topmasts and secure the great guns by strong lashings; they, however, rode out the storm in safety, and finally arrived at Napha on the 25th of July. On the approach to the coast of Lew Chew the weather was so hazy that the land could not be discerned at any distance, and, night coming on, it was thought advisable for the ships to stand off, which they did, and were carried very much to the southward and westward by the current. This current, according to the generally received accounts, should have been setting in a contrary direction, and consequently the allowance for a northeast set was wrongly made.

The atmosphere continued hazy throughout the night, and as the day dawned the land was still concealed from view, and it was some hours before the position of the steamers could be determined by the sight at last of the Amakirima Islands. At some distance from the islands a patch of breakers was observed, which was duly noted in the chart. The discovery of these breakers and other dangers among the Amakirima group show the necessity of a thorough

MEASURES FOR PERMANENT ARRANGEMENTS. 275

survey of the islands lying west of Great Lew Chew, and a surveying expedition could not be better employed than in making the proper investigations.

On coming to anchor in the harbor of Napha, at noon on Monday, (25th July,) the storeship Supply was found there rolling in the swell of the bay like a great log, and the officers stated that the gale had blown with great violence with them and had raged several days, while those upon the land declared that it had been one of the severest storms they had ever experienced.

Upon the Commodore's arrival at Lew Chew he lost no time in advancing the chief purpose of his visit, and prepared at once to enter into negotiations with the authorities for obtaining from them further relaxations in their laws respecting strangers. Having been comparatively successful with the Japanese, the Commodore felt confident of gaining additional concessions from the Lew Chewans, and that too without resort to any act of unkindness, or the adoption of their policy of deceit and falsehood.

The officers of the Supply, which vessel had been left at Napha during the Commodore's visit to Japan, stated that the people had evinced no unfriendly feeling towards them, but were still very much reserved and as tenacious as ever of their system of espionage. Supplies of provisions, however, had been regularly furnished through the agency of Dr. Bettelheim, and payment had been also received through him.

The Commodore had no time to spare, as his present visit was intended to be very short, and he was not disposed to be put off for a moment by the usual temporizing policy of the slow-moving Lew Chewans, so he demanded at once an interview with the regent; the demand was immediately granted, and a day appointed for the meeting. Previous, however, to the interview, the Commodore had caused the regent to be made acquainted with the nature of the propositions, upon a favorable concession to which he had resolutely fixed his mind. Commander Adams was commissioned to lay these propositions before the mayor of Napha and some of the authorities, and accordingly went ashore, accompanied by Dr. Williams, the Chinese interpreter, bearing the following instructions from the hands of the Commodore:

"Establish rate and pay for rent of house for one year. State that I wish a suitable and convenient building for the storage of coal, say to hold six hundred tons. If they have no such building, I desire to employ native workmen to erect one after the fashion of the island; or if the Lew Chewan government prefers, it can be done under the inspection of the mayor, at government expense, and I will agree to pay an annual rent for it. Either one or the other arrangement must be made."

"Speak about the spies, and say if they continue to follow the officers about, it may lead to serious consequences, and perhaps to bloodshed, which I should deplore, as I wish to continue on the most friendly terms with the authorities. That should any disturbance ensue, it will be the fault of the Lew Chewans, who have no right to set spies upon American citizens who may be pursuing their own lawful business."

"We must have a free trade in the market, and the right to purchase articles for the ships."

"It will be wise, therefore, for the Lew Chewans to abrogate those laws and customs which are not suited to the present age, and which they have no power to enforce, and by a persistence in which they will surely involve themselves in trouble."

"Let the mayor clearly understand that this port is to be one of rendezvous, probably for years, and that the authorities had better come to an understanding at once."

"Thank the mayor for the kind act of the authorities in putting a tombstone over the remains of the boy buried from the Susquehanna, and ask the privilege of paying the cost of the same."

"Require prompt and early replies to all these propositions and demands."

The Commodore, in addition to these instructions by which Commander Adams was to be governed in his interview, sent a formal communication to the regent, in these words:

"*To his Excellency the Tsung-li-kwan of the Kingdom of Lew Chew:*

"SIR: The commander-in-chief of the United States naval forces in the East India, China, and Japan seas, having returned to this port from Japan, is about sailing for China, and before leaving is desirous of communicating to his excellency the Tsung-li-kwan a few observations, having reference to the intercourse of persons under his command with the authorities and people of Lew Chew.

"The commander-in-chief, while he thanks the officers of the Lew Chewan government for the services which they have already rendered in furnishing a few supplies to the ships of the squadron, cannot see the necessity of enforcing against strangers a system of restriction which is altogether at variance with the customs and practices of all civilized nations, and which cannot at the present day be recognized as just or proper.

"The commander-in-chief is especially desirous of remaining on the most friendly terms with the government of Lew Chew, and of contributing all in his power to the prosperity and happiness of the people; and he claims that the officers and men under his command shall be received on the same footing as those who arrive from China and Japan; that they shall have the privilege of purchasing in the market and shops whatever they may need, and for which they will pay the prices demanded by the sellers; that the inhabitants, particularly the women and children, shall not fly from us as if we were their greatest enemies; and, finally, that our officers and men shall not be watched and followed by low officials and spies. He declares that if this system of espionage is persisted in, he will on his return to Lew Chew take the necessary steps to stop it.

"It is repugnant to the American character to submit to such a course of inhospitable discourtesy, and though the citizens of the United States, when abroad, are always regardful of, and obedient to, the laws of the countries in which they may happen to be, provided they are founded upon international courtesy, yet they never can admit of the propriety or justice of those of Lew Chew, which bear so injuriously upon the rights and comforts of strangers resorting to the island with the most friendly and peaceful intentions.

"With the highest consideration,

"M. C. PERRY,
"*Commander-in-Chief of the United States Naval Forces,*
"*in the East India, China, and Japan Seas.*"

Upon Commander Adams laying the propositions of the Commodore before the mayor of Napha, he was told by that official that he could do nothing of his own accord, and was obliged to refer all the demands of the Americans to the Tsung-li-kwan, or regent of Lew Chew, as his own powers were entirely subordinate to those of that high dignitary. Captain Adams then told the mayor that he must inform the regent that the Commodore desired to have an interview with him, either the next day or the day after, at any hour or place he, the regent, might appoint; and, moreover, that his excellency must come prepared to answer, unequivocally and without discussion, the propositions just presented. To this the mayor replied that the regent would be immediately notified, and that the Commodore should be informed as to the time and place of meeting.

Next morning, Lieutenant Contee, the Commodore's aid, was sent ashore to call upon the mayor of Napha, from whom he learned that the regent had appointed the ensuing day, (Friday, July 28,) and the Kung-qua at Napha, as the time and place for the interview.

Accordingly, on Friday the interview came off, and its details are minutely given in the following report, prepared by a subordinate officer appointed for that special service:

"By previous arrangement, two o'clock, p. m., had been fixed upon as the hour for the interview, and the regent had sent word that he would leave Shui at noon. About half-past one, however, a boat came off to the Susquehanna with the Pe-ching, Chang-yüen, on board, to inform the Commodore that everything was in readiness for his reception, and the regent already in waiting. The place selected for the purpose was the Kung-qua of Napha, which is used on all official occasions. The Commodore went ashore at two o'clock, accompanied by Captain Adams, captain of the fleet, Lieutenant Contee, flag lieutenant, Captain Lee, of the Mississippi, Captain Kelly, of the Plymouth, and twelve other officers, making a staff of sixteen persons.

"On landing he was received by a deputation of officers, headed by the Pe-ching, and conducted to the place of reception, which is situated on the main street or road leading from Napha to Shui, and about a quarter of a mile from the beach. It is a small but neat building, surrounded by a high wall, which screens it from all observation from without. The mayor of Napha, with some of his attendant officers, stood at the entrance, and the regent advanced to the door of the enclosure to receive the Commodore. Within the building, tables were already prepared for a collation, similar to that given at Shui by the former regent, though not on so extensive a scale. The feast was arranged in precisely the same manner, the Commodore and Captain Adams occupying the first table on the right hand, while the regent and mayor took that on the left, opposite to him. After tea had been brought, the regent made a complimentary remark to the Commodore, hoping that he had returned in good health. Ichirazichi acted as interpreter, and the conversation was carried on by Mr. Williams, through the medium of the Chinese language.

"The Commodore stated that he would leave in a few days for China, but should return again to Lew Chew in a few months. Before he left, however, he wished to have a settlement of all those matters concerning which he had addressed them. His demands were reasonable and proper, and he expected that they would be complied with. The Americans were persons of few words, but they always meant what they said. The regent answered that his reply would soon be ready, and invited the Commodore, in the meanwhile, to partake of some refreshments. He was answered that we preferred business first and the refreshments afterwards. The requests made were fair and simple, and the Commodore was dissatisfied with any delay in granting them. We had been to Japan, where we had been received in a very friendly manner. We had exchanged presents with Japanese governors, and were on friendly terms with the Japanese. We hoped, now, to be on friendly terms also with the Lew Chewans. Mr. Williams then, at the Commodore's request, gave a brief narration of his reception by the princes of Idzu and Iwami, and of our exploration and survey of the bay of Yedo. The regent observed, in return, that his reply would be very soon delivered.

"The dinner then commenced, and seven or eight of the twelve courses of soups had been served, when the letter was brought in and given to the regent, who took it, and, accompanied by the mayor and interpreter, advanced to the Commodore's table, where he presented it with every appearance of submission and humility. His demeanor during the dinner was even more constrained and impassive than on the occasion of his dining on board the Susquehanna, previous to our departure for Japan. The letter was enclosed in an envelope, and stamped with the great seal of Lew Chew. Mr. Williams, at the Commodore's order, opened and read it on the spot.

"It commenced by affirming the small size and poverty of the island, stating that Dr. Bettleheim's residence among them had given them much trouble, and that if we should erect a building for coal their difficulties would be greatly increased. Besides, they said, the temple which they had appropriated to our use was thereby rendered useless to them, and their priests were prevented from performing their worship in it. The productions of the island were few, as they derived all of their teas, silks, cloths, and many other articles from Japan and China. With regard to the shops and markets, that was a matter that depended on the people themselves, and if they chose to keep their shops shut, the regent could not interfere. He declared, moreover, that the persons who had followed us whenever we had gone ashore were not spies, but officers appointed to act as guides, and to prevent us from being annoyed by the people. Since we had not found them to be of service, and objected to them, they would be directed not to follow us in future.

"After the letter had been read, the Commodore ordered it to be delivered back to the regent, stating that it was not at all satisfactory, and could not be received. We had asked, he said, for no more than is accorded to us in other countries—for no more than we already had in China, and expected to have in Japan. With regard to the temple, that they had themselves assigned it to our use, as they invariably had done, for those foreigners who had visited them previous to our arrival. We would pay them rent for it, and expected to pay for everything that we obtained. We had travelled over their island, and knew that the soil was rich, the people thrifty, and supplies of all sorts abundant. As we paid for all we received, our presence was an advantage to the people, who found in our vessels a good market for their productions. If they did not wish to erect a building for coal, we would send a vessel with materials, and put it up ourselves. The regent ventured to say that there were some difficult points in the Commodore's communication, and they had much deliberation concerning them, before the reply was written. The Commodore reiterated what he had previously said, that all his demands were plain and simple, and ought to be granted without hesitation. The Lew Chewans should be satisfied, by this time, that we had no intention to injure them. They had not been molested in any way by any of our men, and if they persisted in following us with spies hereafter he would not be answerable for the consequences.

"The regent attempted to come forward and again present the reply; but the Commodore rose and prepared to leave, declaring that if he did not receive satisfactory answers to all his demands by noon the next day, he would land two hundred men, march to Shui, and take possession of the palace there, and would hold it until the matter was settled. With this declaration, he left, the regent attending him to the gateway, where he remained until all the officers had taken their departure. The Commodore returned to the beach, attended by his staff, and immediately went on board the Susquehanna."

It will be observed that the new regent, Shang-Hiung-Hiun, was a great adept in the temporizing policy of his government, and was ever ready with a thousand crooked arguments for not giving a direct answer to a direct demand.

The Commodore, however, was not to be balked of his purpose by any of the shams and devices of Lew Chew policy, and went straight on to the end proposed, without allowing himself to be diverted from a broad, honest course of fair dealing, into any of the bye-ways of the oriental hide-and-go-seek diplomacy. As to resorting to force, which had been threatened at the close of the conference with the regent, the necessity of violent measures was never seriously contemplated by the Commodore, as it was rightly judged that a resolute attitude would answer all the purpose of a blow. The Commodore, therefore, sent Commanders Adams and Buchanan, accompanied by Dr. Williams, to the mayor of Napha. These gentlemen were instructed to obtain categorical replies to all the demands made upon the regent the previous day. Simultaneously with this mission ashore, an incident occurred, which, however slight in itself, had probably no small effect upon the timid hearts of the Lew Chewans. The Commodore had dispatched his carpenter to look after the sedan chair which had been deposited in the temple at Tumai, since its use on the previous occasion of the grand procession to the palace of Shui. The people of Lew Chew watched, with considerable anxiety, the movements of the carpenter, and their frightened imaginations already, no doubt, fancied the Commodore borne on in his car of state, the aforesaid sedan chair, as a triumphant victor within the walls of their capitol.

Whether this looking after the sedan chair was accidental or not, it happened in the very nick of time, and probably hastened the decision of the Lew Chew authorities. The mayor of Napha was very prompt in complying, to the extent of his authority, with the demands of the Commodore, as urged in his behalf, by his representative Commander Adams, who returned to the ship bearing the message that the regent would be immediately communicated with, and that the Commodore might be assured that a definite answer would be given to his propositions the next day.

Accordingly, at about ten o'clock the following morning, the mayor came on board the Susquehanna, with the information that all the Commodore's propositions had been acceded to, and would be carried out as far as the people could be controlled. He then, in detail, stated the various concessions to which the government had finally yielded. In regard to the coal depot, he said that preparations had already been made for its construction, and that the government had agreed upon the amount of rent, which was to be ten dollars per month. As for access to the market, it having been stated that the difficulty was with the common people, and particularly the women, who were averse to entering into immediate commerce with strangers, a compromise was proposed by the Commodore, and agreed to on the part of the mayor, which was to the effect that a bazaar should be opened in the Kung-qua for the sale of the various products of the country which the Americans might desire to purchase.

The mayor proposed the subsequent Sunday for the opening of the bazaar, when he was told that that was a day kept holy by Christians, when buying and selling were contrary to their religion. It was then proposed, and acceded to, that as the squadron was not to sail until Monday, at nine o'clock, that the market should be opened at six o'clock on the morning of that day.

Although the authorities had soon found that it was necessary to give a favorable answer to the demands of the Commodore, and the mayor of Napha had come on board for the express purpose of giving such an answer, which he accordingly did at once, yet while yielding each point, he still pertinaciously insinuated all sorts of trivial objections to the Commodore's plans. He said that the coal would not be safe on shore, as the natives would probably steal it; in answer to which he was told that the government of Lew Chew would be held responsible for every lump of it. The mayor was then ready with another objection, stating that typhoons blew very severely on the island, and would no doubt sweep away the coal depot; and thus, to the very last, while forced to grant all that was asked, the authorities still clung to their prevaricating policy, as if deceit was so much a part of their nature that they practiced it for its own sake alone.

During the few days in which the steamers remained at Napha a party of the officers and artists of the expedition, at the suggestion of Commodore Perry, availed themselves of the occasion to visit the ruins of the castle of Tima-gusko. The Commodore had requested them to take their supplies with them, that they might be entirely independent of the natives for the satisfaction of their wants. They accordingly set out well provided with a supply of ship biscuit, and some American *saki*, which Japanese word was now pretty generally accepted as the generic term for all that was intoxicating and potable. Trusting to the general direction that the castle was situated at the southern end of the island, and constantly repeating with an interrogatory tone, whenever they met a native, the word "*Tima-gusko?*" the party proceeded on their way. Passing from the little village, on the southern side of Junk river, they got upon a narrow paved road leading eastward along its banks. By the way they reached a large village, where they were hospitably entertained at tea, in a handsome *Kung-qua*, embowered in fruit-bearing lime trees, and succeeded in making friends with the Lew Chewan host, and a party of his neighbors, who just dropped in to get a glance at the strangers, and to share in their supplies of ship biscuit and foreign saki, which were liberally dispensed by the American officers, and highly relished, as usual, by the Lew Chewans.

Tima-gusko? Tima-gusko? which was about the extent of the limited vocabulary of the Americans, seemed quite intelligible, and the interrogatory repetition of the word was responded to by an offer on the part of the Lew Chewan tea party to act as guides. They were, undoubtedly, some of the spies who swarmed everywhere, but it was thought advisable, as it seemed quite impracticable to get rid of them, to turn these fellows to some good purpose, and their services as guides were accordingly accepted. In spite, however, of their assistance, it was a long time before the right road was discovered, and then only after a very tedious tramp through rice fields flooded with water, and the climbing of a steep hill, from which a beautiful view, however, of the palace of *Shui* and its groves, and Napha with its white tombs and red tiled houses, and its inner and outer bays, and of the whole amphitheatre of the verdant hills of the island, proved some compensation for the labor lost.

The true road was only reached at last by turning back, in accordance with the direction of the Lew Chewan guides, or rather spies, in whom it would have been better to have trusted from the first; but these timid-hearted natives had become so impressed with the obstinacy of the self-willed Yankees, and their resolute determination to have their own way, wherever it might lead, that they seemed half afraid of urging the right, when they knew the Americans were pursuing the wrong. It was thus, from the apparent distrust in their own knowledge on the part of the Lew Chewans, that the party from the ship had followed their own bent, but finding at last that it was wrong, they trusted to the leadership of their guides.

On returning through the rice fields towards the bridge of *Ishirashi*, as the natives called it, and which was supposed to be the same as that of *Madaw-darki*, as it had been termed by Dr. Bettleheim, the Lew Chewans pointed up to some ruined walls which stood upon the brink of a lofty and precipitous hill, which overlooked the town of Napha, and a large circuit of the country and the surrounding waters.

The report, as drawn up by one of the party and laid before the Commodore, describes Tima-gusko as distant four miles in a southeast direction from Napha, and as being on a large scale, covering about eight acres, but in a state of utter ruin. It seemed to have no regular plan, and the walls had been erected upon various projecting points of the rock, and often parallel to each other in several lines, for the purpose of strengthening the defences. The neck of the headland connecting it with the hills behind had been separated by a moat, which was, however, hardly perceptible from the profuse growth of vegetation, which filled it up and concealed it from the eye. On a lofty eminence of the headland there was an oblong space shut in with walls, and thickly crowded with a dense thicket of trees and undergrowth. This part of the fortress was in a better state of preservation than the rest, and the original height of the wall, which reached about twelve feet, was discernable. On the western side there was a massive arched gateway, with a wooden door, closed by what appeared to be a Chinese lock. As a large tree, growing on the summit of the arch, had sent down its twisted roots among the stones which formed the sides of the entrance, a natural ladder was thus formed, by which the party succeeded in clambering over into the enclosed space. Following a narrow pathway through the otherwise impenetrable thicket, a heap of ruins was reached, upon the summit of which were two stones marked with Chinese characters, and the remains of some *joss* sticks. From these it was concluded that the present inhabitants of Lew Chew still retain some forms of this worship. *Tima-gusko* is undoubtedly the remains of the southern one of the three castles which were the strongholds of the three several kings who at one time divided the dominion of Lew Chew. The traditional account of the former dynasties, as given by Klaproth in his translation of the "*Kan-to-sits*," seems remarkably confirmed by the observations of our officers at Lew Chew. The two castles of the north and the south were found in ruins, while the central one of Shui, now the habitation of the present supposed young king, was seen to be in a perfect state of preservation, and indicated that the dynasty of Lew Chew had been finally concentrated in a single ruler.

In accordance with the arrangements between the Commodore and the authorities of Napha, the bazaar was opened at six o'clock on the morning of the steamer's departure, (Monday, August 1.) The *Kung-qua*, the place selected for the mart, was found duly prepared, with heaps of Lew Chewan productions, a motley assortment of lacquered cups, plates and boxes, pieces of grass-cloth, and the various articles of Lew Chew costume, such as cotton and silk sashes, sandals of straw, and hair pins of brass and silver, fans, chow-chow boxes, which correspond somewhat with our sandwich cases, smoking pipes and a plentiful supply of tobacco. The interpreter, *Ichirazichi*, was the presiding genius, or, rather, roguish Mercury of this market, who went busily about performing his functions as general broker, accompanied by a group of subordinate officials. The various parties from the ship soon commenced a brisk business, and succeeded in spending, in the aggregate, about a hundred dollars. As the demand increased it was found, in accordance with the usual law of trade, that the supply augmented, and the Lew Chew merchants were not backward in illustrating this principle of political economy. The prices were not very heavy at first, but the natives, in the course of the business, began to improve in this particular, and it was found that some from the ships had paid at least double the sum paid by others for a similar article. The objects obtained were of not much importance, but the chief interest of the occasion arose from the fact that this dealing with foreigners was the first authorized, and was in direct opposition to a fundamental law of the island, the abrogation of which cannot but result in the greatest advantage to the people of Lew Chew. The signal of departure being hoisted, the party of purchasers returned to their respective ships, and at 8 o'clock in the morning (August 1) the Commodore started for Hong Kong.

So prompt had been the effect of the Commodore's resolute demands upon the authorities of Lew Chew, that on the day of sailing, the building for the storage of coal, commenced only two days previous, had been framed and reared, and it was learned afterward that it was entirely finished in two days more. The building is 50 by 60 feet in dimensions, with a water-tight thatched roof, with the eaves projecting beyond the sides, which are boarded up more than half the distance from the ground to the roof, leaving an open space sufficient for purposes of ventilation. It was originally of sufficient capacity to hold 500 tons of coal, and the first cargo placed in it was that of the Caprice, which arrived soon after the departure of the Commodore. Subsequently, the Southampton landed her cargo, shipped at Macao, when it was thought advisable to enlarge the depot, and accordingly the authorities added a wing to each side.

The Commodore, conceiving it to be of the highest importance that a ship of the squadron should be stationed almost constantly at Lew Chew, to keep alive the friendly interest and good feeling then subsisting between the Americans and the islanders, who were becoming daily more cordial, he determined to leave the Plymouth, Commander Kelly, there. He, however, instructed this officer to run over to the Bonin islands, after the termination of the hurricane season, for the purpose both of visiting the settlement at Port Lloyd and of surveying the southern cluster of the Bonins, originally called the Coffin islands, after the first American discoverer in 1823, though, as we have stated before, subsequently appropriated and named by the English Captain Beechy, the Baily group.

The instructions of the Commodore to Commander Kelly referred generally to the conciliatory but firm attitude he desired should be sustained in all the relations of the Americans with the Lew Chewans. It was strictly enjoined upon Captain Kelly that he should receive nothing from the islanders without returning a fair compensation, and always bear himself towards them in such manner as to prove that it was the desire of the United States to cultivate their friendship and secure their confidence. The Commodore, in addition to some detailed instructions in regard to the construction of the coal depot and landing the cargoes from the expected storeships, directed that, in his absence, the survey of Melville harbor and the coast of the island should be made, the investigations already commenced in the waters of Napha be continued, and a boat and officer kept in readiness to pilot in any of the American squadron that might arrive.

In regard to Captain Kelly's visit to the Bonin Islands, he was instructed to proceed with the Plymouth, after the hurricane season, about the 1st of October, provided nothing occurred to detain him at Lew Chew, to Port Lloyd, where he was to enquire into the condition of the settlers, especially with respect to Nathaniel Savory and John Smith, two persons who had been enrolled on the books of the steamer Susquehanna. He was also directed, after obtaining the services of some of the settlers at Port Lloyd as guides or pilots, to visit the group of islands lying south of Peel Island, and named on Beechy's chart Baily's group. Captain Kelly was then to lay out a chart, giving the result of his survey, and to be careful to give the name of

Coffin, the original discoverer, to the group of islands alluded to. The largest single island, or the one containing the best harbor, was to be called Hillsborough, and its port to be termed Newport. To these directions were added general instructions to examine and survey the harbor and coasts, and to investigate the geological formation and the nature and condition of the soil of the Coffin Islands.

In anticipation of the regular course of the narrative, it may be well to give here the result of Captain Kelly's observations and proceedings at the Lew Chew and Bonin Islands, in accordance with the Commodore's instructions. The officer appointed by the commander of the Plymouth for the survey of the middle group of the Lew Chew Islands and the neighboring waters, reports that on September 15, 1853, he and his party encamped on the island of *Kindaka*, the southeastern one of the chain extending along the east coast of Great Lew Chew. Here a bay was discovered, but it was found to be of no practical utility, being filled with coral reefs, which extend, in fact, in an unbroken chain outside of all the islands as far as the northeast point of Ichey, with the exception of a narrow ship channel between the islet off the northeast end of *Kindaka* and the island of *Ta-king*. But as this channel leads to a bay with numerous reefs, it is not safe to enter it. In regard to Barrow's Bay, the survey proved it to be useless for all purposes of navigation, from its exposure to easterly winds and the swell from the ocean.

A port of refuge, however, was discovered on the west side of the island of *Ichey*, which forms the southern point of Barrow's Bay, as well as under *Hanadi*, toward both of which a secure anchorage may be found. This is, in fact, the only harbor of refuge on the eastern coast of the Lew Chew group.

The position of Sidmouth Islands was found to be in latitude 26° 43′ 30″ north, differing 3′ 30″ from that assigned to it by Captain Basil Hall in his sketch of the Lew Chew group.

And the outline of the coast was observed also to run in a direction varying somewhat from that laid down by that navigator. The whole of the island of Great Lew Chew was circumnavigated in the course of this survey, under the directions of Commander Kelly.

On the arrival of the Plymouth at the Bonins, it was found that the settlers on Peel Island, the principal one of the group, had of their own accord organized a municipal government, under the title of "*the Colony of Peel Island.*" Commander Kelly also, in accordance with the instructions of Commodore Perry, visited the islands hitherto termed "Baily's," took formal possession of them in the name of the United States, and gave them their proper name of Coffin, a due record of which was made upon the chart, and upon the spot, by affixing a plate, inscribed with the fact, to a large sycamore tree growing about twenty feet from the beach, near the northwest point of the cove, and burying one also, with some documents placed in a bottle, giving a true history of the discovery of the islands, and assigning the credit to the genuine discoverer, the American whaling captain, Coffin.*

---

* As an interesting specimen of this original effort at constitution-making by wanderers from many lands, civilized and savage, we subjoin a copy of the

"ORGANIZATION OF THE SETTLERS OF PEEL ISLAND."

"We, the undersigned, residents and settlers on Peel Island, in convention assembled, wishing to promote each other's mutual welfare, by forming a government, have ordained and established the following articles, which we solemnly bind ourselves to support for the period of two years."

On leaving Napha, the reflection naturally suggested itself to the mind of the Commodore as to the effect produced upon the Lew Chewans by his visit. It seemed evident that a very marked change had taken place in the deportment of the islanders toward the Americans.

There was less mystery about them, and some of the spies had thrown off a portion of their reserve. The Lew Chew authorities probably conjectured, and with good cause, that the trouble they had taken in their attempts to deceive the Commodore, with respect to the condition of their government, the poverty of the islands, and the harmless innocence of the people, was futile, and so much labor lost. And accordingly it was found that, although they still adhered, as if by instinct, to their system of deception, they were not quite so ready with their misrepresentations.

But, after all, many allowances should be made for these misgoverned people, who have been, doubtless, taught from infancy to practice duplicity and lying as a necessary part of an accom-

---

ARTICLE I.

"The style of our government shall be the '*Colony of Peel Island.*'"

ARTICLE II.

"The government shall consist of a chief magistrate, and a council, composed of two persons; and by virtue of this article, we hereby unanimously elect and appoint Nathaniel Savory, chief magistrate, and James Maitley and Thomas H. Webb, councilmen; each to hold his said office of chief magistrate and councilman for the period of two years from the date of this convention. The said chief magistrate and council shall have power to enact such rules and regulations for the government of this island as to them, from time to time, may appear necessary for the public good; such rules and regulations, to become binding on the residents, must have the approval and concurrence of two-thirds of the whole number of residents."

ARTICLE III.

"Until such time as the chief magistrate and council may be enabled to form a code of regulations, we unanimously ordain and establish the following thirteen sections, under this article, which shall have full force and effect until the adoption of others, and until the expiration of two years."

SECTION 1.

"It shall be the duty of any and all person or persons having claims and demands against each other, or who shall have any dispute or difficulties between themselves, which they cannot amicably settle, to refer the same to the chief magistrate and council, for adjudication and settlement; and their decision to be final and binding."

SECTION 2.

"All penalties in this colony shall be a pecuniary fine; and no penalty for any offence shall exceed the sum of —————."

SECTION 3.

"The chief magistrate and council shall have power to direct the seizure and sale of any property of any offenders, sufficient to pay the same, against whom a fine has been decreed, wherever it may be found within the limits of Peel Island."

SECTION 4.

"It shall be unlawful for any resident, settler, or other person, on the island, to entice anybody to desert from any vessel that may come into this port, or to secrete or harbor any such deserter."

SECTION 5.

"Any person who shall entice, counsel, or aid, any other person to desert from any vessel in this port, or shall harbor or conceal him to prevent his apprehension, shall be liable to a fine, not exceeding $50 (fifty dollars)."

SECTION 6.

"All moneys arising from the levy of fines upon offenders shall be a public fund for the use and behalf of the colony; and the same shall be placed in the hands of the chief magistrate for safe keeping, and to be appropriated to such public purposes as the chief magistrate and council may deem necessary and proper; and a correct account of all expenditures of said moneys shall be kept by them, and a statement of receipts and expenditures published at the end of one year."

SECTION 7.

"All public moneys remaining unexpended at the end of one year shall be equally divided among the present settlers, unless otherwise ordained by a convention of the people."

plished education, and altogether essential to advancement. It is certain that they do not, any more than the Japanese, place the least confidence in each other, and the government in employing their agents invariably send them forth in couples, one to watch the other.

The abominable system of espionage imposes great hardships on all classes, as those in power can never know how soon any of their acts, however harmless they may appear to themselves, may be construed into offences against the state. They thus find their lives in constant jeopardy, and are often compelled to purchase safety by the most servile humility, or a good share of their substance. If, by the most prostrate servility, or by the prodigal forfeit of property, they fail to obtain immunity, they are forced to commit suicide, in order to save their fortunes from confiscation and their families from ruin. The lower classes are by no means the

Section 8.

"*Port Regulations.*—There shall be two regularly appointed and recognized pilots for this port, and, by virtue of this section of article 3, we hereby unanimously appoint James Maitley and Thomas H. Webb as such for a period of two years from the date of this convention. Said pilots may appoint capable substitutes under them; and it shall be unlawful for any other person or persons to perform the duty of pilots. Any one who shall, without the authority of either of the appointed pilots, attempt to pilot any vessel into or out of this port, shall be liable to a fine equal to the amount of the established rate of pilotage."

Section 9.

"It shall be unlawful for any commander of a vessel to discharge any of his crew in this port without permission from the chief magistrate and council, and no commander of a vessel shall leave any sick or helpless man or men upon the island, unless he procure a house for him or them and make suitable arrangements for his or their comfort and subsistence during his or their illness."

Section 10.

"Any person or persons not owning land upon this island who may hereafter enter into partnership in trade with a resident and landholder, or who shall purchase an undivided interest in the land of a resident, must enter into written articles of agreement, and obtain a written title to the undivided interest he may purchase in lands, stock, &c.; and in the event of dissolution of partnership, or death of either party, partition of the property shall be made by the chief magistrate and council, whose duty it shall be to secure and take charge of the property and effects of any deceased person for the benefit of his friends."

Section 11.

"Any person or persons who shall be guilty of trespass or waste upon the lands of any of the inhabitants, shall be fined in a sum equal to the value of the damage or waste he or they may commit thereon, upon a proper adjudication thereof by the chief magistrate and council."

Section 12.

"The chief magistrate and council may, when they deem it necessary, call a convention of the people to propose new, and make amendments to the foregoing, rules and regulations."

Section 13.

"Any and all person or persons who shall hereafter emigrate to or settle in this colony, shall be subject and held amenable to the foregoing rules and regulations."

All the above articles of government having been prepared, concurred in, and adopted by us, in convention assembled, at the house of Nathaniel Savory, in Port Lloyd, Peel Island, on the 28th day of August, A. D. 1853, we solemnly pledge ourselves to each other to support and carry out the same.

In testimony whereof we have hereunto subscribed our names the day and year aforesaid.

NATHANIEL SAVORY,
THOMAS H. WEBB,
JAMES MAITLEY,
WILLIAM GILLY, JR.,
JOHN BRONA,
JOSEPH CULLEN,
GEORGE W. BRUNO,
GEORGE HORTON.

smallest sufferers, for it is their hard-tasked labor which supports the whole system which is carried on by swarms of spies, who infest every corner and nook of the island.

On the second evening after leaving Napha, as the Susquehanna and Mississippi were proceeding on their course to Hong Kong, a sail was seen ahead in the distance, steering in a northeasterly direction. At first there were some doubts as to what she was, but these were soon cleared up by the flashing of her guns, in the approaching darkness of the night, which showed that she was saluting the Commodore's flag on the Susquehanna. It was now certain that she was an American man-of-war, and soon she was discovered to be the long-expected Vandalia. As she lay to, the Susquehanna steered toward her, making a signal for her commander to come on board, and soon a boat came off, bringing Captain Pope, who at once reported to the Commodore. The voyage of the Vandalia had been a remarkably fine one, having left Philadelphia only on the fifth of March, touching at Rio Janeiro by the way. Her commander brought the information of the arrival of the Powhatan from the United States at Hong Kong, and of her proposed departure for Lew Chew. This information made Commodore Perry very anxious to reach port before the sailing of the Powhatan, as her trip to the north would be utterly useless, and the consequent consumption of coal a serious loss to the limited stock of the squadron. The Vandalia being ordered back to Hong Kong, the fleet continued its course to that place, where the steamers arrived on Sunday, August 7, 1853.

The Vandalia, however, did not get back to Hong Kong until the fifteenth. The Commodore was much disappointed to find that the Powhatan had sailed just the day before his arrival, and as she had taken the Formosa passage, he had thus lost the chance of intercepting her. She did not return to Hong Kong until the 25th of August, having been detained ten days at Lew Chew for the repair of her machinery; and similar delays had been found necessary, in the opinion of her chief engineer, at almost every port at which the Powhatan touched on her outward passage.

As the typhoon season was approaching, and the ships all required a general overhauling, the engineers asking for sixty working days for putting the Powhatan alone in order, and the crews needing some relaxation, the Commodore determined, in consideration of these circumstances, to give all his vessels a thorough refitment.

View of Outer Harbor of Napha from the Capstan.

CHAPTER XVI.

ALARM OF AMERICANS IN CHINA.—REQUEST TO COMMODORE THAT HE WOULD SEND A SHIP TO CANTON.—SUPPLY SENT.—THE REST OF THE SQUADRON AT CUM-SING-MOON.—HOSPITAL ESTABLISHED AND HOUSE TAKEN AT MACAO.—SICKNESS IN THE SQUADRON.—WORK KEPT UP IN ALL DEPARTMENTS, NOTWITHSTANDING.—HEALTHINESS OF CANTON.—GLUTTONY OF THE CHINESE.—CHINESE SERVANTS.—CHINESE ENGLISH, OR "PIGEON."—MALE DRESSMAKERS, CHAMBER SERVANTS, ETC.—CHINESE FEMALE FEET.—CHINESE GUILDS.—BEGGARS.—CHARITABLE INSTITUTIONS.—THIEVES.—BOATMEN.—LABORING CLASSES.—DOMESTIC SERVANTS.—POLYGAMY AND ITS MORAL RESULTS.—DECADENCE OF MACAO.—HUMBLED CONDITION OF THE PORTUGUESE.—HARBOR OF MACAO.—COMMODORE ESTABLISHES HIS DEPOT FOR THE SQUADRON AT HONG KONG.—PLEASANT SOCIETY OF MACAO.—POWHATAN STATIONED AT WHAMPOA TO RELIEVE THE SUSQUEHANNA.—SUPPLY STILL AT CANTON.—CHINESE PEACEABLE TOWARD FOREIGNERS.—STEAMER 'QUEEN' CHARTERED TO PROTECT AMERICAN INTERESTS IN CHINA WHILE THE SQUADRON SHOULD GO TO YEDDO.—SUSPICIOUS MOVEMENTS OF RUSSIANS AND FRENCH INDUCE THE COMMODORE TO HASTEN HIS RETURN TO JAPAN.—LEXINGTON ARRIVES.—THE SQUADRON ORDERED TO RENDEZVOUS AT NAPHA, LEW CHEW.—ORDERS RECEIVED, JUST AS THE SQUADRON LEAVES CHINA, TO DETACH A STEAMER FOR THE USE OF MR. MCLANE, AMERICAN COMMISSIONER TO CHINA.—EMBARRASSMENT OF THE COMMODORE IN CONSEQUENCE.—HIS MODE OF PROCEEDING TO ACCOMPLISH BOTH THE OBJECTS OF THE GOVERNMENT.—CORRESPONDENCE WITH SIR GEORGE BONHAM TOUCHING THE BONIN ISLANDS.—COURTESY OF THE ENGLISH ADMIRAL PILLOW.—SQUADRON ASSEMBLES AT NAPHA.

ᴇɴ time had not elapsed after the arrival of Commodore Perry at Hong Kong before the American merchants at Canton applied to him for further protection to their lives and property, which they believed endangered by what appeared to them the imminent prospect of a revolutionary outbreak in the city. These gentlemen addressed a communication to the Commodore, in which they expressed their great satisfaction at his determination to remain upon the Chinese coast with his squadron until he was prepared to resume negotiations with Japan. They moreover stated their belief that the revolution which had commenced in China would result in the overthrow of the *Tartars*, with no immediate prospect for the future but a confused state of anarchy, without a power anywhere to reduce it to the order of a settled government.

While it was acknowledged that the majority of the Chinese people are distinguished by a disposition to cultivate the peaceful pursuits of industry and commerce, and the opinion was expressed that the revolutionists were favorably disposed toward foreign intercourse, thus giving hopes for the future prosperity of trade, still it was declared that the disturbed condition of the country was such that, if continued, foreign commerce would be destroyed, and the importation of American goods, so vastly important to the United States, be entirely extinguished.

The chief purpose, however, of the communication from the American merchants was, as it stated, to urge upon the Commodore to send one or more of his vessels to the immediate neighborhood of the factories at Canton, the whole country about which place was swarming with thieves and desperate fellows, lying in wait for an opportunity to attack and plunder the foreign residences, if not to wreak their vengeance upon the persons of their occupants.

The Commodore promptly answered this communication with assurances of his determination to give his countrymen all the protection required in the prevailing crisis of China affairs. He had already sent the Mississippi to Blenheim Reach to protect the shipping at Whampoa, as also to guard against the numerous pirates; and had directed an examination of the river with a view of moving that steamer nearer Canton; but as for placing her at the point desired by the American merchants, it was impossible, from her draught of water. The Commodore, however, promised that the Supply, which had an efficient armament and accommodations for a hundred and fifty men, should be sent on her arrival, if it were necessary, to the city of Canton itself, and if there was any delay in the arrival of that vessel that the storeship Southampton should take her place. In the meantime the merchants were informed that they could have, if they desired, a guard of marines and one or more pieces of artillery from the Mississippi, which would be landed and stationed at the Factories. Moreover, Commander Lee, of the steamer Mississippi, was instructed to be prepared to land, on the requisition of the acting American vice consul, at a moment's notice, an advanced guard, to be followed, if need be, by a much larger force, composed of detachments from the other ships in the river.

On the arrival of the Supply from Amoy, the Commodore dispatched her, as he had promised, to take her station at the anchorage opposite the city of Canton. Meanwhile the remainder of the squadron were ordered to rendezvous at Cum-sing-moon, a port lying between Hong Kong and Macao. This port was more safe and commodious, as well as more healthful, than any of the other harbors or anchorages in the neighborhood, and, being the rendezvous of the opium vessels belonging to the merchants of Canton, possessed the additional advantage of constant communication with the neighboring towns.

The Commodore, having thus disposed of his squadron, found it convenient, in order to arrange the accumulated results of his voyage to Japan and the Lew Chew and Bonin Islands, to take a house at Macao, for facilitating his own business, and for the accommodation of the surveying officers and artists of the expedition to bring up their work. A hospital was also established in the town under the superintendence of the fleet surgeon. The Commodore found the station he selected much more advantageous than it would have been on board either of the ships, or at Canton or Hong Kong; as Macao was an intermediate, or rather central point between those two places and Cum-sing-moon, and where, with mails arriving and departing daily, and steamers and dispatch boats almost hourly, he was enabled to hold communication with them all.

The hospital soon had a good number of inmates sent from the different ships. Scarcely an officer or man escaped an attack of fever of more or less severity, and some few deaths occurred, among which were those of Lieutenant Adams, of the Powhatan, and the master of the band belonging to the steamer Mississippi. The Commodore himself, worn out by duties which were more than usually heavy, in consequence of the supervision of the labors in connexion with the accumulated results of the expedition, and large correspondence that became necessary from the apprehensions of the danger entertained by the American merchants as likely to result from the disturbed state of China, was finally prostrated and suffered from an attack of illness. Notwithstanding, however, the work of the expedition was not allowed any remission. The surveying officers continued their hydrographical labors and succeeded in preparing fair copies of the charts which had been constructed during the late cruise. The artists and draughtsmen were constantly engaged in making and completing their sketches and drawings, of which more than two hundred were finished. The several apparatus of the magnetic telegraph, the Daguerreotype, and the Talbotype were arranged and put in full operation.

Macao had always hitherto been considered a remarkably salubrious place, and chosen as the usual summer resort of families from Canton and Hong Kong; but the epidemic which prevailed in 1853 proved that it was not always to be exempt from those destructive visitations of disease to which the cities and towns of the east are so much exposed. During the time that so much sickness prevailed at Macao, Canton was comparatively exempt. In fact, this latter city is looked upon, and justly so, as a healthful place when compared with other cities in the neighborhood; and this seems more remarkable when it is considered that the inhabitants are constanly breathing the miasmatic atmosphere arising from the luxuriant and marshy fields of rice and other grains which surround Canton. Many parts of the town itself, in fact, are periodically overflowed by the rising of the river, which makes the circumstance of its comparative healthfulness still more extraordinary. While there was so much sickness at Macao, the public garden of the Factories at Canton was covered with water which approached to the very doors of the merchants, and this too at a season when, in all inter-tropical latitudes, local fevers are to be expected. And notwithstanding all these exciting causes of disease, the officers and crew of the Supply, at anchor off the city, and within the direct influence of them, remained perfectly healthy, while those on board the other ships suffered more or less from the prevailing epidemic.

Various speculations have been advanced to account for the singular exemption of the inhabitants of Canton from the effects of malaria. Some have ascribed it to the vast amount of smoke produced by the burning of wood for domestic purposes, while others have attributed it to the abstemiousness of the people. These reasons seem, however, insufficient to account for it; for if smoke only be effective to dispel the ill influences of malaria, New Orleans should be free from them, for more fuel is certainly burned there than at Canton. As for the abstemiousness of the people, which certainly exists, but from necessity, not choice, it is hardly reasonable to suppose that that would counteract the other habits of their lives, which certainly would appear to be highly unfavorable to health. If narrow, filthy streets, ill-ventilated and crowded houses, and uncleanliness of person, can produce disease, then it would appear that the people of Canton should be sorely afflicted. But yet all these predisposing causes seem to have no effect either upon the myriads who live and die in crowded boats upon the river, or upon those who throng the land, and years pass away without any serious epidemic.

In regard to the abstemiousness of the Chinese, this, as has been remarked, is altogether a virtue of necessity, as they seem to be fond enough of flesh and of all sorts of food, however gross, when they can get it. They are certainly the most inordinate feeders in the world, when supplied with the material necessary for the exercise of their gastronomical propensities. The poorer classes are accustomed to the use of boiled rice only, mixed with small proportions of dried fish, and occasionally with some simple condiments, and they consume enormous quantities of this food, if they have the means of procuring it. Dogs and cats, which are carried about the streets for sale, must be considered delicacies above the reach of the poorer classes, judging from the prices demanded for them. Rats, mice, and other vermin, are also eagerly sought after, and are made up into various savory dishes. To the families belonging to the fast boats attached to the ship a good fat rat was one of the most acceptable of presents, which they cooked and served up with their rice, making a dish very much like the French one of *Poulet-au-riz* in appearance; but as for the taste, that question must be referred to Chinese authorities, as no American or European has yet been found, it is believed, to test it by actual experiment.

Those Chinese employed in the ships of the squadron have always found the navy ration insufficient to satisfy their gluttony, notwithstanding that of the United States vessels is far more abundant and of better quality than the ration of the navy of any other country. A mess of ten American seamen usually stop each two rations, for which they receive the commutation in money. The Chinese, however, although the most sordid of beings, not only devoured the entire ration served out to them, but went about the decks collecting what they could pick up from the leavings of the messes, and invariably beset the ship's cooks for the scrapings of the coppers.

The Chinese servants employed in the Commodore's cabin ate, in miscellaneous food, including rice, bread, beef, pork, and the leavings of the table, three times as much as the other attendants. In fact, the enormous quantities of rice they consumed, with whatever else they could seize upon, is almost incredible. As for sugar and other sweets, there would have been no end to their pilfering, if they had not been carefully watched by the steward. This gross feeding exhibited its effects upon the Chinese servants, as it does upon dumb animals, for they soon became fat and lazy.

Most of the Chinese servants employed in the European and American families settled in China engage to find their own food. Their wages vary from four to six and seven dollars per month; the cooks, however, receive from seven to ten. All articles for household consumption, in the foreign establishments, are procured through the agency of a person called a *comprador*, who hires the servants, pays them their wages, and becomes security for their honesty; he keeps a regular account of the domestic expenditure, and settles with his employers at established periodical seasons. In the large mercantile establishments the profits of these compradors are very considerable. However ample a dinner may have been furnished, it would be difficult to secure at some of the residences, where little attention is paid to the economy of the household by the proprietors themselves, anything for a late guest arriving half an hour after the meats had been served. Scarcely are the dishes taken from the dining room, before they are on their way to the neighboring eating houses, there to be rehashed into stews, and sold to the middle classes. In the hongs of the merchants, who are called upon, as a part of their business, to keep up abundant tables, great waste must necessarily take place, but as the expenditure goes to the profit and loss of the concern, it is of little consequence. The missionaries and others, of small means, are necessarily hard put to it to make both ends meet.

In the houses of the foreign merchants, where there happen to be no ladies, female servants are unknown; and what would appear to be repugnant to our own sense of delicacy, there are even some English and American families without female domestics, although ladies form part of the household. The reason assigned is the difficulty of obtaining trusty maid servants.

Chinese Girl, Showing Female Head Dress.

It was, however, observed, that in all the families containing children, either maid servants or women of Macao, called Amahs or Ayahs, were employed.

The wages of the latter at Macao are four dollars a month, but if taken to Canton or Hong Kong they demand additional compensation. Many of the women speak a little of the lingua called Chinese English, or in the cant phrase, *pigeon*, which sounds very ludicrous to those first hearing it, but one soon finds himself drawn necessarily into this manner of making himself understood. The Macao women possessing this elegant accomplishment demand higher wages.

There is certainly some excuse for employing male attendants about the bed chamber and dressing rooms, when it is known that the Chinese lords of creation are the only tailors, dressmakers, washers, ironers and doers up of fine linen. In Canton, however, there are some women hired by the tailors to do plain sewing, for which they receive nearly as little as our needle workers, and those poor creatures in Great Britain, over whose misery and living death Hood sang his dirge. Their pay is from five to seven cents a day. The male tailors are somewhat better paid, and will go to any house and work for twelve hours at the rate of twenty-five cents a day, they finding their own food, or, as they call it, their "*chow-chow*." It is not uncommon to see a dirty small-footed female sitting at some corner in the street, with a supply of sewing materials and a few rags, ready to stitch up a rent or put a patch upon the garments of any passer by who may want her services. Toward night she may be seen hobbling home, with her stock in trade, on her disgusting stumps, of which she is seemingly very proud.

All the Chinese women, in fact, pride themselves very much on their goat-like hoofs, and have the greatest possible contempt for a natural foot. Little girls are said to importune their mothers with tears in their eyes to compress their feet, as promising them a higher position in society, although females of the lower orders are frequently observed with the aristocratic hoof, but these are those who have, possibly, seen better days. It is difficult for strangers to get a sight of these singular deformities, as the Chinese women manifest the greatest reluctance to show them; but Dr. Parker prevailed upon a girl of thirteen, who was a patient in his hospital, to unbandage in the presence of her mother, in order to satisfy the curiosity of the Commodore, who had quite enough in one glance of that shapeless stump, which appeared more like a specimen of bad surgery, such as Dr. Parker would have been doubtless ashamed of, than, as the Chinese considered it, an elegance of fashion.

These horrid hoofs are very carefully looked after by the Chinese women, and are swathed in gay bandages of all colors, and shod with a high heeled shoe, richly worked and adorned.

A fashionable ladies' dressmaker in China, where all these indispensible servitors of fashion are males, is always greatly in demand among the foreign ladies, and it is as necessary to bespeak his services in time at Canton and Macao as it is those of a Miss Lawson in New York. These man-milliners generally require what they call a *muster*, or pattern, which they, with the usual Chinese imitative skill, reproduce exactly, whether of London, Paris or New York fashion, and adapt it to any form or size. It was by no means an agreeable sight, on passing one of the dark and dirty tailor shops at Macao, to behold the greasy and half naked Chinaman, late at night, busily plying his dirty fingers about a splendid female dress, destined to drape the graceful form of some beautiful woman at the coming ball or dinner party. These male dressmakers are held in such estimation by those resident in China, that some few European and American ladies have been known, on leaving the country, to carry away a China man-milliner with them.

The ordinary compensation for all operatives in Canton, who find their food, varies from twelve to twenty cents a day. Farm hands, when fed, receive six cents for twelve hours work, being at the rate of a farthing an hour. The day laborers, chair bearers, and porters, if not hired by the job, are paid from twenty to twenty-five cents. Boatmen's wages are from one and a half to two and a quarter dollars per month, when found, which latter condition generally includes food, not only for themselves, but for their wives and children, who live with them in the boat.

Porters, and those of other crafts in Canton, form themselves into guilds, and appoint leaders, or headmen, who contract for labor of various sorts. This system of organization is not confined to those who work, but extends to those who beg. The beggars, like the gipsies, have their kings, who assign to their ragged subjects their particular offices of vagabondage and their respective fields of operation; and what is singular, the laws of China secure to these rogues certain rights and privileges. These laws give to them the right of approaching and knocking at the door of any domicile, or to enter the shops, and there to strike together a couple of sticks similar to those used by the watchmen employed by families to guard their premises against thieves; these sticks produce a disagreeable sound, and, however long the beggars keep up this annoyance, they cannot be legally ejected until they are paid the usual gratuity, which is the smallest coin in use, termed a *cash*, and which in value is about the twelfth of a cent; when supplied with this the beggar takes his departure, and repeats the stick striking nuisance next door, and so on until he has completed his daily circuit.

Chinese Beggar—Macao.

It is said that one hundred of these mendicants are assigned by their king to Old China street alone, which is altogether occupied by wealthy shop keepers. Some of these commute with the beggars, by paying them a round sum for exemption from the annoyance of these noisy visitors; others refuse to do this, and hold out as long as their patience will allow, with a view of wasting the time of the suppliant, who, having a right to visit all the shops, desires to make the greatest number of calls possible in the course of the day, and thus be able to pay into the general treasury at night the largest amount of *cash*. The organized beggars have their own benevolent institutions, where provision is made for the sick and needy and the old and infirm. The number of these well disciplined gentry can hardly be estimated by a stranger, but it is undoubtedly very large, if we may judge from the crowds which infest those parts of the city of Canton accessible to foreigners.

Each city has its own laws with respect to mendicants, and its own charitable institutions. In Canton there are four principal benevolent establishments: one for widows, another for foundlings, a third for furnishing coffins for the dead relations of indigent families, and the fourth for "loafers." They are all, however, so badly managed, that they answer very indifferently the purpose intended, for it happens very generally in China, as is too often the case in Christianized countries, that those who have the control of these institutions contrive to embezzle the revenues, and thus make themselves rich by taking care of the poor. Whether thieving is one of the recognized functions of these beggars or not, is not known; but it is quite clear that they can and do turn their hand with great skill to occasional small pilfering, in which they show themselves as great adepts as the most accomplished pickpockets in any part of the world.

The Americans, during the detention of the squadron on the coast of China, had occasion to become practically acquainted with the mode of carrying on business on the part of the lower or laboring classes. Among these, the boatmen and boatwomen were those with whom there was, of course, the most frequent relations. The men-of-war, as in fact do most of the merchant vessels, employ what is called a *fast* boat, which is always in charge of a skipper. This man's family, if he have one, which is almost universally the case, lives with him in his boat, and assists in rowing, steering, managing the sails, and in otherwise conducting the craft. The children are born and grow up in the boat, rarely leaving her, and, in proportion to their number and strength, contribute to the profit of their father, who happens to be the proprietor. The females lend a hand as readily as the males, and both sexes are seen laboring alike. A skipper who has the misfortune to be childless, has to employ six or eight laborers to assist him in the management of his fast boat; while he who has been blessed with a numerous progeny can dispense with these expensive assistants. Forty dollars a month is the ordinary rate paid by ships for the hire of one of these boats.

There are various other descriptions of boatmen and boatwomen plying their curious craft in the Canton river; there are those who manage the flower boats, the *hong* boats, the pull-away boats, the numerous fishing boats, and the Tanka boats. The latter, and their picturesquely costumed female tenders, have been already described somewhat in a previous chapter; but it may not be uninteresting to give some additional details in regard to them. They are used as passenger boats to carry people backwards and forwards from the land to the shipping in the harbor. In construction they are short, but broad in beam. In the centre there is a canopy of matting under which the passengers sit or recline. The crew generally consists of two women, who are often quite young, and who are generally joint proprietors, and a little female apprentice of twelve or thirteen years of age. One of the elder girls sculls and steers the Tanka boat, the other sits in the bow and rows, while the chief function of the youthful apprentice is to collect the fare, see to the comfort of the passengers, and make herself generally useful.

These girls rarely leave their boats except to purchase their simple food of rice, dried fish, and leeks, which they cook on board, except in very boisterous weather, when it becomes necessary to haul their craft on shore. On the latter occasion they are always ready to lend each other a hand, and getting their boats high and dry on the land, and snugly protected, they form quite a group on the shore, like a flock of amphibious marine birds, and avail themselves of the opportunity to gossip and visit each other, which they do on board of their stranded barks.

In regard to the lower or laboring classes of China, of whom the Commodore had an opportunity of forming some judgment, as he was brought in contact with them from the necessity of availing himself of their services, he was agreeably disappointed, as he found them, practically, not so bad after all. It is true honesty is only a conventional virtue with the Chinese; but it can be obtained for money, like anything else among that nation of shopkeepers; and if a Chinese laborer stipulates to be honest for a consideration, he may, in ordinary cases, be depended upon, especially if he furnishes security for the fulfilment of his contract. If, however, honesty has not been made expressly a part of the bargain, a Chinaman thinks he retains the right of lying, cheating, and thieving, to the full extent of his opportunity and the utmost bent of his inclinations. In engaging servants, it is customary to require of them to produce securities who will hold themselves accountable for their honesty and good conduct. Without an endorsement, no foreign merchant would think of taking a Chinese domestic into his household any more than he would receive across the desk of his counting-room an equivocal note without the security of a good house or name.

Chinese Fruit Seller—Macao.

It is difficult to form any just estimate of the higher classes in China without an opportunity, which few can possess, of mixing in intimate social intercourse with them. The foreign merchants, whose relations with the country are entirely commercial, have but little occasion of knowing any others than those engaged in trade. The missionaries have an opportunity, undoubtedly, of extending their observations over a wider range, but their experience is generally confined to the outskirts of society.

There was no very complete account of the social habits and characteristics of the Chinese people until the publication of Père Huc's book of travels, which contains certainly the best account extant of the inner life of China. What is seen by a casual visitor of Chinese society is not calculated to impress him very favorably. The position of women is such as to destroy all the best features of domestic life. Polygamy being allowed by the laws of China, as well as concubinage, women are naturally considered as mere household slaves to gratify the passions and do menial service at the will of their lords and masters. The men do not treat females as equals, and seemingly avoid their society as much as possible, for they are passing their leisure hours at the tea and opium houses, while the women are kept at home in a state of domestic slavery. As among the negroes on the western coast of Africa, the wealth of a king or chief is estimated by the stock of wives he has been enabled to purchase, with all the cocoa-nut oil, gold

Dress of Chinese Lady of Rank.

dust, and elephant's tusks he can muster, so in China, the number of damsels who can be bought to call a man husband, make up the estimate of his wealth and swell his importance. The very wealthy and aristocratic are the exclusive few, however, in China, who can afford the luxury of a multiplicity of wives.

The Commodore's residence at Macao gave him an opportunity of extending his observations of that place, beyond what had been offered by his previous casual visit.

Macao, once so famed for its extensive and profitable commerce and for its wealth, is now entirely divested of them, and seems to be sustained only by a small coasting trade, the expenditures of a limited garrison, and those of the families of the English and American merchants who make it a summer resort, and, having abundance of money, freely disburse it. The Portuguese jurisdiction is confined within very narrow limits. The Chinese settlements seem to be fast absorbing the whole place; in fact, the larger portion of the population of the town is already composed of China men and women, who perform most of the menial duties in the domestic establishments, both of the Portuguese and of other foreigners.

Chinese Barber—Macao.

The Chinese are also the shopkeepers, the mechanics, and the market people. What the native Portuguese have to do it would be difficult to conjecture. They are, with some exceptions of wealthy merchants, mostly very poor and too proud to work; there are some few, however, who are employed as clerks in the various foreign mercantile houses, while the greater portion spend their time in idleness, living upon the remnants of the once princely fortunes of their ancestors, and still occupy, in beggarly poverty, the stately mansions erected in the olden time of Macao's splendid prosperity.

There is still a show of military possession on the part of the Portuguese, who hold the surrounding hills, covering the city with fortified works, constructed after the fashion of the seventeenth century. These seem quite sufficient to keep the Chinese in due awe, who, if they had the least energy, could easily dislodge the Portuguese, for whom they have no great affection, and might drive them altogether from the country. The Portuguese garrison consists of about two hundred regular soldiers and as many local militia, all of whom are under excellent discipline, and better dressed and more orderly men are seldom seen.

It will be, perhaps, recollected that the English East India Company, before the abolition of its charter, made Macao a sort of entrepot for its China trade, and some of the finest residences were erected by that munificent corporation, or by the ostentatious Portuguese in their days of wealth and prosperity. One of these magnificent dwellings, with a garden of more than an acre in extent, tastefully laid out, and still kept in order at considerable cost, could be hired, at

Protestant Grave Yard—Macao.

the time of the Commodore's visit, for the small sum of five hundred dollars a year; and this place has the additional advantage of the romantic association with the name of the poet Camoens, it having been his favorite resort, and the spot upon which, as the reader has already

MACAO FROM PENHA HILL.

seen, a monument to his memory has been erected. It was from Macao, in the days of its opulence, that many of the commercial expeditions of the Portuguese were dispatched to Japan; and at Macao, too, the church of Rome had one of its most powerful ecclesiastical establishments, sustained by the dread might of the inquisition, which, in former times, exercised in the east the full force of its dark and cruel discipline. Now, however, the opulence and enterprise of its merchants are gone, and the awful dominion of the haughty ecclesiastics and their bloody tribunal has lapsed into the weak hands of a few impoverished priests, who meekly appeal to the pity, and barely live upon the bounty, of the reduced Portuguese population.

Since the construction of vessels of greater draught than those of former times, few that visit Macao can enter the inner harbor; it, however, is sufficiently deep for those vessels engaged in the coasting trade, sailing under the Portuguese flag, and called *Lorchas*, which are a sort of nondescript of curious rig and construction. The Chinese junks are also enabled to enter the inner port, as are occasionally a brig or schooner. The storeship Southampton, drawing thirteen and a half feet, anchored inside. Thirteen, and at high tides fourteen, feet can be carried into this inner port, and about as much into a small harbor opposite the city, called the *Typa*. It was in the *Typa* that the Portuguese corvette, Don John the Second, was lying when blown up, when the United States sloop-of-war Marion, being at anchor near by, rendered much service. The Portuguese ship is generally supposed to have been blown up purposely by the gunner, who had been punished in the morning by the captain for neglecting some necessary preparation to do honor to the day, which was some national anniversary.

Ships of war and large merchant vessels, resorting to Macao, anchor, as has been observed in a previous chapter, in the road, at a distance of from three to five miles from the city; this makes the communication with the shore at all times inconvenient, and in blowing weather altogether impracticable. This, together with other reasons, prompted the Commodore to recommend the removal of the naval depot to Hong Kong. Commodore Perry, on this subject, gave his views at length, in a communication to the Secretary of the Navy. He there stated that, in consideration of the inconvenience and consequent delay, with the increased expense of landing and shipping at Macao articles sent from the United States for the use of the squadron, and especially the coal, that he at once saw the necessity of having a depot at Hong Kong, which had been originally the naval station; but as, at the time of the agitation of the Oregon question, a rupture had been supposed to be imminent with Great Britain, it had been removed. No such troubles now threatening, there could be no doubt that government property would be safer at Hong Kong than at the badly defended town of Macao. Hong Kong has all the advantages of anchorage, as vessels of the largest size can be moored in smooth water, within seven hundred yards of the land, allowing of the conveyance of articles of all kinds, in all weather, with great facility, from shore to ship, and ship to shore. The only objection to be urged against Hong Kong was its unhealthfulness; but this did not apply to those afloat, who were exempt from the evil effects of the injurious causes which prevailed on land. Hong Kong has the additional advantage of being the market for all the various provisions which may be required by a naval squadron, and has conveniences for the refitment and repair of vessels. Pending the action of the naval department, the Commodore made every necessary preliminary arrangement, by obtaining depots for coal and other supplies at Hong Kong, and then ordered the coal vessels and storeships to discharge their freight at that port.

The Commodore found Macao an exceedingly agreeable place of residence, as the picturesque beauties of the country were full of interest, and the town, with its pleasant foreign society, presented many attractions. During his stay there he made the acquaintance of many of the residents, among whom were the families of several of the Canton merchants having summer establishments at Macao, to which they are accustomed to retire during the hot months, and where they exercise the kindest and most liberal hospitality. Monsieur de Bourboulon, the French minister to Canton, had a residence at Macao, and with his wife, an American lady, whom he married while secretary of legation at Washington, contributed much toward heightening the charms of social intercourse.

View from Ruins of Jesuit Convent—Macao.

The French commodore, Monsieur de Montravel, came with his squadron and anchored in the outer road, and Commodore Perry had an opportunity of forming his acquaintance and of interchanging with him, as well as with Monsieur de Bourboulon, and, indeed, with all the principal residents of Macao, those acts of hospitality and kindness which are invariably allied to a just appreciation of mutual courtesy.

With Governor Guimaraës, an officer of the Portuguese navy, whom the Commodore had met before on the coast of Africa, there were the most friendly and intimate relations, as well as with Captain Loreiro, of the same service; and it is due to both these officers to acknowledge their courteous deportment in the course of all the official transactions with them. The utmost good feeling prevailed in the intercourse with Sir George Bonham, the British superintendent of affairs in China and governor of Hong Kong, and with the military and naval commanders-in-chief, as well as with the mandarins of the country and the local authorities.

Two events occurred in 1849 at Macao, during the administration of the Portuguese Governor Amaral, an officer of distinction and universally esteemed, which, although they were published at the time of their occurrence in the Hong Kong newspapers, are still so strikingly illustrative of the fallen fortunes and depressed national character of the Portuguese, that it may not be amiss in this place to relate them. The first event alluded to, grew out of one of those acts of folly which are sometimes exhibited by the ill-regulated enthusiasm of fanatics in foreign countries, where the religion happens to differ from their own. A young Englishman, attached to a missionary school at Hong Kong, made a visit to Macao, and shortly after landing he espied one of those religious processions so common in Roman Catholic countries, in which what is called the Host is conducted with great pomp through the principal streets, attended by numerous priests and others in full costume, with lighted candles, the swinging of censers, and all the rich display of Romish ecclesiastical ceremony.

This young man on seeing, for the first time, perhaps, this singular exhibition of what to him seemed nothing but an insult to true Christianity, and making, probably, not sufficient allowance for differences of opinion and religious belief, and for the sincerity, however mistaken, of those of another faith than his own, conceived the idea of showing his contempt for such pageantry. He accordingly placed himself conspicuously in the way of the procession, and refused to take off his hat when the Host passed. This act, if unwilling, from conscientious motives, to perform, he might have easily avoided by turning away and passing down another street. Many Protestants in Romish countries do so. The young man, however, did not act in this very obvious and simple manner, by which he might have readily saved his conscience and allowed others who differed from him to act in accordance with their views. When the Englishman was observed purposely standing in the way of the procession and covered, he was mildly requested by the priests to take off his hat, or move away; but so far from complying with this request, the young enthusiast pressed his hat closer on his head and stood his ground like a martyr. He was now warned by the armed police to uncover or to retire, but being still obstinate, notwithstanding this summons, he was arrested and taken to the guard-house.

Here was now a catastrophe, one of her Majesty's subjects shut up in a Portuguese guard-house. The indignation of Captain Keppel, commanding the British man-of-war Dido, then at anchor in Macao roads, was greatly aroused, and a demand was immediately made upon Amaral, the Portuguese governor, for an unconditional surrender of the Englishman. The governor asked a short delay, for the purpose of consulting the ecclesiastical council. In the meantime, a regatta of boats belonging to the United States ship Plymouth and the vessel commanded by Captain Keppel, who had been appointed one of the judges, was to take place. Governor Amaral and many of the garrison officers were also to be present on the occasion. The day arrived, and Captain Keppel quietly withdrew himself from the place, and with a party of marines and some volunteer officers left the outer roads, the scene of the regatta, pulled on shore, and landed opposite the house of Mr. Patrick Stewart, and thence passing through an unoccupied house and garden, in order to avoid the main street, came suddenly upon the guard of the garrison, and rushing upon the sentinel, rescued by force the Englishman, whose ill-timed enthusiasm had brought about this military outrage.

The second incident, to which allusion has been made, was one of equally surprising character, and resulted in the death of the governor. It appears that Amaral was a man of great energy, and ambitious of improving the town of Macao by opening carriage roads through and about its limited space. In the governor's attempts to effect these improvements, he was charged by the Chinese with desecrating their ancient burial places. He had received several obscure hints to the effect that his life was in danger, but paid little or no attention to them. In accordance with his usual practice, he was riding in the afternoon on the outskirts of the town, the common resort of equestrians, accompanied by his aid-de-camp, Lieutenant Leite, also on horseback, while a number of other horsemen were not far off, when, as he came to a part of the road skirted by a few bushes, a Chinaman, or perhaps more, as the number was never exactly ascertained, rushed upon him from behind them. The governor's bridle was snatched from his single hand, (for he had only one arm, the other having been lost in battle,) and he himself was dragged from his horse behind the ambuscade of bushes, his head cut off and his hand severed, leaving nothing but his maimed and lifeless body for the startled view of the other horsemen who rode up, and eagerly but in vain sought after the assassin. No traces were ever discovered of the dastardly murderer or murderers, and the Portuguese council of Macao, in spite of the strictest investigations, could never get any clue to the authors of the crime. The Chinese authorities, however, it was suspected must have been acquainted with the persons of the villains, as after repeated summons of the Portuguese council of Macao the severed head and hand of the unfortunate governor were sent to the city. This murder occurred only two months after the act of Captain Keppel, which had greatly chagrined the gallant Amaral.

The engineers having reported, towards the latter end of October, that the machinery of the steamer Powhatan was in good working order, she was sent to take the place of the Susquehanna. This latter vessel had previously relieved the Mississippi at Whampoa. Each steamer in turn dispatched an officer of marines with a competent guard and one of the boat howitzers to remain at Canton during her stay at Whampoa. The guard was stationed on board the Supply, then lying off the town, while the officer was a guest at the house of some one or other of the American merchants, that he might be in readiness in case of any disturbance at night. All this time, however, there was not the slightest incident that could in any degree justify an opinion that a revolt was seriously contemplated by the Chinese people, and up to the day of the departure everything remained as quiet in Canton as at the moment of first sending vessels and a guard to the city. Nor had there been any outbreak, at either of the consular cities, which had in the least affected Americans or foreigners of whatever nation, during the presence of the squadron on the Chinese coast.

However the Chinese may have quarrelled among themselves and cut each other's throats, not a foreigner conducting himself properly had been in the least degree molested. Before leaving the Chinese coast, Commodore Perry had succeeded in establishing the most cordial understanding with the Canton merchants, and, in consideration of the necessity of withdrawing the Supply from that city and the Powhatan from Whampoa, had determined, at the request of the merchants, to assume the responsibility of hiring and arming a small steamer for the protection of the American residents during his absence. Conformably to this determination, the Commodore chartered a new and very suitable vessel, the steamboat Queen, for six months, at five hundred dollars a month, with the privilege of extending the term of engagement at the same rate of hire. To this steamer was assigned a sufficient armament, and the command was given to Lieutenant Alfred Taylor, of the Mississippi, with such complement of officers, engineers, sailors, and firemen, as could be spared from the squadron. The Commodore had the satisfaction of receiving from the leading American merchants a communication, in which it was stated that there seemed no immediate danger of an attack, and which contained an expression of satisfaction at the provision made by the Commodore for the protection of their interests during his absence.

About the close of November, the French commodore in the frigate Constantine, then lying at Macao, suddenly put to sea under sealed orders. It was at the time well known, that in a day or two he was to have departed for Shanghai with the French minister, Monsieur de Bourboulon, and his wife, as passengers, but on the arrival of the mail from Europe he hurried away without any one knowing in what direction. The Russian admiral, Pontiatine, in the frigate Pallas, and with three other vessels, was at this time at Shanghai, having just arrived from Nagasaki. The Commodore, suspecting that the Russians contemplated the design of returning to Japan and of ultimately going to Yedo, which might seriously interfere with his operations, and suspecting also that the same place was the destination of the French commodore, became very anxious for the arrival of the storeship Lexington with some articles for presents on board. He determined, therefore, rather than allow either the Russians or the French to gain an advantage over him, to encounter all the inconveniences and exposure of a cruise to Japan in mid-winter. Nor was he to be deterred from his purpose by the terrible accounts given by writers of the storms, fogs, and other dangers to be met with on the inhospitable Japanese coasts during the inclement season.

It had been originally the intention of the Commodore to wait until the spring had set in before going to the north, but the suspicion of the movements of the French and Russians induced him to alter his plans. The expected Lexington having fortunately arrived, after an unusually long passage, she was ordered to Hong Kong, there to land such part of her cargo as would not be required for the Japan service, and to take on board, in place of what she might discharge there, four hundred tons of coal. This being accomplished, the Commodore sailed from Hong Kong in the Susquehanna, on the 14th of January, 1854, for Lew Chew, in company with the Powhatan, Mississippi, and the storeships Lexington and Southampton, the two latter being respectively in tow of the steamers; the Macedonian and Supply having been a few days before dispatched for Lew Chew, there to join the Vandalia. The Plymouth was at Shanghai, and the Saratoga had orders to meet the squadron at Lew Chew.

On the very day and at the precise hour of the Commodore's sailing, the steamer arrived with the overland mail, bringing precise instructions from the Navy Department to detach one of the steamers from the Japan expedition, and place her at the disposal of the Hon. Mr. McLane, recently appointed commissioner to China, and then soon expected to arrive from the United States. As these orders caused Commodore Perry great embarrassment, and would, if executed, injuriously delay his plans and interfere with the success of his mission, he determined not to act upon them immediately and thus weaken his force, but to wait until he had made a preliminary demonstration in Yedo bay.

The Commodore was somewhat surprised to learn from Sir George Bonham, a few days prior to his leaving Hong Kong, that his visit to the Bonin Islands had attracted the attention of the British government. Sir George had called on board the Susquehanna to confer with the Commodore upon the subject, stating that he had been instructed by Lord Clarendon, then minister of foreign affairs, to ask of him some explanations of his designs. The Commodore, in answer, declared his willingness to communicate to Sir George Bonham the information he desired, and accordingly gave him verbally to understand his objects, but at the same time suggested that he would prefer to have the purport of their conversation put in writing. To this proposition Sir George immediately assented, and the following day he wrote a letter recapitulating what he had already personally stated, to which the Commodore replied.*

---

* SUPERINTENDENCY OF TRADE, HONG KONG, *December 22, 1853.*

SIR: With reference to my interview with your excellency, respecting your visit to the Bonin Islands, and to your proposal that I should address you officially on this subject, I have now the honor to enclose, for your information, copy of a letter and its enclosures from a Mr. Simpson, wherein it is stated that you have purchased ground from a resident there for a coal depot, for the use of the government of the United States of America.

After our conversation yesterday your excellency will, I am sure, clearly understand that it is not my desire nor intention to dispute your right, or that of any other person, to purchase land on the Bonin Islands; but as it is generally understood that this group was some time ago taken possession of in the name of the government of Great Britain, I think it desirable to acquaint your excellency therewith, in an official form, that you may, should you see fit, favor me with an explanation of the circumstances referred to by Mr. Simpson.

I have the honor to be, sir, your excellency's most obedient humble servant,

J. G. BONHAM.

His Excellency Commodore PERRY, *United States navy, &c.,*
United States Steamship Susquehanna.

BEAULEY, INVERNESSHIRE, *October 1, 1853.*

MY LORD: I observe it stated in the public prints that the officer commanding the United States Japan expedition had touched at the Bonin group—that he had made purchase from a resident there of land for a government coal depot.

Permit me to call your lordship's attention to the fact that this group of islands, so advantageously situated for opening up intercourse with Japan, really appertains to Great Britain.

Having had some connexion with it while acting temporarily for her Majesty's government in the South Seas, its importance was impressed upon my mind; and I respectfully bring under your lordship's notice the particulars which will be found narrated in the enclosure herewith.

I have, &c.,

ALEX. SIMPSON.

True copy:

H. N. LAY.

LORD CLARENDON, &c., &c., &c.

Extract from a pamphlet published by the writer in 1843.

THE BONIN ISLANDS.

"WOAHOO, SANDWICH ISLANDS, *December 27, 1842.*

"This small but interesting, and, from its situation, valuable group of islands lies in latitude 27° north, longitude 146° east, within five hundred miles distance from the city of Jedo, in Japan.

"It appertains to Great Britain, having been discovered by an English whaling vessel in 1825, and formally taken possession of by Captain Beechey, of her Majesty's ship 'Blossom,' in 1827. There were no aboriginal inhabitants found on the islands, nor any trace that such had ever existed.

"Their aggregate extent does not exceed two hundred and fifty square miles; but their geographical position—so near Japan, that mysterious empire, of which the trade will one day be of immense value—gives them a peculiar importance and interest. The climate is excellent, the soil rich and productive, and there is an admirable harbor, well fitted for the port of a commercial city.

"The first colonists of this eastern group were two men of the names of Millichamp and Mazarro, who, having expressed to Mr. Charlton, the British consul at the Sandwich Islands, their wish to settle on some uninhabited island in the Pacific ocean, were by him recommended to go to this group, of the discovery and taking possession of which he had been recently informed. They sailed accordingly, in 1830, took with them some Sandwich Island natives as laborers, some live stock and seeds, and landing at Port Lloyd, hoisted an English flag which had been given to them by Mr. Charlton.

"The little settlement has been visited by several whaling vessels since that period, and also by a vessel from the British China squadron. Mr. Millichamp returned to England, and Mr. Mazarro, anxious to get additional settlers or laborers to join the infant colony, the whole population of which only numbers about twenty, came to the Sandwich Islands in the autumn of 1842 in an English whaling vessel. He described the little settlement as flourishing, stated that he had hogs and goats in

The following are the copies of the letter of the Navy Department and the Commodore's answer, which latter was necessarily hurried, as it was written and dispatched by the pilot after the squadron was fairly under way and standing out of port:

Secretary of the Navy to Commodore Perry.

NAVY DEPARTMENT, *October* 28, 1853.

SIR: For some months past, the department indulged the hope of being able to dispatch a steamer to China, to be at the service of the commissioner representing our government, and to afford him facilities for accomplishing the great purposes of his mission, rendered much more interesting and important by the startling revolutionary movements in that country. The United States steamer Princeton was especially set apart for that purpose. But the steamers

---

abundance and a few cattle ; that he grew Indian corn and many vegetables, and had all kinds of tropical fruits ; that, in fact, he could supply fresh provisions and vegetables to forty vessels annually.

"Mr. Mazarro, who, in virtue of his first arrival, receives the appellation of governor, finds the task of governing even this little colony no easy matter. He applied to me for assistance in this task, and thankfully received the following document, which I drew up for his assistance and moral support:

"'I hereby certify that Mr. Matthew Mazarro was one of the original leaders of the expedition fitted up from this port, under the protection of Richard Charlton, esq., her Majesty's consul, to colonize the Bonin Islands ; and I would intimate to the masters of all whaling vessels touching at that group, that the said Mazzaro is a sober and discreet man, and recommend them to support him by all means in their power against the troublers of the peace of that distant settlement, recommending, also, to the settlers to receive Mr. Mazarro as their head, until some officer directly appointed by her Britannic Majesty is placed over them.'

"ALEX. SIMPSON,
"*H. B. M. Acting Consul for the Sandwich Islands.*

"God save the queen.

"A small body of enterprising emigrants would find this group a most admirable place for settlement. Its colonization, indeed, I consider to be a national object."

True copy :
H. N. LAY.

UNITED STATES STEAM FRIGATE SUSQUEHANNA,
Hong Kong, December 23, 1853.

SIR : Referring to the conversation which I yesterday had the honor of holding with your excellency, as also to your written communication, with accompanying papers, this moment received, I beg to remark that the account given by Mr. Simpson is far from being correct.

That gentleman has omitted to name *all* the white persons who embarked in the enterprise to form a settlement upon Peel Island. The names and places of birth of these men may be enumerated as follows :

Mateo Mazarro, the leader, a native of Genoa ; Nathaniel Savory, born in Massachusetts, United States ; Alden B. Chapin, also a native of Massachusetts ; John Millechamp, a British subject, and Charles Johnson, a Dane.

These five men, accompanied by about twenty-five or thirty natives of the Sandwich Islands, male and female, landed at Port Lloyd in the summer of 1830. Of the whites, Nathaniel Savory is the only one remaining on the island. Mazarro, Chapin, and Johnson, are dead, as I am informed ; and Millechamp is now residing at Guam, one of the Ladrone group.

It would, therefore, appear, that so far as the nationality of the settlers could apply to the question of sovereignty, the Americans were as two to one, compared with the three others, who were subjects of different sovereigns.

Since the first occupation of the island, the early settlers have been occasionally joined by white persons landing from whaling ships, some few of whom have remained ; and, at the time of my visit there were, I think, about eight whites in the settlement.

These people, after my departure, met together and established a form of municipal government, electing Nathaniel Savory their chief magistrate, and James Maitley and Thomas H. Webb, councilmen.

With respect to any claim of sovereignty that may be founded upon the right of previous discovery, there is abundant evidence to prove that these islands were known to navigators as early as the middle of the sixteenth century, and were visited by the Japanese in 1675, who gave them the name of "Bune Sima."—(See enclosed extracts.)

In 1823, three years before the visit of Captain Beechey, in H. M. ship "Blossom," the group was visited by a Captain Coffin, in the American whaling ship "Transit."*

---

*I have ascertained the name of this vessel from a Captain Morris, commanding an American whaling ship now in this port.

Since the above was written, the Commodore has taken pains to procure evidence, on oath, that Coffin was born in the United States. As to the ship he has no further testimony than that stated above.

Princeton, San Jacinto, and Alleghany, have all proved miserable failures. This accounts, therefore, for the delay of a previous order similar to this.

The President trusts that it may not seriously incommode your operations, in regard to Japan, to co-operate with our commissioner in the interesting undertaking to bring about free intercourse with the government of China; to form commercial treaties of vast benefit to the American people, and introduce a new era in the history of trade and commerce.

The mission in which you are engaged has attracted much attention, and excited much expectation. But the present seems to be a crisis in the history of China, and is considered by many as throwing around China, at least, as much interest and attraction as Japan presents.

To have your name associated with the opening of commercial intercourse with Japan may well excite your pride; but to be identified, also, with the great events that we trust may yet transpire in connexion with China, may be well esteemed a privilege and an honor.

Hoping that it may not interfere seriously with your plan of operations, you will, on receipt of this communication, immediately dispatch one of the war steamers of your squadron to Macao, to meet the Hon. R. M. McLane, our commissioner to China, to be subject to his control until other orders reach you. Mr. McLane will bear with him further instructions to you. In the meantime, however, you will act as heretofore in the matter of your mission—only dispatching the vessel as above mentioned. Mr. McLane will probably leave on the 19th proximo.

Your very interesting dispatches of 25th June last have been received, and the department is much gratified with your successful operations thus far, and indulges the hope, that in regard to Japan and China there is in store for you much additional honor and fame.

I am, very respectfully, your obedient servant,

J. C. DOBBIN.

Commodore M. C. PERRY,
   Commanding United States Squadron, East India and China Seas.

Thus it is plainly shown that the government of her Britannic Majesty cannot claim the sovereignty upon the ground of discovery, and it only remains to determine how far this right may be derived from the ceremony performed by Captain Beechey.

But these are matters only to be discussed by our respective governments, and I refer to them now merely in explanation of our conversation of yesterday.

With respect to my purchase of a piece of ground from Nathaniel Savory, though conceiving myself in no way bound to explain such arrangement, I do not hesitate, in all due courtesy, to say, that the transaction was one of a strictly private character.

In acquiring the fee of the land, I had not the slightest idea of personal profit, but made the purchase for a legitimate object, and to withhold the only suitable position in the harbor for a coal depot from the venality of unprincipled speculators, who might otherwise have gained possession of it for purposes of extortion.

And now let me assure your excellency, that the course pursued by me has been influenced solely by a settled conviction of the necessity of securing ports of refuge and supplies in the north Pacific for our whaling ships, and a line of mail steamers, which sooner or later must be established between California and China.

I have no special instructions from my government upon the subject, and am yet to learn whether my acts will be approved.

The recognized sovereignty of these islands would only entail an expense upon the power undertaking their occupancy and protection, and whether they may ultimately fall under the American, the English, or a local flag, would be a question of little importance, so long as their ports were open to the hospitable reception of all nations seeking shelter and refreshment.

And I may venture further to remark, that it would seem to be the policy, as well of England as of the United States, to aid in every possible way in the accomplishment of an arrangement that would fill up the remaining link of the great mail route of the world, and thus furnish the means of establishing a semi-monthly communication around the entire globe.

With great respect, I have the honor to be, your most obedient servant,

M. C. PERRY,
   Commander-in-Chief United States naval forces, East India, China, and Japan seas.

His Excellency Sir I. GEORGE BONHAM, Bart.,
   H. B. M. Chief Superintendent of Trade, Hong Kong.

Commodore Perry to the Secretary of the Navy.

UNITED STATES STEAM FRIGATE SUSQUEHANNA,
Hong Kong, January 14, 1855.

SIR: On the eve of getting under way for Japan, with all my arrangements made to leave in an hour, and a large portion of my force actually gone, I am placed in possession of the letter of the department of the 28th of October, (which arrived by the mail of last night,) directing me, under certain views of the government with respect to China, to detach one of the steamers of my command, to be placed at the disposal of Mr. R. M. McLane, recently appointed Commissioner to China.

Such an arrangement, at this moment, would be seriously inconvenient and highly injurious to my plans, the execution of which has already commenced; indeed, it could not be done at this time without deranging the operations of the squadron—so intimately are the steamers connected with each other; and I feel assured that, if the department could be made acquainted with the true state of things, and the importance of my carrying the three steamers with me to Japan, as it now knows of the events of my former visit to that Empire, it would at once revoke the order; but, as it is my duty to obey, though it cannot be done at this moment without serious consequences to the success of my mission, I will detach one of the steamers from the Bay of Yedo, and send her to Macao, where only she can be of use in contributing to the convenience of the commissioner, as her great draught of water will render it impossible to ascend, for any useful purpose, the rivers in China.

My various letters to the department will, I think, demonstrate the correctness of this assertion. However, I have no alternative, though I cannot but express the deep disappointment and mortification to which I am subjected.

Although Mr. McLane may not find a steamer waiting for him at Macao when he arrives, I will order her to the coast of China the moment I can do so consistently with the public interests.

I am sure the department will not object to the exercise of this discretion—no possible inconvenience can arise from the delay. Mr. McLane may probably be detained some time in Europe, and the steamer may be back in time to meet him, and before he will be prepared to act.

I must confess that this order has dampened my hopes very much, but I will do the best I can.

I am, sir, very respectfully, your obedient servant,

M. C. PERRY,
*Commander-in-chief of United States Naval Forces
in the East India, China, and Japan Seas.*

Hon. JAMES C. DOBBIN,
Secretary of the Navy, Washington.

The English mail steamer, which had arrived just before the departure of the squadron, had brought the cases and packages expected from Paris, containing presents for the Japanese, but too late to be taken on board any of the ships. They were therefore passed over to the care of some commercial friends at Canton, who were requested to send them to Shanghai by her Majesty's steamer the Rattler, to sail for that place two days after the Commodore's departure, and on board of which they were to be received by the polite permission of Admiral Pellew. They were to be shipped then in the Saratoga, which would carry them to Lew Chew, where they were duly received in time for the second expedition to Japan.

The squadron having set sail from Hong Kong, the course was directed through Lymoon passage. It was thought desirable to get well to the northward before striking over for the south end of Formosa. The northeasterly current, which is constantly setting with great rapidity round the south end of this island, and with decreased velocity along its eastern coast, was especially noticed during the voyage, and careful observations, the results of which will be given in a future chapter, were made upon its force, direction, and other characteristics, which resemble remarkably those of the Gulf stream on our own coast. The monsoon fortunately not having been very strong, a very favorable passage was made, with the two store ships in tow, as far as the northeastern point of Formosa, when they were cast off, with orders to follow the steamers to Napha, where the latter arrived on the 20th of January, and the former on the twenty-fourth of the same month. Here were found the Macedonian, Vandalia, and Supply. The Saratoga, however, had not yet made her appearance.

View on the Pack-shan River.

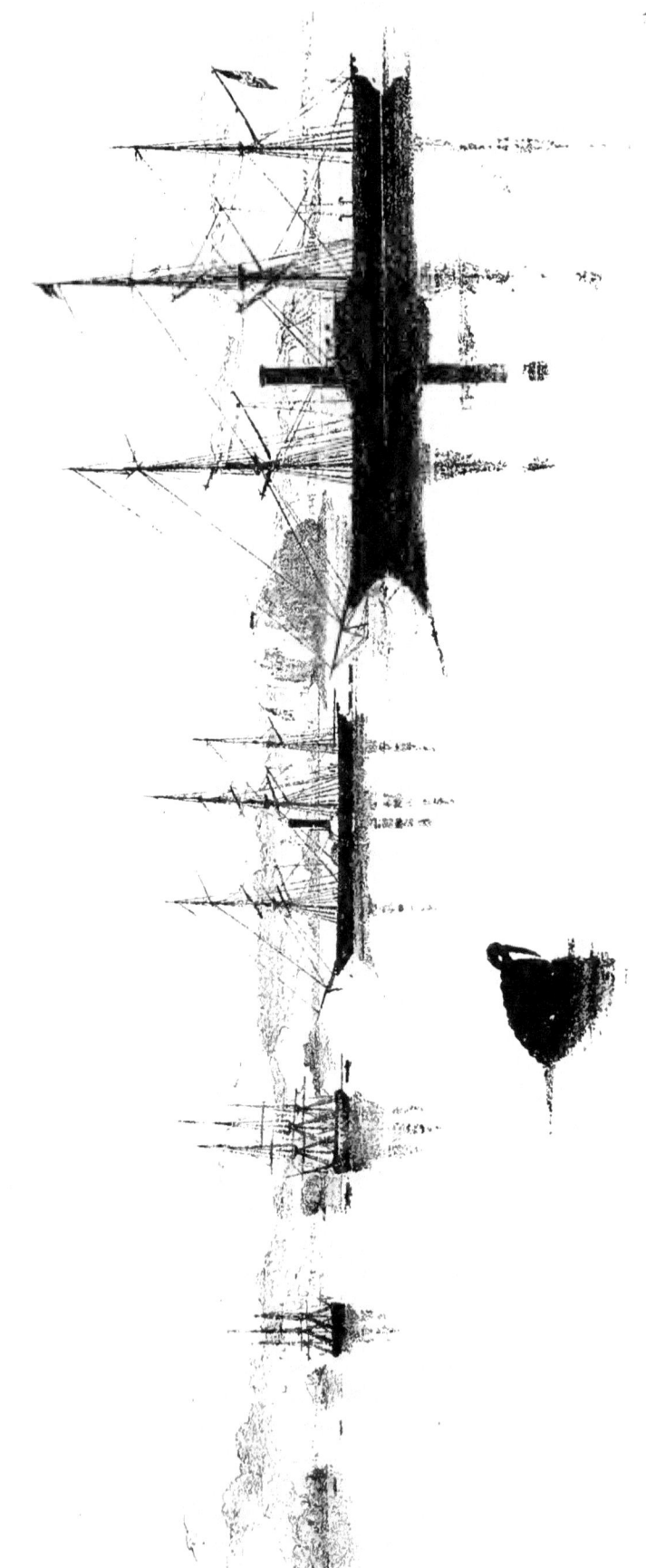

CHAPTER XVII.

INCREASED CORDIALITY AND FRIENDLY INTERCOURSE ON THE PART OF THE LEW CHEWANS.—SECOND VISIT OF THE COMMODORE TO THE PALACE AT SHUI.—ENTERTAINMENT BY THE REGENT.—NO METALLIC COIN OF LEW CHEW TO BE OBTAINED.—REV. MR. JONES' SECOND EXPLORATION IN SEARCH OF COAL.—FINDS IT AT SHAH BAY.—THE MINERAL NOT VALUED BY THE NATIVES.—ADDITIONAL GEOLOGICAL OBSERVATIONS IN LEW CHEW.—REMARKABLE SALUBRITY OF THE ISLAND.—TENURE OF LANDS.—AGRICULTURE.—RICE, POTATOES, SUGAR, COTTON, WHEAT, BARLEY, MILLET, SAGO, BEANS, PEAS, TOBACCO, EDIBLE ROOTS, FRUITS, TREES, FLOWERS, ETC.—SUGAR MILLS.—GRAIN MILLS AND GRANARIES.—POPULATION.—ETHNOLOGY.—COSTUME.—POLITENESS OF MANNER.—GENERAL INTELLIGENCE.—ARCHITECTURE.—RUDE ATTEMPTS IN PAINTING AND SCULPTURE.—AMUSEMENTS.—GOVERNMENT.—RELIGION.—FUNERAL RITES.—JAPANESE SPIES IN LEW CHEW.—DEPARTURE FOR THE BAY OF YEDO.

SIX MONTHS had passed since the Commodore's last departure from Lew Chew, and now, on his fourth visit to that interesting island, he observed a very marked change in the conduct of the Lew Chewans towards the Americans. The authorities readily furnished whatever was required, and received a due price for it, seemingly as a matter of course, while the people had evidently thrown off somewhat of their reserve, and were more disposed to a friendly intercourse. The men in the street grew quite familiar with the sight of the strangers, and did not avoid them, while the women, even, no longer fled from the market places, but remained in charge of their stalls, apparently unmindful of the foreign intruders.

The Commodore, soon after his arrival, gave notice to the regent that it was his intention before leaving Napha to visit the palace of Shui for the second time, thinking it not amiss, as the Lew Chewans seemed to be gradually yielding to American intercourse, to weaken by repetition the very strong opposition at first evinced to opening the gates of the royal residence to foreign visitors. The regent, however, still exhibited a very decided aversion to the admission of the Commodore within the sacred walls of the palace, and in a courteous communication expressed a willingness to receive him, but a very strong preference for Napha as the place of reception. The Commodore, however, holding to his original intention, declared, in answer, that it would be far more respectful toward the empire of Lew Chew to go to the royal palace, and added that he would expect that horses, kagos, and kago-bearers should be in readiness to carry him and his attending party on the day proposed for the visit.

The regent was prepared to meet this demand with all the usual variety of objections, in accordance with the crooked Lew Chewan policy, but they were answered by the Commodore's repetition of his original resolve.

The regent accordingly put the best face possible on the matter, and made all the necessary preparations; and when the Commodore, on the 3d of February, carried his intentions into execution he was received with all proper respect and the usual courtesies. He paid his first visit, as on the previous occasion, to the palace, accompanied by a military guard and a suite of officers, and was received with the same formal ceremonies. Immediately after, as on the former visit, the party proceeded to the regent's house, where they found a handsome feast in preparation, to which the Americans, having now somewhat accustomed their palates to the Lew Chewan cookery, succeeded in doing better justice than on the previous occasion. In the course of the entertainment the Commodore informed the regent that he was desirous of obtaining for the United States mint, in exchange for American coinage of equal value, all coins in use on the island; as it was well known that the imperial money of Japan was in circulation in Lew Chew, although it had hitherto been carefully concealed. Both the regent and the pe-ching or treasurer declared that there were no coins in the island, except a few in the possession of the Japanese residents, who would not part with them. This declaration the Commodore was inclined to believe to be, like most of their very positive assertions, false, and he therefore urged upon them a compliance with his request, and left with them a certain number of American coins, of about fifty dollars in value. The Commodore, at the same time, stated that he should expect to receive a number of Japanese or Lew Chew coins in exchange before his departure. The subject was then dropped; but just on the eve of the squadron's sailing, a formal communication was received from the authorities in the name of Shang-Hyung-Hiun, superintendent of affairs in the Middle Hill prefecture, in the kingdom of Lew Chew, high minister, and Ma-Liang-tsái, treasurer, in which document it was stated, that on several occasions demands had been made for an exchange of Japan coins for American, but that it was impossible to comply.

The reasons given were that all the commercial transactions between Lew Chew and Japan were carried on by the interchange of commodities, and not by the use of coin. That all the gold and silver used by the Lew Chewans themselves for their hair pins were obtained from China. That although every effort had been made to obtain Japanese coins by careful investigations among those in Lew Chew engaged in trade with Japan, it had been in vain, as the Japanese strictly forbade by law the exportation of their money, and that none could accordingly be brought into the island. With this document the authorities returned the American coin that had been deposited with them, but as the Commodore refused to receive it, it was left in their possession.

At the end of the regent's banquet each of the guests was presented, on leaving the hall, with a red card, which was understood to entitle the holder, at Napha, to refreshments and other privileges. This was a curious practice, the object of which seemed to extend the entertainment, and was a very creditable picture of Lew Chewan hospitality, as it appeared to give it an indefinite duration.

Exploring parties had been early dispatched to make further investigations of the condition and resources of the island. These investigations were directed chiefly to the examination of the geological formation, the nature of the soil, and the mineralogical and agricultural resources of Lew Chew. The officers selected for the various duties were Chaplain Jones and several of the surgeons, whose studies and tastes were supposed to fit them especially for making those observations, which had more or less a scientific bearing.

The chaplain concentrated his investigations upon the resources of the island in regard to coal, and the result seemed to prove the interesting and important fact of the existence, at Shah bay, of that combustible, a supply of which might be readily obtained by proper mining. The natives do not seem conscious of the presence of this valuable mineral in their island; they remain, probably, totally unacquainted with its uses.

In the geological features of the island of Lew Chew, the first peculiarity that strikes the eye are the great masses of coral rock abounding everywhere, even on the tops of the highest mountains, four or five hundred feet above the level of the sea. The steep promontories along the coast are generally composed of gneiss, while in the interior some of the loftier eminences show strata of slate. The base of the island is of the two combined, upon which the coral zoophite has built its structures, which by some internal convulsion have been upheaved to their present height. The soil on the surface is composed of the detritus of coral and decomposed vegetable and animal remains. As the streams are free of lime, it is conjectured that their springs take their origin from, and their currents flow through, those strata which are below the coral formation.

The soil varies in accordance with the face of the country, being rich and fertile in the valleys and plains, and comparatively poor upon the mountain tops and their acclivities. The climate is generally favorable to culture, though droughts are said occasionally to occur, and the island must suffer from the typhoons, being in the direct range of their ordinary occurrence. The climate is undoubtedly highly favorable also to health, as may be inferred, not only from the condition of the inhabitants but the topographical characteristics of the island. The entire absence of marshes, together with the pure air constantly wafted over the land in the breezes from the surrounding sea, must exempt it from all miasmatic disease. Although situated near the tropics, the heat is so tempered by the sea winds and the elevation of the land, that it is never excessive.

All the land in Lew Chew is held by government and rented to large tenants, who, in their turn, sub-let it to smaller ones, who are the direct cultivators of the soil. The system of cultivation is rude and primitive, being performed by the hands of men and women, with the occasional aid, however, of the horse and bull. A rude kind of plough, chiefly made of wood but tipped with an iron point, and of the old Roman model, is used. They have harrows, hoes, sickles, and axes, but all of simple and awkward construction. They have but small supplies of iron and evidently employ it with a very strict regard to economy.

As rice is one of the chief products of Lew Chew and requires abundant supplies of water, a very extensive system of irrigation is carried on. The ground is arranged in a series of terraces which succeed each other, from the acclivities of the hills down to the bottoms of the valleys, and the water of the neighboring streams is directed into them from the sides by means of ditches and conduits. There are no dams, properly so called, but the irrigation is so graduated by means of the terrace-like arrangement of the land that the supply of water is gradual, and never in such excess as to produce any of the ill effects of flooding or surface washing. The land, generally, is divided into small allotments appropriated to single individuals, so that the surface of the country has rather the appearance of being divided into highly cultivated gardens than overspread with fertile fields. In preparing the land for the cultivation of rice it is first overflowed, and then the laborer, who goes to work knee deep into the mud and water, hoes it into furrows. The plough is used subsequently for further loosening the soil, and is followed by the application of the harrow. All this process is carried on while the land is overflowed, and although this is considered by our agriculturists as the very worst kind of farming, it seems very well adapted to Lew Chewan husbandry with its inferior implements. The rice is not sown broad-cast over the fields, but first grown in plots and then transplanted by hand. The water was observed always covering the fields, but it was not ascertained whether it was ever drawn off, probably, however, not until the harvest, which takes place before the rice is "dead ripe." When this occurs the plants are cut, gathered into bundles, and then spread out to dry in the air and sun. The product gives something like twenty bushels to the acre, and the head of the grain is remarkably large and full, in consequence, probably, of the mode of growth by transplantation. The rice fields probably yield two crops annually, with an alternation of a supply of taro or sweet potatoes, both of which are extensively cultivated. Sugar cane, wheat, cotton, barley in small quantities, tobacco, several varieties of millet, sago, beans, peanuts, turnips, peas, radishes of very large size, some being three feet in length and twelve inches in circumference, egg-plants, onions, and cucumbers, are all found growing in the island. Of fruits there are the peach, the water melon, the banana, the wild raspberry, and the fig. Grass is not cultivated, but some wild and coarse varieties are occasionally seen. It might be supposed by the casual observer, from the beautiful aspect presented by the rich growth of the island, that the variety of the vegetable kingdom is very great. Close investigation, however, proves the reverse, for there is a remarkable sameness pervading nearly the whole country from north to south. The flora in some respects presents a tropical appearance, but not so much so as might be expected from the position of the island as compared with some others having a higher latitude. The trees that are most abundant, are the pine and the banyan, (ficus indica,) but as these are found growing in regular lines along the highways, forming beautiful avenues, leading to the tombs and villages, it is reasonable to suppose that they have been planted. The banyan is particularly abundant and is much used for hedges, being planted on the tops of the coral walls which surround the houses, and pruned and cut into symmetrical forms. The vegetable ivory tree, the ebony, the mulberry, several varieties of the palm, the orange, the lemon, and the banana, are all found, but many of them are evidently not indigenous. Of flowers there is the camelia, which grows wild and bears a beautiful pink blossom, the dahlia, the morning glory, the marsh mallow, the hibiscus, and some few others.

The bamboo, which grows abundantly, is of the greatest use to the inhabitants, supplying them with food, with material for clothing and for building, and, when in its natural stateliness of growth, with a beautiful shade for their houses and villages. The ferns are exceedingly fine upon the island, and some of them are of the large and spreading tree variety. The agriculture of the island, though of the simplest character, as we have seen, yet seems to answer its purpose admirably. Of the five hundred thousand acres, embraced by the whole area of Great Lew Chew, one-eighth at least is under cultivation, producing, it is supposed, about two hundred thousand bushels of rice, fifty thousand bushels of wheat, with the additional product of thirty-five thousand acres of sweet potatoes, two thousand acres of sugar cane, and a considerable number of acres of beans, taro, and other kinds of grain and vegetables. The implements of labor, as has been observed, are rude in construction, but are handled with great skill and effect. The agricultural machinery is simple in principle but generally effective. The sugar mills consist of three cylinders of hard wood, supported in an upright position by means of a wooden frame. The cylinders are about a foot in diameter, and are arranged in a row, with a mortice between them to regulate the approach and their pressure upon the cane. The central one has a wooden axle or shaft extending through the frame which supports it, to which is attached a curved lever of fifteen feet in length, by which the mill is readily worked. This central cylinder has a row of cogs of hard wood near its upper end, which play into mortices cut into each of the two other cylinders. A single bull or horse is generally used to work the mill, and the animal moves in a circuit of about thirty feet in diameter. The cane is placed first between the central and right cylinders, and before its escape it is caught by the hand of the workman and, being twisted like a rope, is thrust in between the central and left cylinders, by which it is completely crushed and

Sugar Mill in Lew Chew.

its juice expressed, which flows through gutters into a tub placed in a hole near by. The juice is then conveyed to neighboring houses, temporarily constructed for the purpose, and there boiled in iron pans containing about eight or ten gallons. What use is made of all the sugar it is difficult to understand, as the common beverage, which is tea, is never sweetened.

It probably is kept as a delicacy for the palates of the higher classes, who delight in sweetmeats and other confections of sugar, or sent as an export or tribute to Japan. In spite of an abundant product, sugar is evidently a scarce article among the common people, for one of the interpreters begged some from the Americans, as if he esteemed it a rare luxury. The refuse cane, after being pressed, (baggass, as we call it,) is carefully dried and used as fuel. The Lew Chewans have also mills for the grinding of grain. These are made of excellent millstones, and are worked by hand. The flour, however, remains unbolted, but makes a good and sweet bread. The granaries are marked objects in every village throughout the island. They are generally constructed of either woven cane or wood, and in a square form, increasing in width from their base, which is supported upon posts placed upon stones, to their tops, which is covered with a rice straw thatch. They have the advantage of being well ventilated and protected from vermin, of which, especially of rats, there is a great abundance. These granaries often contain as much as five hundred bushels, and as they are grouped together in numbers, amounting sometimes to nearly a score, they are supposed to be the property of the government.*

The population of Great Lew Chew must amount to between one hundred and fifty and two hundred thousand, since there are two large cities, those of Napha and Shui, and some thirty-six towns beside, with an average of about six thousand people each. The island seems to be peopled by two distinct races, the Japanese and the Lew Chewan, properly so called. They both have originally sprung, however, from the same stock. It has been supposed by some that the Lew Chewan people are chiefly allied to the Tagallas, a race which is spread over the Phillipine, Marian, and other Pacific islands, and which originally sprang from the Malays. There is, however, no affinity between the Lew Chew, Malay, and Tagalla languages, nor are the relations of their physical peculiarities such as to favor the opinion of a common origin. From the discovery, during the exploration of the island, of some remains of ancient Hindoo worship, it was surmised that the Lew Chewans might possibly have been originally a colony from southern Asia. Whether these remains are the relics of a people living in Lew Chew previous to the present races, or only the vestiges of a religion once held by one of the present existing races, but now supplanted by the wide-spreading Buddhism, it is not easy to decide. Dr. Fahs, however, (to whom, together with his associate, Dr. Green, we are indebted for the principal facts of this chapter,) inclines to the belief that the Hindoo idolatry was introduced directly by means of priests coming from India as missionaries, or through the medium of the commercial intercourse which has, in all ages, existed between eastern nations.

The Japanese and the Lew Chewans differ slightly from each other, the latter being more effeminate and somewhat less intelligent, but this may be owing to their simple, retired life, upon a remote island, where their wants are few, and nature is generous. They have, however, such strong resemblances that it is almost impossible to resist the conviction of their sameness of origin. They have both the same height, and very similar features. In both, the head is oval, approaching in form that of the European, the frontal bones rounded, and the forehead high, the face oval, and the general expression mild and amiable, the eyes large and animated, though more so in the Japanese than in the Lew Chewans, the irides in both are dark brown or black, the lashes long, and the eyebrows rather heavy and arched.

The long angular form of the internal canthus of the eye is seldom seen, either in the Japanese

---

* A detailed and highly interesting report on Lew Chew agriculture, prepared by the fleet surgeon, Dr. Green, will be found in Appendix, volume 1.

or Lew Chewan. The nose in each is generally handsome, and well proportioned to the other features; the root of it is not depressed, as in the Chinese or Malay, and the nostrils are not so widely dilated. The cheek bones are not very prominent, and consequently there is a want of that squareness of face which is so remarkable in some eastern races. The mouth is rather large, the teeth broad, very white and strong, and the chin neatly cut. One mark the Japanese and Lew Chewans have in common to distinguish them from the Malay or Chinaman; it is the possession of a strong black beard, which both the latter are destitute of to any extent. In other parts of the body the same conformity of organization exists in the Lew Chewan and Japanese.

But it is not in mere physical conformity that we trace the same origin of both races. The identity of the two races is proved by the more satisfactory testimony of affinity of language. Dr. Fahs, while preparing his report upon the ethnology of Lew Chew, gave as much attention as his opportunities afforded to the study of the language, and prepared the following vocabulary, in which some Lew Chewan and Japanese words are placed side by side. It will be observed there is such a similarity between the two, that no doubt can be entertained of the words being the same, with only the difference which may be reasonably put down to peculiarity of dialect.

	Lew Chew.	*Japanese.*		*Lew Chew.*	*Japanese.*
Water,	Mizee,	Mi-dsoo.	Rice,	Kumee,	Ko-me.
Tea,	Chaa,	Ts-ga.	Sweet potato,	Karaemu,	Ka-ran-da-imo.
Sun,	Fee,	Fi.	Pan,	Nudee,	Ko-na-be.
Fire,	Fiee,	Fi.	Wine,	Sakee,	Sa-kee.
Moon,	Sichee,	Ts'ki.	Tobacco,	Tobako,	Ta-ba-ko.
Star,	Huzee,	Ho-si.	Basket chair,	Kagoo,	Ka-go.
Wind,	Hadzee,	Ka-zee.	Silver,	Nanzee,	Si-ro-goone.
Chicken,	Nuatuee,	Ne-wa-ts-ri.	Iron,	Titzee,	Tets'.
Egg,	Tomague,	To-ma-go.	Cap,	Hachee-machee,	Ba-oosi.
Sea,	Oomee,	Oo-mi.	Looking glass,	Ka-ga-me,	Ka-ga-mi.
Eye,	Mee,	Me.	Book,	Soomuzee,	S'yo-mots.
Hand,	Tee,	Te.	Chair,	Tee,	K'yokf'rokf.
Nose,	Hanaa,	Ha-na.	Stone,	Ezaa,	I-si.
Mouth,	Koochee,	Koo-tse.	Swine,	Boobaa,	Boo-ta.
Tree,	Kee,	Ki.			

It will be observed that two-thirds of the words, at least, in the comparative vocabulary, are, with the slight differences of spelling, almost exactly the same. The orthography of a language employed by a foreigner depends more or less upon his capricious estimate of the sounds that the strange words seem to his ear to possess, and accordingly different observers will necessarily employ a variety of spelling. In these words in the comparative lists which seem to differ there will, on investigation, be found considerable affinity, and they will almost invariably show a common derivation from the same root. This lexical comparison is all we can here make. Unfortunately, we have no Lew Chew grammar to compare with that of Japan.

Allusion has already been made to the full beard, as a distinctive mark between the Lew Chewans or Japanese, and Chinese and Malayan. The men in Lew Chew in youth have almost invariably a rich jet black beard, which in age becomes as white as snow. The higher classes allow their beards to grow of great length, and cultivate them with great care and pride, while the inferior people are obliged by law to cut theirs. The moustache is also generally worn, but seldom grows very luxuriantly. The hair is ordinarily of a deep black, and is allowed to grow in long locks behind and at the sides of the head, while the middle of the pate is shaved clean. The hair being well oiled and gathered up from the sides and back, is formed into a large knot and affixed to the bald place in the head with pins either of gold, silver, or brass, according to the rank of the wearer.

The Lew Chewan male has generally a well proportioned figure, with broad and largely developed chest, narrow hips, and a slim waist and neck. A deformed person is a very rare sight in Lew Chew. The costume is neat, graceful, and suitable to the climate, and its flowing outline is particularly becoming to the aged, who, with their long white beards, have quite a patriarchal look. The dress is a loose robe, with very wide sleeves, which falls nearly to the ankles, and is gathered in at the waist with a girdle of silk or grass cloth, to which is attached the invariable pouch containing the pipe and a supply of tobacco. The cap worn by the higher classes, and called in the Lew Chew tongue a *hachee-machee*, is of cylindrical form, and seems to be made of two bands crossing each other in a figure of eight form. The laboring people go invariably barefooted, but the better classes wear a white stocking, to which, when they go out, a straw sandal is added. A band from the front passes between the great and next toe, as is seen in the ancient statues. The peasants in the country go bareheaded as well as barefooted, and are scantily clothed in a coarse cotton shirt, or with a mere cloth about the loins.

The women are kept so secluded, particularly those of the higher rank, that it is difficult for a stranger to obtain a sufficient opportunity to investigate their peculiarities very thoroughly. They are generally short of stature, and by no means handsome, having a great squareness of face, and more depressed noses than the men. Some of the ladies of distinction, the exclusive few, are described as being tolerably good looking, and of fair complexion. The women wear a robe very much like that worn by the men, though without the girdle, while their hair, none of which is shaved, is dressed in the same style, except that the top knot is rather more in front, and somewhat to the side of the head. Woman is by no means as high in the social scale in Lew Chew as she should be, being regarded as a mere slave or chattel, and always slighted by the men, who seem hardly to notice her, either in the houses or in the streets, although the females in their deportment toward strangers show apparently much modesty and amiability.

The Lew Chewans are a remarkably courteous people in their ordinary intercourse with each other, and in their occasional relations with foreigners. Their usual form of obeisance is preposterously polite, they clasp their hands with a spasmodic earnestness of courtesy, and pressing them to their forehead, bow so low that it is a marvel how they preserve their centre of gravity. The ordinary bending of the body, which seems to be to the utmost extent of suppleness of back, is still further extended on coming into the presence of those of very high rank, when the polite but inferior Lew Chewan bows so low as literally to touch if not to fall upon the ground.

The people of Lew Chew are naturally among the most intelligent of the eastern nations, but they are kept in general ignorance by their rulers. The higher classes are well instructed in the learning of China, whither the literati and professional men, and especially the physicians, are sent to finish their education. The literature, whatever they may possess, is derived from the Chinese and Japanese.

The occupation of the Lew Chewans is chiefly agricultural, although they have some little

commerce with China and Japan, to which they send annually a few junks, which carry such articles of clothing and provisions as can be spared, and bring back in exchange the productions of those countries. They have apparently no currency of their own, but in spite of their protestations to the contrary, they are evidently familiar with money, particularly with the Chinese copper coin termed *cash*. Their manufactures are few, and consist of sugar of a coarse kind, salt of inferior quality, large vats for making which are found extending along the bay of Napha, *Sakee*, a spirit distilled from rice, cotton and grass cloth of rude texture, an inferior style of lacquered ware, pottery, hair pins, junks, agricultural tools, and a limited variety of other articles needed for their own simple life.

Salt Flats—Napha.

In the higher arts, the Lew Chewans have not made much progress, although there are specimens among them of rude paintings and sculpture, particularly of the latter, in the coarse figures of their idols, with which they adorn their tombs and temples. In their architecture there is more evidence of advance than in the other branches of the fine arts. The ruins of the castles in the northern and southern parts of the island, and the structure of the palace of Shui, with the various bridges, viaducts and roads throughout the country, show considerable architectural skill. In the arches and massive masonry of the fortresses, and walls of stone, there are marks, not only of artistic design, but of skilful workmanship. Their town houses are all constructed of wood, roofed with earthen tiles, surrounded with verandahs of bamboo, and enclosed within high walls of coral. The cottages in the country are generally thatched with rice straw, and surrounded by either stone walls or bamboo picket fences, within which there is not only the house, but the usual farmer's concomitants of stable, pig pen, and poultry hutch. The furniture is of the simplest kind, consisting of thick mats spread upon the plank floor, upon which the natives sit cross legged, a few stools, a table, and a teapot with a supply of cups. The food of the people is simple, being mostly rice and sweet potatoes. Animal food is but rarely used by the lowest classes, and consists, when enjoyed, chiefly of pork. The higher ranks have a more elaborate cookery, and succeed in spreading occasional banquets, which were found quite appetising. A great variety of soups, with various sweetened confections, and vegetable concoctions of different kinds, are the chief elements of the *recherché* Lew Chewan cuisine of the best tables.

The Lew Chewans are a hard working people, and enjoy but little relaxation from labor. They have certain festivals, but of not frequent recurrence, for the celebration of religious and national holidays. Of their amusements little could be observed, although it was inferred from the existence of large level spaces, handsomely bordered with spreading pines, in the neighborhood of the towns and villages, apparently adapted for racing, wrestling and other athletic sports, that the Lew Chewans occasionally indulged in such exercises and amusements. In the markets there are frequently found for sale certain large balls, adorned with bright colored threads, supposed to be used in a game like that of our football.

Captain Basil Hall, in his interesting but not very authentic account of the Lew Chewans, states that they were unacquainted with war; and in relating, during an interview with Napoleon, at St. Helena, his experiences of travel, startled that great soldier with this unique characteristic of the Lew Chewans, which drew from him, as he shrugged his shoulders, the remark, "No wars; it is impossible!" Hall's statement would seem to be confirmed by the apparent absence of all arms or ammunition, or even of the rudest weapons of attack and defence, such as bows and arrows. The ruins of fortresses and the walled defences of Shui, however, seem to indicate that the island has not always enjoyed this blessed condition of peace, and the Japanese histories record the fact of ancient intestine and foreign wars.*

The government of Lew Chew seems to be an absolute despotism, with a system of administration like that of Japan, to which the island is tributary. The present king is said to be a youth of some eleven years of age, under the immediate personal guardianship of a queen mother, while his government, during the minority, is delegated to a regency, composed of a regent and three chief officers, entitled *pe-chings* or treasurers. As the policy of the government is to keep all foreigners in an absolute ignorance of its character, and as every kind of deception is resorted to for the purpose, it is difficult to acquire a full knowledge of its nature. The very existence of a young king is doubted, since from the time of the visit of Basil Hall, nearly forty years ago, to that of Commodore Perry, the same story has been told about the

---

* Our well known and deservedly distinguished countryman, Doctor John W. Francis, of New York, knew Captain Basil Hall personally, while he was in the United States, and has furnished the compiler with the following memorandum: "On the occasion of an assemblage of literary men, at some entertainment given to Captain Hall, inquiries were put by several of the gentlemen as to the *literal accuracy* of various circumstances related by the Captain in his book on Lew Chew. They wished to know whether they were to understand his statements literally. In my hearing, he made this general remark, by way of answer to all these interrogatories: 'If I were to rewrite the book, I should make of it a different story.'"

minority of the ruling prince, and unless he is endowed with perpetual childhood, or there has been a succession of juvenile kings, it is difficult to reconcile the experiences of the various travellers who have visited Lew Chew in the long intervals of scores of years. The *literati*, as in China and Japan, compose the higher and ruling classes, and, as in these countries, are prepared for official position by a diligent study of the doctrines of Confucius and Mencius. In fact, the young men belonging to families of rank are ordinarily sent to China to complete their education, and fit them for their positions as officers of the government. The exclusive policy of Japan is that also of Lew Chew, and was rigidly adhered to until dissolved by the intercourse of the Americans under Commodore Perry. The system of espionage pervades the whole government from the administration of the highest to the lowest official. Most of the higher classes seem to have little else to do than to watch every word and movement of the people, and form a large body of indolent non-producers, who live idly upon the hard tasked laborers of the lower classes, who are treated with all the rigor of social servitude. The country is supposed to have been conquered, centuries ago, by a Japanese prince of Satsuma, to the successor of whom it is believed to be tributary, although there are some relations not well understood with China.

The religion of Lew Chew is, as we have before stated, the generally prevalent Buddhism of the east, with a mixture of various idolatries peculiar to the island; there are, however, not many temples in Lew Chew, and those which exist do not attract a very large or a very devoted class of worshippers. As in China and Japan, a general skepticism or religious indifference seems to exist, particularly among the *literati*, or higher classes. The Bonzes, or priests, however, are treated with greater reverence in Lew Chew than in most oriental countries, though they have the same forlorn look, and go about, with their shaven crowns and fusty garments, like similar miserable mendicants in China.

Great reverence is paid to the dead in Lew Chew, where they are put in coffins in a sitting posture, and, being followed by the friends and relations and a procession of women in long white veils which cover their heads and faces, are interred in well built stone vaults, or tombs constructed in the sides of the hills. After the body has been interred for a period of seven years and all the flesh is decayed, the bones are removed and deposited in stone vases, which are placed upon shelves within the vaults. The poor people place the remains of their dead in earthen jars, and deposit them in the crevices of the rocks, where they are often to be seen broken and disarranged. Periodical visits are paid by the surviving friends and relations to the burial places, where they deposit offerings upon the tombs. On the first interment of the rich dead, roast pigs and other articles of food are offered, and after being allowed to remain for a short time, are distributed among the poor.

During the explorations of the island of Lew Chew, which were so effectively prosecuted by the Rev. Mr. Jones, Mr. Taylor, Drs. Fahs, Greene, and others, under the direction of the Commodore, and which resulted in the obtaining of so much new information in regard to a singular people, of whom little has been previously known to the world, there were many specimens obtained of their various fabrics and of their natural productions, and particularly of their botany, which have been brought to the United States for the investigation of the scientific and the interest of the curious.

The purposes of the Commodore in regard to the island had been so far effectively carried out. The building for the storing of coal had been completed, the temple appropriated for the accommodation of the sick and others of the squadron, whose duties made it necessary for them to reside on shore, had been secured, and those supplies obtained which were necessary for the squadron. With an occasional faint demur on the part of the authorities, they continued to accept payment for the various articles needed, and with their growing willingness to sell came an increased demand for higher prices. The friendly intercourse of the Americans with the inhabitants of the island had undoubtedly greatly contributed to their advantage. The most scrupulous regard had been observed toward the rights of the authorities and other classes, and they all were becoming less reserved. It was not an unreasonable inference, from the favorable disposition of the Lew Chewan people toward relations with a higher civilization, and from a seeming sense on their part of the oppressive tyranny of their absolute rulers, that they would rejoice in being placed in a political position that might render them independent of Japanese despotism.

A more demonstrative indication of the friendly feeling of the Lew Chewans for their foreign visitors would have been shown probably had it not been for the numerous Japanese agents and spies who were ever on the watch to notice and report to the imperial government every event that transpired, and to make those who manifested any friendship toward the Americans accountable at some future time.

The Commodore, being detained at Napha in negotiations with the authorities, thought it advisable to dispatch some of the sailing vessels of the squadron to Yedo bay, with the intention of following soon after with his steamers. He expected to arrive, with the advantages of steam in his favor, in Japan at about the same time with those who had preceded him in their departure.

Accordingly, Captain Abbot sailed on the first of February in the Macedonian, in company with the Vandalia, Lexington, and Southampton. The Commodore followed on the seventh of February, with the steamers Susquehanna, Powhatan, and Mississippi. The storeship Supply had been got ready, and was ordered to sail on the next day after the Commodore's departure for Shanghai, there to take on board a cargo of coal and some live stock, and proceed to join the squadron in Yedo bay.

It had been arranged that Dr. Bettelheim, who had been superseded by another English missionary, a Mr. Moreton, should have a passage for himself and family in the Supply to Shanghai.

American Grave-yard at Tu-mai, Lew Chew.

CHAPTER XVIII.

LETTER FROM DUTCH GOVERNOR GENERAL OF INDIA ANNOUNCING THE DEATH OF THE JAPANESE EMPEROR.—COMMODORE'S REPLY.—ENUMERATION OF THE SEVERAL OBJECTS IN VIEW.—PROSPECTS OF THEIR ATTAINMENT BY THE MISSION.—OFFICERS AND MEN LEFT IN LEW CHEW.—ARRIVAL OF THE SARATOGA.—RUN TO YEDO BAY.—OHO-SIMA.—CLEOPATRA ISLES.—MIJAKO-SIMA.—ALL BELONG TO LEW CHEW GROUP.—ENTRANCE OF GULF OR OUTER BAY OF YEDO.—JAPANESE CHARTS OF LITTLE VALUE, MADE FOR MERE COASTING.—WINTRY ASPECT OF JAPAN.—MACEDONIAN AGROUND.—HAULED OFF BY THE MISSISSIPPI.—FRIENDLY OFFERS OF THE JAPANESE TO ASSIST THE MACEDONIAN.—SQUADRON PROCEEDS UP THE BAY AND ANCHORS AT THE "AMERICAN ANCHORAGE."—JAPANESE OFFICIALS COME ALONGSIDE.—RECEIVED BY CAPTAIN ADAMS ON THE POWHATAN, PURSUANT TO THE COMMODORE'S ORDERS.—THEY ATTEMPT TO PREVAIL ON THE COMMODORE TO RETURN TO URAGA, STATING THAT THE HIGH JAPANESE FUNCTIONARIES WERE THERE AWAITING HIS ARRIVAL, BY APPOINTMENT OF THE EMPEROR.—COMMODORE DECLINES ON ACCOUNT OF SAFETY OF THE SHIPS.—VISIT ON THE NEXT DAY FROM THE OFFICIALS, WHO REITERATE THEIR REQUEST, WITH AN ASSURANCE THAT THE COMMISSIONERS WERE ORDERED TO RECEIVE THE COMMODORE AT URAGA WITH DISTINGUISHED CONSIDERATION.—COMMODORE AGAIN DECLINES.—JAPANESE ASK THAT AN OFFICER MAY BE SENT TO URAGA TO CONFER WITH THE COMMISSIONERS AS TO A PLACE OF MEETING.—COMMODORE CONSENTS THAT CAPTAIN ADAMS MAY HOLD SUCH A CONFERENCE, BUT THAT THE COMMISSIONERS MUST COME THERE TO HOLD IT.—JAPANESE BECOME ALARMED AS TO THE FRIENDLY FEELINGS OF THE AMERICANS.—THEIR FEARS ALLAYED.—SURVEY OF THE BAY RESUMED WITHOUT INTERRUPTION BY THE JAPANESE.—OUR BOATS FORBIDDEN BY THE COMMODORE TO LAND.—JAPANESE PERSIST FOR SEVERAL DAYS IN DESIRING THE COMMODORE TO GO TO URAGA WITH THE SHIPS.—COMMODORE INVARIABLY REFUSES.—AT LENGTH THE JAPANESE ARE INFORMED THAT THE COMMODORE WILL ALLOW CAPTAIN ADAMS TO MEET A COMMISSIONER ON SHORE NEAR THE SHIPS, OR THAT HE WILL PROCEED UP THE BAY TO YEDO.—NOTE FROM THE COMMISSIONERS TO THE COMMODORE.—HIS REPLY.—CAPTAIN ADAMS SENT DOWN TO URAGA TO COMMUNICATE TO THE COMMISSIONERS THE COMMODORE'S REASONS FOR DECLINING TO TAKE THE SHIPS TO URAGA.—SOME OF THE JAPANESE ACCOMPANY HIM IN THE VANDALIA.—INTERVIEW OF CAPTAIN ADAMS WITH THE COMMISSIONERS AT URAGA.—VISIT TO CAPTAIN ADAMS FROM YEZAIMAN ON BOARD THE VANDALIA.—ASSURES CAPTAIN ADAMS OF THE FRIENDLY DISPOSITION OF THE EMPEROR.—VANDALIA RETURNS, AND PERCEIVES AHEAD THE SQUADRON STANDING UP THE BAY TOWARD YEDO.—THE JAPANESE NO LONGER URGE GOING TO URAGA, BUT SUDDENLY PROPOSE YOKU-HAMA, WHERE THE SHIPS THEN WERE, ABOUT EIGHT MILES FROM YEDO.—COMMODORE IMMEDIATELY ASSENTS.—BUILDINGS CONSTRUCTED AT YOKU-HAMA.—A JAPANESE SEAMAN IN THE SQUADRON SENDS A LETTER TO HIS FAMILY ASHORE, BY YEZAIMAN.—YEZAIMAN DESIRES AN INTERVIEW WITH HIM.—THE INTERVIEW.—CEREMONIALS SETTLED AS TO THE CONFERENCES ON SHORE FOR NEGOTIATION.

PREVIOUS to leaving Napha, Commodore Perry had received a communication from the governor general of Dutch India, conveying information of the death of the Emperor of Japan, soon after the reception of the President's letter. The Japanese government (so said the communication) had requested the Dutch superintendent to communicate the fact to the American government, as this event, according to the laws and customs of Japan, made certain ceremonies of mourning and arrangements for succession to the throne necessary, and the consequent postponement of all consideration of the President's letter for the present. The Japanese authorities accordingly had, as was stated by the governor general, repeatedly requested the superintendent of the Dutch factory at Nagasaki to express the wish of the government of Japan that the American squadron would not return to the Bay of Yedo at the time fixed by Commodore Perry, lest his presence might create confusion. The Commodore answered the communication of the governor general of Dutch India with the usual formal expression of regret at the event of the Emperor's death, and added that he hoped the present rulers of Japan were so well satisfied of the intentions of the President of the United States, as stated in his letter, that they would not be disposed to throw any serious obstacles in the way of accomplishing friendly relations between the American nation and the Japanese.*

The Commodore had previously heard, through the officers of the Russian squadron, of the reported death of the Emperor of Japan, and that similar reasons to those set forth in the communication of the Dutch governor general had been assigned to the Russian admiral for not

---

* [Translation.]

BUETENZORG, *December* 23, 1853.

Mr. COMMODORE: The Dutch ship "Hendrika," master Admiral, which sailed for Japan in July last, has returned to Batavia on the 15th instant.

She brings intelligence from the superintendent of our factory there, up to November 15, 1853, and information of the death of the Emperor of Japan, soon after receiving the letter of the President of the United States.

The Japanese government has requested the Dutch superintendent to communicate to the American government: That this event, according to Japanese laws and customs, makes necessary the performance of many and continuing ceremonies of mourning, and extensive arrangements with respect to the succession to the throne; that during the period of mourning no business of any importance can be transacted; that the letter of the President of the United States can only be taken into deliberation when the time of mourning is over; that previous thereto, the opinions upon the subject have to be obtained from all the governors (lords) in Japan; that for that purpose the governors have to repair to Yedo in succession, (one after the other;) that all that will take much time.

The Japanese authorities have repeatedly requested the superintendent of our factory that he would inform the American government of the wish of the Japanese government not to let the American squadron return to Japan at the time fixed upon by your excellency, for fear that under the circumstances created by the decease of the Emperor, and from the several and unavoidable conferences with the Japanese authorities, and of those authorities among themselves, the American squadron might create *broil*, (confusion,) as the Japanese authorities express themselves.

I believe it not necessary to go beyond informing your excellency of this wish of the Japanese government, to be filed with my letter of September 22, 1852, (No. 134.)

With great respect, I have the honor to be, your excellency's obedient servant,

DUYMAER VAN TWIST,
Governor General of Netherlands, India.

By order of his excellency the governor general:

A. PRINS, *Chief Secretary*

His Excellency COMMODORE PERRY,
Commandant of the United States squadron, destined for Japan.

UNITED STATES STEAM FRIGATE SUSQUEHANNA,
Napha, Lew Chew, January 23, 1854.

SIR: I have the honor to acknowledge the receipt of the letter of your excellency of the 23d ultimo, informing me of a communication you had received from the superintendent of the factory at Dezima, announcing the death of the Emperor of Japan, and detailing the consequences that would result from this event in retarding the progress of the mission with which I have been charged.

Allow me to thank your excellency for the trouble you have taken in conveying to me this sad intelligence. I trust, however, that the present rulers of Japan have become so well satisfied of the intentions of the President in suggesting the propositions which I have had the honor of presenting, that they will not be disposed to throw any serious obstacles in the way of a friendly understanding between the two nations.

With great respect, I have the honor to be, your most obedient servant,

M. C. PERRY,
Commander-in-chief United States naval forces, East Indies, China, and Japan Seas.

His Excellency DUYMAER VAN TWIST,
Governor General of the Netherlands, India.

ENUMERATION OF THE SEVERAL OBJECTS IN VIEW.

replying to the letter from his sovereign, which had been sent to Yedo from Nagasaki. The Commodore was disposed to suspect, at first, as nothing had been said of the illness of the Emperor of Japan during the first visit to the Bay of Yedo, and as so short an interval had elapsed since then, that the statement of the death of the Emperor was a mere *ruse* to obstruct the American negotiations.

And even granting that the Emperor was dead, (which was proved subsequently to be the fact,) there seemed to be no reason for the delay in public business. The laws of China require the eldest son of the highest classes to abstain from pleasure, company, or business, for seven weeks in the event of the death of an Emperor, but the successor to the imperial throne assumes the government immediately, and public business is never interrupted. A similar custom was inferred to prevail in Japan, as none of the books describing the manners and customs of that Empire allude to any different practice on such an occasion.

The Commodore was not, however, to be deterred from the prosecution of his plans by any unfavorable intelligence which those who might be disposed to obstruct them so carefully acquainted him with.

It is well to enumerate here, while the Commodore is on his way to Japan, the leading objects of his mission. He was to demand explanations of the Japanese government respecting its treatment of American citizens who had been accidentally thrown upon its shores, and to make declaration that the United States government will no longer tolerate such acts; to endeavor to obtain, at least, the opening of one or more Japanese ports to American vessels; and to negotiate, if possible, a treaty with the Empire upon a basis just and equitable, and if a general treaty could not be made, to make the best that was attainable for trade. Of course, there was much uncertainty in regard to the successful issue of the mission in this respect, and the Commodore was resolved to do all in his power by firmly insisting upon what was due to the United States, and discreetly urging the establishment of those relations which seemed desirable for the interests of his country. There would be little difficulty, he thought, in bringing about suitable explanations and apologies, with assurances of kind treatment to all strangers who should thereafter fall into the hands of the Japanese, as also a friendly reception and necessary supplies to whaling ships anchoring in the ports of the empire. These results alone, it was believed, would repay the United States government for all the expenses of the expedition. With respect to the accomplishment of the other objects there was some doubt, unless force should be resorted to. This, however, was an alternative that could only be justified by some overt act of wrong or insult on the part of the Japanese government, and, of course, was not contemplated. The Commodore, though he felt confident that the purpose of his mission as regards the demanding of redress for ill-treatment of American citizens would be easily accomplished, nevertheless had made provision against any failure. He had arranged, provided the Japanese government refused to negotiate, or to assign a port of resort for our merchant or whaling ships, to take under surveillance of the American flag the island of Great Lew Chew, a dependency of the Empire of Japan. This, if necessary, was to be done on the ground of reclamation for insults and injuries well known to have been committed upon American citizens. Previously to leaving Napha, Commodore Perry accordingly issued a proclamation to the effect that as a question was pending between the United States and Japan touching certain demands upon the Japanese government, and as it was deemed essential to the security of the just claims of the United States to assume, during the pending negotiations, limited authority on the island of Great Lew

Chew, he had, therefore, detached from the squadron two master's mates and about fifteen men to look after the United States government property and other interests during his absence.

These were merely measures of precaution, which seemed justified by the wily policy of the Japanese, which forbade any confident reliance upon its justice, and by the probability of the Russians, French, or English, in their eagerness to anticipate the Americans, stepping in before them and seizing a dependency like Lew Chew, which might so greatly further their purposes in regard to Japan. It was not proposed by the Commodore to take Lew Chew, or claim it as a territory conquered by, and belonging to, the United States, nor to molest or interfere in any way with the authorities or people of the island, or to use any force, except in self defence. In fact, there was not likely to be any occasion for violence, as the Americans already possessed all necessary influence in Lew Chew, which had been acquired by kindness and non-interference with the laws and customs of the island.

The arrival of the Saratoga from Shanghai had been expected for some days previous to the Commodore's departure from Napha, and, as she had not arrived before his setting out, it was thought probable that the squadron would fall in with her outside the harbor. Accordingly, the steamers' course was directed to the westward of Lew Chew, in view of intercepting the track of the Saratoga, and it so happened that the steamers had scarcely cleared the harbor when a sail was discovered standing toward the island, which, on approaching nearer, was ascertained, by signal, to be the long looked-for ship. Captain Walker, who was in command of the Saratoga, soon came on board the Susquehanna, and received orders to proceed direct to the American anchorage in Yeddo bay. Upon his return to his ship, after sending some live stock brought from Shanghai for the squadron, and three packages containing presents for the Japanese authorities, he bore away with the intention of taking the passage east of Lew Chew.

The passage of the steamers, until the islands lying at the entrance of the great Bay of Yedo were made, was pleasant and by no means protracted. The northern group of the Lew Chew chain, composed of the islands of Oho-sima, or as the Chinese call it Ta-tao, Tok-sima, Ratona-sima, and Kikai-sima, were passed in full view. There was an opportunity, which was improved, of establishing with some accuracy the positions of several of the headlands on the western side of Oho-sima and the islets named by Captain Guerin, of the French corvette Sabine, Cleopatra islands. In passing these islands, Commodore Perry was reminded of an order he had received from the Secretary of the Navy to investigate, and report upon, a question touching the original discovery of Oho-sima, by Commander Glynn, in February, 1846, being at the time in command of the United States sloop-of-war Preble. A diligent investigation was accordingly made, and the results embodied in a communication to the Navy Department. The island represented to have been seen in June, 1849, and described in Commander Glynn's letter to Commodore Jones, dated February 21, 1850, as bearing in a southeasterly direction from the Preble, and as a new discovery, is called in the Japanese charts, Oho-sima, and by the Chinese, Ta-tao. The islets stated to have been discovered at the same time, and described as bearing north-northwest, were examined, in 1846, by Captain Guerin, of the Sabine, and named by him "Cleopatra Isles." The latter, as well as others lying contiguous to Oho-sima, were distinctly seen from the decks of the several ships of the squadron, during the present voyage, on February 8, 1854. Sketches of the islands were taken, and their positions established by cross bearings taken from the steamer Susquehanna, at noon, after good observations. The results were as follows:

South end of Cleopatra Isles, latitude 28° 48′ N., longitude 128° 59′ 30″ E.

North end of Oho-sima, latitude 28° 29′ N., longitude 129° 30′ E.

Oho-sima is the principal of what may be called the northern group of the Lew Chew chain, which, in connexion with the Mijako-sima, and other islands commencing with the Cleopatra, extend from near the north end of Formosa to Kiusiu, the southwestern extremity of Japan proper. The three groups of Mijako-sima, Great Lew Chew, or Okinawa-sima, and Oho-sima, should be denominated the southern, middle, and northern Lew Chew islands, the central government being established at the city of Shui, in the island of Great Lew Chew. Of the people and government of these islands little is known, but it is presumed that they are all subject to an intermediate sovereignty between Lew Chew and the Empire of Japan, or possibly the Japanese prince of Satsuma. This potentate is stated by Von Siebold to receive about 2,240,000 guilders, or nearly $900,000, annually, from the Lew Chew islands. Oho-sima is in circumference nearly one hundred and fifty English miles, and bears in its external aspect, with its mountains and richly verdant valleys, a considerable resemblance to Great Lew Chew. It is represented by various writers to be thickly populated, having all the advantages of cities, towns, villages, and commodious ports. It is surprising that it has never hitherto been visited by any Christian voyager.

The Mijako-sima islands have been more than once visited by foreign vessels, and during the progress of the Japan expedition, by the Saratoga, whose officers described the inhabitants as being in language, manners, customs, and appearance, almost identical with the people of Lew Chew. And it is reasonable to infer that this, in common with the other inhabited islands of the chain, has been peopled for many hundreds of years. The Mijako-sima group was ascertained to be governed by officers appointed by the king and council of Great Lew Chew, who are frequently changed, in conformity with the policy practised throughout Japan and its dependencies.

The Cleopatra islands are only two in number, lying in close proximity to each other, and are small and uninhabited. They are cone-shaped, and evidently of volcanic origin, the craters being clearly visible, the larger one of which has been estimated at 1,650 feet in height. The geographical position of all this chain of islands, extending from Formosa to Japan proper, would seem to be so arranged as to suit the convenience of the commerce of the unskilful Japanese navigators, who sail in their frail open-sterned vessels from island to island, always being careful to have a port under their lee, into which to escape on the least approach of foul weather.

On entering, upon the 11th of February, the outer Bay of Yedo, or as it may be more suitably termed, the Gulf of Yedo, including the space embraced between Cape Nagatsuro on the west, Cape Serafama or Cape King on the east, and Wodawara, Kamakura, and Cape Sagami on the north, the steamers encountered a severe blow from the northward and eastward. They were kept, however, during the night, under the lee of Oho-sima, (*i. e.* Great Island,) and thus avoided the greatest violence of the gale. On the previous afternoon a cluster of three dangerous rocks, showing above the surface of the sea from ten to twenty feet, were passed quite near. These were supposed to be what are called on the charts the Broughton Rocks; and if they were, their position is evidently very erroneously laid down, and if they were not, they have escaped the observation of previous European and American navigators. That these rocks should have been hitherto unnoticed would not be at all remarkable, for few ships have ever visited the southern and eastern coasts of Japan, and it is not reasonable to expect that the very imperfect charts which have been compiled from the meagre information furnished by Broughton,

Gore, King, Krusenstern, and the three or four American and English vessels which have visited the coast within a few years back, should be in any manner correct.

It is true that the Japanese have constructed charts, but they are on a plan peculiar to themselves, and of little benefit to the bold navigators, with their large vessels, of Europe and America. The Japanese charts, without meridian or scale, and totally destitute of any record of soundings, are hardly of any use, except in their own timid navigation. The Japanese never venture, if they can possibly avoid it, beyond sight of land, and always seize upon favorable seasons, weather, and winds, for making their longest runs. Their junks skirt the coasts by touching the land here and there, and going from island to island, and seldom make a run of a longer duration than twenty-four hours. The largest Japanese junks seen did not draw more than eight feet of water, and, as has just been remarked, they run from port to port, invariably seeking shelter on occasions of adverse winds or appearances of bad weather. The pilots, familiar with every rock upon the coast, need no charts, and conduct their vessels, in accordance with their cautious navigation, with general safety. Every harbor, however small, is furnished with conveniences for securing the Japanese craft, holes being artificially made through the angles of the rocks for passing the cables, and where this is not practicable, upright pillars or posts are hewn or morticed in the stone, and all chafings of the moorings provided against by a careful rounding and smoothing of the neighboring projections or detached parts.

On the morning of the 12th of February the weather became more settled, and the steamers stood up the bay. The outlines of the land were recognized from the familiarity of the previous visit, but a change had come over the face of the landscape, in consequence of the difference of season. The lofty summit of Fusi-Yama was distinctly visible as before, but was now completely clothed in its winter garb of snow. The rich verdure of the surrounding land had lost its cheerful summer aspect, and looked withered, bleak and sombre. The rising uplands were no longer reposing in their beds of green, shaded from a summer's sun beneath spreading groves, but were bare and desolate, while the distant mountains stood chill in their snowy drapery and frowned upon the landscape. The weather was cold and blustering. As the steamers approached the land, two vessels were observed close in and apparently at anchor. On approaching them it was discovered that they were the Macedonian and Vandalia. The latter had a signal displayed announcing that the Macedonian was aground. It was soon ascertained that Captain Abbott, on the day previous, had mistaken the indentation in the coast within which his ship was aground for the entrance to the passage to Uraga and Yedo. He had, accordingly, on venturing too near the shore, grounded his vessel on a ledge of rocks not, of course, laid down upon the imperial chart which he had; said chart being nothing more than a copy of one of Von Siebold's maps, which had been copied from the Japanese authorities, with a few notes upon it, made during the first visit of the squadron to the Bay of Yedo. Captain Abbott, finding his ship in this dilemma, adopted the usual means of getting her afloat by starting the water, making her guns ready for throwing overboard, and actually throwing over the side many miscellaneous articles. Commander Pope of the Vandalia, at that time in company, immediately anchored and sent his boats to the assistance of his consort the Macedonian.

The fortunate arrival of Commodore Perry with his three steamers at once gave assurance of effectual aid. Commander Lee of the Mississippi was accordingly ordered to approach with his steamer as near as he could safely venture to the ship on shore, and run a couple of hawsers to her with the view of hauling her off by the power of steam. This duty he executed with his usual promptitude and judgment, and before night the Macedonian was towed into a safe anchorage. Meanwhile the other vessels were brought to anchor for the night, having been joined on the same afternoon by the Lexington, which, it will be recollected, sailed from Napha in company with the Macedonian and Vandalia. In the course of the night a boat came alongside the Commodore's flag-ship, having been dispatched by Lieutenant Commanding Boyle of the Southampton, which vessel, another of Captain Abbott's division, had arrived the day before at the American anchorage in the Bay of Yedo.

Lieutenant Boyle had received information from the Japanese authorities that two ships had arrived off Kama-kura, and that one of them was ashore, and very promptly and properly dispatched the launch of the Southampton, with two officers and a suitable crew, to render all practicable assistance.

The friendly disposition of the Japanese toward the Americans was handsomely illustrated by their offers of assistance as soon as the Macedonian was observed ashore. Such, too, was their courteous and scrupulous regard for the interests and property of their visitors, that they actually took the trouble of sending to the squadron, then at a distance of twenty miles, a hogshead of bituminous coal, which had been thrown overboard on lightening the ship, and subsequently washed ashore.

Next morning (February 13) after the Macedonian had been relieved from her hazardous position, in the bight of Kawatsu, near Kama-kura, the whole squadron moved up the Bay of Yedo, sailing in a line ahead, the Lexington, Vandalia, and Macedonian being in tow respectively of the Susquehanna, Powhatan, and Mississippi. With the experience of navigation acquired during the previous visit, there was no occasion for the ships to feel their way, but they passed along the magnificent bay with confidence, bringing into view at each turn various points of the land on either side, which had now the aspect of familiar ground.

The precipitous coasts of Sagami rose bleakly in the winter atmosphere on the left, while far inland could be seen the lofty ranges of the mountains covered with snow, and the high peak of Fusi-Yama, about the lofty summit of which the clouds were scudding in reckless succession. There was the distant coast of Awa, some twelve miles away on the opposite side, and along the shores everywhere were the numberless villages and towns, though snugly reposing under the cover of the high land which rose behind them, yet looking desolate and exposed, in comparison with their former aspect of rural comfort when nestling in the full-leaved groves of summer. Abreast was the town of Gorihama, the scene of the delivery of the President's letter, and in front extended out from the land the promontory of Uraga, with its harmless forts, and as the ships doubled it and came abreast the city, numerous government boats, with their athletic oarsmen sculling vigorously, and their little striped flags fluttering in the wind, pushed off to intercept the squadron, as on the previous visit. The Japanese officials, however, who had risen from their places midships, and seemed to be directing their boats towards the squadron, were warned off, and the strangers moved majestically on, with their train of formidable men-of-war, without altering their course a line, or lingering a moment in their speed until they reached the anchorage, at three o'clock in the afternoon, (February 13.) The government boats were left in the distance, but were seen sculling rapidly along and following in the wake of the squadron.

The position in which the three steamers and the four ships, including the Southampton, which had preceded the squadron, had anchored was named, in the previous visit, the "American anchorage." It is within the bight embraced within two bold headlands, about twelve miles distant from each other, on the western side of the Bay of Yedo. The anchorage was about twelve miles beyond the town of Uraga, and about twenty miles from the capital city of Yedo. The island which had been called Perry's, and which presented such a picturesque aspect during the summer with its pleasant groves, was seen as the squadron passed up, and the fort which covered its summit could be more distinctly traced through the trees, which had been stripped of their foliage by the frost and winds of winter.

The villages of Otsu and Torigasaki, no longer embowered in green growth, stood out from the land a mile or so distant, in all the sharpness of outline and staring surface of their peak-roofed and boarded houses. The anchorage, though protected by the bounding headlands and the curved shore, had less of that sheltered look which it had previously presented.

The squadron had hardly come to anchor when two of the government boats, which had followed rapidly in the wake of the ships, came alongside the Susquehanna. The Japanese officials requested to be admitted on board, but as the Commodore had caused the extra or captain's cabin to be removed from the steamer Susquehanna to the Powhatan, in view of changing his flag to that ship preparatory to the return of the former to China, and as in accordance with the system of exclusiveness which it was thought politic still to continue, the Commodore could not admit them, as they were of subordinate authority, into his own cabin, he directed Captain Adams to receive the officials on board the Powhatan.

Captain Adams, having been charged by the Commodore with precise and special instructions to hear all the Japanese had to say, but to give them no unnecessary information, nor to promise anything, proceeded to the steamer Powhatan, accompanied by the interpreters, Messrs. Williams and Portman, and the Commodore's secretary, Mr. Perry.

The government boats followed and the Japanese deputation came on board the Powhatan. It consisted of a high dignitary, who was announced as Kura-kawa-kahie, the two interpreters who had formerly officiated, three grey-robed individuals, who seemed to be making excellent use of their eyes, and turned out to be *metske dwantinger*, literally cross-eyed persons, or those who look in all directions, in other words spies or reporters. They were all received with one ceremony and ushered into the cabin, where the object of their visit was set forth at length. Some preliminary conversation took place, in the course of which inquiries having been made about Yezaiman, the governor of Uraga, who had taken so prominent a part in the negotiations on the previous visit, the Japanese stated that that dignitary was unwell, but would probably soon pay his respects to the Commodore. Questions were also asked and answered in regard to the ships, their number, names, and those that were to come. The usual compliments, of which the Japanese officials seemed never weary or forgetful, having passed, they stated that their business was to endeavor to induce the Commodore to return to Uraga, where, they said, there were two high Japanese officials, in waiting, and that more were expected, who had been appointed by the Emperor to meet and treat with the Americans. Captain Adams replied that the Commodore would not consent to go to Uraga. And upon the Japanese rejoining that the Emperor had appointed that town for the place of negotiation, and that it could, in consequence, be nowhere else, he was told by Captain Adams that the Commodore was willing to meet the commissioners on shore, opposite the present anchorage of the squadron; but if the Japanese government would not consent to that, the Commodore would move his ships higher up the bay, even, if it should be deemed necessary, to Yedo itself. The interview was conducted in the most courteous and friendly manner, and after the business was over, the Japanese partook of some refreshments and entered cheerfully into a general conversation.

The Japanese now took their leave, and although they had been impressed with the resolute bearing of the Americans, departed with their usual good humor and polite expressions of friendly feeling.

The next day the Japanese officials came off again to the Powhatan, and were received as before by Captain Adams, under instructions from the Commodore.

The Japanese reiterated their assurances of the friendly disposition of the Emperor, who had given orders, as they said, that the Americans should be treated with the greatest consideration. The commissioners, they declared, would be ready to receive the Commodore in a few days, and upon being asked in what place, they answered at Kama-kura. As Uraga had been specified on the previous day, Captain Adams, with some surprise, demanded how it was that the place had become so suddenly changed. The Japanese, with their usual imperturbable manner, which is schooled to cunning and deceit, promptly answered, without the least mark of emotion or evidence of discomposure, that the Emperor had named both places, so that if the Commodore should not be satisfied with the one, he might perchance with the other.

Kama-kura is a town situated in the outer Bay of Yedo, about twenty miles below Uraga, at the place where the Macedonian had grounded. As the Commodore had had an opportunity when anchored off Kama-kura, while engaged in the extrication of the Macedonian from her perilous position, of seeing enough of that place to satisfy him that it would be absurd to take the ships there, and as he suspected some artful design on the part of the Japanese, when informed that Kama-kura had been specified, he directed Captain Adams to say that it was altogether unsuitable. Captain Adams then conveyed this information to the Japanese, with the statement that neither Uraga nor Kama-kura were proper places, as they were so distant and so insecure as harbors, and that some other locality must be selected. The Japanese then proposed that Captain Adams should go down to Uraga and confer with the high officer there about the place of meeting, when they were told that it would be necessary to receive the instructions of the Commodore before a reply could be given on that point.

The Commodore's secretary, who was present at the interview, was then dispatched to the Susquehanna. The secretary soon returned with the answer that the Commodore would neither go to Uraga, nor allow any of his officers to do so, but that Captain Adams would be permitted to meet any of the high Japanese dignitaries on the shore, near the anchorage of the squadron, to confer upon the subject of a proper place of meeting, but that it was an essential condition of the Commodore's consent that the place should not be remote from his present position.

The Japanese officials, notwithstanding the very explicit answer, which was duly conveyed in Dutch by Mr. Portman to Tatsnoske, (who, as on the first visit, was one of the attendant interpreters,) and by him interpreted to his superiors, still pertinaciously clung to their original proposition, and urged the necessity of making Uraga the place of meeting. As they still persisted in their wearisome efforts to carry their point, Captain Adams cut the matter short by telling them to put in writing their objections to holding the interview in the neighborhood of the American anchorage, to which the Japanese assented, on the condition that Captain Adams would answer a written question which they were about to ask. This being granted, Toksuro, the second interpreter, having conferred for a moment with his superiors, wrote down in Dutch the proposed question, which was translated by the American interpreter, Mr. Portman: "As the President's letter was received at Gorahama, near Uraga, why are you not willing to receive the answer there?" Captain Adams answered that he did not know precisely all the Commodore's reasons, but the principal one was that the anchorage was very unsafe.

The Japanese now seemed somewhat troubled, as if they feared that the Americans were disposed to assume a hostile attitude, and asked, with some anxiety, whether the Commodore was actuated by the same friendly feelings as the Japanese government. Captain Adams did all in his power to reassure them, and declared that the Americans were actuated by no other motives than those of friendship, and that their greatest desire was to be in relations of peace and amity with Japan, and that their chief object in refusing their assent to the Japanese propositions was the fear of endangering the lives of the officers and crews and the safety of the ships by resorting to an insecure place. The Japanese reiterated, several times, that a high officer would come to arrange all business with the Commodore, but that he could not arrive for several days. Upon its being proposed that he should come on board the ships, the Japanese declared that that was quite impossible; and then Captain A. suggested that, as it was the custom to transact all public business at the metropolis, the Commodore should go to Yedo. The last suggestion was opposed by the very emphatic remark: "You cannot be received at Yedo."

The Japanese now requested that the boats of the squadron should be prohibited from landing or surveying the harbor, and were told that could not be promised, but that the Commodore should be informed of the request. After the usual refreshments—tea, wine, cakes, and segars—of which the Japanese always freely partook, and the ordinary interchange of compliments, they prepared to take their departure, saying, as they left, that it would take some six or seven days before they could bring any decision from the high officer in regard to the place of meeting, but promising the earliest dispatch.

A surveying party had been organized on the second day of the arrival of the squadron, under the command of Lieutenant Maury, and ordered to commence operations, which were effectively carried out. There were no positive interruptions on the part of the Japanese authorities, but they evidently looked upon the proceeding with jealous anxiety; and that the subject was uppermost in their mind is clear, from the constant allusion to it in their various conferences with the American officers. The Commodore, however, fully alive to the importance of thoroughly surveying the bay, not only for the convenience of the immediate purposes of the expedition but for the future interests of the United States, and, we may add, those of the whole civilized world, was resolved to omit no opportunity of obtaining a thorough knowledge of the navigation of the bay, and thus complete the hydrographical reports and charts, which are now among the by no means least valuable results of the expedition. The surveying boats were accordingly kept busy day after day, and the protestations of the Japanese authorities, though courteously listened to, were always met with the assertion of the resolute determination of the Commodore to prosecute what he believed so essential to the full development of the objects of his mission. It was now the fourteenth of February, a day which was recorded in the logs as cold and blustering, but with an atmosphere perfectly clear. The land just off the ships, the promontories to the north and south, and the opposite shore, showed a clear and distinct wintry aspect, and the view could be readily extended for a circuit of many miles, far back to the snowy summits of the mountains, which traced their irregular outlines upon the cold grey sky.

Notwithstanding that the Japanese officials had declared that it would require several days before they could bring any answer to the Commodore's protest against moving his squadron to Uraga, they came on board the Powhatan early the next morning, (February 15.) Commodore Perry had suffered since his arrival from a severe indisposition, of which the Japanese had heard, and they now made their visit to inquire, as they said, after the *Admiral's health. They also stated that they had been instructed to lay off the squadron with their boats, in case the Americans had anything to communicate, or desired any supplies. They made an offer to bring off wood, water, or anything else the ships might require; when they were told that nothing was wanted at present, but perhaps some fish, eggs, and vegetables might be acceptable in a few days, and that they would be received provided payment should be taken for them. The Japanese then replied that their proposed supplies were intended as presents, and that they had no authority to receive money for them. They seemed to be very fearful lest some of the boats should land, but they were assured that they would not be allowed to do so. Captain Adams, in the course of the conversation, alluded to the report of the death of the Emperor, but was not very explicit in his question, as there seemed to be some doubt of its truth. He merely stated that when the squadron had sailed for Japan he had heard that a high dignitary had died, and asked whether it was true. To which the Japanese answered, "Yes, a very high man died lately." Captain A.—"What was his rank?" Japanese official.—"He was a prince." It was thus a matter of the greatest difficulty to get at the truth, the Japanese being as indirect and evasive as possible in regard to the simplest matter of fact.

The Japanese dignitaries repeated their official visits day after day, sailing up in their boats from the long distance of Uraga, and consumed the time with offering the most puerile pretexts for coming, and the length of their negotiations. Now they would express the greatest solicitude about the Commodore's health, and showed their courtesy by bringing him presents of bon-bons and confectionary; again they would offer provisions and other supplies; at another time they would enter into explanations about the Americans going ashore, and on one occasion they brought with them a dozen or more naval buttons which had been thrown into their boats, and which they returned with the most formal ceremony. They always recurred, however, to the question of the vessels going to Uraga, and never ceased persisting in their pertinacious solicitations that the Commodore would remove his squadron there, notwithstanding the direct and resolute refusal with which they were invariably opposed. On their visit on the 18th of February they announced that the high officer had arrived at Uraga, and that they had been sent to request the Commodore to meet him there. Upon being told that it was impossible for the Commodore to go to Uraga, Captain Adams then handed them the following document from the Commodore:

"UNITED STATES STEAM-FRIGATE POWHATAN,
"*American Anchorage, Yedo Bay, February* 18, 1854.

"The Commodore expects to be received at Yedo, agreeably to the customs of all countries.

"In consideration of the size of our ships, and their great value, he cannot return to the anchorage at Uraga, nor even remain at this place much longer, but will have to go higher up the bay towards Yedo, where the vessels can be more secure.

"If the great man (chief commissioner) will appoint an officer of proper rank to meet Captain Adams on shore, near where the ships are now lying, to determine when and where the interview with the Commodore shall take place, he must let us know by noon of Tuesday next.

---

* The Japanese officials always spoke of the Commodore as the Admiral, not being acquainted with the former title.

"The Commodore will be happy to place a ship at the disposal of the great man, to bring him up to the place of interview, and take him back again to Uraga, if he wishes it.

"When the officer comes to meet Captain Adams, he had better bring a letter to show that he has proper authority, and a person must be sent to conduct Captain Adams to the place of meeting."

The Japanese received the dispatch from the Commodore without any attempt to discuss it, and bore it away with them, with the intention of consulting, doubtless, with others higher in authority. As they rose to depart, they asked if the Commodore had received a letter, through the Dutch at Nagasaki, which had been sent to him the previous year by the government of Japan. Captain Adams, as he had not been authorized to make any revelations on the subject, answered he had no authority to speak on the subject. They then took their departure.

It was on this day (February 18th) that the Commodore transferred his broad pennant to the Powhatan. The surveying boats, as usual, were busily occupied on duty, but had changed their scene of operations further toward Yedo. The Southampton followed in their wake, in order to facilitate the work of the surveyors, who had hitherto lost much time by being obliged to return, after a day's labor, a great distance to the squadron. The surveying party was now, by being immediately followed by a ship, enabled to go on board of her at night, without losing time, which it was necessary to economise, in order fully to complete the extensive observations they had in view.

The next day was Sunday, (February 19th,) but the Japanese officials, notwithstanding, came on board the Powhatan as usual. They were told that it was a day set apart by the Americans as their Sabbath, but that if they had anything to say, they would be listened to, in consideration of the long distance and inclement weather through which they had come. They brought with them a large quantity of vegetables, oranges, fowls, eggs, and various sweetened confections, which they courteously offered as a present to the Commodore, with a kind inquiry after his health. These were received upon their expressing a willingness to receive something in return, and they accordingly were presented with some ship's bread and a box of tea; the Japanese remarked, as they received them, they had given eatables only, and that it was a Japanese custom to receive eatables only in return. Upon being asked whether the Commodore's propositions had been laid before the high officer, the officials replied that they had, and that he desired to confer about the President's letter at Uraga. The Commodore's objections against going to Uraga were again resolutely pressed, but the Japanese merely answered, that that place had been selected by the order of the Emperor. Captain Adams distinctly declared, that if the Commodore did not receive a favorable answer to his request for an interview with the high officer near his present anchorage, by the subsequent Tuesday, (February 21st,) "he would then know what to do." The Japanese official still reiterated that it was the Emperor's order that the interview should be held at Uraga. The next day there was another visit, with the usual ceremonies, and a present of oysters for the Commodore.

The Japanese brought with them a short dispatch from the high commissioners, addressed to the Commodore, written in Japanese and Dutch, stating their instructions from the government. The translation is as follows:

"We are compelled by the order of the Emperor to meet the ambassador of the President of the United States of America either at Kama-kura or Uraga.

"In the interim we shall talk about the negotiations of commerce and the influence it must exercise upon the well-being of the Japanese and American nations. It is out of the question now. This is all according to truth."

This document having been laid before the Commodore, he submitted the following answer:

"The Commodore, for the reasons before given, cannot return to Uraga. His instructions are to receive the answer of the Emperor to the President's letter at Yedo."

The Japanese having received and perused the answer attentively, conferred with each other, and then promised that it should be submitted to the high officer. Captain Adams now informed them that it was his intention, under orders, to go down to Uraga the next day to declare in person to the high officer what had just been delivered in writing from the Commodore. The Japanese seemed very anxious to know if he would be accompanied by a very large party, and seemed quite tranquilized when told that there would be a few officers only. They promised that a boat should be in readiness, and all other preparations made for the reception. In the course of a general conversation they were told that the following Wednesday would be the anniversary of Washington's birthday, and that a salute would, in consequence, be fired. They seemed perfectly acquainted with the name of the great father of our country, and expressed a desire to participate in celebrating the occasion, asking to be permitted to come off to see the guns fired. They were, of course, politely invited, and requested to bring their ladies with them; the latter part of the invitation they, however, jeered at as a very amusing but quite an impracticable joke.

On Tuesday, the 21st day of February, the Japanese boat came alongside the Powhatan, and the officials, on being received aboard, stated that they had come to show Captain Adams the landing at Uraga. They were then invited to accompany him on board the Vandalia, which ship immediately set sail, and moved down the bay. Captain Adams was the bearer of the following note from the Commodore to the Japanese authorities:

"United States Flag-ship Powhatan,
"*American Anchorage, Yedo Bay, February* 20, 1854.

"The undersigned is highly gratified to learn, through the officers of his Majesty who have visited the flag-ship, that the imperial court has come to the conclusion to respond, in the most cordial manner, to the propositions of the President of the United States which the undersigned had the honor to present in July last.

"Inasmuch as the anchorage at Uraga is unsafe and inconvenient, and considering the great size and value of the steamers composing a part of the command of the undersigned, he does not consider himself justified in removing to that place; on the contrary, he deems it necessary to seek a more commodious harbor higher up the bay; and as his instructions direct him to present himself at Yedo, it is desirable that he should approach as near as possible to that city, as well for the better convenience of communication as with reference, also, to the arrangement and exhibition of the various presents sent by the President to his Imperial Majesty.

"As the mission of the undersigned is of a most friendly character, he is not prepared to anticipate any objection to his reception at the seat of government, conformably to the usages of all the nations of Europe and America, and he hopes that when the steamers shall have reached the vicinity of the city, and secured more suitable moorings, he may have the honor of

334   EXPEDITION TO JAPAN.

receiving on board his ship such distinguished members of the imperial court as may be desirous of viewing the steamers and witnessing the working of their machinery.

"This communication will be presented by Commander H. A. Adams, captain of the fleet, who is empowered to receive any written proposition addressed to the undersigned, and place at the disposal of the commissioners of his Imperial Majesty one of the vessels of the squadron.

"With the highest respect,

"M. C. PERRY,
"Commander-in-chief U. S. Naval Forces East India, China, and Japan seas."

It was calm in the morning, but before the Vandalia had reached Uraga a strong gale from the southwest, and directly ahead, prevented her from reaching the port, and made it necessary for her to anchor under Point Rubicon.* Captain Adams, accordingly, was not enabled to land, until the succeeding day. It being the twenty-second of February, Washington's birthday, the Vandalia commenced at noon firing a salute in honor of the occasion, and amidst the salvo of

Landing at Uraga.

artillery Captain Adams left the ship, accompanied by a score of officers and attendants, and landed at Uraga, where they were met by a large party of Japanese officials, who conducted them to a wooden pavilion, which evidently had been but lately constructed.

Captain Adams and his suite were ushered into a large hall, some fifty feet long and forty

---

* Point Rubicon was a headland, in the bay which had received that name from the Commodore, because it was just abreast of it where the surveying boats, on the first visit to Yedo Bay, had, in spite of some show of opposition on the part of the Japanese, persisted in carrying on the operations with success, and thus passed, as it were, the Rubicon.

wide. The floor was spread with soft mats of very fine texture, and at a distance of several feet from the walls, on either side, were arranged long settees covered with what appeared to be a red felt; in front of them were tables spread with a silken crape.

The Americans were invited, on entering, to take their seats on the left hand, which is esteemed by the Japanese the place of honor; this they had no sooner done than the Japanese prince, accompanied by two other high dignitaries, entered the hall, through a curtained opening which led into another compartment. As soon as these dignitaries presented themselves, the governor of Uraga, the interpreters, and various Japanese subordinates, who had accompanied the Americans, dropped at once upon their knees—a position they retained throughout the interview—and bowed their heads to the ground. The prince and his two associates took their seats on the right, opposite to the American officers, and a file of Japanese soldiers, amounting to half a hundred, marched in and ranged themselves, on their knees, behind the three dignitaries, in the space between their backs and the wall.

The prince, with his robes of richly embroidered silk, his fine presence, his benevolent and intelligent face, and his courtly manners, made quite an imposing appearance.

He first addressed Captain Adams, rising as he spoke, and expressed his pleasure at seeing him. His interpreters translated his Japanese into Dutch, which was then repeated in English by the American interpreter, Mr. Portman. The audience then commenced in form, and was conducted throughout with the most friendly expression of feeling on both sides.

Captain Adams commenced by stating, that it was quite evident that Uraga was not a proper place for the ships, since the anchorage was so much exposed. The Japanese replied, that it had been ordered by the Emperor to receive the Admiral there, and to deliver the answer to the President's letter there. Captain Adams, without at the moment pushing this subject further, handed his card to the prince, and requested his in return. He was told that he should have it in a few minutes, when the Japanese prince, requesting to be excused for a few moments, retired through the curtained door into an adjacent apartment. In the meantime the attendants handed round tea, in small China cups handsomely adorned, and borne upon wooden trays beautifully lacquered. The Japanese interpreters apologised for the meagreness of the repast, and entered into an informal conversation, in the course of which they asked for the names of the American officers who were present, and inquired whether they were satisfied with Uraga as a proper place for the reception of the President's letter.

This subject was uppermost in their minds, and they seemed resolved to press it on all occasions, as they were very desirous of preventing any nearer approach of the squadron to Yedo; being instructed, no doubt, to attempt to accomplish this purpose at all hazards. They were told that Captain Adams had a letter upon the subject from the Commodore, and were reminded of the severe weather to which the Vandalia had been exposed, and how impossible it was to place the squadron in a position so little protected against the stormy season then prevailing.

The prince now entered and his card was handed to Captain Adams, upon which was recorded his full name and title, thus: Hayashi-Daigaku-no-kami, *i. e.*, Hayashi, prince of Daigaku.

Captain Adams now handed the Commodore's letter, which has already been given in full, to the prince, accompanying it with a statement in regard to the insecure anchorage at Uraga, and the necessity of having shelter, space, and smooth water, for mooring the squadron, and repairing one of the ships which had become leaky. He also emphatically declared that it was quite impossible for the Commodore to come to Uraga, but that he would be very happy to send one of his steamers to convey the prince up the bay to a place of meeting, near the anchorage of the American ships.

The prince and his two coadjutors now retired to consider the Commodore's letter. In the meantime refreshments were presented, consisting of tea, of a cake resembling our sponge cake, candy, various fruits, and their saki.

A general conversation ensued in regard to the building which the Japanese said had been especially constructed for the meeting with the Commodore, the depth of the harbor, and other points of no material interest.

The Japanese interpreters, in answer to the objections urged against the security of the port of Uraga, insisted that it was perfectly safe, and requested Captain Adams to make a survey of it, in order to convince himself; and again and again earnestly urged upon him to entreat the Commodore to bring his ships there, and meet the Japanese high officers, who had been appointed to treat with him; saying that if he would come the whole treaty might be arranged before night. Captain Adams, in answer, said that he would inform the Commodore, when the conversation was interrupted by the reappearance of the three Japanese high dignitaries. Upon entering they announced that they had carefully perused the Commodore's letter three or four times, but were not prepared to give an answer, as they would be obliged to consult the other high officers appointed by the Emperor, and who were now in waiting at Uraga. On being asked when the answer would be ready, they appointed the third day after the interview. Captain Adams strove to impress upon them the necessity of dispatch, in consequence of the insecurity of the ship in the prevailing stormy weather at Uraga, and of explicitness in their answer, as the Commodore was anxious to bring matters to a conclusion, and to send to America one of his ships to report progress in the negotiations, and prevent others from coming out. The conference now being at an end, the prince and his coadjutors bowed politely and retired.

The weather being stormy and the water in the bay very rough, the American officers delayed their return to the Vandalia, and occupied the interval in strolling about and viewing the neighborhood. Hardly anything could be seen, however, of the town and the people, as the Japanese authorities had, in accordance with their usual custom, hemmed in the shore, on both sides of the audience hall, with cotton screens of some eight feet in height, which excluded the houses from the sight of the strangers. Crowds of men, women, and children could be observed, however, in the distance, thronging upon the surrounding hills, and gazing eagerly at the Americans. When the storm had somewhat abated, Captain Adams and his party, having been presented, in accordance with Japanese practice, with paper parcels containing the remains of the refreshments which had been left upon their plates or salvers, returned to their ship lying off the harbor. Some went back in the Vandalia's boats, while others accepted the offers of the Japanese officials, and put off in their craft. The superior excellence of the Japanese boats, in a sea, was admirably proved, by the fact that those on board of them reached the ship with dry jackets while the others were wet through and through by the dashing spray. The use of the scull instead of the oar, may partially account for this advantage of the Japanese boats, although their construction has something to do with it. The sculls never leave the water, while the oars are constantly in and out, dipping up considerable spray, which at every stroke is blown, in case of a high wind, all over the persons in a boat of our usual construction.

On the next morning (February 23) the Vandalia was still lying off Uraga, when our old acquaintance, Yezaiman, the governor of Uraga, presented himself. This, it will be remembered, was the dignitary who had figured so conspicuously during the first visit of the squadron to the Bay of Yedo. His absence hitherto had created great surprise, and it was naturally feared that his conduct on the previous occasion had not been approved of by his government, and that he had fallen into disgrace, or possibly had been reduced to the disagreeable necessity of disembowelling himself. He however explained his long absence on the score of illness, and the immense pressure of public business. He expressed great pleasure in seeing his old acquaintances, and proved himself the same affable, courteous gentleman, as on all previous occasions. Yezaiman explained the object of his visit by presenting a letter from himself, in which he informally, as he stated, though undoubtedly with the connivance of the government, repeated the assurances of the friendly disposition of the Emperor, and earnestly solicited Captain Adams to use his influence with the "Admiral" to prevail upon him to concede the point in regard to Uraga. Everything, of course, was referred to Commodore Perry, although the belief was expressed that he would resolutely adhere to his original determination. Yezaiman, having promised that the answer of the high officers to the Commodore's letter should be brought on board the next day, took his departure.

Accordingly early the next morning (February 24) the Japanese, having brought the dispatch in answer to the Commodore's letter, and having taken the occasion of urging their views about Uraga, for their first and last word was perpetually Uraga! Uraga! the Vandalia got under way to join the squadron at the American anchorage. The ship, however, had not proceeded far, when the steamers and sailing vessels were observed in the distance ahead, standing up the bay.

The Commodore, having little hope of any favorable result from the visit of Captain Adams to Uraga, had determined to put his threat into execution, and had actually removed the squadron, during the absence of the Vandalia, to a spot whence Yedo might be seen from the masthead. So near, indeed, did he approach to that capital, that the striking of the city bells during the night could be distinctly heard. As a measure of precaution, the surveying boats always sounded in advance of the ships, and when the Vandalia was seen to approach with Captain Adams on board, bearing the dispatch of the high officers at Uraga, the surveying party was absent engaged in further explorations toward Yedo. Next morning (February 25) while the squadron was anchored off the town of Kanagawa, one of the Vandalia's boats arrived, and came alongside the flagship, bringing Captain Adams, who handed the Commodore the following letter from the high officer:

"*To Admiral M. C. Perry:*

"The undersigned, ambassadors of the Emperor of Japan, have perused and understood the letter of the Lord Admiral, and in reply may remark:

"The Lord Admiral is right in going up to Yedo, to be received there according to the custom in Europe and America. According to the Japanese custom ambassadors are commissioned, and a building erected, for the reception of ambassadors from foreign countries in a friendly manner and with high consideration.

"The Emperor has sent us to Uraga to receive the Admiral with the highest honor, and to extend the Japanese hospitality towards him, and have the interview at that place in compliance with the order of the Emperor, regardless of the customs of foreign countries.

"We wish this to be well understood: we desire the Admiral to come to Uraga, there to have the interview with us in the building aforesaid, and would gratefully acknowledge the friendly meeting of the Lord Admiral in complying with this order of the Emperor and our own wishes.

"Our best wishes for the health of the Admiral.

"HAYASHI-DAIGAKU-NO-KAMI.

"*The 27th Siogoots*, 1854.

The arrival of Captain Adams was soon followed by that of Keyama Yezaiman, the governor of Uraga, who made his appearance with the alleged object of receiving a reply to the high officer's letter, but, as it will appear, for another purpose. Yezaiman commenced by inquiring whether the Commodore was still determined not to return to Uraga, and being answered in the affirmative, he again offered supplies, and was again told that wood and water would be received. Yezaiman replied that these articles would be cheerfully furnished, but that they could only be obtained at Uraga. He was then informed that it was a matter of indifference whence they came, but that the Commodore would not go to Uraga, and if the Japanese did not bring water to the ships, the Commodore would send on shore and procure it by some means.

Finding that the Commodore was immovable in purpose, and evidently inclined to approach nearer to Yedo, Yezaiman suddenly abandoned the previously pretended ultimatum of the Japanese commissioners, as to the place of meeting, and suggested a spot in the immediate neighborhood of the village of Yoku-hama, directly opposite to where the ships then were anchored.

Thus, after having interposed for the last ten days all possible objections to the squadron's moving further up the bay, and having used every inducement to prevail upon the Commodore to return to Uraga, they suddenly abandoned the position from which they had so frequently declared they could not possibly be moved. They had discovered that the Commodore was not to be shaken from his resolution, and finding that the ships had already approached within eight miles of their capital, they thought it politic to stop them there, while it was practicable, by a conciliatory concession.

The motive of the Commodore for thus persisting, with what may seem obstinacy, in his determination not to go to Uraga, is best explained by himself. In his communication to the honorable Secretary, on this subject, he thus writes:

"I was convinced that if I receded in the least from the position first assumed by me, it would be considered by the Japanese an advantage gained; and, finding that I could be induced to change a predetermined intention in one instance, they might rely on prevailing on me, by dint of perseverance, to waver in most other cases pending the negotiations; therefore, it seemed to be the true policy to hold out at all hazards, and rather to establish for myself a character for unreasonable obstinacy, than that of a yielding disposition. I knew that upon the impression thus formed by them would in a measure hinge the tenor of our future negotiations; and the sequel will show that I was right in my conclusions. Indeed, in conducting all my business with these very sagacious and deceitful people, I have found it profitable to bring to my aid the experience gained in former and by no means limited intercourse with the inhabitants of strange lands, civilized and barbarian; and this experience has admonished me that, with people of forms, it is necessary either to set all ceremony aside, or to out-Herod Herod in assumed personal consequence and ostentation.

"I have adopted the two extremes—by an exhibition of great pomp, when it could properly be displayed, and by avoiding it, when such pomp would be inconsistent with the spirit of our institutions; and by resolving never to recognise, on any occasion, the slightest personal superiority, always meeting the Japanese officials, however exalted their rank, with perfect equality, whilst those of comparative distinction, of their own nation, were cringing and kneeling to them; and from motives of policy, and to give greater importance to my own position, I have hitherto studiously kept myself aloof from intercourse with any of the subordinates of the court, making it known that I would communicate with none but the princes of the Empire. Up to this time, I have succeeded far beyond my expectations in maintaining this extreme point of diplomacy, and, as I believe, to very great advantage.

"It is probable that arrogance may be charged against me for persisting as I did, and against the judgment of all about me, in changing the place of conference, and thus compelling four princes of the Empire to follow the squadron, and subjecting the government to the trouble and expense of erecting another building; but I was simply adhering to a course of policy determined on after mature reflection, and which had hitherto worked so well."

The Commodore expressed a willingness to accede to the last proposition of the Japanese, provided his officers, on examining the place selected, should find it suitable. Captains Buchanan and Adams accordingly, having visited the spot in company with Yezaiman, returned with a favorable report. The situation was suitable in all respects, being near to Yedo, with safe and commodious anchorage at a mile distant from the shore, and affording abundant space for landing and exhibiting the presents intended for the Emperor. The Commodore accordingly determined to concur in the choice of the place now selected, and notified his resolution in the following communication:

"UNITED STATES FLAG-SHIP POWHATAN,
"At anchor off the town of Yoku-hama, Yedo Bay, March 1, 1854.

"YOUR EXCELLENCY: The letter of your excellency from Uraga was duly delivered by Captain Adams; and shortly after, when it was ascertained that I could not agree to return to Uraga, Keyama Yezaiman suggested that the negotiations might be conducted at a village opposite the present anchorage of the squadron.

"Being exceedingly desirous of meeting the wishes of your excellency, in every way consistent with the honor and interest of my country, and learning that the place pointed out was in all respects convenient for the purpose, I at once consented to defer my visit to Yedo until after the completion of the negotiations.

"I the more readily entered into this arrangement, as, on examination of the port by the surveying boats, it has been found that the ships can approach near to the city, where I propose at some future time to anchor them, as well to do honor to his Imperial Majesty by salutes, &c., as to be in full view of the palace, and convenient to be visited by such of the court as may desire to examine the steamers and their machinery, and I hardly need say that they will be kindly and politely received.

"With the most profound respect,
"M. C. PERRY,
"*Commander-in-chief United States Naval Forces East India, China, and Japan Seas, and Special Ambassador to Japan.*
"His Highness HAYASHI-DAIGAKU-NO-KAMI, &c., &c., &c."

The surveying boats had been kept busy during the progress of all this negotiation, and immediately after the Commodore had signified his intention of accepting the proposition of the Japanese offering Yoku-hama as the place of meeting, the party of surveyors returned to the Powhatan, and reported that they had found six fathoms of water within four or five miles of Yedo. This near approach to their capital was supposed to be the clue to the sudden change in the policy of the Japanese, as they doubtless feared that the Commodore would proceed at once to execute his threat of moving his squadron to Yedo, if the authorities still persisted in their demands for him to return to Uraga.

The Japanese now commenced constructing at once a wooden building for the proposed conference, and great numbers of workmen were seen busily engaged in bringing materials and putting them together in the form of a large and irregular structure. The ship's boats were sent out to examine the anchorage opposite the place, and the Commodore, after receiving a favorable report, directed (February 27) the squadron to be moored in a line abreast, and within a mile of Yoku-hama, covering with their guns an extent of shore of five miles. Captains Buchanan and Adams went ashore, soon after the anchoring of the ships, to see the buildings in progress of erection, and to instruct the Japanese workmen how to make the wharf for the landing of the Commodore and his party. Accordingly, when Yezaiman came on board the Powhatan, on March 3d, he alluded with some expression of anxiety to the fact of some of the Americans having landed, fearing, he said, lest some trouble might ensue, if this should be continued, between our people and the natives. As soon, however, as he was told the purpose of the visit, and of the Commodore's order that no one of his men should be allowed to land, he seemed satisfied.

Captain Adams now gave the governor of Uraga a letter which had been written to his friends by a Japanese who belonged to the squadron, and was generally known among the sailors by the soubriquet of Sam Patch. Sam was one of the crew, consisting of sixteen men, of a Japanese junk which had been driven off in a storm from the coast of Japan. An American merchant vessel, having fallen in with the junk, took the Japanese on board and conveyed them to San Francisco, where they were removed to a revenue cutter. They remained on board the cutter twelve months, when they were taken by the United States sloop-of-war St. Mary's to China, and there transferred to the Susquehanna. When this steamer joined Commodore Perry's squadron, bound to Japan, the Japanese all preferred to remain in China, lest if they returned home they should lose their lives, with the exception of Sam Patch, who remained on board, and being regularly shipped as one of the crew, was with the squadron on the first, as he was now on the second, visit to Japan. Upon his letter being presented to Yezaiman he was requested to deliver it in accordance with the direction, which he promised to do, but the Japanese seemed very much surprised at the fact of one of their countrymen being among the crew, and expressed an earnest desire to see him. Yezaiman was accordingly promised that his request should be complied with in the course of a few days.

Yezaiman and his interpreters, to whom there was now added a new one, of the name of Moryama Yenoske, who spoke a little English, which he was said to have acquired from an American sailor who had been a captive in Japan, and was one of those taken away by the Preble, came off daily to the ships. As the building on shore was in progress, the details of its erection, and the prospective interview ashore, were naturally daily topics of conversation. The coming ceremonies were spoken of, and the rank and number of those who were to participate in them discussed. Yezaiman, in accordance with the request of the Commodore, submitted the names and credentials of the high commissioners who were to represent the government of Japan at the approaching conference. The following is a translation of the letter of credence of the imperial officers:

HAYASHI DAIGAKU-NO-KAMI, IDO-TSUS-SIMA-NO-KAMI, IZAWA MEMA-SAKI-NO-KAMI, UDONO MIMBUSCO:

You are hereby empowered to hold interviews with his excellency the American ambassador on his arrival, and to negotiate concerning the business which has been communicated to you.

SIOGOOTS.　　　　　　　　　　　　　　KA-EI-SILSI-NEU. [SEAL OF THE EMPEROR.]

Yezaiman having said, that now as his government knew the Americans better, and had entire confidence in them, there would be no Japanese soldiers brought out at the coming interview at Yoku-hama, as before at Gora-hama, he was assured that the guard that would accompany the Commodore was only intended to do honor to the occasion. A conversation then ensued which, as it refers to the important subject of the resources of Japan, in regard to coal and other supplies, is thought of sufficient importance to give verbatim, as reported by the Commodore's secretary. Captain Adams, it will be observed, was still acting in behalf of Commodore Perry, as the latter continued his policy of seclusion.

Yezaiman (having first alluded to the fact of the President's letter stating that coal would be probably wanted by American steamers touching on the coast of Japan) asked, "How much shall you need annually?"

Captain Adams. "It is quite impossible now to say what amount will be needed; ships will call and get what they want. The Commodore, however, will speak on this point with the commissioners."

Yezaiman. "We have plenty of coal, but a port is asked for to get it from—that is, a port where a ship can take it in conveniently."

Captain Adams. "Yes: a port lying along the southern shores of Nippon would be most convenient, but the Commodore will arrange that. Where is the best coal found?"

Yezaiman. "The most abundant supply and the best coal come from Kiusiu. I do not know how much there is in Nippon, but there is none in Sikok." Yezaiman then changed the subject by asking, "What sort of provisions do you want? We have the greatest abundance of wheat and vegetables at Nagasaki."

Captain Adams. "Our ships will only take such supplies as you can furnish."

Yezaiman. "Our principal supplies are pork, beef, sheep, poultry, and vegetables of many kinds, but no Irish potatoes."*

Captain Adams. "Did you give the Russians any coal?"

Yezaiman. "Yes: a little from time to time, and they said it was very good." Yezaiman then promised to bring a specimen of their coal, which he said was a fuel seldom used by the Japanese.

The arrival of the Saratoga, on the fourth of March, was quite an event to all the officers and men in the squadron, who, confined to the narrow limits of an anchored ship, month after month, with no variety in the daily routine of duty, and no change of scene from the monotonous view of the same look-out from deck, gladly welcomed anything that could break up for

---

* Yezaiman means at Nagasaki, where limited supplies of these articles are kept for strangers. The Japanese, in general, do not use the meats here named.

a moment the tedium of their life. The Saratoga had experienced very severe weather, which those in the squadron, although sheltered in a safe anchorage, could readily understand, for the season, even in the bay, had given evidence enough of its rude inclemency. Frequently the wind was so high and the waters of the bay so disturbed, that the surveying boats were obliged to intermit their labors. The frequent recurrence of rain, alternating with an occasional snow-storm, and a cold temperature more penetrating to the sensations, from its moisture, gave all a very disagreeable experience of a Japan winter. The hard-working Japanese boatmen seemed alone insensible to the weather, and, as they worked vigorously at their long sculls, sung cheerily, as if their half-naked bodies were as much proof against cold wind and boisterous weather, as their tight built craft.

According to agreement, Sam Patch was brought forward and presented to the Japanese officials, and no sooner did he behold these dignitaries than he prostrated himself at once, apparently completely awe-stricken. Sam had been frequently laughed at during the voyage by his messmates, and teazed by statements of the danger to which his head would be exposed on his arrival in his own country, and the poor fellow possibly thought his last hour had come. Captain Adams ordered him to rise from his knees, upon which he was crouching with the most abject fear and trembling in every limb. He was reminded that he was on board an American man-of-war, perfectly safe as one of her crew, and had nothing to fear; but it being found impossible to reassure him while in the presence of his countrymen, he was soon dismissed. But more of Sam hereafter.

The eighth of March had been appointed by the Commodore as the day for the conference ashore; and, as crowds of Japanese laborers kept busily at work upon the building, there seemed every prospect of its being ready in time. When the building was finished, the usual Japanese deputation, headed by Yezaiman, came off to the Powhatan, and, announcing the fact, asked if the Admiral would be ready to land on the next day, (March 8.) They were told that, provided the weather should be suitable, the Commodore and his party would leave the squadron at twelve o'clock on the morrow. Yezaiman entered into some preliminary explanations in regard to the ceremonies on the occasion. He asked the number and names of all the officers in the squadron, with the purpose, as he said, of providing presents for each. Upon being asked whether the chief of the commissioners appointed to negotiate with the Commodore was next in rank to the Emperor, Yezaiman answered that he was, and at the same time corrected a previous statement, saying that, instead of four dignitaries in addition to the high commissioner, there would be five. With the usual courtly assurances of kindly feeling, Yezaiman and his suite took leave, saying, as he departed, that he would send a person on board next day to conduct the Commodore and his party to the land.

Yoku-hama, Bay of Yedo.

CHAPTER XIX.

SHIPS ANCHORED IN YOKU-HAMA BAY SO AS TO COMMAND THE SHORE.—KANAGAWA "TREATY HOUSE."—IMPERIAL BARGE.—LANDING OF THE COMMODORE.—DESCRIPTION OF THE JAPANESE COMMISSIONERS.—INTERPRETERS.—SERVILITY TO SUPERIORS.—NEGOTIATIONS COMMENCED.—COMMODORE SUBMITS A COPY OF THE TREATY OF THE UNITED STATES WITH CHINA FOR CONSIDERATION.—DEATH OF ONE OF OUR MEN.—COMMODORE PROPOSES TO BUY A BURIAL GROUND FOR AMERICANS.—COMMISSIONERS PROPOSE TO SEND THE BODY OF THE DECEASED TO NAGASAKI FOR INTERMENT—COMMODORE REFUSES AND PROPOSES TO BURY THE DEAD ON WEBSTER'S ISLAND.—COMMISSIONERS CONSENT TO THE INTERMENT AT YOKU-HAMA.—THE BURIAL BY CHAPLAIN JONES.—INTEREST OF THE JAPANESE IN THE CEREMONY.—THEY AFTERWARD PERFORM THEIR OWN RITES OVER THE COVERED GRAVE.—THE JAPANESE BUILD AN ENCLOSURE AROUND THE SPOT.—JAPANESE ARTISTS ATTEMPT THE PORTRAITS OF OUR OFFICERS.—ANSWER TO THE PRESIDENT'S LETTER.—INFORMAL CONFERENCE BETWEEN CAPTAIN ADAMS AND YENOSKE.—LANDING AND DELIVERY OF THE PRESENTS.—JAPANESE WORKMEN ASSIST THE AMERICANS IN PREPARING FOR THEIR EXHIBITION.—NEGOTIATIONS CONTINUED.—SURPRISE AND DELIGHT OF THE JAPANESE AT THE TELEGRAPH AND RAILROAD.—CURIOSITY OF THE JAPANESE IN EXAMINING MECHANISM.—PASSION FOR BUTTONS.—NOTE-TAKING OF EVERYTHING STRANGE TO THEM.—LOVE OF PICTURES.—DRAWINGS.—COMMON PEOPLE DISPOSED TO SOCIAL INTERCOURSE WITH THE AMERICANS.—EXCITEMENT ON CHAPLAIN BITTINGER'S ATTEMPT TO REACH YEDO BY LAND.—WRITTEN REPLY OF COMMISSIONERS, DECLINING TO MAKE A TREATY LIKE THAT OF THE UNITED STATES WITH CHINA.—FURTHER NEGOTIATIONS.—ACCURACY OF THE JAPANESE IN NOTING ALL THE DISCUSSIONS.—PORTS OF SIMODA AND HAKODADI AGREED TO, BUT WITH GREAT DIFFICULTY ON THE PART OF THE JAPANESE.

ALONG the western side of the Bay of Yedo, from its mouth, where it opens into the Gulf of Yedo, to the capital, there is almost a continuous range of towns and villages. The only breaks in this otherwise uninterrupted scene of populousness are the projecting spurs of the highlands, which, presenting less advantage for habitation, naturally prevent the erection of dwelling houses. These promontories, however, are covered with batteries, which are more formidable in aspect than in reality, for their guns are but of small calibre, and the defences slight in construction. Yoku-hama is one of these numerous and populous villages, and is situated at the head of a bay called on the American charts "Yoku-hama Bay," which is formed by Point Hope, on the southeast, and the neck of land extending northeast from Kanagawa to the suburb of the city of Yedo, termed Sinagawa, and near to which the junks resorting to the capital usually anchor. At the position in front of Yoku-hama there was just sufficient room to anchor in a line of battle the whole squadron; the guns of the several ships commanding an extent of shore equal to their entire range. It was in this position that the Commodore had placed his nine ships—the steam frigates, the Powhatan, which was the flag-ship, the Susquehanna, and the Mississippi, and the sailing ships, the Macedonian, the Vandalia, the Saratoga, the Southampton, the Lexington, and the Supply, the latter having subsequently joined the squadron.*

Kanagawa is quite a large town, and was the residence of the Japanese commissioners pending the negotiations of the treaty, and it would have been selected by Commodore Perry for the place of conference, had it not been for the impossibility of the ships approaching within gunshot of its front towards the bay. He therefore preferred to select Yoku-hama, to confirm the choice of Captains Buchanan and Adams, who had been sent to examine and report upon the most eligible anchorage for the squadron.

The building erected for the accommodation of the Japanese commissioners and the Commodore, and the numerous persons in attendance, and which was called by the Americans the "treaty house," was placed upon a level plain near to the shore, and contiguous to the village of Yoku-hama, being distant from Kanagawa three, from the southern suburb of the capital five, and from Yedo itself probably nine miles. The treaty house had been hastily erected of unpainted pine wood, with peaked roofs, and covered a large extent of ground, having a reception hall of from forty to sixty feet in area, and several adjoining apartments and offices. From each side extended yellow canvas screens divided into panel-like squares by black painted stripes. On the exterior walls of the building was spread a dark cloth, upon which was represented in bright colors some device which was said to be the arms of the third commissioner, Izawa, prince of Mimasaki.

At an early hour on the 8th of March, the day appointed for the conference with the Japanese commissioners, there was an unusual stir ashore preparatory to the ceremonies of the occasion. The Japanese workmen were busily engaged in adorning the treaty house with streamers and other gay paraphernalia. Two poles were erected, one on either side of the entrance, to which were hung long oblong banners of white cotton cloth with a bright red stripe across the centre. On the peaked roof of the building was placed a tall staff, surmounted with a circular ornament in shape like the upper part of a chandelier, from which was suspended a heavy silken tassel. In the preparation of the place it had been surrounded by the usual enclosure of cloth, which completely excluded it from the view of those without, and, in fact, seemed to enclose it within a sort of prison yard. The Commodore, who saw this arrangement from his ship before he landed, immediately sent an officer on shore to demand what it meant, and, in answer to some frivolous pretext about preventing intrusion and doing honor to the occasion, informed the Japanese that he would forego the honor, and that, until it was completely removed, he could not think of landing. It was immediately taken down by the Japanese.

Bands of flag-bearers, musicians and pikemen manœuvred in order here and there, glistening with their lacquered caps, bright colored costumes, crimson streamers, showy emblazonry, and burnished spears. There was no great military display as on the first visit at Gora-hama, and the few who had the look of soldiers were merely a small body guard, composed of the retainers of the various high dignitaries who were to officiate on the occasion. Crowds of people had

---

* The Supply arrived with coal and stores for the squadron on the 19th of March.

gathered from the neighboring towns and villages, and were thronging in curious eagerness on either side of a large open space on the shore, which was kept free from intrusion by barriers, within which none of the spectators were allowed to enter. Two or three officials were seen busily moving about, now directing the workmen, and again checking the disorder among the Japanese multitude.

Soon a large barge came floating down the bay, from the neighboring town of Kanagawa. This was a gaily painted vessel, which, with its decks and open pavilion rising high above the hull, had very much the appearance of one of our western river steamboats, while streamers floated

Imperial Barge at Yoku-hama.

from its three masts, and bright colored flags and variegated drapery adorned the open deck above. This barge bore the Japanese commissioners, and when it had reached to within a short distance of the shore, these dignitaries and their suites disembarked in several boats and hurried to the land. An immense number of Japanese craft of all kinds, each with a tassel at its prow and a square striped flag at its stern, gathered about the bay. The day was fresh and clear, and everything had a cheerful aspect, in spite of the lingering wintry look of the landscape.

The Commodore had made every preparation to distinguish the occasion of his second landing in Japan by all necessary parade, knowing, as he did, the importance and moral influence of such show upon so ceremonious and artificial a people as the Japanese. He had, accordingly, issued orders to the effect that all the marines who could be spared from duty should appear on the occasion in full accoutrement, that the bands of music from the three steamers should be present, and all the officers and sailors that could possibly leave. The officers were to be in undress uniform, frock coats, cap and epaulets, and equipped with swords and pistols. The sailors were to be armed with muskets, cutlasses and pistols, and dressed in blue jackets and trowsers and white frocks. The musicians were each to be supplied with cutlass and pistol, and every man of the escort provided with either musket or pistol cartridge boxes.

At half-past eleven o'clock the escort, consisting of about five hundred officers, seamen and marines, fully armed, embarked in twenty-seven boats, under the command of Commander Buchanan, and forming a line abreast, pulled in good order to the shore. When the escort had landed, the marines were drawn up in a hollow square, leaving a wide open space between them, while the naval officers remained in a group at the wharf. The ship's boats were arranged in two separate divisions of equal numbers on either side of the landing, with their bows pointing in regular order from the shore. The Commodore now embarked from the Powhatan in his barge, under a salute from the Macedonian of seventeen guns. The Commodore, on landing, was received by the group of officers, who, falling into a line, followed him. The bands now struck up a lively tune, and the marines, whose orderly ranks in complete military appointment, with their blue and white uniforms, and glistening bayonets, made quite a martial and effective show, presented arms as the Commodore, followed in procession by his immediate staff, his guard of fine looking sailors and a number of his subordinate officers, proceeded up the shore. A group of richly costumed Japanese guards, or retainers, with banners, flags and streamers, were gathered on each side of the entrance of the treaty house. As the Commodore and his party passed up between these they were met by a large number of Japanese officials who came out, and uncovering, conducted them into the interior of the building. As they entered, by a preconcerted arrangement, howitzers which had been mounted on the bows of the larger ship's boats, that were floating just by the shore, commenced firing in admirable order a salute of twenty-one guns in honor of the Emperor, which were succeeded by a salute of seventeen for Hayashi Daigaku-no-kami, the high commissioner, and the hoisting of the Japanese striped flag from the masthead of the steamer Powhatan in the bay.

The apartment into which the Commodore and his officers first entered was a large hall, arranged in a similar manner to that at Gori-hama. Thick rice-straw mats carpeted the floor, long and wide settees, covered with a red cloth, extended along the sides, with tables spread with the same material arranged in front of them. The windows were composed of panes of oiled paper, through which a subdued and mellow light illuminated the hall, while a comfortable temperature was kept up—for, although the spring, which is early in Japan, had already opened, the weather was chilly—by copper braziers of burning charcoal, which, supported upon lacquered wooden stands, were freely distributed about. Hangings fell from the walls around, with paintings of trees, and representations of various animals and birds, particularly of the crane, with its long neck in every variety of strange involution.

The Commodore and his officers and interpreters had hardly taken their seats on the left, the place of honor, and the various Japanese officials, of whom there was a goodly number, theirs on the right, when the five commissioners entered from an apartment which opened through an entrance at the upper end of the hall. As soon as they presented themselves the subordinate Japanese officials prostrated themselves on their knees, and remained in that attitude during their presence.

The commissioners were certainly august looking personages, and their grave but courteous manners, and their rich flowing robes of silk, set them off to the highest advantage. Their costume consisted of an under garment somewhat similar to the antique doublet, and a pair of very wide and short trowsers of figured silk, while below the legs were encased in white cotton

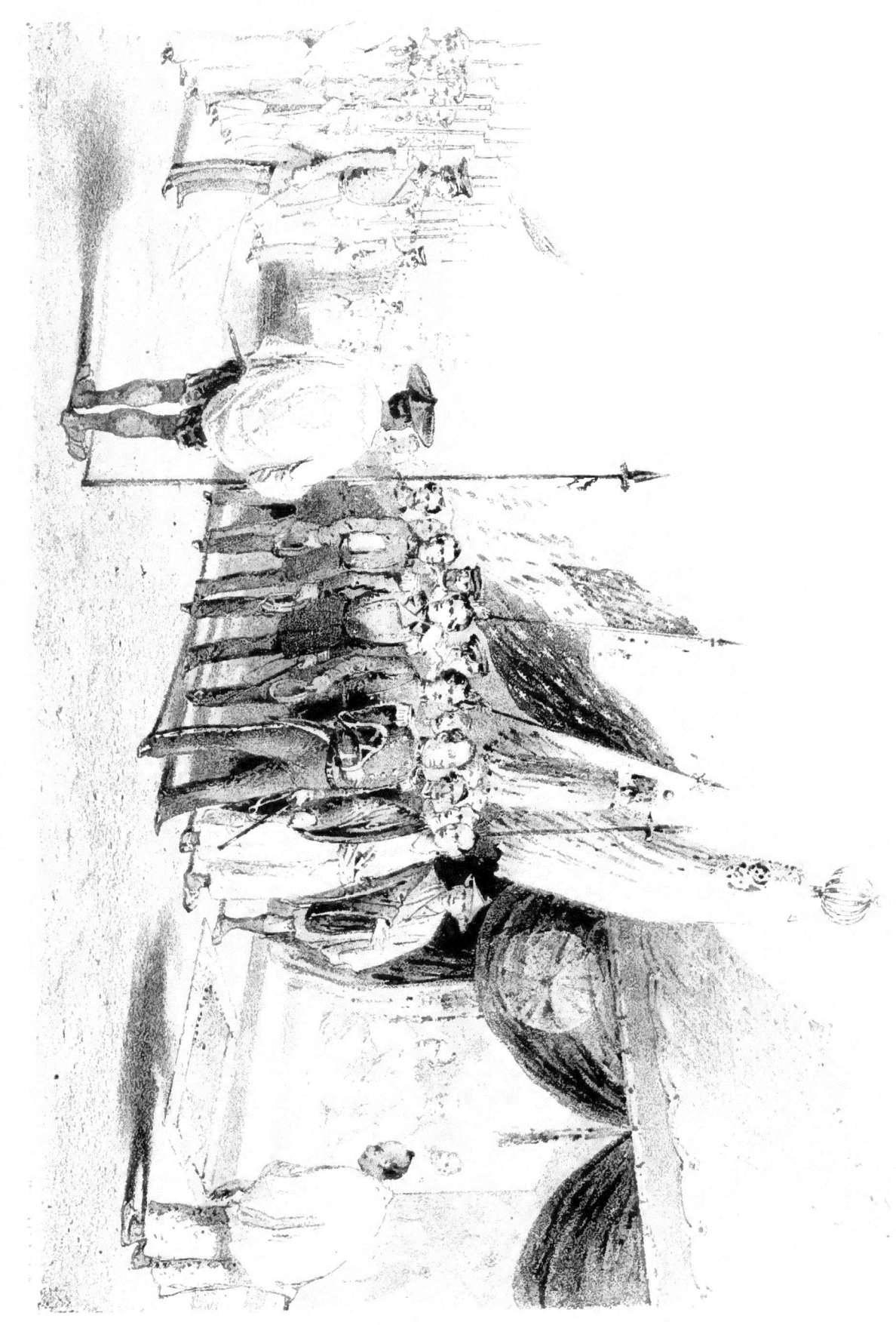

or woollen socks, laced to some distance above the ankles. The socks were so contrived that the great toe was separated from the other four for the passage of the band which attached to the sandal, and joined another from the heel at the ankle, where the two were tied together. Over the doublet and trowsers a loose gown of embroidered silk, something in the shape of the clerical robe, with loose sleeves, was worn. This was secured to the waist by a sash, in which are usually thrust the two swords which mark the dignitaries of higher rank. The three princes alone, of all the commissioners, were observed to wear a white inner shirt, or vest, which was exposed at the breast. This was a mark of the very highest rank, and belongs exclusively to princes and the loftiest dignitaries of the Empire.

Hayashi Daigaku-no-kami, prince councillor, was evidently the chief member of the commission, for all matters of importance were referred to him. He was a man of about fifty-five years of age, was handsomely formed, and had a grave and rather saturnine expression of face, though he had a benevolent look and exceedingly courtly manners. Ido, Prince of Tsusima, was probably fifty, or thereabout, and was corpulent and tall in person. He had a rather more vivacious expression than the elder Hayashi. The third and youngest of the princes was the Prince of Mima-saki, who could hardly be much beyond forty years of age, and was far the best looking of the three. He was quite gay, fond of fun and frolic, and had the reputation of being a Lothario. According to the interpreters, Mima-saki entertained more liberal views with respect to foreign intercourse than any of his coadjutors, and seemed to be a great favorite with the Japanese, as he certainly was with all the Americans. His gaiety of heart manifested itself very apparently in his fondness for the music of the bands of the squadron, and he could not keep his hands and feet quiet whenever they struck up a lively air.

Udono, who, though not a prince, was a man of high station, and was known by the title of Mimbu-shiyoyu, or member of the board of revenue, was a tall, passable looking man, but his features were prominent and had much of the Mongolian caste. The fifth and last one of the five commissioners was Matsusaki Michitaro, whose rank and title were not discovered. Indeed, he had not been originally named to the Americans as one of the commissioners. In reply to the inquiries made, they at first said there were four; and afterward, at a subsequent interview, the interpreter remarked, as if casually, that a fifth commissioner had been added. Possibly he was the official public spy appointed to remind the others, by his presence, of their duty, and we may add, danger. Whatever may have been his official position, his precise business in the commission it was difficult to fathom; he was always present at the conference, but took his seat constantly at rather a remote distance from the other dignitaries, on the further end of the sedan. By him there was continually crouched, upon his knees, a scribe, who was constantly employed in taking notes of what was passing, and occasionally under the promptings of his superior. Matsusaki was rather an equivocal character, difficult to understand. As far as could be observed, he did not seem to be called into consultation, at least publicly, and from the circumstance of not sitting with the other commissioners, his rank and powers seemed to be inferior to theirs. This, however, is but conjectural. Our officers, of course, asked no questions, though all agreed in the decidedly unfavorable impression made upon them by Matsusaki. For aught they knew, he might have been the Emperor himself, though it is most unlikely; and if he were, all that can be said is that he was much less polished and agreeable than his prince commissioners. He was, as we have intimated, probably the court spy. He was a man of sixty years of age at least, had a long, drawn-out meagre body, a very yellow bilious face, an uncomfortable dyspeptic expression, which his excessive short-sightedness did not improve, for it caused him, in his efforts at seeing, to give a very wry distortion to a countenance naturally not very handsome.*

Moryama Yenoske was the principal interpreter who officiated on the occasion; the same man who figured so conspicuously during the visit of Captain Glynn in the Preble. As soon as the commissioners had taken their seats, Yenoske took his position on his knees, at the feet of Hayashi, the chief, and humbly awaited his orders. The Japanese are never forgetful of the respect which they think due to rank, and graduate their obeisance according to its degrees. From the Emperor to the lowest subject in the realm there is a constant succession of prostrations. The former, in want of a human being superior to himself in rank, bows humbly to some Pagan idol, and every one of his subjects, from prince to peasant, has some person before whom he is bound to cringe and crouch in the dirt. One is reminded, as he looks upon a universal nation on their knees, "in suppliance bent," of a favorite amusement of childhood, where a number of blocks are placed on end in a row, one shoves the other, and the first being knocked down, topples over the second, and so on in succession until all are tumbled upon the ground. The crouching position in which an inferior places himself, when in the presence of his superior in rank, seems very easy to a Japanese, but would be very difficult and painful for one to assume who had not been accustomed to it. The ordinary mode pursued is to drop on

---

* It may not be without interest to the reader to present the heraldic devices of the Emperor and commissioners, as well as that of Lew Chew.

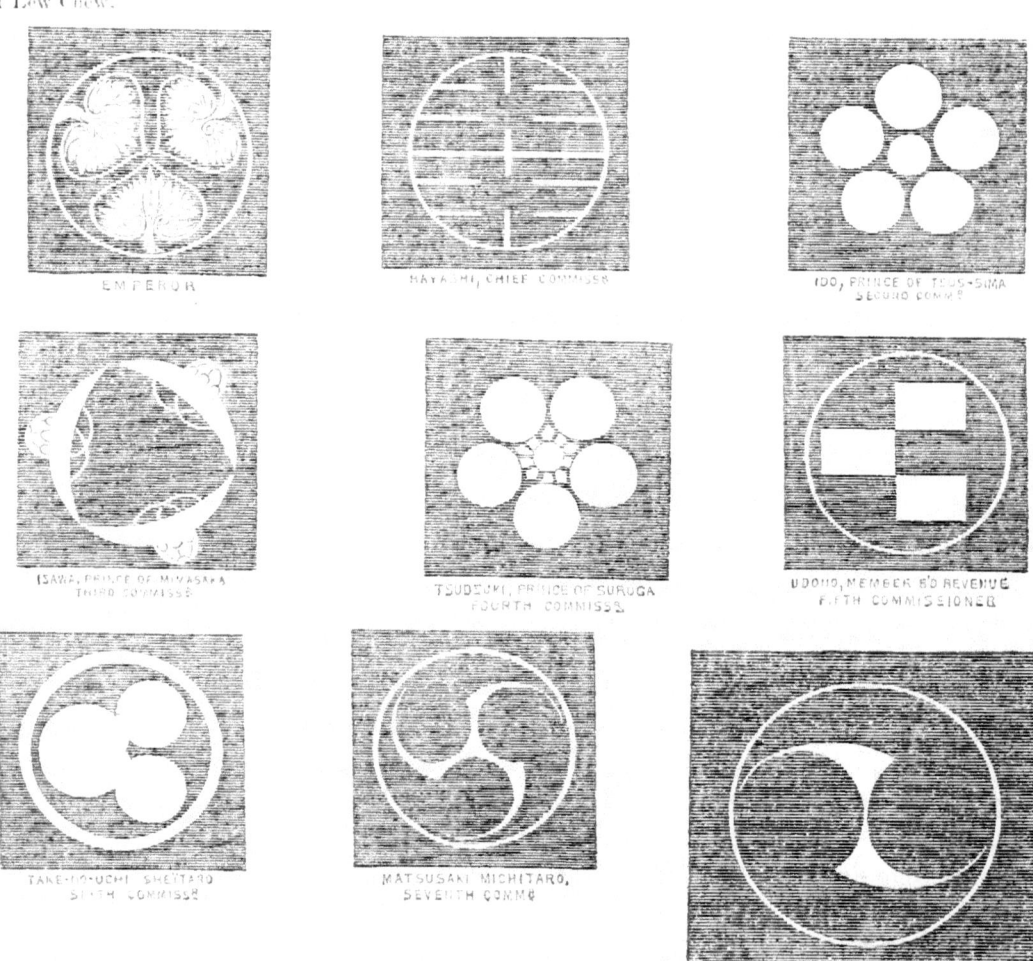

the knees, cross the feet, and turn up the heels, with the toes, instep, and calves of the legs brought together into close contact.

Sometimes it is mere squatting down with the soles firm upon the ground, the knees bent, and the body crouched low. Yenoske was quite an adept in these manœuvres, as were his coadjutors, and especially the prefect, Kura-kawa-kahei, who was one of the subordinate functionaries present during the conference. They all showed a wonderful elasticity of muscle and suppleness of joint which could only have been acquired by long practice, and reminded one of those skilful contortionists or clowns, who exhibit their caoutchouc accomplishments to the wonderment of the spectators. These worthies, humble as they were in the august presence of the commissioners, had their worshippers in turn, who were more humble still, and who outdid them, even, in their bowings and prostrations. Every Japanese is thus by turns master and slave, now submissively with his neck beneath the foot of one, and again haughtily with his foot upon the neck of another. The commissioners, after a momentary silence, spoke a word to the prostrate Yenoske, who listened an instant, with downcast eyes, and then by a skilful manœuvre, still upon his knees, moved toward the commissioners' interpreter, and having communicated his message, which proved to be merely the ordinary compliments, with an inquiry after the health of the Commodore and his officers, returned with an appropriate answer to his former position. An interchange of various polite messages having been thus borne backward and forward for several minutes, through the medium of the humble but useful Yenoske, refreshments, consisting of the invariable pipe, tea in porcelain cups, served on lacquered trays, cakes, and some confectionary were handed round.

It was now proposed by the commissioners that an adjournment should take place to another room, which they stated would accommodate comfortably about ten persons. Accordingly, the Commodore having assented, he, accompanied by the captain of the fleet, his two interpreters and secretary, were conducted into another and much smaller room, the entrance to which was only separated from the principal hall by a blue silk flag, ornamented in the centre with the embroidered arms of Japan. On entering, the commissioners were found already seated on the right, they having withdrawn previously to the Commodore, and arranged themselves in rank upon one of the red divans, which extended along the sides of the apartment.

The Commodore and his party took their seats on the left, and business commenced, the commissioners having preliminarily stated that it was a Japanese custom to speak slowly. They were evidently very anxious to proceed with deliberation, and weigh every word with the exactness of cautious diplomatists.

The chief commissioner now handed the Commodore a long roll of paper, which proved to be an answer to the President's letter, delivered on the previous visit at Gori-hama in July.

Translation of answer to the letter of the President to the Emperor of Japan.

"The return of your excellency, as ambassador of the United States to this Empire, has been expected according to the letter of his Majesty the President, which letter your excellency delivered last year to his Majesty the Emperor of this Empire.

"It is quite impossible to give satisfactory answers at once to all the proposals of your government, as it is most positively forbidden by the laws of our Imperial ancestors: but for us to continue attached to the ancient laws, seems to misunderstand the spirit of the age; however, we are governed now by imperative necessity.

"At the visit of your excellency last year to this Empire, his Majesty the former Emperor was sick, and is now dead. Subsequently, his Majesty the present Emperor ascended the throne; the many occupations in consequence thereof are not yet finished, and there is no time to settle other business thoroughly. Moreover, his Majesty the new Emperor, at the succession to the throne, promised to the princes and high officers of the Empire to observe the laws. It is therefore evident that he cannot now bring about any alteration in the ancient laws.

"Last autumn, at the departure of the Dutch ship, the superintendent of the Dutch trade in Japan was requested to inform your government of this event, and a reply in writing has been received.

"At Nangasaki arrived recently the Russian ambassador to communicate a wish of his government. He has since left the said place, because no answer would be given to any nation that might communicate similar wishes. However, we admit the urgency of, and shall entirely comply with, the proposals of your government concerning coal, wood, water, provisions, and the saving of ships and their crews in distress. After being informed which harbor your excellency selects, that harbor shall be prepared, which preparation it is estimated will take about five years. Meanwhile a commencement can be made with the coal at Nangasaki by the next Japanese first month, (Siogoots,) (16th of February, 1855.)

"Having no precedent with respect to coal, we request your excellency to furnish us with an estimate, and upon due consideration this will be complied with, if not in opposition to our laws. What do you understand by provisions, and how much coal?

"Finally, anything ships may be in want of that can be furnished from the production of this Empire shall be supplied. The prices of merchandise and articles of barter to be fixed by Kurakawa Kahei and Moryama Yenoske. After settling the points before mentioned, the treaty can be concluded and signed at the next interview.

"Seals attached by order of the high gentlemen.

"MORYAMA YENOSKE."

The Commodore having returned the document, requesting it should be signed by the high commissioner, and delivered to him next day, entered at once upon the subject which was uppermost in his mind, the negotiation of a treaty. He remarked that it would be better for the two nations that a treaty similar to the one between the United States and China should be made. He had been sent, he continued, by his government to make a treaty, and if he did not succeed, the United States would probably send more ships to make one; but he hoped that everything would be soon settled in an amicable manner, and that he would be enabled to send two of his ships, as he desired, to prevent others from coming. A copy of the Chinese treaty, written in English, Chinese, and Dutch, accompanied by two notes from the Commodore, and a letter in answer to one sent by the high commissioner from Uraga, were now handed to the Japanese, when they asked for time to have the documents translated into their own language.

Notes handed to First Commissioner on Wednesday, March 8, 1854.

The American ambassador learns with pleasure that the Japanese government is disposed to enter into some friendly arrangement with the United States. As such is happily the case, it would be much more advantageous to both nations, and especially to Japan, if a treaty is agreed upon, even if it be of short duration; for reason that the citizens and subjects of both the contracting powers would be mutually bound by law to conform to all its stipulations, and thus prevent mistakes and consequent disputes.

This is the practice with all other nations; and such is the present condition of the world, that these treaties have become necessary to avert contention and war. The obligations to conform to them are enjoined as well by considerations of honor, as the preservation of the peace and prosperity of the respective countries; and it would be impossible for the western nations to preserve friendly intercourse if it were not for similar treaties.

Although we have abundance of prepared provisions in the squadron, it would be desirable to obtain daily supplies of fresh meat, vegetables, &c., for which we would pay the prices demanded. Wood and water will, of course, be wanted, and for a supply of which we shall be thankful.

The health of the officers and men require that they should have exercise on shore; and though I have hitherto, out of respect to the Japanese laws, forbidden any one to land except for purposes of duty, I feel assured that some arrangement will be made to admit of some reasonable intercourse with the neighborhood.

Copies of the surveys which the officers are employed in making will be presented to the Imperial government; and, to make them more perfect, it will be necessary to place signal-poles at some points on shore by which to measure the angles; therefore it is requested that the officers landing for such purposes may not be molested.

It is thought that the business of the negotiation would be facilitated by submitting the several questions and replies that may arise in writing.

M. C. PERRY.

UNITED STATES FLAG-SHIP POWHATAN,
Yedo Bay, off the town of Yoku-hama, March 1, 1854.

YOUR EXCELLENCY: In presenting for the consideration of your highness the accompanying draught of a treaty, which, in all its essential features, is identical with that at present subsisting between the United States and China, I again venture to urge upon the Imperial government of Japan the importance of establishing a friendly understanding with the nation which I have the honor on this occasion to represent.

It would be needless in me to reiterate the arguments already advanced in support of a measure so fraught with the best interests of the two nations, and so necessary to the peace and prosperity of Japan.

I have in a former communication remarked that the President of the United States entertains the strongest desire, and cherishes a most fervent hope, that the mission which he has intrusted to my charge may result in the accomplishment of a treaty mutually beneficial, and tending to avert, by timely negotiation, the consequences that would otherwise grow out of collisions certain to arise, should the present undefined relations between the two countries much longer continue.

In the increasing number of American ships almost daily passing and repassing the territories of Japan, the President is apprehensive of the occurrence of some further act of hostility towards the unoffending citizens of the United States who may be thrown by misfortune upon your shores, and hence his wish to establish a treaty of friendship, which shall give assurance of the discontinuance of a course of policy, on the part of the Japanese, altogether at variance with the usages of other nations, and no longer to be tolerated by the United States.

As an evidence of the friendly intentions of the President, and to pay the highest honor to his Imperial Majesty, he has sent me in command of a number of ships—to be increased by others which are to follow—not only to bear to his Majesty the letter which I have already presented, but to evince, by every suitable act of kindness, the cordial feelings entertained by him towards Japan.

That there might be sufficient time allowed for a full consideration of the just and reasonable demands of the President, I took upon myself to withdraw the ships in July last from the coast, and have now, after an absence of seven months, returned, in the full expectation of a most satisfactory arrangement.

Another proof of the friendly disposition of the President has been given in his sending for exhibition to the Imperial court three of the magnificent steamers of the United States, of which there are many thousands, large and small, in America; and he has also sent, for presentation to the Emperor, many specimens of the most useful inventions of our country.

Therefore, after all these demonstrations of good will, it would be strange if the Japanese government did not seize upon this very favorable occasion to secure a friendly intercourse with a people anxious to prevent, by wise and prudent foresight, all causes of future misunderstanding and strife.

It will be observed that there is no western nation so intimately connected with the peace and welfare of Japan as the United States, a part of whose territory lies opposite the Imperial coast, and whose commerce covers the Pacific ocean and Japan seas; not less than five hundred large ships being engaged exclusively in those regions in pursuit of whales, the crews of many of which suffer for want of water and other refreshments; and it would seem nothing more than common humanity to receive those who may seek shelter in the ports of Japan with kindness and hospitality.

The government of China has derived much benefit from its treaty with the United States. The purchase of teas by the Americans during the present year will amount to three million six hundred thousand (3,600,000) taels, and of raw and manufactured silks to nearly three millions (3,000,000) of taels.

Nearly thirty thousand subjects of the Emperor of China have visited America, where they have been kindly received, and permitted by the American laws to engage in whatever occupation best suited them. They have also been allowed to erect temples, and to enjoy in all freedom their religious rites. All have accumulated money, and some have returned to China, after a short absence, with sums varying from 300 to 10,000 taels.

I have adverted to these facts merely to show the advantages that would grow out of such a treaty as I now propose, and to remark again that some amicable arrangement between the two nations has become positively necessary, and for reasons already explained.

Indeed, I shall not dare to return to the United States without carrying with me satisfactory responses to all the proposals of the President, and I must remain until such are placed in my possession.

With the most profound respect,

M. C. PERRY,
Commander-in-chief U. S. Naval Forces East India,
China, and Japan Seas, and special Ambassador to Japan.

His Highness HAYASHI-DAIGAKU-NO-KAMI, &c., &c.

One of the marines belonging to the Mississippi had died two days previous to the conference, and the suitable interment of his body now came up in course of discussion. The Commodore proposed to buy a piece of ground from the Japanese for the burial of the man then lying dead, and for any other American who might die. This proposition seemed to perplex the commissioners, and, after some consultation, they retired to discuss the question alone, and, on leaving, invited the Commodore and his officers to partake of some refreshments, consisting of saki, fruit and cakes, soups and fish, which were immediately served. This invitation was accepted, with the remark that it would be more consonant with American notions of hospitality if the commissioners were to join the Commodore and his officers, as the breaking of bread together was, in the United States, as among many other nations, considered an evidence of friendship. The Japanese replied that they were unacquainted with foreign customs, but would cheerfully join. They then all retired; but, shortly after, the second and third in rank of the number returned and participated socially in the repast that had been served, one of the dignitaries filling a cup of saki at once, drinking it off to the dregs, and, turning it bottom upward, remarked that it was a Japanese custom for the host to drink first.

It was not long before the whole board was again in session, and a written reply to the Commodore's request respecting the burial of the marine presented by the chief commissioner, and to the purport that, as a temple had been set apart at Nagasaki for the interment of strangers, it would be necessary to send the body to Uraga, whence, at a convenient season, it might be conveyed in a Japanese junk to the former place. To this the Commodore objected that undisturbed resting places were granted by all nations, and then proposed to send boats and inter the body at Webster island. Webster island, as it is named on the American charts, is a small island lying convenient to the "American anchorage;" and the Commodore had determined, if the Japanese had persisted in forbidding the interment within any of their numerous burial places, to have effected it at all hazards upon that island, being perfectly satisfied that the Japanese respect for the dead would leave the body undisturbed. The commissioners evinced strong objections to the choice of the spot, and, after considerable discussion among themselves, finally consented to allow the burial to take place at Yoku-hama, at a place adjoining one of their temples, and in view of the squadron. They observed, however, that, as the novelty of the scene might attract an inconvenient crowd, the authorities would send on board the Mississippi, in the morning, an officer to accompany the funeral party.

The Commodore now prepared to depart, having first stated that he would be happy to see the Japanese dignitaries on board his vessel as soon as the weather should become warmer. They expressed courteously the pleasure they would have in accepting the invitation, and, bowing, retired. The subordinate American officers had been entertained with refreshments in the large outer hall during the conference, and amused with the rude efforts of Japanese artists, who had been sent from Yedo, at delineating their portraits. The Commodore now passed out, followed by his suite and the procession of officers as before, and marching down, to the music of the bands, between the files of marines on either side, embarked in his barge and pulled for the ship. The other boats soon followed, filled with the numerous officers, sailors, marines, and others, who had shared in the ceremonies of the day.

Early next day, (Thursday, March 9,) as had been arranged, a Japanese official went on board the Mississippi, to accompany the funeral party on shore, for the purpose of pointing out the burial place selected for the interment of the dead marine. At five o'clock in the afternoon the boats left the ship with the body, attended by the chaplain, Mr. Jones, Mr. Williams, the interpreter, and a party of marines. The flags of every vessel in the squadron were hoisted at half mast as the boats pushed off. The body was borne to a very picturesque spot at the foot of a hill, at a short distance from the village of Yoku-hama. The chaplain, Mr. Jones, was robed in his clerical gown, and on landing was received in the most courteous manner by some of the Japanese authorities, who showed none of their supposed repugnance to the Christian religion and its ministers. Crowds of the people had also gathered, and looked on with great curiosity,

Buddhist Priest in Full Dress.

but with decorous respect, as the funeral procession moved slowly along to the sound of the muffled drum. The road lay through the village, and its inhabitants came out from their houses and open shops to behold the novel scene. The place chosen for the burial was near a Japanese place of interment, with stone idols and sculptured headstones, and as the procession came up a Buddhist priest, in robes of richly embroidered silk, was observed already on the ground.

Mr. Jones read the service of the Protestant Episcopal church, and while he was officiating the Buddhist priest sat near by on a mat, with an altar before him, on which was a collection of scraps of paper, some rice, a gong, a vessel containing saki, and some burning incense. The service having been read, the body lowered, and the earth thrown in, the party retired from the grave. The Buddhist priest then commenced the peculiar ceremonies of his religion, beating his gong, telling his rosary of glass and wooden beads, muttering his prayers, and keeping alive the burning incense. He was still going through his strange formulary when the Americans moved away, and crowds of Japanese continued to linger in the neighborhood, about the crests and acclivities of the hills which bounded the scene. Mr. Williams, the interpreter, who had lived long in China, and was familiar with the Buddhist worship, recognized its peculiarities in the precisely similar ceremonies performing at the grave by the Japanese priest. A neat enclosure of bamboo was subsequently put up about the American grave by the authorities, and a small hut was erected near, for a Japanese guard to watch the grave for a time, according to their custom.

On the same day the prefect, Kura-Kawa-Kahei, and the chief interpreter, Yenoske, came on board the Powhatan with a copy of the Imperial reply to the President's letter, duly certified and signed by the four commissioners. The two Japanese officials subsequently repaired to the Mississippi, where they conferred for some time with Captain Adams. They appointed the Monday following (March 13th) for the reception of the presents, and it was arranged that those persons who had the supervision of the telegraph, the Daguerreotype apparatus, and steam engine, should land on the previous Saturday, to arrange a place for their suitable exhibition. The Japanese stated that two of the commissioners would be in attendance, with a scribe, to receive and record the various presents, and the names of the persons for whom they were intended. Upon Captain Adams saying that all the presents received by the officers of the United States were, by law, the property of the government, Yenoske remarked that a similar law existed in Japan. To the inquiry of the Japanese as to when the Commodore's reply to the answer to the President's letter would be ready, it was promised for the subsequent Saturday.

Captain Adams now asked what ports the commissioners had selected for the trade of the Americans, and where they were, and remarked that five years, the time appointed for the opening of them, was deemed by the Commodore much too long, and that he would never submit to having a place so restricted as Dezima for the use of the Americans. The prefect waived all immediate consideration of the subject, saying that it was one upon which the commissioners would negotiate and deliberate, and that it would necessarily require time. Yenoske, the interpreter, was then told that he could forward the purposes of the expedition, since he was familiar with them; he promised to do so to the utmost of his power, but he declined, although a map was placed before him, to name the ports for American intercourse, saying, as he refused, that the whole matter was so new, and so opposed to the laws of the Empire, that time would be required to bring matters to such an issue. In regard to the question of going ashore, which had been submitted to the commissioners, Captain Adams asked for some explicit reply, stating that the surveying party, which was at the time at work in the bay, would require to plant signals along the shore, but would not go into the interior. To this the prefect answered that the views of the commissioners had not been yet fully matured, but seemed to concur in the necessity of the signals, if the Commodore had so ordered it. He, however, expressed his fear of trouble and confusion, if the officers, engaged in their duty, should enter the villages, and hoped they would go down the bay, and not northward. The subject of supplies was next spoken of, and the question of payment seemed to be conceded by the Japanese, who proposed that as soon as a port was selected, certain compradors should be appointed for the sale of articles of every kind, but in the meantime, they said a single person would be chosen, whose duty it would be to supply what was necessary, and receive in payment the American coin, to be estimated weight for weight with the Japanese money. They would prefer, they said, that Nagasaki should be the place for such transactions, but granted the necessity of carrying them on for the present where they were. The hours for the future meetings being settled at from eleven o'clock to one, instead of the previous irregular mode, the Japanese took their departure.

On the next day (March 11) a short conference was held by Captain Adams with the same Japanese officials in the treaty house on shore. He also bore a communication of the date of the 10th of March from the Commodore, addressed to the commissioners, in which the answer to the President's letter was acknowledged. The Commodore, while he expressed his satisfaction at the determination of the Japanese government to alter its policy in regard to foreign governments, at the same time stated that the concessions proposed were not enough, and that a written compact or treaty, with wider provisions, was essential. The chief points talked of were, the answer to the Commodore's notes in reference to the proposed treaty, and the privilege of going ashore. In regard to the former, they stated that a reply was not yet prepared; but as for the latter, the interpreter remarked, unofficially, that there would be no objection to the Commodore and his officers going ashore; but that if the permission should be general, difficulty with the people might ensue. Some general conversation followed in regard to the necessity of dispatch in the negotiations, Captain Adams stating that it was the Commodore's intention to send one of his ships to the United States, in the course of a week or so, to inform the government at home of the progress of the negotiations, that it might know whether it was necessary to send more vessels or not. The Japanese evinced some uneasiness at this statement, and asked, "Whether the Americans are friendly?" "Certainly we are," was the answer, and the conference closed in the most amicable manner.

The day agreed upon had arrived (Monday, March 13) for the landing of the presents, and although the weather was unsettled, and the waters of the bay somewhat rough, they all reached the shore without damage.*

---

* The following is a list of some of the various presents landed on the occasion:

1 box of arms, containing—
    5 Hall's rifles, ⎫
    3 Maynard's muskets, ⎪
    12 cavalry swords, ⎪
    6 artillery swords, ⎬ Emperor.
    1 carbine, ⎪
    20 army pistols, ⎭
    2 carbines, cartridge boxes, and belts, containing 120 cartridges.
    10 Hall's rifles.
    11 cavalry swords.
    1 carbine, cartridge box and belts, and 60 cartridges.
    60 *ball cartridges.*
1 box books, Emperor.
1 box dressing-cases, Emperor.
1 box perfumery, 2 packages, Emperor.
1 barrel whiskey, Emperor.
1 cask wine, Emperor.
1 box for distribution.
1 box containing 11 pistols, for distribution.
1 box perfumery, for distribution.
A quantity of cherry cordials, distribution
A quantity of cherry cordials, Emperor.
A number of baskets champaigne, Emperor.
A number of baskets champaigne, commissioners.
1 box China ware, commissioners.
A quantity of maraschino, commissioners.
1 telescope, Emperor.
Boxes of tea, Emperor.
1 box of tea, commissioners.

DELIVERY OF THE PRESENTS. 357

The presents filled several large boats, which left the ship escorted by a number of officers, a company of marines, and a band of music, all under the superintendence of Captain Abbott, who was delegated to deliver the presents, with proper ceremonies, to the Japanese high commissioners. A building adjoining the treaty house had been suitably constructed and arranged for the purpose, and on landing Captain Abbot was met by Yezaiman, the governor of Uraga, and several subordinate officials, and conducted to the treaty house. Soon after entering, the high commissioner, Prince Hayashi, came in, and the usual compliments being interchanged, Captain Abbott, with the interpreters, were led into the smaller room, where a letter from the Commodore and some formalities on the delivery of the presents were disposed of. The Japanese commissioner, after some discussion, fixed the ensuing Thursday (March 16) for an interview with the Commodore on shore, when they promised to deliver a formal reply to his notes in regard to the opening of the various Japanese ports insisted upon.

The presents having been formally delivered, the various American officers and workmen selected for the purpose were diligently engaged daily in unpacking and arranging them for exhibition. The Japanese authorities offered every facility; their laborers constructed sheds for sheltering the articles from the inclemency of the weather; a piece of level ground was assigned for laying down the circular track of the little locomotive, and posts were brought and erected for the extension of the telegraph wires, the Japanese taking a very ready part in all the labors, and watching the result of arranging and putting together the machinery with an innocent and childlike delight. The telegraphic apparatus, under the direction of Messrs. Draper and Williams, was soon in working order, the wires extending nearly a mile, in a direct line, one end being at the treaty house, and another at a building expressly allotted for the purpose. When communication was opened up between the operators at either extremity, the Japanese watched with intense curiosity the *modus operandi*, and were greatly amazed to find that in an instant of time messages were conveyed in the English, Dutch, and Japanese languages from building to building. Day after day the dignitaries and many of the people would gather, and, eagerly beseeching the operators to work the telegraph, watch with unabated interest the sending and receiving of messages.

Nor did the railway, under the direction of Engineers Gay and Danby, with its Lilliputian locomotive, car, and tender, excite less interest. All the parts of the mechanism were perfect, and the car was a most tasteful specimen of workmanship, but so small that it could hardly carry a child of six years of age. The Japanese, however, were not to be cheated out of a ride, and, as they were unable to reduce themselves to the capacity of the inside of the carriage, they betook themselves to the roof. It was a spectacle not a little ludicrous to behold

---

2 telegraph instruments.	1 box coast charts.
3 Francis's life-boats.	4 bundles telegraph wires.
1 locomotive and tender, passenger car, and rails complete.	1 box gutta percha wires.
4 volumes Audubon's Birds of America.	4 boxes batteries.
3 volumes Audubon's Quadrupeds.	1 box machine paper.
Several clocks.	1 box zinc plates.
10 ship's beakers, containing 100 gallons whiskey.	1 box insulators.
8 baskets Irish potatoes.	1 box connecting apparatus.
3 stoves.	1 box machine weights.
Boxes standard United States balances.	1 box acid.
Boxes standard United States bushels.	1 box seed.
Boxes standard United States gallon measures.	Large quantity of agricultural implements, &c., &c., &c.
Boxes standard United States yards.	

a dignified mandarin whirling around the circular road at the rate of twenty miles an hour, with his loose robes flying in the wind. As he clung with a desperate hold to the edge of the roof, grinning with intense interest, and his huddled up body shook convulsively with a kind of laughing timidity, while the car spun rapidly around the circle, you might have supposed that the movement, somehow or other, was dependent rather upon the enormous exertions of the uneasy mandarin than upon the power of the little puffing locomotive, which was so easily performing its work.

Although the Japanese authorities were still very jealous of any intercourse on the part of the Americans with the people, and did all they could to prevent it, still there was necessarily a good deal of intermingling. The ships of the squadron were being daily supplied with water and provisions, for which the officials of the government had now consented to receive payment, but they insisted upon conducting all the regulations, and provided their own boats and laborers for the purpose. There was, however, what with the necessary passing to and from the ships with the supplies, and the arranging and working the telegraphic apparatus, and the toy railway, almost daily intercourse between the American officers, sailors, and marines, and the Japanese mandarins, officials, and laborers.

The Japanese always evinced an inordinate curiosity, for the gratification of which the various articles of strange fabric, and the pieces of mechanism, of ingenious and novel invention, brought from the United States, gave them a full opportunity. They were not satisfied with the minutest examination of all these things, so surprisingly wonderful as they appeared to them, but followed the officers and men about and seized upon every occasion to examine each part of their dress. The laced caps, boots, swords, and tailed coats of the officers, the tarpaulins, jackets, and trowsers of the men, all came in for the closest scrutiny, and a tailor in search of a new cut or a latest fashion could not have been more exacting in his observations than the inquisitive Japanese as he fingered the broadcloth, smoothed down the nap with his long delicate hands, pulled a lappel here, adjusted a collar there, now fathomed the depth of a pocket, and again peered curiously into the inner recesses of Jack's loose toilette. They eagerly sought to possess themselves of anything that pertained to the dress of their visitors, and showed a peculiar passion for buttons. They would again and again ask for a button, and when presented with the cheap gift, they appeared immediately gratified, and stowed it away as if it were of the greatest value. It is possible that their affection for buttons and high appreciation of their value, may be owing to the rarity of the article in Japan, for it is a curious fact, that the simple convenience of a button is but little used in any article of Japanese dress, strings and variou bindings being the only mode of fastening the garments. When visiting the ships the mandarins and their attendants were never at rest, but went about peering into every nook and corner, peeping into the muzzles of the guns, examining curiously the small-arms, handling the ropes, measuring the boats, looking eagerly into the engine-room, and watching every movement of the engineers and workmen as they busily moved, in and about, the gigantic machinery of the steamers. They were not contented with merely observing with their eyes, but were constantly taking out their writing materials, their mulberry-bark paper, and their Indian ink and hair pencils, which they always carried in a pocket within the left breast of their loose robes, and making notes and sketches. The Japanese had all apparently a strong pictorial taste, and looked with great delight upon the engravings and pictures which were shown them, but their own performances appeared exceedingly rude and unartistic. Every man, however, seemed

anxious to try his skill at drawing, and they were constantly taking the portraits of the Americans, and sketches of the various articles that appeared curious to them, with a result, which, however satisfactory it might have been to the artists, (and it must be conceded they exhibited no little exultation,) was far from showing any encouraging advance in art. It should, however, be remarked, that the artists were not professional. Our future pages will show more artistic skill than the rude specimens here alluded to would have led one to suppose existed in Japan. The Japanese are, undoubtedly, like the Chinese, a very imitative, adaptative, and compliant people, and in these characteristics may be discovered a promise of the comparatively easy introduction of foreign customs and habits, if not of the nobler principles and better life of a higher civilization.

Notwithstanding the Japanese are so fond of indulging their curiosity, they are by no means communicative about themselves. They allege, as a reason for their provoking reserve, that their laws forbid them to communicate to foreigners anything relating to their country and its institutions, habits, and customs. This silence on the part of the Japanese was a serious obstacle to acquiring that minute information about a strange people of whom curiosity is naturally on the alert to know everything. Much progress will, however, never be obtained toward a thorough knowledge of Japan, until some of our men of intelligence are established in the country in the character of consular agents, merchants, or missionaries, who may thus be enabled to acquire the language and mingle in intimate social relations with the people.

The common people were found much more disposed to fraternize than were the Japanese officials. It seemed evident that nothing but a fear of punishment deterred the former from entering into free intercourse with the Americans; but they were closely watched by their superiors, as in fact the latter were by their equals.

In Japan, as in Lew Chew, probably, a closer intimacy would have ensued, during the visits of the squadron, with all classes, if they had been allowed to follow their own natural inclinations, and had not been so jealously guarded by the numerous spies. No one, even of the highest dignitaries, is entrusted with public business of importance, without having one or more associated with him, who is ever on the alert to detect and take note of the slightest suspicion of delinquency.

Kura-Kawa-Kahei, the prefect, and Yenoske, the interpreter, paid almost daily visits to the ships, and had always something to communicate in regard to the supplying of the vessels with water and fresh provisions, the arrangements for which were under their especial care. When they came on board, as they were subordinate dignitaries, they were not received by the Commodore himself, but by some of his chief officers, who were delegated for the purpose, and acted as his medium of communication with them. After one of these interviews, (March 14,) as Kura-Kawa and Yenoske were about taking leave, a Japanese official hurried aboard from Kanagawa, and, in a state of considerable excitement, reported that an American officer had passed through that town, and was walking very fast toward Yedo. His appearance, so said the messenger, was causing great excitement, and it was feared that unpleasant consequences might ensue. The Japanese officials, on hearing this, declared that the conduct of the American officer was in violation of their laws and of the promises made to them by the Admiral. The Commodore, when informed of the fact, directed guns to be fired immediately, and a signal made recalling all boats and officers to their respective ships. He also prepared written orders, which were sent in different directions, commanding all persons belonging to the squadron to repair immediately on board. A copy of these orders was, on the instant, dispatched by the Japanese officials, then in the Powhatan, in pursuit of the American officer, reported to be on his way to Yedo. The Commodore's prompt action was handsomely acknowledged by the authorities, who sent to him, next day, a formal expression of their gratitude.

The American officer, whose intrusion had created so great an excitement, was Mr. Bittinger, the chaplain of the steamer Susquehanna. While taking a walk on shore, this gentleman's curiosity prompted him to extend his observations somewhat beyond the usual circuit of some four or five miles, within which the Japanese authorities had contracted the movements of their visitors. Starting from Yoku-hama, opposite to where the squadron was anchored, the enterprising investigator pushed on to the town of Kanagawa, some three miles further up the bay, where he was accosted by some of the Japanese officials and the interpreter, Gohatsiro, who urgently solicited him to return. He was not, however, to be so easily balked of his purpose, and continued his journey, followed by the Japanese officers, who dogged his steps at every turn until he reached Kamasaki. Here there was a river to cross, and he tried to prevail upon the Japanese boatmen to ferry him to the opposite side, but they refused in spite of bribes and threats, in the course of which the chaplain, if the Japanese accounts are to be believed, drew his sword. He now pursued his way higher up the river with the hope of finding a place that might be forded, and had just reached a very promising looking crossing, the depths of which he was about trying, when the messenger, who had hurried in rapid dispatch, from the steamer Powhatan accosted him with the written order of the Commodore. "He," thus reported the Japanese authorities, with their usual minuteness of description, "read it, walked four steps further, read it again, then suddenly returned and intimated his intention of going back to the ship." The chaplain, in the course of his wanderings, had an opportunity of seeing one of the largest towns of Japan, that of Kanagawa, which, with its numerous wide streets, and its crowded population, had quite an imposing appearance. He penetrated into several of the dwellings and temples, and, by his pertinacious perseverance, succeeded in obtaining, in one of the shops, some Japanese money in exchange for American coin. The native authorities seemed particularly worried in regard to this last matter, as it was so great an offence against their laws. The Japanese, in their report of the occurrence, stated that the American officer had gone into a shop by the roadside and asked the keeper to allow him to see some coins. The Japanese shopman complied with the request, but as he seemed somewhat chary in the display of his treasure the chaplain insisted upon seeing more, which demand was also granted. Scales were now asked for, which being brought the chaplain took out some silver pieces, and weighing them in one balance against the Japanese gold and silver coins, mixed indiscriminately in a heap, in the other, transferred the latter to his pockets and left his American coin to console the shopman for the loss of his Japanese change. The authorities further reported that the chaplain was not content with gentle exhortations and mild persuasions, but had used threatening gestures, in which his drawn sword had figured conspicuously. They, however, mildly and courteously added in their report, "that they supposed that it was with no intention to do harm, but for his own amusement." There was a gentle and graceful charity in the suggestion of an apology for the conduct of the American officer, which showed an example in beautiful accordance with the precepts of the faith of the intruder, and well worthy of imitation. On the next day Yenoske brought back the sum of three dollars and a half in American silver coin, which had been left in compulsory exchange with the Japanese shopman, and stated that six pieces of gold, six of silver, and the same number of copper, were in possession of the chaplain. Yenoske requested that the Japanese money should be returned, and was told it should be restored.

The day appointed for the conference, on shore, with the Commodore (March 16) proved very stormy, and, accordingly, the interview was postponed until the next morning. In the meantime, a communication had been received from the commissioners, in answer to several notes of the Commodore, in regard to a proposed treaty with Japan, on the basis of that between the United States and China:

Note from the Japanese Commissioners to Commodore Perry.

At our personal interview, on the 8th, you presented us a paper in which the President's views were expressed; and, on the 11th, we received a reply to our letter, in which the same views were given as at the interview in relation to the commerce your country now has with China; both of which we have carefully examined, and learn that you wish to ascertain whether we are ready to adopt the same that the Chinese have. The burden of that which you presented on the 8th is similar to that which was sought in the President's letter, and you gave it, to learn whether we would adopt it or not. In our letter, it was plainly stated that our Emperor had but lately acceded to his throne, and all the numerous affairs of government required to be quietly settled, and that he had no leisure for extraneous negotiations. Consequently, he last autumn sent, through the superintendent of the Dutch shipping, to make this known to you, for you to communicate it to the United States.

Among those points which you now propose for adoption, the two items of extending succor and protection to the distressed and wrecked vessels on our coast, and of furnishing coal to passing ships and supplying provisions and other necessaries to those who may be in need of them, are founded in reason, and ought to be granted without hesitation. But as to opening a trade, such as is now carried on with China by your country, we certainly cannot yet bring it about. The feelings and manners of our people are very unlike those of outer nations; and it will be exceedingly difficult, even if you wish it, to immediately change the old regulations for those of other countries. Moreover, the Chinese have long had intercourse with western nations, while we have had dealings at Nagasaki with only the people of Holland and China. Beside them, it mattered not for us to trade with those of any other land; and this has made our exchange of commodities very small.

The ships of your country must, therefore, begin your trade at Nagasaki during the first moon of our next year, where they can procure fuel, water, coal, and other things; but as our ideas of things, and what we each like, are still very dissimilar, as are also our notions of the prices or worth of things, this makes it indispensable that we both first make a mutual trial and examination, and then, after five years, we can open another port for trade, which will be convenient for your ships when passing.

The points of the treaty you have now presented for our deliberation, and this now given to you can be retained by each as evidence of our separate views.

KAYEI, *7th year, 2d moon, 17th day.* (*March 15, 1854.*)

                                                  HAYASHI.
                                                  IDO.
                                                  IZAWA.
                                                  UDONO.

The next day, (March 17th,) the Commodore, accompanied by his interpreters, secretary, and two or three of his officers, met the commissioners at the treaty house, and after some preliminary compliments in regard to the presents, he was conducted as before from the hall of reception to the inner room of conference. The Commodore, on the present occasion, had dispensed with the military display, and much of the ceremony of the former visit, (which, as we have intimated in a previous chapter, was merely for effect,) as had the Japanese commissioners, although the negotiations were carried on with the usual formalities.

Hayashi, the chief dignitary, opened the day's business by asking whether the Commodore was satisfied with the Japanese propositions for a treaty, which had been sent on the previous day, alluding to those embodied in the note printed above. The Commodore having replied that their communication was not accompanied with a Dutch translation, the Japanese presented one immediately, and the discussion began. The various propositions of the Japanese, and the answers have been thus formularised:

PROPOSITIONS OF JAPANESE COMMISSIONERS, WITH REPLIES OF COMMODORE PERRY.

First Japanese proposition.

From the next first month, wood, water, provisions, coal, and other things, the productions of this country, that American ships may need, can be had at Nagasaki; and after five years from this, a port in another principality shall be opened for ships to go to.

NOTE.—Those articles to be charged at the same prices that are charged to the Dutch and Chinese, and to be paid for in gold and silver coin.

Commodore Perry's reply.

Agreed to; but one or more ports must be substituted for Nagasaki, as that is out of the route of American commerce; and the time for the opening of the ports to be agreed upon must be immediate, or within a space of sixty days. The manner of paying for articles received shall be arranged by treaty.

Second Japanese proposition.

Upon whatever part of the coast people may be shipwrecked, those people and their property shall be sent to Nagasaki by sea.

NOTE.—When, after five years shall have expired, and another harbor shall be opened, those shipwrecked men will be sent either there or to Nagasaki, as may be most convenient.

Commodore Perry's reply.

Agreed to, excepting as to the port to which the shipwrecked men are to be carried.

Third Japanese proposition.

It being impossible for us to ascertain who are pirates and who are not, such men shall not be allowed to walk about wherever they please.

Commodore Perry's reply.

Shipwrecked men and others who may resort to the ports of Japan are not be confined, and shall enjoy all the freedom granted to Japanese, and be subject to no further restraints. They shall, however, be held amenable to just laws, or such as may be agreed upon by treaty.

It is altogether inconsistent with justice, that persons thrown by the providence of God upon the shores of a friendly nation should be looked upon and treated as pirates, before any proof shall be given of their being so; and the continuance of the treatment which has hitherto been visited upon strangers will no longer be tolerated by the government of the United States, so far as Americans are concerned.

Fourth Japanese proposition.

At Nagasaki they shall have no intercourse with the Dutch and Chinese.

Commodore Perry's reply.

The Americans will never submit to the restrictions which have been imposed upon the Dutch and Chinese, and any further allusion to such restraints will be considered offensive.

Fifth Japanese proposition.

After the other port is opened, if there be any other sort of articles wanted, or business which requires to be arranged, there shall be careful deliberation between the parties in order to settle them.

Commodore Perry's reply.

Agreed to, so far as it applies to ports other than Nagasaki.

Sixth Japanese proposition.

Lew Chew is a very distant country, and the opening of its harbor cannot be discussed by us.

Commodore Perry's reply.

As there can be no good reason why the Americans should not communicate freely with Lew Chew, this point is insisted on.

Seventh Japanese proposition.

Matsmai is also a very distant country, and belongs to its prince; this cannot be settled now, but a definite answer on this subject shall be given when the ships are expected next spring.

Commodore Perry's reply.

The same with respect to the port of Matsmai, for our whaling-ships, steamers, and other vessels.

These propositions and replies were consecutively discussed, the commissioners interposing with great pertinacity all possible difficulties, and contending that the laws of the Empire were of such a character as positively forbade the concessions demanded. They insisted that Nagasaki was the place set apart for strangers; they stated that the inhabitants and authorities of that city had been trained to enforce the laws with respect to foreigners, and declared that if the Americans were to have another port assigned to them, five years would be required to make similar preparations. The Commodore replied that the fact of Nagasaki having been especially appropriated to foreigners was one of the grounds of his objections to it; that its inhabitants and authorities, having been so long accustomed to the servility of the Dutch, would doubtless exact more from the Americans than they would be inclined to submit to, and serious consequences might follow. Moreover, the Commodore declared that he desired it to be well understood that his countrymen visiting Japan must be free from all those oppressive laws which have been hitherto imposed upon strangers. In a word, he declared emphatically that he would not think of accepting Nagasaki as one of the ports.

The Commodore then informed the commissioners that he should expect, in the course of time, five ports to be opened to the American flag. He would, however, he said, be content for the present with three: one on the island of Nippon, say either Uraga or Kagosima; another in Yesso, suggesting Matsmai, and a third in Lew Chew, that of Napha. In regard to the remaining two he was willing to defer all discussion to some future time.

After many evasions, and their usual protestations of legal difficulties, they at last answered that, as the Commodore positively refused to accept Nagasaki, and as they themselves objected to Uraga, that Simoda accordingly was formally proposed. In regard to Lew Chew, the commissioners declared that, as it was a distant dependency, over which the Emperor of Japan had but limited control, they could entertain no proposition. And as for Matsmai, that also stood in similar relations to the Japanese government.

Notwithstanding all these objections, the Commodore still persisted in his demands, as he had always to be on his guard against the deceitful diplomacy of the people with whom he was negotiating. Finding that the Commodore was resolute, and that all their cunning devices to bend him from his purpose were of no avail, the commissioners proposed to consider the matter, and retired to another apartment for private consultation. After an absence of an hour they returned and reported as the result of their deliberations that a longer time would be required before their decision could be given in regard to the opening of Matsmai. They remarked, in addition, that it was not in the power of the Emperor to grant the use of this port without consulting the prince under whose hereditary right it was governed, and that to do this would require a year, at the expiration of which time they would be prepared to give a reply. The Commodore then told them that he could not leave Japan without an answer of some kind, and that if the prince to whom they referred was an independent sovereign, he would go himself to Matsmai and negotiate with him.

This point was finally settled for the time by the Japanese saying that they would give a definite answer on Thursday, the twenty-third of March. In regard to Simoda, it was agreed that the Commodore should dispatch one or more vessels to that port, and the commissioners a Japanese officer of rank to meet them, in order that the harbor might be examined, and its fitness for the required purposes determined, it having been clearly understood that if it did not answer the expectations of the Americans in all respects, another place, somewhere in the southern part of Nippon, would be insisted on. The Vandalia and Southampton were accordingly dispatched, on the twentieth of March, to examine the harbor of Simoda.

The day after the conference on shore, Moryama Yenoske, the chief interpreter, accompanied by two Japanese officials, came on board the Powhatan and submitted a paper, in the Dutch language, containing a report by the Japanese themselves of the propositions made by the

Commodore, and it proved that the commissioners were perfectly cognizant of his views.* On the occasion of this visit Yenoske asked for the Japanese coins which had been obtained by the chaplain of the Susquehanna in the course of his wanderings on shore, and they were delivered to him. On the interpreter and his companions taking leave, presents were given to them, as they had been also to the commissioners after the last interview at the treaty house. These gifts consisted of Colt's pistols, and various articles of American manufacture of no great value.

On one of these visits, which were regularly kept up almost without the intermission of a single day, the Japanese officials were asked what had been the result of the expedition of the Russians to Nagasaki? They replied that no treaty of any kind whatever had been made with them; but they had been told that the Emperor had so many affairs to dispose of that their propositions could not be entertained at that time; although, perhaps, in the course of a few years, circumstances might be more favorable for negotiation. This they declared was the constant answer to their repeated demands. The Russians had been, however, supplied with wood, water, and provisions. One of the chief objects of their visit, said the Japanese, was to define with precision the frontier of Yesso.

On the twenty-third of March the usual deputation visited the Powhatan, bearing with them the final answer of the commissioners in regard to the opening of the port of Matsmai. The document presented was written in the Japanese, Chinese, and Dutch languages; of the latter of which the following is a translation:

"Ships of the United States of North America, in want of provisions, wood, and water, shall be supplied in the harbor of 'Hakodadi,' as has been desired. Some time will be required to make preparations, inasmuch as this harbor is very distant; consequently a commencement can be made the 7th month of next year, (the 17th September, 1855.) Kaei Sitzinen Nigoats. (March 23, 1854.)

"Seals attached by order of the high gentlemen.

"MORYAMA YENOSKE."

---

* This Japanese report is curious as an evidence of the precision with which the commissioners conducted the negotiations, and of the exactitude with which their reporter, who was constantly present, noted the proceedings of the conference:

Japanese statement of points agreed upon in the interview of Commodore Perry with the Japanese commissioners, March 17, 1854.

1st. The citizens of the United States will not submit to degradations like those imposed upon the Dutch and Chinese, in their confinement at Nagasaki; that place is not convenient for ships to resort to, and does not answer the purpose.

2d. Lew Chew is a very distant country, and a definite answer cannot be given.

3d. Matsmai is a very distant place, and belongs to a prince. This point cannot be settled now; some time will be required for negotiation, until the first month of our next year; because the concurrence of the central government and of the prince of that country are both necessary to effect a result; a negotiation of the admiral with that prince, therefore, would be to no purpose.

It was stated that an answer had better be given at once. There was time enough to have that harbor opened by the above-mentioned time; that it was not probable that in the first year that harbor would be resorted to by many ships, because some time would be required to communicate this decision to the government and to have it generally known.

In consideration thereof, it was agreed that a final answer should be given on the 23d of March, (the 26th of the Japanese month.)

It being mentioned that, besides Lew Chew and Matsmai, more harbors in Nippon would be required, it was suggested that the harbor of Simoda could be opened for the ships of the United States, and agreed that two ships of the squadron would sail on the 19th of March to make a survey of that harbor; and, further, that some Japanese officers, to go by land, would arrive at that place on the 22d instant, and that the captains of those ships would await the arrival of those officers before proceeding to survey, permit any one to land, &c.

That shipwrecked men should meet with kind treatment, and be free as in other countries.

Agreement made upon due consideration.

The Commodore assented to the proposition of the commissioners assigning the port of Hakodadi, which was near the city of Matsmai, and was reported to have a better harbor, on the condition that, on examination, it proved equal to the favorable description given of it. He, however, expressed his desire that it should be opened at an earlier date than that proposed.

This concession of Hakodadi betokened a favorable prospect for a successful issue to the great purpose of the expedition; and the Commodore now looked forward with sanguine expectations to an early consummation of his labors in the formation of a satisfactory treaty.

Japanese grave-yard at Yoku-hama.—Grave of the Marine on the right.

CHAPTER XX.

CORDIALITY BETWEEN JAPANESE AND AMERICANS.—PRESENTS FROM THE JAPANESE.—COINS.—SINGULAR CUSTOM OF INCLUDING RICE, CHARCOAL, AND DOGS, IN A ROYAL JAPANESE PRESENT.—JAPANESE WRESTLERS.—THEIR IMMENSE SIZE AND STRENGTH.—EXHIBITION IN THE RING.—CONTRAST IN THE EXHIBITION OF THE TELEGRAPH AND LOCOMOTIVE.—PARADE OF THE MARINES.—YENOSKE VISITS THE FLAG-SHIP, AND SEEKS TO DRAW THE COMMODORE OUT.—FAILURE.—ENTERTAINMENT OF CHINESE COMMISSIONERS ON BOARD THE FLAG-SHIP.—GREAT CORDIALITY.—PERFORMANCE ON SHIP BOARD OF "ETHIOPIAN MINSTRELS" TO THE GREAT AMUSEMENT OF THE JAPANESE.—NEGOTIATIONS CONTINUED.—JAPANESE OBJECT TO THE IMMEDIATE OPENING OF THE PORTS.—FINALLY CONCEDE THE POINT TO A CERTAIN EXTENT.—ABSOLUTE AND PERSISTENT REFUSAL TO ALLOW AMERICANS PERMANENTLY TO ABIDE IN JAPAN.—RELUCTANT CONSENT, AFTER MUCH DISCUSSION, TO ALLOW ONE CONSUL TO RESIDE AT SIMODA.—TREATY FINALLY AGREED ON AND SIGNED.—PRESENTS BY COMMODORE TO THE COMMISSIONERS, THAT TO THE CHIEF BEING THE AMERICAN FLAG.—ENTERTAINMENT OF THE COMMODORE AND HIS OFFICERS BY THE COMMISSIONERS.—PECULIARITIES OF THE MISSION TO JAPAN.—OBSTACLES TO MAKING ANY TREATY AT ALL.—DISPOSITION OF THE JAPANESE SHOWN IN THE CONFERENCES.—PARTICULAR REFUSAL TO MAKE A TREATY ALLOWING AMERICAN FAMILIES OR FEMALES TO LIVE IN JAPAN.—ANALYSIS OF THE TREATY.—COMMODORE CAREFUL TO SECURE FOR THE UNITED STATES ALL PRIVILEGES THAT MIGHT THEREAFTER BE GRANTED BY TREATY TO OTHER NATIONS.—CASE OF THE AMERICAN SCHOONER FOOTE.

AFTER the concessions made by the Japanese, related in the last chapter, the greatest good feeling prevailed on both sides, and there seemed every prospect of establishing those national relations which had been the purpose of Commodore Perry's mission. In accordance with the harmony and friendship which existed, there was an interchange of those courtesies by which mutual good feeling seeks an outward expression. The Japanese had acknowledged, with courtly thanks, the presents which had been bestowed on behalf of the government, and now, on the 24th of March, invited the Commodore to receive the various gifts which had been ordered by the Emperor in return, as a public recognition of the courtesy of the United States.

The Commodore, accordingly, landed at Yoku-hama, with a suite of officers and his interpreters, and was received at the treaty house, with the usual ceremonies, by the high commissioners. The large reception room was crowded with the various presents. The red-covered settees, numerous tables and stands, and even the floors, were heaped with the different articles. The objects were of Japanese manufacture, and consisted of specimens of rich brocades and silks, of their famous lacquered ware, such as *chow-chow* boxes, tables, trays, and goblets, all skilfully wrought and finished with an exquisite polish; of porcelain cups of wonderful lightness and transparency, adorned with figures and flowers in gold and variegated colors, and exhibiting a workmanship which surpassed even that of the ware for which the Chinese are remarkable. Fans, pipe-cases, and articles of apparel in ordinary use, of no great value, but of exceeding interest, were scattered in among the more luxurious and costly objects.

With the usual order and neatness which seem almost instinctive with the Japanese, the various presents had been arranged in lots, and classified in accordance with the rank of those for whom they were respectively intended. The commissioners took their position at the further end of the room, and when the Commodore and his suite entered, the ordinary compliments having been interchanged, the Prince Hayashi read aloud, in Japanese, the list of presents, and the names of the persons to whom they were to be given. This was then translated by Yenoske into Dutch, and by Mr. Portman into English. This ceremony being over, the Commodore was invited by the commissioners into the inner room, where he was presented with two complete sets of Japanese coins, three matchlocks, and two swords. These gifts, though of no great intrinsic value, were very significant evidences of the desire of the Japanese to express their respect for the representative of the United States. The mere bestowal of the coins, in direct opposition to the Japanese laws, which forbid, absolutely, all issue of their money beyond the Kingdom, was an act of marked favor.

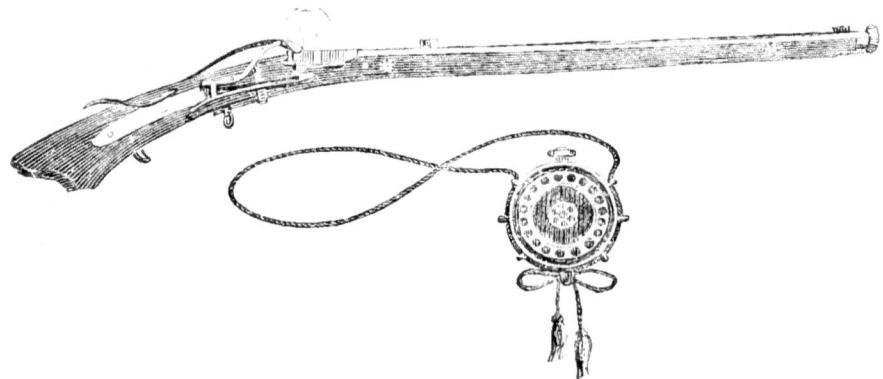

Japanese Match-lock.

As the Commodore prepared to depart, the commissioners said that there was one article intended for the President which had not yet been exhibited. They accordingly conducted the Commodore and his officers to the beach, where one or two hundred sacks of rice were pointed out, heaped up in readiness to be sent on board the ships. As that immense supply of substantial food seemed to excite some wonder on the part of the Americans, Yenoske, the interpreter, remarked that it was always customary with the Japanese, when bestowing royal presents, to include a certain quantity of rice, although he did not say whether that quantity always amounted, as on the present occasion, to hundreds of immense sacks.*

---

* The Commodore, upon subsequent inquiry, learned that there are three articles which, in Japan, as he understood, always form part of an Imperial present. These are rice, dried fish, and dogs.

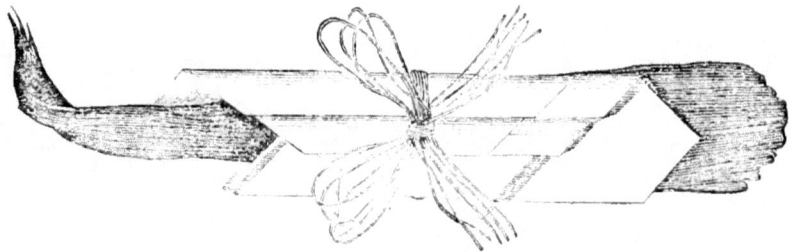

Fish Present of Japan.

[What is seen protruding at either end of the paper cover is a species of dried sea-weed, used as food. The fish is placed upon it, and covered by the paper.]

JAPANESE PRESENTS.

As illustrative of the usages of the country, we subjoin, in a note, the list of articles presented by the Japanese.*

While contemplating these substantial evidences of Japanese generosity, the attention of all was suddenly riveted upon a body of monstrous fellows, who tramped down the beach like so many huge elephants. They were professional wrestlers, and formed part of the retinue of the princes, who kept them for their private amusement and for public entertainment. They were some twenty-five in number, and were men enormously tall in stature, and immense in weight of flesh. Their scant costume, which was merely a colored cloth about the loins, adorned with fringes and emblazoned with the armorial bearings of the prince to whom each belonged, revealed their gigantic proportions in all the bloated fulness of fat and breadth of muscle. Their

---

Some also said that charcoal was always included. Why these should have been selected, or what they particularly symbolize, he did not learn. The charcoal was not omitted in the gifts on this occasion, and four small dogs of a rare breed were sent to the President, as part of the Emperor's gift. We have observed also in the public prints that two were put on board of Admiral Stirling's ship for her Majesty of England. The fact that dogs are always part of a royal Japanese present suggested to the Commodore the thought that possibly one species of spaniel now in England may be traced to a Japanese origin. In 1613, when Captain Saris returned from Japan to England, he carried to the King a letter from the Emperor, and presents in return for those which had been sent to him by his Majesty of England. Dogs probably formed part of the gifts, and thus may have been introduced into the Kingdom the Japanese breed. At any rate, there is a species of spaniel in England which it is hard to distinguish from the Japanese dog. The species sent as a present by the Emperor is by no means common even in Japan. It is never seen running about the streets, or following its master in his walks, and the Commodore understood that they were costly.

* *List of the articles received from the Japanese government, March 24, 1854:*

1st. For the government of the United States of America, from the Emperor—
- 1 gold lacquered writing apparatus.
- 1 gold lacquered paper box.
- 1 gold lacquered book-case.
- 1 lacquered writing table.
- 1 censer of bronze, (cow-shape,) supporting silver flower and stand.
- 1 set waiters.
- 1 flower holder and stand.
- 2 brasiers.
- 10 pieces fine red pongee.
- 10 pieces white pongee.
- 5 pieces flowered crape.
- 5 pieces red dyed figured crape.

2d. From Hayashi, 1st commissioner—
- 1 lacquered writing apparatus.
- 1 lacquered paper box.
- 1 box of paper.
- 1 box flowered note paper.
- 5 boxes stamped note and letter paper.
- 4 boxes assorted sea-shells, 100 in each.
- 1 box of branch coral and feather in silver.
- 1 lacquered chow-chow box.
- 1 box, set of three, lacquered goblets.
- 7 boxes cups and spoons and goblet cut from conch shells.

3d. From Ido, 2d commissioner—
- 2 boxes lacquered waiters, 4 in all.
- 2 boxes, containing 20 umbrellas.
- 1 box 30 coir brooms.

4th. From Izawa, 3d commissioner—
- 1 piece red pongee.
- 1 piece white pongee.
- 8 boxes, 13 dolls.
- 1 box bamboo woven articles.
- 2 boxes bamboo stands.

5th. From Udono, 4th commissioner—
- 3 pieces striped crape.
- 2 boxes porcelain cups.
- 1 box, 10 jars of soy.

6th. From Matsusaki, 5th commissioner—
- 3 boxes porcelain goblets.
- 1 box figured matting.
- 35 bundles oak charcoal.

7th. From Abe, 1st Imperial councillor—
- 14 pieces striped-figured silk, (taffeta.)

8th—12th. From each of other 5 Imperial councillors—
- 10 pieces striped-figured silk, (taffeta.)

13th. From Emperor to Commodore Perry—
- 1 lacquered writing apparatus.
- 1 lacquered paper box.
- 3 pieces red pongee.
- 2 pieces white pongee.
- 2 pieces flowered crape.
- 3 pieces figured dyed crape.

14th. From commissioners to Capt. H. A. Adams—
- 3 pieces plain red pongee.
- 2 pieces dyed figured crape.
- 20 sets lacquered cups and covers.

15th—17th. From commissioners to Mr. Perry, Mr. Portman, and Mr. S. W. Williams, each—
- 2 pieces red pongee.
- 2 pieces dyed figured crape.
- 10 sets lacquered cups and covers.

18th—22d. From commissioners to Mr. Gay, Mr. Danby, Mr. Draper, Dr. Morrow, and Mr. J. P. Williams—
- 1 piece red dyed figured crape.
- 10 sets lacquered cups and covers.

23d. From Emperor to the squadron—
- 200 bundles of rice, each 5 Japanese pecks.
- 300 chickens.

proprietors, the princes, seemed proud of them, and were careful to show their points to the greatest advantage before our astonished countrymen. Some two or three of these huge monsters were the most famous wrestlers in Japan, and ranked as the champion Tom Cribs and Hyers of the land. Koyanagi, the reputed bully of the capital, was one of them, and paraded himself with the conscious pride of superior immensity and strength. He was especially brought to the Commodore, that he might examine his massive form. The commissioners insisted that the monstrous fellow should be minutely inspected, that the hardness of his well-rounded muscles should be felt, and that the fatness of his cushioned frame should be tested by the touch. The Commodore accordingly attempted to grasp his immense arm, which he found as solid as it was huge, and then passed his hand over the monstrous neck, which fell in folds of massive flesh, like the dewlap of a prize ox. As some surprise was naturally expressed at this wondrous exhibition of animal development, the monster himself gave a grunt expressive of his flattered vanity.

They were all so immense in flesh that they appeared to have lost their distinctive features, and seemed to be only twenty-five masses of fat. Their eyes were barely visible through a long perspective of socket, the prominence of their noses was lost in the puffiness of their bloated cheeks, and their heads were almost set directly on their bodies, with merely folds of flesh where the neck and chin are usually found. Their great size, however, was more owing to the development of muscle than to the deposition of fat, for, although they were evidently well fed, they were not less well exercised, and capable of great feats of strength. As a preliminary exhibition of the power of these men, the princes set them to removing the sacks of rice to a convenient place on the shore for shipping. Each of the sacks weighed not less than one hundred and twenty-five pounds, and there were only a couple of the wrestlers who did not carry each two sacks at a time. They bore the sacks on the right shoulder, lifting the first from the ground and adjusting it without help, but obtaining aid for the raising of the second. One man carried a sack suspended by his teeth, and another, taking one in his arms, turned repeated somersaults as he held it, and apparently with as much ease as if his tons of flesh had been only so much gossamer, and his load a feather.

After this preliminary display, the commissioners proposed that the Commodore and his party should retire to the treaty house, where they would have an opportunity of seeing the wrestlers exhibit their professional feats. The wrestlers themselves were most carefully provided for, having constantly about them a number of attendants, who were always at hand to supply them with fans, which they often required, and to assist them in dressing and undressing. While at rest they were ordinarily clothed in richly-adorned robes of the usual Japanese fashion, but when exercising they were stripped naked, with the exception of the cloth about the loins. After their performance with the sacks of rice, their servitors spread upon the huge frames of the wrestlers their rich garments and led them up to the treaty house.

A circular space of some twelve feet in diameter had been enclosed within a ring, and the ground carefully broken up and smoothed in front of the building, while in the portico, divans covered with red cloth were arranged for the Japanese commissioners, the Commodore, his officers and their various attendants. The bands from the ships were also present, and enlivened the intervals during the performance with occasional lively strains. As soon as the spectators had taken their seats, the naked wrestlers were brought out into the ring, and the whole number, being divided into two opposing parties, tramped heavily backward and forward, looking defiance at each other, but not engaging in any contest, as their object was merely to

parade their points, to give the beholders, as it were, an opportunity to form an estimate of their comparative powers, and to make up their betting-books. They soon retired behind some screens placed for the purpose, where all, with the exception of two, were again clothed in full dress and took their position on seats in front of the spectators.

The two who had been reserved out of the band, now, on the signal being given by the heralds, who were seated on opposite sides, presented themselves. They came in, one after the other, from behind the screen, and walked with slow and deliberate steps, as became such huge animals, into the centre of the ring. Then they ranged themselves, one against the other, at a distance of a few yards. They crouched for a while, eyeing each other with a wary look, as if each were watching for a chance to catch his antagonist off his guard. As the spectator looked on these over-fed monsters, whose animal natures had been so carefully and successfully developed, and as he watched them, glaring with brutal ferocity at each other, ready to exhibit the cruel instincts of a savage nature, it was easy for him to lose all sense of their being human creatures, and to persuade himself that he was beholding a couple of brute beasts thirsting for one another's blood. They were, in fact, like a pair of fierce bulls, whose nature they had not only acquired, but even their look and movements. As they continued to eye each other they stamped the ground heavily, pawing as it were with impatience, and then stooping their huge bodies, they grasped handfuls of dirt and flung it with an angry toss over their backs, or rubbed it impatiently between their giant palms, or under their stout shoulders. They now crouched low, still keeping their eyes fixed upon each other, and watching every movement, until, in an instant, they had both simultaneously heaved their massive forms in opposing force, body to body, with a shock that might have stunned an ox. The equilibrium of their monstrous frames was hardly disturbed by the concussion, the effect of which was but barely visible in the quiver of the hanging flesh of their bodies. As they came together, they had thrown their brawny arms around each other, and were now entwined in a desperate struggle, each striving with all his enormous strength to throw his adversary. Their great muscles rose with the distinct outline of the sculptured form of a colossal Hercules, their bloated countenances swelled up with gushes of blood which seemed ready to burst through the skin of their reddened faces, and their huge bodies palpitated with emotion as the struggle continued. At last, one of the antagonists fell, with his immense weight, heavily upon the ground, and being declared vanquished, was assisted to his feet and conducted from the ring.

The scene was now somewhat varied by a change in the kind of contest between two succeeding wrestlers. The heralds, as before, summoned the antagonists, and one, having taken his place in the ring, assumed an attitude of defence with one leg in advance, as if to steady himself, and his bent body, with his head lowered, placed in position, as if to receive an attack. Immediately after, in rushed the other, bellowing loudly like a bull, and, making at once for the man in the ring, dashed, with his head lowered and thrust forward, against the head of his opponent, who bore the shock with the steadiness of a rock, although the blood streamed down his face from his bruised forehead, which had been struck in the encounter. This manœuvre was repeated again and again, the same one acting always as the opposing, and the other as the resisting, force; and thus they kept up their brutal contest until their foreheads were besmeared with blood, and the flesh on their chests rose in great swollen tumors, from the repeated blows. This disgusting exhibition did not terminate until the whole twenty-five had, successively, in pairs, displayed their immense powers and savage qualities.

From the brutal performance of these wrestlers, the Americans turned with pride to the exhibition—to which the Japanese commissioners were now in their turn invited—of the telegraph and the railroad. It was a happy contrast, which a higher civilization presented, to the disgusting display on the part of the Japanese officials. In place of a show of brute animal force, there was a triumphant revelation, to a partially enlightened people, of the success of science and enterprise. The Japanese took great delight in again seeing the rapid movement of the Lilliputian locomotive; and one of the scribes of the commissioners took his seat upon the car, while the engineer stood upon the tender, feeding the furnace with one hand, and directing the diminutive engine with the other. Crowds of the Japanese gathered around, and looked on the repeated circlings of the train with unabated pleasure and surprise, unable to repress a shout of delight at each blast of the steam whistle. The telegraph, with its wonders, though before witnessed, still created renewed interest, and all the beholders were unceasing in their expressions of curiosity and astonishment. The agricultural instruments having been explained to the commissioners by Dr. Morrow, a formal delivery of the telegraph, the railway, and other articles, which made up the list of American presents, ensued. The Prince of Mamasaki had been delegated by his coadjutors ceremoniously to accept, and Captain Adams appointed by the Commodore to deliver, the gifts; and each performed his separate functions by an interchange of suitable compliments and some half dozen stately bows. After this, a detachment of marines from the squadron were put through their various evolutions, drills, &c., while the bands furnished martial music. The Japanese commissioners seemed to take a very great interest in this military display, and expressed themselves much gratified at the soldierly air and excellent discipline of the men. This closed the performances of the day; and, the commissioners having accepted an invitation from the Commodore to dine with him on the twenty-seventh, the Japanese retired to the treaty-house, and the Americans returned to the ships. The Japanese presents were all boxed up and sent, together with the rice and charcoal, on board the storeship Supply, when, after being duly addressed to the proper department of the government, they were stored away for future shipment.

On the next day, (March 25,) Yenoske, accompanied by Kenzeiro, his fellow interpreter, came on board the Powhatan to acknowledge, formally, in behalf of the commissioners, their gratitude for the exhibition of the marines, the locomotive, and the telegraph, with all which they declared themselves highly delighted. Yenoske and his coadjutor were invited to seat themselves in the cabin of the Commodore, and, after some expressions of courtesy, which the Japanese officials were careful never to intermit, proposed to talk over some points in connexion with the projected treaty. The Commodore said he had no objections to the discussion of the matters informally; but he protested against considering the interpreters as the official representatives of the commissioners, with the latter of whom only, he declared, could he treat authoritatively.

Yenoske then commenced by stating that Hakodadi, which the commissioners had desired not to have opened before September, 1855, might be ready for American ships as early as March of that year, and added that Simoda, also, would be prepared by that date. The Commodore replied that, in regard to Hakodadi, although it was his intention to visit it during the summer, he was willing to accept it without a preliminary survey; but, as for Simoda, it must first be examined before it could be adopted. The Japanese now expressed the hope that the Commodore would not go to Hakodadi for a hundred days yet, as it was necessary to send to Nagasaki for an interpreter, who would be obliged to go to Yedo previous to going to Hakodadi. The Commodore stated that he could not wait so long a time, but would be obliged to pay his contemplated visit in about a month; and, as for an interpreter, he would take with him Namoura, one of those who was occasionally present in behalf of the commissioners.

Namoura, Third Interpreter, Yoku-hama.

The Japanese replied that it would be necessary to retain Namoura, and, beside, that the dialect at Hakodadi was so different another interpreter would be required. The Commodore finally declared that, as for Simoda, he would consider that port opened, in accordance with his express understanding with the commissioners, as soon as he should receive a favorable report of it from Captain Pope, who had been dispatched to make the proper investigation.

He also stated that, though he wished all the ports to be opened at once, none of them could be practically available for more than a year, since the necessary preliminary action of his government would require at least that time before ratifying the agreement with the Japanese. The Commodore then cut the discussion short by saying that he desired to refer these points in detail to the commissioners, which he would do, in writing, at the next interview.

Yenoske, who had evidently been delegated by the commissioners to test the firmness of the

Commodore in regard to various points in the proposed treaty which they were loth to concede, now alluded to the establishment of an American consular agent. He said that they would not be required, as the governors of the towns could carry on all the business of supplying the ships with coals, provisions, and other necessaries, without the intervention of any consul, and that, consequently, the commissioners proposed a delay of four or five years before consenting to the appointment of any such officer among them, that they might, in the meantime, discover how the new intercourse with the Americans worked. In reply, the Commodore explained to Yenoske the nature and duties of the consular office, and urged the residence of such an officer as a consul upon the ground of its advantage to the Japanese themselves; and finally declared that this feature must be in the treaty, though he was willing there should be but one consul who should *reside* at Simoda.

The Commodore now informed the interpreters that he wished a junk, loaded with a thousand peculs of coal, to be in readiness for him at Simoda, after his return from Hakodadi. He also desired various other supplies at the same time and place, the whole to be accompanied with a list of prices, as he insisted upon paying for everything. He also insisted that the Americans should be permitted to purchase any articles of Japanese manufacture they might desire, and should have the liberty of going on shore and rambling about the country, under such proper restrictions as the Japanese authorities might be inclined to impose. The interpreters seemed to admit the propriety of these concessions on their part, but were evidently apprehensive of the consequences, remarking that their government had been obliged to make severe regulations in regard to the English and Portuguese, and animadverting with anger upon the conduct of Captain Pellew at Nagasaki some years before.

Monday, March 27, was the day appointed for the entertainment to which the Commodore had invited the commissioners and their attendants. Accordingly, great arrangements were made in the flag-ship preparatory to the occasion. The quarter-deck was adorned with a great variety of flags, and all parts of the steamer put in perfect order, while the officers, marines, and men dressed themselves in their uniforms and prepared to do honor in every respect to their expected visitors.

The Commodore was determined to give the Japanese a favorable impression of American hospitality, and had accordingly spared no pains in providing most bountifully for the large party expected, which was understood to comprise no less than seventy, exclusive of the boatmen and menials. As it was known that the strictness of Japanese etiquette would not allow the high commissioners to sit at the same table with their subordinates, the Commodore ordered two banquets, one to be spread in his cabin for the chief dignitaries, and another on the quarter-deck. The Commodore had long before made up his mind to give this entertainment as soon as the negotiations with the Japanese took a turn sufficiently favorable to justify some degree of convivial rejoicing. He had accordingly reserved for it live bullocks, some sheep, and a supply of game and poultry. The ordinary cabin stores of preserved meats, fish, vegetables, fruits, and a choice supply of the best wines, furnished every requisite for the preparation of a generous feast. These abundant materials, under the cunning hands of the Commodore's *chef de cuisine*, assumed nearly every variety of dish attractive to the eye and appetising to the taste.

Previous to coming on board the Powhatan, the commissioners visited the sloop-of-war Macedonian, being saluted as they stepped on her deck by seventeen guns from the Mississippi, lying near. The great guns and boarders having been exercised for their entertainment, the

DINNER GIVEN TO THE JAPANESE COMMISSIONERS ON BOARD U.S.S. POWHATAN

commissioners, with their numerous attendants, left for the Powhatan, the Macedonian firing a salvo in their honor, as they took their departure. On arriving on board the flag-ship, they were first conducted through the different departments of the steamer, and examined with minute interest the guns and the machinery. A boat was lowered, with a howitzer in its bows, and this was repeatedly discharged, much to their amusement; for, although not a very warlike people, (at least in their modern history,) the Japanese evidently had a great fondness for martial exercise and display. The engines were next put in motion, and they evinced the usual intelligence of the higher class of Japanese in their inquiries and remarks. After satisfying their curiosity, dinner was announced, and the five commissioners were conducted to the Commodore's cabin, where a very handsome banquet awaited them. The subordinate officials, amounting to about sixty, were provided for under the awning on the quarter-deck, where a large table had been spread with an abundant supply.

The Commodore had invited the four captains of the squadron, his interpreter, Mr. Williams, and his secretary, to join the commissioners at his table. Yenoske, the Japanese interpreter, was allowed the privilege, as a special condescension on the part of his superiors, to sit at a side-table in the cabin, where his humble position did not seem to disturb either his equanimity or his appetite. Hayashi, who always preserved his grave and dignified bearing, ate and drank sparingly, but tasted of every dish, and sipped of every kind of wine. The others proved themselves famous trencher-men, and entered more heartily than their chief into the conviviality of the occasion. Matsusaki was the soul of the party, and showed at once a very decided appreciation of American fare, and a special fondness for the champaigne, with no marked aversion, however, to the other wines and beverages. The liqueurs, particularly the maraschino, seemed to suit the tastes of the Japanese exactly, and they drank unnumbered glasses of it. Matsusaki, who was a jovial fellow, soon showed the effects of his copious libations, and became very particularly happy. Hayashi, the grave prince, was the only one, in fact, whose sobriety was proof against the unrestrained conviviality which prevailed among his bacchanalian coadjutors.

The Japanese party upon deck, who were entertained by a large body of officers from the various ships, became quite uproarious under the influence of overflowing supplies of champaigne, Madeira, and punch, which they seemed greatly to relish. The Japanese took the lead in proposing healths and toasts, and were by no means the most backward in drinking them. They kept shouting at the top of their voices, and were heard far above the music of the bands that enlivened the entertainment by a succession of brisk and cheerful tunes. It was, in short, a scene of noisy conviviality, and of very evident enjoyment on the part of the guests. The eating was no less palatable to them than the drinking, and the rapid disappearance of the large quantity and variety of the viands profusely heaped upon the table was quite a marvel, even to the heartiest feeders among the Americans. In the eagerness of the Japanese appetite, there was but little discrimination in the choice of dishes and in the order of courses, and the most startling heterodoxy was exhibited in the confused commingling of fish, flesh, and fowl, soups and syrups, fruits and fricassees, roast and boiled, pickles and preserves. As a most generous supply had been provided, there were still some remnants of the feast left, after the guests had satisfied their voracity, and most of these, the Japanese, in accordance with their usual custom, stowed away about their persons to carry off with them. The Japanese always have an abundant supply of paper within the left bosom of their loose robes in a capacious pocket. This is used for various purposes; one species, as soft as our cotton cloth, and withal exceedingly tough, is used for a pocket handkerchief; another furnishes the material for taking notes, or for wrapping up what is left after a feast. On the present occasion, when the dinner was over, all the Japanese guests simultaneously spread out their long folds of paper, and gathering what scraps they could lay their hands on, without regard to the kind of food, made up an envelope of conglomerate eatables in which there was such a confusion of the sour and sweet, the albuminous, oleaginous, and saccharine, that the chemistry of Leibig, or the practised taste of the Commodore's Parisian cook, would never have reached a satisfactory analysis. Nor was this the result of gluttony, or a deficiency of breeding; it was the fashion of the country. These unsavory parcels they stowed away in their pockets, or in their capacious sleeves, to carry away with them. The practice was universal, and they not only always followed it themselves, but insisted that their American guests, when entertained at a Japanese feast, should adopt it also. Whenever the Commodore and his officers were feasted on shore, they had paper parcels of what was left thrust into their hands on leaving, which they were obliged to take away with them, as it seemed an important part of Japanese hospitality, which could not be declined without giving offence.

After the banquet, the Japanese were entertained by an exhibition of negro minstrelsy, got up by some of the sailors, who, blacking their faces and dressing themselves in character, enacted their parts with a humor that would have gained them unbounded applause from a New York audience even at Christy's. The gravity of the saturnine Hayashi was not proof against the grotesque exhibition, and even he joined with the rest in the general hilarity provoked by the farcical antics and humorous performances of the mock negroes. It was now sunset, and the Japanese prepared to depart with quite as much wine in them as they could well bear. The jovial Matsusaki threw his arms about the Commodore's neck, crushing, in his tipsy embrace, a pair of new epaulettes, and repeating, in Japanese, with maudlin affection, these words, as interpreted into English: "Nippon and America, all the same heart." He then went toddling into his boat, supported by some of his more steady companions, and soon all the happy party had left the ships and were making rapidly for the shore. The Saratoga fired the salute of seventeen guns as the last boat pulled off from the Powhatan, and the squadron was once more left in the usual quiet of ordinary ship's duty.

The following day the Commodore landed to have a conference in regard to the remaining points of the treaty previous to signing. He was met, as usual, at the treaty house by the commissioners, who had more than their ordinary share of gravity, probably, owing to the natural effects of the previous day's conviviality.

As soon as the Commodore had taken his seat, a letter was handed to him, which the Japanese stated they had just received from Simoda. It was from Commander Pope, and had been transmitted through the authorities over land. Its contents gave a satisfactory report of Simoda, and the Commodore at once said that he accepted that port, but declared that it must be opened without delay. Hakodadi, he added, would do for the other, and Napha, in Lew Chew, could be retained for the third. In regard to the other two, he was willing, he said, to postpone their consideration to some other time.

The Commodore now proposed to sign the agreement in regard to the three ports, and directed his interpreter to read it in Dutch. When the document had been thus read and afterwards carefully perused by the Japanese, they stated that they were prepared to concur in everything except as to the *immediate* opening of Simoda. After discussion, it was finally settled that though the port might be opened, the Japanese would address a note to the Commodore, stating that everything which might be wanting by ships could not be furnished there before the expiration of ten months, but that wood and water, and whatever else the place possessed would be supplied immediately; and to this note the Commodore promised to reply, and express his satisfaction with such an arrangement.

The question now came up with respect to the extent of privileges to be granted to Americans who might visit Simoda, in the discussion of which it was perfectly plain that the Japanese meant to be distinctly understood as prohibiting, absolutely, at least, for the present, the *permanent* residence of Americans, with their families, in Japan. The distance, also, to which Americans might extend their excursions into the country around the ports of Simoda and Hakodadi was settled; and it is observable, that, at the special request of the Japanese, the Commodore named the distance, they assenting, at once, to that which he mentioned.

The proposition to have consular agents residing in Japan was one which evidently gave great anxiety to the commissioners, and the same grounds were taken and answered as have already been related in the narrative of the Commodore's conversation with the interpreters on a previous page of this chapter. The Commodore was firm in saying there must be such agents for the sake of the Japanese themselves as well as for that of our own countrymen, and it was finally conceded that there should be one, to live at Simoda, and that he should not be appointed until a year or eighteen months from the date of the treaty.

Two more articles, including the new points which had been discussed were now added to the transcript of the proposed treaty, and the Japanese having promised to bring on board the Powhatan next day a copy, in Dutch, of their understanding of the agreement as far as concurred in, the Commodore took his departure.

During the next two days several notes passed between the Commodore and the Japanese commissioners, in the course of which various questions that had been already considered were more definitively settled; and the American interpreters were occupied, in coöperation with the Japanese, in drawing up the treaty in the Chinese, Dutch, and Japanese languages. On the twenty-ninth, the ships Vandalia and Southampton arrived from Simoda with a confirmation of what Commander Pope had already stated in his dispatch which had been transmitted by the Japanese authorities, over land, to the Commodore, namely, that the harbor and town of Simoda had been found, on examination, suitable in every respect for the purposes of the Americans. All was now in readiness for the final signing of the treaty.

Accordingly, on Friday, the 31st of March, 1854, the Commodore proceeded to the treaty house with his usual attendants, and immediately on his arrival signed three several drafts of the treaty written in the English language, and delivered them to the commissioners, together with three copies of the same in the Dutch and Chinese languages, certified by the interpreters, Messrs. Williams and Portman, for the United States. At the same time, the Japanese commissioners, in behalf of their government, handed to the Commodore three drafts of the treaty written respectively in the Japanese, Chinese, and Dutch languages, and signed by the four of their body especially delegated by the Emperor for that purpose. The following is the treaty as agreed upon.

The United States of America and the Empire of Japan, desiring to establish firm, lasting, and sincere friendship between the two nations, have resolved to fix, in a manner clear and positive, by means of a treaty or general convention of peace and amity, the rules which shall in future be mutually observed in the intercourse of their respective countries; for which most desirable object the President of the United States has conferred full powers on his commissioner, Matthew Calbraith Perry, special ambassador of the United States to Japan; and the august sovereign of Japan has given similar full powers to his commissioners, Hayashi-Daigaku-no-kami, Ido, Prince of Tsus-Sima, Izawa, Prince of Mimasaki, and Udono, member of the Board of Revenue.

And the said commissioners, after having exchanged their said full powers, and duly considered the premises, have agreed to the following articles:

ARTICLE I.

There shall be a perfect, permanent, and universal peace, and a sincere and cordial amity, between the United States of America, on the one part, and the Empire of Japan on the other, and between their people, respectively, without exception of persons or places.

ARTICLE II.

The port of Simoda, in the principality of Idzu, and the port of Hakodadi, in the principality of Matsmai, are granted by the Japanese as ports for the reception of American ships, where they can be supplied with wood, water, provisions, and coal, and other articles their necessities may require, as far as the Japanese have them. The time for opening the first named port is immediately on signing this treaty; the last named port is to be opened immediately after the same day in the ensuing Japanese year.

NOTE.—A tariff of prices shall be given by the Japanese officers of the things which they can furnish, payment for which shall be made in gold and silver coin.

ARTICLE III.

Whenever ships of the United States are thrown or wrecked on the coast of Japan, the Japanese vessels will assist them, and carry their crews to Simoda or Hakodadi, and hand them over to their countrymen appointed to receive them. Whatever articles the shipwrecked men may have preserved shall likewise be restored, and the expenses incurred in the rescue and support of Americans and Japanese who may thus be thrown upon the shores of either nation are not to be refunded.

ARTICLE IV.

Those shipwrecked persons and other citizens of the United States shall be free as in other countries, and not subjected to confinement, but shall be amenable to just laws.

ARTICLE V.

Shipwrecked men, and other citizens of the United States, temporarily living at Simoda and Hakodadi, shall not be subject to such restrictions and confinement as the Dutch and Chinese are at Nagasaki; but shall be free at Simoda to go where they please within the limits of seven Japanese miles (or *ri*) from a small island in the harbor of Simoda, marked on the accompanying chart, hereto appended; and shall in like manner be free to go where they please at Hakodadi, within limits to be defined after the visit of the United States squadron to that place.

ARTICLE VI.

If there be any other sort of goods wanted, or any business which shall require to be arranged, there shall be careful deliberation between the parties in order to settle such matters.

ARTICLE VII.

It is agreed that ships of the United States resorting to the ports open to them shall be permitted to exchange gold and silver coin and articles of goods for other articles of goods, under such regulations as shall be temporarily established by the Japanese government for that purpose. It is stipulated, however, that the ships of the United States shall be permitted to carry away whatever articles they are unwilling to exchange.

ARTICLE VIII.

Wood, water, provisions, coal, and goods required, shall only be procured through the agency of Japanese officers appointed for that purpose, and in no other manner.

ARTICLE IX.

It is agreed, that if, at any future day, the government of Japan shall grant to any other nation or nations privileges and advantages which are not herein granted to the United States and the citizens thereof, that these same privileges and advantages shall be granted likewise to the United States and to the citizens thereof without any consultation or delay.

ARTICLE X.

Ships of the United States shall be permitted to resort to no other ports in Japan but Simoda and Hakodadi, unless in distress or forced by stress of weather.

ARTICLE XI.

There shall be appointed by the government of the United States consuls or agents to reside in Simoda at any time after the expiration of eighteen months from the date of the signing of this treaty; provided that either of the two governments deem such arrangement necessary.

ARTICLE XII.

The present convention, having been concluded and duly signed, shall be obligatory, and faithfully observed by the United States of America and Japan, and by the citizens and subjects of each respective power; and it is to be ratified and approved by the President of the United States, by and with the advice and consent of the Senate thereof, and by the august Sovereign of Japan, and the ratification shall be exchanged within eighteen months from the date of the signature thereof, or sooner if practicable.

In faith whereof, we, the respective plenipotentiaries of the United States of America and the Empire of Japan, aforesaid, have signed and sealed these presents.

Done at Kanagawa, this thirty-first day of March, in the year of our Lord Jesus Christ one thousand eight hundred and fifty-four, and of Kayei the seventh year, third month, and third day.

Immediately on the signing and exchange of the copies of the treaty, the Commodore presented the first commissioner, Prince Hayashi, with an American flag, remarking that he considered it the highest expression of national courtesy and friendship he could offer. The prince was evidently deeply impresssed with this significant mark of amity, and returned his thanks for it with indications of great feeling. The Commodore then presented the other dignitaries with the various gifts he had especially reserved for them. All formal business being now concluded to the mutual satisfaction of both parties, the Japanese commissioners invited the Commodore and his officers to partake of an entertainment which had been particularly prepared for the occasion.

The tables were now spread in the large reception hall. These were nothing more than wide divans, such as were used for seats, and of the same height. They were covered with a red-colored crape, and arranged in order, according to the rank of the guests and their hosts, an upper table, raised somewhat above the rest, being appropriated to the Commodore, his superior officers, and the commissioners. When all were seated, the servitors brought in a rapid succession of courses, consisting chiefly of thick soups, or rather stews, in most of which fresh fish was a component part. These were served in small earthen bowls or cups, and were brought in upon lacquered stands, about fourteen inches square and ten high, and placed, one before each guest, upon the tables. Together with each dish was a supply of soy or some other condiment, while throughout there was an abundant quantity, served in peculiar vessels, of the Japanese national liquor, the saki, a sort of whiskey distilled from rice. Various sweetened confections, and a multiplicity of cakes, were liberally interspersed among the other articles on the tables. Toward the close of the feast, a plate containing a broiled cray fish, a piece of fried fish of some kind, two or three boiled shrimps, and a small square pudding with something of the consistence of blanc mange, was placed before each, with a hint that they were to follow the guests on their return to the ships, and they were accordingly sent and duly received afterward.

The feast of the commissioners did not make a strikingly favorable impression on their guests; but they were greatly pleased with the courtesy of their hosts, whose urbanity and assiduous attentions left nothing to desire on the score of politeness. They left, however, it must be confessed, with appetites but scantily gratified by the unusual fare that had been spread before them. It is true that apologies were made, and this, by the way, proved to be an habitual feature of their entertainments, and causes were assigned for the poorness of the repast on the score of the difficulty of obtaining the best articles of food at Kanagawa. The dinner given to the commissioners on board the Powhatan would have made, in quantity, at least a score of such as that offered by the Japanese on this occasion. To dispose of the subject in one word, the entertainments of the Japanese, generally, while full of hospitality, left but an unfavorable impression of their skill in cookery. The Lew Chewans evidently excelled them in good living.

After the feast, which passed pleasantly and convivially, mutual compliments being freely exchanged, and healths drunk in full, though Lilliputian, cups of saki, the commissioners expressed great anxiety about the proposed visit of the Commodore to Yedo. They earnestly urged him not to take his ships any higher up the bay, as, they said, it would lead to trouble, by which the populace might be disturbed, and their own lives, perhaps, jeoparded. The Commodore argued the matter with them for some considerable time, and, as they still pertinaciously urged their objections to his visit to the capital, it was agreed that the subject should be further discussed by an interchange of notes. The meeting then broke up.

Before proceeding further with the narrative, it may be well here briefly to pause and define with precision what had been accomplished by means of the treaty that had been signed.

When it was determined by our government to send an expedition to Japan, those in authority were not unmindful of the peculiar characteristics of that singular nation. Unlike all other civilized people, it was in a state of voluntary, long-continued, and determined isolation. It neither desired nor sought communication with the rest of the world; but, on the contrary, strove to the uttermost to prevent it. It was comparatively an easy task to propose to any power, the ports of which were freely visited by ships from every part of the world, the terms of a commercial treaty. Such powers have recognized commerce itself as part of their national system, and the principle of permitting it is freely avowed by their usage: a treaty, therefore, had but to define its privileges, and state the conditions on which they might be enjoyed in the case of any nation seeking to make such a treaty. But not so, when, by any power, commerce itself was interdicted and made contrary to law. Before general conditions of commerce could be proposed to such a power, it was necessary to settle the great preliminary that commerce would be allowed at all. Again, if that preliminary were settled affirmatively, a second point, of great moment, remained to be discussed, viz., *to what degree* shall intercourse for trading purposes be extended? Among nations accustomed to the usages of Christendom, the principles and extent of national comity in the interchanges of commercial transactions have been so long and so well defined and understood, that, as between them, the term, "commercial treaty," needs no explanation; its meaning is comprehended alike by all, and in its stipulations it may cover the very broad extent that includes everything involved in the operations of commerce between two maritime nations. All ports are open, all commodities may be imported or exported, subject only to such regulations as may have been agreed upon between the contracting parties. The foundation for the contract existed before its terms were adjusted. But in a kingdom which, in its polity, expressly ignored commerce and repudiated it as an evil instead of a good, it was necessary, as we have said, to lay the very foundation as well as adjust the terms.

Hence the instructions to Commodore Perry covered broad ground, and his letters of credence conformed to his instructions. If he found the Japanese disposed to abandon, at once and forever, their deliberately adopted plan of non-intercourse with foreigners (an event most unlikely) his powers were ample to make with them a commercial treaty as wide and general as any we have with the nations of Europe. If they were disposed to relax but in part their jealous and suspicious system, formally to profess relations of friendship, and opening some only of their ports to our vessels to allow a trade in those ports between their people and ours, he was authorized to negotiate for this purpose, and secure for his country such privileges as he could, not inconsistent with the self respect which, as a nation, we owed to ourselves. It must not be forgotten, in the contemplation of what was accomplished, that our representative went to a people who, at the time of his arrival among them, had, both by positive law and an usage of more than two hundred years, allowed but one of their harbors, Nagasaki, to be opened to foreigners at all; had permitted no trade with such foreigners when they did come, except, under most stringent regulations, to the Dutch and Chinese; were in the habit of communicating with the world outside of them at second hand only, through the medium of the Dutch, who were in prison at Dezima; and a people who, as far as we know, never made a formal *treaty* with a civilized nation in the whole course of their antecedent history. To expect such a people to make a compact such as would be made between two great commercial nations, England and ourselves, for instance, would have been simply ridiculous. There were, in fact, but two points on which the Commodore's instructions did not allow him a large discretion, to be exercised according to circumstances. These two were, first, that if, happily, any arrangements for trade, either general or special, were made, it was to be distinctly stipulated that, under no circumstances, and in no degree, would the Americans submit to the humiliating treatment so long borne by the Dutch in carrying on their trade. The citizens of our country would be dealt with as freemen, or there should be no dealings at all. The second point was, that in the event of any of our countrymen being cast, in God's providence, as shipwrecked men on the coast of Japan, they should not be treated as prisoners, confined in cages, or subjected to inhuman treatment, but should be received with kindness and hospitably cared for until they could leave the country.

It will easily be seen, therefore, that, from the circumstances of the case, there was novelty in the features of the mission on which Commodore Perry was sent. Little or no guidance was to be derived from our past diplomatic experience or action. The nearest approach to such guidance was to be found in our treaty with China, made in 1844. This, therefore, was carefully studied by the Commodore. It purports to be "a treaty or general convention of peace, amity, and commerce," and to settle the rules to "be mutually observed in the intercourse of the respective countries." So far as "commerce" is concerned, it permits "the citizens of the United States to frequent" five ports in China, "and *to reside with their families* and trade there, and to proceed at pleasure with their vessels and merchandise to or from any foreign port, and from either of the said five ports to any other of them." As to duties on articles imported, they are to pay according to a tariff which is made part of the treaty, and in no case are to be subjected to higher duties than those paid, under similar circumstances, by the people of other nations. Consuls are provided for, to reside at the five open ports; and those trading there are "permitted to import from their own or any other ports into China, and sell there, and purchase therein, and export to their own or any other ports all manner of merchandise, of which the importation or exportation is not prohibited by" the treaty. In short, so far as the five ports are concerned, there exists between us and China a general treaty of commerce; and accordingly the twenty-second article expressly declares that "relations of peace and amity between the United States and China" are "established by this treaty, and the vessels of the United States" are "admitted to trade freely to and from the five ports of China open to foreign commerce."

It certainly was very desirable to obtain, if possible, similar privileges from Japan, and the Commodore resolved that, if the Japanese would negotiate at all, his first efforts should be directed to that end. Accordingly he caused to be prepared, in the Chinese character, a transcript of the treaty, with such verbal alterations as would make it applicable to Japan, with the view of exhibiting it to the Imperial commissioners of that country should he be so successful as to open negotiations. He was not sanguine enough to hope that he could procure an entire adoption of the Chinese treaty by the Japanese. He was not ignorant of the difference in national characteristics between the inhabitants of China and the more independent, self-reliant, and sturdy natives of the Japanese islands. He knew that the latter held the former in some degree of contempt, and treated them, in the matter of trade, very much as they did the Dutch. He was also aware that the Chinese, when they made their treaty, did know something of the advantages that might result from an intercourse with the rest of the world; while as to the Japanese, in their long-continued isolation, either they neither knew nor desired such advantages; or, if they knew them, feared they might be purchased at too high a price in the introduction of foreigners who, as in the case of the Portuguese, centuries before, might seek to overturn the empire. It was too much therefore to expect that the Japanese would in *all* the particulars of a treaty imitate the Chinese. Still, they might be disposed to adopt some of its most important features when suggested to them by a knowledge of what other orientals had done.

But of the difficulties encountered, even after the Japanese had consented to negotiate, the best account we think may be given from the conferences and discussions between the respective negotiators, of all which most accurate reports were kept on both sides, in the form of dialogue. At the first meeting of the Commodore with the Imperial commissioners, on the 8th of March, he acted on the plan he had proposed to himself with respect to the treaty with China, and thus addressed them:

"*Com. Perry.* I think it would be better for the two nations that a treaty similar to the one between my country and the Chinese should be made between us. I have prepared the draft of one almost identical with our treaty with China. I have been sent here by my government to make a treaty with yours; if I do not succeed *now*, my government will probably send more ships here; but I hope we will soon settle matters amicably."

"*Japanese.* We wish for time to have the document translated into the Japanese language."

This was but one among a hundred proofs of their extreme suspicion and caution; for there was not one of the imperial commissioners, probably, who could not have read, without the least difficulty, the document as furnished by the Commodore; and certain it is that their interpreters could have read it off into Japanese at once.

The Commodore, whose wish it was to do as far as possible everything that might conciliate, of course, made no objection to a request so seemingly reasonable, though he knew it to be needless, and was content to wait patiently for their reply. In one week that reply came in writing, and was very explicit: "As to opening a trade, such as is now carried on by China with your country, we certainly cannot *yet* bring it about. The feelings and manners of our people are very unlike those of outer nations, and it will be exceedingly difficult, even if you wish it, to immediately change the old regulations for those of other countries. Moreover, the Chinese have long had intercourse with western nations, while we have had dealings at Nagasaki with only the people of Holland and China."

This answer was not entirely unexpected, and put an end to all prospect of negotiating a "commercial treaty," in the European sense of that phrase. It only remained, therefore, to secure, for the present, admission into the Kingdom, and so much of trade as Japanese jealousy could be brought to concede. At length, after much and oft repeated discussion, the point was yielded that certain ports might be opened to our vessels; and then, in the interview of March 25th, came up the subject of consuls.

"*Japanese.* About the appointment of consuls or agents, the commissioners desire a delay of four or five years to see how the intercourse works. The governor of the town and the official interpreter will be able to carry on all the business of supplying provisions, coal, and needed articles, with the captain, without the intervention of a consul."

"*Com. Perry.* The duties of a consul are to report all difficulties between American citizens and Japanese to his government in an authentic manner, assist the Japanese in carrying out their laws and the provisions of the treaty, and recovering debts made by the Americans; and also communicating to the government at Washington whatever the Japanese wish, as no letters can be received after this through the Dutch; and if no consuls are received, then a ship of war must remain in Japan constantly, and her captain do the duties of a consul."

"*Japanese.* If we had not felt great confidence in you, we should not have consented to open our ports at all. Consuls may be accepted by and by, after experience has shown their need; and we hope that all American citizens obey the laws of their country, and behave properly."

"*Com. Perry.* True; and I hope no difficulty will arise: and this appointment of consuls in Japan, as they are in China, Hawaii, and everywhere else, is to prevent and provide for difficulties. No American will report his own misdeeds to his own government, nor can the Japanese bring them to our notice, except through a government agent. This provision must be in the treaty, though I will stipulate for only one, to *reside* at Simoda, and he will not be sent, probably, for a year or two from this time."

And thus it was that the Commodore had to explain everything, and feel his way, step by step, in the progress of the whole negotiation.

"*Japanese.* The commissioners wish every point desired by the Admiral to be stated clearly, for the Japanese are not equal to the Americans, and have not much to give in exchange."

"*Com. Perry.* I have already stated all my views as regards our intercourse in the draft of the treaty you have." [This was one prepared by the Commodore after the rejection of the transcript of the Chinese treaty.] "Let the commissioners state their objections to it. This treaty now to be made is *only a beginning*; and as the nations know each other, the Japanese will permit Americans to go anywhere, to Mount Fusi, all over the country."

"*Japanese.* We have found restrictions necessary against the Portuguese and English." Then followed observations by the Japanese on Pellew's entry into Nagasaki harbor, which showed how much dislike of the English that event had occasioned. A strong proof of their remarkable caution was furnished by the Japanese at the conference held on the 28th of March, when most of the terms of the treaty had been agreed upon.

"*Com. Perry.* I am prepared now to sign the treaty about these three harbors."

[Mr. Portman, interpreter, then read in Dutch that portion of the treaty which contained such points as had been already agreed upon.]

"*Japanese.* It is all correct except that we have objection to opening the port of Simoda *immediately*; if any vessels were to go there in distress, we would be glad to furnish them with provisions, wood, and water."

"*Com. Perry.* You have already consented, in one of your letters to me, to open that port immediately. I am very desirous of settling that matter now, as I wish to dispatch the Saratoga home to inform the government, before Congress adjourns, how matters are advancing; that will take some time, and there is no probability that any ships will come here before ten or twelve months have expired; so that it will make no difference to you whether you put it in the treaty to be opened now or in ten months."

"*Japanese.* We are willing to put it in the treaty 'to be opened now,' if you will give us a letter or promise that no ships will come here before the President gives his permission."

"*Com. Perry.* I cannot do that very well, but I am willing to put it off ninety days; that will be about the time I shall return from Hakodadi; it was your own proposition yesterday to open that port immediately. I consent to this, however, to show you how desirous I am to do what I can to please you. I cannot consent to a longer time."

"*Japanese.* If we put it in the treaty to be opened now, we would like you to give us an order that no ships shall enter that port before ten months."

"*Com. Perry.* I cannot do that. But there is no probability that any ships will come here before that time, as I shall not leave here for three months, and they will not hear of it before that time; and when they do hear of it, it will take several months for ships to make the voyage here. If you choose, I will keep one of the ships at Simoda for several months."

"*Japanese.* If ships go there before that time, we shall not be able to give them other than provisions, wood, and water."

"*Com. Perry.* The ships that may go there will want such things only as you may have; if you have them not, of course you cannot and will not be expected to furnish them; but, as I said before, there is no probability that ships will go there before the expiration of ten months."

"*Japanese.* When you come back from Matsmai, we will have a plenty of provisions at Simoda for the whole squadron; but to other ships we cannot furnish more than wood, water, &c."

"*Com. Perry.* When we return from Matsmai we shall not want many provisions, as we shall be going to a place where we can get a plenty. It is only the principle I wish settled now. I have come here as a peacemaker, and I want to settle everything now, and thus prevent trouble hereafter; and I wish to write home to my government that the Japanese are friends."

"*Japanese.* We will write you a letter stating that we cannot furnish everything before ten months, but that we can furnish wood and water immediately, and that we will furnish such other things as we possibly can. This letter we would like you to answer."

"*Com. Perry.* Very well; I will."

"*Japanese.* [Entering on another part of the terms agreed on.] We will not confine Americans, or prevent them from walking around; but we would like to place a limit to the distance they may walk."

"*Com. Perry.* I am prepared to settle that matter now, but they must not be confined to any particular house or street. Suppose we make the distance they may walk, the same distance that a man can go and come in a day. Or, if you choose, the number of *lis* or *ris* may be agreed upon."

"*Japanese.* We are willing that they shall walk as far as they can go and come in a day."

"*Com. Perry.* There is no probability that sailors would want to go on shore more than once from curiosity; beside, they will have their daily duties to attend to on board ship, and will not be able to go on shore."

"*Japanese.* We do not want any women to come and remain at Simoda."

"*Com. Perry.* The probability is but few women will go there, and they only the wives of the officers of the ships."

"*Japanese.* When you come back from Matsmai we would like *you* to settle the distance Americans are to walk. It is difficult for *us* to settle the distance."

"*Com. Perry.* Say the distance of seven Japanese miles in any direction from the centre of the city of Simoda."

"*Japanese.* Very well. A few miles will make no difference. You are requested not to leave agents until after you have experienced that it is necessary."

"*Com. Perry.* I am willing to defer the appointment of a consul or agent one year or eighteen months from the date of signing the treaty; and then, if my government think it necessary, it will send one."

In fact, not an article of the treaty was made but upon the most serious deliberation by the Japanese. In answer to a question from Captain Adams, in the very first stages of the negotiation, they replied: "The Japanese are unlike the Chinese; they are averse to change; and when they make a compact of any kind they intend it shall endure for a thousand years. For this reason it will be best to deliberate and examine well the facilities for trade and the suitableness of the port before any one is determined on." Probably nothing but the exercise of the most perfect truthfulness and patience would ever have succeeded in making with them a treaty at all; and from the language of one of their communications, it is obvious that, with characteristic caution, they meant that their present action should be but a *beginning* of intercourse, which might or might not be afterward made more extensive according to the results of what they deemed the experiment. Thus they say: "As our ideas of things and what we each like are still very dissimilar, as are also our notions of the prices or worth of things, this makes it indispensable that we both first make a mutual trial and examination." This shows the spirit in which they negotiated. The treaty has already been laid before the reader. A brief analysis of it is all that is here necessary. And it is to be remarked first, that it evidently implies, in its language and proper construction, future and more enlarged regulations as to commerce. Thus, in article VI, it is declared: "If there be any other sort of goods wanted, or any business which shall require to be arranged, there shall be careful deliberation between the parties in order to settle such matters." And again, in article VII, "It is agreed that ships of the United States, resorting to the ports open to them, shall be permitted to exchange gold and silver coin and articles of goods for other articles of goods, under such regulations as shall be *temporarily* established by the Japanese government for that purpose." In both these articles the Japanese substituted the word "goods" for "merchandise," as from their ignorance of the customs and terms used in foreign trade, they did not know what might be included in the technical meaning of the word "merchandise;" while "goods" had, to their minds, a well defined and perfectly intelligible signification. The words "shall be," in the sixth article, point to the probable necessity of *future* treaty-making with us, to "settle" "*any business* which shall require to be arranged." This, it must be remembered, was the first formal treaty they ever made on the subject of foreign trade, at least since the expulsion of the Portuguese, and they evidently meant to proceed cautiously by single steps. Again, in article VII, the word "*temporarily*" is used, inserted by them, and meant to imply some future action toward a more complete commercial arrangement or treaty, for which, at the present, they were not prepared. They meant, therefore, their action to be initiative only now, but contemplating, prospectively, a more enlarged commercial intercourse.

Secondly. There is observable throughout, the predominating influence of the national prejudice against the permanent introduction of foreigners among them. The word "reside" is but once used in the whole treaty, and that in the eleventh article relative to consuls. The details of conferences, already given, show how anxiously they sought to avoid having consuls at all. Indeed, Commodore Perry says, "I could only induce the commissioners to agree to this article, by endeavoring to convince them that it would save the Japanese government much trouble, if an American agent were to *reside* at one or both of the ports opened by the treaty, to whom complaints might be made of any mal-practice of the United States' citizens who might visit the Japanese dominions." They wanted no *permanent* foreign residents among them, official or unofficial. This was shown most unequivocally in the remark already recorded in one of the conferences: "*we do not want any women to come and remain at Simoda.*" Simoda was one of the ports open for trade with us, they knew that our people had wives and daughters, and that a man's family were ordinarily resident with him in his permanent abode, and that if the head of the family lived in Simoda as a Japanese would live, there would certainly be women who would "come and remain at Simoda." But more than this. It will be remembered that the Commodore had submitted to them our treaty with China, and they had held it under consideration for a week, at the end of which time they said, "as to opening a trade, such as is now carried on by China with your country, we certainly cannot yet bring it about. The Chinese have long had intercourse with western nations, while we have had dealings at Nagasaki with only the people of Holland and China." Now what was "such a trade" as we carried on with China? The Japanese read in our treaty that five ports were open to us, that permission was given "to the citizens of the United States to frequent" them; and further, "*to reside with their families and trade there.*" This they deliberately declined assenting to when they refused to make a treaty similar to that with China. They surely would not afterward knowingly insert it in any treaty they might make with us. The only *permanent* residence to which they gave assent, and that most reluctantly, was the residence of a consul. *Temporary* residence was allowed to our shipwrecked citizens, as well as to those who went to Simoda or Hakodadi on commercial business. They are allowed to land, to walk where they please within certain limits, to enter shops and temples without restriction, to purchase in the shops, and have the articles sent to the proper public office duly marked, where they will pay for them, to resort to public houses or inns that are to be built for their refreshment, "when on shore" at Simoda and Hakodadi; and until built, a temple, at each place, is assigned "as a resting place for persons in their walks." They may accept invitations to partake of the hospitality of any of the Japanese; but they are not permitted to enter "military establishments or private houses *without leave.*" Without leave, our citizens cannot enter them within the territories of any nation with which we have a treaty. In short, the whole treaty shows that the purpose of the Japanese was to try the experiment of intercourse with us before they made it as extensive or as intimate as it is between us and the Chinese. It was all they would do at the time, and much, very much, was obtained on the part of our negotiator in procuring a concession even to this extent.

But, as he knew that our success would be but the forerunner of that of other powers, and as he believed that new relations of trade once commenced, not only with ourselves, but with England, France, Holland, and Russia, could not, in the progress of events, fail effectually and forever to break up the old restrictive policy, and open Japan to the world, but must also lead gradually to liberal commercial treaties, he wisely, in the ninth article, secured to the United States and their citizens, without "consultation or delay," all privileges and advantages which Japan might hereafter "grant to any other nation or nations." And the Commodore's comments on this article, conclusively show, that *he*, at least, did not suppose he had made a "commercial treaty."

"ARTICLE IX. This is a most important article, as there can be little doubt that, on hearing of the success of this mission, the English, French, and Russians will follow our example; and it may be reasonable to suppose that each will gain some additional advantage, *until a commercial treaty is accomplished*. Article IX will give to Americans, without further consultation, all these advantages."

As far as we have yet learned, all other powers have been content to obtain just what we, as pioneers, have obtained. Their treaties are like ours.* That of Russia is copied from ours, with

---

* In a note to page 63, we have said intelligence had reached us of a commercial treaty between England and Japan. We have reason to think this is a mistake. If there be such a treaty, we are entitled, under our 9th article, to all its privileges and advantages, at once.

no change but that of the substitution of the port of Nagasaki for Napha in Lew Chew. We respectfully submit, therefore, that all, and indeed, more than all, that, under the circumstances, could reasonably have been expected, has been accomplished. Japan has been opened to the nations of the west, and it is not to be believed, that having once effected an entrance, the enlightened powers that have made treaties with her will *go backward*, and, by any indiscretion, lose what, after so many unavailing efforts for centuries, has at last been happily attained. It belongs to these nations to show Japan that her interests will be promoted by communication

---

Since the foregoing was written the treaty with England has reached us. We subjoin it, with the expression of our regret that Admiral Stirling could obtain no more than he did, as all he might obtain beyond what we had, would, under article IX of our treaty, have inured at once to our benefit, as well as that of England.

[From the London Gazette, of January 15.]

CONVENTION BETWEEN HER MAJESTY QUEEN VICTORIA AND THE EMPEROR OF JAPAN.

CONVENTION BETWEEN HER MAJESTY AND THE EMPEROR OF JAPAN, SIGNED AT NAGASAKI, IN THE ENGLISH AND JAPANESE LANGUAGE, OCTOBER 14, 1854, RATIFICATIONS EXCHANGED AT NAGASAKI, OCTOBER 9, 1855.

Convention for regulating the admission of British ships into the ports of Japan.

It is agreed between Sir James Stirling, knight, rear admiral, and commander-in-chief of the ships and vessels of her Britannic Majesty in the East Indies and seas adjacent, and Mezi-no Chekfusno Kami, Obm yo of Nagasaki, and Nagai Evan Ocho, Omedski of Nagasaki, ordered by his Imperial Highness the Emperor of Japan to act herein, that—

1. The ports of Nagasaki (Fisen) and Hakodadi (Matsmai) shall be open to British ships for the purposes of effecting repairs and obtaining fresh water, provisions, and other supplies of any sort they may absolutely want for the use of the ships.

2. Nagasaki shall be open for the purposes aforesaid from and after the present date, and Hakodadi from and after the end of fifty days from the admiral's departure from this port. The rules and regulations of each of these ports are to be complied with.

3. Only ships in distress from weather, or unmanageable, will be permitted to enter other ports than those specified in the foregoing articles, without permission from the Imperial government.

4. British ships in Japanese ports shall conform to the laws of Japan. If high officers or commanders of ships shall break any such laws, it will lead to the ports being closed. Should inferior persons break them, they are to be delivered over to the commanders of their ships for punishment.

5. In the ports of Japan, either now open or which may hereafter be opened to the ships or subjects of any foreign nation, British ships and subjects shall be entitled to admission and to the enjoyment of an equality of advantages with those of the most favored nation, always excepting the advantages accruing to the Dutch and Chinese from their existing relations with Japan.

6. This convention shall be ratified, and ratifications shall be exchanged, at Nagasaki, on behalf of her Majesty the Queen of Great Britain, and on behalf of his Highness the Emperor of Japan, within twelve months from the present date.

7. When this convention shall be ratified, no high officer coming to Japan shall alter it.

In witness whereof we have signed the same, and have affixed our seals thereunto, at Nagasaki, this 14th day of October, 1854.

JAMES STIRLING.

N. B. The Japanese text was signed by the Japanese plenipotentiaries.

Exposition of the Articles of the Convention of Nagasaki of the 14th of October, 1854, agreed to on the 18th of October, 1855, by their Excellencies the Rear-Admiral Commanding-in-Chief and the Japanese Commissioners.

1. The ports of Nagasaki (Fizen) and Hakodadi (Matsmai) shall be open to British ships for the purposes of effecting repairs and obtaining fresh water, provisions, and other supplies of any sort they may absolutely want for the use of the ships. may be repaired. Workmen, materials and supplies will be provided by the local government according to a tariff to be agreed upon, by which, also, the modes of payment will be regulated. All official communications will hereafter, when Japanese shall have time to learn English, be made in that language. A British burying ground shall be set apart on Medsume Sima, fenced in by a stone wall and properly protected.

The first article of the convention opens the ports of Nagasaki and Hakodadi to British ships for repairs and supplies. It opens the whole and every part of those ports; but ships must be guided in anchoring by the directions of the local government. Safe and convenient places will be assigned where ships

2. Nagasaki shall be open for the purposes aforesaid from and after the present date; and Hakodadi from and after the end of fifty days from the Admiral's departure from this port. The rules and regulations of each of these ports are to be complied with.

The second article provides that at each of the ports of Nagasaki and Hakodadi the port regulations shall be obeyed; but the Japanese government will take care that they shall not be of a nature to create embarrassment, nor to contradict in any other way the general tenor and intent of the treaty, the main object of which is to promote a friendly intercourse between Great Britain and Japan.

with them; and, as prejudice gradually vanishes, we may hope to see the future negotiation of commercial treaties, more and more liberal, for the benefit, not of ourselves only, but of all the maritime powers of Europe, for the advancement of Japan, and for the upward progress of our common humanity. It would be a foul reproach to Christendom now to force Japan to relapse

---

3. Only ships in distress from weather, or unmanageable, will be permitted to enter other ports than those specified in the foregoing articles, without permission from the imperial government.

The third article declares that only ships in distress from weather, or unmanageable, shall enter other ports than Nagasaki and Hokadadi without permission from the imperial government; but ships of war have a general right to enter the ports of friendly powers in the unavoidable performance of public duties, which right can neither be waived nor restricted; but her Majesty's ships will not enter any other than open ports without necessity, nor without offering proper explanation to the imperial authorities.

4. British ships in Japanese ports shall conform to the laws of Japan. If high officers or commanders of ships shall break any such laws, it will lead to the ports being closed. Should inferior persons break them, they are to be delivered over to the commanders of their ships for punishment.

The fourth article provides that the British ships and subjects in Japanese ports shall conform to the laws of Japan; and that if any subordinate British subjects commit offences against the laws, they shall be handed over to their own officers for punishment; and that if high officers or commanders of ships shall break the laws, it will lead to the closing of the ports specified.

All this is as it should be; but it is not intended by this article that any acts of individuals, whether high or low, previously unauthorized or subsequently disapproved of by her Majesty the Queen of Great Britain, can set aside the convention entered into with her Majesty alone by his Imperial Highness the Emperor of Japan.

5. In the ports of Japan, either now open, or which may hereafter be opened, to the ships or subjects of any foreign nation, British ships and subjects shall be entitled to admission, and to the enjoyment of an equality of advantages with those of the most favored nation, always excepting the advantages accruing to the Dutch and Chinese from their existing relations with Japan.

The fifth article secures in the fullest sense to British ships and subjects in every port of Japan, either now open or hereafter to be opened, an equality in point of advantage and accommodation with the ships and subjects or citizens of any other foreign nation, excepting any peculiar privileges hitherto conceded to the Dutch and Chinese in the port of Nagasaki. If, therefore, any other nation or people be now or hereafter permitted to enter other ports than Nagasaki, and Hakodadi, or to appoint consuls, or to open trade, or to enjoy any advantage or privilege whatever, British ships and subjects shall, as of right, enter upon the enjoyment of the same.

6. This convention shall be ratified, and the ratification shall be exchanged at Nagasaki on behalf of her Majesty the Queen of Great Britain, and on behalf of his Highness the Emperor of Japan, within twelve months from the present date.

7. When this convention shall be ratified no high officer coming to Japan shall alter it.

ARRANGEMENT REGARDING STAMPS.

An arrangement made subsequently to the convention requires that British ships intending to visit Japan shall be provided with a document in proof of their nationality, and as a check upon the conduct of vessels in Japanese ports; and her Majesty's government has directed a form of certificate of registration to be adopted, which has been accepted as satisfactory by the Japanese authorities; and merchant ships arriving in Japanese ports are to submit their certificate of registration to the officers to be appointed by the Japanese authorities, and to permit them to make such extracts from it as may seem good to them before such ships can be admitted to obtain repairs and supplies. Her Majesty's ships of war will not be provided with such documents, but the officers in command, upon proper application, will afford all reasonable information regarding their ships.

REGULATIONS FOR THE PORT OF NAGASAKI, COMMUNICATED TO REAR ADMIRAL SIR JAMES STERLING BY THE GOVERNOR OF NAGASAKI, OCTOBER, 1854.

Standing port regulations.

Art. 1. Ships shall anchor within two sima, and there await the direction of the governor.

Art. 2. No fire arms to be discharged.

Art. 3. No person to land on any of the islands.

Art. 4. No soundings to be taken, nor boats to be pulling about.

Art. 5. Should any communication be desired, a boat of the upper officers shall be called; but no communication shall be held with merchant boats, and no exchange of articles take place, or trading of any sort.

The above being according to the law of Great Japan, all commanders and other officers shall obey the same, and orders shall be given to the crew that the aforesaid law shall not be broken.

No regulations for the port of Hakodadi have yet been communicated.

Of the Dutch treaty, all we know is contained in the following newspaper paragraph:

THE DUTCH TREATY WITH JAPAN.

In reference to the treaty between the Dutch and the Emperor of Japan, a private letter from Batavia, under date of December 5, to a party in Boston, says: "The Dutch royal commissioners have returned from Japan, and Captain Fabins is off

into her cheerless and unprogressive state of unnatural isolation. She is the youngest sister in the circle of commercial nations; let those who are older kindly take her by the hand, and aid her tottering steps, until she has reached a vigor that will enable her to walk firmly in her own strength. Cautious and kindly treatment now will soon lead to commercial treaties as liberal as can be desired.*

---

with this steamer to take the treaty overland. By favor of a private friend I have seen a copy of it, and a more silly, stupid document I have never read. Things remain as they have done for the last two hundred years, only the Dutch resident of Decima may enter and circulate freely in the town of Nagasaki without the usual *guard of honor*. The ground on which the factory buildings stand and the buildings themselves become the property of the Dutch by purchase. No concessions are to be made by the Japanese to other nations without the Dutch participating in them. The only clause which appears distantly to hint to any future change is when the opperhoofd, (or chief agent of the government,) at Decima, is appointed and recognised as representing the Dutch government, in the event of the Japanese seeing fit, at any time, to desire to treat for further concessions. The treaty is not, I believe, to be published."

It will thus be seen that all other powers have encountered difficulties similar to those we met, and none have made a treaty more liberal than ours.

---

*Note.—Scarcely had this chapter been completed, before the public prints of the country brought to our notice the results of the first voyage made to Hakodadi after the signing of the treaty. The facts appear to be substantially as follows: On the 13th of February, 1855, the American schooner C. E. Foote sailed from Honolulu for Japan, via the Bonin islands. The vessel was fitted out by Messrs. Reed and Dougherty, American citizens, and was loaded, for the most part, with articles of ship chandlery, chains and anchors, pork and beef; sails, tar, cordage, &c. The purpose of the voyage was to fulfil a contract "to establish at Hakodadi a supply depot for American whale ships, so that they may winter at that place instead of Honolulu." Among the passengers were Mr. Reed and his family, and Mr. Doty and his family. These families included three American ladies and some children. On the 15th of March the vessel arrived at Simoda. She there found some of the officers and crew of the Russian frigate Diana, which had been wrecked by the effects of an earthquake at Simoda in the previous December. The Foote had touched at Simoda in the expectation of meeting there the United States ships Powhatan and Vandalia, to which she carried letters, and also to consume the time that had to elapse, some few weeks, before, under the treaty, the port of Hakodadi would be open to our vessels. On the arrival of the vessel, guard and shore boats surrounded her, and great curiosity was manifested to see the American ladies. The Russians were anxious to get away, and the owners of the American vessel at once negotiated with them to take them to Petropaulowski. This made it necessary to land all the passengers and a part of the cargo at Simoda. The schooner having been chartered, and her provisions sold to the Russians, Mr. Reed and Mr. Doty, with the three ladies of the party and the children, landed, and were assigned a residence in one of the temples named in the treaty to be used for that purpose until inns should be built, and carpenters were employed to make it convenient. The Japanese were very curious to see the ladies and children; but the temple and grounds were considered as exclusively the Americans. No Japanese, Mr. Reed states, in a communication to the "Alta Californian," except the officers, were permitted to enter but by special permission. "To guard against intrusion," (thus he writes,) "four officers are stationed at the gate, and are relieved every few hours. The watch is kept up day and night. Near the gate is a small house in which are stationed five other officers, who transmit all messages to or from us, introduce to us all who are allowed to enter, and make for us all the purchases we require." The list of articles of food furnished is both varied and extensive. Nor were the Americans confined to the temple. Mr. Reed thus writes: "In walking into the country, we found that pleasing views invited us from one point to another, from mountain peak to mountain peak, as we admired the strangeness and richness and beauty, until, though we started only for a morning walk, we often wandered too far to return the same night." The amusements of the party were not disturbed; for, on the evening of the 22d of March, the Americans united with the Russian officers in celebrating, in the temple, by music and dancing, the birthday anniversary of one of their number. Nor was this all: the time of the sojourn of our countrymen was about two months and a half; and, during this period, as appears from Mr. Doty's communication to the "San Francisco Herald," "Mr. Reed spent his time in selecting and purchasing a cargo of Japan goods for San Francisco, composed of lacquer ware, rice, silks, &c., &c.," which cargo, the California papers inform us, was afterward sold at San Francisco at a large profit.

It would appear, therefore, briefly to recapitulate, that our countrymen were permitted to land in Japan, were furnished with a house which was made comfortable for their residence, were permitted to store part of the cargo of their vessel, were plentifully supplied with necessary food, were permitted to walk about the country, were not molested in their amusements, and were allowed to purchase a cargo from the Japanese and take it away. Now, not one of these things could any American have done but for the treaty made by Commodore Perry.

Mr. Reed further writes, in the columns of the "Alta Californian:" "The Japanese began early to interrogate us upon our intentions, and we told them in writing that we came there *to live*." In the letter of Reed and Dougherty, addressed to the governor of Simoda, on the 22d of April, 1855, as published in the "New York Herald" of the 15th of October, 1855, they thus state their intentions: "We touched here, expecting to meet the Powhatan and Vandalia, to which we had letters, and also to consume time, knowing that, by the treaty, we could not go to that place (Hakodadi) before the middle or last of this month."

"We found the officers and crew of the wrecked ship Diana here, and anxious to go away, and we at once negotiated to transport them to Petropaulowski. On this account it became necessary for us to come on shore, and also to land part of our cargo and all the passengers."

"It was not our design to land here, nor is it our intention now to remain here longer than till our vessel returns, which we now expect in fifteen or twenty days. Should our schooner be lost and never return, our plans may be changed altogether; and should we not hear from her for two months to come, we then may seek other means of conveyance from this place."

"Our object is not to mingle or trade with the Japanese, but to trade with and assist our own people and ships that visit Japan."

As to the treaty, the letter proceeds: "We know well the interpretation and meaning given to it by our government." "We shall never compromise our government by saying that we have no right to remain here a week, a month, a year, or even five years, for we know, by the treaty, we have a perfect right so to do."

Mr. Doty, in his letter to the authorities of Simoda, dated the 23d of April, as published in the "New York Herald" of October 15, 1855, thus writes:

"I give you in writing the following reason for my sojourn at this place:

"I arrived in this port on the 15th ult., on board the American vessel C. E. Foote. Soon after our arrival, I was informed that the vessel would sail hence to Heda, and from thence to a foreign port, with officers and men of the late Russian frigate Diana. Not wishing to make the above voyage with my family, I came on shore, and now must necessarily remain here until the return of our vessel, when it is my intention to leave Simoda.

"If the vessel should not return after a reasonable time for making the voyage has elapsed, I shall avail myself of the first opportunity that offers to sail direct for the United States of America.

"In answer to the question of right of Americans to reside here, I would most respectfully beg leave to represent that, in my opinion, it is a matter to be settled by our respective governments, and, therefore, decline making any further communication upon this subject."

A proclamation was then issued by the authorities of Simoda, as follows:

"PROCLAMATION.

"To the Americans at Yokuseu Temple:

"About your leaving this place, your intention is heard, which you have declared that staying in this place is not properly your intention. But because the Russians have engaged the vessel manned by you, with which they have gone home, you have been compelled to stay here, and that you will, on the return of the vessel, leave this place, or should she not return in the intended time, to await the arrival of a vessel that sails for your country, and with that vessel to leave this place.

"According to this declaration, you must, on the return of your vessel, leave this place; or should she not return in the declared time, then, upon the arrival of an American ship, you must leave this place, without, at that time, expressing any excuse to delay you.

"Your present stay among us is found necessary, but it cannot in future be taken as an example.

"Never let it be asked again to stay. It is not only so in this place, but also at Hakodadi, which you and all Americans are obliged to observe.

"The foregoing is communicated by word of mouth from the governor of Simoda."

Soon after this, Commander Rogers, of the United States surveying expedition to the North Pacific, arrived at Simoda in the Vincennes, and to him the Americans appealed. This officer, taking distinctly the ground that the proper interpretation of the treaty was not confided to him, but could be settled only by the two governments of Japan and the United States, still endeavored, by a temperate and judicious letter to the authorities of Simoda, to induce them to put a different construction from that they had adopted upon the "temporary residence" allowed to Americans under the treaty; his effort, however, was fruitless.

But the object of Messrs. Reed and Dougherty, as they have stated it in the "San Francisco Herald" of the 18th of September, 1855, was to transport goods, and to *establish* themselves in Hakodadi for the purpose of supplying our whale ships that designed to winter there instead of at Honolulu. In other words, their object was to make at Hakodadi a permanent commercial agency and supply depot for whale ships; to live in Japan with their families, just as they would live in any European foreign port where they might establish a storehouse. They, therefore, while yet at Simoda, on the 20th of May, addressed the following letter to the governor of Hakodadi, and forwarded it by the Vincennes, that was about to sail for Hakodadi:

"To His Excellency the Governor of Hakodadi:

"We have the honor to communicate with you, through Commodore Rodgers, commanding the United States surveying expedition, and who visits your place to meet a part of his squadron, and also to survey and make a chart of your harbor. We are merchants on our way to your place, to make a temporary residence there, in order that we may receive and supply a certain number of our ships that are daily expected there. The supplies we intend to furnish are necessary, and cannot be furnished by the Japanese, for they have them not, such as chains and anchors, pork and beef, sails, tar and cordage, and ship chandlery generally. We have our families with us, and shall require or want a house for them to live in, and also a building to store our goods, for which we expect to pay a reasonable compensation or sum of money. We have been living here (at Simoda) for the past three months, awaiting the return of our vessel to take us to your place. When it returns, (and we expect it every day,) we shall leave this place for Hakodadi. On our arrival there, we trust your excellency, in the absence of hotels and inns, will have selected a suitable place for our families to reside, and also to store our goods. Suffer us, also, to ask of your honor to inform any of our ships which may arrive there before us that we are at this place, and expect soon to be at Hakodadi."

To this an answer was sent through Commander Rodgers, the purport of which will be seen from the following communication, sent by that gentleman to Messrs. Reed and Dougherty:

"United States Ship Vincennes, Hakodadi, *June* 19, 1855.

"Gentlemen: The governor of Hakodadi has replied to my application for permission for you to reside on shore, in accordance with the stipulations of the treaty of Kanagawa, that temporary, used in the treaty means a short time—he thinks five or ten days, or, at the utmost, a few months. Unless I will consent to his definition, by asking for some short definite period, after which you may be sent away, he utterly refuses to permit you to sleep on shore a single night. I have replied that I dare not define temporary residence in other than the usual manner. That if two governments, in their wisdom, preferred to give you permission to "live temporarily" in Hakodadi, I would not so circumscribe the meaning of the treaty.

"I apprehend no difficulty in obtaining permission for you to live for a few months in Hakodadi; but I must say how long you may remain. After the time expires, the Japanese will consider that you cease to be temporary residents, and that you commence to live permanently. If permanent residence is not in the treaty, they will then have a right to send you away. I have been officially informed of the fact, and, therefore, say to you officially that the government of Japan will not suffer you to sleep a night on shore while I persist in claiming temporary residence to mean an indefinite period of time.

"If the government of the United States decides that the treaty has been broken to your prejudice, I believe it will demand the proper redress for you. Should the government decide that the Japanese are right, your coming here was rash."

Subsequently Messrs. Reed and Dougherty, with their families, left Simoda in their schooner, and proceeded to Hakodadi, arriving at that port eight days after the arrival of the Vincennes, and being the first American merchant vessel which had entered the port under the treaty. In fact the port had but just been opened. Mr. Doty states that they "were refused permission to land, and ordered away."

These seem to be substantially the facts connected with the voyage of the Foote, and it will be perceived, that the question involved in them is one of interpretation of the treaty merely. The conduct of the Japanese at Simoda certainly showed no unwillingness to comply with the treaty stipulations, for everything they did was performed by reason of the treaty, and, but for its existence, would not have been performed at all. The only question raised by them was whether the treaty, by "temporary residence," meant a residence which might be made "permanent" by continuance for an indefinite period. As to Hakodadi, it must be remembered that the port is at a long distance from the capital on the island of Nippon, being, in truth, on another island, (Jesso,) and ordinarily has but little communication with its more populous neighbor. The authorities at Hakodadi did not refuse to let the Americans land—for under the treaty they had a right to do this for "temporary residence"—but asked them to name, before landing, some definite period which should be considered as being "temporary" in the sense of the treaty. They did, however, object to Americans coming on shore, with their wives and children, to *live* at Hakodadi as long as they pleased, just as a Japanese would live there; they did object to their opening a warehouse and making a permanent depot of supply, and establishing a commercial house in Japan, as our merchants do in China; and it will probably be conceded, after reading the conferences of negotiation which we have detailed, that they never meant to bind themselves by the treaty to the concession of such privileges. If they did not, and if, as at Simoda, they carried out all their stipulations touching the temporary sojourn and personal comfort of our countrymen, then it would seem they are not chargeable with any wilful breach of faith. Some may think they misinterpret as to the extent of what they did concede; but this, as Commander Rogers very truly said, is a point which can be settled only by the two governments. One thing seems very certain from the records of the negotiation, that both Commodore Perry and the Japanese commissioners supposed that the treaty they were making was but "a beginning" of friendly relations, and a partial agreement for trade; but neither party could have believed they were framing a general "commercial treaty," inasmuch as the Japanese had, in the beginning, expressly declined to enter into such a compact. It is understood, though we know not that the fact has been officially promulgated, that the interpretation of the treaty by our government agrees with that of the Japanese.

Yedo and Simoda dogs presented to Commodore M. C. Perry by the Japanese commissioners.

CHAPTER XXI.

DEPARTURE OF COMMANDER ADAMS FOR THE UNITED STATES, WITH THE TREATY.—VISITS OF THE COMMODORE AND OFFICERS ON SHORE.—IMPERTURBABLE COMPOSURE OF YENOSKE WHEN CHARGED WITH FALSEHOOD.—CALL UPON THE MAYOR OF YOKU-HAMA.—THE LADIES OF HIS HOUSEHOLD.—DISGUSTING FASHION OF DYEING THEIR TEETH.—USE OF ROUGE.—ENTERTAINMENT OF THE COMMODORE.—THE MAYOR'S BABY.—THE COMMON PEOPLE VERY COMFORTABLE.—FIELD LABORS SHARED BY THE WOMEN.—STRAW GREAT COAT FOR RAINY WEATHER.—PAPER UMBRELLAS.—PEOPLE NOT INDISPOSED TO INTERCOURSE WITH FOREIGNERS.—RESPECTFUL TREATMENT OF THE FEMALE SEX.—JAPANESE UN-ORIENTAL IN THIS RESPECT.—POLYGAMY NOT PRACTISED.—JAPANESE WOMEN NATURALLY GOOD-LOOKING.—SOME STRIKINGLY HANDSOME.—GIRLS HAVE GREAT VIVACITY, YET DIGNIFIED AND MODEST.—SOCIAL HABITS.—VISITS.—TEA PARTIES.—SQUADRON, AFTER NOTICE TO THE JAPANESE AUTHORITIES, PROCEEDS UP THE BAY WITH SOME OF THE OFFICIALS ON BOARD.—POWHATAN AND MISSISSIPPI GO WITHIN SIGHT OF THE CAPITAL.—ITS IMMENSE SIZE.—SEA FRONT PROTECTED BY HIGH PALISADES.—CHANGE OF JAPANESE POLICY ON THE SECOND VISIT TO YEDO.—ALL SHOW OF MILITARY RESISTANCE STUDIOUSLY AVOIDED.—THE COMMODORE ASSURES THE JAPANESE OFFICIALS THAT HE WILL NOT ANCHOR THE STEAMERS NEAR THE CITY, AND, AFTER A GLANCE, AT THEIR REQUEST, RETURNS.—GREAT JOY OF THE OFFICIALS THEREAT.—PREPARATIONS FOR DEPARTURE.—MACEDONIAN ORDERED TO PEEL ISLAND.—SOUTHAMPTON, SUPPLY, VANDALIA, AND LEXINGTON SENT TO SIMODA.—WEBSTER ISLAND.—DEPARTURE OF THE COMMODORE FOR SIMODA.—HARBOR EXAMINED.—THE TOWN AND ADJACENT COUNTRY.—SHOPS AND DWELLINGS.—PUBLIC BATHS.—FOOD.—MODE OF CULTIVATION.—BUDDHIST TEMPLES.—GRAVE YARDS AND TOMBS.—STATUES OF BUDDHA.—OFFERINGS OF FLOWERS ON THE GRAVES.—EPITAPHS OR INSCRIPTIONS.—CHARMS FOR KEEPING AWAY FROM THE DEAD MALIGNANT DEMONS.—A TEMPLE APPROPRIATED FOR THE OCCUPANCY OF OUR OFFICERS.—A SINTOO TEMPLE.—MARINER'S TEMPLE.—SALUBRITY OF SIMODA.—MADE AN IMPERIAL CITY SINCE THE TREATY.

HE treaty having been signed and exchanged, the Commodore sent it, together with the necessary communications, to our government at Washington, under the especial charge of Commander H. A. Adams, commissioned as bearer of dispatches, who left in the Saratoga. This vessel got under way on the morning of the 4th of April, (1854,) and sailed for the Sandwich Islands, homeward bound. As she passed the squadron anchored at Kanagawa, the Saratoga saluted the flag of the Commodore with thirteen guns, which were returned from the Powhatan. The wind and weather prevented her, however, from getting out of the bay, and she was obliged to anchor at the "American anchorage" on the first night, and did not stand out for sea until the next day.

The Japanese interpreters still visited the ships almost daily, and came on board the Powhatan on the day after the departure of the Saratoga, bringing with them a number of trifling presents of lacquered ware, porcelain, and other articles for several of the subordinate officers. On the following morning, one of the small brass howitzers was landed from the Mississippi as a present for the Emperor, as well as several boxes of tea brought from China, to be distributed as gifts to the interpreters and some of the Japanese dignitaries. Soon after, the Commodore went ashore, accompanied by several of his officers, for the purpose of taking a survey of the country. After having been entertained at the treaty house with the usual refreshments, the party set out on their walk, attended by Moryama, Yenoske, the chief interpreter, and several of the Japanese officials. A circuit embracing some five miles was the extent of the field of observation, but this gave an opportunity of seeing a good deal of the country, several of the villages, and large numbers of the people.

Farm Yard, Yokohama.

The early spring in that temperate latitude had now much advanced, and the weather, though never very severe, the thermometer having varied during the stay of the squadron from 38° to 64°, had become more warm and genial. The fields and terraced gardens were now carpeted with a fresh and tender verdure, and the trees, with the full growth of renewed vegetation, spread their shades of abounding foliage in the valleys and on the hill sides of the surrounding country. The camelias, with the immense growth of forty feet in height, which abound everywhere on the shores of the bay of Yedo, were in full bloom, with their magnificent red and white blossoms, which displayed a purity and richness of color, and a perfection of development, unrivalled elsewhere. As soon as a village or hamlet was approached, one of the Japanese attendants would hurry in advance and order the women and the rabble to keep out of the way. This did not suit the purposes of the Commodore, who was desirous of seeing as much as possible of the people, and learning all he could of their manners, habits, and customs. He accordingly spoke to the interpreter and took him to task, particularly for dispersing the women. Yenoske pretended that it was entirely for the benefit of the ladies themselves, as their modesty was such that it could not withstand the sight of a stranger.

The Commodore did not believe a word of this interpretation, however adroit, and plainly told Yenoske so. The imputation, though it expressed a doubt of his truthfulness, did not offend the interpreter in the least, but was rather taken as a compliment to his duplicity, which is one of the most cherished accomplishments of a Japanese official. Finding that the Commodore was quite alive to the Japanese cunning, and was not to be balked of any of his privileges as a sight-seer, Yenoske promised that at the next town, where some refreshments had been ordered, the women should not be required to avoid the party. Accordingly, on entering this place, every one crowded out to see the strangers, men, women, and children.

The Commodore and his officers were conducted to the home of the mayor or chief magistrate of the town. This dignitary, with great cordiality, met and welcomed them to the hospitalities of his establishment. The interior was quite unpretending, consisting of a large room, spread with soft mats, lighted with oiled paper windows, hung with rudely executed cartoons, and furnished with the usual red-colored benches. The wife and sister of the town official soon entered with refreshments, and smiled a timid welcome to the visitors. These women were bare footed and bare legged, and were dressed very nearly alike, in dark colored robes, with much of the undress look of night gowns, secured by a broad band passing round the waist. Their figures were fat and dumpy, or at any rate appeared so, in their ungraceful drapery, but their faces were not wanting in expression, for which they were very much indebted to their glistening eyes, which were black as well as their hair; this was dressed at the top of the head, like that of the men, although not shaved in front. As their "ruby" lips parted in smiling graciously, they displayed a row of black teeth, set in horribly corroded gums. The married women of Japan enjoy the exclusive privilege of dyeing their teeth, which is done with a mixture of vile ingredients, including filings of iron and sakee, termed *Oha gur* or *Camri*. This compound, as might be naturally inferred from its composition, is neither pleasantly perfumed nor very wholesome. It is so corrosive, that in applying it to the teeth, it is necessary to protect the more delicate structure of the gums and lips, for the mere touch of the odious stuff to the flesh burns it at once into a purple gangrenous spot. In spite of the utmost care, the gums become tainted, and lose their ruddy color and vitality. We should think that the practice was hardly conducive to connubial felicity, and it would be naturally inferred that all the kissing must be expended in the extacy of courtship. This compensation, however, is occasionally lost to the prospective bridegroom, for it is not uncommon for some of the young ladies to inaugurate the habit of blacking the teeth upon the popping of the question.

The effects of this disgusting habit are more apparent from another practice which prevails with the Japanese, as with our would-be civilized dames, that of painting the lips with rouge. The ruddy glow of the mouth brings out in greater contrast the blackness of the gums and teeth. The rouge of the Japanese toilet, called *bing*, is made of the *carthamus tinctorius*, and is prepared in cups of porcelain. When a slight coat is applied, it gives a lively red color, but when it is put on thick, a deep violet hue, which is the most prized, is the result.*

---

* Thunberg.

The worthy mayor had some refreshments prepared for his guests, consisting of tea, cakes, confectionary, and the never absent saki. With the latter was served a kind of hot waffle, made apparently of rice flour. The civic dignitary himself was very active in dispensing these offerings, and he was ably seconded by his wife and sister, who always remained on their knees in presence of the strangers. This awkward position of the women did not seem to interfere with their activity, for they kept running about very briskly with the silver saki kettle, the services of which, in consequence of the smallness of the cups, were in constant requisition. The two ladies were unceasingly courteous, and kept bowing their heads, like a bobbing toy mandarin. The smiles with which they perseveringly greeted the guests might have been better dispensed with, as every movement of their lips exposed their horrid black teeth and decayed gums. The mayoress was uncommonly polite, and was good natured enough to bring in her baby, which her guests felt bound to make the most of, though its dirty face and general untidy appearance made it quite a painful effort to bestow the necessary caresses. A bit of confectionary was presented to the infant, when it was directed to bow its shaven head, which it did with a degree of precocious politeness, that called forth the greatest apparent pride and admiration on the part of its mother and all the ladies present.

On preparing to depart, the Commodore proposed the health, in a cup of saki, of the whole household, which brought into the room, from a neighboring apartment, the mayor's mother. She was an ancient dame, and as soon as she came in she squatted herself in one corner, and bowed her thanks for the compliments paid to the family, of which she was the oldest member.

As the Japanese officials no longer interfered with the curiosity of the people, there was a good opportunity of observing them, though hurriedly, as the Commodore and his party were forced to return early to the ships. The people, in the small towns, appeared to be divided into three principal classes,—the officials, the traders, and laborers. The inferior people, almost without exception, seemed thriving and contented, and not overworked. There were signs of poverty, but no evidence of public beggary. The women, in common with many in various parts of over-populated Europe, were frequently seen engaged in field labors, showing the general industry and the necessity of keeping every hand busy in the populous Empire. The lowest classes even were comfortably clad, being dressed in coarse cotton garments, of the same form, though shorter than those of their superiors, being a loose robe, just covering the hips. They were, for the most part, bareheaded and barefooted. The women were dressed very much like the men, although their heads were not shaved like those of the males, and their long hair was drawn up and fastened upon the top, in a knot, or under a pad. The costume of the upper classes and the dignitaries has been already described. In rainy weather, the Japanese wear a covering made of straw, which being fastened together at the top, is suspended from the neck, and falls over the shoulders and person like a thatched roof. Some of the higher classes cover their robes with an oiled paper cloak, which is impermeable to the wet. The umbrella, like that of the Chinese, is almost a constant companion, and serves both to shade from the rays of the sun, and keep off the effects of a shower. The men of all classes were exceedingly courteous, and although inquisitive about the strangers, never became offensively intrusive. The lower people were evidently in great dread of their superiors, and were more reserved in their presence, than they would have been if they had been left to their natural instincts. The rigid exclusiveness in regard to foreigners is a law merely enacted by the government from motives of policy, and not a sentiment of the Japanese people. Their habits are social among themselves, and they frequently intermingle in friendly intercourse. There is one feature in the society of Japan, by which the superiority of the people, to all other oriental nations, is clearly manifest. Woman is recognised as a companion, and not merely treated as a slave. Her position is certainly not as elevated as in those countries under the influence of the Christian dispensation, but the mother, wife, and daughter of Japan, are neither the chattels and household drudges of China, nor the purchased objects of the capricious lust of the harems of Turkey. The fact of the non-existence of polygamy, is a distinctive feature, which pre-eminently characterizes the Japanese, as the most moral and refined of all eastern nations. The absence of this degrading practice shows itself, not only in the superior character of the women, but in the natural consequence of the greater prevalence of the domestic virtues.

Japanese Women—Simoda.

The Japanese women, always excepting the disgusting black teeth of those who are married, are not ill-looking. The young girls are well formed and rather pretty, and have much of that vivacity and self-reliance in manners, which come from a consciousness of dignity, derived from the comparatively high regard in which they are held. In the ordinary mutual intercourse of friends and families the women have their share, and rounds of visiting and tea parties are kept up as briskly in Japan as in the United States. The attitude assumed by the women, who prostrated themselves in the presence of the Commodore and his party, should be considered rather as a mark of their reverence for the strangers than as an evidence of their subordination. That in the large towns and cities of Japan there is great licentiousness, it is reasonable to suppose, for such seems, unhappily, a universal law in all great communities; but it must be said to the credit of the Japanese women, that during all the time of the presence of the squadron in the bay of Yedo, there was none of the usual indication of wantonness and license on the part of the female sex in their occasional relations with the miscellaneous ships' people.

On the 9th of April, notwithstanding a note received from the commissioners, in which they urgently remonstrated against the movement, the Commodore sent word that he would on the following day approach with the steamers as near to Yedo as the depth of water would allow. Accordingly, on the next morning, the whole squadron got under way from the anchorage at Kanagawa, and moved up the bay. The Japanese interpreters came on board the Powhatan just as she started, and were evidently in great dismay. They earnestly begged the Commodore to desist from his purpose, urging that the safety of the Empire, perhaps, and certainly that of their own lives, depended upon the issue. Not being able to dissuade the Commodore, the Japanese remained on board to mark his movements. The steamers Powhatan and Mississippi advanced beyond the other vessels and doubled the point near Sinagawa, the southern suburb of the capital, and came so close to the far-famed Yedo that, if it had not, unfortunately, been for a fog, so common on that coast, the capital would have been distinctly visible. The general outline of the city could, however, be made out, showing an immense and thickly crowded number of houses and buildings covering a large surface. Though there was every indication of the great size of the town, there was a general similarity in the low peaked houses and the terraced gardens to the other populous settlements on the bay. Upon the heights and projecting points commanding the capital there were the usual forts, with canvas outworks, and other fortified places. The Buddhist temples, however, which are generally the highest and most conspicuous buildings in these Japanese towns, may possibly, from the prevailing haze which confined the view, have been mistaken for fortifications.

Along the whole sea front of the city there appeared to be a row of high palisades, with occasional openings for the admission of boats or small junks. Whether these were arranged to protect the landing places from the washing of the sea, or to defend the city from an attack, it was impossible to decide. It was quite probable, however, that they had been put up in consequence of the visit of the squadron, to prevent the approach of the armed boats in case of an attempt on the part of the Americans to land by force. One thing, however, seems quite certain, that the city of Yedo can be destroyed by a few steamers of very light draught of water and with guns of the heaviest calibre.

Considerable preparation had evidently been made at first by the Japanese to impress the Americans with a great idea of their military power. New works of defence were commenced, and large numbers of troops paraded ostentatiously within sight of the squadron, during the first visit to Yedo bay, and it is probable that it had been seriously discussed in the Japanese councils whether or not to resist by force all intercourse with the Americans. On the second visit there was evidently a change of policy, and a studious avoidance of all show of military resistance. An extensive fortified work that had been begun in the neighborhood of Yedo was discontinued, and a fire which destroyed it and the large wooden shed which had been built for the accommodation of the numerous workmen, was suspected to have been applied at the instigation of the authorities, in order to efface every vestige of an erection, which might provoke by its show of hostility an unfriendly feeling on the part of the formidable visitors.

In consequence of the strong ebb tide, the boats which were pulling ahead, engaged in sounding the channel towards the city, made but little headway, and the steamers with difficulty stemming the current could not be kept under safe steerage. The sailing ships had already anchored some distance astern. The Commodore having promised the commissioners, in order to allay their apprehensions, that he would not anchor the steamers near the capital, but only advance them sufficiently to take a glance at it, felt himself bound to return. The men in the boats were exhausted with hard pulling, and as it was not safe to keep the steamers where they were without dropping anchor, the surveying party were accordingly summoned back, and the ship's head pointed down the bay again. The fears of the commissioners, as they stated, and as the interpreters who were present never failed to continue to suggest, were founded upon the supposition that if the squadron should anchor near to, and in full view of the capital, its immense populace would become greatly excited. This, they declared, might result in the most disastrous consequences; and though they did not particularly name the Emperor and his household, they evidently felt deeply concerned about their safety. In consequence, therefore, of the very courteous and friendly conduct of the princes and their coadjutors, and trusting to their asseverations that they would be held personally responsible for any catastrophe that might ensue from anchoring the steamers off the city and saluting the palace, as was the original intention, the Commodore determined to yield to their remonstrances. A direct appeal was also made by the commissioners to the generosity of the Commodore in the statement that having, in the treaty, conceded more than had been originally designed, and thus shown their confidence and friendship, they hoped the Commodore would not subject them to a possible injury and probable death. The Commodore yielded at once. He thought it was better not to bring about an issue that might endanger the very friendly position in which he had placed himself in relation to the Japanese. It would have been a source of endless regret, too, if to gratify a profitless curiosity misfortune should have been brought upon the commissioners, whose friendly conduct deserved every kind return that might be given in consonance with duty. The squadron, therefore, now returned and anchored at the "American anchorage." The anxiety of the Japanese interpreters, who remained on board during the whole trip, was thus much relieved, and they participated with the greatest conviviality in a collation which was spread for their entertainment in the Commodore's cabin.

There being no further reason for the detention of the squadron in the upper bay of Yedo, the Commodore prepared to depart. He accordingly dispatched in advance the Macedonian for Peel island, on the 11th of April; the ships Southampton and Supply on the fourteenth, and the Vandalia and Lexington on the sixteenth, for Simoda. During the two days preceding his own departure, the Commodore took the opportunity of inspecting the island near the "American anchorage," which had been called by him Webster, and the neighboring shores. The beauty of the country, now developed in all its picturesque charms of rich verdure, shaded groves, fertile fields, and cultivated gardens, was a source of never-ending pleasure, and as the time approached for taking leave of the attractive shores of the upper bay of Yedo, there was no little feeling of regret. The scenery in the neighborhood of the American anchorage was now very familiar to all on board ship, and had a double interest, as well that of association from long residence as from its intrinsic beauties. Webster island is a charming spot, shaded with the thickest groves of green growth, and varied with hill and dale, wild mountain top and cultivated slope. Between it and its neighboring isle, called by the surveyors Perry, after the Commodore, is a little bay, upon the inland shores of which there is a considerable quarry of stone that the Japanese have extensively worked. Large blocks were lying about, and the rocky precipices of the shore were hewn into good walls of a smooth surface, from which the masses of stone had been cut with a regularity that showed much skill. There were other evidences about of the busy industry of the Japanese; there were various boat building yards, with junks dragged ashore for repairs, with workmen actively at work over their hulls, and various docks and landing places constructed of stone, and showing the careful industry and no little skill of the people.

Mia or Road Side Chapel, at Yoku-hama.

At four o'clock in the morning of the 18th of April the Commodore finally got under way for Simoda, in the Powhatan, accompanied by the Mississippi, and anchored in that port at ten minutes past three in the afternoon of the same day. The Mississippi dropped her anchor off

the mouth of the harbor, but soon after took her position within, in the neighborhood of the Powhatan. The Vandalia, Southampton, Supply, and Lexington, were found anchored there. The Commodore had purposely dispatched the several ships in succession, in order to enable those which arrived first, time for examining the harbor and selecting convenient anchoring places for their consorts which were to follow. This turned out to be a well-timed precaution, as the Southampton, in warping into the inner harbor, came upon a rock lying in the middle of the channel, with only twelve feet of water upon it at low water, a danger which had escaped the hasty examination of the surveyors. If it had not been for this timely discovery, one or both the steamers would have probably struck upon the rock, as it lies directly in the way, and is all the more dangerous from its being only thirty feet in diameter, and cone-like in shape. Lieutenant Commandant Boyle had very prudently placed a buoy upon it, which enabled the steamers to avoid the danger, and pass in without inconvenience, although the channel at that point is only six hundred yards wide. Both steamers found sufficient room to moor without interfering with the Southampton and Supply, already in the inner harbor. The Lexington subsequently came in also and anchored, but Captain Pope preferred a position further out for his ship, the Vandalia.

Simoda from the Creek.

There can be no better harbor than that of Simoda for a limited number of vessels; "when its contiguity to the sea, its easy and safe approach, its convenience of ingress and egress are considered, I do not see," says Commodore Perry, "how a more desirable port could have been selected to answer all the purposes for which it is wanted."

The town of Simoda, or Shimoda, is on the island of Nippon, near the mouth of the lower bay or gulf of Yedo; latitude 34° 39' 49" north; longitude 138° 57' 50" east. It is within the prefecture of Kamo, one of the eight, into which Idzu is divided, and occupies the southern termination of that principality. The town is situated at the western end of the harbor, on a plain at the opening of a fertile valley. Its name is probably derived from its low position, *Simoda*, meaning *Low field*. Through the valley a small stream, called Inodzu-Gawa, flows, and empties at the town into the harbor. This river is navigable for the flat bottomed boats, which are used by the inhabitants for transporting stone, timber, grain, and other produce.

The country surrounding the town is extremely picturesque and varied. Undulating hills, covered with trees and verdure, rise from the water's edge and extend back into the lofty mountains, rock-ribbed and bare.

Valleys divide the mountain ranges, with their richly cultivated fields and gardens, stretching up to the very summit of the hill sides. Streams of water, shaded with groves, wind through the level bottoms, and beautify and enrich the land. The snow-capped Fusi is visible in the distance, pointing its cone-like summit high into the clouds, and far above the elevation of the blue mountains which surround it. On entering the harbor, the town, with its groups of low houses, does not present a very imposing appearance, but, with its back ground of hills, wooded with spreading pines and yew trees, and the verdant valleys which open between them, it has an air of sheltered repose, and an appearance of secluded rusticity which are quite attractive.

Landing Place at Simoda.

Simoda is said to be the largest town in the principality of Idzu, and was at one time a m... of considerable importance. It was founded centuries ago, and some two hundred years since, was the port of entry for vessels bound to the capital, but Uraga, further up the bay, having

succeeded to this important function, Simoda has declined and become comparatively a poverty stricken place. There is not much appearance of commercial activity in the port, but there still is some inconsiderable business carried on through it, between the interior of the country and various places on the Japanese coast. In front of the town there is a depot for small junks and boats, artificially constructed by means of dykes and a breakwater. This is connected with the river, which flows through the valley, that extends into the interior, and the boats are thus enabled when the tide, which rises about five feet, is at its height, to float in, and sail up the stream. Rude docks exist for building and launching vessels, and these show some evidence of activity in the numbers of junks, about which there are always numerous laborers, more or less busy at work, constructing and repairing. Near these docks, picturesquely bordered by a row of stately pine trees, in the shade of which stands a small shrine, there is a landing place which, however, is not very easily reached by ships boats when the tide is low.

The town of Simoda is compactly built, and regularly laid out. The streets intersect each other at right angles, and most of them are guarded by light wooden gates, with the names of the streets marked upon their hollow posts, within which are the stations of the watchmen. Through the town a small stream passes, the sides of which are walled with stone, and across it are thrown four small wooden bridges, which connect the opposite banks. The streets are about twenty feet in width, and are partly macadamized and partly paved. Simoda shows an

Street and Entrance to Chief Temple, Simoda.

advanced state of civilization, much beyond our own boasted progress in the attention of its constructors to the cleanliness and healthfulness of the place. There are not only gutters, but sewers, which drain the refuse water and filth directly into the sea or the small stream which divides the town.

The shops and dwelling houses are but slightly built, many of them being merely thatched huts. A few of the houses of the better classes are of stone, but most are constructed of a framework of bamboo or laths, and then covered with a tenacious mud. This latter, when dry, is again covered with a coat of plaster, which is either painted or becomes black by exposure. Mouldings are afterwards arranged in diagonal lines over the surface of the building, and these being painted white and contrasting with the dark ground behind, give the houses a curious pie-bald look. The roofs are often of tiles colored alternately black and white, and their eaves extend low down in front of the walls, and protect the inmates from the sun, and the oiled paper windows from the effects of the rain. On the tops of some of the houses wires are stretched in various directions to keep off the crows, it is said; but whether on account of their being birds of ill omen, or only in consequence of their bad habits, was not very apparent. These houses have no chimneys, and there being occasional fires for cooking and other purposes, the smoke is left to force its way through the various crannies and cracks which may chance to exist, unless, as is sometimes the case, there are certain holes in the upper part of the walls prudently left for the purpose. The buildings are generally but a single story in height, though many of the houses and shops have attics for the storage of goods and refuse articles.

Some of the residences stand back from the front of the streets, with yards before them, although generally the latter are in the rear, and are variously appropriated, some for kitchen gardens and others for pleasure grounds, with flowering shrubs, ponds for gold fish, and other ornamental appliances. There are a few buildings fronted with stone, while the main structure is of dried mud or adobe, these are used for the storage of valuable goods, as they are supposed to be better protected against fire. The fronts of the shops and houses have movable shutters, which at night are fastened to the posts which support the projecting roofs. Behind these are sliding panels of oiled paper, which are closed when privacy is sought, and opened for the purpose of seeing in the houses what may be passing, or displaying the goods in the inside of the shops. In lieu of the paper windows there are occasional lattices of bamboo. The title of the shop is displayed over the door or window, generally in some fanciful device, significant of the kind of business carried on. There are but few signs distinctly recording the trade or occupation, although there was one shop which bore on its front, in the Dutch language, the name in full of a Dutch nostrum, which seemed to be a popular remedy in Japan, for the same was observed in Kanagawa. The finer goods were generally kept secluded from view in boxes and drawers, and seemed to be of a kind which indicated no great affluence on the part of the community.

The internal arrangements of the houses and shops of Simoda is simple and uniform, though somewhat modified according to the position and business of the inmates. The door is on the right or left side, and is protected by the overhanging roof, under which the coarser goods are sheltered, and the customers when driving a bargain. From the front door a pathway leads directly to the rear, where there are various dwelling and out-houses, among which there is often the shrine for private worship. In the shops this passage way is crowded with baskets, stands, and trays, laden with various merchandise; and the walls on either side are provided with shelves, upon which goods are also heaped. In the best establishments articles for sale are seldom displayed beyond turning the opened ends of the boxes which contain them towards the street.

In the interior of the houses there is a large frame work, raised two feet above the ground.

JAPANESE WOMAN
from Simoda

It is spread with stuffed mats, and is divided into several compartments by means of sliding panels. This house within a house may be applied to all the various purposes of trading, eating, sleeping, and receiving company, according to the pleasure or necessities of the proprietors. This cage or platform is used as the workshop by some of the various handicraftsmen, as, for example, the carpenters and lacquer varnishers; the blacksmiths and stonecutters, however, perform their heavier work upon the ground.

The houses intended for lodgers are generally clean and neatly spread with the usual soft and thick mats, which serve the double purpose of seats by day and beds by night. The names of the guests are recorded as with us, but somewhat more publicly as they are affixed to the door posts on the street. The aristocratic gentry have their coats of arms emblazoned in full and displayed upon wide banners, stretched in front of their stopping places. The interiors of these hotels are by no means very magnificent in appearance or complete in appointment. The entire absence of tables, chairs, sofas, lamps, and other essentials to comfort, interfere very seriously with a guest taking his ease at his Japanese inn. Moreover, the want of pictures, looking-glasses, and other pleasing appeals to the eye, gives to the establishment a very naked, cold look to a traveller who has a vivid recollection of the warm snugness of an English inn or the luxurious completeness of an American hotel.

The whole number of houses in Simoda is estimated at about a thousand, and the inhabitants are supposed to amount to nearly seven thousand, one-fifth of whom are shopkeepers and artisans. There are in the town, as elsewhere in Japan, a disproportionate amount of officials, soldiers, and retainers, of the various princes and dignitaries, who add nothing to the productive resources of the country, but are great consumers of the results of the labor of the lower classes, who are forced to do much work and are allowed to enjoy but little of the profit. The people have, notwithstanding, a tolerably thriving appearance, and it is seldom that a beggar is seen. The streets, with the exception of the few shops which do but little business, show no signs of trading activity. There is no public market place, and all the daily transactions of buying and selling are conducted so privately and quietly that, to a passing stranger, Simoda would appear as a place singularly devoid of any regard to the concerns of this world.

The people have all the characteristic courtesy and reserved but pleasing manners of the Japanese. A scene at one of the public baths, where the sexes mingled indiscriminately, unconscious of their nudity, was not calculated to impress the Americans with a very favorable opinion of the morals of the inhabitants. This may not be a universal practice throughout Japan, and indeed is said by the Japanese near us not to be; but the Japanese people of the inferior ranks are undoubtedly, notwithstanding their moral superiority to most oriental nations, a lewd people. Apart from the bathing scenes, there was enough in the popular literature, with its obscene pictorial illustrations, to prove a licentiousness of taste and practice among a certain class of the population that was not only disgustingly intrusive, but disgracefully indicative of foul corruption.

The chief diet of the inhabitants of Simoda consists of fish and vegetable food. There are poultry, chickens, geese and ducks, and some few cattle, but the latter are used only for beasts of burden, and their flesh is never eaten. Rice, wheat, barley, and sweet potatoes are the chief articles raised in and about Simoda, although Irish potatoes, buckwheat, Indian corn, taro, beans, cabbages, cresses, and egg plants are produced to some extent. The wheat and barley are reaped in May, and the rice, which is first sown and then transplanted, as in Lew Chew, is ready for the latter operation in the middle of June, and these crops succeed each other year after year. During the winter, part of the rice fields, that which lies low, is left fallow, while the terraces are turned into wheat fields. In preparing the fields for the reception of the young shoots of rice, they are overflown with water, and then reduced by ploughing and harrowing into a soft well mixed mud. Subsequently, a substratum of grass and small bushes is trodden down below the surface by the feet. The laborer putting on a couple of broad pieces of wood, like a pair of snow shoes, goes tramping over the grass and bushes, laboring until they all disappear below the surface of the mud. This operation over, the small plants are transferred from the plot where they have been sown, to the fields, where they are allowed to remain until maturity. The rice crop is ready for harvesting in the latter part of September or early in the ensuing month. Oxen and horses are occasionally used in agricultural operations, but the labor is mostly performed by hand.

Whatever may be the moral character of the inhabitants of Simoda, it might be supposed, from the great number of places of worship, that they are a highly devotional people. Though the peculiar religions of the Japanese seem to be sustained in a flourishing condition, the people are rather remarkable for their toleration of all kinds of worship, except that of the Christian, for which, in consequence of the political intrigues of the Roman priesthood, centuries ago, they have an intense hatred, carefully inculcated by those in authority, who keep alive the traditional enmity engendered at the epoch when the Portuguese were expelled the Empire. The Buddhist and Sintoo worships are those most prevalent in Japan, and the lower classes are strict but formal devotees, while it is suspected that the higher and better educated are indifferent to all religions, and entertain various speculative opinions, or seek refuge in a broad skepticism.

There are no less than nine Buddhist temples, one large *Mia*, or Sintoo temple, and a great number of smaller shrines. Those devoted to the worship of Buddha have strange fanciful titles: the largest is called Rio-shen-zhi, or Buddha's obedient monastery; and there are Dai-an-zhi, or great peace monastery; the Hon-gaku-zhi, or source of knowledge monastery; the Too-den-zhi, or rice field monastery; the Fuku-zhen-zhi, or fountain of happiness monastery; the Chio-raku-zhi, or continual joy monastery; the Ri-gen-zhi, or source of reason monastery; and lastly, the Chio-me-zhi, or long life monastery. Twenty-five priests and a few acolytes are attached to these temples, and are supported by fees bestowed by devotees for burial services, and the various offices peculiar to Buddhism. The buildings are of wood, and although generally kept in tolerable repair, show the effects of weather upon the unpainted surface. The roofs are tiled and project, as in the houses, beyond the walls. The posts which support the superstructure are, together with the rest of the wood work, covered with the famous Japanese lacquer. The floors, which are raised four or five feet above the ground, are neatly covered with matting. At the door of the main apartment there is a drum on the left and a bell on the right, the former of which is beaten, and the latter tingled, at the commencement of worship, to awaken the attention of the idols to the prayers of the devout. Between the door and the central shrine there are several low lecterns, or reading desks, near each of which there is conveniently placed a piece of wood carved in the shape of a fish, which is used to beat time during the chanting, which forms an important part of the religious services.

The shrine, in which are arranged the ancestral tablets, in niches, seems to be an object of particular attention, for it was kept always in perfect order, and the monuments and idols were

not allowed to suffer from want of repair or of a decent regard to cleanliness. The sculpture of the various images was no better in art or more imposing in appearance than the ordinary figures of *Joss* in the Chinese temples. An occasional picture is hung up as a votive offering upon the walls, representing, rather rudely, some event in the life of the worshipper, in the course of which he had reason, as he piously believed, to be grateful for the services of Buddha or some of his numerous progeny of subordinate deities. Certain boxes, distributed about the temple, remind the Christian visitor of the duties of charity, and he thinks with a pious recollection of the claims of the poor, which are suggested by a practice similar to that in the old churches of his own faith. His charitable feelings, however, are suddenly repelled when he learns the object of the boxes, for the label upon them reads: "For feeding hungry demons," and the promise which follows that, "his merit will be consolidated," is hardly inducement enough to contribute toward the necessities of the devil, or any of his voracious legion. In front of some of the temples pillars are found, upon which are inscribed an edict forbidding any liquors or meats to be carried within the sacred precincts.

Connected with each monastery is a grave-yard, in which there is a great variety of monuments and tombstones. They are generally made of a greenstone found in the neighborhood of Simoda, and have the various forms of simple slabs, raised tombs, and obelisks. Among the

Grave-yard and Temple at Simoda.

monuments are distributed statues of Buddha, varying in size from the largeness of life to that of only a foot or less. They are represented in various attitudes, some erect and others in a sitting posture, while many are carved in relief upon slabs of stone, where Buddha is seen issuing from an opening shell, and is figured sometimes with his hands clasped, or holding a lotus flower, a fly-trap, or some other symbol. A pleasant feature in the aspect of the otherwise gloomy burial places, disfigured by the coarse and grotesque art of a corrupt superstition, is the abundance of flowers which are plentifully distributed about. These are placed, freshly culled from day to day, in cups and troughs of water, which are deposited before the tombs and idols. Offerings of other kinds are also frequently found near the various statues of Buddha and his kindred deities.

The tombs and monuments, as with us, are inscribed with epitaphs; but such is the moisture of the climate, that they are soon covered with moss and rendered illegible. Some of the fresher ones, however, could be deciphered, and it was observed that, as in our own practice, the rank, merits, and date of death of deceased, were usually recorded. That the good deeds of the departed may live after them, there is often a summary of their meritorious works during life, among which we read that some have recited one thousand, two thousand, and even three thousand volumes of the canonical books, an amount of pious performance which entitles them, say the eulogistic Japanese epitaphs, to heavenly felicity. An invocation, "Oh, wonderful Buddha!" generally prefaces the inscriptions. In the grave-yard of the Rio-shen-zhi, there is a sort of pantomimic record of the deceased, where, in a fenced enclosure of bamboo, there is a sepulchre of two personages of rank. Their statues and those of their families and servants are represented as if holding an audience, which indicates the rank of the deceased.

Near the recent graves and tombs narrow boards or wooden posts are placed, on which extracts from the canonical books are written, exhorting the living to add to their stock of good works by diligently repeating the pages of those excellent volumes, or vicariously performing that necessary duty, by getting the priests to do it for them, and not neglecting to pay the customary charges. The canonical books supply many of the other inscriptions with various quotations, aptly chosen to extol the felicity of the departed, or to inculcate the shortness of life and the vanity of this world; one of the latter, when translated, read thus:

> "What permanency is there to the glory of the world?
> It goes from the sight like hoar-frost before the sun.
> If men wish to enter the joys of heavenly light
> Let them smell a little of the fragrance of Buddha's canons."

Another was this: "Whoever wishes to have his merit reach even to the abode of the demons, let him with us, and all living, become perfect in the doctrine." And again: "The wise will make our halls illustrious and the monuments endure for long ages." To them all was added a significant hint, that these hopes and aspirations were to be secured in their objects by the prompt payment of the contributions levied on the living. At Yoku-hama, in addition to these various Japanese inscriptions, there were boards upon which were written charms in the Thibetan or complicated Chinese characters, the purport of which the writers themselves do not profess to understand, but all appeared to believe they were effectual in warding off malignant demons from disturbing the dead.

The nine Buddhist temples are all situated in the suburbs, back of the town; and on the acclivities or summits of the hills, which bound them in the rear, there are shrines and pavilions erected within groves of trees, which are approached by a flight of stone steps. In the interior of these pavilions and shrines are rude images, or merely inscriptions, dedicated to the tutelary deities of the spot. Their purpose is to afford facility to those living near, or to

4

the passer by, of appeasing and imploring the good and evil spirits which are supposed to frequent the neighborhood. At the doors and before the shrines there are always bits of paper, some rags, copper cash, bouquets of flowers and other articles, which have been placed there as propitiatory offerings by different devotees.

The Rio-shen-zhi, the largest of the nine Buddhist temples, was set apart by the government authorities for the temporary use of the Commodore during the stay of the squadron. It is situated on the south side of the town, and has quite a picturesque aspect, with a precipitous rock of over a hundred feet on one side, and a burial ground on the other, extending up the acclivity of a thickly wooded hill. Connected with the temple is a kitchen garden, which supplies the priests with vegetables, and pleasure grounds with beds of flowers, tanks containing gold fish, and various plants and trees. A small bridge, neatly constructed, leads from the gardens to a flight of steps, by which the hill in the rear is ascended. Adjoining the ecclesiastical part of the establishment there is a room used for lodgers, which is so constructed with sliding doors that it may be separated into several rooms for the accommodation of many persons, or left as one large apartment. The officers of the squadron were comfortably provided for in another building, and with an abundant supply of mats to sleep upon, good wholesome rice and vegetables to eat, plenty of attendants, and everything clean, there was very little reason for complaint on the score of the material necessities of life.

The large *Mia*, or Sintoo temple, is situated in the same part of the town as the Buddhist establishments. A wide street, the broadest in Simoda, leads to an avenue of fir and juniper trees, the vista through which is closed by the temple. As the visitor approaches he comes to a bridge which is thrown over an artificial fish pond, which breaks the continuity of the street, and as he enters the shaded avenue he passes over another miniature bridge beautifully constructed of finely carved greenstone. Two grim statues of armed men, whose fierce aspect is heightened by the covering of moss and lichen which, with their irregular growth, roughen the rude sculpture, and, by their mottled color, give an increased savageness to its look, stand, one on either side, as guardians of the temple. Several pairs of candelabras in stone are arranged near by, towards the termination of the avenue, and on their right is a square belfry of open woodwork resting upon a high foundation of masonry. From the roof swings a beam, which is used to strike the bell which hangs within. To the left is a low shed covering six small stone images of deified heroes, the flowers and coins lying before which indicate the worship of devotees. As the visitor advances he passes under a pavilion built over the pathway, and finds within various offerings, some paintings, coarsely executed, of junks, and shipwrecks, a bow or two, and scores of queues, cut off by shipwrecked sailors, and hung up as testimonials of gratitude for the preservation of their lives.

Leaving the pavilion the visitor reaches a flight of stone steps beyond, which lead to the principal hall, which is elevated some six feet above the ground. Two stone lions, whose small heads and enormous ungainly bodies show that the artist was equally unacquainted with the grace of art and the truth of nature, guard the entrance. The porch is sustained by posts which are carved with grotesque representations of tigers and elephants' heads, and other adornments, showing neither skill of hand nor beauty of design. The temple itself is constructed of wood, with a covering of thatch. The interior is not, like the Buddhist monasteries, supplied with sliding panels, but contains two compartments—the main hall and an inner shrine, partitioned by a latticed bamboo screen. Within the latter is the image of Hachiman, the deified hero to whom the temple is dedicated. Standing in a niche, on either side, is the figure of an attendant dressed in ancient Japanese official costume, armed with a bow, as if awaiting the orders, as in life, of their superior. Before the god-like Hachiman there is the usual variety of devotional offerings. A large number of paintings of no great artistic skill, a frame containing the representation of a pagoda constructed of copper cash, a sword, bow and arrows, and a subscription list of at least thirty feet in length, hung from the walls of the shrine. This gigantic subscription list contains the names and donation of the contributors towards the expenses of the temple services. The Japanese priests find, we suppose, as we fear it is sometimes found elsewhere, that an imposing display of the munificence of their benefactors is a useful reminder of duty to the benevolent, and a great encouragement of generosity. The idol of Hachiman is honored annually with a festival, termed *matzouri*, which occurs on the fifteenth day of the eighth month, when the subscribers are expected to pay up the amount of their contributions, for which their names are down upon the enormous list. Before the image there is a box provided for the alms of those who are too modest to publish their names, or whose donations are too small to make much of a figure on paper.

As the Japanese structures are unpainted, the wood work soon turns brown and decays, requiring frequent repair and removal. There is always a sort of guardian or superintendent living on the premises, whose duty it is to keep in order the temple and grounds, and most of them are creditable evidences of the care of the overseers. There are, however, some of these establishments which show either a careless superintendence or a low state of the exchequer, for several show signs of ruin and neglect.

In addition to the one great Sintoo temple, there are various smaller shrines of the same faith dedicated to certain deified heroes, whose services are called into requisition by those of some particular occupation, or on the occasion of a special emergency. The sites of these humbler places of worship have been picturesquely selected on the acclivities, or the summits of the wooded hills which bound the town of Simoda landward. The pathways which lead to them are handsomely constructed, often with causeways, bridges of a single Roman arch, and flights of steps, all of stone, carefully sculptured and substantially built. Various gateways, guarded by stone statues of lions, or sometimes merely by pillars, upon which an inscription warns off intruders, divide at intervals the approach, while the sides of the avenues are shaded with fine trees of vigorous growth and abundant foliage. Some of the temples are so embosomed in groves, that they are completely hidden from the sight, until their shaded thresholds are reached unexpectedly by the stranger. One of these was especially noticed for the beauty of its position and the perfection of its structure. It was particularly devoted to a patron saint of the sailors, and was called by the Americans "the mariners' temple," and those engaged in occupations connected with the sea constantly resort there, to invoke the aid of, or to return thanks to the enshrined deity. Groups of fishermen, with their baskets laden with the successful hauls of the day, gathered within the precincts of the sacred place, and gratefully symbolized, according to prescribed form, the gratitude of their hearts. Shipwrecked mariners prostrated themselves before the idol, and fulfilled their vows by the sacrifice of their queues, and other exercises of self-imposed penance, which they had pledged for their lives in the agony of impending danger. Within the shade of the grove boatmen and fishermen were busy repairing their nets, and surrounded with their long oars, their baskets, and all the paraphernalia of their business, seemed to be invoking a blessing upon their labors, and propitiating the deity

for good luck to the next day's fishing. The mariners' temple is one of the handsomest structures in Simoda. A solid stone causeway, leading over an arched bridge, with a low, well-constructed wall on either side, leads to the steps of the building. The temple is built in the usual style, with a projecting roof of tiles ornamentally arranged in cornices of flowers and graceful scrolls, and supported by lacquered pillars. Over the door-way there is a fine specimen of carved wood work, representing the sacred crane, on the wing, symbolizing as it were the unsettled life of the mariner. The body of the building is closed partly with wall and partly with oiled paper casements. The usual stone lantern is found on the left, and from the door hangs a straw rope, which, being connected with a bell inside, is pulled by the devotee to ring up the deity, that he may be aware of the call, and be wide awake to the spiritual necessities of his visitor.

The expense of these numerous religious establishments must be very great, and the tax upon the people of Simoda proportionately burdensome, but it was impossible to obtain any very exact data in regard to the amount. As the voluntary system prevails to a great extent, and ecclesiastical prosperity depends chiefly upon the generosity of the pious, the priests are very naturally stimulated into a very vigorous exercise of their functions, and are undoubtedly indefatigable laborers in their peculiar field.

The country about Simoda is beautifully varied with hill and dale. There are the usual signs of elaborate Japanese culture, although from the more sparse population of the neighborhood there is more land left in a comparatively barren condition than further up the bay towards the capital. The bottoms and sides of the valleys are covered with gardens and fields, which are well watered by the streamlets which flow through every valley, and which, by artificial arrangement, are diverted from their course, and pour their fertilizing waters over the land from terrace to terrace. There are four principal villages near Simoda. Kaki-zaki, or Persimmon point, lies at the end of the harbor and contains barely two hundred houses. One of its monasteries, known by the name of Goku-zhen-zhi, was set apart, like the Rio-zhen-zhi in Simoda, as a place of resort for the foreigners; and within the ground attached is the burial place appropriated to Americans. There is a good anchorage at Kaki-zaki for junks, and many of them take in their cargoes there rather than at Simoda.

Passing over the hills in a southeasterly direction, we come to the village of Susaki, which, with its two hundred houses or so, hangs upon the acclivity of a wooded hill side, with its front extending down to the beach and facing the waters of the inlet. Its inhabitants are generally fishermen, and their boats, and even larger vessels, can approach the shore at all states of the tide. From Susaki a good road leads in a northeasterly direction to the village of Sotowra, a small hamlet, also situated on the seaside, but with a pleasing landscape inland, varied by cultivated fields and an undergrowth of dwarf oaks. A larger place, the town of Shira-hama, or White Beach, extends its houses along a sandy beach some three miles distant from Sotowra, and is comparatively a flourishing settlement. Several quarries of trachyte, or greenstone, are worked in the neighborhood, and large quantities of charcoal are prepared on the forest-crowned hills in the rear.

Turning westwardly and ascending the hill beyond Shira-hama, the highest summit within five miles of Simoda is reached, from which the whole southern area and breadth of the peninsula of Idzu can be seen at one glance. Barren peaks rise to the view out of thickly wooded hills, whose sides open into valleys, down which the wild vegetation throngs until checked by the culture of the fields that surround the busy hamlets at the bottom. Where the beholder stands on the summit of the hill there is a small wooden shrine, almost hidden in a grove of pines. The numerous pictures, flowers, rags, copper cash, and decapitated queues found within, attest the popularity of the Zhi-zo-bozats, the deity of the place.

Valley above Simoda.

Descending the hill by its northwestern slope, the largest valley of the country round is entered. The river Inodzu-gama, which flows into the harbor of Simoda, passes through this, irrigating the cultivated banks and sustaining the commerce of the various villages and towns in the interior. The hamlet of Hongo, containing about one hundred and fifty houses, is situated on the river, which has been dammed at that spot, and turns five undershot mills for cleaning rice. This operation is performed by a very simple machine, which consists of a projecting piece of wood or stone attached at right angles to the end of a long lever, which plays upon a horizontal axis, and is moved up and down, like a pestle working in a mortar.

This rude machinery is occasionally worked by water, as at Hongo, but more frequently by a man, who steps alternately off and on, the long end of the beam. The river at Hongo is navigable for flat bottomed boats, which frequent the place for charcoal, grain, stone, and other products. The country about is beautifully diversified, and the culture of the land is carried on to an extent that would hardly be believed by one who was not familiar with the populous countries of the east. Every hill is but a succession of terraces, rising one above the other, from the base to the summit, and green with the growth of rice, barley, wheat, and other grain.

At the opening of a smaller valley, which branches off from the main one near Hongo, is a small village, called Rendai-zhi, from the Lotus terrace monastery near by.

Japanese Rice Cleaner and Spade.

From Hongo the valley widens more and more until it reaches Simoda, where it forms an open expanse, like an alluvial plain. Along the base of the range of hills, and up their slopes, in the direction of the harbor, the numerous farm houses and abounding granaries, many of them of stone, and with substantial walls of the same material, exhibit a cheerful prospect of thrift and comfort. Nor are there wanting evidences of luxuriant enjoyment in the handsome structure of the dwelling houses, with their pleasure grounds adorned with pastures of variegated flowers, artificial ponds of gold fish, and fancy dwarf shade and fruit trees. West of Simoda the villages are smaller, and the hills which flank them of less height. In that direction there are no villages of a shorter distance than five miles from the town of Simoda. Near two seaside settlements, towards the southwest, the inhabitants have excavated large chambers in the cliffs, some hundred feet above the shore, in which they store the sea weed, which is a favorite article for chewing, as tobacco is used with us, and where the fishermen occasionally resort for shelter. The lower hills in every direction are covered with wood, from which large supplies of charcoal are made, which is extensively used as fuel for domestic and manufacturing purposes.

The topographical characteristics of Simoda are such as to indicate a healthful climate. Its situation on the extremity of a peninsula, looking seaward, and the elevated ground which surrounds the town, secure the fresh breezes of the sea and a freedom from miasmatic influences. Simoda itself lies low, but the soil is dry, and the stream which passes through it flows rapidly and with a clear current of pure water. It cannot be very cold, as Simoda is at the level of the sea, by the equable temperature of which the winter season is necessarily tempered. The hills from under which the town snugly reposes protect it from the full severity of the blasts from the snowy summits of the distant mountains. The climate is more or less variable in the winter and spring. The presence of snow upon the lofty peaks, although there is seldom frost or snow at Simoda itself, and the not unfrequent rains with the ever recurring fogs, give an occasional humidity and rawness to the atmosphere, which are chilling to the senses, and must be productive of occasional inflammatory diseases, such as are frequent in the spring and winter with us. The change of the wind alternates often between the warm sea breezes from the south, and the cold blasts from the snow-capped mountains inland, and produces the usual effects, doubtless, of such variations. In the summer it is occasionally very hot in the day time, but the nights are refreshed by the sea breezes. From April 19th to May 13th, a record of the thermometer gives 72° as the highest, and 58° as the lowest point, and of the barometer 29.38 and 30.00. As the season advances the mercury rises, no doubt, much higher, reaching probably 85° of Fahrenheit, or more. Simoda is liable to the ordinary affections of temperate climates, but there seems no reason to suspect that it has a special tendency to any epidemic diseases.

Since the treaty of Kanagawa, by which the port was opened to intercourse with the Americans, Simoda has been separated from the jurisdiction of the principality of Idzu, and constituted an imperial city, the authorities of which are appointed directly by the government at Yedo. There is a governor or general superintendent of the municipal and commercial affairs of the place, with a fiscal assistant or treasurer, whose particular function has regard to the revenues. Subordinate to these two officials, there are the same number of prefects or *bugio*, who again have under them various collectors and interpreters, whose business is the practical administration of affairs in the various departments of government and trade. The limit of the jurisdiction of the imperial officers is marked by six guard stations, neither of which is more than a mile and a half from the town, placed on all the principal roads leading to Simoda. Beyond these, the inhabitants of the country are amenable as before to their own local government, while within them all persons are under the newly appointed authorities.

Gongs and Musical Instruments for Worship.

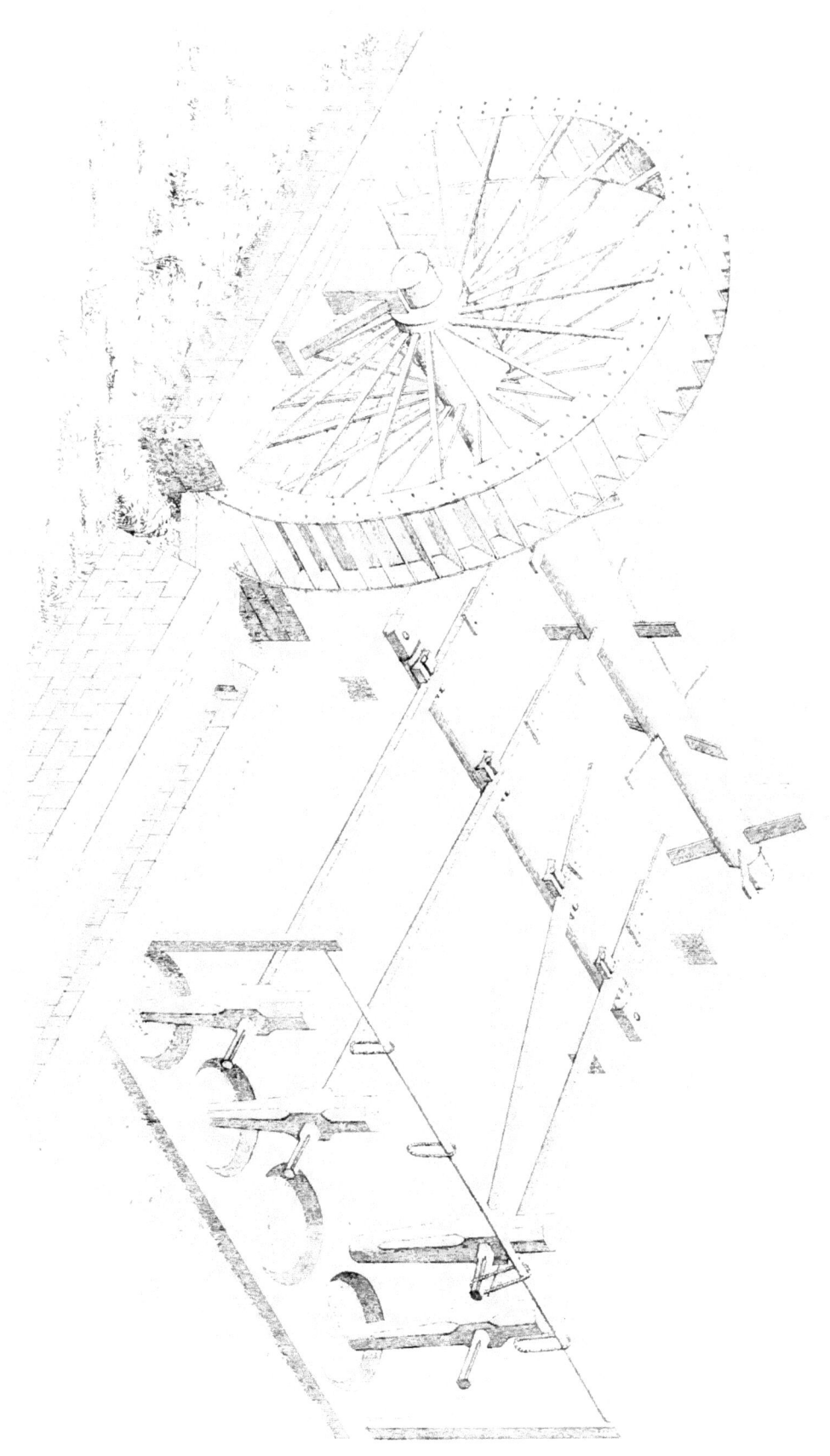

JAPANESE RICE MILL.

CHAPTER XXII.

SURVEY AND DESCRIPTION OF THE HARBOR OF SIMODA.—DISCIPLINE IN THE SQUADRON.—INTERCOURSE WITH THE AUTHORITIES OF SIMODA.—KURA-KAWA-KAHEI, THE PREFECT.—HIS DISPOSITION TO PRODUCE TROUBLE.—TREATMENT OF THE AMERICAN OFFICERS.—REMONSTRANCES OF THE COMMODORE.—EQUIVOCATION OF THE PREFECT.—HE IS FRIGHTENED INTO PROPRIETY.—EFFORTS OF TWO JAPANESE GENTLEMEN CLANDESTINELY TO LEAVE THEIR COUNTRY IN THE SQUADRON.—COMMODORE'S CONDUCT.—BUDDHIST TEMPLES AT SIMODA.—PREFECT AGAIN SHOWS HIS PETTY HOSTILITY.—HIS PREVARICATIONS AND FALSEHOODS.—FUNERAL OF AN AMERICAN ON SHORE.—INSULT OFFERED TO AMERICAN OFFICERS ON SHORE.—PREFECT'S FURTHER FALSEHOODS.—COMPELLED TO APOLOGIZE, AND INFORMED THAT HIS INSOLENCE WOULD NOT BE BORNE IN FUTURE.—FRIENDLY INTERCOURSE WITH THE PEOPLE.—DEPARTURE FOR HAKODADI.—VOLCANO OF OHO-SIMA.—THE KURO-SIWO, OR JAPANESE "GULF STREAM."—STRAITS OF SANGAR.—FOGS.—HARBOR OF HAKODADI.—DIRECTIONS FOR ENTERING.

ON THE Commodore's arrival at the port of Simoda, he immediately organized a surveying party for the complete examination of the harbor, and, during his stay, succeeded in obtaining a thorough knowledge of all the points of nautical interest to the navigator. The harbor of Simoda is near the southeastern extremity of the peninsula of Idzu, which terminates at the cape of that name, and bears S. W. by W., at a distance of forty-five miles from Cape Sagami, at the entrance of the lower bay or gulf of Yedo. To the northward of the harbor, a high ridge of mountains intersects the peninsula, and south of this, all the way to the cape, the land is broken by innumerable peaks of less elevation. There are several islands and prominent rocks, which are picturesque features in the view, and important indications, which require to be carefully considered by those approaching Simoda from the sea. Rock island, in latitude 34° 33′ 50″ N., longitude 138° 57′ 16″ E., is about one hundred and twenty feet high, and a third of a mile long, with precipitous shores, and a surface of irregular outline. Covering the top there is a thick growth of shrubs, grass, weeds, and moss. From the summit of this island overfalls were seen, bearing N. ½ W., distant a mile or a mile and a half, which may have been caused by rocks or reefs. An effort was made to investigate the cause, but without success, in consequence of the strong current and the fresh winds. The Japanese fishermen, however, deny that there is any danger to navigation in that direction. North by west from Rock island, distant two miles, are the Ukona rocks, which are really two in number, though at a distance they generally appear as one. The larger reaches a height of seventy feet. Between these rocks and Rock island there is a current setting east northeastwardly, and running at a rate of quite four miles an hour. From Rock, Centre island, so called from its being the point from which the treaty limits are measured, bears N. ½ E., at a distance of five and a half miles, and from the two Ukona rocks, N. by E. ½ E., distant three and a half miles. Centre island is high, conical in shape, and is covered with a full growth of trees, while through its base passes, from one side to the other, a natural cave. Its latitude was found, by careful observation, to be 34° 39' 49" N., and its longitude 138° 57' 50" E., with a variation of 52' westwardly. High water, full and change, five hours. The extreme rise of the tide is five feet seven inches upon the shores of the island, and the mean rise three feet. Buisako is the name of an islet which, covered with trees and shrubs, and about forty feet in height, lies N.N.E. from Centre island. Off the village of Susaki, at a distance of one-third of a mile from the shore, is a ledge of rocks upon which the swell is always breaking.

Vessels bound to the harbor of Simoda from the southward and westward should make Cape Idzu, latitude 34° 32' N., longitude 138° 51' E., from which Rock island bears E.S.E. ½ E., distant about six miles. If the weather is at all clear, the chain of islands at the entrance of the lower bay or gulf of Yedo will, at the same time, be plainly visible. Between Rock island and the main land there are a number of rocks projecting above water, among which the Japanese junks freely pass; but a ship should not attempt the passage inside the island, unless in case of urgent necessity, as the northeasterly current, which sweeps along this coast, seems to be at this point capricious both in direction and velocity. Giving Rock island the berth of a mile, the harbor of Simoda will be in full view, bearing N. ½ W., distant five miles. Vandalia bluff, on the east side of the entrance, may be recognized by a grove of pines on its summit, and the village of Susaki, which is situated about one-third of the way between the bluff and a sharp point called Cape Diamond, making out to the eastward of the entrance to the harbor. A vessel standing in from Rock island will probably pass through a number of tide-rips, but soundings will not be obtained by the hand-lead until near the entrance of the harbor, when the navigator will find himself in from seventeen to twenty-four fathoms. Should the wind be from the northward and fresh, it would be expedient to anchor at the mouth of the harbor until it lulls or shifts, or until the vessel can be conveniently warped in, as the breezes usually blow in flaws and are always baffling.

Approaching from the northward and eastward, a vessel can pass on either side of the island of Oho-sima, from the centre of which Cape Diamond bears W.S.W. ¾ W., distant about twenty miles. The navigator approaching from the east will not find the harbor opening until he is well inside of Cape Diamond. Between Oho-sima and Simoda no dangers are known to exist, but the northeasterly current must be borne constantly in mind, particularly at night and in thick weather. Its general strength is from two to three miles per hour; but as this, as well as its direction, is much influenced by the local winds, headlands, islands, rocks, and other causes, neither can be relied on.

Should Oho-sima be obscured by thick weather before reaching Cape Diamond, the pilot should endeavor to sight Rock island, for there are no very conspicuous objects on the main land by which the stranger can recognize the harbor at a distance, and the shore appears as one unbroken line. To the northward of Cape Diamond is the bay of Sira-hama, which is quite deep, and as it has several sand beaches it may be taken for Simoda; but as this bay is

approached, Cape Diamond will shut in the Ukona rocks and Rock island to the southward, while in the Simoda roads they are both visible from all points. To the westward of the harbor there are several beaches and banks of sand, which, as they can be plainly discerned at the distance of six or eight miles, will serve as good land marks.

A vessel from the southward and eastward should pass to the west of the island of Meac-sima, which may be known by a remarkable snow-white cliff on its western side, and a patch on the summit toward the north. To the southward and westward of the island there are two groups of dangerous rocks, some fifteen or twenty feet high, which were called by the Commodore, Redfield, after the well-known scientific investigator of that name. One set is in latitude 33° 56′ 13″ N., and longitude 138° 48′ 31″ E.; the other in latitude 33° 57′ 31″ N., and in longitude 138° 49′ 13″ E.

There are but two hidden dangers in the harbor. The first is the Southampton rock, so called from the ship which touched upon it, and lying in mid-channel, bearing N. ½ W. from Vandalia bluff, between which and Centre island it is situated about three-fourths of the way. The rock is estimated to be about twenty-five feet in diameter, and has two fathoms of water covering it. It was marked by the surveyors with a white spar-buoy. The other concealed danger is the Supply rock, which bears S. by W., at a short distance from Buisako islet, and has a sharp edge with eleven feet of water upon it. A red spar-buoy indicates its position.

The general discipline of the squadron had been excellent during the whole expedition, and under circumstances calculated to test, with some degree of severity, the government of the officers and the obedience of the men. From the necessity of conciliating the strange people of Japan, and conforming, in some respects, to their habits of non-intercourse with foreigners, it required great tact, on the part of those having authority on board ship, to reconcile the natural desire of occasional liberty on the part of the sailors with the rigid reserve of the Japanese. This was, however, accomplished with general success, and there was but little occasion for any but the ordinary exercise of the rules of discipline to secure the preservation of that good order which was the characteristic of all the ships of the squadron. Neglect of duty and small offences were promptly rebuked and punished by the usual penalties, and great severity was rarely called for. On the 19th of April, however, it was found necessary to convene a general court martial on board the Mississippi for the trial of several seamen, and the result was the finding of two of the men guilty of desertion. It was, however, but technical desertion, consisting in what Jack calls "French," meaning "taking French leave," by wandering off from a boat ashore, without permission, to look for drink. The laws of the service, however, properly enough, deem such conduct desertion. The sentence was duly read in all the ships of the squadron, and the delinquents suffered the usual penalty of confinement for a time and stoppage of pay.

On the third day after reaching Simoda, April 21st, the Commodore, accompanied by a small suite of officers, landed, and paid an official visit to Kura-Kawa-Kahei, the prefect. The party was received with the usual formal courtesies by the Japanese official and Moryama Yenoske, who had come to Simoda to exercise his functions as an interpreter, and to aid, by his experience, in carrying out the conditions of the treaty just negotiated at Kanagawa. The Commodore, after partaking of refreshments, walked through the town to take a general survey, and entered various temples, which are the chief objects of interest to the stranger at Simoda. On his

418   EXPEDITION TO JAPAN.

return to the ship he was accompanied by several of the Japanese officials, who proposed to make some arrangement for the supply of such provisions as might be required by the squadron.

Presuming upon the privileges secured by the treaty, the officers began now to frequent the shore and stroll freely about the streets of the town and the neighboring country. The common people, as had been elsewhere observed, seemed very much disposed to welcome the strangers and engage in friendly converse with them. They exhibited their usual curiosity, and thronged about the Americans, examining their dress, and, with almost childish eagerness and delight, fingered the officers' buttons, swords, and gay accoutrements, and, pointing to them, would ask, in their pantomimic way, the English names for each article which struck their fancy. It was soon discovered, however, that the Japanese authorities were not disposed to allow of this free intermingling of the people with the Americans, and no sooner was it observed than various armed soldiers or policemen came up and dispersed their countrymen. Not satisfied with the exercise of this severe discipline upon the poor Japanese, the officials seemed determined to practice their authority upon the American officers. It was found that, wherever the latter went, they were followed by a squad of soldiers, who watched every movement, and dogged

Group of Japanese Women—Simoda.

their steps with the pertinacity of a pack of hounds. The people, under the orders of the local authorities, fled, and the town, with its shops closed and its streets deserted, was as sad as if it had been devastated by the plague. Even in their strolls into the country, the American officers found that they could not divest themselves of the perpetual presence and jealous watchfulness of the Japanese spies, who were evidently resolved to restrict the freedom of their visitors, and put them under the most rigid surveillance.

JAPANESE WOMEN SIMODA

The Commodore, upon being made aware of this treatment of his officers, felt greatly indignant, as it was in violation of the stipulations of the treaty, and he determined to bring the authorities of Simoda, whom he held responsible, to account. He accordingly dispatched his flag lieutenant and his two interpreters on shore, to call upon the prefect and lay before him certain complaints, which were specified in a memorandum in which the Commodore expressed his dissatisfaction at the manner in which his officers were treated on going ashore, and protested against their being followed by soldiers, the dispersion of the people, and the closing of the shops. These, he declared, were at variance with the stipulations of the treaty; and threatened, if the annoyances should continue, that he would sail to Yedo with his whole squadron and demand an explanation. The Commodore also took occasion to insist upon a suitable place being set apart on shore for a resort for himself and officers; and as he proposed a visit to the island of Oho-sima, requested that proper provisions should be made for the journey, a junk be provided, and certain Japanese officials selected to accompany the American expedition.

The prefect, upon hearing this protest of the Commodore, replied, that the Dutch at Nagasak were always followed by twelve or fourteen Japanese soldiers, and seemed to think that such a precedent should be a rule of conduct for the Americans. He was, however, told, that the treatment of the Dutch was not to be taken for a moment as a criterion by which the Japanese authorities were to judge of what was proper in their relations with the Americans, who had a "treaty of amity and intercourse" with Japan; and coming, as they did, to Simoda as friends, they would insist upon being treated as such, and suffer no infringement of privileges which had been guarantied by a solemn compact. The prefect, moreover, was told that the Americans intended no harm to the people, but, on the contrary, desired the most friendly relations with them, and the freest intercourse, without being watched and restrained by soldiers, acting under the orders of their superiors. Such a surveillance as had hitherto been practised was what Americans were not accustomed to, and particularly as it would seem to indicate that they were intent upon the commission of some outrage.

This resolute language produced its desired effect upon the prefect, who excused his conduct upon the plea that he had left Yoku-hama before the signing of the treaty, and had, in consequence, not been aware that it contained the clause "free intercourse." He would be obliged, he continued, to refer to his superiors at Yedo for instructions on this point, and ascertain how they construed that article; but, in the meanwhile, he would give orders that the houses should not be closed, and try the experiment of allowing the officers to visit the shore without being followed by soldiers.

The prefect then readily acceded to the Commodore's demands in regard to a place of resort and the visit to Oho-sima, saying that any of the temples were at his disposition, where the best accommodation Simoda afforded would be prepared for him, and that a junk, two boats, and certain Japanese attendants would be immediately provided for those persons of the squadron the Commodore wished to send to Oho-sima. After an expression from the prefect of courtesy, and the hope that trifles would not be permitted to interrupt the friendly feeling subsisting between the Americans and the Japanese, the interview closed.

The various officers of the squadron now visited the shore daily, and for a time there was apparently less disposition to interfere with their movements, or watch their proceedings. On one of these occasions a party had passed out into the country beyond the suburbs, when they found two Japanese following them; but, as they were supposed to be a couple of spies on the watch, little notice was at first taken of them. Observing, however, that they seemed to be approaching as if stealthily, and as though desirous of seeking an opportunity of speaking, the American officers awaited their coming up. On being accosted, the Japanese were observed to be men of some position and rank, as each wore the two swords characteristic of distinction, and were dressed in the wide but short trowsers of rich silk brocade. Their manner showed the usual courtly refinement of the better classes, but they exhibited the embarrassment of men who evidently were not perfectly at their ease, and were about doing something of dubious propriety. They cast their eyes stealthily about as if to assure themselves that none of their countrymen were at hand to observe their proceedings, and then approaching one of the officers and pretending to admire his watch-chain, slipped within the breast of his coat a folded paper.* They now significantly, with the finger upon the lips, entreated secresy, and rapidly made off.

During the succeeding night, about two o'clock, a. m., (April 25th,) the officer of the mid-watch, on board the steamer Mississippi, was aroused by a voice from a boat alongside, and upon proceeding to the gangway, found a couple of Japanese, who had mounted the ladder at the ship's side, and upon being accosted, made signs expressive of a desire to be admitted on board.

They seemed very eager to be allowed to remain, and showed a very evident determination

---

* This paper proved to be a letter in Japanese, of which the following is a literal translation by Mr. Williams, the interpreter of the squadron:

"Two scholars from Yedo, in Japan, present this letter for the inspection of 'the high officers and those who manage affairs.' Our attainments are few and trifling, as we ourselves are small and unimportant, so that we are abashed in coming before you; we are neither skilled in the use of arms, nor are we able to discourse upon the rules of strategy and military discipline; in trifling pursuits and idle pastimes our years and months have slipped away. We have, however, read in books, and learned a little by hearsay, what are the customs and education in Europe and America, and we have been for many years desirous of going over the 'five great continents,' but the laws of our country in all maritime points are very strict; for foreigners to come into the country, and for natives to go abroad, are both immutably forbidden. Our wish to visit other regions has consequently only 'gone to and fro in our own breasts in continual agitation,' like one's breathing being impeded or his walking cramped. Happily, the arrival of so many of your ships in these waters, and stay for so many days, which has given us opportunity to make a pleasing acquaintance and careful examination, so that we are fully assured of the kindness and liberality of your excellencies, and your regard for others, has also revived the thoughts of many years, and they are urgent for an exit.

"This, then, is the time to carry the plan into execution, and we now secretly send you this private request, that you will take us on board your ships as they go out to sea; we can thus visit around in the five great continents, even if we do in this, slight the prohibitions of our own country. Lest those who have the management of affairs may feel some chagrin at this, in order to effect our desire, we are willing to serve in any way we can on board of the ships, and obey the orders given us. For doubtless it is, that when a lame man sees others walking he wishes to walk too; but how shall the pedestrian gratify his desires when he sees another one riding? We have all our lives been going hither to you, unable to get more than thirty degrees east and west, or twenty-five degrees north and south; but now when we see how you sail on the tempests and cleave the huge billows, going lightning speed thousands and myriads of miles, skirting along the five great continents, can it not be likened to the lame finding a plan for walking, and the pedestrian seeing a mode by which he can ride? If you who manage affairs will give our request your consideration, we will retain the sense of the favor; but the prohibitions of our country are still existent, and if this matter should become known we should uselessly see ourselves pursued and brought back for immediate execution without fail, and such a result would greatly grieve the deep humanity and kindness you all bear towards others. If you are willing to accede to this request, keep 'wrapped in silence our error in making it' until you are about to leave, in order to avoid all risk of such serious danger to life; for when, by-and-bye, we come back, our countrymen will never think it worth while to investigate bygone doings. Although our words have only loosely let our thoughts leak out, yet truly they are sincere; and if your excellencies are pleased to regard them kindly, do not doubt them nor oppose our wishes. We together pay our respects in handing this in. April 11."

A small note was enclosed, of which the following is a translation: "The enclosed letter contains the earnest request we have had for many days, and which we tried in many ways to get off to you at Yoku-hama, in a fishing boat, by night; but the cruisers were too thick, and none others were allowed to come alongside, so that we were in great uncertainty how to act. Hearing that the ships were coming to Simoda we have come to take our chance, intending to get a small boat and go off to the ships, but have not succeeded. Trusting your worships will agree, we will, to-morrow night, after all is quiet, be at Kakizaki in a small boat, near the shore, where there are no houses. There we greatly hope you to meet us and take us away, and thus bring our hopes to fruition. April 25."

not to return to the shore, by the desire they expressed of casting off their boat, utterly regardless of its fate. The captain of the Mississippi directed them to the flag-ship, to which, on retiring to their boat, they pulled off at once. Having reached her with some difficulty, in consequence of the heavy swell in the harbor, they had hardly got upon the ladder and mounted to the gangway, when their boat got adrift, either by accident, or from being let go intentionally. On their reaching the deck, the officer informed the Commodore of their presence, who sent his interpreter to confer with them and learn the purpose of their untimely visit. They frankly confessed that their object was to be taken to the United States, where they might gratify their desire of travelling, and seeing the world. They were now recognised as the two men who had met the officers on shore and given one of them the letter. They seemed much fatigued by their boating excursion, and their clothes showed signs of being travel worn, although they proved to be Japanese gentlemen of good position. They both were entitled to wear the two swords, and one still retained a single one, but they had left the other three in the boat which had gone adrift with them. They were educated men, and wrote the mandarin Chinese with fluency and apparent elegance, and their manners were courteous and highly refined. The Commodore, on learning the purpose of their visit, sent word that he regretted that he was unable to receive them, as he would like very much to take some Japanese to America with him. He, however, was compelled to refuse them until they received permission from their government, for seeking which they would have ample opportunity, as the squadron would remain in the harbor of Simoda for some time longer. They were greatly disturbed by this answer of the Commodore, and declaring that if they returned to the land they would lose their heads, earnestly implored to be allowed to remain. The prayer was firmly but kindly refused. A long discussion ensued, in the course of which they urged every possible argument in their favor, and continued to appeal to the humanity of the Americans. A boat was now lowered, and after some mild resistance on their part to being sent off, they descended the gangway piteously deploring their fate, and were landed at a spot near where it was supposed their boat might have drifted.

On the afternoon of the next day, Yenoske, the chief interpreter, who had come to Simoda from Yedo for the express purpose of requesting the postponement of the expedition to Oho-sima, which was conditionally granted by the Commodore, came on board the Powhatan, and requested to see the flag-lieutenant, to whom he stated, that "last night a couple of demented Japanese had gone off to one of the American vessels," and wished to know if it had been the flag-ship; and if so, whether the men had been guilty of any impropriety. The flag-lieutenant replied, that it was difficult to retain any very precise recollection of those who visited the ships, as so many were constantly coming from the shore in the watering boats and on business, but he assured the interpreter that no misdemeanor could have been committed, or he would have been aware of the fact. The interpreter was then asked, whether the Japanese he referred to had reached the shore in safety, to which the very satisfactory answer that "they had" was received.

The Commodore, upon hearing of the visit of the interpreter and the apparent anxiety of the Japanese authorities in regard to the conduct of the two strange visitors to the ships, sent an officer on shore in order to quiet the excitement which had been created, and to interpose as far as possible in behalf of the poor fellows, who it was certain would be pursued with the utmost rigor of Japanese law. The authorities were thanked for the solicitude they had expressed lest the Americans should have been inconvenienced by any of their people, and assured that they need not trouble themselves for a moment with the thought that so slight a matter had been considered otherwise than a mere trivial occurrence unworthy of any investigation. The Japanese were further informed that they need give themselves no anxiety for the future, as none of their countrymen should be received on board the American ships without the consent of the authorities, as the Commodore and his officers were not disposed to take advantage of their confidence or act in any way that would be inconsistent with the spirit of the treaty. If the Commodore had felt himself at liberty to indulge his feelings, he would have gladly given a refuge on board his ship to the poor Japanese, who apparently sought to escape from the country from the desire of gratifying a liberal curiosity, which had been stimulated by the presence of the Americans in Japan. There were other considerations which, however, had higher claims than an equivocal humanity. To connive at the flight of one of the people was to disobey the laws of the Empire, and it was the only true policy to conform, in all possible regards, to the institutions of a country by which so many important concessions had already been reluctantly granted. The Empire of Japan forbids the departure of any of its subjects for a foreign country under the penalty of death, and the two men who had fled on board the ships were criminals in the eye of their own laws, however innocent they might have appeared to the Americans. Moreover, although there was no reason to doubt the account the two Japanese gave of themselves, it was possible they were influenced by other and less worthy motives than those they professed. It might have been a stratagem to test American honor, and some believed it so to be. The Commodore, by his careful efforts to impress upon the authorities how trifling he esteemed the offence, hoped to mitigate the punishment to which it was amenable. The event was full of interest, as indicative of the intense desire for information on the part of two educated Japanese, who were ready to brave the rigid laws of the country, and to risk even death for the sake of adding to their knowledge. The Japanese are undoubtedly an inquiring people, and would gladly welcome an opportunity for the expansion of their moral and intellectual faculties. The conduct of the unfortunate two was, it is believed, characteristic of their countrymen, and nothing can better represent the intense curiosity of the people, while its exercise is only prevented by the most rigid laws and ceaseless watchfulness lest they should be disobeyed. In this disposition of the people of Japan, what a field of speculation, and, it may be added, what a prospect full of hope opens for the future of that interesting country!

Some days subsequently, as a party of officers were strolling in the suburbs, they came upon the prison of the town, where they recognized the two unfortunate Japanese immured in one of the usual places of confinement, a kind of cage, barred in front and very restricted in capacity. The poor fellows had been immediately pursued upon its being discovered that they had visited the ships, and after a few days they were pounced upon and lodged in prison. They seemed to bear their misfortune with great equanimity, and were greatly pleased apparently with the visit of the American officers, in whose eyes they evidently were desirous of appearing to advantage. On one of the visitors approaching the cage, the Japanese wrote on a piece of board that was handed to them the following, which, as a remarkable specimen of philosophical resignation under circumstances which would have tried the stoicism of Cato, deserves a record:

"When a hero fails in his purpose, his acts are then regarded as those of a villain and robber. In public have we been seized and pinioned and caged for many days. The village elders and head men treat us disdainfully, their oppressions being grievous indeed. Therefore, looking up while yet we have nothing wherewith to reproach ourselves, it must now be seen whether a hero

will prove himself to be one indeed. Regarding the liberty of going through the sixty States as not enough for our desires, we wished to make the circuit of the five great continents. This was our hearts' wish for a long time. Suddenly our plans are defeated, and we find ourselves in a half sized house, where eating, resting, sitting, and sleeping are difficult; how can we find our exit from this place? Weeping, we seem as fools; laughing, as rogues. Alas! for us; silent we can only be.
"ISAGI KOODA,
"KWANSUCHI MANJI."

The Commodore, on being informed of the imprisonment of the two Japanese, sent his flag lieutenant on shore to ascertain unofficially whether they were the same who had visited the ships. The cage was found as described, but empty, and the guards of the prison declared that the men had been sent that morning to Yedo, in obedience to an order from the capital. They had been confined, it was stated, for going off to the American ships, and as the prefect had no authority to act in the matter, he had at once reported the case to the imperial government, which had sent for the prisoners, and then held them under its jurisdiction. The fate of the poor fellows was never ascertained, but it is hoped that the authorities were more merciful than to have awarded the severest penalty, which was the loss of their heads, for what appears to us only liberal and a highly commendable curiosity, however great the crime according to the eccentric and sanguinary code of Japanese law. It is a comfort to be able to add, that the Commodore received an assurance from the authorities, upon questioning them, that he need not apprehend a serious termination.

The large Buddhist temple, the Rio-shen-zhi, or great peace monastery, was the place appropriated by the authorities, in accordance with the demands of the Commodore, for his use, and another was provided for that of his officers. Most of the Japanese temples have apartments separate from the ecclesiastical part of the establishment, which are used for lodging and entertaining strangers and distinguished visitors. They are also employed occasionally for various public gatherings, on festival and market days; and bazaars, for buying and selling, are not unfrequently opened; thus converting the temple into a place for the free exercise of all the roguery of trade, if not literally into a "den of thieves." As the supply of furniture was scant in the lodging department of the Rio-shen-zhi, chairs and other appliances of comfort were brought from the ships, and the quarters were made tolerably luxurious. In order to familiarize the Japanese people with their presence, the Commodore and his officers frequently resorted to their apartments on shore, and found a walk in the pleasure grounds which surrounded them, and on the wooded hills at the back, a pleasant diversion from the routine of ship's duty.

There was, notwithstanding the promise of the prefect, very little improvement in the conduct of the authorities, and the Americans still found their liberty much restricted, and their privacy interrupted by the jealous watchfulness and intrusive officiousness of the soldiers and spies. The Commodore himself, on one occasion, when proceeding through the town in company with several of his officers, found that he was constantly preceded by two Japanese functionaries, who ordered all the people they met to retire within their houses and close the doors. The shopmen were evidently forbidden to sell their wares to the strangers, for the most trifling articles which they might desire to purchase could not be obtained on any terms. The Commodore found it necessary again to protest against this illiberal treatment, and sent his flag-lieutenant to the prefect to lay before him certain complaints and to insist upon their causes being immediately removed. The prefect was accordingly called upon, and informed that it appeared that he was determined to evade the full execution of the stipulations of the treaty, since, by allowing his spies or soldiers to follow the Americans, and by ordering the people to withdraw from the streets and to close their houses, he was placing every obstruction in the way of that friendly intercourse with the Japanese which was guarantied by the compact solemnly entered into between Japan and the United States. The prefect was then assured, that if these annoyances should continue, the Commodore would stop all relations with the town and return to Yedo, as, although he had been eight days at Simoda, there had been very little improvement in the conduct of the authorities, and his patience was exhausted.

The prefect excused himself by averring that the Commodore was mistaken in his allegations, and that the soldiers were present for the protection of the visitors, and were engaged, not, as was supposed, in ordering the people to withdraw and close their houses, but in directing them to welcome the Americans, and open their doors to them. Upon the flag-lieutenant, however, urging that his personal experience proved the contrary, the prefect said then that his orders had been misunderstood, and he would renew them and see that they were executed, that the Commodore might have no reason to complain thereafter. In regard to trading with the Americans, the prefect declared that he had received no instructions to allow of it until the opening of a bazaar. He was then answered that the officers merely wanted some small articles for their own use, and any purchases they might make could not be considered as coming within the technical understanding of the term "trade." It was then agreed, after some resistance on the part of the prefect and a long discussion, that whenever an American wished to buy any article he should give an order for it to the shopman, who would be directed to take the order and the purchase to the interpreter, by whom the article would be sent to the ships. The prefect then referred to the case of the two Japanese who had clandestinely visited the steamers, and seemed solicitous of obtaining some information in regard to their conduct, but his enquiries were abruptly checked by the answer that the Commodore was not to be questioned by any of the subordinates of the government.

As the Americans, subsequent to this last interview with the prefect, began to frequent the shops and select articles for purchase, it was found necessary to establish some temporary currency. It was accordingly arranged, since the Japanese money, from the strict laws which governed its circulation, could not be used in dealings with foreigners, that United States coins should be received by the shopmen at Simoda. The value of these was estimated comparatively with the Chinese copper cash, with which the Japanese were familiar, at the rate of 1,600 Chinese cash to one silver dollar. This the Japanese readily assented to, and became soon as eager as any other trading people to become possessed of the money of the Americans.

On the 2d of May the Macedonian arrived from the Bonin Islands with a very welcome supply of fine turtles, which were distributed among the several ships of the squadron and greatly enjoyed. The market of Simoda was not well supplied with fresh meats, for, in consequence of the prevailing Buddhism and the simple habits of the people, there were but few animals which could be obtained for food. The poultry were very scarce, and the few cattle in the place were too much valued as beasts of burden to be readily offered for sacrifice to the carnivorous propensities of strangers; so the arrival of the turtles was very gratefully welcomed by those on board ship who, with the exception of a supply of fish and vegetables, had been so long confined to a sea-diet of biscuit and salt junk.

Two days subsequent to the arrival of the Macedonian the Lexington was dispatched for Lew

Chew, and on the 6th of May the Macedonian, Vandalia, and Southampton preceded the steamers and sailed for Hakodadi.

One of the sailors on board the Powhatan having unfortunately fallen from aloft and died soon after, it became necessary to make some provision for his burial.

The Japanese authorities readily assented to the request that he should be buried ashore. A place of interment was accordingly selected in the neighborhood of the village of Kaki-zaki, and thenceforward appropriated as the burial place for Americans. On the day of the funeral several Japanese officials came on board ship, and saying that their laws required it, asked to inspect the body. They, however, politely prefaced their demands with the remark that it was a formality about which the prefect and they themselves could exercise no discretion, but that they had no doubt it might be dispensed with for the future, on a requisition being made to the commissioners. As the coffin was still unnailed, and there seemed no good reason for refusing to grant the request of the Japanese officials, they were allowed to see the body. The burial then took place, according to the usual Christian ceremonies, in the place on shore which had been appropriated for the purpose.

Everything seemed now to be on the most friendly footing, and it was with no little surprise and vexation that the Commodore heard, from the reports of some of his officers, of an outrage which called for a prompt rebuke, and the demand for an apology from the local authorities. The Commodore's first impulse, in fact, was to dispatch a guard of marines on shore to arrest the Japanese officials who had been guilty, but, upon reflection, he determined to send his lieutenant to call upon the prefect and to lay before him the facts of the outrage, and to insist upon the fullest explanation and apology. The occurrence was simply this: three of the officers went ashore to amuse themselves in the neighborhood of Simoda with their fowling-pieces, and, after a day's shooting, which was prolonged to a late hour, they betook themselves to one of the temples as a resting place. As the evening was too far advanced to think of returning to the ships, it was proposed that the sportsmen should spend their night in the lodging apartment connected with the monastery. With a view courteously to avoid any misunderstanding, the officers first informed Tabroske, the interpreter, of their intention, which was supposed to be in perfect conformity with the understanding with the authorities, who had specifically declared that either of the temples was at the disposition of the Commodore and his officers for a resting place. The three gentlemen had hardly, however, entered and prepared themselves for a night's rest upon the soft mats of the apartment, when a great noise at the entrance and the subsequent thronging in of a troop of soldiers, led by Tatsnoske and a number of Japanese officials, disturbed their prospect of repose, and greatly aroused the indignation of the officers. The Japanese intruded themselves unceremoniously into the sleeping apartment, and rudely insisted on the Americans leaving on the instant and returning to the ships.

Tatsnoske and another official, finding that their urgent appeals were unheeded, left with the intention, as they said, of going to see the Commodore in reference to the matter. In their absence, the remaining officials and soldiers became still more rude and insolent, but were soon brought to a civil silence and driven in fright from the apartment by the formidable attitude of the three officers, who stood to their arms, and significantly cocked their revolvers. There was no further interruption to the tranquillity of the officers, but a guard was stationed in another part of the temple, where they remained during the whole night.

The prefect was disposed at first to justify the conduct of his subordinates when the case was laid before him. He declared that the American officers were in the wrong for not having given previous notice of their intention to stay on shore, and because they had gone to a temple which had not been especially designated for their use.

When the prefect was set right in regard to these false countercharges, he shifted his ground and urged that, as the treaty had not yet gone into effect, the Americans could not yet claim the advantages it was supposed to secure. This view was, of course, emphatically objected to, and the prefect, moreover, informed that the Commodore was not willing to discuss with him the subject of the interpretation of the treaty, as it did not concern him. It was then proposed by the prefect that the matter complained of should be submitted to the commissioners for their arbitration. This was peremptorily declined, and an immediate apology for the outrage, or a categorical refusal, insisted upon. The Japanese official was not yet willing to come directly to the point, and lingered in the discussion of the minor details of the question, in the course of which he stated that it was a Japanese custom to appoint guards for the *protection* of strangers. He was then indignantly told that the Americans required no such protection, as they were well able to protect themselves on all occasions, and that one of the articles of the treaty was framed for the express purpose of securing freedom from that very surveillance alluded to. The prefect was then emphatically assured that the Americans would never submit with impunity to such treatment, as it was not only an infringement of the stipulations of the treaty, but a violation of the laws of hospitality and an outrage. The prefect now disavowed the whole proceeding, saying that his subordinates had acted upon their own responsibility and without his knowledge, and that he regretted its occurrence. This apology was, of course, accepted, with a reminder, however, that for the future the Commodore could make no distinction between the prefect's own acts and those of his subordinates, but that the former would be held responsible in all cases.

The prefect then expressed a desire to restrict the stay of officers during the night on shore to cases of necessity, but any such qualification of the privilege was positively denied; and as the Japanese "could not, of course, judge of the necessity which might require the American officers to remain on shore, they must decide that for themselves."

All difficulty now being removed, there was no further interruption to the friendly intercourse between the people of Simoda and their American visitors. There were daily and most intimate relations with the authorities, who seemed anxious to facilitate the views of the Commodore, and superintend the supplying of his vessels with water, and all the provisions their scant resources afforded. As the day was now approaching the 9th of May, which had been appointed for meeting the Japanese officials at Hakodadi, the Commodore took his departure for that place in his flag-ship, the Powhatan, accompanied by the steamer Mississippi. The Macedonian, Vandalia, and Southampton had sailed previously for the same port. The store-ship Supply was left at Simoda. Previous to the Commodore's departure, he had offered a passage to the interpreter Tatsnoske, or any other Japanese personage whose presence might be required at Hakodadi; this offer, however, was declined, as, with their usual ceremonious obedience to their superiors, they were fearful of taking any step, however trifling in itself, without being fortified by the authority of the imperial government. The Commodore had now been twenty-five days in the harbor of Simoda, and as much of his time had been spent in tedious negotiation with the local authorities, who pertinaciously disputed at every step what had been previously conceded by their superiors, he was glad to vary the dull business in which he had been necessarily

involved by the disputatiousness of the prefect of Simoda and his satellites. He had, however, succeeded in making a thorough survey of the harbor, had acquired a considerable knowledge of the place and its resources, and, above all, impressed the people with a just idea of the friendly relations he wished to establish with them, and taught the authorities that no infringement, in the slightest degree, of the stipulations of the treaty of Yoku-hama would be allowed to pass with impunity.

On leaving the outer harbor, Oho-sima and other islands of the cluster, lying at the entrance of the Gulf of Yedo, came into full sight. For the sake of examining the former, and observing more closely the volcano on it, the steamers were steered so as to pass near its southern end. The volcano was in a state of active eruption, and there seemed to be either several craters, or one of great extent, as the vapor and smoke could be seen rising at short intervals and at different places along the crest of a ridge of mountains which extended to a distance of four or five miles. After passing Oho-sima, the steamers hauled up for Cape King, for the purpose of establishing the position of that important headland by the meridian observations. Up to the southern end of Oho-sima there was but little current discovered, but after reaching the channel between that island and Cape King it was observed to run with considerable rapidity in a direction nearly east, and on doubling the Capes its velocity increased still more.

In running along the coast between Capes Susaki, Serofama, and Firatatsi, or as the last is most generally called, Cape King, the three prominent southern headlands of the promontory of Awa, there was a good view of the land, and every one was struck with the extraordinary extent and perfection of its cultivation. Every portion of earth, from the base to the very summits of the mountains was terraced and planted with grain, and innumerable towns and villages were seen crowding, in all directions, the hill sides and the valleys.

Cape King, Firatatsi, the southeastern extremity of the island of Nippon, and included within the district of Awa, is in latitude 34° 53' 15" north, and in longitude 140° 18' 50" east, according to the observations taken on board the steamers Powhatan and Mississippi during the voyage. The headland, which forms the cape, runs off in an easterly direction to a low point that rises gradually inland, and about two miles from the extremity of this point is a cone-shaped elevation crowned by a tuft of trees. A little more than half way between Cape King and Cape Sirofama, near the shore, is another conical hill, also topped with trees, which offers a good land-mark. A strange navigator, first making this part of the Japanese coast, might mistake Cape King for an island. Vessels bound to Simoda from the east should endeavor to make Cape King, and after getting it to bear north, at a distance of six miles, should steer for the southern end of Oho-sima, which can be seen, in this position, in clear weather. After passing the southern end of Oho-sima, the navigator should steer west for the harbor. No specific account is here given of the currents, which are rapid and irregular throughout the Gulf of Yedo. The only sure guides, therefore, are the charts, the cross-bearings of the more prominent islands, and a good look-out. Along this part of the coast, the influence of the stream, called by the Japanese, *Kuro-siwo*, was quite perceptible. It never ceases to run in a northeasterly direction.

On this current the observations of our officers are particularly interesting. A detailed report thereon, made by Lieutenant Bent, will be found in the Nautical Appendix. We will therefore here present merely the general results attained by the gentlemen of the expedition. They found on the coast of Japan a stream analogous, in many respects, to the "gulf stream" on our Atlantic coast.

This commences on the south end of the island of Formosa, and is undoubtedly part of the great equatorial current of the Pacific. The larger portion of this current, when it reaches the point just named, passes off into the China sea; while the other part is deflected to the northward, passing along the eastern coast of Formosa, where its strength and character are unequivocally shown, and extending itself, at times, as far to the eastward as the Lew Chew islands, where the increased temperature of the water shows the presence of a torrid current. Its northwardly course, however, continues as far as the parallel of 26°, when it bears off to the northward and eastward, washing the whole southeastern coast of Japan as far as the Straits of Sangar, and increasing in strength as it advances. At the chain of islands south of the Gulf of Yedo, about the meridian of 140° E., its maximum strength on one occasion was observed to be seventy-two, seventy-four, and eighty miles per diem, respectively, on three successive days. From the south end of Formosa to the Straits of Sangar, its average velocity was found to be from thirty-five to forty miles per day, at all seasons when our ships traversed it. Its precise width south of the Gulf of Yedo was not satisfactorily ascertained, but enough was discovered to make it certain that it reaches to the southward of Fatsicio, and it extends perhaps even to the Bonin Islands in latitude 26° N.

In the latitude of 40° N. and to the eastward of the meridian 143° E. the stream turns more to the eastward, and thus allows a cold counter-current to intervene between it and the southern coast of the island of Yesso. Our hydrographers could not positively ascertain the fact, but they believed that this hyperborean current, found on the coast of Yesso, passes to the westward through the Straits of Sangar down through the Japan sea, between Corea and the Japanese islands, finding an outlet through the Formosa channel into the China sea. The data they had, together with the known fact that a strong southwardly current prevails between Formosa and the coast of China, particularly during the northeast monsoon, when the northwardly current along the east coast of Formosa continues unimpeded, would seem to give probability to this conjecture of the gentlemen. The southwest monsoon may possibly affect this counter-current, and force it to mingle its waters with those of the Kuro-siwo, or "Japanese gulf stream," between the north end of Formosa and the southwest extremity of Japan. The Vandalia was ordered from Hakodadi, to pass westward through the Straits of Sangar and proceed to China, on the western side of Japan. One object of this was to make observations on current and temperature; but, unfortunately, the Commodore left China before the report was made, and it has never reached him.

The existence of this counter-current, however, is so well known by vessels trading on the coast of China, that they seldom attempt to *beat* to the northward through the Formosa channel, but usually make the passage to the eastward of Formosa during adverse winds, even though such winds may be stronger on the east side of the island than in the Formosa channel. Lieutenant Bent traced also some striking analogies between this Kuro-siwo (great stream) of Japan, and our gulf stream. His observations were strikingly confirmatory of the views that have been expressed both by Mr. Redfield and Lieutenant M. F. Maury, as to the cause of the deflection of the Atlantic gulf stream to the eastward, and the cold counter-current below or between it and the shore. The first is not caused by the water impinging on land, and being thereby turned to the east, but by the greater rotative velocity of the latitudes at and near the equator, which throw the gulf stream eastward; and the second is produced by the tardy rotation of the high latitudes operating on the cold counter-current setting southward from the pole and throwing it to the west, along the shores and soundings of our Atlantic coast. The Grand Bank itself, Mr. Redfield thinks, is less a cause than an effect. Now there are precisely similar currents, warm and cold, with the same relative position too, on the coast of Japan. It may be that the first *northward* direction of both currents may be produced by the configuration of the eastern sides of America and Asia respectively, but their turn to the eastward afterwards is probably not influenced by any agency of the land in its shape or position.

There are other analogies which Mr. Bent remarked. These are found in the strata of cold water in the gulf stream, marked by Professor Bache on the charts of the coast survey in the report of 1853, and corresponding strata, derived entirely from the observations made on our Japan expedition. A comparison of temperatures of the two streams (Atlantic and Pacific) showed a striking coincidence. The maximum was the same; but in the Kuro-siwo, the difference between its temperature and that of the ocean, proper to the latitude where taken, was somewhat greater than in the gulf stream.

There is also a sea-weed floating in the Kuro-siwo, similar in appearance to the *fucus natans* of the gulf stream; specimens of it were collected, but unfortunately lost before reaching the hands of the scientific botanists to whom it was to be submitted. We cannot therefore say it was the same plant in the classifications of science; but to a sailor's eye there was no difference between it and the weed of the gulf stream. Lieutenant M. F. Maury is of opinion that this current in the Pacific has its origin in the Indian ocean, where the temperature is much greater than in the Caribbean sea, and where the waters, obstructed on the north by tropical lands, must somewhere make a current by which to escape, but this supposition appears to us questionable.

While steering along the shore to the northward the steamers, being about six miles from the land, and off Isomura, approached a fleet of fishing-boats, where there was noticed a discoloration of the water and an unusual drift of sea-weed. Soundings were then taken with the deep-sea-lead, and seventy-four, and then eighty fathoms, with a bottom of fine black sand, were found. The vessels still continuing to run along the shore within five or six miles, and Dai-ho-saki or White Cape being made, another cluster of fishing-boats was noticed under sail, apparently trailing for fish. About them the water was observed broken and discolored, and when the steamers had reached within a mile of the spot, their engines were stopped, and the lead again thrown, when soundings were obtained in thirty fathoms, coral bottom. The ships' course being changed from northeast by east to southeast, and running slowly and cautiously, they came suddenly on the eastern edge of the broken water into twenty-one fathoms, with what is called overfalls, and a bottom of coral as before. There seemed every reason to believe, from these indications, that there was a dangerous ledge lying directly in the way along the coast, at a distance from the land where such a danger would be hardly looked for. The Commodore would have anchored and examined this ledge had it not been for the near approach of night; and as for waiting until next day, the necessity of being at Hakodadi on the 19th of May, made it advisable not to lose any time by delay. It is true, with good weather, there was every reason to expect that the voyage might be accomplished in a day or two before the time appointed, but with the frequency of fogs about the Straits of Sangar, and the experience of the vexatious detentions caused by those annoyances, there could be no certainty in the calculation.

During the day time the course was kept along the coast, although at night the ships were hauled a little off. On the 15th of May, Cape Kurosaki came into sight, with its elevated peaks in the interior covered with snow. The atmosphere was fresh and invigorating, the mean temperature of the air being 59° of Fahrenheit, and that of the water 55°. The water was perfectly smooth, with an oily aspect from the surface, being covered with a substance which was supposed to be the excrement of whales, of which large numbers of various kinds, as well as of porpoises, were seen. At daylight, on the 16th, the course was shaped at an angle approaching the coast, and although the land had been for awhile out of sight, it was now again made and traced along until the ships reached the northeastern extremity of Nippon, called by the Japanese Sirija Saki. The southern and eastern coast of Japan from Cape Sirofama, as far as was observed, is not so high as that on the western side of the Gulf of Yedo. It is, however, of sufficient height to be observed, in tolerably clear weather, at a distance of forty miles. On getting abreast of Cape Sirija Saki, the Strait of Sangar, which separates Nippon from Yesso, was full in view, with the high land of the latter island distinctly visible ahead. The course was now steered directly for Hakodadi, but on getting into the middle of the strait a current or tide was encountered, which probably accelerated the eastern one, until the two reached a combined velocity of six knots. This powerful current prevented the steamers from reaching port that night, and it was thought advisable to put the heads of the steamers seaward. This would not have been necessary if any reliance could have been placed upon the continuance of clear weather. The engines were so managed as to expend little coal, and still to retain the position of the vessels; consequently, on taking the cross-bearings at daylight, it was found, notwithstanding the current, that the ships had not shifted their places a mile from where they had been when night set in.

Scarcely, however, had the steamers stood again for their destined port when a dense fog came on and obscured every object from sight, so that it was found necessary to head the steamers towards the east. The sun, however, on approaching the zenith, cleared away the fog, and fortunately bearings were distinguished which served as a guide to the port. As the cape, called by the Japanese Surro-kubo, and which the Commodore named Cape Blunt, in honor of his friends Edmund and George Blunt, of New York, was approached, there could be discerned over the neck of land which connects the promontory of Treaty Point* with the interior, the three ships of the squadron which had been previously dispatched, safely at anchor in the harbor of Hakodadi. At the approach of the steamers, in obedience to the previous instructions of the Commodore, boats came off from the ships with officers prepared to pilot in the Powhatan and Mississippi, which finally came to anchor at nine o'clock on the morning of the 17th of May.

The spacious and beautiful bay of Hakodadi, which for accessibility and safety is one of the finest in the world, lies on the north side of the Strait of Sangar, which separates the Japanese islands of Nippon and Yesso, and about midway between Sirija-saki,† the northeast point of the former and the city of Matsmai. The bay bears from the cape N.W. ½ W. distant about forty-five miles, and is four miles wide at its entrance and runs five miles into the land.

The navigation of the Strait of Sangar, as far as it was examined by the officers of the expedition, proved to be safe and convenient, and the entrance to the port of Hakodadi as accessible as that of Simoda, which is saying everything in its favor. Like Simoda, Hakodadi has an outer and inner harbor, the former being formed by the bay, which is somewhat of

---

* So called on the American charts.

† Saki, in the Japanese language, means "cape;" consequently it should more properly be called Cape Sirija.

horse-shoe shape. And here, too, as at Simoda, a dangerous obstruction was timely discovered and buoyed out, consisting of a long spit of shoal water, making out from the centre of the town to an extent of about twelve hundred yards. The inner harbor is the southeastern arm of the bay, and is completely sheltered, with regular soundings and excellent holding ground.

Hakodadi from the Bay.

For expansiveness and safety from all winds it has not its superior in the world, with anchorage of five to seven fathoms, and room to moor a hundred sail. The inner harbor is formed by a bold peaked promontory standing well out from the high land of the main, with which it is connected by a low sandy isthmus, giving it, consequently, in the distance, the appearance of an island. It may be readily recognized by the navigator from the outline of the land, and, on approaching from the eastward, after passing Cape Surro-kubo, or Cape Blunt, which forms a conspicuous headland, twelve miles east by south from the town, the junks at anchor in the harbor will be visible over the low isthmus.

To enter the harbor the navigator must, after rounding the promontory of Hakodadi, and giving it a berth of a mile to avoid the calms under the headland, steer for the sharp peak of Komaga-daki, bearing about north, until the east peak of the saddle, bearing about N.E. by N., opens to the westward of the round knob on the side of the mountain; then haul up to the northward and eastward, keeping them open until the centre of the sand hills on the isthmus, which may be recognized by the dark knolls upon them, bears S.E. by E. ¾ E. This will clear a spit which makes out from the western point of the town in a north-northwesterly direction, two-thirds of a mile. Though this spit would be a danger in entering the harbor, it, in fact, makes the anchorage more safe by its forming a natural breakwater, sheltering vessels at anchor inside of it from all inconvenient swell. Then bring the sand hills a point on the port bow, and stand in until the western extremity of the town bears S.W. ½ W., when the best berth will be secured, with five-and-a-half or six fathoms water. If it should be desirable to get a little nearer in, haul up a little to the eastward of south for the low rocky peak which will be just visible over the sloping ridge to the southward and eastward of the town. A vessel of moderate draught may approach within a quarter of a mile of Tsuki Point, where there is a building yard for junks. This portion of the harbor is generally crowded with native vessels, and unless the want of repairs, or some other cause, renders a close berth necessary, it is better to remain further out.

If the peak or saddle should be obscured by clouds or fog after doubling the promontory, it will be necessary to steer N. by E. ½ E., until the sand hills are brought upon the bearing previously given, when it will be proper to proceed as there directed. A short distance from the tail of the spit is a detached sand bank, with three-and-a-half fathoms of water upon it, the outer edge of which was marked by the officers of the expedition with a white spar buoy. Between this and the spit there is a narrow channel, with five or six fathoms depth of water. Vessels may pass on either side of the buoy, but it is more prudent to go to the northward of it. Should the wind fail before reaching the harbor, there will be found a good anchorage in the outer roads, with a depth of from ten to twenty-five fathoms.

Kamda Creek, Bay of Hakodadi.

CHAPTER XXIII.

VISIT FROM THE AUTHORITIES AT HAKODADI.—THEIR IGNORANCE THAT A TREATY HAD BEEN MADE.—VISIT TO AUTHORITIES AND EXPLANATION OF AFFAIRS TO THE JAPANESE.—ANSWER OF THE OFFICIALS AT HAKODADI.—THEIR FRIENDLINESS AND COURTESY.—VISITS AND RAMBLES OF THE AMERICANS ON SHORE.—HOUSES ALLOTTED FOR THEIR TEMPORARY ACCOMMODATION.—DESCRIPTION OF HAKODADI.—RESEMBLANCE TO GIBRALTAR.—CLEANLINESS OF STREETS.—PAVEMENTS AND SEWERS.—DIVISION INTO DISTRICTS UNDER OTTONAS.—PACK HORSES USED, NO WHEEL CARRIAGES.—TOWN VERY THRIVING.—BUILDINGS DESCRIBED.—PREPARATIONS AGAINST FIRES IN THE CITY.—SKILL OF CARPENTERS AND HOUSE-JOINERS.—SHOPS, THEIR CONSTRUCTION AND GOODS.—CARVINGS IN WOOD.—FURNITURE.—CHAIRS AND TABLES.—FASHION IN EATING.—TEA, HOW PREPARED, FIRE FOR BOILING THE KETTLE.—KITCHENS, STABLES, AND GARDENS.—FIRE-PROOF WAREHOUSES.—TRAFFIC AT THE SHOPS.—BUDDHIST TEMPLES.—GRAVE-YARDS.—PRAYING BY MACHINERY.—INSCRIPTIONS ON TOMBS.—SINTOO TEMPLES.—SHRINES BY THE WAY SIDE.—GATEWAYS ON THE ROADS.—PROSPECTS FOR CHRISTIANITY IN JAPAN.—WEAK MILITARY DEFENCES OF HAKODADI.—SURROUNDING COUNTRY.—LOOK-OUT FOR SHIPS APPROACHING.—JAPANESE TELESCOPE.—GEOLOGY OF THE COUNTRY.—MINERAL SPRING.—NATURAL CAVE.—CULINARY VEGETABLES.—COMMERCE AND FISHERIES.—JAPANESE JUNKS.—SHIP YARDS.—FEW BIRDS.—FISH ABUNDANT.—WILD QUADRUPEDS.—FOX CONSIDERED AS THE DEVIL.—HORSES MUCH USED.—KAGOS.—CLIMATE OF HAKODADI.—POPULATION AND PHYSICAL CHARACTERISTICS OF THE PEOPLE.—AINOS OR HAIRY KURILES.—MECHANICAL SKILL OF THE JAPANESE.—CARPENTRY AND MASONRY.—COOPERS.—IRON ORE WORKERS.—BLACKSMITHS, THEIR BELLOWS.—COPPER MUCH USED IN JUNK BUILDING.—SPINNING AND WEAVING.—DYED COTTONS.—SILK FABRICS.—LACQUERED WARE.—PRINTING, DRAWING, AND PAINTING.—SCULPTURE.—ARCHITECTURE.—GENERAL INTELLIGENCE.—INFORMATION, DERIVED THROUGH THE DUTCH AT NAGASAKI, FROM EUROPEAN PUBLICATIONS.—JAPANESE GAME OF CHESS.—CARDS.—LOTO.—BALL AND JACKSTRAWS AMONG THE CHILDREN.

HE steamers had been at anchor but a few hours when a boat, which, from the usual black striped flag and emblazoned standard at the stern, was known to be a government craft, was seen slowly to approach the flag-ship. Her build was very much like those boats elsewhere seen, but of a heavier make and clumsier model. Her eight boatmen were dressed in the livery—dark blue and white—and marked on the back with the arms of the dignitary in whose service they were. Their boat was rowed instead of being sculled, and made less speed than was usual with the Japanese government boats. As soon as it arrived alongside of the Powhatan several Japanese officials came on board. On their arrival they were presented with the letter the Commodore bore from the Japanese commissioners, and a copy of the treaty in the Chinese language. They stated that the officers from Yedo, who had been delegated to meet the Americans at Hakodadi, had not yet come; and that the people had been greatly alarmed at the arrival of the ships, as there had been no previous intimation of the intended visit of the squadron, and they had not even heard of the treaty, or of the opening of Simoda. The Japanese officials were then informed that on the next day a delegation of his officers would be sent by the Commodore on shore to confer with the authorities.

Preparations were immediately made, on the arrival of the steamers, for a complete survey of the harbor, and this having once been begun was carried on diligently during the stay of the ships, until a very effectual examination of the whole harbor was made, as had been the case at Simoda.

On the succeeding morning, (May 18,) as had been appointed, the flag-lieutenant, accompanied by the two American interpreters, Mr. Williams and Mr. Portman, and the Commodore's secretary, paid a visit to the governor. On their arrival at the government house, the governor Yendo Matzaimon presented himself, in company with Ishuka Konzo and Kudo Mogoro, two of the principal personages of his suite. The Americans were received with the usual ceremonious courtesies, and, being seated in a handsome hall with the ordinary appointments of a Japanese apartment, were ready to proceed at once to business. The governor was a middle-aged man, with a very benevolent expression of face, and of the characteristic mild and courteous manners; and his companions, though obsequious in the presence of their superiors, were also very creditable specimens of Japanese gentlemen. The conference hall was large, and opened by a wide open doorway from a narrow courtyard, in which could be seen various entrances with carved wood cornices, and staircases leading to other apartments of the building. Windows and doorlights, constructed in form like our own, but with paper panes, lighted the place, and handsome mats carpeted the floor, while there was but the ordinary meagre supply of furniture, consisting only of a half dozen camp stools. A shallow recess at one end of the room, with an elaborate carved moulding along the border, contained the usual arm-chair and idols, showing it to be dedicated to the rites both of hospitality and of family worship. Attendants frequently passed in and out with supplies of tea, cakes, confectionary, pipes, and tobacco, and the governor and his companions were never forgetful of their duties as hosts, but politely pressed their guests at every moment to refresh themselves.

The American officers now explained the object of their visit, and stated in effect that the Commodore had come to Hakodadi with his squadron to carry out the stipulations of the treaty between the United States and Japan, agreed upon on the 31st of March, and that any deviation from the spirit and letter of that treaty on the part of the authorities of Yesso would lead to serious consequences. It was then demanded that arrangements should be made at Hakodadi, as had been at Simoda, securing to the Americans the privilege of going where they chose, through the streets or out into the country, into the shops and public buildings. It was further required that the shopkeepers and market people should be allowed to sell their articles, and that a temporary currency be established for the mutual convenience of buyer and seller; that three different houses or temples be appropriated by the authorities as places of resort severally for the Commodore, the officers, and the artists of the expedition; that such supplies as the country afforded be furnished to the ships according to a fixed tariff of prices, and that not only articles of necessity, but those productions of Yesso and specimens of natural history which might be objects of curiosity and interest in America, be also provided, for which a just price would be paid.

The governor, on hearing these demands, asked for a delay until the officers appointed by the commissioners, whom the Commodore had stated he expected, should arrive with instructions from Yedo. The governor accounted for the delay in the arrival of the Japanese officials by the long distance of the capital from Hakodadi, saying that it was a journey of thirty-seven days length in winter and thirty in summer. He also declared that he had no special commands himself but what were contained in the letter presented by the Commodore, which merely commended the Americans to the ordinary welcome and good treatment, and enjoined upon the authorities to supply the ships with provisions and water. After some discussion, in the course of which the American officers reiterated their demands and the governor his objections, it was agreed that the views of the authorities of Hakodadi should be stated at length in writing, and submitted next day for the consideration of the Commodore.

Accordingly, on the succeeding morning, the following communication was received from the governor and his coadjutors: "Hakodadi is an outlying, remote region, and its population sparse and ignorant, so that when your honorable ships arrived recently in this place, all, both old and young, fled away into the interior, although the local officers ordered them not to scatter."

"You have come to this place under the impression doubtless that it was an extensive region and well settled, not with the least desire to rob or rudely force your way into it without permission. The common people here being ignorant and easily alarmed, we have been unable to get them to come before us, so that we could instruct them in this matter personally, for such is their waywardness; and it accounts for their timidity, as you saw yesterday when you and other officers went through the streets, and for there being no business doing. But after this you may go on shore, no obstructions will be put in the way of your walking, nor will the people be rude to you."

"This place is as it were no bigger than a pill or a speck, and the country in its vicinity is sterile, and produces almost nothing. The provisions and other necessaries are brought from other principalities, quite unlike the rich regions of Simoda and Uraga, and we fear the list now given, (deer skins, dried fish, fish oil, salt salmon, surume, a sort of fish, saccharine fucus laminaria, and roe of salmon,) meagre as it is, will by no means meet your desires after you have examined it, but rather dissatisfy you. As for what has been hitherto supplied no prices are asked."

"Yesterday you spoke of maintaining friendly relations with us, and this surely involves the duty on both sides of adhering to right, and nothing should be done to hinder amicable feelings. We are placed here in charge of the public halls, and to rule the people, as our chief duty, which cannot be evaded; and though to let you have the halls as you desire might be agreeable to you, yet the result would be very heavy and serious to us, and the people would hardly know to whom to look as their rulers. If you press the matter to this degree, and insist on three buildings, will it be consistent with your professions of friendship?"

"Yesterday, your gentlemen explained to us several particulars having reference to intercourse with us, to wit: that on the 31st of March a treaty was formed at Yoku-hama, between the high officers of our respective countries, and in compliance with that, you had come to Hakodadi to carry its provisions into effect, in the same manner as had been done at Simoda respecting trade and procuring three houses for resting at, and wherein to make drawings."

"It is a matter of great surprise to us that, since a treaty has been formed at Yoku-hama, no orders or letters have reached us from court on this matter, nor did the communication you brought us from Uraga contain any reference or explanation on these points, which we now learn from yourselves for the first time. Yet, to follow out a course of action ourselves, before receiving any directions from the throne, is a very serious matter, we can assure you: for the undeviating usage of all our principalities is first to attend to those commands, and can we here be expected to transgress it? Whether the matter be of great or small moment, if it appertain to the state, it must be referred to the prince, and he makes a clear statement to the Emperor, and acts after he obtains special commands. You yourselves, gentlemen, after all your experience at Yokuhama and Simoda, cannot but be aware that such is the usage and law in this country. Yet such articles of provisions as we have here, eggs, fowls, green fish, ducks and other commodities, as well as rambling about the country, going into villages, markets and shops, albeit they are contemptible and dilapidated, mean and rude, quite beneath the slightest regard or care, are temporarily allowed, and that which you require will be furnished."

After the flag-lieutenant, who had been delegated to receive the above communication, had explained in regard to the "hall" alluded to, that it was only desired by the Commodore to use those parts of the temples usually appropriated to lodgers, as temporary places of resort, and not to take possession of their ecclesiastical establishments, the governor seemed greatly relieved, as he evidently supposed that it was the intention in some way to interfere with their national worship. The governor then having announced that it was the intention of "Matsmai Kangeayou, great officer of the family of the Prince of Matsmai," to call upon the Commodore next day, the American officers took their leave.

After this preliminary negotiation, the officers of the ships began daily to visit the land, and they walked freely through the streets, frequented the shops and temples, and strolled without interference into the neighboring country. Three houses were finally, after several conferences, assigned, one for the accommodation of the Commodore, another for his officers, and a third for the artists, and a bazaar opened daily, where the various articles of Japanese art and manufacture could be obtained at fair prices, a dollar, which is equal to about three of their silver coins, called *itchaboo*, passing current for 4,800 copper cash. With this greater freedom of intercourse on shore, the Americans soon became tolerably acquainted with Hakodadi and its people, and we may here appropriately introduce some description of them, while we intermit for the present the relation of the further progress of the tedious negotiations with the authorities.

The town of Hakodadi, or Hakodate,* lies on the southern coast of the island of Yesso, in latitude 41° 49′ 22″ north, and longitude 140° 47′ 45″ east, being situated on the western bank of a small peninsula, which forms one side of the harbor. The meaning of the Japanese word Hakodadi is "box shop," but what gave rise to the name it is not easy to understand, as some of the best informed inhabitants themselves seem unacquainted with the origin of the term. The appearance of the place on entering the harbor is striking and picturesque. The town stretches for the space of three miles along the base of a lofty promontory, divided into three principal peaks, which reach a height of from six hundred to a thousand feet. Their lofty summits are bare, and often covered with snow; their upper slopes are but scantily clothed with underwood and some scattered pines, while below, where the mountains begin to rise from the level land, there is a rich profusion of verdant growth, with groves of wide-spreading cypresses, tall forest maples, and fruit-bearing trees, the plum and the peach. This abundant vegetation

---

* Golownin, in his "Recollections," calls the town Chakodade, but erroneously.

presents a pleasing contrast to the bolder and more barren aspect of the higher acclivities and summits of the surrounding hills. The town thus appears to be nestling in repose under the cover of the shade of the trees in the midst of a scene of rural beauty, while all around in the distance is the wild, bleak massiveness of nature. A low, sandy isthmus, scantily verdant here and there with a few patches of kitchen gardens, connects the peninsula upon which the houses are built to the main land. Coarse, hard rocks of trachyte, thrown up by volcanic agency, separate the alluvial sand from the mountainous region in the interior, and add to the wildness of the scene. The Japanese have quarried the rocks here and there, and various hewn surfaces, with cut blocks lying about, prove the art and busy industry of the people. These quarries supply them with stone for constructing their sea walls, jetties, dykes, foundations for their houses, and other building purposes.

The town contains over a thousand houses, which mostly stretch along in one main thoroughfare near the seaside, while the remainder, forming two or three parallel streets, hang upon the ascent of the hill in the rear. Every one on board the ships who had visited Gibraltar was struck with the resemblance of Hakodadi, from its position and general aspect, to that famous fortified town. There was the isolated hill, on the base and acclivity of which the houses were built corresponding to the rock of Gibraltar; there was the low neck of land reaching to the elevated region beyond, like the neutral ground which separates the English fortress from the Spanish territory, and a receding country and capacious bay surrounding Hakodadi, as well as Gibraltar, to strengthen the resemblance between the two. Moreover, the position of the Japanese town on the Strait of Sangar, with the high land of Nippon and its towns of Say and Mimaga at the south, like that of Gibraltar, overlooking the narrow channel which connects the Atlantic and Mediterranean and commands the opposite and elevated coast of Africa, with the towns of Tangier and Ceuta clothing its heights, served to confirm the similarity of features with which every one whose travelled experience allowed of comparison was greatly impressed.

Hakodadi belongs to the imperial fief of Matsmai, and is the largest town on the island of Yesso, with the exception of Matsmai, from which it is distant about thirty miles in an easterly direction. An excellent road not far from the seacoast connects the two places, and a large trade is carried on between them and by both with several small towns on the island of Nippon, on the southern side of the Strait of Sangar, or, as it should be properly called, Tsugara.

The town of Hakodadi is regularly built, with streets running at right angles with each other. They are between thirty and forty feet in width, and are carefully macadamized to allow of the proper draining of water. There are open gutters on each side, which receive the drippings of the houses and the washings of the street, and also well constructed sewers through which the surplus water and the refuse are poured into the bay. The side walks, which are frequently paved, are curbed with stone planted on edge as with us, but as no wheeled carriages are found in the town, the middle of the street is used indiscriminately in dry weather by the pedestrian. Hakodadi, like all the Japanese towns, is remarkably clean, the streets being suitably constructed for draining, and kept, by constant sprinkling and sweeping, in a neat and healthful condition. Wooden picket fences with gates cross the streets at short intervals; these are opened for the passage of the people during the day, but closed at night. The same municipal regulations obtain in Hakodadi as in all the other towns of Japan; the inhabitants of the several streets form so many separate communities, as it were, responsible for the conduct of each other, each governed by an official called "ottona," who is also held responsible for the good order of the people under his especial charge, and these *ottonas* are also made responsible for the conduct of each other. The gates and picket fences would seem to mark out the separate fields of duty of these officials. At one side of the street, among the houses, there is ordinarily a sentry-box for a watchman, whose duty it is to guard the town against disturbance, and give early notice of the occurrence of fire. A general quiet pervades the streets, without those ordinary signs of busy activity which belong to a trading city. No carriages or laden wagons rumble along the road, no clamorous dealers claim the preference of the purchase of their wares, no busy pedlars or itinerant hucksters cry their articles for sale, and no turbulent mob disturbs the general peace and tranquillity. An almost universal quiet prevails in the streets, broken only at times by a stout horse-boy yelling to his obstinate beast of burden, either an unruly nag or lumbering ox, and an officious attendant of some great man shouting out to the people to prostrate themselves before his coming master, or perhaps the clanging of the hammer of a workman busy in some neighboring forge. Still the stranger is impressed with the idea that Hakodadi is a thriving town when he beholds the occasional droves of laden pack-horses slowly pacing through the streets, the hundreds of junks at anchor in the harbor, the numerous boats rapidly gliding across the bay, and the many richly dressed two-sworded Japanese gentlemen and officials pompously stalking about or riding richly caparisoned horses.

The buildings in Hakodadi are mostly of one story, with attics of varying heights. The upper part occasionally forms a commodious apartment, but is ordinarily merely a dark cockloft for the storage of goods and lumber, or the lodging of servants. The height of the roofs is seldom more than twenty-five feet from the ground. They slope down from the top, projecting with their eaves beyond the wall, are supported by joints and tie-beams, and are mostly covered with small wooden shingles of about the size of the hand. These shingles are fastened by means of pegs made of bamboo, or kept in their places by long slips of board, which have large rows of cobble stones put upon them to prevent their removal. The stones are, however, said to have the additional advantage of hastening the melting of the snow, which during the winter season is quite abundant at Hakodadi. The gable ends, as in Dutch houses, face towards the street, and the roofs projecting to some distance, serve as a cover and a shade to the doors. All the roofs of the houses in front are topped with what at first was supposed to be a curious chimney wrapped in straw, but which upon examination turned out to be a tub, protected by its straw envelope from the effects of the weather, and kept constantly filled with water, to be sprinkled upon the shingled roofs, in case of fire, by means of a broom which is always deposited at hand, to be ready in an emergency. The people would seem to be very anxious on the score of fires, from the precautions taken against them. In addition to the tubs on the tops of the houses, there are wooden cisterns arranged along the streets, and engines kept in constant readiness.

These latter have very much the general construction of our own, but are deficient in that important part of the apparatus, an air chamber, and consequently they throw the water, not with a continuous stream, but in short, quick jets. Fire alarms, made of a thick piece of plank, hung on posts at the corners of the streets, and protected by a small roofing, which are struck by the watchman, in case of a fire breaking out, showed the anxious fears of the inhabitants, and the charred timbers and ruins still remaining where a hundred houses had stood but a few months before, proved the necessity of the most careful precautions.

A few of the better houses and the temples are neatly roofed with brown earthen tiles, laid in gutter form. The poorer people are forced to content themselves with mere thatched hovels, the thatch of which is often overgrown with a fertile crop of vegetables and grass, the seeds of which have been deposited by vagrant crows. The walls of the buildings are generally constructed of pine boards, fastened lengthwise, with a layer inside and out, to the framework, which is jointed with admirable skill. The boards in front and rear are made to slide horizontally in grooves like shutters. At night they are barred fast, and in the day-time entirely removed, to allow of the light to pass freely through the paper screens behind them. As in Simoda, the roofs project beyond the walls of the houses, and serve as a shelter, in front for the display of goods, and in the rear for the carrying on of various domestic operations. The Japanese wood-work is never painted, although in the interior of the houses it is occasionally varnished or oiled; the buildings consequently have a mean and thriftless look. In the wintry, moist climate of Hakodadi, the effect of weather upon the unpainted pine boards was strikingly apparent, causing them to contract mould and rot, so that the whole town had a more rusty, ruined appearance than its age should indicate.

Previous to building a house the ground is beaten smooth, and the floor is raised about two feet above it, leaving a space in front and by one of the sides, which serves for a path to the rear, and a place to store heavy goods, as the roof projects over and protects it from the weather.

In the shops the whole front is often taken out to display their contents, but in the dwellings and the mechanics' establishments, there is usually a barred lattice of bamboo to hide the inmates from passing observation. Each house has a charm placed over the lintel or doorpost, consisting of the picture of a god, a printed prayer or a paper inscribed with some complicated characters, designed to protect the dwelling from fire or any other calamity.

Japanese Pillow and Cushion.—Drawer open.

The raised floor which covers nearly the whole area of the house is covered with white mats made soft and thick by being lined at the bottom with straw. These are very neatly woven and bound with cloth, and are all of the uniform size prescribed by law, being three feet by six, and placed in rows upon the floor so neatly as to have the appearance of one piece. Upon these mats the people sit to take their meals, to sell their wares, to smoke their pipes, to converse with their friends, and lie down at night without undressing themselves to go to sleep, adding, however, a quilted mat for a cover, and the equivocal comfort of a hard box for a pillow. The houses are generally lighted, as has been frequently observed, with windows of oiled paper, though mica and shells are occasionally used instead.

The interior of the houses is plain and simple in arrangement, but always scrupulously neat and clean. There are in some of the better mansions occasional wood carvings of exquisite workmanship, though not very elaborate in design. The paper windows and sliding screens which divide the apartments are often adorned with paintings of landscape and birds. In addition to the panels the walls of the room are frequently hung with gaily painted paper, which being arranged as rolling maps are with us, is moveable at pleasure. The stork or crane, a bird held sacred by the Japanese, and the winged tortoise, and the porpoise, or dolphin of the ancients, are favorite designs in all these decorations, whether of wood, carving, or painting, in the various buildings.

The furniture of a Japanese house is particularly meagre, consisting invariably of nothing but the floor mats and the household utensils, which are few and simple. As squatting, not sitting, is almost the invariable practice, there seems no occasion for chairs, although they were sometimes found, and invariably supplied on state occasions. These are clumsy contrivances with coarse leathern seats, and a framework like that of the common camp stool, which is readily folded up when not used. At the conferences with the authorities, the subordinate officers, both American and Japanese, were seated on sedans or benches covered with a red crape, while the Commodore and the highest native dignitaries were honored with stools, which occasionally had the comfortable addition of arms and backs to them. The national posture of all classes, however, in Japan, when at rest, is crouching either upon the knees, or on the haunches with their legs crossed. The latter is common among the lower classes, and is pronounced by the fashionables as decidedly vulgar, who invariably assume the former.

Tables are not generally used, but on the occasion of the public entertainments given to the American officers, the narrow red crape covered benches were appropriated for the spread of the feast, the dishes being raised to the proper height for the guest by means of the ordinary lacquered stands of a foot in height and fourteen inches square. The Japanese eat from these raised trays while squatting upon their mats, and the unsocial practice thus obtains of each person taking his food by himself. Some lacquered cups, bowls, and porcelain vessels, the invariable chopsticks, and an occasional earthenware spoon, comprise the ordinary utensils used in eating. They drink their soups directly out of the bowl, as a hungry child might, after seizing with their chopsticks the pieces of fish which are generally floating in the liquid. Their tea-kettles, which are always at hand simmering over the fire in the kitchen, are made of bronze, silver, or of fire-proof earthenware. In the centre of the common sitting room there is a square hole built in with tiles and filled with sand, in which a charcoal fire is always kept burning, and suspended above is the tea-kettle supported by a tripod. There is thus constantly a supply of hot water for making tea, which is invariably handed to the visitor on his arrival. The beverage is prepared as with us, but very weak. The cup is generally of porcelain, with a wooden lacquered cover. The tea is not ordinarily sweetened, though at Hakodadi sugar was often used. The better houses are warmed, but very imperfectly, by metal braziers placed on lacquered stands containing burning charcoal, which are moved readily from room to room as they may be required. In the cottages of the poor, there being but little ventilation from their contracted size, and no places of issue for the smoke, the burning charcoal in the fixed central fire places becomes a great nuisance. In the more pretentious establishments, where there is plenty of space and holes in the roof or in the walls for the escape of smoke, while the charcoal is not brought in until perfectly ignited, this mode of heating the apartments is more endurable. At Hakodadi the people seemed to suffer a great deal from the wintry weather, the poorer classes kept much within doors huddled about their meagre fires in their hovels, which, without chimneys, and with but a scant light from the paper windows, were exceedingly cold, gloomy, and comfortless. The richer people strove to make themselves more comfortable by enveloping their bodies in a succession of warm robes, but succeeded indifferently, as they were constantly complaining of the severity of the weather.

It is by the charcoal fires in the centre of the sitting apartment where the water for tea is boiled, the saki heated, and sundry small dishes cooked; but in the larger establishments there is a kitchen besides, where the family cooking is got up. These are generally provided with a stove, like an ordinary French cooking apparatus, in which wood is often burned, but this is an article they are very economical in using.

Japanese Kitchen, Hakodadi.

Connected with most of the dwellings in Hakodadi there is a yard in which there are out-houses used for kitchens or stables. There is also frequently a garden where vegetables in small quantities are raised, flowers cultivated, and shade-trees and ornamental shrubs planted. Some of the leading men of the place have handsome residences upon elevated situations, a little back of the town. Their houses are of the ordinary construction, but much larger in dimensions. The superior wealth and luxurious tastes of their proprietors are shown chiefly in the handsome gardens and pleasure grounds. These are tastefully planted with fruit and shade trees, and bounded with green hedges, while beds of variegated flowers contrast their bright hues with the green verdure of the foliage and the lawns of grass. There seems, in the high fences which guard from the eyes of the passer by the sight of these luxurious delights, a desire for that privacy which betokens a love of retirement and a fastidious appreciation of the reserved comforts of home.

As in Simoda, there are large fire-proof warehouses, used for the storage of valuable goods. They are built with a great deal more care than the ordinary shops and other buildings, and have walls two feet thick, made of dried mud and cobbles, and faced with stone, while their roofs are securely constructed of earthen tiles. These warehouses are generally two stories in height, the upper one having window shutters of wood sheathed with iron. Their exterior is sometimes covered with a coat of fine plaster, which, with their substantial structure, gives them a neatness and solidity of aspect which contrast greatly with the flimsy stained look of the ordinary houses. They are probably depots for the storage of goods which belong to the government, and are kept with great care and guarded watchfully.

The shops in Hakodadi generally contain such goods as are of a cheap sort, and adapted to the restricted wants of a poor population. The stock is made up of a miscellaneous assortment of coarse, thick cottons, inferior silks, common earthen and China ware, lacquered bowls, cups, stands and chop sticks, cheap cutlery, and ready made clothing. Furs, leather, felted cloths, glass-ware, or copper articles are rarely seen, nor are books and stationery very common. The provision shops contain rice, wheat, barley, pulse, dried fish, seaweed, salt, sugar, sackee, soy, charcoal, sweet potatoes, flour, and other less necessary articles, and all apparently in abundant quantities. There is no public market in the town, as neither beef, pork, nor mutton are eaten, and very little poultry. Vegetables, and a preparation made of beans and rice flour, which has the consistency and appearance of cheese, are hawked about the streets, and form a considerable portion of the diet of the people. The signs of the shops, in accordance with the general practice in Japan, are inscribed on the paper windows and doors, in various well known devices and cyphers, either in Chinese or Japanese characters. The shopmen were at first very shy, and showed but little disposition to sell their goods to the Americans; but when they became somewhat more familiar with the strangers, the characteristic eagerness of tradesmen developed itself to the full, and the Hakodadi merchants showed themselves as clever at their business as any Chatham street or Bowery salesman with us. They bustled about the raised platform upon which they were perched, pulled out the drawers arranged on the walls, and displayed their goods to the greatest advantage when they thought there was a chance of catching the eye and pleasing the taste of a passing American. They were always very jealous, however, of their prerogatives, and were exceedingly annoyed if any of their purchasers stepped upon the platform, which was their trading sanctum, and as carefully guarded against intrusion as the "behind the counter" of a New York shopman. The purchaser ordinarily stood under the roof, on the ground, in the space which intervened between the sidewalk and the elevated shop floor. Some of the more impatient and intrusive Yankees, however, would occasionally spring up, and pulling out the goods, handle them very unceremoniously, not, however, without a serious protest on the part of the sellers, who sometimes were so annoyed that official complaints were made by them to the authorities. The shopkeepers had always a fixed price for their goods, and all attempts to beat them down were useless, and generally rebuked by an expression of displeasure.

There are four large Buddhist temples in Hakodadi, one of which, called the Zhiogen-zhi, or the country's protector, is a good specimen of Japanese architecture. It was built by the townspeople about twenty years since, and is kept in excellent repair. The tiled roof rises fully sixty feet from the ground, and is supported by an intricate arrangement of girders, posts, and tie-beams, resting upon large lacquered pillars. This temple is one of the most conspicuous objects seen when entering the harbor. The principal apartment in the interior is elaborately carved and richly gilded. The carving and sculpture about the altar, the niches, and cornices, are of wood and brass, and show very skilful workmanship. The designs are dragons,

phœnixes, cranes, tortoises, and other subjects associated with the religious worship of Buddha. The main floor is elevated six feet above the ground, and covered, as usual, with thick mats. There are three separate shrines, each containing an image, the one in the nave being the largest and most highly adorned. A sort of architrave descends between the pillars, so contrived that, with the aid of folding screens, the shrines may be readily partitioned off. There are six priests attached to the establishment, and their quarters and those which are provided for visitors were models of neatness and cleanliness. The temples in Japan, as in China, are often used for places of concourse or entertainment, and on such occasions the altars and shrines are covered or removed, which so changes the aspect of the interior that no one would suspect that he was in a house of worship. On the visit of the American squadron one of the temples was appropriated for a bazaar—a worldly use that the ecclesiastics, so far from objecting to, highly approved of, as it added considerably to their revenue, the rent of the apartments being the perquisite on the occasion.

In the enclosure before the Zhiogen-zhi there is a grove of large spreading cypresses, in the shade of which there are several outer buildings, and a shed which covers six small stone images of deities. On either side of the avenue which leads to the temple there are pairs of stone candelabras, and near by the statue of a goddess with a child in her arms. A copper nimbus or glory surrounds the heads of all these idols, and reminds the Christian visitor of what he may have seen in some churches of his own country.

Next to the Zhiogen-zhi, in a southerly direction, is the Zhetsa-zhi or True-acting monestary, an older and somewhat dilapidated building. There are several small sheds in the yard in front of this temple, one of which protects from the weather a subscription-box and a handsomely sculptured stone candelabra. The priests have shown considerable taste in the cultivation and arrangement of the garden and pleasure grounds in the rear of the building.

Idols near a Buddhist Temple, Hakodadi.

Near the main street, which extends along the bay, in an enclosure beautifully shaded with willows and firs of remarkable growth, is the Kono-zhi, or High Dragon temple, so called from a large dragon carved along the entablature in front; there is also a carp fish, some six feet long, skilfully cut out of wood, extending in an upright direction on the right side of the porch. This temple is a large edifice, and, although now falling to decay, bears in its elaborate ornaments and its expensive appointments signs of having been once in great esteem. Within the grounds which enclose it are various richly adorned gateways, stone statues, candelabras, and shrines, all showing more or less skilful design and workmanship. The fourth and last of the Buddhist temples is called the Shiomio-zhi, or the monastery of Buddha's name, but presents nothing of especial interest to distinguish it from the others.

Each of these temples has its adjoining grave-yard, filled with tombs and monuments characteristic of the Japanese people and their religious belief. Near each grave, as at Simoda, there are square posts and boards, with the names of the dead, quotations from the canonical Buddhist books, lines of poetry, and moral and religious apothegms, generally referring to the vanity of this world and the felicity of Buddha's heaven in the next. There was a curious contrivance found in one of the burial places, consisting of a tall post, in which an iron wheel was attached. The post was placed upright, and being square presented four surfaces, on each of which was one or two of the following inscriptions or prayers:

"The great round mirror of knowledge says, 'wise men and fools are embarked in the same boat;' whether prospered or afflicted, both are rowing over the deep lake; the gay sails lightly hang to catch the autumnal breeze; then away they straight enter the lustrous clouds, and become partakers of heaven's knowledge."

"The believing man Hanyo Shenkaman, who no longer grows old."

"The believing woman, once called Yuenning: Happy was the day she left."

"Multitudes fill the graves."

"To enable to enter the abodes of the perfect, and to sympathize fully with the men of the world, belongs to Buddha. It is only by this one vehicle, the coffin, we can enter Hades. There is nought like Buddha; nothing at all."

"We of the human race with hearts, minds, and understandings, when we read the volumes of Buddha, enjoy great advantages."

"He whose prescience detects knowledge, says: as the floating grass is blown by the gentle breeze, or the glancing ripples of autumn disappear, when the sun goes down, or as the ship returns home to her old shore, so is life: it is a smoke, a morning tide."

"Buddha himself earnestly desires to hear the name of this person, (who is buried,) and wishes he may go to life."

"He who has left humanity is now perfected by Buddha's name, as the withered moss is by the dew."

"The canon of Buddha says, all who reach the blissful land will become so that they cannot be made to transmigrate, (or change for the worse.)"

The square post upon which these inscriptions were cut was nearly eight feet in length, and near the centre, at a convenient height to be reached by the hand, was affixed, vertically, a wheel, which moved readily on an axle that passed through the post. Two small iron rings were strung upon each of the three spokes of the large wheel. Every person who twisted this instrument in passing was supposed to obtain credit in heaven for one or more prayers on the post, the number being graduated according to the rigor of the performer's devotion, and the number of revolutions effected. The jingle of the small iron rings was believed to secure the attention of the deity to the invocation of the devotional, and the greater the noise, the more certain of its being listened to. This praying by wheel and axle would seem to be the very perfection of a ceremonious religion, as it reduces it to a system of mechanical laws, which, provided the apparatus is kept in order, a result easily obtained by a little oil, moderate use, and occasional repairs, can be readily executed with the least possible expenditure of human labor, and with all that economy of time and thought which seems the great purpose of our material and mechanical age. Huc, in his interesting account of his travels in Thibet, speaks of an improvement on the machine we have described, where the apparatus was turned by

water-power, and very appropriately styles it a prayer mill. In the course of the progress of the Japanese in the mechanical arts, this, with their usual readiness in adopting new improvements, will no doubt be introduced, or perhaps the more effective power of steam will be applied to their praying machines, and with the introduction of steamboats and railroads may commence an era of locomotive devotion.

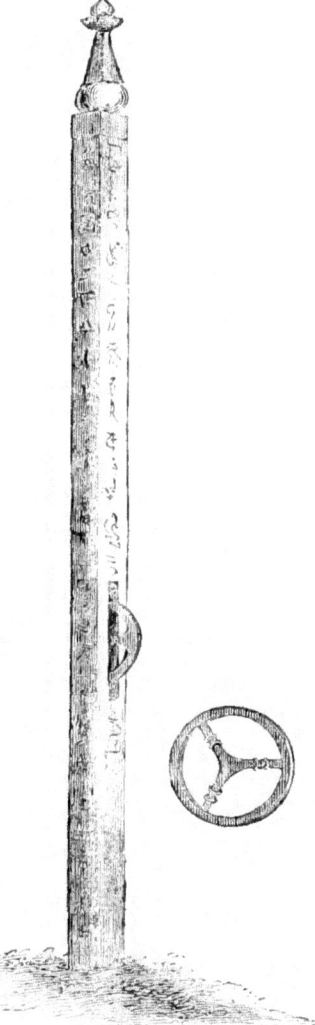

Prayer Wheel.

There are three large *Mia*, or Sintoo temples, in Hakodadi, called respectively the Sheumei, the Hachiman, and the Penten, dedicated to national deified heroes and gods. They are not in so flourishing condition as their competitors, the Buddhist temples, which have gained the ascendancy, and are fast absorbing the whole devotional interests of the Japanese people. The Sintoo places of worship are generally got up on a cheaper scale, and are much less resorted to. They have no burying grounds attached, and are not surrounded by any defined enclosure. There are, however, several gateways, with ornaments sculptured on stone spanning the approach, but the area which surrounds the temples is open and the public road passes through it. A curator with his family, whose duty it is to keep the idols polished up and the sacred grounds in a tidy condition, generally resides on or near the premises. The Hachiman house of worship presents a peculiarity in its architecture not elsewhere observed, which consists of a projection from the roof like a dormer window, underneath which there is an entablature adorned with a few carvings in wood. The effect, in an architectural point of view, is good, as it relieves the blankness of a great expanse of roof, and is in harmony with the ornaments of the eaves below.

Upon the summits and acclivities of the hills in the neighborhood of Hakodadi, and in niches and small shrines under shadow of groves of cypress and other trees by the wayside, are frequent stone statues of Buddha, venerable with age and moss-grown, about four feet high, elevated upon small pedestals, and the innumerable offerings of copper cash, rags, flowers, and written papers, strewed before them, prove the large number of devotees and the attention of the people to their devotional duties. The Japanese resort frequently to these roadside deities, and the higher they are perched, and the more inaccessible their approach, the greater is esteemed the merit in invoking them. These idols are supposed to have great power in warding off the storms or disasters to which mariners on that inhospitable coast are exposed, and most of the offerings are made with a view to propitiate Buddha and his associate deities in the event of an approaching danger. In addition to the statues there are distributed along the roads and pathways frequent stone slabs with inscriptions and a gallows-shaped gateway, fancifully carved and ornamented beams, with two vertical and a single horizontal one crossing them at the top. These are never passed by the pious Japanese without a genuflexion and the utterance of a passing prayer; and so frequent are the stoppages in consequence, that the American officers, when strolling into the country under the guidance of a native, found their journey indefinitely prolonged, and their patience sorely taxed.

The question naturally arises, what, upon a survey of the whole ground, are the prospects of now presenting Christianity to the Japanese mind with any hope of a favorable reception? To this subject Mr. Jones, the chaplain, naturally directed his thoughts, and his sound judgment, added to his known pious zeal, entitles his opinions to the respect of Christians of all denominations. He thus writes:

"Apart from governmental influence, I think there would be no great difficulty in introducing Christianity; *but the government would interfere most decidedly.* I performed funeral services on shore four times: once at Yoku-hama, twice at Hakodadi, and once at Simoda; in every instance in the presence of the Japanese, and, in most, when large numbers were collected. They always behaved well. Japanese officers were present, with their insignia, on all occasions. I thus became known among the people everywhere as a *Christian clergyman*, or, to follow their signs for designating me, as 'a praying man.' Instead of this producing a shrinking from me, as I had supposed it would, I found that I had decidedly gained by it in their respect, and this among officials as well as commoners. At our last visit to Simoda we found a new governor, it having now become a royal instead of a provincial town. This governor was an affable, yet dignified, man, of very polished manners, and would compare favorably with the best gentlemen in any country. At the bazaar, amid the buying, &c., I was led up to him by one of the officials and introduced *as a clergyman*. The governor's countenance brightened up as my office was announced, and his salutation and treatment of me became additionally courteous. I mention this, however, for what it may be worth. There was no seeming aversion to me because I was a minister of Christianity. The government, however, beyond all doubt, is exceedingly jealous about our religion; but the Japanese officials, as well as the people, are so inquisitive, and so observant of all that comes within their reach, that, doubtless, after a time, they might be brought to see the difference between ourselves and the Romanists. Against the latter they have a deep-seated dislike. Until they do understand that difference, no form of Christianity can probably get foothold in Japan."

There is little appearance of military defence about Hakodadi, though its position would seem to offer advantages for rendering it almost impregnable. Beyond the town, however, in an easterly direction, there are two earthen forts dug out of the ground, and intended, apparently, to guard the entrance to the harbor. Stakes or palisades are driven in along the cuttings to prevent the earth from caving in, and to aid in the defence. Two wooden buildings stand near by, which are connected with magazines underneath the excavated area of the forts. Within these latter is a pavement of stone, and embrasures of four feet in width, opening in the eastern embankment looking seaward, and made apparently for only two guns. On the beach, at the eastern end of the main street, there is a building, with a broad enclosure, which seems to be intended for purposes of fortification, although, from the absence of cannon and other warlike appointments, it may be only used for a parade ground. There are better specimens of military defence in Japan than those rude constructions, as, for example, at Uraga, where several stone forts exist, built according to better principles of art, although there are probably none in the whole country which could withstand a slight cannonading from European or American ships of war, or even an attack from a few well armed boats.

The country about Hakodadi, though picturesque to the view, did not present such attractions

for the pedestrian as that in the neighborhood of Simoda. The environs are comparatively rude and uncultivated, and the land is so broken by the hills and mountainous elevations, that the roads are necessarily steep, irregular, and toilsome to the traveller. The isolated rock at the base, and on the side of which the town is built, is steep and rough, but is ascended by a winding path to the top. The summit commands a fine view of the harbor, and was often scaled by the officers of the expedition, where they were reminded of the high advance in art of the country by finding an observatory, or look-out for vessels, supplied with a telescope of Japanese manufacture, being arranged with glasses like our own inserted in a tube of bamboo.

The geological features of the hill itself are of considerable interest. It is composed of a variety of granite, the syenite, generally gray, though occasionally of a reddish tint, in which crystals of tourmaline are more or less abundantly diffused. On the southwestern side of the promontory the rock has been first torn apart by some subterranean force, leaving a crevice about twenty feet in width, and subsequently another upheaving movement has forced up, so as to fill the space partially, a rocky substance, similar to the mountain in kind, but with no tourmaline, and a softer feldspar, having the character of the porphyritic formation. At this point a mineral spring issues from the crevices of the rock. It is considerably impregnated with sulphuretted hydrogen gas, as was very evident from its taste and odor, is warm to the touch, and one of the surgeons reports it as "sitting lightly on the stomach." Its gases and odor are lost, however, by being kept even for a short time. The water contains chloride of sodium, and probably some mineral sulphate or sulphuret. The intelligent medical officer Dr. Green, to whose account we are indebted for our information, further reports it to be medicinally somewhat diuretic and slightly aperient, and infers that it would be probably beneficial in some cutaneous diseases and chronic complaints, where the secretions are disordered or suppressed. The natives, who accompanied the Americans to the spring, made signs that the water was not good to drink, but excellent to bathe in; and the erection of a presiding deity in its neighborhood, and the frequent use of it by the inhabitants for washing themselves, proved a high appreciation of its qualities.

A few hundred yards west of the sulphur spring, at the back of the town, is a natural cave in the mountain. It opens from the sea into a steep, perpendicular cliff, and can be entered only by means of a boat. It is about thirty feet high, a dozen or so in width, and the water at the entrance has a depth of nearly twenty feet. A party from the ships penetrated it until the darkness of the interior became so great that objects could no longer be distinguished; it was found, however, by groping along, that the cave branched off to the right and left, with apparently the same depth of water and the same height of roof as at the entrance. Within, a perfect calmness reigned, the water being almost motionless, and the atmosphere close and undisturbed by a breath of wind. When the light was sufficient, the bottom could be seen glistening brightly with a deposit of white sand. When storms prevail, there must be a great rushing of waters, and war of the winds, through this cavernous channel. The entrance to the cave is arched, and the rocky cliff in which it opens has a columnar formation, extending from the curve of the arch, high up the rock. At first sight it was supposed to be basalt, as it had a similar appearance to the columns of the Giant's causeway in Ireland; but on further investigation, the geological formation proved to be the syenitic form of granite, like the main body of the mountain.

The peninsula on which the town stands affords but a few score of acres of arable land lying on the eastern slope of the highest hill, near the fishing village of Shirasawaki on the seashore. It is cultivated in vegetables, principally for the consumption of the people of Hakodadi. Onions, a few sweet potatoes and radishes, are the chief products, the last of which are a very favorite article of food, and are served up raw, being grated and used as a condiment with fish, and cooked by stewing and boiling. The low isthmus which connects the site of the town with the main land is mostly left uncultivated, although it might be by proper tillage rendered tolerably productive. Further in the interior, the soil is more worked, and large crops are obtained, but with very little profit to the farmer, as the country in that direction is composed of a flat, sandy plain, which can only be made productive by immense labor, and a great expenditure of manure, which is extensively used.

There are several beautiful copses of pines and maples near the town, some fruit trees and flowering shrubs, and the vegetation upon the lower acclivities of the surrounding hills is vigorous. A large variety of northern plants, birches, spiræas, laburnums, wake-robins, and others clothe the sides, and afford a scant fuel to the poor.

The inhabitants of Hakodadi and its neighborhood, gaining their livelihood chiefly from commerce and the fisheries, necessarily pay but little attention to agricultural pursuits. They carry on a large trade with the interior of the island of Yesso, with Matsmai, and other of the numerous towns and villages, which are supplied with the various products of Japan by means of the brisk commerce which exists between Hakodadi and the shipping ports on the coasts of Nippon, Sikok, and Kiu-siu. The junks engaged in this shipping trade take from Hakodadi cargoes of dried and salted fish, prepared seaweed, charcoal, deers' horns, timber, and other produce of Yesso, and bring back rice, sugar, tea, various grains, sweet potatoes, tobacco, cloths, silks, porcelain, lacquered ware, cutlery, and whatever else they may need. More than a hundred of the native vessels sailed for different southern ports of the Empire during the short stay of the Commodore, and all had cargoes almost exclusively made up of productions of the sea. They generally travel along the western coast, as being less boisterous, and affording a greater number of safe anchoring places. These junks are all nearly of the same dimensions in burden, corresponding to about a hundred tons of our measurement, and in construction, rig, and equipment, precisely alike. More than a thousand of these vessels are occasionally seen at one time at anchor in the port of Hakodadi. The principal places with which this commerce is carried on are Sado, lying south of Matsmai, Yedo, Yetchigo, Nagasaki or Simonosaki, and with Osaka and Owari. Of the craft in which this commerce is carried on the Commodore has furnished the following account:

"The ramifications of the laws of Japan leave nothing unnoticed, and it has been more than once remarked, that in no part of the world are the established laws and municipal regulations more thoroughly enforced, and so in respect to the construction of vessels or junks as they are called. The builder is not permitted to deviate from a uniform rule, as well in model, size, rig, as in the interior arrangement.

"In the time of Kempfer, the authorized dimensions of Japanese merchant vessels were, as he tells us, 'fourteen fathoms long and four fathoms broad,' (length 84 and breadth 24 feet;) he says nothing of the depth, but from their flatness I should judge that the hold could not exceed six or eight feet under deck. These proportions have not, in all probability, changed for a long period before Kempfer's book appeared, (which was published in the early part of the last century,) down to the present time.

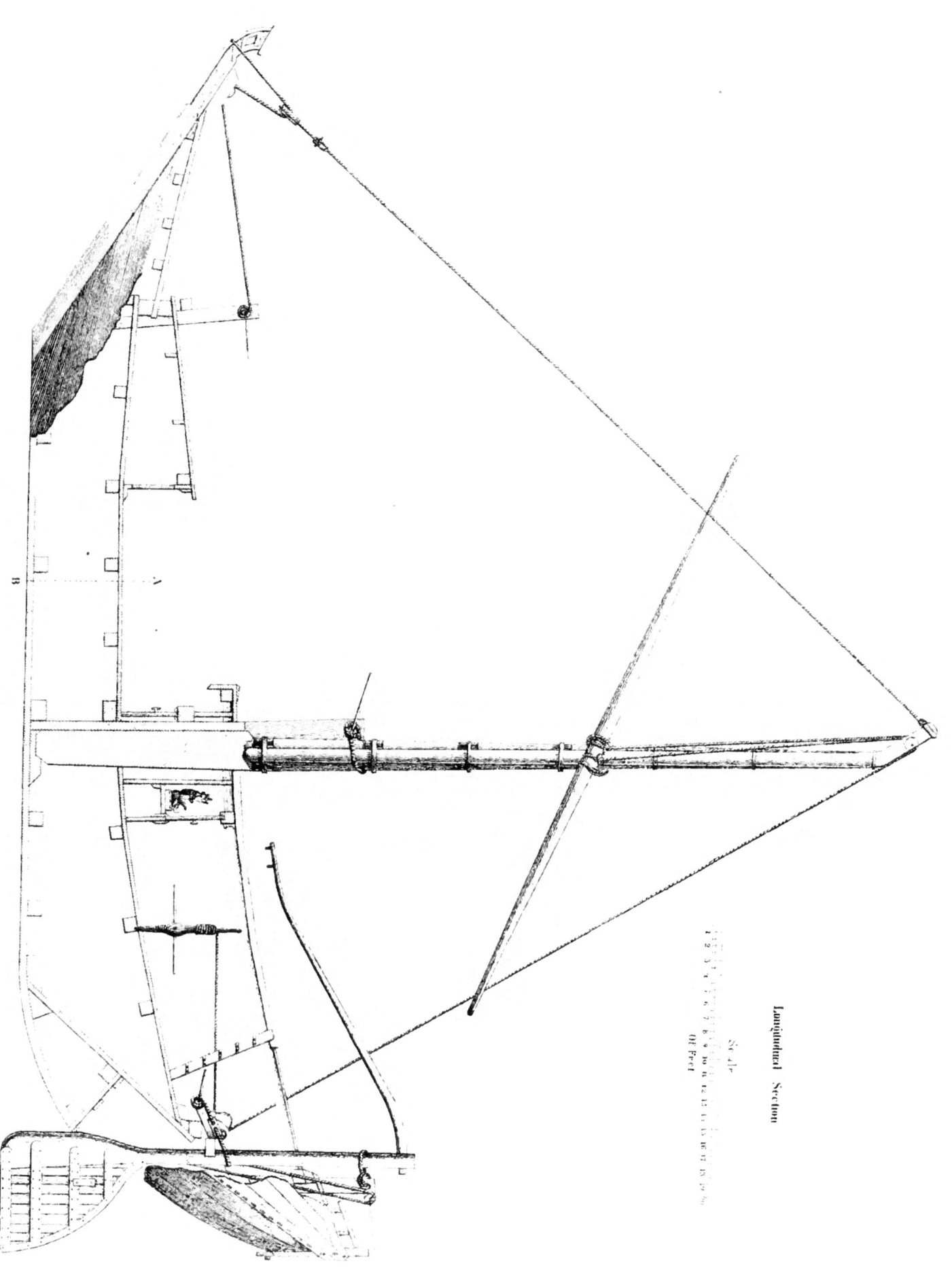

Longitudinal Section

Scale
Of Feet

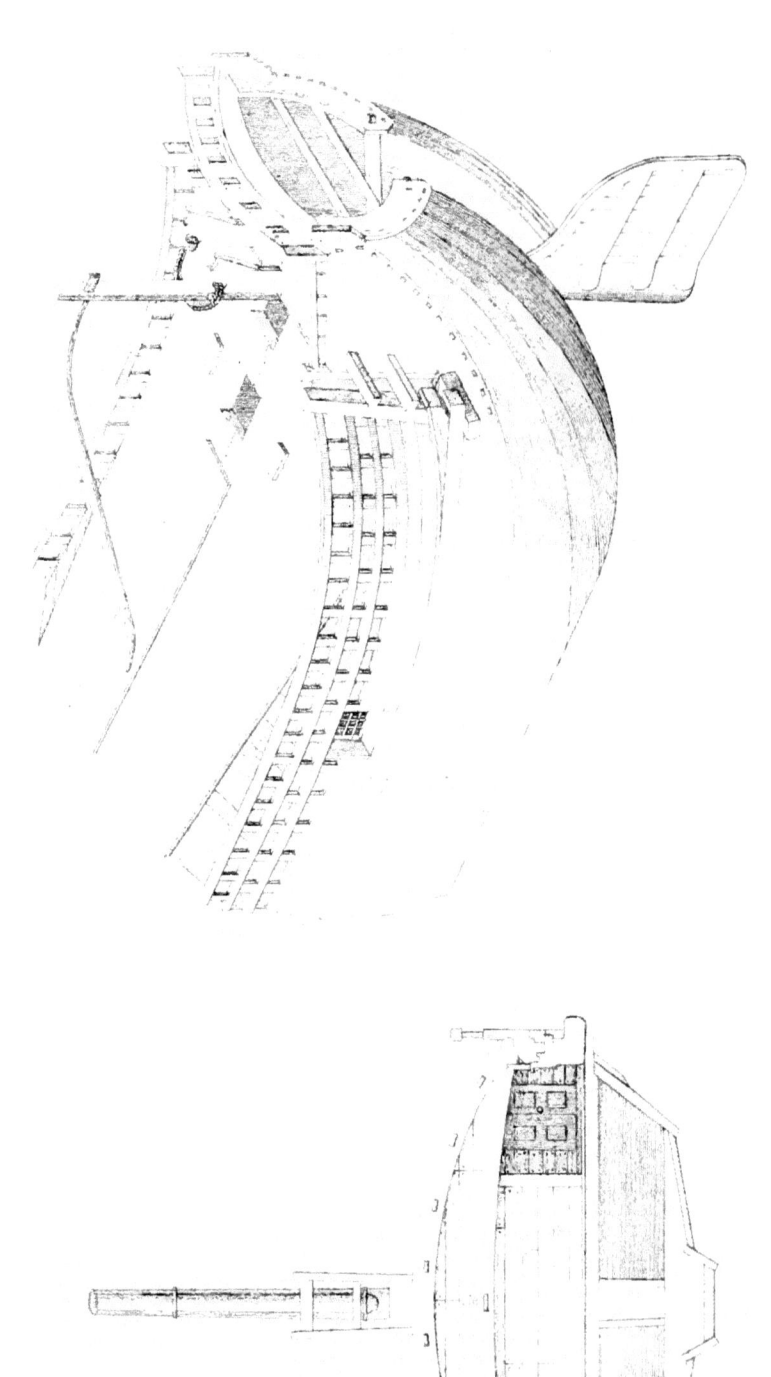
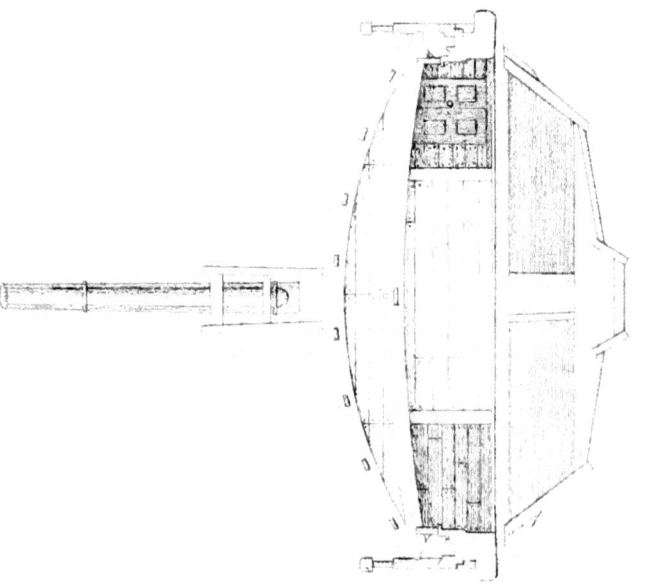

JAPANESE JUNK

"Those which came within my observation, and I certainly could not have seen less than a thousand, were all of somewhat similar dimensions and appearance: the drawings to which the reader is referred are so accurate that any precise description is rendered unnecessary, and it is only requisite to say that they all have at this time open sterns, with a strong bulkhead aft to keep the water from flowing into the hold. The rudder is of large and unwieldy size, and is hoisted up or lowered by means of runners worked by a windlass fitted in the cabin, which latter is also used in connexion with one on the forecastle for hoisting and lowering the mast and sail.

"The reasons assigned for requiring the sterns of all vessels to be constructed in this way, has been to render more convenient the management of the rudder; Kempfer and other writers ascribe it to the suspicious policy of the government, which forbids any of its vessels to visit foreign countries; and, until the period of my negotiations, the punishment of death was adjudged against all who, by design or accident, were thrown upon a strange land; and hence they very naturally assumed that the navigators of these frail and open stern craft would not venture beyond the sight of land. It is known, however, that the Chinese junks usually have sterns and rudders somewhat similar, and a presumption may be reasonably advanced that this description of rudder was the first substitute for the paddle oar or sweep used in early times for steering, and the recess in the stern has been left for the sole convenience of taking the rudder out of the water.

"It will be seen by the drawings that these vessels have a sharp tapering bow with a straight projecting stern. They have but one mast, and that is placed considerably abaft the centre beam; one sail only is used, and that a lug with a square head. This is worked by braces to the yard and by the usual tacks and sheets, and a number of bow lines attached to both leaches, and extending well up towards the head; these are intended to keep the sail flat, when on a wind; but with all these contrivances it cannot be prevented from bellying to such a degree as to render it impossible for the vessel to work nearer the wind than seven points on either tack; and, to make the sail still more clumsy and unsuitable, the material of which it is made, either cotton or grass cloth, is laced together in vertical breadths, instead of being closely sewed, as with us.

"The main or lower deck is flush, and intended to be sufficiently strong and water tight to secure the cargo; over this and abaft the mast, is a sort of half deck, which covers the cabin, and is also of tolerable strength. In this cabin the officers, passengers, and servants are quartered, the different apartments being formed of moveable bulkheads or screens; here also is the altar, surmounted by an image of some patron god. Forward of the mast, and above the main or only flush deck, is a sort of pitched roof, with sides resting upon the gunwales. This is covered with boards or thatch, and serves as a shelter for the crew, averaging about thirty in number, and the stowing of the least valuable part of the cargo; forward of this is the cable windlass and a space for working the runner forestay; here also the anchors are stowed when on board."

By this description one may well judge of the unfitness of these vessels even for navigating the coasts and islands of Japan, made, indeed, more dangerous by the prevalence of boisterous and foggy weather in those regions; doubtless many of them are lost, but their pilots (for each has an under officer of this class) rarely venture more than a few miles from the land, excepting when running from island to island; and in these passages they never leave port without favorable weather and a fair wind.

The boats are large and commodious, and in model not unlike the junks; they are usually propelled by sculls, which are worked at the sides on projections from the gunwales, the oars or sculls being long and somewhat bent. At Hakodadi we noticed that some of the boatmen used their oars in the American fashion, excepting that they dropped and raised their starboard and port oars alternately, and not uniformly together as we do. In sculling, the Japanese stand, and keep perfect measure or stroke with their sculls, which is the better preserved by their chaunting a monotonous refrain, every alternate man swinging his body in opposite directions, one pushing the other pulling. The rowers thus vibrating half of them one way, and half the other, the boat is kept perfectly upright as she dashes through, or rather over, the water.

We saw nothing remarkable in the manner or workmanship of the Japanese shipbuilders. It is doubtful whether they have any scientific rules for drafting or modelling, or for ascertaining the displacement of their vessels; nor perhaps has it been necessary, as the law confined them all to one model and size.

The tools with which they work are of primitive description, and the finest of their work is not remarkable for its neatness; copper is preferred to iron in fastening, when it can be advantageously used, and this is doubtless owing to the great abundance of the former as a native production.

It is a singular fact, strongly illustrative of the effect produced upon the people of this strange country by our friendly and social communications with them, that the law already mentioned, which restricted the construction of their vessels to one particular model, and that inflicting death upon those of their nation who should return to the Empire after having once left it, no matter how, were both suspended; whether annulled or not, I cannot say.

Kayama Yesaiman, the governor of Uraga, was authorized, as we have heard, and instructed to build a vessel after the model of the storeship Supply, a very pretty vessel, and the Japanese commissioners who negotiated with me invited a native we had on board the flag-ship, to whom the sailors had given the *sobriquet* of "Sam Patch," to land and rejoin his family, pledging themselves, in my presence, that he should be treated kindly and provided for, under the immediate protection of one of them. Since then there has been, as I understand, no objections made to the return of any of the shipwrecked Japanese; but how far they have improved in ship building, I have not heard.

We saw no war junks, and it is probable they have none of any size, the country not having been engaged for a long period in war. They content themselves, most likely, in putting light swivels or howitzers on the larger of their boats, whenever they cannot depend entirely upon their many land batteries.

A very large portion of the population is engaged in the fisheries, which supply an abundant product. While the American squadron was in the harbor, the seine was frequently drawn by the sailors of the ships, and large quantities of excellent fish obtained, consisting of salmon, salmon trout, groupers, white fish, porgies, perch, flounders, herrings, whitings, mullets, and various other kinds. The salmon we took are not more than half the size of those obtained in the United States, but are superior to them in flavor. (Specimens of smoked salmon from further north were as large as ours.) Crabs, clams of the genus *Venus*, with beautifully-marked shells, and the large blue muscle, are found in great abundance. The crabs are of considerable size, and proved excellent eating, quite equal to the famous ones of the Chesapeake.

The sportsmen of the expedition, in their occasional rambles, succeeded in obtaining but few

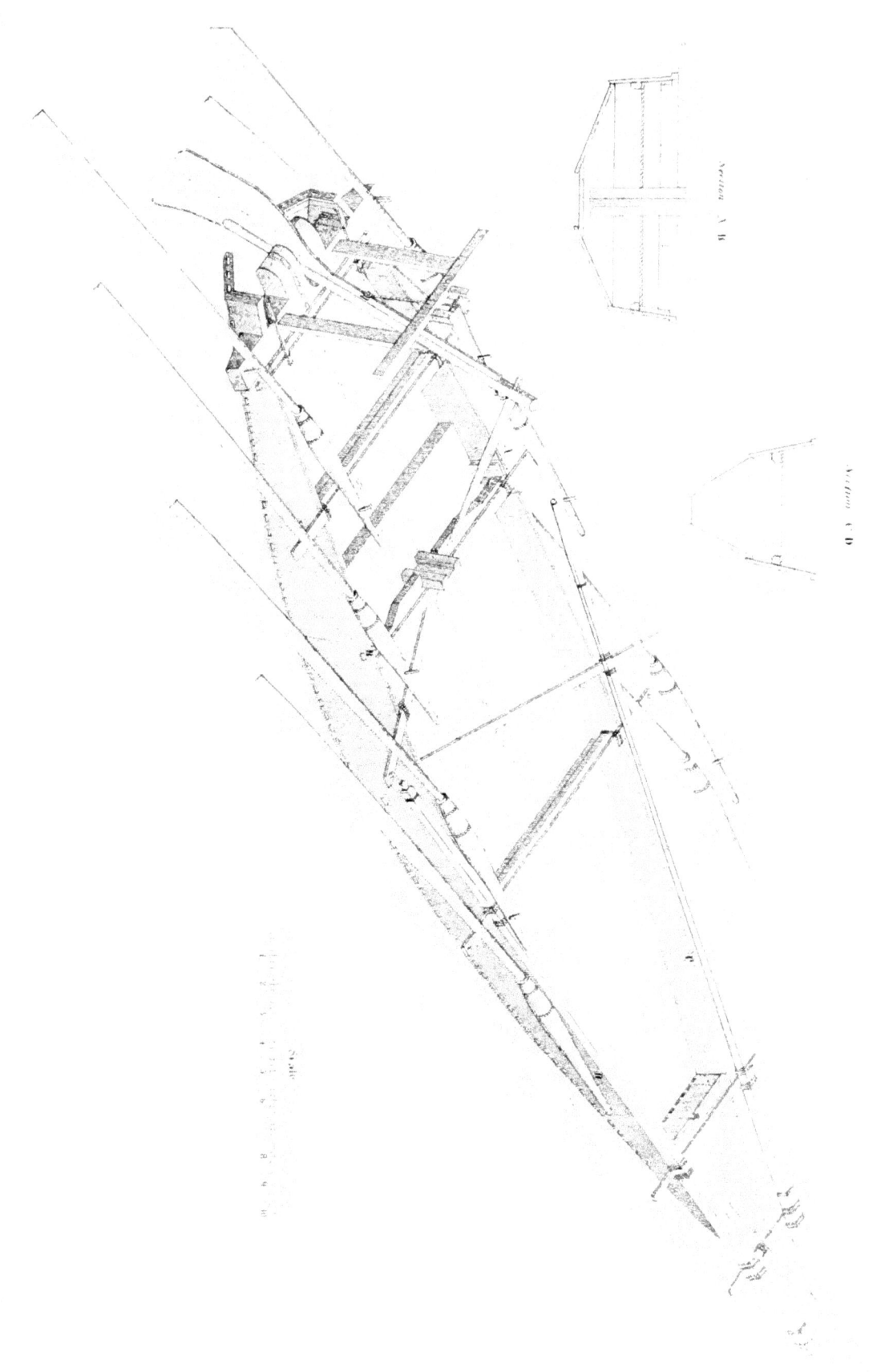

JAPANESE BOAT

specimens of birds or animals. Wild geese, ducks, quail, and other descriptions of game are, however, abundant in their seasons, but the pheasant is rarely seen; of common birds there were found some curlew, plover, and snipe. The fox, the wild boar, the deer, and the bear, are occasionally hunted. The fox is looked upon by the Japanese as possessed of an evil spirit, and is represented in their allegories as a willing agent of the devil, and with this belief the animal is pursued to the death. The people do not attempt to deprecate the wrath and cunning of his satanic majesty and his brood, as in some countries, but manfully hold them in defiance, and boldly give them battle. A male and female fox, with another animal allied to them in species, were shot, and their skins preserved.

Fishing at Hakodadi.

Hakodadi, in the future, will probably be frequented by our whalers, as it is conveniently situated to their usual resorts. Von Siebold states that sixty-eight square-rigged vessels were counted by the Japanese as passing Hakodadi and Matsmai in one year, and probably nearly all these were American, and most of them engaged in the whale fishery. Von Siebold, moreover, significantly adds, "and not one daring to approach the shore within gunshot." The treaty has, however, dispelled these alarms, and American vessels are now secured a safe retreat and a place for obtaining necessary supplies.

Hakodadi will not probably soon become a place of much trade with American vessels, but it can readily supply to the whalers and other ships good water and abundance of fish, poultry, vegetables, and some timber, and other articles, the varieties and quantities of which will no doubt increase with the demand. Fish, however, is the great staple food of the people throughout the Empire of Japan, and is justly called by them their staff of life; and to express their appreciation of its value, they invariably wrap up a bit of it in paper and send it with each gift. Cattle are only used for the plough and as beasts of burden, so it is almost impossible to obtain a supply of beef. Horses are used a good deal in Hakodadi and the neighborhood for carrying burdens, and also for riding purposes. These animals seem of an excellent breed, and though small are neatly limbed, spirited, and of good bottom. The roads, which, by-the-bye, are provided with roadside conveniences answering to the French *cabinets d'aisances*, are excellent throughout the country, and are occasionally wide and paved, though most frequently they are mere bridle paths, but kept in good order for the horsemen, the pack animals, and the sedans or kagos.

Japanese Kago.

These latter are most generally used for travelling, and consist of small wooden boxes, supported by poles, which are carried upon the shoulders of the bearers. They are adorned and enriched according to the distinction of the proprietors, but are never very comfortable conveyances.

Hakodadi is several degrees further north than Simoda, and is surrounded like it with mountains, which are, however, more numerous and lofty, though at a further distance from the town. These were found to be covered at their summits and on their upper acclivities with snow, as late as the month of June. The climate of Hakodadi is, therefore, colder than that at Simoda in winter and spring, and the fogs are both frequent and dense. The range of the

JAPANESE JUNK.

thermometer from May 18 to June 3 was from 51° to 66°, and that of the barometer 29° 45′ to 30° 05′.

The changes of temperature and humidity are sudden and extreme, and therefore render the inhabitants liable to inflammatory diseases, but probably not more so than in the northern cities with us.

There are apparently no sources of miasma, as the town is situated at the base and on the side of a considerable mountain; while such is the careful cultivation and draining of the Japanese farmers, there probably can be no causes of ill health from the low sandy isthmus and the level plains which connect the peninsula, upon which Hakodadi is situated, with the distant range of mountains. It may, then, be reasonably inferred, that both Hakodadi and Simoda are

Sub-prefect of Hakodadi with Attendants.

free from malignant endemic diseases, and may be resorted to with advantage by our ships of war on the China station, particularly at that period of the year—the latter part of summer and autumn—when dysentery and fevers are usually prevalent there. This opinion has, however, more particular reference to the climate; for, if true, as Golownin says, that the inhabitants of the island of Yesso are subject to scurvy, it will be necessary for vessels to provide against the chances of this disease. It is quite probable that the statement of Golownin may be correct, as occasionally a scarcity of vegetable food—a frequent source of scurvy—might occur towards spring, as the winters are so long, and the space so short for culture, which, moreover, is the exceptional occupation of the people along the coast, who are mostly engaged in commerce and the fisheries. Vessels, therefore, on a long cruise, should make provision for the possible want of vegetable supplies at Hakodadi.

The town contains from six to eight thousand inhabitants, and, from their manly occupations in connexion with the sea, are a comparatively vigorous and spirited people.

There are still some of the indigenous race of Ainos existing upon the island of Yesso, but they are rarely seen in the neighborhood of Hakodadi. There was, however, during the expedition sent by the Commodore to Volcano Bay, an opportunity of obtaining a casual glance at these strange people, who are described as being of a stature less than that of Europeans, averaging a little over five feet in height, but well proportioned and with intelligent features. Their color is quite dark and their hair black and coarse, which is clipped behind but allowed to straggle in thick matted locks down in front, in a confused cluster with their long beards, which are never

Water-boats and Junks, Hakodadi.

cut or shaven. Their legs are bare of artificial covering, but are grown over with a plentiful crop of coarse hair, which, together with the abundant growth on their heads and faces, has given them the name, by which they are better known, of "Hairy Kuriles." Their dress was a coarse and ragged blue undergarment reaching below the knees, over which was thrown carelessly a brown sack with wide sleeves, made of grass or skins. Their dishevelled hair and rude costume gave them a wild look, and they had a dirty, poverty-stricken aspect. Their chief occupation is that of fishing, which they carry on under the eye and for the benefit of their Japanese taskmasters, to whose absolute will they are subject.

Though the people of Hakodadi are generally engaged in the fisheries and occupations connected with a nautical life, there are, of course, to be found in the town persons of all classes, trades, and businesses.

In speaking, moreover, in the course of the following remarks, upon Japanese life, as illustrated by manners, habits, customs, and occupations, chiefly observed at Hakodadi, it must not be inferred that what is said applies exclusively to the inhabitants of that place, as a more general bearing is intended.

In the practical and mechanical arts, the Japanese show great dexterity; and when the rudeness of their tools and their imperfect knowledge of machinery are considered, the perfection of their manual skill appears marvellous. Their handicraftsmen are as expert as any in the world, and, with a freer development of the inventive powers of the people, the Japanese would not remain long behind the most successful manufacturing nations. Their curiosity to learn the results of the material progress of other people, and their readiness in adapting them to their own uses, would soon, under a less exclusive policy of government, which isolates them from national communion, raise them to a level with the most favored countries. Once possessed of the acquisitions of the past and present of the civilized world, the Japanese would enter as powerful competitors in the race for mechanical success in the future.

Every American admired the skillful workmanship of the carpenters as displayed in the construction of the wood-work in the houses, the nice adjustment and smooth finish of the

Japanese Cooper.

jointing, the regularity of the flooring, and the neat framing and easy working of the window casements and movable door panels and screens. The general designs of the houses and public buildings were very inferior to the execution of the details of construction. The former were uniform, and probably in accordance with the ancient models, and showed a constraint of inventive power within rules doubtless prescribed by government, while the latter evinced that perfection of finish which belongs alone to progressive experience. As in the carpentry, so in the masonry, there was no freedom nor boldness of conception, but the most complete execution. Their stone was well cut, and their walls strongly and regularly built, generally in the massive cyclopean style.

The coopers were found to be very expert at Hakodadi, where a large number of barrels was constantly in the process of manufacture for packing the dried and salted fish. The barrels are firkin-shaped, bulging at the top, and are rapidly and skilfully hooped with plaited bamboo. There are many workers in metal for ornamental and useful purposes. The Japanese understand well the carbonizing of iron, and the temper of much of their steel is good, as was proved by the polish and sharpness of their sword blades. The cutlery, however, in common use at

Blacksmith's Shop.

Hakodadi was of an inferior kind, and the barber of one of the ships pronounced a razor, purchased in the town, as abominably bad, neither cutting nor capable of being made to cut. The blacksmiths are numerous and busy in the town, but their work is of a small kind, as they do not use the base metals in large masses, but chiefly as parts of various implements and articles, of which wood forms the larger portion.

Their bellows are peculiar, being a wooden box with air chambers, containing valves and a piston, which is worked horizontally at one end like a hand pump, while the compressed air issues from two outlets at the sides.

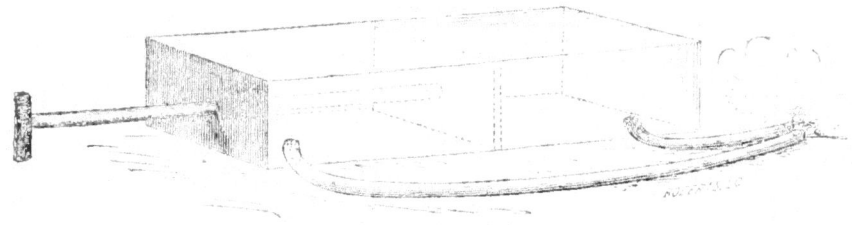
Blacksmith's Bellows.

Charcoal is generally used as the fuel, of which large quantities are made in the forests of the mountains of the interior, and brought to the town by droves of pack-horses, which are seen constantly trotting through the streets.

As the commerce of Hakodadi is extensive, the ship, or rather junk yards, showed much activity, and great numbers of vessels were constantly seen there in progress of construction. Pine is the material of which the vessels of all sizes are built, and copper is used extensively for bolting and for other purposes. The models are much superior to those of the Chinese; but of this department of industry we have already spoken fully.

Ship-yard.

Nothing was seen of the higher and more complicated branches of industrial art in operation, although the shops were supplied with fabrics which proved no little skill and perfection in various manufactures. The people seemed, however, to be unacquainted with woollen tissues, and exhibited great curiosity in examining the cloth dresses of the Americans. Cotton is much worn by the lower classes, and is generally coarsely woven, being ordinarily made in private looms at home. Every Japanese woman is more or less an adept at handling the wheel, the spindle, and shuttle, and they were often seen busy in preparing the threads and weaving the rude fabric of which the garments of the poorer classes are commonly made.

Their cottons are occasionally printed with colors, forming neat calico patterns, but their tints readily fade and will not bear washing. The width of the calico pieces, like that of the silks and crapes, is uniformly eighteen inches. This is not suited to an American or European market. Their silks are rich and heavy, and somewhat like our brocade in texture, but stouter

Spinning and Weaving.

and less flexible. They are often of very elaborate figured patterns, interwoven with golden threads and exceedingly beautiful. These are mostly used for the state robes of the high officials and dignitaries of the land. A very high price was generally demanded for these silks, though, in one instance, one of the officers, from some cause or other, purchased a piece at Hakodadi at thirteen cents per yard. The various colored crapes are some of them very flimsy, and are an essential part of Japanese upholstery, being often seen as coverings to divans or seats, and hangings to apartments. Other pieces are superior to Chinese crapes.

The lacquered ware has all the lightness, neatness of cabinet-work structure, and exquisite polish, that seems possible in work of that description, and the porcelain is equal to the

choicest specimens of similar Chinese work. The forms and ornamentation of the various articles, although frequently grotesque, showed much grace and skill, and proved great advancement in the application of the arts of design to manufacturing purposes.

In examining into the character of art exhibited by the Japanese in the illustrated books and pictures brought home by the officers of the expedition, of which several specimens are now before us, the same surprising advancement of this remarkable people, as they have shown in so many other respects, is strikingly observable. To the archaeologist there is presented in these illustrations a living example of the archaic period of a national art, when the barbaric character of the past seems to be fast losing its rude features in the early and naive beginnings of a sober and cultivated future. We are reminded, in a degree truly surprising, of the monochromatic designs upon the Etruscan vases. We find simplicity of expression rather than, as might be expected, extravagance and grotesqueness; and a soberness of coloring so far removed from the gaudy tendencies of oriental taste, that, as we look, we are almost persuaded that we have here a beginning of that unextravagant expression of nature which, in the early Greek efforts, though crude, is so interesting to the antiquarian and artist. The character and form in these Japanese illustrations, though apparently much in advance of Chinese art, are still typical rather than naturalistic; yet they are marked by an observation of nature which removes them from anything like conventionalism or manner.

One of these specimens is a book in two volumes, written by the Prince Hayashi, the chief member of the imperial commission appointed to negotiate the treaty, and presented by him to

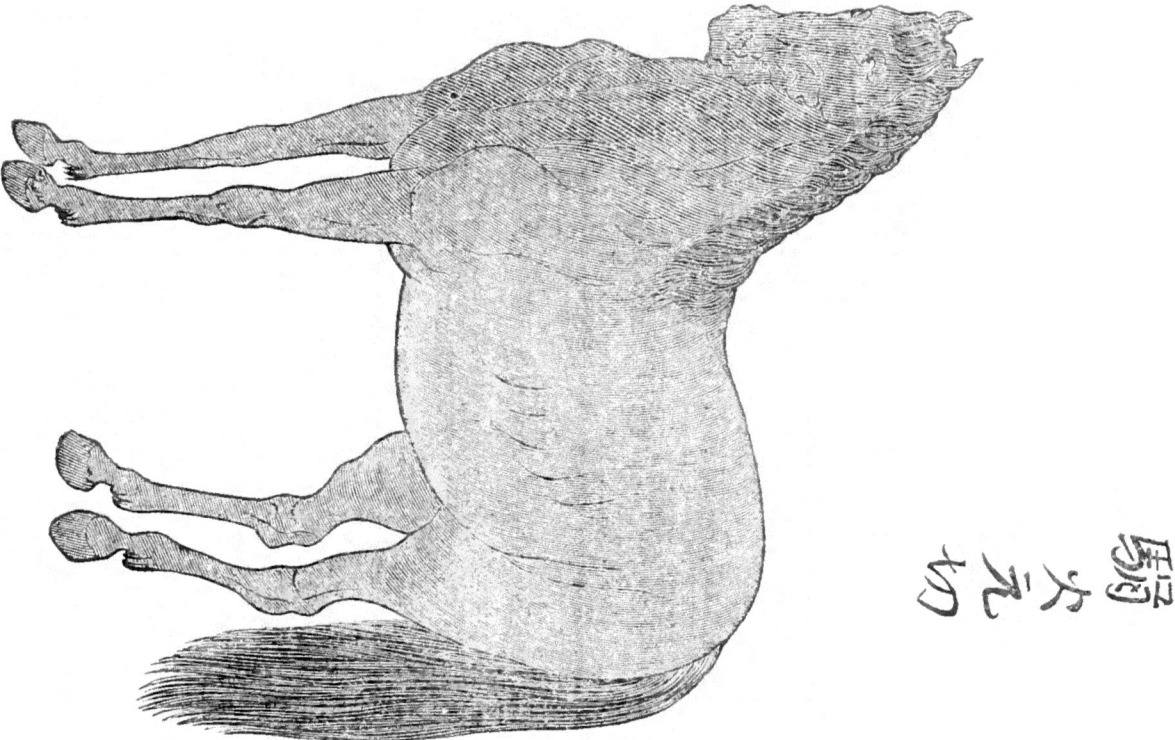

Fac Simile of Horse, from Japanese Drawings.

Commodore Perry. The subject treated of is "The Points of a Horse," and the work is illustrated by a large number of pictures. These illustrations are from woodcuts of bold outline, and apparently printed with a tint to distinguish each in the various groups of the animal, by sober greys, reds, and blacks. The style might be classed as that of the mediæval, and the horses might pass for those sketched in the time of Albert Durer, though with a more rigid adherence to nature. They exhibit, what may be noticed in the Elgin marbles, a breed of small stature and finely formed limbs, such as are found in southern countries. There is great

freedom of hand shown in the drawing. The animals are represented in various attitudes, curvetting, gambolling, and rolling upon the ground, positions requiring and exhibiting an ability in foreshortening, which is found, with no small surprise, in Asiatic art.

Another example of Japanese art before us is a species of frieze, if we may so call it, cut in wood and printed on paper in colors. It presents a row or line of the huge wrestlers of whom we have spoken on a previous page. The chief point of interest in this illustration, considered in an artistic sense, is, that, apart from its being a successful specimen of printing in colors—a process, by the way, quite modern among ourselves—there is a breadth and vigor of outline compared with which much of our own drawing appears feeble, and, above all things, undecided. Whatever the Japanese may lack as regards art, in a perception of its true principles, the style,

grace, and even a certain mannered dexterity which their drawings exhibit, show that they are possessed of an unexpected readiness and precision of touch, which are the prominent characteristics in this picture of the wrestlers. There is no stiffness or angularity about it. There is also a picture of an amphitheatre, in which the wrestlers appear, which serves to correct an error found in former writers as to Japanese ignorance of perspective.

In illustration of the rapidity and dexterity with which the Japanese artists work we have the testimony of the chaplain of the Mississippi, the Rev. Mr. Jones, who employed an artist at Hakodadi to paint for him a set of screens. Mr. Jones sat by the painter and watched him at his work. He made no previous sketch, but drew at once the various portions of the landscape, putting in his houses, ships, horses, trees and birds, with wonderful readiness, the whole being a fancy piece; and when he came to paint the foliage of some pines, he used two brushes in one hand at the same time, so as to expedite his work. The result was, though not a production of high art, yet a much better specimen of ornamental screen than could readily be found in the most pretentious manufacturing establishment of our own country. And here we may add, that a very remarkable specimen of Japanese linear drawing in perspective fell under Mr. Jones' observation. On the first visit of the squadron to Japan, as we have stated, intense interest was excited among the natives by the engines of the steamers. Their curiosity seemed insatiable, and the Japanese artists were constantly employed, when they had opportunity, in making drawings of parts of the machinery, and seeking to understand its construction and the principles of its action. On the second visit of the squadron, Mr. Jones saw, in the hands of a Japanese, a perfect drawing, in true proportion, of the whole engine, with its several parts in place, which he says was as correct and good as could have been made anywhere. The Japanese artist had made it, and valued it very highly, being unwilling to part with it at any price; Mr. Jones would have gladly bought it, and offered to do so, that he might bring it home as a specimen of Japanese skill.

In regard to anatomical markings, there is, in the specimens of Japanese drawings we have before us, no lack of such a degree of correctness as may be obtained by close *outward* observation of the parts. The muscular development of the horses, both in action and at rest, is shown in lines sufficiently true to nature to prove a very minute and accurate observation, on the part of the artist, of the *external* features of his subjects. This is very striking in the frieze of the wrestlers alluded to above. It is characterized by remarkable precision in this respect, and while preserving in the figures all the peculiar features of the Asiatic stock, the outer angle of the eye running upward, the small corneas, &c., there is distinctive expression, yet with similarity, and a height of art is reached in the drawings corresponding, as regards naturalistic characters, with what has been found in some of the Ninevah fragments.

The third example of Japanese art is afforded by an unpretending, illustrated child's book, purchased in Hakodadi for a few Chinese copper "cash." This humble little primer suggests a thousand points of interest in connexion with the Japanese, and acquaints us at once, as we turn over the very first page, with an important fact as regards their advance in art. We here find evidence that, unlike the Chinese, the artists of Japan have, as we have already hinted, a knowledge of perspective. There is a balcony presented in angular perspective, with its rafters placed in strict accordance with the principle of terminating the perspective lines in a vanishing point abruptly on the horizon. On another page there is what appears to be some Tartar Hercules, or Japanese St. Patrick clearing the land of reptiles and vermin, and the doughty destroyer is brandishing his sword in most valiant style. This is drawn with a freedom and humorous sense of the grotesque and ludicrous that are rarely found in similar books prepared for the amusement of children with us. In one of the illustrations there is a quaint old shopman peering through a pair of spectacles stuck upon his nose, and made precisely like the double-eyed glasses just now so fashionable, without any side wires or braces to confine them to

the head. A number of tea-chests are heaped one above another at his side, and the perspective of these is perfectly correct. A glass globe of gold fish, which have awakened the hungry instincts of a cat that wistfully watches their movements in the water, is among the pictures. A couple of chairmen, who have put down their sedan to take their rest, are engaged lighting their pipes; and a professor, seemingly, of phrenology is standing amid the paraphernalia of his art, whatever it be, and is taking the measure with a pair of compasses of a bald-headed disciple. All these scenes occur among the illustrations of this little book. All show a humorous conception and a style of treatment far in advance of the mechanical trash which sometimes composes the nursery books found in our shops. A people have made some progress worth studying who have a sense of the humorous, can picture the ludicrous, and goodnaturedly laugh at a clever caricature. The constant recurrence on the margin of the pages of these Japanese books of what is usually called by architects "the Greek fret or border," is certainly curious. We are surprised by a classic form that we would not have expected to find an established feature in Oriental art. Not less surprising also is it to find another architectural form belonging to what is usually termed the "Gothic" style. If the reader will turn to the end of chapter XXI, he will find, delineated on a gong, the perfect representation of the trefoil of the modern architect; it is an accurate copy from the original. Our artist has also sketched another, in which the "Gothic" pattern is plainly seen. These are singular coincidences.

There is great scope for sculpture in the image-worship of the religion of the Japanese, and, accordingly, statues of stone, metal, and wood, abound in the temples, shrines, and by the way-sides. The mechanical execution of these generally exhibits much manual skill, but none of them are to be named as works of art. The wood carving is often exquisitely cut, and when representing natural objects, particularly the lower animals and familiar parts of vegetation, is often remarkably close to truth. The sculptured cranes, tortoises, and fish, which are among the most frequent subjects carved upon the entablatures and cornices of the houses and temples, were continually admired for their fidelity to nature.

With the exception of a temple or a gateway here and there, which, in comparison with the surrounding low houses, appeared somewhat imposing, there were no buildings seen which impressed the Americans with a high idea of Japanese architecture. The most creditable specimens of this branch of art are found in some of the stone causeways and bridges which are often built upon single bold Roman arches, and in design and masonry are equal to the most scientific and artistic structures anywhere.

There were no printing establishments seen either at Simoda or Hakodadi, but books were found in the shops. These were generally cheap works of elementary character, or popular story books or novels, and were evidently in great demand, as the people are universally taught to read and are eager for information. Education is diffused throughout the Empire, and the women of Japan, unlike those of China, share in the intellectual advancement of the men, and are not only skilled in the accomplishments peculiar to their sex, but are frequently well versed in their native literature. The higher classes of the Japanese with whom the Americans were brought into communication were not only thoroughly acquainted with their own country, but knew something of the geography, the material progress, and contemporary history of the rest of the world. Questions were frequently asked by the Japanese which proved an information that, considering their isolated situation, was quite remarkable, until explained by themselves in the statement that periodicals of literature, science, arts, and politics, were annually received from Europe through the Dutch at Nagasaki; that some of these were translated, republished, and distributed through the Empire. Thus they were enabled to speak somewhat knowingly about our railroads, telegraphs, daguerreotypes, Paixhan guns, and steam-ships, none of which had they ever seen before Commodore Perry's visit. Thus, too, they could converse intelligently about the European war, about the American revolution, Washington, and Buonaparte. As strikingly illustrative of the extent of their information as to passing events out of the Empire, Lieutenant Bent relates that when he was there in the Preble in 1849, after the close of the war with Mexico, the interpreters, in their very first interview with Captain Glynn, said: "You have had a war with Mexico?" "Yes." "You whipped them?" "Yes." "You have taken a part of their territory?" "Yes." "And you have discovered large quantities of gold in it?" And after the seamen, whom Captain Glynn went to demand, were given up, they stated to our officers that, from the guards of their prison in Matsmai, (many hundred miles from Nagasaki,) they had heard of every battle we had with the Mexicans, and of every victory we gained. The Japanese learned the facts from the Dutch.

As the better classes showed an intelligent interest in all they saw on board the ships and steamers that was novel to them, so the common people exhibited an importunate curiosity about

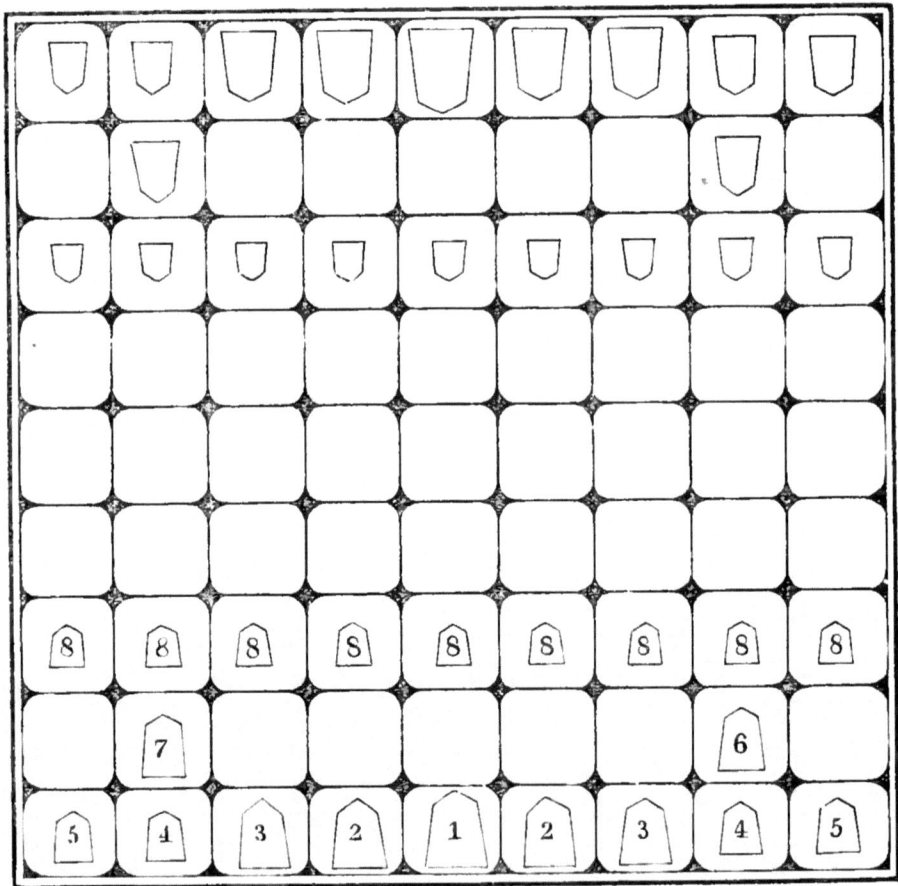

1. *Oho-shio*, (King,) centre square, first row.
2. *Kin-shio*, (Gold, or chief councillor,) upon first row, and on either side of *Oho-shio*.
3. *Gin-shio*, (Silver, or sub-councillor,) upon first row, and one on each square, next outside *Kin-chio*.
4. *Kiema*, (Flying horse,) upon first row, and one on each square, next outside *Gin-shio*.
5. *Kioshia*, (Fragrant chariot,) one upon each corner square, first row.
6. *Hishia*, (Flying chariot) on second square, second row, on right side of the board.
7. *Kakuku*, (The horn,) on second square, second row, left side of the board.
8. *Ho-hei*, (The soldiery,) on all the nine squares of the third row.

all that pertained to the dress and persons of the Americans whenever they visited the land. The Japanese were constantly besetting the officers and sailors in the streets, making all kinds of pantomimic inquiries about the English names of some part of their persons and apparel, from hat to boots, taking out their paper and pencil and making memoranda of the newly acquired English words.

The Japanese are hard workers, but they compensate themselves with occasional holidays, and in the evenings and hours of leisure with frequent games and amusements. One day, at Hakodadi, Dr. Green, the fleet surgeon, and Mr. Jones, the chaplain, were strolling through the streets, when a shower of rain drove them for shelter into a sort of military station or guard house, at hand. On entering, they found some of the inmates playing at a game very similar, as it appeared, to chess. This interested the Doctor, who forthwith set about studying it, until, finally, with the aid of the interpreters, he succeeded, after some sittings, in mastering its mysteries. The game is called *Sho-Ho-Ye*, and is a great favorite among the Japanese. The Doctor's account of it will be found below.*

Besides this, they have a game analogous to ours with cards. They play with flat pieces of horn, ivory, or bone. These are about an inch and two-thirds long, and little more than an

---

* JAPANESE GAME OF SHO-HO-YE, ANALOGOUS TO OUR GAME OF CHESS.

This game is played by two persons, with forty pieces, (twenty on either side,) and upon a chequer board of eighty-one squares, (nine upon each side.) The board is of one uniform color, though the squares might be colored, as with us, for the sake of convenience. The pieces are also of one uniform color, as they are used, (at pleasure,) by either party, as his own, after being captured from the adversary. They are of various sizes, are long and wedge-shaped, being at the same time sharpened from side to side, in front, and the names of each piece are inscribed upon it, both the original, and the one assumed, upon being reversed or turned over, (as below.) Each player knows his men, or pieces, by their pointed and thin end being always forward or from him. But they would be more readily distinguished if the back parts of all were painted with some decided and striking color, as that part of his own men is seen by each player only—and if the fronts of all the men were painted of some other color, as that part of the adversary's pieces is seen by either player only. They are laid flat upon the board, (front forward,) and thus their names are plainly visible. They capture, as in chess, by occupying the places of the captured pieces. The King, *Oho-shio*, being the chief piece, cannot remain in check, and when checkmated, the game is lost.

The pieces are named, and are placed upon the board, as follows, viz:

Oho-shio, (King,) centre square, first row.

Kin-shio, (Gold, or chief councillor,) upon first row, and one on either side of *Oho-shio*,

Gin-shio, (Silver, or sub-councillor,) upon first row, and one on each square, next outside *Kin-shio*.

Kiema, (Flying horse,) upon first row, and one on each square, next outside *Gin-shio*.

Kio-shia, (Fragrant chariot,) one upon each corner square, first row.

Hishia, (Flying chariot,) on second square, second row, right side of the board.

Kakuko, (The horn,) on second square, second row, left side of the board.

Ho-hei, (The soldiery,) on all the nine squares of the third row.

The moves and powers of the pieces are as below, only noting, that in capturing, there is no deviation from them, as with us, in the case of pawns.

Oho-shio moves and takes on one square in any direction.

Kin-shio, as the *Oho-shio*, except that he cannot move diagonally backward.

Neither of the above are ever reversed or acquire different powers; but all the pieces below may be reversed, (at the option of the player,) when they move *to* or *from* any square, in any of the adversary's three first rows, and thereby they acquire different powers, as well as different names.

Gin-shio moves and takes as the *Oho-shio*, except that he cannot move directly on either side, or directly backward. When reversed, or turned over, he becomes a *Gin-Nari-Kin*, and acquires all the powers (and those alone) of the *Kin-shio*.

Kiema has the move of our knight, except that he is strictly confined to two squares forward and one laterally, and can in no case make more than four moves as a *Kiema*. When reversed he becomes a *Kiema-Nari-Kin*, with all the powers (and those alone) of the *Kin-shio*.

Kioshia moves directly forward *only*, but that may be any number of steps. He may be reversed upon either of the first three rows of the adversary, and then becomes a *Kioshia-Nari-Kin*, with all the powers (and those alone) of the *Kin-shio*.

Hishia has the entire powers of our castle, and when reversed, he assumes the name of *Rioho*, (the dragon,) and acquires, in addition to his former moves, all those of the *Oho-shio*.

Kakuko has the entire powers of our bishop, and when reversed, he assumes the name of *Riome*, (the dragoness,) and acquires, in addition to his former moves, all those of the *Oho-shio*.

inch wide. There are forty-nine pieces, marked by three different colors, blue, red, and white, to indicate the different suits, and also by lines and dots to signify the value of the piece. The games played with these are, as with our cards, numerous, and are generally played for money. The Japanese shuffle and cut them precisely as is done with us, sometimes by lifting off a part of the pack, and at others expressing satisfaction with them as they are, by tapping the knuckle on the top of the heap. Another common game is played with small black and white stones, and seems to be somewhat of the character of loto, so much played in the gardens and estaminets of Paris and Hamburgh, frequented by the lower classes. It was a cheerful reminder of one's childhood, and another bond of sympathy between the various branches of the human race, however remotely separated from each other, to find the little shaven-pated lads playing ball in the streets of Hakodadi, or jackstraws within the domestic circle at home.

NOTE.—For the remarks made in this chapter on the specimens of Japanese art alluded to, we would make our acknowledgments to the accomplished instructor in drawing, &c., in the Free Academy of New York, Professor Duggan. The specimens were submitted to him with a request that he would examine them artistically, and favor the compiler with his opinion.

Ho moves forward one step only at a time, and may be reversed upon either of the first three rows of the adversary; when so reversed, he becomes a *Ho-Nuri-Kin*, and acquires all the powers of the *Kin-shio*.

Besides the preceding moves and powers, any piece which has been taken may be replaced upon the board, at the discretion of the captor, as follows, viz: when it is his move, instead of moving one of his men, he can replace any one of the captured pieces upon any unoccupied square whatever, observing to keep that side up to which it was entitled originally; but it may be reversed at any move thereafter, if *to* or *from* any square in the before-mentioned three first rows of the adversary, and observing further, that he cannot replace a *Ho*, or (soldier,) on any column upon which there is already one of his own, i. e., he cannot double a *Ho*, or (soldier.)

It may be further stated, that no piece can pass over the head of any other piece in its move, except the *Kiema*.

Some of the problems of this game, prepared by Dr. Green, will be found in vol. 1 of the Appendix.

CHAPTER XXIV.

INTERVIEW BETWEEN THE COMMODORE AND THE REPRESENTATIVE OF THE PRINCE OF MATSMAI.—SOUTHAMPTON SENT TO EXPLORE VOLCANO BAY, INCLUDING ENDERMO HARBOR.—REPORT OF THE SURVEY.—POVERTY OF THE REGION AROUND THE BAY.—ERUPTION OF A VOLCANO AT MIDNIGHT.—AINOS.—BOUNDARIES OF AMERICANS AT HAKODADI LEFT TO BE SETTLED WITH THE IMPERIAL COMMISSIONERS.—GOOD UNDERSTANDING BETWEEN THE AMERICANS AND PEOPLE OF HAKODADI.—JAPANESE DELIGHTED WITH THE EXHIBITION OF THE "ETHIOPIAN MINSTRELS" ON BOARD SHIP.—SQUADRON THEATRICALS.—INTEREST OF JAPANESE IN THE MACHINERY AND FIRE-ARMS OF THE SHIPS.—ANSWER OF HAKODADI AUTHORITIES TO COMMODORE'S ENQUIRIES AS TO EUROPEAN OR AMERICAN VESSELS WRECKED IN JAPAN DURING THE LAST TEN YEARS.—ANSWER OF THE IMPERIAL COMMISSIONERS TO SIMILAR ENQUIRIES.—MACEDONIAN SAILS FOR SIMODA.—VANDALIA DISPATCHED FOR CHINA BY THE WESTERN PASSAGE.—JAPANESE OFFICERS DESIRE A CONFERENCE WITH THE COMMODORE.—FLAG-LIEUTENANT SENT ASHORE TO BRING THEM ON BOARD.—DISRESPECTFUL CONDUCT OF THE OFFICERS —FLAG-LIEUTENANT RETURNS WITHOUT THEM.—JAPANESE OFFICERS FINALLY COME OFF IN THEIR OWN BOAT.—NOT ALLOWED TO SEE THE COMMODORE UNTIL THEY APOLOGIZE FOR THEIR BEHAVIOR.—APOLOGY ACCEPTED.—CONFERENCE RESULTS IN NOTHING BUT A FURTHER ILLUSTRATION OF JAPANESE FINESSE.—BURIALS OF AMERICANS AT HAKODADI.—RESPECT SHOWN FOR THE CEREMONIES BY THE JAPANESE.—BUDDHIST PRIEST PERFORMS HIS FUNERAL CEREMONIES AFTER THE AMERICANS RETIRE.—SERVICES IN A BUDDHIST TEMPLE.—JAPANESE ERECT A FENCE AROUND THE AMERICAN GRAVES.—SAILOR'S EPITAPH COMPOSED BY HIS SHIPMATES.—BLOCK OF GRANITE PRESENTED BY THE JAPANESE AT HAKODADI FOR THE WASHINGTON MONUMENT.—VOLCANO OF OHO-SIMA.—ARRIVAL AT SIMODA.—MEETING WITH THE COMMISSIONERS.—BOUNDARIES AT HAKODADI SETTLED.—APPOINTMENT OF PILOTS AND HARBOR-MASTER AGREED ON.—VALUE OF JAPANESE AND AMERICAN MONEY RESPECTIVELY FIXED.—ADDITIONAL REGULATIONS BETWEEN THE COMMISSIONERS AND COMMODORE AGREED TO AND SIGNED.—COAL SUPPLIED AT SIMODA.—ITS COMPARATIVE QUALITY AND VALUE.—COST OF VARIOUS ARTICLES FURNISHED TO THE SHIPS.—ANOTHER BLOCK OF STONE FOR THE WASHINGTON MONUMENT PRESENTED BY THE IMPERIAL COMMISSIONERS AT SIMODA—JAPANESE PRESENT OF DOGS TO THE PRESIDENT.—SAM PATCH HAS AN INTERVIEW WITH THE OFFICIALS OF HIS COUNTRY.—REFUSES TO GO ON SHORE OR LEAVE THE SHIP.—PRAISEWORTHY CONDUCT OF A MARINE TOWARD SAM.—"DAN KETCH."—JAPANESE PUNISHMENT OF CRUCIFIXION.—PRACTICE OF THE "HARI KARI," OR "HAPPY DISPATCH."—DEPARTURE FROM SIMODA.—MACEDONIAN AND SUPPLY SENT TO FORMOSA AND PHILLIPPINES.—REDFIELD ROCKS.—PARTY SENT ON SHORE FOR OBSERVATION OF OHO-SIMA.—ARRIVAL AT LEW CHEW.—SOUTHAMPTON ORDERED TO HONG KONG.—POWHATAN AND MISSISSIPPI COME TO ANCHOR AT NAPHA.

ON the afternoon of May 19, the Commodore, having shifted his flag temporarily to the Mississippi, received on board of that ship Matsmai Kangsayu, the great officer of the family of the prince of Matsmai, who had come, as had been announced, to meet the Americans on behalf of his superior. He was accompanied by Yendo Matazaimon, the *bungo* or governor of Hakodadi, Ishuko Kenso, the Chinese interpreter, and several attendants. After the usual interchange of compliments, the Commodore asked when he was to expect the arrival of the Prince of Matsmai himself. Kangsayu replied, that it was impossible to say, as he was at Matsmai, and no communication had been received from him in reference to his coming. The Commodore then remarked, that if the prince did not come to see him he would be obliged to go and see the prince, since there was no one at Hakodadi with whom a conference could be held in regard to the treaty. Upon this the Japanese rejoined, that, as the prince could not leave Matsmai himself, he had delegated his highest officer to meet the Commodore as his substitute, who was ready to put the treaty in operation. It was, however, added, that the Americans were asking for some things not specified, inasmuch as the treaty was not to go into effect before the lapse of a year from its date. It was then explained to the Japanese, that this condition had reference to merchant vessels, but that the Commodore had made subsequent arrangements with the high commissioners about his present visit, the objects of which he was now desirous of accomplishing if Kangsayu had full powers to act in the matter. This dignitary then answered that he was clothed with complete local authority, but that neither he nor his prince could settle the boundary within which American intercourse was to be restricted without instructions from the court at Yedo.

The wind now commenced blowing very hard, and the bay was so rough that the Japanese preferred remaining for some time on board the Mississippi, where they were handsomely entertained and shown all the points and novelties of the steamer. After a long stay, in the course of which the Japanese were evidently gratified by all they saw (manifesting therein their usual intelligent interest) and by the attentions they received, they returned to the shore.

On the next day the Southampton was dispatched by the Commodore to make a survey of Volcano Bay, including Endermo harbor, about seventy miles from Hakodadi, at the southeastern end of Yesso; and it may be here appropriate, though somewhat anticipating the chronological order of events, to dispose of this part of our story, by giving a general report of the result of the survey. The ship arrived off the southern promontory of Volcano Bay at five o'clock on the afternoon of the day of her departure from Hakodadi. The wind soon lulled to a dead calm, and the bay was not entered until the next morning. The weather being very thick the ship bore away for the harbor of Endermo, and shortly after noon made the land ahead, which, being approached to within two miles, was coasted in ten fathoms of water, taking care to keep off when shoaling in that depth. The fog was so thick, and the breakers were so far off the shore, that it was not deemed prudent to approach too near the land; and, consequently, the entrance to the harbor of Endermo, which is quite narrow and shut in by adjacent points, could not be seen. Its position, however, having been passed, and the ship continuing to run along the land by the lead until seven o'clock in the evening, came then to anchor in front of a small village. As the night advanced the atmosphere cleared, for a moment, sufficiently to allow of the sight of several junks anchored near a large town about three miles distant. The fog soon gathered again and continued so thick all the rest of that night and the next day, with fresh breezes from E.S.E., that it was deemed more prudent to remain at anchor, and the ship did not again get under way until the 27th of May.

At sunrise on that day, the fog having partly dispersed, the Southampton stood for the eastern coast, sounding with a boat in five fathoms to within a mile and a half of the shore, and also running a line of soundings in the ship. As the morning advanced the fog cleared off, and revealed to view a charming scene of picturesque beauty. The land rose from the sandy beach in undulating heights, covered with trees of dark green foliage, interspersed here and there with yellow spots of culture, while innumerable houses were seen everywhere grouped at the openings of the ravines toward the sea, into which streams of fresh water poured, after irrigating the cultivated fields on the hill sides and the fertile bottoms of the valleys, and passing through the villages.

The meridian observation having been taken, which gave the latitude 42° 17′, the ship,

heading east, made for an indentation in the land, supposed to be the entrance to the harbor of Volcano Bay, and with a depth of water of seventeen fathoms and a fair wind, before which she was going at nine knots, the whole circuit of the large bay soon opened to the sight. An amphitheatre of lofty mountains, with summits covered with snow, surrounded the land, which gradually lessened in height as it descended toward the hills and uplands that rose immediately from the shore. To the northeast were two volcanoes in active eruption, throwing out convulsively their thick smoke, which, as it swept before the breeze, darkened with its passing but ever recurring shadow the snow which glittered like silver upon the sunlit summits of the neighboring mountains.

Passing a small island, called Olason, from one of Captain Broughton's men who was buried there, the Southampton stood up the channel of Endermo, and anchored in the evening near the land, where a few houses, a fortification upon an adjacent hill, and some sheds upon the shore, indicated a settlement. Soon two officials came off in a boat, rowed by a number of Indians, (as they are called,) the native *ainos*, and upon reaching the ship the Japanese functionaries produced a bit of paper in which was wrapped some rice and a piece of wood, and displaying the contents, pointing at the same time to some water, asked, by signs, if either of these was required. The chief dignitary, who, in addition to the usual Japanese official costume, wore an outside coat with a red collar and a great deal of embroidery, and seemed to be a military personage, was not apparently disposed to be very friendly toward his visitors. Upon his being made to understand that if any fish, vegetables, eggs, or poultry could be obtained from the land, the Americans would be glad to purchase them, the Japanese officer sent his boat ashore, apparently with the view of ascertaining. Upon its return, the only article brought back was a bundle of stems, looking like those of the rhubarb plant, with the information that, in consequence of the weather, there were no fish, and only three chickens in the place.

Next morning a surveying party commenced their operations in the bay, and continued them during the stay of the ship. Little was to be had from the shore in the way of provisions, but the bay abounded in clams, muscles, and fish, and large supplies were obtained. The inhabitants, who were mostly *ainos*, had been very much alarmed at the arrival of the Southampton, and were seen hurrying away from the harbor and village with all their property heaped upon their backs, so that the land was quite deserted. The few Japanese officials became gradually more friendly, and frequently visited the ship and partook of its hospitalities. Nothing occurred of especial interest during the visit to Endermo bay beyond the blazing up one night of another volcano, making three which were seen from the ship in a state of active eruption at the same time. The sudden starting up of a broad and vivid flame from the summit of a mountain in the midst of the night, dispelling at once the darkness which enveloped sea and land, produced a grand effect. The other two volcanoes merely emitted smoke, while the third continued in a blaze.

Lieutenant Boyle, commander of the Southampton, visited Olason island, at the mouth of Endermo Bay, previous to his departure, and found the grave of the buried sailor left there by Captain Broughton. The Japanese authorities had respected the remains, though they had been interred more than three-fourths of a century, and built on the spot where they rested one of the usual tombs of the country, with the ordinary marks of mourning. The survey having been completed, the ship sailed to join the squadron at Simoda, pursuant to orders.

The Commodore, on the next day after the visit from Kangsayu, went on shore to call upon this dignitary, who, after having presented his credentials from the Prince of Matsmai, and emphatically declared that the latter could not possibly come to Hakodadi, was officially recognized as the representative of his superior. He, however, refused to settle definitively the question of the boundary within which the Americans, in their intercourse with the place, were to be restricted, and the subject was finally disposed of by a mutual agreement that it should be referred to the commissioners who were to meet the Commodore at Simoda. During the frequent visits of the Americans on shore, occasional disagreements arose in regard to their relations with the shopkeepers and the extent and freedom of their walks in the town and about the country. These little troubles, which, although they gave rise to much tedious negotiation, were uniformly settled by mutual explanations, produced in the end the establishment of an excellent understanding and the most friendly feelings between our countrymen and all classes of the Japanese.

The governor and his attendants continued to visit the ships frequently, when they were uniformly entertained with refreshments, and sometimes invited to a more ceremonious dinner, of which they always partook with a proper appreciation both of the viands and the courtesy. On one occasion, some of the sailors got up a concert of "Ethiopian minstrels," which seemed to give as much delight to the natives at Hakodadi as it had done to the commissioners in the bay of Yedo. The performance undoubtedly showed that talent for grotesque humor and comic yet sentimental melody which are, as some think, characteristic of the sailor, the monotony of whose life on ship-board is often compensated by that hearty flow of animal spirits with which natures, invigorated by a hard and hazardous occupation, console themselves for its risks and privations. The sentimental strain, too, in which the sailor sometimes indulges, is naturally the antagonistic tone with which the mind, surrounded by its rude associations, opposes their petrifying influence. All the sailors' rough humor is hence toned down by a gentler touch of feeling. The negro minstrelsy, which not only wrinkles the face with a broad and noisy laugh, but also can moisten the eye with a tear, is consequently a great favorite with Jack. The sailors performed their parts with a sympathetic interest and an earnest intensity, which would have carried with them the frequenters of Christy's, and produced a marked effect even upon their sedate Japanese listeners, and thus confirmed the universal popularity of "the Ethiopians" by a decided hit in Japan. Everything was arranged appropriately as to dresses and scenery, much as it would have been at home. Bills of the performance, too, were printed by the aid of the press, which was on board one of the ships of the squadron, and freely worked within the dominions of the Emperor of Japan, without regarding any censorship that he might possibly be disposed to establish. American like, our men stuck to the principle of a "free press," on the ground that the press itself and popular opinion are about the best correctives of the abuse of the press. And here we may remark, that theatrical performances in the squadron were not confined to "Ethiopian minstrelsy." Histrionic ambition took a higher flight, and ventured on the "legitimate drama." There was more than one company of Thespians in the squadron, composed of the men, who acquitted themselves very creditably. They generally selected some good natured officer, known to have a taste for theatricals, to give them some general instructions, and help them at rehearsals, and with such aid, added to natural cleverness and quickness of parts, they succeeded very well. The female characters were allotted to boys, and all the appliances of scenery and appropriate costume were called in to give greater effect.

The Japanese officials took especial interest, on the occasion of their frequent visits to the

ships, in the inspection of the armament, and were often gratified with the exercise of the guns, the filling of the shells, and other matters of military discipline and practice. Though, in their later history a pacific people, the Japanese, as we have already said, are fond of military display, and seemed particularly desirous of scrutinizing all the warlike appointments which made their visitors so formidable; as if they felt the necessity, in the new relations which were opening with foreigners, of studying and adopting the best means of attack and defence, should either ever become necessary by any future collision with the great powers of the west. With proper training, no people would make better soldiers. Every opportunity was afforded them, without restriction, of satisfying their curiosity, which was naturally directed towards those points in which they were conscious of their greatest weakness; and this liberality of the Americans, in the free exposition of their power, deeply impressed the Japanese with a conviction of the pacific intentions of their visitors, who desired to show that they looked to a friendly intercourse, and not to a violent invasion, for those mutual benefits which were to accrue from more intimate relations between the United States and Japan.

A valuable communication was received from the authorities at Hakodadi, in answer to certain enquiries made by the Commodore in regard to the various American and European vessels which were supposed to have been wrecked at different times upon the coast of the Empire. There was reason to suppose that several vessels which had been lost, and never heard of in the countries from which they had sailed, had been wrecked on the shores of the island of Yesso; and it was thought possible, from the hitherto inhospitable conduct of the Japanese government towards foreigners, that some who had been cast by calamity upon its mercy might yet be held in captivity. It was, therefore, a great satisfaction to receive the following answer from the Hakodadi officials:

"From the third year of Ohoka to the third of Kayee, [1847 to 1851,] there were five foreign vessels wrecked by storms on our coasts, whose crews have all been sent on to Nagasaki, thence to be sent by the Dutch back to their homes; not one now remains in Japan.

"In 1847, June, seven American sailors were drifted ashore at Yetoroop in a boat.

"In 1847, June, thirteen American sailors in three boats were thrown ashore at Yeramachi, N.W. of Matsmai.

"In March, 1849, three men from an American ship went ashore at Karafto, the south end of Saghalien, and then went off.

"In May, 1850, an English ship was wrecked at Mabiru, in Yesso, from which thirty-two men came; but where they came from we know not."

The Commodore also addressed to the imperial commissioners, with whom the terms of the treaty were negotiated, a communication on the same subject, and received the following reply:

"*To His Excellency Commodore Perry:*

"The undersigned have well understood your written communication in reference to ships navigating the Pacific, the Chinese, and Japanese seas, which have never been heard of at their ports of destination; and the probable fate of their crews being uncertain, his majesty the President has ordered enquiries to be made on the subject, and ships-of-war have been sent to Borneo, Formosa, and other islands; and that two ships were again to sail to Formosa, by your order, for a similar purpose.

"In reply to your request for a list of all the ships which have been wrecked in Japan for the last ten years, we have the honor to state as follows:

"In 1847, some Americans, shipwrecked in the principality of Matsmai, were sent to Nagasaki to take passage in the Dutch trading ships.

"In 1848, some Americans, shipwrecked in the same principality, were sent to Nagasaki, and thence taken away by an American ship-of-war. [This was the Preble.]

"In the year 1850, some Americans and Englishmen, shipwrecked, were sent to Nagasaki, to go in the Dutch trading ships.

"Beside the three instances just mentioned, there has been no shipwreck, and there are no foreigners now in Japan. The local authorities having settled this business, we are not able to give you the names of the shipwrecked persons.

"We have the honor to be, with great respect,

"BY THE IMPERIAL COMMISSIONERS.

"Seal attached by order of the high gentlemen.

"MORYAMA YENOSKE."

On the morning of the 31st of May the Macedonian sailed for Simoda, and the Vandalia for Shanghai, the latter vessel being directed by the Commodore to take the western passage by passing through the Straits of Sangar, the Japan sea, and China gulf. The steamers still remained at Hakodadi to await the arrival of those personages whom the commissioners had promised to send there to meet the Americans and settle the stipulations of the treaty in regard to that place. The Commodore was naturally somewhat impatient at the delay in the coming of the expected delegation, as, in accordance with his agreement to that effect, he was obliged to return to Simoda on the 15th day of June, and the last day of the previous month had now passed. On the morning of the 1st of June, however, a communication was received by the Commodore, written in Japanese, Chinese, and Dutch, of which the following is an English translation:

"The Japanese imperial government officers, Amma Zhium-noshin and Hirayama Kenzhiro, and others, desire a conference with his excellency the plenipotentiary of the United States and other officers.

"They have received orders from the court to go to Karafto, and, learning that your ships were at Hakodadi examining its harbor, in accordance with the treaty of Kanagawa, have come, as these distant frontier places are not fully apprized of all these matters, and perhaps there may be some mistake or misapprehension. We have requested of our superior officer presently to come and deliberate upon such matters as may come up, as was done at Yoku-hama; but he has taken a passage by sea, and has already gone on to Karafto. We are unable, therefore, to tarry behind him for more than three days in order to confer with your honor.

"We wish you much peace."

This was not very explicit, but it seemed apparent that, although these dignitaries affected, in their letter, merely to have called, as it were, in passing, they were delegated by the government to make the visit. In accordance, however, with the indirect policy of Japanese diplomacy, it was deemed expedient to make use of a subterfuge, by which the intention of the government, of deferring all negotiation until the meeting of the commissioners, might be accomplished and yet concealed, for fear of offending the sensibilities of the Americans by this change in the original arrangement. The flag-lieutenant, Mr. Bent, was sent by the Commodore to meet the Japanese delegates, and inform them that they would be received on board the Powhatan at any time they might appoint. One o'clock was accordingly named, and at that hour the boat was sent ashore to receive the Japanese officials and bring them to the ship. On the flag-lieutenant's arriving at the government house and sending word that he was in waiting to conduct the deputies to the Commodore, he was told that these gentlemen were at luncheon. After a due exercise of patience for more than an hour, the chief deputy and two of his suite presented themselves, and very deliberately, instead of proceeding to the boat, took their seats in the custom-house, and leisurely refreshed themselves with tea and pipes. The flag-lieutenant very courteously reminded them that it was time to go, but these dignitaries, with the greatest self-composure imaginable, continued to sip their tea and smoke their pipes, and showed by their manner that, such was the idea of their own importance, that not only time and tide, but flag-lieutenants, should wait their leisure. This conduct was the more remarkable from a people so habitually ceremonious and polite. The officer, therefore, very properly said that the boat sent by the Commodore was at the steps, and was then going off to the ship, and if they chose to take passage in it he would be pleased to have their company; if not, they would be obliged to find their own conveyance; but, as the appointed hour had long since passed, it was doubtful whether they would be received by the Commodore at all. They then replied, without, apparently, making any effort to hurry themselves, that they were waiting for their companions.

The flag-lieutenant now, without more ado, took his departure, and, getting into the boat, put off for the ship. On his way thither he was met by a messenger from the Commodore, with the command to wait no longer for the deputies, unless they had some good reason for their delay. On the flag-lieutenant's making his report, orders were given to prepare for another visit to the land, with a stronger demonstration of earnestness. The deputies, however, in the mean time arrived, and, as they presented themselves at the gangway of the Powhatan, the flag-lieutenant demanded, in the name of the Commodore, an explanation of their delay. The Japanese functionaries then having offered as an apology that they had been delayed in purchasing a few articles as presents for the American ambassador, were treated as if they told the truth, and conducted to the Commodore's cabin, where they held a short conference, and refreshments were hospitably set before them. They repeated in conversation the tenor of their note, and said they had no authority to settle the boundaries in Hakodadi. Of course there was no occasion to confer further with them, and the Commodore no longer pressed the matter, but determined to postpone all negotiations until he should meet the imperial commissioners at Simoda, the appointed time for which meeting was now rapidly approaching.

On parting with these Japanese officials, the Commodore took occasion, while expressing his gratification at the general kindness and courtesy of the authorities and people at Hakodadi, to remark, that the inhabitants still seemed suspicious of the Americans, as they continued to shut their houses and remove the women from observation. To this the deputies returned a written reply, which, as it presents a document singularly characteristic of the gentle, conciliatory tone of the Japanese, and of their ingenuity in the work of self-justification, and also exhibits the moderate style of their official communications, we give at length:

"To hear from the Commodore that, since his arrival in Hakodadi, he has been much pleased with his intercourse and communications with the local authorities, is truly a great gratification to us. With regard to going through the streets, and seeing shops and houses shut, with neither women nor children in the ways, let it be here observed, that at Yoku-hama this very matter was plainly spoken of by Moryama, the interpreter, at that place. The customs of our country are unlike yours, and the people have been unused to see people from foreign lands; and though the authorities did what they could to pacify them, and teach them better, they still were disinclined to believe, and many absconded or hid themselves. If the Commodore will recall to mind the day when he took a ramble to Yoku-hama, in which some of us accompanied him, he will recollect that in the villages and houses we hardly saw a woman during the whole walk. If he saw more of them at Simoda, as he went about, it was because there the people were gradually accustomed to the Americans, and their fears had been allayed, so that they felt no dread.

"On these remote frontiers, many miles from Yedo, the usages of the people are so fixed that they are not easily influenced and altered; but, pray, how can the inhabitants here think of regarding Americans with inimical feelings? Even when they see their own officers, with the persons of whom they are not familiar, they also run aside, and, as from fear, seek to escape *us*. This is the custom of our country that officers should accompany visitors about—a custom not to be so soon changed. Still, the disposition of the men here is ingenuous, brave, upright, and good, and that of the women retiring and modest, not gazing at men as if without bashfulness. Such characteristics and such usages must be considered as estimable, and we think that you also will not dislike them.

"In general, when upright, cordial propriety marks intercourse, then peace, good feeling, and harmony are real between the parties; but if harshness, violence, and grasping characterize it, then hate and distrust with collision arise, and love will not be found to bring the hearts of the people together. This is a rule of heaven, concerning which no one can have any doubt."

The authorities of Hakodadi had set apart and fenced off, for the interment of the American dead, a portion of a small, neglected burial ground, situated in an easterly direction, beyond the town and near the forts. The spot is exceedingly picturesque, and commands a fine view of the harbor, the Straits of Sangar, and the adjacent coasts. It was the melancholy duty of our countrymen to deposit there the remains of two of their shipmates, who, after a long illness, died during the stay of the squadron in that port. The funerals were conducted with the usual naval and religious ceremonies. After a short preliminary service on board ship, the escort, consisting of several officers, a number of seamen and marines, in four boats, conducted the bodies ashore, the boats and all the ships with flags at half-mast. On reaching the land, the procession was formed, and as it marched with slow step and muffled drums to the burial place, a large concourse of Japanese collected and followed it to the grave. The chaplain, the Rev. Mr. Jones, read the burial service of the Protestant Episcopal church, and, after the services had terminated, many of the natives gathered around him, and, although they evinced much curiosity, they never forgot the respect which they seemed to think due to his religious office. This was the fourth funeral among the Americans in Japan, and knowing the very strong prejudice against Christianity, and, indeed, the very violent opposition to it manifested by the Japanese, Mr. Jones had felt uncertain, when his duty required him to officiate at the first interment, how far he would be permitted to proceed unmolested. He accordingly asked the Commodore for directions, and was told, "Do exactly as you always do on such occasions, no more, nor no less;" and in answer to his inquiry how he should act if interrupted, the answer was, "still go on and have your usual service." No opposition, however, was made, and the chaplain felt that it was a day to be remembered, that, after the lapse of centuries, a minister of Christ stood, in his person, upon the soil of Japan, and, unmolested, performed one of the rites of his faith. He could not but remember, that, more than two hundred years before, it had been written in Japan, "so long as the sun shall warm the earth, let no Christian be so bold as to come to Japan; and let all know that the king of Spain himself, or the Christian's God, or the great God of all, if he violate this command, shall pay for it with his head." The first funeral was at Yoku-hama, the second at Simoda, and the last two at Hakodadi. Respect for the ceremonies was shown by the Japanese at all; and at the latter place the natives often alluded, in their intercourse with Mr. Jones, to his officiating at the grave, and called him, in their language, "the praying man;" and instead of losing standing among them from his office, as he expected to do, he found himself treated with increased friendliness and attention.

By the burial ground at Hakodadi, which was allotted to our countrymen and had been long used by the Japanese themselves, there is a Buddhist temple surrounded with an enclosure containing large roughly carved stones, intended to represent deities, and inscribed with various devices and religious apothegms. There are also several of the rotary praying machines, already described, and when the chaplain turned enquiringly to the apparatus, the Japanese put their hands together, signifying that it was intended for prayer, and then pointed to the prayer-book in Mr. Jones' hands, implying that it was used for the same purpose, an explanation which the good chaplain felt to be anything but a compliment to his much valued manual of devotion. By the way, on the subject of prayer, the chaplain had an opportunity to obtain further information. One day he wandered into a Buddhist temple when the Japanese were at worship. There was a large altar exactly similar to that in a Romish church, with a gilt image in its recess; two handsome lamps lighted, two large candles burning, artificial flowers, &c., with an abundance of gilding; there were also two side altars with candles on them burning. Before the principal altar, within an enclosure, were five priests, robed and on their knees, the chief one striking a small saucer-shaped bell, and three others with padded drumsticks striking hollow wooden lacquered vessels, which emitted a dull sound. They kept time, and toned their prayers to their music in chanting: after chanting, they knelt again, and touched the floor with their foreheads; after which they repaired to the side altars and had a short ceremony before each of them. When all was over, one of the priests approached, and, pointing to an image, asked Mr. Jones what it was called in America. He answered: "Nai," "we have it not." He then pointed to the altars and asked the same question, to which he received the same reply. When the chaplain left the temple, as he walked on, his official attendant asked him 'if the people prayed in America?' He was answered in the affirmative, and Mr. Jones, dropping on one knee, joined his hands, and, with upturned face, closed his eyes, and pointed to the heavens, to intimate by signs that we pray to a being there. He then asked his attendants if they prayed to that being? He replied: "Yes; we pray to Tien," their word for heaven or God.

To return to our narrative of matters connected with the funeral, it was found, in a few days after the interment of our countryman, that the Japanese authorities had caused to be erected a neat picket fence around the American graves, before it was known to our officers.*

After a farewell visit of ceremony on shore, and an interchange of courtesies and presents, (among which was a block of granite for the Washington monument,) the Powhatan and Mississippi, which were the only vessels of the squadron left, took their departure for Simoda

---

* The seamen of the Vandalia, to the crew of which ship the deceased had belonged, with a pious reverence for their departed shipmates sleeping in that distant land, erected a gravestone, upon which was inscribed an epitaph of their own composition, in the following words, cut by the Japanese in English letters from a copy furnished them:

"Sleeping on a foreign shore,
Rest, sailor, rest! thy trials o'er;
Thy shipmates leave this token here,
That some, perchance, may drop a tear
For one that braved so long the blast,
And served his country to the last."

The want of poetic inspiration in this humble tribute may well be forgiven for the sake of its mingled affection and patriotism. Poor Jack may not be able to *write* poetry, and yet his heart may feel as strongly as another man's those deep emotions of our nature which underlie the poet's work, when, "with his singing-robes about him," he soars aloft with his impassioned gushes of spirit-stirring song, or, it may be, in gentler mood, breathes, as it were, on Æolian harp-strings, making the sadder " music hat can move to tears."

on the 3d of June, 1854. The steamers, however, had hardly got under way at early sunrise, when they were obliged to anchor again at the mouth of the bay, in consequence of a dense fog. It was providential that the weather had remained clear a sufficient time to allow of securing some bearings for a safe anchorage. As the day advanced the fog was dissipated, and the two steamers, weighing again, got clear of the straits before night.

On the fifth day out, the smoke of the volcano of Oho-sima was discovered in the distance, and the land was soon distinctly made; but the weather becoming very thick from the rain and mist, it was found necessary to put the ships' heads off shore and continue under low steam during the night. The fog continuing while the ships were among the islands in the Gulf of Yedo, caused a delay of full twenty-four hours, and they consequently did not arrive at Simoda until the 7th of June, which, however, was one day before the time appointed for a meeting of the Commodore with the commissioners. Nothing of especial interest occurred during the passage. A very large number of whales was observed, and the strong eastward current was remarked as before.

At noon, the Powhatan, passing Vandalia bluff at the entrance of Simoda harbor, ran in and came to anchor in her former berth, followed by her consort the Mississippi. The store-ship Supply was found at anchor in the harbor. Shortly after anchoring, some of the Japanese officers came on board the flag-ship, and cordially welcoming the Commodore on his return to Simoda, informed him that the commissioners had arrived from Yedo with an addition of two to their number. As the Commodore was very desirous of completing his business with these functionaries, who, judging from past experience, would probably be somewhat slow in all their movements, he sent his flag-lieutenant on shore to propose an immediate interview. It was ascertained by this officer that the commissioners were out of town, but very soon after a message arrived, to the effect that they would return at once, and be in readiness to meet the Commodore the next day at noon.

The Commodore landed with a suitable escort on the next day, and was received at the temple by the commissioners, with the usual formal compliments. The two new members of the commission were presented by name and title as Tzudsuki, Suraga-no-kami, (prince of Suraga,) and Take-no-uchisetaro, comptroller of the revenues: the chief commissioner then stated that Simoda had been made an imperial city, and that Izawa, Prince of Mimasaki, and Tzudsuki had been appointed its governors, with Kura-kawa-kahei and Ise-sin-toheiro as lieutenant-governors. In consequence of this new organization the commissioners declared that it would be necessary to establish certain boundaries to the city by means of walls and gates, in order to define the limits of the imperial jurisdiction; and asked whether the Commodore would object to the erection of such, with the understanding that the Americans should have the privilege of going where and when they pleased within them, and beyond them, *on asking permission*, which permission would always readily be granted. The Commodore replied that he had no desire to interfere with any plans of the government, provided they did not violate the stipulations of the treaty; and, reminding them that the Americans had a perfect right, guarantied to them by that document, of moving unmolested within the limits of seven *li* or *ri*, said that, of course, he would leave what was beyond that distance to be governed by their own regulations.* It

---

* A *ri* is equal to $2\frac{153}{1000}$ English statute miles; 6 feet is equal to 1 ken; 60 kens make 1 choo; 36 choos make 1 ri. The fans of the Japanese are of uniform size, six of them making five English feet. They are used as measures, recognised by the laws.

was then mutually agreed that three American officers should accompany the Japanese officers appointed to affix the boundaries, and regulate the erection of the walls and gates at Simoda. The Commodore, however, positively refused to consent that Americans should ask any permission of the Japanese officers, or of any one else, to go anywhere within the limits of the seven *ri* fixed by the treaty, they, of course, conducting themselves properly and peaceably.

The great discussion, however, was concerning the boundaries within which our countrymen might go at Hakodadi. These had not yet been settled at all. The Japanese wished to confine Americans within the city itself; but as the Commodore protested most strongly against this, the subject was postponed for future consideration. The commissioners having stated that a special place had been set apart for the burial of Americans, asked permission to have the body of the man buried at Yoku-hama removed to Simoda. This was granted, and a promise made that proper persons from the squadron should be selected to assist in the removal.

The suggestion of the Commodore that pilots and a harbor-master be appointed was readily acceded to by the commissioners, who promised that suitable persons should be chosen and made acquainted with their duties. The conference then closed and was resumed on the following day, in the course of which the question again came up in regard to the limits at Hakodadi, but its settlement was, for the second time, postponed. A general conversation ensued over the refreshments with which the Japanese entertained their guests, in which the commissioners showed, by their enquiries, that lively interest which was uniformly exhibited among the educated classes in the events transpiring in different parts of the world. They were very curious to know something about the products and manufactures of the United States, and asked our views in regard to China and its revolution, and concerning the war between Russia and Turkey.

Another conference took place on the succeeding day, but without any definite result in regard to the limits at Hakodadi, although the question was discussed for several hours. An attempt was made by the commissioners to obtain the consent of the Commodore to a regulation prohibiting the Americans from remaining on shore after sunset, which was positively refused. Two (the newly appointed commissioners) had been chosen expressly to settle the question in regard to the comparative value of the Japanese and United States currencies, and Pursers Speiden and Eldridge were selected by the Commodore to confer with them on that subject. An important result ensued, embodied in an interesting and valuable report made by those gentlemen to the Commodore.*

After a succession of daily conferences, which continued from the 8th to the 17th of June, a mutual agreement was finally adjusted on the latter day, in regard to the various disputed

---

* The following correspondence embraces the official action on this point :

United States Flag-ship Powhatan, *Simoda, June* 12, 1854.

Gentlemen : You are hereby appointed to the duty of holding communication with certain Japanese officials delegated by the imperial government, in conformity with the treaty of Kanagawa, to arrange with officers, alike delegated by me, the rate of currency and exchange which shall for the present govern the payments to be made, by the several ships of the squadron, for articles that *have* been and *are* to be obtained ; also to establish, as far as can be, the price at which coal, per picul or ton, can be delivered on board at this port of Simoda.

It is not to be understood that the rate of currency or exchange which may be agreed upon at this time is to be permanent ; on the contrary, it is intended only to answer immediate purposes. Neither you nor myself are sufficiently acquainted with the purity and value of the Japanese coins to establish a fixed rate of exchange, even if I had the power to recognise such arrangement.

It will, however, be very desirable for you to make yourselves acquainted with all the peculiarities of the Japanese currency,

points of detail not specified in the treaty. These are embodied in the following additional regulations:

Additional regulations, agreed to between Commodore Matthew C. Perry, special envoy to Japan from the United States of America, and Hayashi Daigaku-no-kami; Ido, Prince of Tsus-sima; Izawa, Prince of Mimasaki; Tsudzuki, Prince of Suruga; Udono, member of the board of revenue; Take-no-uchi Sheitaro, and Matsusaki Michitaro, commissioners of the Emperor of Japan, on behalf of their respective governments.

ARTICLE I.—The imperial governors of Simoda will place watch stations wherever they deem best, to designate the limits of their jurisdiction; but Americans are at liberty to go through

---

and also, if practicable, with the laws appertaining thereto, as the information will be valuable in facilitating all future negotiations upon the subject.

You will, of course, before entering into any agreement which may be considered binding, refer to me.

Very respectfully, your obedient servant,

M. C. PERRY,
Commander-in-chief of the United States Naval Forces in the East India and China Seas.

Purser WILLIAM SPEIDEN, *United States Navy.*
Purser J. C. ELDRIDGE, *United States Navy.*

UNITED STATES STEAM-FRIGATE POWHATAN, *Simoda, June* 15, 1854.

SIR: The committee appointed by you, in your letter of the 12th instant, to confer with a committee from the Japanese commissioners in reference to the rate of exchange and currency between the two nations in the trade at the ports opened, and to settle the price of coal to be delivered at this port, beg leave to report:

The Japanese committee, it was soon seen, came to the conference with their minds made up to adhere to the valuation they had already set upon our coins, even if the alternative was the immediate cessation of trade. The basis upon which they made their calculation was the nominal rate at which the government sells bullion when it is purchased from the mint, and which seems also to be that by which the metal is received from the mines. The Japanese have a decimal system of weight, like the Chinese, of catty, tael, mace, candareen, and cash, by which articles in general are weighed; but gold and silver are not reckoned above taels. In China, a tael of silver, in weight, and one in currency are the same, for the Chinese have no silver coin; but in Japan, as in European countries, the standard of value weight and that of currency weight differ. We were told that a tael weight of silver has now come to be reckoned, when it is bullion, as equal to 225 candareens, or 2 taels, 2 mace, 5 candareens; but, when coined, the same amount in weight is held to be worth 6 taels, 4 mace. It is at the bullion value that the government has decided to receive our dollar, the same at which they take the silver from the mines; asserting that, as its present die and assay give it no additional value, it is worth no more to them. In proportion to a tael a dollar weighs 7 mace, 1 1-5 candareen, which, at the rates of bullion value, makes it worth 1 tael, 6 mace, or 1,600 cash. Thus the Japanese government will make a profit of 66⅔ per cent. on every dollar paid them of full weight, with the trifling deduction of the expense of re-coining it. The injustice of this arrangement was shown, and the propriety of paying to the seller himself the coin we gave at this depreciated rate urged, but in vain.

For gold the rate is more, as the disparity between the value of bullion and that of coin, among the Japanese, is not so great. A tael weight of gold is valued at 19 taels in currency, and a mace at 1 tael, 9 mace. The gold dollar weighs almost 5 candareens, but the Japanese have reckoned it as the twentieth part of a $20 piece, which they give as 8 mace, 8 candareens; and, consequently, the dollar is only 4 candareens, 4 cash. This weight brings the gold dollar, when compared with the tael of bullion gold worth 19 taels, to be worth 836 cash, and the $20 piece to be worth 16,720 cash, or 16 taels, 7 mace, 2 candareens. Thus, when converted into a silver value, makes a gold dollar worth 52¼ cents, and a $20 piece worth $10.45, at which the Japanese propose to take them. But this valuation of the gold dollar at 52¼ cents, when reckoned at 836 cash, its assessed value by the Japanese government, suffers the same depreciation as our silver; and its real value, when compared with the inflated currency in use among the people, is only about 17¼ cents. Consequently, by this estimate, gold becomes 50 per cent. worse for us to pay in than silver. The currency value of a gold dollar, taking the *ichibu* as of equal purity, and comparing them weight for weight, is only 1,045 cash, or nearly 22 cents in silver; so that the actual depreciation on the part of the Japanese is not so great as silver—being for the two metals, when weighed with each other, for silver as 100 to 33⅓, and for gold as 22 to 17. The elements of this comparison are not quite certain, and therefore its results are somewhat doubtful; but the extraordinary discrepancy of both metals, compared with our coins and with their own copper coins, shows how the government has inflated the whole monetary system in order to benefit itself.

The parties could come to no agreement, as we declined to consent to the proposals of the Japanese, who were decided to adhere to their valuation of a silver dollar at 1 tael, 6 mace, or 1,600 cash; neither would they consent to do justly by us in relation to the moneys paid them at this place before our departure for Hakodadi, at the rate of only 1 tael, 2 mace, or 1,200

them, unrestricted, within the limits of seven Japanese ri, or miles; and those who are found transgressing Japanese laws may be apprehended by the police and taken on board their ships.

ARTICLE II.—Three landing-places shall be constructed for the boats of merchant ships and whale-ships resorting to this port; one at Simoda, one at Kakizaki, and the third at the brook lying southeast of Centre Island. The citizens of the United States will, of course, treat the Japanese officers with proper respect.

ARTICLE III.—Americans, when on shore, are not allowed access to military establishments or private houses without leave; but they can enter shops and visit temples as they please.

ARTICLE IV.—Two temples, the Rioshen at Simoda, and the Yokushen at Kakizaki, are assigned as resting-places for persons in their walks, until public houses and inns are erected for their convenience.

ARTICLE V.—Near the temple Yokushen, at Kakizaki, a burial-ground has been set apart for Americans, where their graves and tombs shall not be molested.

ARTICLE VI.—It is stipulated in the treaty of Kanagawa, that coal will be furnished at Hakodadi; but as it is very difficult for the Japanese to supply it at that port, Commodore Perry promises to mention this to his government, in order that the Japanese government may be relieved from the obligation of making that port a coal depot.

ARTICLE VII.—It is agreed that henceforth the Chinese language shall not be employed in official communications between the two governments, except when there is no Dutch interpreter.

ARTICLE VIII.—A harbor-master and three skilful pilots have been appointed for the port of Simoda.

ARTICLE IX.—Whenever goods are selected in the shops, they shall be marked with the name of the purchaser and the price agreed upon, and then be sent to the Goyoshi, or government office, where the money is to be paid to Japanese officers, and the articles delivered by them.

ARTICLE X.—The shooting of birds and animals is generally forbidden in Japan, and this law is therefore to be observed by all Americans.

ARTICLE XI.—It is hereby agreed that five Japanese ri, or miles, be the limit allowed to Americans at Hakodadi, and the requirements contained in Article I, of these Regulations, are hereby made also applicable to that port within that distance.

ARTICLE XII.—His Majesty the Emperor of Japan is at liberty to appoint whoever he pleases to receive the ratification of the treaty of Kanagawa, and give an acknowledgment on his part.

---

cash, to the dollar, by which they had made a profit of 75 per cent. on each dollar, stating that the money paid them at this rate had passed out of their hands; and, moreover, that the prices placed upon the articles furnished had been charged at reduced prices with reference to the low value placed upon the dollar.

For the amount due and unsettled, for supplies received at Yoku-hama, and on account of which Purser Eldridge paid Moryama Yenoske, imperial interpreter, $350 in gold and silver, that they might be assayed and tested at Yedo, they consent to receive the dollar at the valuation now placed on them; that is, at the rate of 1,600 cash for the silver dollar.

We carefully investigated the price of the coal to be delivered to vessels in this port. We learn that 10,000 catties or 100 piculs have arrived; and this, at the rate of 1,680 catties to a ton of 2,240 pounds, or 16 4-5 piculs, costs 262 taels, 6 mace, 5 candareens, 3 cash, or $164 16; making the rate to be $27 91 per ton. The Japanese state that the price of coal would be considerably reduced as the demand for it increased, and their facilities for mining became more perfect.

In conclusion, we take pleasure in expressing our thanks to Messrs. Williams and Portman, whose services as interpreters were indispensable, and from whom we received important aid in our investigations.

We have the honor to be, respectfully, your obedient servants,

WILLIAM SPEIDEN, *Purser United States Navy.*
J. C. ELDRIDGE, *Purser United States Navy.*

Commodore M. C. PERRY,
Commander-in-chief of the United States Naval Forces in the East India and China Seas.

It is agreed that nothing herein contained shall in any way affect or modify the stipulations of the treaty of Kanagawa, should that be found to be contrary to these regulations.

In witness whereof, copies of these additional regulations have been signed and sealed in the English and Japanese languages by the respective parties, and a certified translation in the Dutch language, and exchanged by the commissioners of the United States and Japan.

SIMODA, JAPAN, *June* 17, 1854.

M. C. PERRY,
Commander-in-chief of the U. S. Naval Forces, East India, China, and Japan Seas, and Special Envoy to Japan.

These regulations were agreed to on the part of the commissioners only after a very hard struggle. The question of limits to the Americans, both at Simoda and Hakodadi, was the one most difficult of adjustment, in consequence, as it appeared, of the trouble in reconciling the imperial and local jurisdictions. The commissioners urged that the authority of the Empire did not extend as far as the seven Japanese *ri*, or sixteen English miles, guarantied to the Americans by the treaty of Kanagawa. The Japanese officers had pointed out three positions to the American officers, who had been designated by the Commodore to be present, as the sites for the gates and walls. Neither of these was distant more than a mile and a half from Centre Island, the starting point agreed upon from which to mark the boundary. The gates were finally erected at the spots indicated, when the commissioners formally proposed that the Commodore should now assent to a regulation making it necessary for Americans desiring to pass beyond them to obtain permission first from the Japanese officer on duty. But the Commodore peremptorily refused, and was firm in resisting all efforts, great or small, to weaken, in the slightest degree, the concessions already made to the Americans by the treaty. He intimated, however, a willingness to assent to such regulations as were undoubtedly necessary to govern the Japanese authorities as well as the Americans; but as for modifying or in any way altering the treaty, he wished them distinctly to understand that it was entirely impossible. In regard to the limits at Hakodadi, the commissioners at first wished to confine them to one street, then to the whole town, then to the projecting promontory extending toward the sea, next to three Japanese ri, and then to three and a half. They thus contested the ground, inch by inch. The Commodore proposed that the Americans should enjoy the same extent of boundary as had been granted at Simoda; but this was so pertinaciously opposed that it was thought expedient to compromise for five Japanese *ri*, or twelve English miles; and as the country in the neighborhood of Hakodadi is mountainous and sparsely settled, this restriction will prove of no great consequence. Nothing, however, was more apparent than that the Japanese, admonished by their old Portuguese experience, were exceedingly reluctant to allow Christian foreigners to come among them at all, even for temporary purposes.

The Japanese authorities had, in accordance with their agreement, supplied the steamers at Simoda with some of their native coal. It had been brought from their mines, at considerable trouble and expense, in hampers made of rice-straw. Notwithstanding the country is said to produce large quantities of this mineral, and the people are reported to have been long familiar with its uses, the coal they supplied appeared to be surface coal, and to have been obtained from mines which had not been opened thoroughly and worked. On being tried on board the steamers, the engineers reported that it was of a quality so inferior that they were unable to keep up steam with it. They have, however, very good coal, and the experiments practically made on specimens brought home by the squadron give the following results. A careful chemical analysis made at the navy yard laboratory, Brooklyn, will be found in the Appendix.

"NAVY YARD, NEW YORK, *January* 8, 1856.

"SIR: In compliance with your order of November 5, to subject to suitable tests samples of Japan and Formosa coals, with a view to ascertain their respective qualities as fuel, we respectfully report, as follows, viz:

"As both the Japan and Formosa coals are of bituminous character, we have used, as a standard of comparison, the best quality of Cumberland coal, and conducted the test upon a scale sufficiently large, that incidental causes, of a minor character, always attending experiments, would not be likely to materially affect the correctness of the results obtained.

"The test was made in a boiler of the drop-flue form, having thirty-nine square feet of grate surface. The engine worked from this boiler has a cylinder of thirty-six inches diameter, with four feet length of stroke, and operates the machinery in the machine shop of this yard; the work is so nearly equal, at each moment of time, that the resistance may be considered constant.

"The experiments were conducted for consecutive days with the different kinds of coal, and the quantity consumed at the expiration of each day's work accurately noted, which was required to maintain as nearly an equal pressure of steam as possible.

"The following table embraces the results obtained of the comparative evaporative effect of the two coals, and also the comparative stowage:

CUMBERLAND COAL.

Date.	Hour.	Steam pressure.	Remarks.	Date.	Hour.	Steam pressure.	Remarks.
1855. Dec. 27	8 A. M.	14		1855. Dec. 28	8 A. M.	15	
	9 A. M.	15			9 A. M.	16	
	10 A. M.	15			10 A. M.	15	
	11 A. M.	13			11 A. M.	14	
	12 A. M.	14			12 A. M.	15	
	1 P. M.	15	Coal consumed, 1,900 lbs.		1 P. M.	13	Coal consumed, 1,950 lbs.
	2 P. M.	13			2 P. M.	15	
	3 P. M.	14			3 P. M.	14	
	4 P. M.	14			4 P. M.	14	
	4.30 P. M.	15			4.30 P. M.	13	40 cubic feet displaced for one ton of coal.

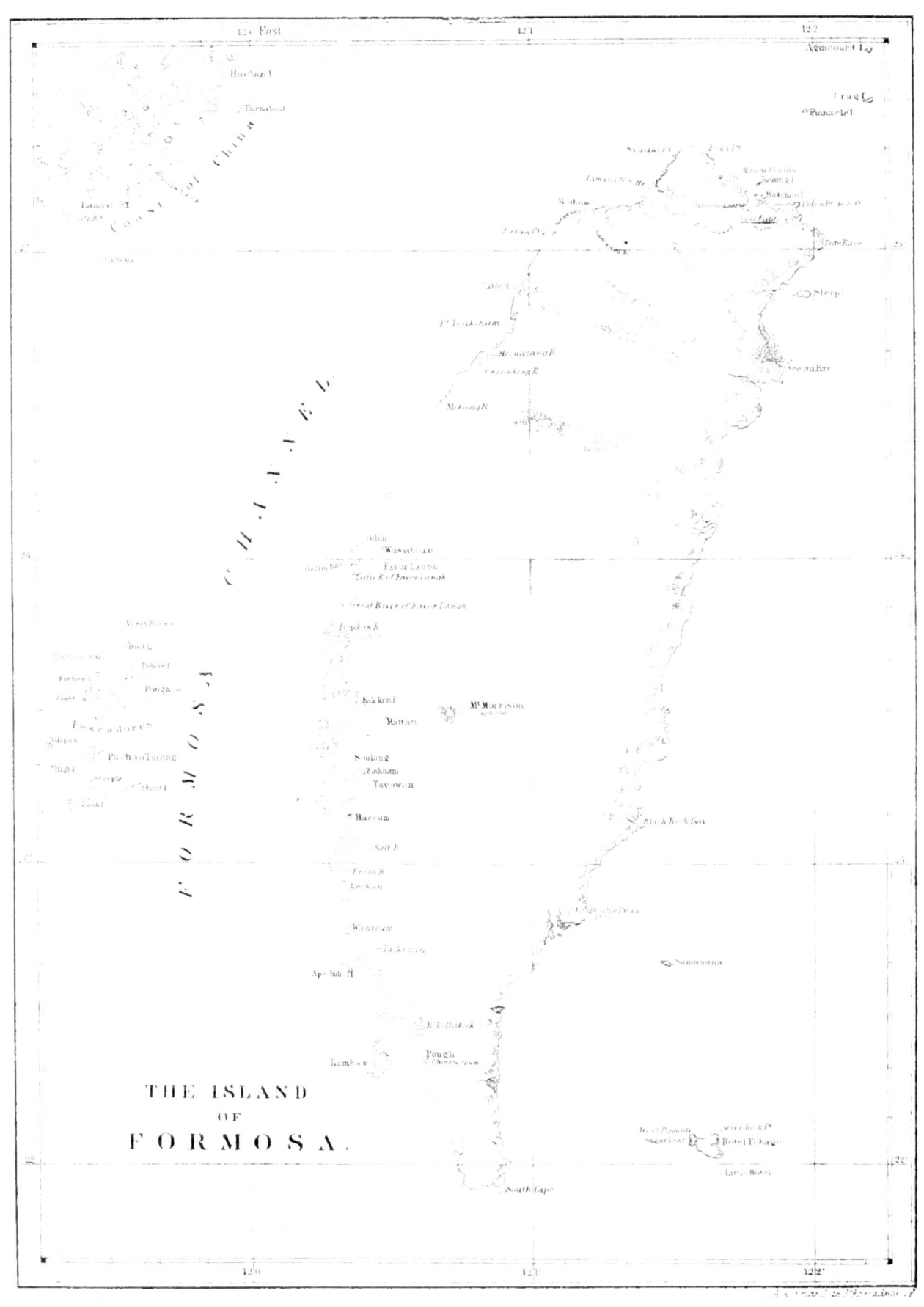

FORMOSA COAL.

Date.	Hour.	Steam pressure.	Remarks.	Date.	Hour.	Steam pressure.	Remarks.
1855. Dec. 29	8 A. M.	16		1855. Dec. 31	8 A. M.	16	
	9 A. M.	14			9 A. M.	15	
	10 A. M.	13			10 A. M.	14	
	11 A. M.	15			11 A. M.	14	
	12 A. M.	13			12 A. M.	13	
	1 P. M.	14	Coal consumed, 2,957 lbs.		1 P. M.	15	Coal consumed, 3,036 lbs.
	2 P. M.	16			2 P. M.	14	
	3 P. M.	13			3 P. M.	14	
	4 P. M.	14			4 P. M.	13	
	4.30 P. M.	14			4.30 P. M.	14	40 cubic feet displaced for one ton of coal.

JAPAN COAL.

Date.	Hour.	Steam pressure.	Remarks.	Date.	Hour.	Steam pressure.	Remarks.
1856. Jan. 2	8 A. M.	14		1856. Jan. 3	8 A. M.	12	
	9 A. M.	13			9 A. M.	13	
	10 A. M.	13			10 A. M.	14	
	11 A. M.	12			11 A. M.	13	
	12 A. M.	14			12 A. M.	14	
	1 P. M.	13	Coal consumed, 3,700 lbs.		1 P. M.	15	Coal consumed, 3,643 lbs.
	2 P. M.	15			2 P. M.	14	
	3 P. M.	14			3 P. M.	14	
	4 P. M.	14			4 P. M.	15	
	4.30 P. M.	13			4.30 P. M.	14	37 cubic feet displaced for one ton of coal.

"The Formosa coal burns freely, leaving but a small amount of ashes and scoria.

"The Japan coal produces considerable scoria and ashes. The sample of this coal was taken from the out-croppings of the vein, and will, undoubtedly yield a much superior quality at a greater depth.

"JESSE GAY, *Chief Engineer*.
"WILLIAM E. EVERETT, *Chief Engineer*.

"Captain ABRAHAM BIGELOW,
"*Commandant Navy Yard, New York.*"

Whether the shrewd Japanese supplied an inferior quality to deceive their visitors, or whether from ignorance of the article and want of mining skill they innocently brought that which was inferior, cannot be certainly decided; but as good coal certainly exists in Japan, and as the natives not only use it, but, according to Von Siebold, know very well how to mine it, the probabilities are that they purposely furnished the poorest samples. When the Preble was at Nagasaki, and they saw the armorer on board at work at his forge, they pretended that they did not know what coal was, and actually took a piece on shore as a curiosity, expressing, with well feigned astonishment, their surprise at seeing a "stone" that would burn. The coal that was obtained was charged at the enormous rate of about $28 per ton; but the Japanese stated that the price would be probably much reduced as the demand for it increased, and their facilities for obtaining it improved. We are inclined to think, after a careful examination of the particulars of the interviews and conferences with them on all topics, that on no one subject did they misrepresent more unscrupulously than on that of coal. There is no doubt that they have an abundance, and some of it very good.

As the negotiations with the commissioners had now terminated, the Commodore prepared for his final departure, and accordingly was desirous of settling the accounts of the ships with the local authorities. Proper officers were accordingly sent on shore to receive from the governor a statement, with the prices of the various articles with which the squadron had been furnished.*

Among other accounts was a bill for spars, which had been ordered previous to leaving for Hakodadi; but upon investigation it was found that, although charged, they had not yet been prepared or delivered, and that even the trees from which they were to be made had not yet been cut down. The bazaar had also been opened for several days, and was supplied with the various articles of Japanese manufacture which the Americans desired to purchase and take home as memorials of the expedition. The prices charged, however, were so exorbitant that the Commodore was obliged to protest against the conduct of the authorities in this respect, and to rebuke them for the neglect, not to call it by a harsher term, in not having the spars ready, although they had been charged for as if furnished.

The protest and complaints of the Commodore having been laid before the governor, Prince Agawa, that functionary sent Moryama Yenoske, the interpreter, on board the flag-ship with a respectful rejoinder to the effect that the prices of articles offered for sale in the bazaar had been arranged at Yedo, and that they were not above the usual market valuation. It was then explained by the flag-lieutenant that, although the prices in Chinese "*cash*" might not appear exorbitant to the Japanese, yet that they were really so to the Americans, who were obliged to pay in dollars, at a depreciation much below their value. Moryama Yenoske explained the affair of the spars by declaring that *he* was responsible for what he was pleased to term the error, as he supposed that all the Commodore had asked for was the *cost* of spars, and did not understand that an order had been given for a supply of them. Subsequently, the Commodore

---

* The cost of the various supplies, which are those ordinarily required by foreign vessels, is here given, as it may be of interest and value to future navigators.

PRICES OF SUPPLIES AT SIMODA.

1,200 Cash = $1.		Six fans = 5 English feet.	
Wood	$6 75.	1 spar, 82 fans long, diameter 1 fan 3.6-10 inches	$108 80
Eggs	7 for 10 cents.	2 spars, 50 fans 6 inches long, diameter 8 inches	27 00
Chickens	39 cents each.	2 ditto, 73 fans 7 in. long, diameter 1 fan 2.8-10 in.	176 10
Fish	from 17½ to 89 cents each.	2 ditto, 47 fans 3 inches long, diameter 8 inches	25 50
Cray-fish	3½ cents each.	2 ditto, 52 fans 8 inches long, diameter 8 inches	27 00
Ditto	11½ cents per cattee.	2 ditto, 39 fans 6 inches long, diameter 6.4-10 inches	10 40
Cabbage	18 cents per sack.	2 ditto, 55 fans long, diameter 8 inches	30 00
Radishes	12½ cents per sack.	1 ditto, 66 fans long, diameter 1 fan 1.2-10 inches	54 40
Potatoes	38 cents per sack.	1 ditto, 44 fans long, diameter 7.2-10 inches	7 80
Onions	10 cents per sack.	2 ditto, 49 fans long, diameter 8 inches	25 50
(The sack holds a little more than an English bushel.)		2 ditto, 46 fans long, diameter 7.2-10 inches	19 50
		2 ditto, 30 fans 8 5-10 in. long, diameter 7.2-10 in.	13 00
		2 ditto, 49 fans 5 in. long, diameter 1 fan 1.2-10 in.	95 20
		2 ditto, 33 fans long, diameter 4 8-10 inches	71 49
		2 ditto, 55 fans long, diameter 1 fan 2.8-10 inches	163 20

TATSNOSKÉ AND HIS INTERPRETER.

and some of his officers went on shore and partook of a handsome collation, at the earnest solicitation of the commissioners, who, on the occasion, made an ample apology for the various errors and misunderstandings which had interrupted the friendly intercourse between the Americans and the authorities. The Commodore explained that it was a principle he had been contending for, and not the comparatively unimportant consideration of a few hundred dollars, more or less, as his government had placed ample means in his hands, and he was disposed to pay liberally for all he had; but neither the United States nor he were at all willing to be imposed upon. Moryama Yenoske, who was always the most active of all the officials, and was now the chief spokesman, said that the Americans might purchase any articles they pleased at their own valuation. This offer was, of course, rejected; and Yenoske then assumed, in behalf of himself and his fellow-interpreter, Tatsnoske, the whole blame, not only in regard to the spars, but the exorbitant prices and all the other wrongs which had given rise to complaint. Indeed, these two worthy gentlemen seemed to be convenient mediums through which their superiors might render a vicarious expiation for their offences. They were ever ready to shoulder all the responsibility for anything wrong. Yenoske, however, was very civilly told that, although the Commodore could appreciate the self-sacrificing devotion with which he shouldered all the blame, yet that it was not a victim that was sought, but merely a correction of certain evil practices which, if not checked in the beginning, might lead to disaffection and serious quarrel. A perfect reconciliation then ensued, which was appropriately sealed by a present from the commissioners of a block of stone for the Washington monument, which was to be carried to the United States as a tribute from Japan to the memory of the great father of our republic. Nothing afterwards occurred to interrupt friendly relations, and frequent intercourse, which grew more and more intimate as the day of departure approached, took place with all classes on shore. Handsome presents were exchanged, and some choice articles of Japanese manufacture were received from the authorities as gifts for the President and for the officers of the ships. Among the gifts were three Japanese dogs, sent to the President. These were of the small spaniel breed, already alluded to, very highly esteemed in Japan, and purchasable only at a very large price. The Commodore succeeded in bringing them to the United States, and they now thrive at Washington. The Commodore obtained two for himself, one only of which reached the United States.

A few days previous to the departure of the Commodore, Moryama Yenoske, in company with several other officials, came on board the Powhatan to request that the Japanese "Sam Patch," of whom we have spoken, should be allowed to remain in Japan. They were told that the Commodore had no objection whatever to the man's remaining, if he wished; but that it must be by his own free will, and that the commissioners must give a written pledge that the man should not, in any way, be punished for his absence from Japan. Moreover, as he had suffered shipwreck, and had been thrown, by God's providence, on American protection, and had entered on board an American ship by his own choice, he was entitled to all the protection and security of an American citizen; consequently the Commodore could allow of no coercion being resorted to to make the man remain in Japan. The Japanese officials ridiculed the idea of his suffering any harm or hurt by his remaining in Japan, and said that the commissioners would cheerfully give any guarantee required that he should in no way be molested, but be allowed at once to return to his friends, who were very anxious to see him. Sam was now called up, but all the eloquence and persuasiveness of the Japanese were insufficient to induce him to leave the ship. The truth is that Sam never, during the whole stay of the squadron in Japan, appeared fully to understand the independence and safety of his position. Long habit had so impressed upon him the cowardice of trembling servility before his superiors in Japan, that it was very obvious the interview with the officials produced no emotion but abject fear. He fell on his knees before them after the manner of his country, and would have remained in that position if Lieutenant Bent, who was determined that no such obsequiousness should be shown on the deck of an American man-of-war, and under the flag of the United States, to anything wearing the human form, had not peremptorily ordered him immediately to rise to his feet.

Sam had taken his place as one of the crew, and had won the goodwill of his shipmates generally by his good nature. All pitied his misfortunes, and one of the marines named Goble, a religious man, had taken a special interest in him; finding in his docility and intelligence promise of good fruit from a properly directed religious training, Goble had begun with him a system of instruction which he hoped would not only make the Japanese a fair English scholar, but a faithful Christian. Sam came to the United States in the Mississippi, and accompanied his benevolent shipmate and devoted teacher to his home in the interior of New York, where Goble has property. At the last accounts they were living there together, and it is not unreasonable to hope that Sam, with the education of his faithful American friend, may be an instrument, in the event of his return to Japan, under a further development of our relations with that Empire, of aiding in the introduction of a higher and better civilization into his own country.

It will be recollected that, of the several Japanese who had been picked up on the coast of California and taken to Shanghai, with the view of restoring them to their own country, Sam Patch was the only one who accompanied the expedition to Japan. The rest were all afraid, and Sam went with fear and trembling. On the return of the Mississippi to China, on her way home, another of the Japanese expressed a wish to visit the United States, and was gratified in his desire; this was the young man whom we have mentioned on a former page. His Japanese name is something like *Dans-Kevitch*; but the sailors, with their usual fondness for christening those adopted into their roving family, soon called him *Dan Ketch*. It was fortunate for the poor fellow that he escaped the more usual nautical cognomen of *Jack*; for that, however respectable in itself, would have made a much less reputable combination in union with the Americo-Japanese *Ketch*; and poor Dan might have found himself undesirably elevated to the office of a hangman, without precisely understanding the process which conferred the unenviable rank. Dan is under the protection of the Commodore, and evinces great intelligence with an eager desire for knowledge. Should he ever return to Japan, as at present he purposes, after learning more about us, he will doubtless carry home with him no small amount of information about our country.

The Commodore now transferred his broad pennant from the Powhatan back to the Mississippi, and the two steamers got under way and moved down to the outer roads of Simoda, where they anchored preparatory to their final departure. Moryama Yenoske, in company with some of the other officials, paid a farewell visit to the Commodore on that day, bringing with him the closing accounts of the ships, and some specimens of natural history as presents. A handsome entertainment was spread before the visitors in the cabin, and in the course of the friendly conversation around the table, a Japanese picture, representing the punishment of crucifixion, was shown to Yenoske. This had been purchased at Simoda, by some of our officers, and

FROM AN ORIGINAL JAPANESE DRAWING OBTAINED IN CHINA.

its presence turned the conversation on the subject of capital punishments in Japan. The Commodore was glad of the opportunity to procure accurate information on this point, inasmuch as some writers, later than Kaempfer, have denied his statement that crucifixion is a Japanese mode of execution. Yenoske said that the picture itself was illustrative merely of a scene in one of their popular farces; but, he added, that regicides were executed somewhat in the manner represented in the picture, being first nailed to a cross and then transfixed with a spear. In the picture, the man was merely *tied* to the cross. Decapitation, however, he said, was the usual mode of capital punishment for murderers, but never strangulation or hanging. Upon Yenoske being asked if the practice of the Hari-kari or "Happy dispatch" still prevailed, he replied that one of his fellow interpreters had committed suicide in that way, in his presence, while at Nagasaki. The Commodore then inquired if it were true that the governor of Nagasaki had destroyed himself, after the visit of Captain Pellew in 1808; and Yenoske declared that not only the governor had done so, but that two other high officers and ten subordinates had followed his example. The Japanese, after a prolonged conviviality, took their farewell of the Americans, with many expressions of warm attachment to their visitors, and pulled off for the land.

The ships were now all in readiness for departure. The Southampton, which had arrived from Volcano Bay on the tenth of June, and had discharged her cargo of coal into the steamers, the Macedonian, which reached Simoda on the eleventh, and the store-ship Supply that had been stationary in that port for several months, with the Mississippi, now the flag-ship, and the Powhatan, composed the whole squadron, and were anchored in the outer bay, preparatory to sailing for their respective destinations. Arrangements had been made to carry out the regulations agreed to with the authorities in regard to the appointment of a harbor-master and three pilots, and these now, at the last moment, were completed by the signature of Kura-kawa-kahei, the deputy-governor, to a written contract,* copies of which were made in English and Dutch,

---

* *Regulations respecting pilots, and the supplying of American vessels entering the port of Simoda.*

A look-out place shall be established at some convenient point, from which vessels appearing in the offing can be seen and reported, and when one is discovered making apparently for the harbor, a boat shall be sent to her with a pilot.

And in order to carry this regulation into full effect, boats of suitable size and quality shall always be kept in readiness by the harbor-master, which, if necessary, shall proceed beyond Rock island, to ascertain whether the vessel in sight intends entering the harbor or not. If it may be the desire of the master of said vessel to enter port, the pilot shall conduct her to safe anchorage, and during her stay shall render every assistance in his power in facilitating the procurement of all the supplies she may require.

The rates of pilotage shall be: for vessels drawing over 18 American feet, fifteen dollars; for all vessels drawing over 13 and less than 18 feet, ten dollars; and for all vessels under 13 feet, five dollars.

These rates shall be paid in gold or silver coin, or its equivalent in goods, and the same shall be paid for piloting a vessel out as well as into port.

When vessels anchor in the outer harbor, and do not enter the inner port, only half the above rates of compensation shall be paid to the pilot.

The prices for supplying water to American vessels at Simoda shall be fourteen hundred cash per boat-load, (the casks being furnished by the vessel.) And for wood delivered on board, about seven thousand two hundred cash per cube of five American feet.

SILAS BENT, *Flag Lieutenant.*
KURA-KAWA-KAHEI, *Lieutenant Governor.*

UNITED STATES STEAM-FRIGATE MISSISSIPPI, *at Sea, June 28, 1854.*

Approved:
M. C. PERRY,
Commander-in-chief United States Naval Forces East India, China, and Japan Seas.

UNITED STATES STEAM-FRIGATE MISSISSIPPI, *Simoda, Japan, June 23, 1854.*

Bepalingen met betrekking tot loodsen, en het leveren van benodigdheden aan Amerikaansche schepen in den haven van Simoda.

Op eene daartoe geschikte plaats zal een uitkyk worden opgerigt van waar schepen in de nabyheid komende kunnen worden

and deposited with the Japanese officials at Simoda. The harbor-master and the pilots, after having been selected by the local authorities, were brought to the Commodore for his confirmation of their appointment. The Commodore, having signified his approval of the choice, gave to the harbor-master a spy-glass, to be kept always at the look-out place and to

---

gezien, alsdan zal de overheid daarvan verwittigd, en een boot met een loods aan boord naar het schip afgezonden worden als hetzelve naar deze haven schynt te komen.

Ten einde deze bepaling ten volle uit te voeren zullen booten van genoegzame grootte altyd door den havenmeester in gereedheid worden gehouden, welke booten als zulks nodig mogt zyn zoover als Rots eiland (Mikomoto Sima) zullen gaan om te onderzoeken of het schip in gezigt al of niet in den haven zal komen. Als nu de schipper van zulk een schip den haven wil binnen loopen, zal de loods hetzelve naar een veilige ankerplaats brengen, en gedurende deszelfs verblyf aldaar al het mogolyke aanwenden, om het verkrygen van wat hetzelve nodig mogt hebben, gemakkelyk te maken.

Het loon van den loods zal zyn voor schepen meer den achttien Amerikaansche voeten diep in het water, vyftien dollars ; voor schepen meer dan dertien en minder dan achttien voeten diep in het water, tien dollars ; en vyf dollars voor schepen minder dan dertien Amerikaansche voeten diep in het water.

Dit loon zal betaald worden in gouden of zilveren munt, of met eene gelyke waarde in goederen en eveneel zal betaald worden voor het uitloodsen, als voor het naar binnen loodsen.

Als schepen niet in den binnen haven komen, doch in den buiten haven ten anker gaan, zal alleen de helft van de hierboven vastgestelde loonen worden betaald.

Amerikaansche schepen in den haven van Simoda, zullen kunnen verkrygen water aan boord tegen veertien honderd pitjes (cash) voor een volgeladen boot, (de watervaten door het schip geleend wordende) en brandhout aan boord geleverd voor ongeveer zeven duizend twee honderd pitjes per kubiek iki, of kubick van vyf Amerikaansche voeten.

SILAS BENT, *Luitenant Adjudant.*
KURAKAWA KAHEI, *Luitenant Gouverneur.*

Goedgekeurd : M. C. PERRY,
Opperbevelhebber van de Oorlogsmagt van de Vereenig de Staten in de zeeen van Oost Indie, China, en Japan.

Eene ware vertaling, A. L. C. PORTMAN.
V. S. Stoom-Fregat Mississippi, *Simoda, Japan, den 23sten Juny,* 1854.

United States Steam-Frigate Mississippi, *at Sea, June* 27, 1854.

This is to certify that Yohatsi, Hikoyemon, and Dshirobe have been appointed pilots for American vessels entering or departing from the port of Simoda, and that the following rates for pilotage have been established by the proper authorities, viz:

For vessels drawing over eighteen American feet.. $15 00
For vessels drawing over thirteen and less than eighteen feet............................ 10 00
For vessels drawing under thirteen feet... 5 00

These rates shall be paid in gold or silver coin, or its equivalent in goods ; and the same shall be paid for piloting vessels out as well as into port.

When vessels anchor in the outer roads, and do not enter the inner harbor, only half the above rates of compensation shall be paid to the pilots.

By order of the Commander-in-chief:

SILAS BENT, *Flag Lieutenant.*

Approved : M. C. PERRY,
Commander-in-chief of the United States Naval Forces in the East India, China, and Japan Seas.

United States Steam-Frigate Mississippi, *Simoda, Island of Niphon, Japan, June* 22, 1854.

Dit dient om te verklaren, dat Yohatsi, Hikoyemon, en Dshirobe benoemd zyn als loodsen voor schepen van de Vereenigde Staten de haven van Simoda binnenkomende, of uitgaande ; en dat het loon voor de loodsen door de bevoegde overheid is vasgesteld geworden als volgt :

Voor schepen over 18 Amerikaansche voeten diep in het water............................... $15 00
Voor schepen over 13 en minder dan 18 voeten diep.. 10 00
Voor schepen onder 13 Am: voeten deip.. 5 00

Dit loen zal betaald worden in gouden of zilveren munt of met eene gelyke waarde in goederen ; en hetzelfde zal betaald worden voor het binnen komen als wel als voor het uitgaan.

Als schepen in den buitenhaven ankeren er niet naar binnen gaan, zal alleen de helft van de hierboven vastgestelde loonen worden betaald.

Op last van den Opperbevelhebber :

SILAS BENT, *Luitenant Adjudant.*

M. C. PERRY,
Opperbevelhebber van de Oorlogsmagt van de Vereenig de Staten in de zeeen van Oost Indie, China, en Japan.

Eene ware vertaling, A. L. C. PORTMAN.
V. S. Stoom-Fregat Mississippi, *Simoda, Japan den 22sten Juny,* 1854.

pass to his successor in office; to each of the pilots a comfortable overcoat and two American ensigns, to be displayed on board the pilot-boats when going to any vessels that may appear off the harbor. The surveyors had marked the rocks, buoys, and prominent headlands with signal flags, but as the Japanese authorities objected to them as seeming to imply some evidence of right to possession, it was readily conceded that the Japanese should substitute for them their little white and black striped flags.

On the morning of the 28th of June, 1854, the whole squadron got under way; but the wind shifting to the southward, the Macedonian and Supply were obliged to anchor again. The Commodore, accordingly, ordered these vessels to warp into a safe berth, and sail when the wind and weather should permit, and to keep company, if possible, to Kelung, in Formosa, where they were bound. There seemed no occasion to wait for them, as their destination was different, and any further delay on the part of the steamers would only result in an unnecessary consumption of coal; so the Mississippi and the Powhatan, with the Southampton in tow, stood out to sea and shaped a course to the southward and westward.

In passing out beyond Rock Island, a high sea was encountered, which gave additional proof that the outer as well as the inner harbor of Simoda is perfectly safe. The violence of the sea being in a considerable degree broken by the ledge of rocks extending, though not continuously, from Rock Island to Cape Idzu—but these channels were not thoroughly explored by the officers of the expedition—"I should not like," says the Commodore, "to venture through either of them, and would not recommend others to do so. It is more prudent to go outside of Rock Island, by which ships will not be so much endangered by the influence of the rapid current seemingly setting at all times to the eastward."

After leaving Simoda, the Commodore directed the steamers to be steered to the southward, in order to obtain another observation of the Redfield rocks, discovered on the passage during the previous month of February. On coming up with them it was found that their positions had been very correctly established by former notes, but care was taken to verify these by fresh observations. From the Redfield rocks a course was made for the northeast end of Oho-sima, the island claimed to have been discovered by Commander Glynn. On the previous passage to Japan, the western shore of Oho-sima and the adjacent islands had been carefully observed. It was now determined to examine very closely the eastern coast, and, consequently, on the morning of the 29th of June, the northern point of Oho-sima was made with this view. It was found that this part of the island bore N. 82° W., and that the bearings, therefore, on the chart, were erroneous. The steamers continuing their course, passed between Oho-sima and Kikai-sima, or Bungalow Island, and traversed the eastern coast of the former so closely, that all its sinuosities, bays, inlets, could be marked with much accuracy. Having at meridian obtained excellent observations of latitude and longitude, as the result of the notes of the three ships, it was practicable to determine the positions of the most prominent headlands by a series of angles deduced from these observations.

Before the visit of the United States squadron to these seas, a French chart, constructed by Monsieur N. Guerin, capitaine de vaisseau, and published in Paris in 1848, was the most approved guide. This chart has been improved by the observations and notes of the officers of the expedition, and, although there are doubtless many hidden dangers yet to be discovered and accurately reported, it can be said, with honest pride, that the Americans have contributed very much towards the hydrographical information of that part of the world, and especially of the gulf and bay of Yedo, waters hitherto almost unknown to foreign navigators.

After the meridian observations had been calculated, Commodore Perry dispatched two of the boats of the Mississippi, in charge of Lieutenants Maury and Webb, to visit a little bay of the island of Oho-sima, about two miles distant abreast the ships. These officers landed, and found only a small hamlet and a squad of miserably clad natives drawn up on the shore to meet them, armed with clubs, stones, and one old firelock. The inhabitants, however, notwithstanding their warlike aspect, were very civil, and gave, in exchange for bread and pork, some fowls and vegetables. A few botanical specimens were also obtained, but there was no time, or, what is even more important, no coal to spare for any lengthened exploration. This was probably the first time a Christian had ever landed upon Oho-sima. These islands, however, deserve a more complete examination, and it is hoped that our government will, ere long, send suitable vessels for such a purpose. One small steamer and a schooner of about a hundred and twenty tons, with a store-ship for carrying coals and provisions, would be adequate for the work.

Keeping as near as safety would permit to the chain of islands lying between Oho-sima and Lew Chew, the steamers were steered southward and westward during the night, and at daylight made the northern end of Great Lew Chew and the other islands in the neighborhood. On rounding the former a ship was discovered, about five miles distant, steering north with a fair wind. As soon, however, as she saw the steamers approaching, she tacked and stood to the southward and westward. The Commodore ordered two blank cartridges to be fired as a signal for the ship to heave to. At first she did not seem inclined to do so, but finding that the squadron was closing in upon her very fast, she tacked again, and, running down towards the steamers, she finally hove to. The flag-lieutenant then boarded her in a boat from the Mississippi, and learned that the vessel was an English ship from Shanghai bound to England. The captain explained the cause of his suspicious movements by saying that, having heard of the war with Russia, he had supposed at first that the American ships were the Russian squadron, and was greatly alarmed until he succeeded in making out distinctly the United States colors. He showed his friendly disposition by sending to the Commodore an English paper. Within ten miles of Napha, and as night approached, it became so dark that it was deemed imprudent to enter the harbor, and the vessels were accordingly kept merely under steerage-way until daylight, when the Powhatan cast off the Southampton, which had orders to proceed direct to Hong Kong. Both steamers then entered the port of Napha, and came to anchor on the 1st of July, 1854.

CHAPTER XXV.

PREPARATIONS FOR FINAL DEPARTURE FROM THE JAPANESE WATERS.—MACEDONIAN AND SUPPLY ORDERED TO FORMOSA.—INSTRUCTIONS TO CAPTAIN ABBOT, OF THE MACEDONIAN, TO TOUCH AT THE PHILIPPINES ON HIS WAY FROM FORMOSA TO CHINA.—MISSISSIPPI, POWHATAN, AND SOUTHAMPTON PROCEED TO LEW CHEW.—STATE OF AFFAIRS IN LEW CHEW.—SUPPOSED MURDER OF AN AMERICAN BY LEW CHEWANS.—TRIAL OF LEW CHEWANS FOR MURDER BY THEIR OWN AUTHORITIES ON THE COMMODORE'S DEMAND.—DESCRIPTION OF A LEW CHEW COURT OF JUSTICE.—ACCUSED MADE TO PLEAD BY PUNCHES IN THE RIBS.—ACCUSED CONVICTED AND BROUGHT TO THE COMMODORE FOR PUNISHMENT.—HE HANDS THEM OVER TO THEIR OWN AUTHORITIES—THEY ARE BANISHED.—NEW YEAR'S CUSTOMS.—COAL REMOVED FROM THE DEPOT TO THE SHIPS.—COMPACT OR TREATY MADE WITH LEW CHEW.—PRESENT FROM THE LEW CHEWANS TO THE COMMODORE—A STONE FOR THE WASHINGTON MONUMENT.—EFFORT OF A JAPANESE TO COME OFF IN THE SQUADRON TO THE UNITED STATES.—PARTING ENTERTAINMENT TO LEW CHEW AUTHORITIES.—DEPARTURE OF THE SQUADRON FOR CHINA.—MACEDONIAN'S VISIT TO FORMOSA.—UNAVAILING SEARCH FOR AMERICANS SUPPOSED TO HAVE BEEN WRECKED ON THE ISLAND.—EXPLORATIONS BY CHAPLAIN JONES FOR COAL.—FOUND IN ABUNDANCE AND OF GOOD QUALITY.—SURVEY OF THE HARBOR OF KELUNG.—LYING AND CUNNING OF THE FORMOSANS.—RUN TO MANILLA.—VERY STORMY PASSAGE.—MARINE VOLCANOES IN THE NEIGHBORHOOD OF FORMOSA.—INQUIRIES AT MANILLA INTO THE MURDER OF CERTAIN AMERICANS.—SATISFACTORY CONDUCT OF THE SPANISH AUTHORITIES IN THE MATTER.—DELIVERY BY CAPTAIN ABBOT TO THE GOVERNOR OF SIX SILLIBABOOS THAT HAD BEEN PICKED UP AT SEA BY LIEUTENANT COMMANDING BOYLE, OF THE SOUTHAMPTON, FLOATING IN AN OPEN BOAT.—REMARKABLE DISTANCE THAT THEY HAD DRIFTED.—PHYSICAL APPEARANCE OF THE SILLIBABOOS.—VOYAGE OF MACEDONIAN TO HONG KONG.—CAPTAIN KELLY'S HANDLING OF THE CHINESE PIRATES AND IMPERIAL TROOPS; FORCES THEM TO MAKE REPARATION.—CHASTISEMENT OF THE CHINESE BY THE JOINT ACTION OF THE OFFICERS AND MEN OF THE PLYMOUTH AND OF THOSE OF HER BRITANNIC MAJESTY'S SHIPS ENCOUNTER AND GRECIAN.—THE COMMODORE, BY LEAVE FROM THE NAVY DEPARTMENT, TURNS OVER THE COMMAND TO CAPTAIN ABBOT, AND RETURNS HOME BY THE OVERLAND ROUTE.—ON THE ARRIVAL OF THE MISSISSIPPI IN NEW YORK, ON THE 23D OF APRIL, THE COMMODORE REPAIRS ON BOARD, AND FORMALLY HAULING DOWN HIS FLAG, TERMINATES THE EXPEDITION.

HE story we are telling will perhaps be better understood if, before proceeding further, we recapitulate as to the disposition that had been made of the several ships of the squadron. The Saratoga sloop-of-war was on her way home, as we have stated, with the copy of the treaty in the custody of Captain Adams, who had been dispatched on the 4th of April, as a special messenger by the Commodore, to deliver the important document into the hands of the proper authorities. The steamer Susquehanna had been sent on the 24th of March, just one week before signing the treaty, and at the first moment at which she could be spared, to place herself at the disposal of the Hon. Mr. McLean, our minister to China. The Vandalia sloop-of-war, instead of returning with the other ships from Hakodadi to Simoda, had been ordered to make her way from the former port to China, by passing through the Straits of Sangar, and down on the western side of Japan to Shanghai. The store-ship Southampton having surveyed Volcano bay, and Endermo bay within it, just on the northern or Yesso side of the eastern entrance of the Straits of Sangar, had rejoined the squadron, and was now ordered to China.

The Plymouth, it will be remembered, had been left at Shanghai to protect American interests there, and was not with the squadron on the second visit to the Bay of Yedo; while the store-ship Lexington was sent back from Simoda to Lew Chew, during the previous month of May. There were, therefore, collected at Simoda, after the visit to Hakodadi, but five ships of the squadron, viz: the steamers Mississippi and Powhatan, the Macedonian sloop-of-war, the Southampton, which, having finished the survey of Volcano bay, there rejoined the squadron, and the store-ship Supply, the last named having remained at Simoda during the absence of the others.

As the discovery of coal was an important object, and as, beside, there were various causes making a visit to Formosa necessary, the Commodore, as has been said, ordered the Macedonian and Supply to that island, with instructions to Captain Abbot, in command of the former vessel, to stop at the Philippines on his way back, to join the squadron in China. As to the steamers, he proceeded with them and the Southampton direct to Lew Chew. This was the fifth and last visit to Napha; we shall first speak of that, reserving for a future page the results of the voyage of the Macedonian to Formosa.

When the squadron left Lew Chew on its last visit, two master's mates, named Randall and Bierbower, had been left in charge of the coal depot established at Tumai, and now, on the Commodore's return, he found that matters during his absence had not proceeded quite as amicably as he could have wished. Randall had his little complaints to make, and had preferred them to his superior, Lieutenant Commanding Glasson, when he arrived in the Lexington in May, and this latter officer now reported them to the Commodore. They amounted to but small grievances, however; one consisted of a complaint that some of the children in Lew Chew had thrown stones, which fell near some of the American seamen who were walking on shore; another was, that a Lew Chew butcher had quarrelled with one of the seamen while engaged in traffic with him, and beaten him with a club. Lieutenant Glasson had called on the mayor of Napha to ask an explanation. As to the first, the mayor stated that it was an accident, occurring while the children were engaged in sport, and was not an intentional act of aggression toward the seamen. As to the case of the butcher, the mayor stated that one of the sailors attempted in the market to take from the butcher certain of his meats without paying for them. The butcher naturally endeavored to secure his property, when the sailor struck at him with his knife; a scuffle ensued, in which the sailor was beaten with a club. Lieutenant Glasson told the mayor that the butcher, instead of resorting to force, should have reported the sailor; that he (the mayor) well knew the Commodore, on such a state of things, would have caused the man to be punished, and would have amply reimbursed the butcher for his loss; but that the latter should not have violated the law of Lew Chew and resorted to such desperate remedies. To this the mayor readily assented. These, however, were minor matters, and the probability is that the general feeling on board the ships was that the sailor got no more than his deserts, as the matter seems to have gone no further.

But there was a far more serious incident to be reported by Lieutenant Glasson; this was no less than the supposed murder of one of his crew by the Lew Chewans. It seems that, on the 12th of June, a man named Board was found dead in Napha, under circumstances which justified a strong suspicion that he came to his end by violence. The Commodore had not yet reached the island, and Lieutenant Glasson appointed five officers of the ship to investigate the circumstances and report thereon to him. These gentlemen, after making a post-mortem examination and hearing witnesses, reported as their opinion that the man came to his death from blows inflicted on his head by some person or persons unknown to them, and by subsequent immersion in the water for a considerable time while insensible from the blows he had received. They further added, that the testimony of the Lew Chew witnesses was very equivocal and unsatisfactory. Soon after this the Commodore arrived, when Lieutenant Glasson immediately reported to him all the facts and documents in his possession connected with the case; and, among the rest, that he had demanded a full and fair investigation by the local authorities of Lew Chew, to which demand he had received no satisfactory answer.

The Commodore, upon enquiry, soon became convinced that the man's death, though unlawfully produced, was probably the result of his own most gross outrage on a female, and, in such case, not undeserved: still he felt that, for the security of others, both Europeans and Americans, who might subsequently visit the island, it was important to impress upon the authorities the necessity for the full investigation and proper punishment, by the local authorities, of acts of violence committed upon strangers who might visit them. He therefore made a peremptory demand upon the regent or superintendent of affairs to cause a judicial trial to be instituted, conformably to the laws of Lew Chew.

This demand was at once complied with, the court consisting of six superior judges, and the regent and first treasurer giving their constant personal attendance during the entire proceedings.

The facts, as well as they could be ascertained, appeared to be these. On the 12th of June three American sailors, one of whom was named Board, passing through the streets of Napha, forcibly entered the house of one of the inhabitants, and taking therefrom some saki soon became intoxicated. Two of them found a sleeping place in the gutter, but Board, clambering over a wall, entered a private house, where he found a woman, named Mitu, and her niece, a young girl. He brandished his knife, threatened the woman, and attempted the foulest outrage; she cried out until she fainted and became insensible. Her cries brought some Lew Chew men to the spot, and the circumstances clearly showed the purpose of Board. Some of the Lew Chewans seized him and threw him to the ground. More than half drunk, he rose and fled towards the shore, seeking to escape. Many persons had by this time assembled, and pursued Board, throwing stones at him, some of which struck him, and, according to the statements of the native witnesses, in his drunkenness he *fell* into the water and was drowned. Whether this latter particular was precisely in accordance with the fact was somewhat doubtful.

At any rate, the Lew Chew authorities, declaring that it was "altogether illegal to throw stones and wound persons, causing them thereby to fall into the water and be drowned," convicted six persons, one as principal and the others as accessories. After the conviction the regent and first treasurer appeared on board the Mississippi with the ringleader bound, and desired to deliver him to the Commodore to be dealt with according to the laws of the United States. The Commodore, of course, declined to receive him, and explained to the Lew Chewans that it was not his wish or purpose to interfere in any mode with the administration or execution of the Lew Chew laws; that he only wished them to enforce them on proper occasions, when wrong or injury was done to any foreigners who might chance to visit the island. He accordingly remanded the prisoner to the regent, who expressed many thanks to the Commodore for the act. The end of the matter was that the accessories were banished to a neighboring island for a time, and the principal was banished for life. It seems doubtful, however, whether these sentences were rigorously executed, although the authorities solemnly promised the Commodore that they should be.

The Commodore, however, ordered the trial by a court martial of the two surviving Americans, who commenced the disturbance, and they were dealt with according to their deserts. The whole affair was a subject of deep regret to the Commodore, and was the only instance of any seriously unpleasant occurrence during the whole intercourse of the Americans with the Lew Chewans, in their five visits to the island.

It may not be uninteresting to lay before the reader the forms of a Lew Chew judicial proceeding, as the customs of a country, in so grave a proceeding, are necessarily illustrative of the national character. The flag-lieutenant, Mr. Bent, and Mr. Williams, the interpreter, had been selected by the Commodore to attend the trial, in accordance with the request of the Lew Chew authorities that some of our officers should be present. These gentlemen, on reaching the hall, were furnished with seats at the head of the room, immediately opposite to the regent and treasurer; on their left sat three of the judges on mats; and opposite to them, on a line with the regent and treasurer, were the three other judges similarly seated. The prisoner on trial knelt on the ground outside of the hall, (which was open on that side,) with his head just above the flooring of the balcony, and facing the interior of the hall. Questions were put to him by the judges, and if he proved intractable or stubborn in responding his elbows were tied together behind his back, and, on the slightest hesitation, a policeman on either side of him punched him severely in the ribs with large sticks about two inches in diameter and four feet in length. These never failed to loosen the fellow's tongue, but whether to utter truth or falsehood was, to our gentlemen, very questionable. This, if not equal in severity to the old "*peine forte et dure*" of our ancestors, proceeds on the same principle.

On each successive visit to the island the gentlemen of the expedition gathered additional scraps of information as to customs, one of which is so similar, in the feeling which prompts it, to our own new year's congratulations, that it is worthy of a passing notice. In the spring, when the new year opens in Lew Chew, and perhaps in Japan also, (though of the latter we cannot speak certainly,) the usage of the islanders is to offer the expression of their good wishes and friendly feelings in the form of inscriptions attached to the houses of each other, or sent to the inmates. Mr. Williams translated several of these, a few of which we subjoin as specimens:

"*Gay clouds meet the rising, glorious sun; ten thousand joys greet the opening spring.*"

"*Let all sing these days of general peace, and rejoice together in the opening spring.*"

"*May all joys clamber about your happy abode; may a thousand lucks collect at this gate.*"

"*May every door have luck and joy, and every land be blessed with peace.*"

"*May your felicity be as broad as the eastern sea; your age enduring as the southern hills.*"

"*The peach tree in fairy land ripens in thirty centuries; may the seaside house be blessed with ninety more autumns.*"

"*We joyfully hope the brightening year will meet a flourishing time, as the bloom of spring begins to shine upon this humble door.*"

"*May the three stars, peace, office, age, enter your door; and sons, riches, honors, bless your gate.*"

"*Happiness descends from heaven.*"

"*As the wind and light go their circuits through the world, so does the gladsome spring from heaven to us come down.*"

While the judicial proceedings in the case of Board's death were in progress, the Commodore, who was anxious to lose no time, employed, with the aid and approval of the Lew Chew authorities, native lighters to transport to the steamers all the coal remaining in the coal-shed at Tumai; and causing the building itself to be put in order, left it in charge of the native authorities, with an assurance that they would look carefully to its preservation for future use, and the reception of any deposit of coal the United States might wish to make there in time to come.

There remained, however, one important piece of business yet to be done. This was the making of a compact or treaty between our government and that of Lew Chew. Accordingly, the flag-lieutenant, Mr. Bent, and the interpreter, Mr. Williams, were deputed by the Commodore, under suitable instructions as to terms, to confer with the regent of Lew Chew; and these gentlemen, on the 8th of July, met that official on shore by appointment, and discussed with him the proposed compact, a rough draft of which they presented. The preamble to this recognized Lew Chew as an independent nation. To this recognition the regent objected, saying that such an assumption on their parts would get them into trouble with China, to which country they owed allegiance; that, as to the articles of the compact, they would cheerfully assent to them, and faithfully fulfil them, nor would they hesitate to affix their seals to the instrument, but that it had better not bear on its face the assertion or appearance of their claiming absolute independence. There was none of the delaying, crooked policy of the Japanese in these negotiations. The Lew Chewans were made fully to understand what had transpired in Japan, and probably derived confidence and candor from their knowledge of the Japanese treaty, which was shown to them.

After the discussion our officers returned on board to report to the Commodore their proceedings, and submit the terms proposed and accepted. On the 10th, the same gentlemen were sent to hold another interview with the regent, when they soon succeeded in arranging all the terms of the compact satisfactorily to both parties, and obtained from the regent a promise that a bazaar should be opened on shore, on the succeeding Wednesday and Thursday, for the officers of the ships. It was also arranged that the Commodore would visit the regent at an appointed hour on the morrow. On the next day, in the morning, the Commodore sent on shore a number of presents for the regent, treasurer, and other officers of the island, consisting of revolvers, lorgnettes, a dressing case, and numerous valuable agricultural implements. He was also particularly careful to send a handsome present to the poor woman who had been the subject of Board's outrage. At noon he landed himself, and, with a small escort of marines, visited the regent at the town-hall.

After the usual compliments, and a formal delivery of the presents he had sent on shore, the articles of agreement or compact that had been made was produced, written in the English and Chinese languages, and read, and the instruments were duly signed and sealed, and copies exchanged, by the Commodore, regent, and treasurer of Lew Chew, the English version being as follows:

"*Compact between the United States and the kingdom of Lew Chew, signed at Napha, Great Lew Chew, the* 11*th day of July,* 1854.

"Hereafter, whenever citizens of the United States come to Lew Chew, they shall be treated with great courtesy and friendship. Whatever articles these persons ask for, whether from the officers or people, which the country can furnish, shall be sold to them; nor shall the authorities interpose any prohibitory regulations to the people selling; and whatever either party may wish to buy shall be exchanged at reasonable prices.

"Whenever ships of the United States shall come into any harbor in Lew Chew they shall be supplied with wood and water at reasonable prices; but if they wish to get other articles they shall be purchaseable only at Napha.

"If ships of the United States are wrecked on Great Lew Chew, or on islands under the jurisdiction of the royal government of Lew Chew, the local authorities shall dispatch persons to assist in saving life and property, and preserve what can be brought ashore till the ships of that nation shall come to take away all that may have been saved; and the expenses incurred in rescuing these unfortunate persons shall be refunded by the nation they belong to.

"Whenever persons from ships of the United States come ashore in Lew Chew they shall be at liberty to ramble where they please, without hindrance, or having officials sent to follow them, or to spy what they do; but if they violently go into houses, or trifle with women, or force people to sell them things, or do other such like illegal acts, they shall be arrested by the local officers, but not maltreated, and shall be reported to the captain of the ship to which they belong, for punishment by him.

"At Tumai is a burial-ground for the citizens of the United States, where their graves and tombs shall not be molested.

"The government of Lew Chew shall appoint skilful pilots, who shall be on the look-out for ships appearing off the island; and if one is seen coming towards Napha they shall go out in good boats beyond the reefs to conduct her in to a secure anchorage; for which service the captain shall pay the pilot five dollars, and the same for going out of the harbor beyond the reefs.

"Whenever ships anchor at Napha the local authorities shall furnish them with wood at the rate of three thousand six hundred copper cash per thousand catties; and with water at the rate of six hundred copper cash (43 cents) for one thousand catties, or six barrels full, each containing thirty American gallons.

"Signed in the English and Chinese languages, by Commodore Matthew C. Perry, commander-in-chief of the United States naval forces in the East India, China, and Japan seas, and special envoy to Japan, for the United States; and by Sho Fu Fing, superintendent of affairs (Tsu-li-kwan) in Lew Chew, and Ba Rio-si, treasurer of Lew Chew, at Shui, for the government of Lew Chew; and copies exchanged this 11th day of July, 1854, or the reign Hien Fung, 4th year, 6th moon, 17th day, at the town hall of Napha."

As soon as this business was thus happily completed, a handsome entertainment, furnished by the Lew Chew authorities, was served, of which the Americans partook, and great kindness and cordiality characterized the festivities. At four o'clock the Commodore returned to his ship. On the next day, the 12th, there was sent off to the Commodore a large bell, as a present from the regent; whether of Lew Chew casting is not known, though the probability is it was made in Japan, and, at any rate, it is no discreditable specimen of foundry work. A little circumstance that occurred on this last visit to Lew Chew was highly gratifying to the feeling with which every American thinks of the character of Washington. Various parts of the world, as is known, have testified their appreciation of the exalted virtues of the father of our country, by contributing a stone to be wrought into the monument which is rising at Washington to perpetuate the memory of one who presented a specimen so rare of the qualities which ennoble humanity. There is something at once impressive and beautiful in such a tribute, coming from the men of various lands and tongues, as if all were anxious to claim their kindred share in a glorious possessor of human nature, and to attest their respect for such an illustration of human purity. It serves to show that as a *man* Washington belonged to the world, and men every where are justly proud of their brotherhood; such pride is their tribute to human virtue; as the leader of our army who periled all he had on earth for his country, and as the head of our republic, he belonged indeed to us; but we are willing and glad that good men everywhere should seek to catch inspiration from his virtues. When these poor Lew Chewans knew that a stone from their far distant island would be acceptable, even they understood what it meant, they had heard of "the great mandarin," as they called him, and the stone was sent. So, too, the rocks of Japan and Formosa have furnished their quota of material, and thus the broad lands of earth's continents and the remote islands of oriental seas have alike brought together their enduring tributes to a memorial which is meant

"To give the *world* assurance of a MAN!"

It was during this last visit, also, that a circumstance occurred which served to show that some of the common Japanese, at least, had seen enough of the world and of other people than their countrymen to make them desirous of seeing more. While the squadron was lying at anchor at Napha, a native of Japan, who was in Lew Chew, in what capacity we know not, swam from the shore to the Lexington with a bundle of clothing, and begged to be received on board and to be brought to the United States. The officer in command of the Lexington sent him to the flag-ship; and while the Commodore would have made no objection provided the assent of the Japanese authorities had been obtained, yet, knowing their severe restrictions on the subject of natives leaving the kingdom, and, scrupulously anxious not to give offence, he declined, as before, receiving the man, and ordered him to be set on shore again. The only Japanese who came home in the squadron were part of the shipwrecked crew of a junk, of which we have already spoken. These men were taken from San Francisco to China, and there two of them shipped themselves as landsmen on board the Susquehanna, and both are now in the United States. Frequent intercourse with one of them—a young man of some twenty-two years—enables us to say that he is remarkably intelligent, reads and writes Japanese, both Kata-kana and Hira-kana, has learned to speak (though imperfectly) and to write English, is very desirous of information, conforms to our customs and fashion in dress, and is most scrupulously clean and tidy. His wish is to learn more of our country and language, and then to return to Japan.

On the evening of the 14th the Commodore gave a parting entertainment on board his ship to the authorities of Lew Chew. All passed off pleasantly, and at nine o'clock the guests returned on shore, after uttering many thanks for the attentions the Commodore had shown them on his repeated visits, and expressing and seemingly feeling great gratification in the courtesies that had been shown them. On the next day the Lexington was ordered to Hong Kong and sailed immediately; and on the 17th the Commodore left in the Mississippi, accompanied by the Powhatan, these being the only remaining vessels of the squadron, and the harbor of Napha was left to the quiet in which it reposed when our ships first anchored in its waters.

Whatever satisfaction their departure may have afforded the Lew Chewans was doubtless enhanced by the fact that the ships took away Dr. Bettelheim. This gentleman had been superseded by the Rev. Mr. Moreton, who was on the ground; and Dr. Bettelheim's family had left some time before for China in the Supply. The earnestness of application to the Commodore to take Dr. Bettelheim away with him forcibly demonstrates the very little prospect there was of any useful labors, on his part, among the natives; and, indeed, their desire to be rid of Mr. Moreton also, would seem to hold out but small hope, at present, of evangelizing Lew Chew. The letter addressed by the authorities to the Commodore will be found below.*

The Powhatan, pursuant to orders, took her course for Ning-po-fou, Fuh-chow-fuh, and Amoy, on the coast of China, to inquire into the interests of Americans resident in those places, and was instructed to proceed from Amoy to Hong Kong. The Mississippi proceeded direct to the last named port.

And now, while she is on her passage, we will return in our narrative to the expedition to Formosa, the incidents of which occurred simultaneously with those which form the subject of the previous part of this chapter. It will be remembered that the Macedonian, Captain Abbot, and the Supply, Lieutenant Commanding Sinclair, had been sent from Simoda, before the squadron left that port, with instructions to visit Formosa, and the former ship was also ordered on her way thence to China, to stop at the Philippines. There was more than one object contemplated in the visit to Formosa. Certain of our countrymen, as our authorities at home had been informed, navigating near Formosa, had been shipwrecked and thrown upon that island, where they remained, either in a state of captivity or because they were unable to get away. Instructions were therefore given by the navy department to the Commodore to make research and inquiry into this matter. Again, the importance of an abundant supply of coal for the use of steamers, not only of our own, but of other nations that may reasonably be expected ere long to throng these seas, furnished another motive for the visit to Formosa, as there was reason to think the mineral existed in abundance on that island. There was also a particular reason for touching at the Philippines, which we will detail presently.

On the 29th of June, the Macedonian and Supply left Simoda. On the second day out the Supply disappeared, and was not seen again until she entered the harbor of Kelung in Formosa, on the 21st of July, ten days after the arrival at that place of the Macedonian, which had made the run from Simoda in about twelve days, encountering an opposing current, head winds, and

---

* *From the authorities of Lew Chew to Commodore Perry:*

A prepared statement Sho Fu-ting, general superintendent of affairs in the kingdom of Lew Chew, and Ba Rio-si, treasurer at Shui, earnestly beg your excellency's kind consideration of some circumstances; and that, to show compassion on our little country, you will take away back to their own land Bettelheim and Moreton, who have remained here long. * * *

In the years 1844 and 1846 some French officers came, and the Englishman Bettelheim also brought hither his wife and children to reside, and they all required something to be daily given them, to our continual annoyance and trouble. Whenever an English or French ship came in, we earnestly represented these circumstances to them, and besought them to take these people away with them. The Frenchmen, knowing our distresses, went away in the year 1848 to their own country, and have not hitherto returned; but Bettelheim has loitered away years here and not gone, and now, further, has brought Moreton with his family to take his place and live here, greatly to the discomfort of the people, and distress and inconvenience of the country.

We have learned that your excellency has authority over all the East Indian, China, and Japan seas, and not a ship of any western country can go from one of these seas to the other but you know and regulate its movements. Wherefore we lay before you our sad condition in all its particulars, humbly beseeching your kind regard upon it, and requesting that, when your fine ships return, you will take both Bettelheim and Moreton away with you. This will solace and raise us up from our low condition, and oblige us in a way not easy to be expressed. We wish your life may be prolonged to a thousand autumns, in the enjoyment of the highest felicity.

July 10, 1854.

tempestuous weather through nearly the entire voyage. The island was made at its northern end, and the entrance to Kelung was not very plain. Certain landmarks, however, were noted by the officers, upon further acquaintance with the locality, and by these and the charts made by the surveying party during the stay of the ship, information was obtained which may be relied on, and which is recorded in the nautical appendix. Very violent currents were found at the north end of the island, though these may have been stronger than usual at the arrival of the Macedonian, as there had then been a tempest of some days' continuance. A pilot came off and took the ship safely into the harbor.

As to our supposed shipwrecked and captive countrymen, Captain Abbot made the most diligent investigation, through the medium of his Chinese steward, but could gain no intelligence, although his inquiries were made, not only of the mandarins or officials in and about Kelung, but also of all classes of the people. The report from all was uniform; they declared that they neither knew nor had heard of any shipwreck of any American or European vessel on any part of the island; nor had they ever known or heard of the existence of the crew, or any part thereof, of any such vessel anywhere in Formosa, and Captain Abbot became quite convinced that, in this particular, they told the truth, and reported to the Commodore accordingly, that he had "no belief that any of our missing countrymen are alive on the island of Formosa."

But after this conclusion had been reached, and no doubt correctly, a specimen of cunning was exhibited, on the part of the island authorities, such as meets us at every turn in the story of our intercourse with all the eastern people, and indeed seems characteristic of oriental negotiation. The chief mandarin of Kelung came to Captain Abbot, just as he was about sailing, (he had doubtless purposely deferred his visit until that moment, to forestal the possibility of strict inquiry,) and informed him that he had been making more particular investigations concerning shipwrecks, and had learned that some six or seven years before a ship had been wrecked, forty or fifty miles from Kelung, on the *western* side of the island, having a number of black men on board as well as white; that the white men took the boat and went off to an adjacent island, while the black men were left, and all died on board the ship; and that he would send some of his war-junks with the Macedonian to show Captain Abbot the place. This story was a lie too transparent to deceive Captain Abbot for a moment, and was evidently a ruse by which he hoped to induce the commander of the Macedonian to do what, for several days, he had been unavailingly persuading him to perform. He had been endeavoring to prevail on him to take the ship, in company with some of his war-junks, to the western side of the island, a run that, in going and returning, would occupy, he said, four or five days only, and there assist him in driving off the rebels who were there collected, with whom his troops had lately had a fight and been beaten, with a loss of thirty men killed and wounded. The fact was that he lived in constant fear of an invasion from Amoy. He told Captain Abbot that if he would render him this assistance, he would, immediately on his return, make him a present of a large ship-load of coal. It is needless to say that Captain Abbot paid no attention to his proposals for a moment; he then seemed very anxious that the ship should prolong her stay at Kelung, as he supposed her presence there would insure the place from any attack by the rebels during her stay.

As to another object of the mission to Formosa, the search for coal, this was confided to the chaplain, Mr. Jones, of the Mississippi; and Midshipmen Breese and Jones, with Mr. Williams, master's mate, all of the same ship, were detailed for special duty as assistants. The full results of Mr. Chaplain Jones' labors will be found in his very interesting report in the Appendix. Suffice it here to say, that he found an abundance of coal, of excellent quality, admirably situated for transportation from the mines to the water at very little expense; and that he had reason to believe that a considerable part of the island, around Kelung, at least, was underlaid with coal. Several tons were purchased and brought away, though in the negotiation the Formosans, high and low, showed themselves to be such adepts in falsehood and cunning, that even the equanimity of the good chaplain was disturbed, and his really mild and amiable spirit was roused to meet the prevarications of the chief mandarin, by bidding the interpreter say to him, "that he had trifled with us, had *lied*, and tried to deceive us from the beginning, and that we would be trifled with no longer;" and this, from the lips of Mr. Jones, will appear to those who know his eminently peaceful temper to be terribly energetic language. It may well be doubted whether he ever before told any body, in good wholesome English, that "he lied;" and yet the squadron, probably, did not contain a more resolute and fearless man.

On the 23d of July, the Macedonian left Kelung, for Manilla, in the island of Luconia. The Supply was ordered to remain, to take in the coal and sail, as soon as she could, for Hong Kong. On this part of her voyage, the Macedonian encountered terrible weather, having met with the border of a typhoon soon after getting clear of the northern shores of Formosa. This providentially carried the ship very rapidly on her course to the southward of the south end of the island before the tempest became so violent that she could not run. In the long experience of Captain Abbott, (so he reports,) he never before encountered such weather at sea. "We had," says he, "a constant succession of heavy, tempest squalls, with hard drenching rains, some of them peculiarly severe and frightful in appearance. The ship suffered more, during this short passage, in her sails and rigging, than on her whole passage out from the United States."

But this is emphatically the region for phenomena and convulsions of nature. The vessels of the squadron had a varied experience in these waters. Some met typhoons and some suddenly found themselves along side of marine volcanoes. It was within ten miles of Formosa that Lieutenant Commanding Boyle, in the store-ship Southampton, when on his way from the United States to join the squadron at Hong Kong, came near a marine volcano. He thus describes it: "On the 29th of October, 1853, near the island of Formosa, I discovered a volcano, distant from the land about ten miles, in a violent state of eruption, throwing out columns of vapor to a great height, resembling in appearance a similar phenomenon to which I was witness some years ago on the coast of Sicily; this, however, was of greater magnitude and force than that, although no lava was visible by reason of the dense bank of vapor which hung around it. The depth of water here is much greater than on the Sicilian coast, and hence my conclusion as to the cause of not seeing lava. When last seen, at 3 p. m., it was in a lively state of activity, and bore N.N.W., distant about ten miles. It was in latitude about 24° N., and longitude 121° 50′ E.; there was no sail in sight.

"Shortly after passing the neighborhood of the volcano, we passed through a very heavy over-fall or rip, so much so, that the executive officer and others, at first, supposed that there were breakers. I had seen such an appearance before, and decided that it was, what it proved to be, an effect of the volcano merely. On arriving, a few days afterwards, at Lew Chew, I found that they had had a few shakes. * * * * * * *

"On my discovery of the phenomenon off Formosa, I had at the mast-head, in addition to the usual look-out, a seaman, called Gilbert Lee, in whom I had great confidence, who at first thought the appearance was caused by a steamer. One of the petty officers, A. L. Benton, also took particular notice of it; several on deck said they did not know what to make of it. As I have before stated, it had the same appearance as when Graham's island rose from the ocean off the coast of Sicily."*

As no opportunity was ever lost by the squadron of obtaining accurate information that might benefit nautical men of all countries, while the Macedonian was at Kelung, Lieutenant Preble was employed, under Captain Abbot's orders from the Commodore, in making a survey of the harbor; in this work Passed Midshipman Jones volunteered as an assistant, and a chart was prepared by these gentlemen, the correctness of which may be relied on. The object of the Commodore in directing the Macedonian to proceed from Kelung to the Philippines was twofold. In the month of March, 1853, a shocking murder had been committed by several Spaniards on two Americans, at a rope factory at Santa Mesa, within the jurisdiction of the governor and captain general of the Philippines. Captain Abbot was instructed respectfully to ask of the authorities what measures, if any, had been taken to discover and bring to punishment, under the Spanish law, the perpetrators of the homicide. The Marquis de Novaleches, the governor general, in reply to Captain Abbot's inquiries, very promptly informed him that the courts had been employed, ever since the murder occurred, in ferreting out and punishing the guilty; that some of those concerned had been detected and sentenced; that two of the criminals had not yet been found, but that, if in the islands, the court, which had not relaxed its zeal and diligence, would find and punish them; that instructions had been received from the government at home most earnestly to prosecute the matter to the fullest penalties of the law on all who were guilty; and finally, that all which had been done had been fully reported to the government of her Catholic majesty, and probably through that channel to the authorities of the United States.

The other cause for Captain Abbott's visit was occasioned by an act of humanity on the part of our countrymen. On the morning of the 5th of August, 1853, in about latitude 18° 46' N., longitude 124° E., the store-ship Southampton, Lieutenant Commanding Boyle, was steering S.W. by W., the wind blowing from the northward and westward a fresh top-gallant breeze, with considerable swell, when a boat was discovered to windward. The ship was hove to, and presently succeeded in getting on board the boat and its contents. When hoisted in and measured, the craft was found to be twelve feet long, four wide, and seventeen inches deep. On

---

* It would seem that this part of the ocean exhibits this phenomenon with considerable frequency. We have before us a letter from Lieutenant Jones, addressed to Lieutenant Bent, in which he describes a similar convulsion, to which he was a witness, in January, 1850, and not far from the spot designated by Lieutenant Commanding Boyle. Mr Jones was, at the time, an officer of the United States sloop-of-war St. Mary's, and thus writes: "It was in latitude about 20° 56' N. and longitude 134° 45' E. I was in the St. Mary's. We were bound from the Sandwich Islands to Hong Kong. The wind at the time was moderate from the eastward, and the sea smooth. At about 11 p m., the ship going seven or eight knots, the wind suddenly died away, the sea became troubled, the air heated, and a sulphurous smell was, to some of the men, very apparent. There were puffs of wind from different quarters, but before the yards could be braced around, it would be calm again. This lasted about twenty-five minutes, when the wind came out as before from the eastward, and when I came on deck, at midnight, there was nothing unusual in the appearance of the weather or sea. Unfortunately, the officer of the deck did not take the temperature of the air or the water, nor did he think of sounding.

"My information was derived immediately after the watch, from the officers and men of the watch. All noticed the wind dying away suddenly, and most of them the heated air. A number observed the sea and thought they were in a tide-rip, but a larger one than they had ever before seen. Only a few remarked the sulphurous smell, but they were positive and to be relied on; they were intelligent men. The officer of the deck I think was one, also the quartermaster. Though all did not give the same account, there was no contradiction."

502   EXPEDITION TO JAPAN.

board of the boat, when the ship thus picked her up, were six males, four of whom were adults and two were boys, the one about ten and the other fourteen years of age. They were all of healthy appearance, of medium stature, of a dark color, the hair cut close, not tattooed, and did not appear to be much exhausted. Captain Boyle supposed, from their appearance, that they might have been adrift some two or three days. They had in the boat about two or three dozen ears of Indian corn, (maize,) a few sweet potatoes, some prepared betel nuts, a cask, two gongs, a fishing net, an axe, a small piece of grass cloth as a sail, and a colored piece of cloth supposed to be a flag. Of water they had none; but, from the frequent showers encountered by the ship, Captain Boyle concluded they had not suffered much from the want of it.

To what nation or people these poor creatures belonged no one could tell, as nobody on board could understand their language. It was observed, however, that the word most frequently on their lips was *Sil-li-ba-boo*. The nearest land to the ship was Cape Engano, the N.E. point of Luconia, distant about one hundred miles. The Babuan and Bashee group were about one hundred and eighty miles directly to windward; and the first conjecture was that possibly they might belong to these. Their dress consisted of wide-legged trowsers extending a little below the knee, with a dark-colored gown enveloping the entire person, and secured around the neck by a drawing string; their heads they would sometimes bind around with a cotton handkerchief, after a fashion not unlike that used by the blacks of the southern States. Though seemingly not much exhausted when they were taken on board the ship, yet they evidently experienced great difficulty in walking, from their long confinement in a cramped position. Sleep, with suitable diet, however, soon restored them to their usual condition.

Boat with sillibaboos, picked up by the Southampton.

When the ship came near and passed through the group of islands just named, the commander watched closely to observe if they showed any mark of recognition. Their attention was called to them by signs, and they seemed to understand the pantomimic inquiry, for they invariably shook their heads as if to imply that their home was not there, and pointing towards the eastward, said "*Sil-li-ba-boo*." Soon after the ship arrived at Cum-sing-moon, in China, and here great pains were taken to discover, if possible, where these poor adventurers belonged. There were many ships lying there, and the Commodore directed that diligent search should be made among them all, in the hope that, perchance, some one might be found who could communicate with them. They were visited by many from the various vessels, and, from their timidity, they fell at first under the suspicion that they were anxious to remain unknown; but Captain Boyle became quite convinced that their shyness, and repugnance to leave the ship, proceeded from fear alone. They were taken on board each of the trading ships at Cum-sing-moon, and out of the numerous tongues spoken on board not one was found like that spoken by these men. At length they uttered some words when on the deck of the English ship Bombay, which Captain Jamieson, the commander, thought he recognized as belonging to the language of the natives of the Bentinck Isles. On perceiving that their words were attracting notice, they made their usual salaam, and uttering *Sil-li-ba-boo*, afterwards held their peace. There is an island called by that name, and mentioned by Horsburg as being in latitude 4° N., longitude 127° E., but this is so remote from the spot where they were picked up, some twelve or fifteen hundred miles, that Captain Boyle could not suppose it possible they had drifted such a distance. The wind had, indeed, for several days been strong from the southward and eastward, just before the boat was seen, though at the time they were picked up it was from the northward and westward. Notwithstanding this, however, it seemed most improbable that in their frail craft they could have floated so many miles. Captain Jamieson and his crew interested themselves much for these poor creatures, and persevered in their efforts to communicate with them by means of the slight vocabulary they had acquired in their voyagings; and though such communication was very imperfect, of course, yet it was plain some words were understood, and the unfortunate men were evidently pleased, and sought opportunities of mingling with those who could comprehend any portion, however small, of their language. With these imperfect means of knowledge, the best account Captain Jamieson could gather from them was, that they did come from Sil-li-ba-boo, distant as it was; that they left the land in their boat with some articles of food for a vessel in the offing, met a fresh breeze which carried them out to sea, and, by its continuance, prevented their return to land, and that they had been in the boat fifteen days when the Southampton picked them up. By direction of the Commodore, two of the surgeons of the squadron made a minute examination of these Sil-li-ba-boos, and reported in substance as follows:

"The Sil-li-ba-boos are of medium height and well set, with moderate muscular development, and, though possessed of no great strength, are active in movement. Destitute of the fatty tissue beneath the skin which generally gives roundness and fullness to the forms of northern races, the Sil-li-ba-boos have, from this deficiency, a sharp and angular contour that deprives them of all claim to physical beauty. Their features have the irregular expression of the negro, though their color resembles that of the mulatto. Their heads are small and round, with a large disproportionate development of the posterior part of the skull; their faces are oval, their foreheads moderately high, their eyes dark, but not very brilliant or intelligent, and their chins broad and massive. Their noses are long and flat, their lips thick and prominent, and their large mouths display strong well-formed teeth, which, however, are generally blackish, from the use of the betel nut. The skin is smooth, with a small supply of black coarse hair in those parts where it is usually found, except on the head; there it grows profusely and straight, but is worn short. Their limbs are lithe, and their hands and feet small. Their language is soft and agreeable to the ear, but, although it is supposed to be a derivation from the Malayan, it is not intelligible to those on board familiar with the ordinary dialect of the Malays. They are, however, believed to be of Malay origin, much modified by the effects of climate and accidental causes. The intelligence of the Sil-li-ba-boos is so far blunted as to place them within the category of the savage races, to which, in habits and social characteristics, they are closely allied."

One purpose of the visit of the Macedonian to Manilla was to hand over the Sil-li-ba-boos to the governor general of the Philippines, that they might be protected and sent home. The governor, with many expressions of gratitude for the kindness that had been shown toward these involuntary wanderers, received them; and we may indulge the hope that, long ere this, they have reached their native island, there to tell to their wondering countrymen the story of their providential preservation and marvellous adventures.

On the 17th of August, the Macedonian (her officers having been shown the greatest civility and kindness both by the authorities and the American residents) left Manilla for Hong Kong, and her voyage presented a strong contrast to what she had experienced in the run from Formosa to Manilla. Captain Abbot reported that for the first five days he had either a dead calm, or light, baffling winds from the north and northwest, which did no more than enable him to make an offing from the land; and after that, either calms or moderate breezes had prevailed, with pleasant weather, and the very unusual circumstance of scarcely any *southing* in the winds. On the 26th, the Macedonian was at her anchorage at Hong Kong.

It will be remembered that we left the flag-ship, the Mississippi, on her way from Lew Chew to Hong Kong. She arrived after a short passage, and the Commodore now turned his attention to affairs in China. The reader will not have forgotten that the Plymouth, Commander Kelly, had been left at Shanghai to watch over the interests of our countrymen there, and did not accompany the squadron on the second visit to the Bay of Yedo. And now it was found that the Chinese imperial troops had given both the English and ourselves some work to do during the Commodore's absence. The first acts of aggression were shown in the latter part of February and beginning of March, very soon after our squadron had left for Japan on the second trip. The imperial troops were at that time encamped around the settlement of the foreigners at Shanghai, and the imperial fleet was anchored off the place. They soon began their acts of violence and robbery on the land, by tearing down buildings that the foreigners were erecting, and stealing the materials; while their fleet, without the slightest previous notice, commenced firing upon and searching all boats passing up or down the river. Complaints were made in the first instance to the general commanding the Chinese troops, and to the *Taoutae*, or commander-in-chief of the fleet. These functionaries at length acknowledged their inability to prevent such acts of aggression, and said that the foreigners would have to protect themselves.

It so happened that on the 6th of March a pilot boat, under the American flag, and belonging to three of the foreign residents, Ayers, Linklater, and Donaldson, all American citizens, was passing on the river with her ensign flying, when, without hail or warning, she was fired upon by one of the imperial fleet, the Sir H. Compton, and ordered alongside. The order was perforce complied with. On reaching the Compton she was immediately boarded from that vessel by a body of armed men, who forthwith hauled down the American ensign, dragged the crew of the boat up the side of the ship, and made them fast by lashing their long Chinese queues to the mainmast. Commander Kelly was informed of these facts by the American consul at seven o'clock that evening, when, in a very few minutes, Lieutenant Guest had his orders, and was under way for the Compton, in one of the ship's cutters, manned by eleven men, armed, and accompanied by the owners of the pilot boat. His instructions were to release the boat and crew, and demand of the captain by what authority he had dared thus to insult the American flag. Lieutenant Guest, of course, interpreted his instructions to mean that, if necessary, he should use force to release the boat and her crew. He was soon alongside of the Compton, and, pursuant to orders, inquired first for her captain, to whom Commander Kelly had addressed a note on the subject of the outrage. He was told that the captain was on board the Agnes, another Chinese vessel of war; he pulled to her, and was there told that he was on shore. Lieutenant Guest did not suppose it to be his duty to seek for him any further, and was soon back to the Compton. This vessel was anchored in the middle of the Chinese fleet, mounted some ten or twelve guns, and had about forty men on her deck, renegades and scoundrels of all nations. On getting alongside, the lieutenant immediately ascended the vessel's side, accompanied by the owners of the boat, ordering his eleven men to remain in the cutter, and to come when he called them, but not before. On reaching the deck he asked for the officer in command, when a Portuguese stepped forward and claimed that rank. Lieutenant Guest then asked him how he dared to fire upon and make prisoners of men under the protection of the American flag, and demanded that they should be immediately released and their boat given up. He replied that he did not do it, and that in the captain's absence he had no authority to release either men or boat. He then conferred with another official, (a Chinaman,) and he confirmed his decision. Lieutenant Guest then called out to his men, "come on board," and with wonderful alacrity and speed they were on the deck, each with cutlass in hand, and in a moment had released the prisoners from their confinement to the mainmast. About this time the crew of the Compton had assumed a menacing attitude, and Mr. Donaldson called out to the lieutenant that some of the men on the poop-deck were levelling their muskets at the Americans. Fortunately the Portuguese commanding officer was at that moment very near Lieutenant Guest. Instantly drawing and cocking his pistol, the American officer levelled it at the Portuguese, and told him that on the first shot fired he would blow out his brains. On hearing this threat, he called loudly to his men on the poop to desist, and no further obstacle was interposed to the taking away of either boat or men. One of the owners examined the pilot boat before her removal, and reported to the lieutenant that his property was all safe, and she was then taken with her crew to a place of safety, within gun-shot of the Plymouth.

The next morning (the 7th) Commander Kelly informed the *Taoutae*, or commander of the imperial fleet, through our consul, that as the Compton had insulted the American flag, she had an act of public atonement to render, which consisted in her hoisting our national colors at her fore-royal masthead in open day, and saluting them with twenty-one guns; and he made a demand accordingly. The Taoutae seeming not disposed to make this act of reparation for unprovoked insult, Commander Kelly, after the allowance to him of a reasonable time, got under way and proceeded to the anchorage of the imperial fleet for the purpose of enforcing his demand by arguments, less gentle indeed, but probably more effective than any he had yet used. The Plymouth, however, had scarcely gained her position, before the captain of the Compton came on board and informed Commander Kelly that he was ordered by the Taoutae to make any concession he, the American captain, might demand, and that on the following day he would hoist the American flag at the fore, and at noon salute it with twenty-one guns. Commander Kelly thought he might as well stay where he was and see it done, as he was determined it should be, and on the next day, at noon, it was done according to promise, when the Plymouth returned to her old anchorage off the American consulate.

One would have supposed that the Chinese might have learned from this transaction that there was a limit to the patience and forbearance of the foreigners at Shanghai; but, though we hear of no more of their insolence on the water, the aggressions of the land troops still continued in the outskirts of the settlement; and although they were frequently warned by the consul of every nation of the probable consequences of such conduct, it availed nothing, and at last the old reply came, that the foreigners must take care of themselves. The foreigners then resolved to take the Chinese at their word, and protect themselves.

The marauding celestials were not long in forcing them to execute their resolution. On the third of April some of the imperial troops commenced destroying a building, which one of the foreigners was erecting, and carrying off the timbers. The owner, on hearing of it, repaired with a friend to the spot, where his remonstrances were answered by an attack on both the gentlemen *with swords*. Providentially one of them had a revolver, with which he defended himself and wounded two of his assailants, who then retreated. Very soon after, however, they began to assemble from the different camps, and attacking a lady and gentleman, compelled the former to flee for her life, pursued by these miscreants, and inflicted several wounds on the latter. It was now obvious that the time had come to deal with these vermin, and the alarm was given. Her Britannic Majesty's ships Encounter and Grecian were in the harbor, as well as the Plymouth, and from the former a small body of marines had been previously put on shore for the purpose of giving protection. As soon as the alarm was given, these repaired to the race course, where the Chinese were assembled in large numbers, and were immediately fired upon. The ground in the vicinity is literally covered with tombs, and behind these the little handful of marines were obliged to seek temporary shelter until reinforcements could arrive. The blue jackets and marines were soon landed from the English ships and from ours, and the Chinese were driven back to their encampments, one of which was captured and destroyed. The English and Americans then retired for the night, keeping up strong patroles. The next morning early a conference was held by the English and American consuls, Captain O'Callaghan, of the English service, and Commander Kelly, who came to the conclusion that it was necessary for the safety of the foreign settlement and population that the entrenched encampments of Chinese, in the vicinity of the race course, should be abandoned by them; and the gentlemen resolved to inform the Chinese general and the commander of their fleet that they must be so abandoned by four o'clock on that day, failing which they would be destroyed. To this communication no reply had been received at half past three, when the foreigners proceeded to their work. Captain O'Callaghan, with about one hundred and fifty sailors and marines from the English ships, and the Shanghai volunteers, occupied the right; the sailors and marines from the Plymouth, in number about sixty, together with thirty men from the American merchant ships, and two private field pieces, worked by American citizens, who placed themselves under Captain Kelly, occupied the left, the whole of this detachment being under the orders of Commander Kelly. This detachment had also a twelve-pound howitzer, with which at four o'clock it commenced throwing shells into the encampment. This was continued for some fifteen or twenty minutes, when, no return being made from the entrenchment, Commander Kelly ordered the firing to cease, with the view of charging into the camp. The men advanced accordingly, when they found themselves separated from the encampment, at a distance of about thirty yards from it, by a creek twenty feet wide and seven deep. Here the Chinese opened a smart fire of musketry and gingals from behind their mud walls, while our men were totally unprotected. The fire continued here about ten minutes, when Commander Kelly directed a flank movement to the left, where were numerous mounds, which would afford the assailants some protection, and whence they could also throw their shot into the enemy's camp. In about eight minutes the Chinese fled in great disorder, leaving behind them a number of wounded and dead.

While these things were passing on the left Captain O'Callaghan had assaulted them on the right, captured their entrenchments on that side, and set their encampment on fire. He then marched up to the rear of that entrenchment which Commander Kelly had attacked in front, so that it was between the two detachments, and set fire to that encampment also. The English and Americans then retired for the night. The next morning at daylight they were again on the spot, when a hundred Chinese coolies were set to work, and soon levelled all the embankments. The casualties to the English and Americans were equal; each had one man killed and three wounded. After this the Chinese behaved themselves quietly.

Our artists, as usual, busied themselves in sketching scenes and objects of interest on this their last visit to China, and directed their attention particularly to the manipulations connected

Chinese Rice Hulling Machine.

with the preparation of agricultural products for market. The rice hulling machine falls far behind that of the Japanese worked by water.

Nor is the mode of whipping cotton, which fell under their observation, more worthy of admiration. It is a coarse and laborious contrivance, which Yankee ingenuity would soon supersede, provided the Emperor of the celestials would grant a "patent for the invention," which could be protected. Without that, Jonathan will not tax his ingenuity.

Cotton Whipping, Hong Kong.

And now the Commodore, having finished the work assigned him by his country, and worn down by long-continued anxiety of mind, ill health of body, aggravated, doubtless, by his solicitudes and cares for many months, and an increasing debility, began to look toward the rest of home, which he so much needed. He had written to the Hon. Secretary some time before, asking leave, when his work was done, to turn over the command to the officer next in rank, and return to the United States. At Hong Kong he found awaiting him dispatches from the Navy Department, conveying the leave he asked, leaving it optional with him to return in the Mississippi, or by the overland route from India. He chose the latter, and, delivering to Captain Abbot the command of the squadron, now composed of the Macedonian, Powhatan, and Vandalia only, (the rest having all been ordered home,) after a most friendly acknowledgment of his services by his countrymen living in China, and a kind farewell expressed in a correspondence between himself and the commercial houses of Russel, Nye, Wetmore, King, and indeed all the American firms and residents, which will be found at length in the Appendix, he embarked, in company with his flag lieutenant, in the English mail steamer Hindostan, and arrived in New York on the 12th day of January, 1855, having been absent from the United States two years and two months.

On the 23d of April, 1855, the Mississippi reached the navy yard at Brooklyn, and on the next day the Commodore, repairing on board and formally hauling down his flag, thus consummated the final act in the story of the United States Expedition to Japan.

SUPPLEMENTARY CHAPTER.

COMMANDER ADAMS ARRIVES IN THE UNITED STATES WITH THE TREATY.—SUBMITTED BY THE PRESIDENT AND RATIFIED BY THE SENATE.—COMMANDER ADAMS SENT BACK WITH AUTHORITY TO EXCHANGE RATIFICATIONS.—ARRIVES AT SIMODA AFTER AN ABSENCE OF LITTLE MORE THAN NINE MONTHS.—ALTERED ASPECT OF THE PLACE FROM THE EFFECTS OF AN EARTHQUAKE.—JAPANESE ACCOUNT OF THE CALAMITY.—LOSS OF RUSSIAN SHIP-OF-WAR DIANA.—RUSSIANS MAKE A TREATY EXACTLY LIKE OURS, WITH A SUBSTITUTION MERELY OF NAGASAKI FOR NAPHA AS ONE OF THE THREE PORTS.—FRENCH SHIP BRINGS IN TWO SHIPWRECKED JAPANESE.—AUTHORITIES REFUSE TO RECEIVE THEM EXCEPT FROM UNDER OUR FLAG—HAVING NO TREATY WITH FRANCE.—MEN TAKEN ON BOARD THE POWHATAN, AND THEN RECEIVED BY THEIR COUNTRYMEN.—ENERGY OF JAPANESE IN REBUILDING SIMODA.—FREEDOM OF INTERCOURSE WITH THE PEOPLE.—NO MORE ESPIONAGE.—BRISK TRAFFIC AT THE SHOPS.—DELIVERY TO CAPTAIN ADAMS OF SOME RELIGIOUS TRACTS LEFT AT SIMODA BY MR. BITTINGER.—JAPANESE HAD LEARNED TO MANAGE THE LOCOMOTIVE, BUT NOT THE TELEGRAPH.—MORYAMA YENOSKE PROMOTED.—MESSAGE FROM THE COMMISSIONERS TO COMMODORE PERRY.—RATIFICATIONS EXCHANGED.

HE Narrative of the Japanese Expedition, properly speaking, ended with the act recorded in the closing sentence of the last chapter; but for the completion of the story, it is thought it will prove not unacceptable to our countrymen to present the subsequent transactions connected with the treaty up to the exchange of ratifications by the respective representatives of Japan and our own government.

Commander Adams, it will be remembered, was dispatched home with the copy of the treaty, on the 4th of April, 1854, in the Saratoga. On the 1st of May, he reached Honolulu, and took the first vessel that offered for San Francisco, and thence, taking the usual route, via Panama, reached the City of Washington on the 12th of July, thus making the travel from Japan to our seat of government in three months and eight days. The treaty was submitted by the President to the Senate, and was by that body promptly and unanimously ratified; and on the 30th of September Commander Adams left New York with the ratified copy for Japan. On reaching England, he took the overland route, and arrived at Hong Kong on the 1st of January, 1855. The Powhatan was ordered by Commodore Abbot immediately to convey Commander Adams to Simoda, where he arrived on the 26th of January, 1855, with full powers as the representative of the United States to exchange with the Japanese authorities the ratifications of the treaty. The journey back to Simoda occupied three months and twenty-seven days, and the whole time that elapsed between the signing of the treaty and the arrival of it in Japan, duly ratified by the President and Senate, was nine months and twenty-two days.

On the arrival of Commander Adams at Simoda, he found a great and sad change in the physical aspects of the place. In the interval during his absence from Japan, (on the 23d of

510   EXPEDITION TO JAPAN.

December, 1854,) an earthquake had occurred which was felt on the whole coast of Japan, doing some injury to the capital, Yedo, completely destroying the fine city of Osaca on the southeastern side of Niphon, and leaving abundant evidences of its ruinous effects at Simoda. One who should now visit the place would find the description of it given in our narrative and the pictured illustrations of our artists no longer appropriate. They represent Simoda *as it was*. Every house and public building on the low grounds had been destroyed: a few temples and private edifices that stood on elevated spots were all that escaped, and but sixteen structures were all that was left of what was once Simoda. The inhabitants told Commander Adams that

Temple of Ben-ting, Simoda.

the destruction was not caused by the immediate agitation of the earth, but by the action of the sea which it occasioned, and which regularly followed the shocks. According to the statements of the Japanese, the waters in the bay and near the shore were first observed to be violently agitated; they soon began rapidly to retreat, leaving the bottom of the harbor, where usually there were five fathoms of water, nearly bare. The sea then rushed in upon the land in a wave five fathoms above its usual height, and, overflowing the town up to the tops of the houses, swept everything away. The frightened inhabitants fled to the hills for safety, but before they could reach their summits they were overtaken by the climbing waters and hundreds were drowned. The waters retreated and returned in this manner five several times, tearing down everything, and strewing the adjacent shores with the wrecks and ruins of houses prostrated, and vessels torn from their anchorage. The Russian frigate Diana, bearing the flag of Admiral Pontiatine, was lying in the harbor at the time. The Russian officers told Commander Adams that, when the waters retreated, the mud boiled up from the bottom in a thousand springs. When they came in they boiled like a maelstrom, and such was their velocity and force that the frigate actually made forty-three complete revolutions in the space of thirty minutes. The officers and crew were made giddy by this rapid turning. Their anchor had been let go in six fathoms; when the waters retreated they could see it, and had but four feet of water alongside. The ship's rudder, stern-post, and a great part of her keel, were knocked off and lost, and her bottom was very much injured. After the effects of the earthquake had somewhat subsided, and the sea became comparatively tranquil, she was found to leak badly. Her guns were landed, and as there was no suitable place in Simoda to heave her down, Admiral Pontiatine sent to look for some contiguous spot fit for the purpose; and it may subserve the interests of navigation here to record that he informed Commander Adams that he found a most excellent and sheltered harbor, resembling that of Hakodadi, but smaller, and completely land-locked with an abundance of water. It is about sixty miles from Simoda, at a place called *Hed-do*, situated at the head of the bay which lies westward of the peninsula of Idzu. Here the Russian admiral attempted to take his disabled ship and repair her, but a gale came on, and she foundered near the shore, the officers and crew with difficulty saving their lives. They were all in Japan during the stay of Commander Adams, and, at that time, with little prospect of getting away. They, however, subsequently chartered the American schooner Foote, as we have related on a previous page, and sailed in her for Petropaulowski. The Russians were in distress, and Captain McCluney, of the Powhatan, generously supplied them with all the provisions he could spare from his ship. The object of the admiral was to make for his country a treaty with Japan, and it was concluded after the loss of his ship and during the stay of Commander Adams, who was informed by the admiral that it was *exactly like that made by Commodore Perry for us*, with the single change of a substitution of the harbor of Nagasaki for that of Napha in Lew Chew; this, we venture to suggest, is no improvement, inasmuch as the long continued and tame submission of the Dutch at Dezima has taught the Japanese officials there to be very arrogant and insolent toward foreigners. But, although Admiral Pontiatine thus succeeded in making a treaty, to Commander Adams the Japanese " appeared to entertain no goodwill toward the Russians." They are probably suspicious of their ultimate purposes.

While the Powhatan was at Simoda, a French ship arrived there and anchored in the outer harbor, having on board two Japanese seamen who had been taken off the wreck of a junk about three years before by an American whale-ship. The authorities ordered the vessel off, would permit none of their people to go on board of her, and positively refused to receive the shipwrecked seamen. They had, they said, no treaty with France, and French vessels had no right to come there under any pretext. At the intercession, however, of Commander Adams and Captain McCluney, they agreed to receive their shipwrecked countrymen from the Powhatan, if Captain McCluney would first receive them on board his ship, and then deliver them as coming from an American man-of-war. This plan was adopted. The men were kept all night on board the Powhatan, and landed the next morning. They were immediately, however, compelled to lay aside their European clothing, and conform in all respects to the Japanese costume; besides which they were placed under a strict surveillance, which continued, at any rate, as long as the ship remained.

Notwithstanding the calamities caused by the earthquake, there was shown a resiliency in the Japanese character which spoke well for their energy. They did not sit down and weep over their misfortunes, but, like men, went to work, seemingly but little dispirited. They were busily engaged, when the Powhatan arrived, in clearing away and rebuilding. Stone, timber, thatch, tiles, lime, &c., were coming in daily from all quarters, and, before the Powhatan left, there were about three hundred new houses nearly or quite completed, though occasional and some pretty strong shocks, during the ship's stay, were admonishing them of a possible recurrence of the calamity.

The outlines of the harbor of Simoda, Commander Adams states, were not altered at all by the earthquake, but the holding ground seems to have been washed out to sea, leaving no bottom scarcely but naked rocks. This, however, will be resupplied, as it was furnished in the first instance, by the washings from the land, which will probably accumulate rapidly. The Powhatan, for want of holding ground, dragged with three anchors ahead, the wind blowing across the harbor, and no sea. Indeed, she was obliged to rely on her steam to keep off the rocks.

From the place we now turn to the people. The Japanese were much more disposed to be friendly and sociable than on the former visit. The officers of the ship roamed over the country undisturbed, went into the villages, and were received with a welcome everywhere. Espionage seemed to have been laid aside, for there was no attempt to follow or watch them. The shops having all been destroyed, and not yet replaced, a bazaar was opened in a temple repaired for the purpose, and was soon filled with a variety of beautiful articles brought from Yedo and the interior towns. The officers were not only invited but importuned to buy, which they did very freely. An anxious wish was expressed by the people to Commander Adams, that trading vessels from America would soon begin to visit them, and the governor of Simoda (who was one of the commissioners that made the treaty) intimated to the commander that it would be very agreeable to him, personally, if a consul from the United States should be appointed to reside at Simoda.

The Japanese were exceedingly desirous of obtaining English books, particularly on medical and scientific subjects; and many valuable works were given to them by our officers. But they coveted our books on any subject except religion. One circumstance occurred which, says Commander Adams, "made me feel a little ashamed." "The governor of Simoda sent off a bundle of religious books which he said 'Bittinger' (one of the chaplains of Commodore Perry's squadron) had left there clandestinely, which was contrary to Japanese law, and 'not right;' and he begged me to take them away with me, which I agreed to do."

Commander Adams found that they had learned to manage the locomotive which the President had sent to the Emperor; they had also the life-boat afloat with a trained crew, but the magnetic telegraph they said was too hard for them yet. Every day, when Commander Adams was not employed on shore, the lieutenant governor or some official of high rank came off to visit him, and their meetings were those of old friends. Some of them indeed were old acquaintances; the governor of Simoda was Isawa, Mimasaki Nokami, one of the treaty commissioners, and our old friend the interpreter, Moryama Yenoske, who assisted in making our translation of the treaty, (he understood English,) was also at Simoda, having been very deservedly promoted; others of the commissioners were also there for the purpose of exchanging ratifications, and Commander Adams was not allowed to feel as if he were among strangers. The commissioners inquired with great interest about Commodore Perry, sent many messages of friendship and remembrance, and charged Commander Adams to say to him that his "name would live forever in the history of Japan."

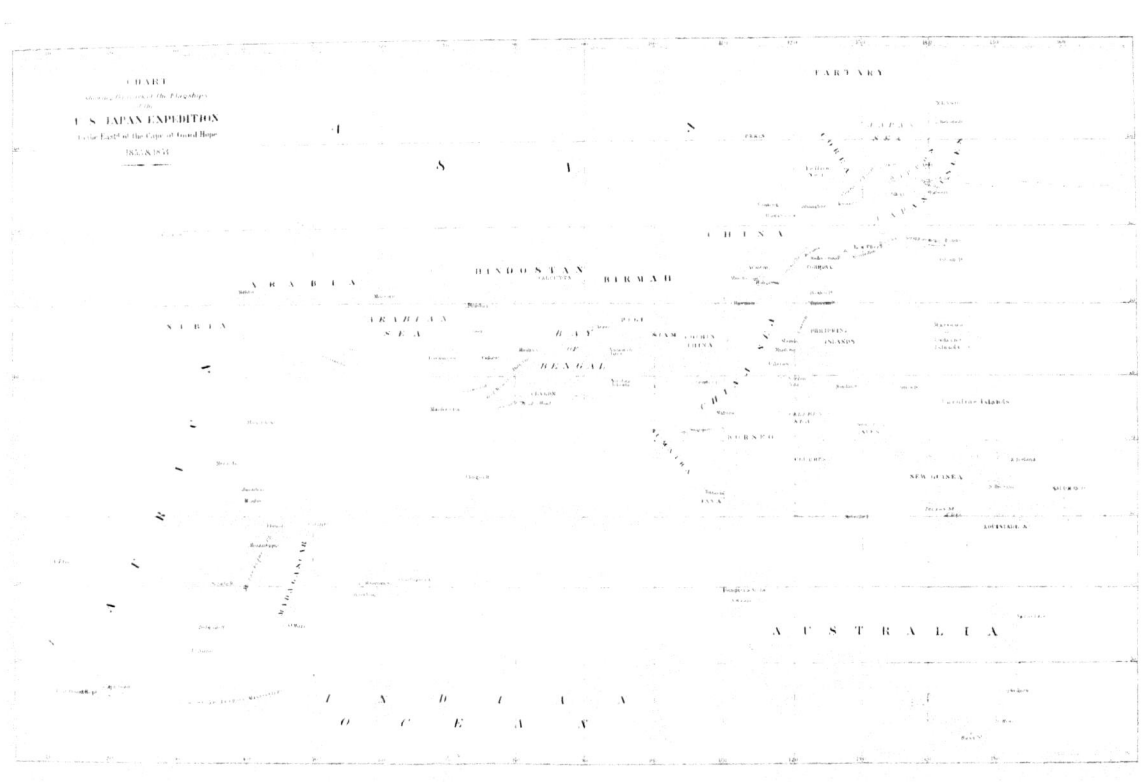

As to the exchange of ratifications, the Japanese, at first, interposed two objections; these, however, did not arise from unwillingness to abide by their engagements, but were rather technical, and founded upon their scrupulous interpretation of the terms of a written contract, and upon their profound respect for ceremonials. The objections were, first, that their copy of the treaty said it was to be ratified *after* eighteen months; ours said *within* eighteen months; but as the Dutch and Chinese translations agreed with our English copy, and as that had been taken as the original, from which all the translations, including their Japanese version, had been made, they became convinced that the discrepancy arose from the ignorance of their translator, and having had explained to them what was meant by our English word "within," as here used, they very gracefully withdrew all objection on this score. The other objection was to the Emperor's affixing his sign manual to the Japanese copy for our government. They said the Emperor never signed any document, but the supreme council only. Commander Adams represented to them that the President and Secretary of State had signed the copy he had brought for them, and beside, the Emperor was the party named in the instrument as having made the treaty, and therefore he wished his signature. Finally, it was concluded that both the Emperor and supreme council should sign it, and it was accordingly done. On the 21st of February the exchanges were formally made, and as soon as it was done, the Powhatan immediately showed the Japanese flag at the fore, and fired a salute of seventeen guns.

The commissioners also gave Commander Adams a *ratified* copy of the "additional regulations" made between the Commodore and the Japanese commissioners, which they seemed to consider part of the treaty, with a request that he would deliver it to the President, and ask him to send out, by some American ship, the American ratification as soon as it was completed. On the day after the ratification, *February* 22, the Powhatan left Simoda, and our new and, as we trust, enduring friendly relations with Japan are thus associated, in date at least, with the name of WASHINGTON.

Graves of American Dead in Japan.

INDEX.

	Page.
Abbott, Captain, misled by Von Siebold's charts	326
inquiries at Formosa	499
report of squalls near Formosa	500
Abbey Point, Lew Chew	152, 195
Adams, William, pilot of the Dueth fleet, his account of his visit to Japan	27
his letters sent to England	34
Adams, Commander, his MS. journal	iv
interview with the governor of Uraga	237
interview with the governor of Uraga	241
interview with the mayor of Napha	276
conversation with Japanese officials respecting the death of the Emperor	331
discussion respecting Uraga	332
interview with the Japanese officials at Uraga	333
conversation with Yezaiman	341
conferences with Japanese officials	355, 356
delivers American presents to the Japanese	372
bearer of the treaty to the United States	393
arrives home	509
returns with the ratified treaty to Simoda	509
his numerous visitors at Simoda	512
leaves Simoda	513
Admiral, title of used for that of commodore, in treating with the Japanese	246
Agriculture of the Japanese, their grains	52
tea	52
Advanced state of Lew Chew	220
Agriculturist, his share in the products of the land	220, 226
Ainos, Yesso	454, 469
Alexander the Great, fleet of, visits Ceylon	116
Althea, Lew Chew	168
Amahs, Chinese nurses	291
Amakirima islands, near Lew Chew	274
Amaral, Portuguese governor, Macao plot against	301

	Page.
America, Japanese knowledge of	464
American commercial houses, high character of among the Chinese	136
merchants at Shanghai claim protection	148
anchorage, the bay of Uraga	265
anchorage, bay of Yedo	328
merchants at Hong Kong, application of the to Commodore Perry	287
sailor captive in Japan	340
ships, intercourse of, with Japan	351
limits in Japan	385, 387
ships in Japan, supplies for	385
intercourse with the Japanese	474
intercourse with Japan, treaty regulations respecting	479
Americans shipwrecked at Formosa	498, 499
Amphitheatre, Japanese drawing of an	461
Anatomical drawing, Japanese	462
Antidote for poison in use in the Indian seas	119
Arch, peculiar, at Nagaguska, Lew Chew	171
Architecture, Japanese	463
Areca tree, Bonin islands	198
Argonaut, visit of the ship, to Japan	39
Arms of Izawa, emblazoned	344
Arrack tree, Bonin islands	198
Art, Japanese	459
Arts of design in Japan	59
Arzobispo, a name given to the Bonin islands	200
Astronomical knowledge of the Japanese	57
Awa, province of Japan	232
capes of	427
Ayahs, Chinese nurses	291
Baby, Japanese	396
Bache, Professor, charts of the coast survey	429
Baggass, or crushed sugar-cane	314
Bailey islands	197, 199, 283
Ballastier, Mr., visit to Siam	121
Bamboo range of mountains, Mauritus	108
Bamboo, Lew Chew	312
fences, Lew Chew	178
Banner Rock, Lew Chew	168
Banyan, Lew Chew	175, 312
Barometrical observations in the Indian ocean	104
Barrels, Hakodadi	456
Barrow's bay, Lew Chew	165, 167, 173, 176

516 INDEX.

	Page.
Bastions, substitutes for in the fort of Nagagnska, Lew Chew	171
Baths, public, Simoda	405
Battas, a tribe of the Malays, their dainty cannibalism	130
Batteries, Japanese, bay of Yedo	343
Beacon-fires, Japanese, bay of Uraga	236
Beard, a full black, a distinctive mark of the Japanese and Lew Chewans	315
Beech tree, Peel island	210
Beechey, Captain, names the Bonin islands	197
his nomenclature of the islands disowned	199
position of Port Lloyd in his chart, erroneous	202
account of the Lew Chewans	221
Beggars, commutation with, Canton	292
Begging, mode of, Canton	293
Belcher, Captain, account of the Lew Chewans	221
Bell, a large, presented to Commodore Perry by the regent of Lew Chew	496
Bellows, Napha, in blacksmith's shop	220
Japanese	456
Bent, Lieutenant, his MS. journal	iv
pilots the expedition in Napha harbor	150
survey of the bay of Uraga	238, 241
conversation with Japanese respecting America	464
rebukes servility of "Sam Patch"	486
commissioner of treaty with Lew Chew	495
Bettelheim, Dr., a missionary at Lew Chew	152
visits Commodore Perry	153
remark on the old regent of Lew Chew	215
believes Lew Chew a part of Japan	222
remarks respecting education in Lew Chew	223
history of, and of his missionary operations in Lew Chew	225
a layman	225
removal of	320
leaves Lew Chew	498
Lew Chew, official communication respecting	498
Bing, Japanese rouge	395
Birds, scarcity of, Lew Chew	175
Bonin islands	203
Bishop's bay, Macao	140
Bittinger, Rev. Mr., visits Kanagawa, Japan	360
his exchange of American for Japanese coin	360
his kind treatment by the Japanese	360
coins obtained by, returned	365
Blacksmiths, Japanese	456
Blacksmith's shop, Napha	220

	Page.
Blunt, Cape, near Hakodadi	430
Boar, wild, Lew Chew	182
Peel island	206
Board, supposed murder of, at Napha	492
Boas of Ceylon	119
Boatmen, Canton	294
Boats, Japanese	450
Bocca Tigris, Canton river	137
Bonaparte, Napoleon, remark on war to Basil Hall	318
Bonham, Sir George, conference with Commodore Perry respecting the Bonin islands	303
Bonin islands	196, 197
discovery of the, by the Japanese	197
advantages of establishing a naval station at the	212
described	200
sovereignty of the	213
Captain Kelly's visit to the	282
English claim to the	304
Books in Japan	58, 59
in Lew Chew, Chinese	224
Japanese	463
Borodino islands	211
Bosquette, M., a writer on hurricanes	113
Boundaries, American, Simoda	477
Hakodadi	478, 481
Boundary of American intercourse in Japan	468
Bourboulon, M. de, French minister to Canton	300, 303
Boyle, Lieutenant, assists the Macedonian, aground in the bay of Yedo	327
places a buoy on a rock, bay of Yedo	401
visits Olason island	469
report of a marine volcano near Formosa	500
treatment of the Sillibaboos	503
Brabant mountains, Mauritius	108
Broom-corn, Lew Chew	173
Broughton rocks, bay of Yedo	325
Brown, Mr., daguerreotypist	154
Buchanan, Commander, conducts regent of Lew Chew over the Susquehanna	216
interview with the governor of Uraga	237
interview with governor of Uraga	244
leads the escort of Commodore Perry	253
first American who lands in Japan	254
conversation with the governor of Uraga	263
Buddha, statues of, in grave-yard, Simoda	407
Buddhism, extent of its influences	21
in Ceylon	120
Buddhist priest at a funeral, Japan	354
temples, Simoda	406
offerings	409

INDEX. 517

	Page.
Buddhist gardens	409
apartments	409
religious services	476
temples, Hakodadi	442
occasionally used as places of concourse	443
Building erected to receive the letter of the President, Japan	254
Burial customs, Lew Chew	319
of a sailor at Kaki-Zaki	425
Butting a part of Japanese wrestling	371
Buttons, Japanese taste for American	358
Cabinets d'aisance, public, Japan	452
Caffre war, consequences of the	99, 103
Caffres, description of	101
Camelias, bay of Yedo	394
Camoens, history of	143
cave of	142
monument to	299
Camp Perry, Lew Chew	167
Camphor tree in Japan	61
Cannibalism, daintiness in	130
Canton, visit to	135
annual trade of	138
charitable asylums of	294
river	135
Cape Colony, population of	101
Cape de Verde islands, the Harmattan observed at	89, 90
Cape of Good Hope, route to, from England	98
Cape Town, visit to	98
Cards, Japanese game of	465
Cassa sent to Japan by Sir Stamford Raffles	44
Castles of Lew Chew	185
Cats and dogs, wild, hunted in the Bonin islands	203
Catherine, Empress of Russia, directs shipwrecked Japanese to be sent home	45
Cattle at Simoda	424
Cecille, Admiral, explores Lew Chew	229
Cedars, Japanese, large size of	61
Centipede boats	158
Centre island, Simoda harbor	416
Ceylon, visit to	116
Chairs, Lew Chew	190
Chama gigas, Bonin islands	202
Chang-Yuen, the Lew Chew guide	172
Chapin, Aldin B., visits the Bonin islands	200
an early settler of the Bonin islands	305
Charcoal, Japanese custom respecting	369
Charitable institutions, Canton	294
Charms on grave-stones, Yoku-hama	408
Charts of Japanese waters in use, incorrect	325
Chess, Japanese game of	465
Chimneys, absence of, Simoda	404
Chin-Chin to Commodore Perry	153
China, laws regulating etiquette on the death of an emperor	323
benefit of American trade to	352
American treaty with	382
sea, navigation of the	132

	Page.
China street, Canton	136
China, imitation of, in Lew Chew	223
Chinese, their claims to have colonized Japan	8
language not understood by the Japanese	8
commerce with Singapore	125
traders, activity of, at Hong-Kong	135
coolies, inefficient	174
coolie, treatment of a sick	181
lack of sympathy for a dying comrade	195
emigrants, Commodore Perry's remarks on the transportation of, to California	212
claim sovereignty over Loo-Choo	221
account of the origin of the Lew Chewans	221
treated as strangers in Lew Chew	222
emigrants to Lew Chew	223
books in Lew Chew	224
handwriting in use in Lew Chew	224
revolution, inquiry of a Japanese respecting	261
abstemiousness of the	289
servants	290
comprador	290
feet, women averse to showing	292
higher classes	295
preponderance in Macao	297
treaty with the U. States, a copy of furnished to the Japanese commissioners	350
imperial troops, conduct to American citizens	504
imperial troops, assaults on American merchants, Shanghai; English and American attack upon	506
Chow Hwang, his account of the origin of the Lew Chewans	221
Christianity, its early introduction into Japan doubtful	22
early introduced into Ceylon	120
the common people of Lew Chew favorably disposed towards	225
introduction of, into Japan	446
in Japan	475
Chung Ching, castle of, Lew Chew	185
Cleanliness of Lew Chew	193
Cleopatra islands, Lew Chew	324, 325
Clergyman, treatment of a, in Japan	446
Clifford, Lieutenant, forms the Lew Chew naval mission	225
Climate of St. Helena	92
Climate of Simoda	413
Clipped Camelia, Lew Chew	176
Clock, Japanese	54
Contee, Lieutenant	155
Coal, abundant in Japan	60
supplies of, a prominent object of the Japanese expedition	75, 77
depots	97
opportune supply of	114
depot at Singapore	129
at Lew Chew	280

518   INDEX.

	Page.
Coal depot at Bonin islands	304
the U. States desirous to procure, from Japan	257
building for storing, Lew Chew	282
at Shah bay, Lew Chew	311
Japan	341, 350
at Simoda	484
analysis of	482
supply of, from Formosa	498, 499
Cockes, Richard, first director of the English factory in Japan	36
Cocoa-nut in Ceylon	117
Coffin, Captain, visits the Bonin islands	197, 199
Coffin islands	199, 283
Color printing, Japan	460
Columbus, examines Marco Polo's writings	5
Columbus, visit of the, to Japan	233
Commercial treaty, the Japanese decline making a	383
Comprador, a household official	140
Compradors of European households in China	290
Compton, the Sir H., of the Chinese imperial fleet, attack on an American pilot-boat	504
forced to make reparation	505
Conference at Hakodadi	434
Confucian temples, schools at	223
writings, text-books in Lew Chew	224
remark of the Bishop of Victoria on	224
Congress water at Shanghai	145
Constantia vineyards, visit to	100
Consul, American, in Japan	374, 383
date of appointment of	385
Consular fees of the United States often insufficient for support	116
Consuls, American, in Japan	377
Contee, Lieutenant, his MS. journal	iv
conference with the deputy governor of Uraga	234
conversation with the governor of Uraga	263
Coolies at Mauritius	109
of Lew Chew commended	163, 164, 174, 179
Coopers, Hakodadi	456
Copper abundant in Japan	60
mode of casting	60
Coral in Napha harbor, Lew Chew	154
reef, China sea	132
reefs	429
rock, Lew Chew	311
walls, Lew Chew	312
Corpse, Japanese official inspection of a	425
Costume of the sexes similar in Lew Chew	158
Cotton weaving, Japan	458
whipping, Hong Kong	508
Courses of a Japanese entertainment	191
Courteous deportment of Japanese officials	247
Crows, precautions against, Simoda	404
Crucifixion, Japanese, punishment of	486
Crumeno, a tree, Bonin islands	210
Crustacea, Bonin islands	202

	Page.
Cultivator, an American, at the Cape of Good Hope	103
Cumberland coal, analysis of	482
Cum-sing-moon, China	503
near Hong Kong, rendezvous of the squadron at	288
Cung-qua, or Khan, Lew Chew	163, 174, 179
Cunning of Mandarin of Kelung	499
of the inhabitants	500
Currency, the Lew Chewans do not possess a	227
Current at sea observed	81
at the Cape of Good Hope	103
between Lew Chew and Japan	230
southeast of Formosa	308
near Hakodadi	430
Currents	90
near Japan	272
Custom dues, Uraga	237, 242
Cutlery, Japanese, inferior	456
Cyclone near Mauritius	113
Daguerreotypists of the expedition	194
Dai-ko-saki, or White Cape	429
Dairi, or ecclesiastical Emperor of Japan	270
Dans Kevitch, a Japanese	486
Dead, respect for the, in Lew Chew	226
Death of a Chinese opium eater	193
Decorations of the Treaty House, Japan	344
Defences, military, at Uraga	239, 240
Demons, boxes for feeding hungry, Simoda	407
Dezima, factory at	4
the residence of the Dutch in Japan	7
described	32
Diamond, Cape, Simoda harbor	416
Diana, the Russian frigate, at Simoda	390
Diaz, discovery of the Cape of Good Hope	98
Diet, Simoda	405
Dinner to the regent of Lew Chew, on board the Susquehanna	217
Dinners, Japanese, unsubstantial	380
Disappointment island, position of	213
Discipline of the expedition in Japan	417
Disembowelment, practice of, among the Japanese	17
Dishes served up in Lew Chew	191
Divine service at sea	196
Docks, Simoda	403
Doeff, a writer on Japan	4, 7
his intrigues against the English in Japan	64
his treatment of the expeditions of Raffles	42, 44
Dogs, Peel island, poor hunters	206
presented by the Japanese	369
Japanese	369
introduced in England	369
Dogwood, tree resembling the, Peel island	210
"Dollar boats," Whampoa	135
Domestic animals running wild, Bonin islands	203, 211
Domestic life, Lew Chew	172
Dosia, a preparation imparting flexibility to a corpse, also administered to the living	57
Doty, Mr., his letters respecting the treatment of Americans at Simoda	390

INDEX.

519

	Page.
Drainage, Japanese	453
Drawings, Japanese	462
Dress of dignitaries at Lew Chew	217
the Japanese	396
Duer, Lieutenant, observation of a meteor, bay of Uraga	236
Duggan, Professor, remarks on Japanese art	466
Dutch, intercourse of the, with Japan	4, 27, 381
extent of their knowledge of Japan	7
expedition to Japan, W. Adams's account of	27
deny the authority of papal grants	27
and English carry on joint buccaneering enterprises	27
aid the Japanese in making war on the native Christians	31
removed to Dezima	32
concessions to Japanese opinion	32
do not trample on the cross	33
officials formerly visited the Emperor of Japan	33
intercourse out of their factory with the Japanese	33
induce Japanese to refuse intercourse with the English	39
their foothold in India destroyed by Clive and Hastings	39
answer to their claim to have assisted the Japanese expedition	63, 67
in 1844 recommend Japan to abolish her exclusive system	64, 65
proposed treaty	65
possession of St. Helena	91
possession of Mauritius	107
possessions in Ceylon	116
treaty with Japan	389
nostrum for sale in Japan	404
Duyong, alleged mermaid of Singapore	131
Dwarf trees of the Japanese	53
Earthquake, Japan	510
East India Company construct roads in St. Helena	92
Education in Japan	58
of the Lew Chewans, Dr. Bettelheim's evidence respecting	223
Ehrenberg, his examination of the Harmattan	90
Eldridge, J. C., purser, report on Japanese currencies	478
Elephants of Ceylon	118
hunting	118
"Elevated enclosure of fragrant festivities," Shui, Lew Chew	190
Emperor of Japan, death of the	321, 331
the new	350
reception of his reply to the letter of the President of the United States	346
his official signature	513
Endermo harbor, survey of; beauty of its shores	468
Engines, disconnecting	105

	Page.
English, intercourse of the, with Japan	4, 31
deny the authority of Papal grants of newly discovered countries	27
trade with Japan at first unprofitable	36
trade closed voluntarily in 1623	36
attempts to reopen trade	37
refused intercourse with the Japanese	39
colonial policy hinders their progress in Japan	40
in 1808 send a man-of-war to Japan in pursuit of Dutch ships	40
treaty with Japan	63, 387, 388
possession of Mauritius	107
possessions in Ceylon	116
temporary possession of the Bonin islands	200
Japanese restrictions upon the	384
ship encountered by the Expedition	490
Epitaphs, Simoda	408
Escort of Commodore Perry at Uraga chosen by lot	252
Espionage, official, in Japan	15
effects of	16
anecdote of	16
Ethiopian Minstrels, Japanese interest in their performances	470
Ethnological resemblances between Lew Chew and Japan	223
European periodicals read and translated in Japan	463
Everett, Edward, his reply to Commodore Perry	87
Exchange, rate of, established with the Japanese	424
Exclusive policy of the Japanese, its origin	19
Executioners in Japan, how selected	14
Factories at Canton	136
Fahs', Dr., exploration of Peel island	204
survey of Peel island	209
report on the ethnology of Lew Chew	315
Fans, Japanese	268
Farm-houses near Simoda	413
Fatsicio island, Japan	271
Fateisko Tokushuuo, Japanese interpreter	244
Fees at "show places"	112
Feki, a prince, story of	20
Female servants in China	291
Ferns, Lew Chew	312
Fertility of Peel island	206, 209
Fi-ija, a stream in Lew Chew	183
Filial reverence, the chief of virtues in Lew Chew and China	224
Fillmore, Millard, his Japanese diplomacy	74
letter of, to the Emperor of Japan	256
letter of credence of Commodore Perry from, as President of the United States	259
Fine arts, Lew Chew	317
Fingoos, of the Cape of Good Hope, described	101
Fir trees forced to an enormous size	53
Firando, first factory of the Dutch at	30
Firatatsi, Cape	427

520 INDEX.

	Page.
Fire-arms, astonishment of the Lew Chewans at the American	182
Fischer, a writer on Japan	4, 7
account of the ingenuity of a Japanese fisherman	55
Fish in Napha harbor, Lew Chew	154
Japanese mode of presenting	368
in Japanese waters	450
a favorite gift	452
Fisherman, Lew Chew	219
Fishing boats, near Macao	133
Fishing at Port Lloyd, Bonin islands	202
Flora of Peel island	210
Flowers, Lew Chew	175
in grave yard, Simoda	408
Fogo, indistinct view of	89
Fogs off the Chinese coast	144
common on the Japanese coast	231, 249
Foot-balls, Lew Chew	318
Foote, C. E., the American schooner at Simoda	390
Forcade, Father, remark of Siebold on	72
Foreigners, Japanese, jealousy of	386
Forks, bamboo sticks used as, Lew Chew	191
Formosa coal, analysis of	483
expedition to	498
Fortifications, Japanese	398
Fortress of Nagaguska, Lew Chew	169
Forts, Chinese, at the mouth of Canton river	137
bay of Uraga	237, 239
Fourth of July, 1853, celebration of by the Expedition	230
Fox, Japanese ideas respecting the	451
Francis, John W., anecdote of Basil Hall	518
Frassinet, his opinion on Pinto's visit to Japan	23
acquits the Dutch of persecuting the Japanese Christians	31
Frederick, visit of the ship, to Japan	39
Free negroes at the Cape of Good Hope	103
at Mauritius	109
French, intercourse of the with Japan	4
possession of Isle of France, or Mauritius	107
inhabitants of Mauritius	110
Fryers, Lieutenant, a writer on hurricanes	113
Fudsi-Jamma, a mountain of Japan	7
Funchal	82, 84
Funeral, American, at Hakodadi	475
of a marine, Japan	353
Fusi the Great, a mountain, Japan	231, 232
Mount, Japan	271
Fusi-Yama, bay of Jedo, summit of	326
Gale experienced by the expedition on entering Yedo	325
Garden seeds distributed to settlers, Bonin islands	211
Geological features of Lew Chew	311
formation of the Bonin islands	202
Geology of Lew Chew, Rev. Mr. Jones's report on	184
of Peel island	209
Gingerbread, tough, Shui, Lew Chew	190
Giumaraës, governor of the Portuguese navy, Hong Kong	300

	Page.
Glass, manufacture of, by the Japanese	51
Glasson, Lieutenant, at Napha	492
Glynn, commander, enforces release of American seamen in Japan	48
urges intercourse with Japan	77
discovery of Oho-Sima in 1846	324
Gneiss, Lew Chew	175
Goats, wild, number of, on Stapleton island, Bonins	211
Goble, Mr., his interest in "Sam Patch"	486
Goebroken Eilander	230
Gohei, an ornament of the Japanese temples	19
Gokai, or "five laws" of Buddism	21
Goku-zhen-zhi, a monastery, Simoda	411
Gold abundant in Japan	60
Golownin, Captain, his account of Japan	7
his visit to Japan	47
says scurvy is prevalent in Yesso	451
Gomara indistinctly seen	87
Gordon, Captain, of the British navy, visits Japan in 1818	44
Gori-Hama, village of, Japan	253
Government of Japan	15
Gozeman, a book-keeper of the Dutch factory, carried off by the English	40
released	41
Grades, classification of the Lew Chewans into four	219
of Lew Chewan population	226
Granaries, Lew Chew	311
Grand Port, Mauritius	111
sea fight at	105
Granite, Lew Chew	178
Grass-cloth robes worn by dignitaries at Napha	216
jackets, Lew Chew	184
Grasses, Peel island	210
Grave yards, Simoda	407
Hakodadi	411
Green, Dr., account of mineral water, Hakodadi	447
Green turtle, Bonin islands	202
Guerin, N., chart of Japanese seas	489
Guest, Lieutenant, his course with the Chinese vessel of war the Sir H. Compton	505
Guilds of porters, Canton	292
of beggars	292
Gulf Stream, analogy with the Kuro-siwo	428
Gutzlaff, remark of Siebold on	72
Hachiman, a Sintoo deified hero	409
Sintoo temple, Hakodadi	445
Hail Columbia, at Shui, Lew Chew	190
Hair, Lew Chew, mode of wearing the	223
pin, Lew Chew	225
Hakodadi, opened to trade by the United States	69, 365
governor of, reply to Messrs. Reed and Dougherty	391
harbor of	431
survey of	434
negotiations respecting the reception of the expedition at	435
products of	435

INDEX. 521

	Page.
Hakodadi, environs of	436
stone quarries, resemblance to Gibraltar	437
streets quiet and cleanly	437
buildings, roofs, precaution against fire, fire-engines	438
wells, sliding partitions, shops	439
fire-engines	438
internal decorations of houses, furniture, stools, tables, cooking-apparatus, tea and tea-cups, fuel	440
kitchens, stoves, out-houses, gardens, fire-proof warehouses	441
shops, commodities, signs, shopmen, fixed prices, Buddhist temples	442
grave yard, epitaphs, prayer wheel	444
Sintoo temples, roadside shrines	445
defences of	446
environs, observatory, telescope	447
geology of, mineral spring, cave	447
vegetables, trees, trade, junks	448
birds, animals, a depot for whalers	451
cattle, horses, roads, sedans, mountains, climate, fogs	452
temperature, healthy climate	453
ship yards	457
Ha-koo-shoo, peasants, Lew Chew	226
Hall, Captain Basil, occupies a house at Lew Chew	158
erroneous statements of	169
erroneous description of the Lew Chewans	220
remark on the Lew Chewans to Napoleon Bonaparte	318
his remark on his account of Lew Chew	318
Hampton, Mr., taken sick during the exploration of Peel island	206
Hansiro, a Japanese convert to Christianity	24
Hara-kiri, or dis-endowelment	215
Harmattan, a wind passing over Africa	89
its alleged effects	89
Harris, Purser, his MS. journal	iv
Hatchee-matchee, or red cap, Lew Chew	189, 216
Haya-hi-daijaku-no-kami, prince of Daijaku, Japan	335
letter of to Com. Perry	337
Japanese commissioner	317
distribution of Japanese presents by	368
at the dinner given by Commodore Perry	375
enjoys negro minstrelsy	376
Haze noticed at sea	89
Hed-do, harbor of, Japan	511
Heine, Mr., artist of the expedition	149
sketches Pino	165
Heraldic devices of the Japanese Emperor and commissioners	348
Hide-yosi, or Fide-yosi, his history	12
Higher classes in China	295

	Page.
Hindoo idolatry in Lew Chew	314
Hirakawa, Japanese	224
Hog lane, Canton	136
Honesty, a conventional virtue with the Chinese	295
Hongo, near Simoda	412
Hongs, at Canton	136
Hong Kong	133
Horsburgh, remark on the action of the barometer in the Indian ocean	104
sailing directions	124
remark on tides in the tropics	132
mention of Sillibaboo island	503
Horse, the points of a, Japanese drawings of	459
Horses, humane treatment of, at Singapore	130
of Lew Chew	158
Lew Chew	192
Japanese	254
Horticulture of the Japanese	53
Hospitality at English colonial settlements to United States officers	110
of foreign merchants in the East	139
Host, incident of disrespect to the at Macao	301
Hot water drunk in Lew Chew	179
House at Lew Chew refused to the expedition	159
House court yards, Simoda	404
Houses, construction of, Uraga	210
at Simoda	404
interior arrangements of, Simoda	405
number of, Simoda	405
uniformity of, in Japan	456
Howland & Aspinwall, acknowledgment of their services by Commodore Perry	111
Huc, M., account of the Portuguese settlement at Macao	140
travels in China	296
description of a praying machine	444
Humboldt, Baron, remark on Teneriffe	88
Hurricanes at Mauritius	105, 112
Huts of natives, Lew Chew	167
Hydrographic survey of the harbor of Lew Chew	161
report on the bay of Uraga	239
Ichirazichi, court interpreter, Lew Chew	192, 216, 284
Ido-Iwami-no-kami, (Prince of Iwami,) Japanese commissioner	255
Ido, prince of Tsusima, Japanese commissioner	317
Idsu or Negatsu cape, Japan	230
Ingenuity of the Japanese	55
Inodzu-gawa, the river Japan	412
Inquisition at Macao	299
Internal trade of the Japanese	53
Interpreter, court, Lew Chew	192
Iron in Japan	60
Irrigation, Lew Chew	220, 311
Ischirazchi, bridge of, Lew Chew	284
Ishee, or Lingam, Lew Chew	173
Isitza, Lew Chew	175
Isomura, Japan	429
Itchaboo, a Japanese coin	436
Iyeyas, his history	12

522 INDEX.

	Page.
Iyeyas, his letter to the King of England	35
Jamestown, St. Helena	92
anchorage at	95
Jamieson, commander of the English ship Bombay	503
Japan, derivation of the name	6
its extent	7
divisions	7
objects of curiosity relative to	3
writers on	4
physical aspect of	7
rivers of	7
roads	8
bridges	8
canals	8
climate	8
colonized by the Chinese	8
duplicate sovereignty of	11
its political subdivisions	15
its Council of State	15
its governor of the Empire	15
introduction of Christianity into	22
visited by Pinto	22
Portuguese intercourse with	24
missions	24
letter of Emperor of, to the King of England	35
progress of industrial arts in, as workers in metal work	50
silver, copper, quicksilver, lead, tin, iron, coal, sulphur, precious stones, pearls, found in	60
Russian expedition to, in 1853	62
Admiral Sterling concludes a treaty with	63
treaty between and other nations, proposed by the Dutch	65
supposed laws regulating etiquette on the death of an emperor	323
an American sailor captive in	340
coal abundant in	341
polygamy unknown in	397
Japanese people, origin of	8
language not understood by the Chinese	8
alphabet or syllabarium	9
dialects	9
construction of language	9
pronunciation	9
Kæmpfer's theory of their origin	9
language, its analogies with other languages	10
color of the	10
of rank resemble Europeans in color	10
resemblance to the Tartar family	10
their claims to antiquity as a nation	11
hereditary rank among the	13
priests, rank of; merchants; peasantry; leather manufacturers; executioners	14
government secretaries; official espionage among the	15

	Page.
Japanese, disembowelment; reason of their unchangeable customs; interdiction of intercourse with Europeans; falsehood among officials a result of their system; not common to the people in general	17
severity of their laws; mode of trial; cage; prisons	18
religion, known as Sintoo; difficulty of obtaining information respecting	19
liberal in their religious views; number of sects among; refusal to banish Jesuits and monks	21
proclamation expelling the Portuguese	26
their reception of the Dutch	28
extirpate the native Christians	31
officials dealing with the Dutch required to trample on the cross	33
intercourse with the English; license to East India Company	34
intercourse with Russia	41
refuse to take back their sailors shipwrecked on the Russian coast	45
decline the overtures of Resanoff	46
officials, conversation with the leaders of the English expedition to that country in 1673	37
refuse intercourse with the English	39
imprison Golownin; intercourse with the United States; refuse to take back their sailors shipwrecked on the United States coast	47
treatment of the ships Morrison, Vincennes, and Prebble; refuse trade with any nation but Holland; imprison United States seamen	48
tabular view of the attempts at intercourse with the	49
their skill in lacquered wood-work and carving	50
manufacture of glass, porcelain, paper-woven fabrics, and leather; shoes of straw	51
agriculture; live stock	52
horticulture; dwarfed trees	53
marine navigation; vessels; compass	53
their scientific knowledge; clock	54
ingenuity; mermaids	55
knowledge of medicine; *post mortem* examination not permitted	56
medical works	56
Dozia	57
their astronomical knowledge	57
similar to that of the Muiscas, of Bogota	58
colleges; schools	58
books, music, drawing, painting, wood-engraving, bas-reliefs, architecture; syaktilo, or enamel	59
cedars	61
camphor tree	61

INDEX. 523

	Page.
Japanese, conduct to be observed towards the, by the expedition	150
embassy at Lew Chew	153
junks	153
official, Lew Chew conversation with	158
possess fire-arms; spies	160
guide, Lew Chew	162
cultivation, Lew Chew	165
discovery of the Bonin islands	197
account of the Bonin islands	198
junk driven into Port Lloyd; wrecked on Stapleton island; survivors taken off by a French ship; wreck seen by officers of the Susquehanna	199
garrison at Napha, Lew Chew; domesticated at Lew Chew; officials, conjectured at; inform Commodore Perry that they claim jurisdiction over Lew Chew	222
expedition makes the first full exploration of the coast of the northern Lew Chew islands	230
at Yedo, admiration of the Susquehanna by the	231
coasting vessels, bay of Yedo	232
guard-boats	233
crews	233, 243
oars	233, 243
flag	233
forts	237, 239
uniform	237
artists	237
diplomacy	238
soldiers, Uraga	239
defences, Uraga	239, 240
junks, Uraga	241
attempt to interrupt the survey of the bay of Uraga	244
officials, courteous deportment of	247, 249
fond of whiskey and brandy	248
their geographical knowledge	248
officials, their inspection of the Susquehanna	248
swords	248
internal trade, activity of	249
official etiquette	251
preparations for the reception of the letter of the President of the U. States	251
standards; official uniform	252
screens of painted cloth	252
oarsmen, dexterity of	254
army, appearance of the; horses	254
cannon; uniform	255
concession of the, in the reception of the letter of the President at Uraga	263
friendly intercourse with Americans of the squadron; intercourse with, forbidden by Japanese officials; officials carry away remnants of a collation in their sleeves	267

	Page.
Japanese lacquered ware; silks; fans; pipes	268
curiosity respecting steam-vessels	271
comparison of the, with the Lew Chewans	314
black beards of the; vocabulary compared with that of Lew Chew; harbors, provision for securing vessels; charts, slight value of; mode of navigation	326
courtesy and scrupulous honesty, instance of; offers of assistance to the Macedonian; officials prevented from boarding the American ships	327
officials received by Captain Adams	328
officials change the place of delivery of the Emperor's letter	329
commissioners endeavor to prevent a survey of the bay of Yedo	330
officials, frequent visits of the; return naval buttons; urge removal of the American squadron to Uraga; offer supplies as presents	331
etiquette respecting presents; officials refuse to receive Commodore Perry, except at Kama-kura or Uraga	332
officials treat invitation to "bring their ladies with them" to the celebration of Washington's birth-day as a joke	333
boats steady in a rough sea; curiosity respecting the Americans; present remnants of feasts to their guests	336
intercourse with Americans	340
crew rescued by an American merchantman	340
ambassadors, credentials of	341
winter; boatmen, rugged health of	342
batteries, bay of Yedo	343
commissioners, arrival of, at Yoku-hama	345
their personal appearance	346
deference to rank; heraldic devices; mode of obeisance; interpreter	348
reply to the letter of the President of the United States	349
drinking custom	353
respect for the dead	355
interest in the American railroad and telegraph	357
curiosity respecting American dress; taste for pictures; taste for sketching; intercourse with the American squadron; taking notes	358
non-communicative; common people more disposed than the officials to intercourse with the Americans; imitative like the Chinese	359
commissioners, note of the, to Commodore Perry	361
report of conference relative to the treaty with the United States	365

524 INDEX.

	Page.
Japanese neatness	368
wrestlers	369
interest in the American railroad and telegraph; presents to the United States placed in the store-ship Supply	372
use of paper; officials, conviviality of, at the dinner given by Commodore Perry	375
officials carry away fragments of a feast; officials' appreciation of negro minstrelsy	376
entertainment in honor of the treaty; dinners unsubstantial	380
commissioners, notes of their conferences with Commodore Perry	383
unlike the Chinese	385
qualifications of the treaty	386
jealousy of foreigners	386
treaty with Russia	387
treaty with England	387, 388
treaty with the Dutch	389
curiosity respecting American women; treatment of Americans and Russians at Simoda	390
proclamation to the Americans at Simoda	391
tooth dye; women	395
women rouge their lips	395
women work in the fields; dress; baby; common people; courtesy of the common people	396
women good looking	397
women, social position of	397
policy towards the expedition	398
stone dressing, boat building yards	400
buildings unpainted	410
inclined to intercourse with the members of the expedition, restrained by their officials	418
scholars, two, request to sail with the expedition	420
confined in a cage	422
official inspection of a corpse	425
officials' insult to American officers	425
apology for	426
boat, Hakodadi	433
vessels, Commodore Perry's account of	448
navigation	449
boats, sculling, rowing, ship models, tools, war junks, fisheries	450
ideas of the fox, of demoniacal influence	451
cabinets d'aisance, public; cattle, horses, roads, sedans	452
drainage	453
dexterity in the mechanical arts, curiosity respecting, neat workmanship	455
houses, carpentry, masonry, stone cutting, coopers' barrels, steel, swords, cutlery, razors, blacksmiths' bellows	458

	Page.
Japanese cotton fabrics, silks, lacquered ware, porcelain	458
art	459
spectacles, drawings	462
drawings of steam-engine	462
screen painter	462
prints	462
sculpture	463
architecture, books, knowledge of European periodicals	463
of America	464
curiosity	464
chess cards	465
game of Loto	466
official uniform	469
respect to the dead	469
officials, their interest in the armament of the expedition	471
embassy respecting boundaries at Hakodadi, official communication	473
respect for the dead	476
currencies, exchange of	478
commission, Simoda	477
knowledge of European affairs	478
coal	481
mining	483
pretend to be ignorant of coal	483
prices, accounts	484
dogs sent to the President of the United States	485
in the United States	486, 497
capital punishments	487
treaty with Russia; shipwrecked seamen; energy	511
friendliness to Americans; anxious for trade; for English books; send away religious tracts	512
technicalities respecting ratifications	513
(See *Hakodadi* and *Simoda*.)	
Jesuits endeavor to destroy the Dutch visitors to Japan	28
Jewels in Japan	60
Johnson, Charles, visits the Bonin islands	200
an early settler of the Bonin islands	305
Jones, Lieut., report of volcanic phenomena at sea	501
Jones, Rev. Mr., his MS. journal	iv
observations of the zodiacal lights	91
zodiacal observations	132
sketches a plan of the fortress of Nagaguska	170
report on geology of Lew Chew	184
conducts an exploration of the interior of Lew Chew	311
reads the burial service in Japan	354
views on the introduction of Christianity into Japan	446
observations on Japanese paintings	462

INDEX.

	Page.
Jones, Rev. Mr., applies for directions respecting funeral service	475
conversation with Japanese on prayer	476
exploration for coal at Formosa	500
Journal kept by the pecking of the exploration of Lew Chew	176
Journals, MS., of the expedition	iii
officers of the expedition invited by Commodore Perry to prepare	88
prohibition of the publication of by members of the expedition	79, 88
"Judge," the Peel island	205
Jungle-weed, Peel island	210
Junks, Japanese	153, 231, 241
large number of in the bay of Uraga	248
Ka-ei-silsi-neu, letter of	341
Kœmpfer	7
a writer on Japan	4
his theory of the derivation of the Japanese	9
remark on profits of Portuguese commerce with Japan	25
agency of the Dutch against Japanese Christians	31, 32
concessions of the Dutch in religious observances	32
remark on the population of Japan	53
account of Japanese minerals	60
account of the Bonin islands	197
account of Japanese vessels	448
on Japanese crucifixion	487
Ka-goo, or Lew Chew chair	172, 181, 310, 452
Kakekigo, a general, story of	20
Kaki-zaki, Simoda	411
Kama-kura, Japan	329
Kami, divinities of	19
Kami-musi, or priests of the temple	20
origin of	20
Kanagawa, bay of Yedo	267, 343, 344
Kanaka inhabitants of the Bonin islands	204
Kangsayu, Matsmai, interview with Commodore Perry	467
Kan-to-sits, chronicles, accuracy of the	281
Kelly, Lieutenant, harbor-master of Port Louis	106
Kelly, Commander, of the Plymouth, forces the Sir H. Compton to salute the American flag; attacks Chinese intrenchments at Shanghai	506
Kelung, Formosa	498
survey of the harbor	499, 501
mandarin of	499
Keppel, Captain, British navy, rescue of an Englishman from justice at Macao	301
Kettal-tree of Ceylon	118
Kikai-sima, or Bungalow island, survey of	489
Kindaka, Lew Chew	283
King, C. W., account of the visit of the "Morrison" to Japan	47
King, Cape, near the Gulf of Yedo	427

	Page.
Kings of the central, southern, and northern hills, Lew Chew	221
Kingfisher described	119
Kiu-siu, an island of Japan	7
color of the inhabitants of the coast of	10
Kiyemon, a Japanese fisherman, raises a sunken vessel	55
Klaproth, comparison of the Japanese with other languages	10
translation of a Japanese account of the Bonin islands	198
account of the sovereignty of Lew Chew	221
Kockebecker, a Dutch director, aids the Japanese against the native Christians	31
Komaga-daki, near Hakodadi	431
Konazaki, bay of Yedo	267
Kono-zhi, a Buddhist temple, Hakodadi	443
Koyanagi, a Japanese wrestler	370
Koye, the Chinese dialect of Japan	9
Kuan-tong	137
Kung-Kwas, no schools in the	223
Kura-kawa-kahie, a Japanese official	328, 349
visits the American squadron	355
frequent visits to the expedition	359
Kuriles, hairy	454
Kurosaki, cape	429
Kuro-siwo, a current, Lieut. Bent's report on	427
Laboring classes of China	295
Laboring class, Lew Chew	219
Lacquered ware, Japanese	50, 268, 367, 458
Lampaçao, Portuguese merchants of, settle Macao	110
Land, tenure of, Lew Chew	311
held by the government, Lew Chew	220
Land crabs, Peel island	205
Language of Lew Chew	221
Latham, Dr., remark on the origin of the Japanese	10
Laxman, a Russian officer, his visit to Japan	45
Lead in Japan	60
Leather manufacturers, treatment of, in Japan	11
Lennox, Lieut., of the garrison at Point de Galle, his elephant hunting	118
Letter of credence of the Emperor of Japan to Toda, Prince of Idzu	250
of the President of the United States	254
delivery of, to the Japanese commissioners	256
Lew Chew islands, Com. Perry proposes the occupation of the ports of the	85
acceded to by the United States	87
visit to	151
officers startled by report of cannon	155
exploration of	158
view from the summit ridge of the island	167
exploration of, by a gentleman attached to the Saratoga	218
origin of the population of	220
sovereignty of	221
their statement of	222

526 INDEX.

	Page.
Lew Chew, Japanese garrison at, trade confined to Japan	222
pay tribute to China	223
invitation of the Chinese in	223
authorities endeavor to drive Dr. Bettelheim from the island	225
naval mission	225
agricultural products, live stock, and fertility of	227
condition of the laboring classes in	227
a portion of the coast unvisited	229
its northern islands first fully explored by the Japanese expedition	230
regent of, letter to Commodore Perry	277
Commodore Perry's fourth visit to	309
explorations of the interior of	311
its soil, climate, temperature, salubrity, tenure of land, agriculture, irrigation	311
products	312
sugar mills	313
granaries, rats, population, origin, comparison with the Japanese	314
vocabulary compared with that of Japan	315
commerce of, Sakee, fine arts, architecture, dwellings	317
furniture, food, amusements, football, unarmed, government	318
youth of, sent to China for education	319
espionage, literati, religion, Bonzes, burial customs, fabrics	319
spies	320
contemplated "surveillance" of, by the American expedition	324
islands, northern group of	324
Japanese control over	364
trial at	493, 494
New Year compliments	494
treaty with the United States	495
Lew Chewan, a, desires to join the American squadron	497
Lew Chewans induced to accept pay for provisions	194
inexpert in the use of knives and forks	217
appreciation of a European dinner	217
social grades among	219
terror of spies	219
their personal appearance	223
black beards of the	315
good figures, courtesy, learning, commerce	316
Licentiousness of Japanese towns	398
of Japanese	405
Licou Kieou, or Lew Chew	151
Light-house Board of the United States, remark on	106
Lignite, Lew Chew	173
Lingam, Lew Chew	173
Literary men, Lew Chew	219
Literati of Lew Chew wear gold and silver hair pins	226

	Page.
Literature in Japan	58
Live stock in Japan	52
Lodgers, arrangements respecting, Simoda	405
Leather, manufacture and use of by the Japanese	51
Lee, Commander, services to the Macedonian aground in the bay of Yedo	326
Left hand, the Japanese place of honor	335
Leite, Lieutenant, attack on, at Macao	302
Lemons, Peel island	206
Longwood, St. Helena, visited	92
Loo rock, anchorage at the	82
Loom, Lew Chew	173, 219
Lorchas, Macao, Portuguese boats	299
Loreiro, Captain, of the Portuguese navy, Hong Kong	300
Loto, Japanese game of	466
Lutke, Captain, of Russian navy, takes possession of the Bonin islands	200
MacFarlane, remark on Japanese deception	18
on the Sintoo worship	19
McLane, R. M., United States commissioner to China	306, 307
McLeod, Captain, of the Alceste, inaccurate account of the Lew Chewans	221
Macao, visit to	140
salubrity of	289
population of	297
Macarenhas discovers Mauritius	106
Macedonian, the, run aground in the bay of Yedo	326
Machinatoo, Lew Chew	184
Madeira, coast of	81
Mahommedans in Ceylon	120
Mail routes from England and the United States to China, letter of Commodore Perry on	212
Malabars of Ceylon	120
Malacca	126
straits of, passage through	122
Malaria, burning wood a defence against	289
Malay race, extent of	131
Mamasaki, Prince of, receives the American presents to the Japanese	372
Man milliner, China, much esteemed by American residents	292
Mandarin, Japanese, enjoying a railroad ride	358
dialect understood by the educated classes in Japan	8
Mangusteen, fruit of the, Singapore	130
March, J. H., his hospitality	83
Marco Polo, his account of Lipangu	4
account of	5
visits Ceylon	116
Marine volcano near Formosa	500
"Mariners' Temple," Simoda	410
Market, Lew Chew	281
Marquesas, native of the, at Peel island	205
Marshall, Humphrey, his intercourse with the expedition	148
Marshes unknown in Lew Chew	311
Mats used as floor-cloths and beds, Lew Chew	218

INDEX.

	Page.
Matsmai, a port of Yesso	7
incident in the history of	16
discussion relative to opening the port of	364, 365
road to	437
Matsusaki, Michitaro, Japanese commissioner	347
his conviviality	375
friendly in his cups	376
Matzaimon, Yendo, governor of Hakodadi	434
Matzoori, a religious festival, Simoda	410
Mauritius, visit to	105
Maury, M. F., observations on the Gulf Stream	428, 429
Maury, Lieut., survey of the bay of Yedo by	330
Mazara, Mattheo, visits the Bonin islands	200
an early colonist of the Bonin islands	304, 305
Meac-Sima, island of	417
Medical knowledge of the Japanese	56
Men the drones of Lew Chew	219
Merchandise, a term not understood in Japan	386
Merchants, rank of, in Japan	14
Mermaid manufacture in Japan	55
Metal workers, Hakodadi	456
Metals found in Japan	50
wrought by the Japanese	50
Meteor, bay of Uraga	236
Meylan	4, 7
description of a Japanese clock	54
on the Japanese religion	19
speaks of a fourth Japanese religion	22
Mia, or Sintoo temples, Hakodadi	445
Simoda	406, 409
Miako, the chief seat of learning in Japan	58
Mijako-sima, Lew Chew	325
Mikados, the founder of the	11
mode of government	11, 13
history of the dynasty	11
Mildtchamp, Richard, visits the Bonin islands	200
an early colonist of the Bonin islands	304
Mills, Lew Chew	314
Mima-saki, prince of, Japanese commissioner	347
Minerals of Japan	60
Ming dynasty, China	221, 222
Missikya, Lew Chew	174
Missionary station, an American colony at Port Lloyd would form a desirable	213
Missionaries at Lew Chew	225
in China, their observations	295
Mississippi, the, her good conduct at sea	81
Molva, Lew Chew	168
Monasteries, Buddhist, Simoda	406
Money value of foreign coins understood in Lew Chew	160
Monsoons at Ceylon	117
Montravel, M. de, French commodore at Canton	300
Mooring vessels, mode of, at Port Louis, Mauritius	105
Moreton, Rev. Mr., succeeds Dr. Bettelheim at Lew Chew	498
Moro, a Portuguese, plots against the Japanese	26

	Page.
Mosquitoes, annoying at Lew Chew	167
Moustache worn in Lew Chew and Japan	315
Music in Japan	59
Muster, or Chinese pattern	292
Mijako-sima islands, Lew Chew	325
Nagagusko fortress, Lew Chew	169
castle at	221
Nagasaki	4, 7
first occupied by the Portuguese	30
Japanese endeavor to restrict American commerce to	363
port regulations of	389
Nagazima Saboroske, vice-governor of Uraga	234
appearance of, in his state dress	253
Napha, Lew Chew	154
visit to	156
mayor of, visits the Expedition	155
the mayor of, invites Commodore Perry to a feast	187
return to	214, 215, 274
new regent of	214
school at	223
interview of Commander Adams with the mayor of	277
view of	280
difficulties with the inhabitants of	492
Napoleon at St. Helena	92
conduct of England to	93
tomb of	94
Navigation of the Japanese by sea, inland	53
of the Chinese coast	144
of the Japanese close in-shore	449
Navy of the United States, backward in adopting improvements in steam-vessels	105
Negatsu, or Idsu, cape, Japan	230
Negro guards of Commodore Perry	255
New Year congratulatory phrases, Lew Chew	494
Night signals of the Expedition, picturesque effect of	196
Nippon, a work on Japan by Siebold	4
volcanoes of	7
the modern Zipangu	4
Dai, Japanese name of Japan	6
an island of Japan	7
Novaleches, marquis of, governor of the Philippine Islands	501
Ny-komma, Lew Chew	179
Oars, Japanese management of	243
Observatory, Japanese	447
O'Callaghan, Captain, of British navy, attack on Chinese intrenchments, Shanghai	506
Officers of state, Lew Chew	219
of the expedition requested to keep journals	88
Oho-sima	229, 231, 271, 325, 416, 427
discovery of	324
Commodore Perry's visit to	419
visit to	490
Oki-nawa-sima, or Great Lew Chew	325

528 INDEX.

	Page.
Olason island, Endermo harbor	469
Oo-bang, public slaves, Lew Chew	226
Opium eater, death of a Chinese	195
Orsa, a Japanese village	268
Osaca, Japan, destruction of, by an earthquake	510
Otaheitan at Peel island	205
Otsu, village of, Bay of Yedo	328
Overfalls, Simoda harbor	415
Owari, the prince of, his history	12
Oxen used in drawing carriages in Funchal	84
teams of at the Cape of Good Hope	100
Oysters, presented by the Japanese to Com. Perry	332
Pacific mail routes	242
Palace, Shui, Lew Chew	190
Pallisades in front of Yedo	398
Palma latina, Peel island	206
Palmer, Aaron H., an early advocate for an expedition to Japan	77
Palms, Peel island	210
Palmyra palm in Ceylon	117
Panama, isthmus of, interoceanic communication at the, known to the Japanese	248
Pandanus, Peel island	205
Lew Chew	174, 176
Paper, manufacture of, by the Japanese	51
burnt by the Lew Chewans	186
Paps, the mountains on the Bonin islands	209
Parasitic plants, thick growth of, Peel island	204
Parker, Dr., Canton	292
Patriarchal authority the basis of the government of Lew Chew	225
Paul and Virginia, foundation of the story of	111
Pavement, Lew Chew	185
Payment made for supplies, Lew Chew	194
Peacock, visit of the, to Siam	121
Pearl fishery of Ceylon	118
Pearls found in Japan	61
Peasantry of Lew Chew	193
rank of, in Japan	14
Pe-ching, or Lew Chew guide	166
the, escort of Com. Perry	189
or guide, Lew Chew, keeps a journal	177
presents to the	194
Peel island	196
European settlers at	203
colony of, Bonins	283
Pellew, Capt., Japanese remarks on	381
visit to Japan	487
Perry, Com. M. C., wishes in regard to this publication, his MS. journals	iii
his revision of the narrative	iv
attestation	v
declines admitting Russian ships in the American squadron	62
avoided intercourse with the Dutch in Japan	67, 69
declines giving Siebold a place in the expedition	70
never saw Siebold's letter of advice	73

	Page.
Perry, Com., expresses the wish to the Japanese commissioners that other nations should share in the benefits of the treaty	74
first to formally propose an expedition to Japan	77
aids in the adjustment of the fishery question	78
declines applications from at home and abroad for situations in the expedition	78
departure from Annapolis	79
letter written at Madeira to the Secretary of the Navy	85
his view of the objects of the expedition	85
order forbidding the transmission home of journals	88
requests officers to prepare journals	88
shows how St. Helena could be attacked	95
economy in the use of coal	97
visits a Constantia vineyard	100
remark on treatment of savage aborigines	101
visits a captive chief at the Cape of Good Hope	102
opinion as to the best course from the Cape to Mauritius	104
hospitality extended to, at Mauritius	11
letter of to Phar-Pen-Clow-Chow-Yon-Hon, a prince of Siam	121
endeavors to open communication with Siam	122
visits a Chinese temple at Singapore	128
remark on hospitalities of foreign nations, and "table money"	133
remark on Canton river; disappointed in the appearance of the city	135
hospitable treatment of at Canton	139
opinion of Shanghai as a naval depot	144
his visit to the Taou-tai of Shanghai	147
his views on the revolution in China	148
admits Bay'd Taylor in the expedition	152
receives a chin-chin at Lew Chew; visited by Mr. Bettelheim, by Whang-cha-ching	153
directs an exploration of Lew-Chew	154
receives the mayor of Lew Chew	155
announces an intention to return the visit	156
directs a sick officer to occupy a house at Tumai	159
letter of Shang-ta-mu to	159
declines invitation of the mayor of Lew Chew; receives banquet sent on board ship	187
refuses to abandon his visit to Shui	187
his progress to Shui	188

INDEX.

	Page.
Perry, Com., curiosity of the Lew Chewans to witness, with his escort	189
his interview with the regent of Lew Chew	190
healths proposed by, at Shui	192
remark on the cleanliness of Lew Chew	193
happy effects of his determination	193
reliance of the Japanese on	193
remark on acceptance of payment by the Lew Chewans	194
sends presents to the queen, regent, and other dignitaries of Lew Chew	194
attends a burial at sea	195
observations on the anchorage of Port Lloyd harbor	202
leaves live stock on Peel and North islands, Bonin island	203
orders an exploration of Peel island	204
orders an exploration of Stapleton island, Bonins	211
recommends Peel island as a stopping place for steam-vessels between California and China	211
distributes garden-seeds to settlers, Bonin islands	211
purchases land for a landing-place and coal depot	211
letter of to the Navy Department, on steam navigation and mail-routes in the Pacific	211
remark on the commercial importance of Shanghai	212
note on the advantages of establishing a naval station at the Bonin islands	212
proposes the establishment of an American colony at Port Lloyd, Bonin islands	213
determines the position of Disappointment island	213
dinner to the new regent of Lew Chew on board of the Susquehanna	215
presents garden-seeds to the regent of Lew Chew	218
entertains him with the music of the band	218
classifies the Lew Chewans in four grades	219
remarks on the misery of the Mexican peons, of the lower classes of the Lew Chewans	219
remark on the investigations of Hall, McLeod, Beechey, Belcher, and the Japanese expedition, respecting the origin of the Lew Chewans	221
information obtained by, respecting the ownership of Lew Chew	222
his opinion on the mixed origin of the Lew Chewans	223

	Page.
Perry, Com., leaves Napha for Japan	228
prepares for action on entering the bay of Yedo	231
forbids the Japanese to visit the squadron at Japan	233
prevents the Japanese from boarding or surrounding the squadron in the bay of Uraga	233, 234, 235
his reception of the deputy governor of Uraga	234
his policy towards the Japanese	235
remark on a meteor, bay of Uraga	236
reception of Keyamon Yezaimen, governor of Uraga	237
enforces a survey of the bay of Uraga	238
refuses to go to Nagasaki	238
threatens to land at Yedo	238
despatches the Mississippi towards Yedo	240
his letter to the Emperor of Japan	244
refuses to communicate with the Japanese through the Dutch or Chinese	244
refuses to go to Nagasaki	244
stipulations with the governor of Uzama relative to the delivery of the letter of the President of the United States	244, 245
preparations for the delivery of the letter of the President of the United States	251
delivery of his credentials and the letter of the President to the Japanese	254
letters to the Emperor of Japan	258, 259
letter of credence	258
announces his departure and return	261
orders the squadron up the bay of Uraga, after the reception of the letter of the President	263
insists on his right to take soundings in the bay of Uraga	266
advances to within ten miles of Yedo	267
presents American seeds and cases of wine to the governor of Uraga	269
refuses presents from the Japanese unless they receive presents in return	269
desirous of protecting American commerce in China	270
his reasons for not waiting for a reply from the Emperor of Japan	270
names islands near the coast of Japan	271
departure from the bay of Uraga	271
concessions obtained by, from the Japanese	272
orders the Saratoga to Shanghai	272
orders the Plymouth to explore the shore of Oho-Sima	272

67 J

530 INDEX.

	Page.
Perry, Com., his policy respecting etiquette, presents	273
negotiations at Lew Chew respecting intercourse with strangers	275
propositions to the authorities of Lew Chew	275
letter to the Tsungli-kwan of Lew Chew	276
interview with the regent of Napha	277
directs survey of Melville harbor	282
instructions to Com. Kelly respecting Lew Chew	282
his remarks on the effects of his intercourse upon the Lew Chewans	284
his arrangements for the protection of American commerce in China	288
takes a house at Macao	288
examines foot of a Chinese woman	292
his opinion of the laboring classes of China	295
favorable opinion of Chinese honesty	295
residence at Macao	297
proposes forming a naval station at Hong Kong	299
his sojourn at Macao	300
arrangements for the protection of American interests at Japan	302
recognition of this service by the American merchants at Canton	302
departure from Hong Kong	303
his letter to Sir J. G. Bonham respecting the Bonin islands	305
letter to the Secretary of the Navy	307
his second visit to Shui	309
endeavors to obtain Japanese coins in exchange at Lew Chew	312
objects accomplished by him in Lew Chew	319
receives information of the death of the Emperor of Japan	321
letter respecting the death of the Emperor of Japan	322
suspects the rumor to be a ruse	323
course contemplated by him in case of a refusal by the Japanese to negotiate	323
objects of his mission to Japan	323
return to the bay of Yedo	324
directions for the relief of the Macedonian, aground in the bay of Yedo	326
refuses to go to Kama-kura, or to Uraga	329
refuses to interrupt the exploration of the harbor of Yedo	330
letter respecting removal of the squadron to Uraga	331
proposes to visit Yedo	333
letter to the Japanese authorities	333

	Page.
Perry, Com., refuses to go to Uraga	333
asks for wood and water from the Japanese	338
refuses to go to Uraga, his letter on the subject	338
policy adopted by, in his intercourse with the Japanese	339
consents to receive the Emperor's letter at Yoku-hama	339
letter of, to the Japanese commissioner	339
refuses to allow the men of the expedition to land in Japan	340
causes screens surrounding the "treaty-house" to be removed	344
preparations for the reception of the Emperor's letter	345
his interview with the Japanese commissioners	349
proposes the formation of a treaty to the Japanese commissioners	350
notes by, handed to the Japanese commissioners	350
requests permission for the members of the expedition to land in Japan	350
reasons presented to the Japanese in favor of a treaty	351
arrangements for the burial of a marine	353
proposes to purchase a burial-place for Americans in Japan	353
communication respecting a treaty with the Japanese government	356
meets Japanese commissioners at the treaty-house	362
his replies to the terms proposed for the Japanese treaty	362
discussion of the treaty with the Japanese commissioners	364
assents to the substitution of Hako-dadi for Matsmai	366
reception of the presents of the Emperor of Japan	367
presents to Japanese	368
presents of the Japanese government to	369
remarks upon Japanese dogs	369
examines Koyanagi, a Japanese wrestler	370
conversation on the treaty with Yenoske	372
claims privileges for members of the expedition	374
dinner to the Japanese commissioners	374
conference respecting the treaty	376
signs the treaty between the United States and Japan	377

INDEX. 531

	Page.
Perry, Com., proposes the American limits in Japanese ports	377
presents Hyashi with an American flag	379
Japanese entertainment to, in honor of the treaty	380
scope of his instructions	381
circulates a Japanese translation of the China treaty	382
novelty of his position	382
notes of his conferences with the Japanese commissioners	383
refuses to allow communications to pass through the hands of the Dutch	383
his proposals to the Japanese respecting an American consul	385
remark on Japanese jealousy of foreigners	386
looks forward to a commercial treaty with Japan	387
does not interpret the treaty as a commercial treaty	392
sends the treaty to the United States	393
his walk in the neighborhood of Kanagawa	394
his visit to a Japanese mayor	395
sails towards Yedo	398
his reasons for not visiting Yedo	399
explores Webster island	399
leaves the bay of Yedo	400
remark on the bay of Simoda	401
lodged in a Buddhist temple at Simoda	409
orders a survey of the harbor of Simoda	415
visit to Kura-Kawa-Kahei, at Simoda	417
his visit to Oho-Sima	419
remonstrance against the spy system	419
declines to allow two Japanese scholars to sail with the expedition	421
incommoded by Japanese officials	423
lodged in the Rio-shen-zhi, Buddhist temple	423
sails for Hakodadi	427
account of Japanese vessels	448
interview with Matsmai Kangsayn	467
visits Matsmai Kangsayn	470
directions respecting funeral services	475
returns to Simoda, interview with Japanese commissioners	477
suggests appointment of pilots, Simoda	477
letter respecting Japanese currencies	478
his course respecting American boundaries, Japan	481

	Page.
Perry, Com., resists imposition at Simoda	484
his course respecting "Sam Patch"	485
approves Japanese pilots, Simoda; presents the harbor-master with a spyglass	488
remark on navigation near Rock island	489
course regarding Lew Chewan criminals	493
proceedings respecting the killing of Board, a seaman	493
repairs coal depot at Tumai	495
presents to the regent of Lew Chew, signs treaty with Lew Chew	495
parting entertainment to the authorities, Lew Chew	497
exertions in behalf of the Sillibaboos	503
directs a surgical examination of the Sillibaboos	503
correspondence with American merchants, China; returns home	508
respect for, in Japan	512
Perry, Mr., his MS. journal	iv
Perry island, bay of Uraga	268, 400
Persimmon point, Simoda	411
Perspective, Japanese knowledge of	462
Petrel, Bonin islands	203
Phaeton, British ship-of-war, visit to Japan	40
Phalic worship, emblems of, Lew Chew	173
Physical conformity of the Japanese and Lew Chewans	314
Pickering, Dr., considers the Japanese of Malay origin	10
Pictures, Simoda	407
Pigs, sacred, at Canton	137
Pi-ko, Lew Chew	183
Pilotage, rates of, Simoda	488
Pilots, danger of trusting entirely to	123
Pine, Lew Chew	163
Pines, large, Lew Chew	181
Pino, Lew Chew	164
Pinto, his visit to Japan	22
Pipes, Japanese	268
Pirate, the, land crab, Bonin islands	202
Pirates, Chinese, on Canton river	137
Plains, fertile, Bonin islands	209
Plymouth, the, left at Shanghai	149
Point de Galle, Ceylon, visit to	114
Polygamy, non-existent in Japan	397
Pontiatine, admiral of the Russian navy in Japan	511
Pope, Commander, letter respecting Simoda	376
Population of Lew Chew, origin of	220
Porcelain, Japanese	51, 458
Port, the United States desirous to obtain access to a Japanese	257
Ports, Japanese, open to Americans	355
Port Lloyd, Bonin islands	202
the crater of an extinct volcano	209
Port Louis, Mauritius	111

532 INDEX.

	Page.
Port Louis, Mauritius, visit to	105
Portman, Mr., Dutch interpreter, conversation of, with a Japanese	234
Portuguese, intercourse of the, with Japan	4
missionaries, their information respecting Japan	7
discovery	22
intercourse with Japan	23
how interrupted	25
insult the Japanese	26
their naval system	27
attribute their expulsion to Dutch intrigues	27
possession of Mascarenhas, afterwards Mauritius	107
possession of St. Helena	91
possession of Ceylon	116
possession of Macao	140
in Macao	297
fortifications, Macao	298
Japanese restrictions upon the	384
Postal service of the Japanese	54
Prayer, Japanese	476
wheel, Hakodadi	444
Praying machine, Japanese	476
"Praying man," Japanese respect for a	446
Preble, United States man-of-war, her visit to Japan	48
Preble, Lieutenant, survey of harbor of Kelung	501
Precipices, Peel island	207
Presents to the Japanese, quality of, proposed by Commodore Perry	86
of Japanese, refused	155
from the United States to the Emperor of Japan	257
of the American government to the Emperor of Japan	270
policy of the expedition respecting	273
law respecting Japan	355
to the Japanese, list of	356
delivery of	357
of the Japanese to the United States	369
President of the United States, letter of the, to the Emperor of Japan	238, 245
Prices of labor in Canton	292
Priests, support of, Simoda	411
Priesthood, Lew Chew	219
Primer, Japanese	462
Prince, young, of Lew Chew	190
Princeton, the, unable to join the squadron	78
Prisons in Japan	18
Proas of Malacca, beauty of models of	126
Queen dowager, Lew Chew	188, 190, 193
Quicksilver in Japan	60
Raffles, Sir Stamford, attempts, as governor of Java, to oust the Dutch from Japan	42
his services to Singapore	127, 128
Railroads of the United States known to Japanese officials at Uraga	248

	Page.
Rajah of Jahore and Singapore	129
Rank indicated by dress in Lew Chew	225
Rats, how served up in China	290
abundance of, Lew Chew	314
Raven with a broad beak, Lew Chew	167
Razor, Japanese	456
Receipt, the Japanese, for the letters transmitted to the Emperor	260
Red card, presentation of a	310
Redfield, W. C., observations on the Gulf Stream	428
Redfield rocks, near Simoda	417
survey of	489
Reed and Dougherty, Messrs., communication to the governor of Hakodadi	391
Reed, Mr., his letters respecting the treatment of Americans at Simoda	390
Regent, Lew Chew, his reception of Commodore Perry	189
entertainment by the, to Com. Perry	191
dignity of proof against the effects of good liquors	218
new, of Lew Chew	214
Religion, Simoda	406
Resanoff, a Russian officer, his visit to Japan	45
orders a hostile attack	46
Residence, American, in Japan	377
Reviews and military exercises of the expedition at Lew Chew	194
Rhubarb, plant resembling	469
Rice, Japanese custom respecting	368
bearded, Lew Chew	163
cultivation of, Lew Chew	311
cultivation, Simoda	406
fields, Lew Chew	168
hulling machine, China	507
mills, Hongo	412
Rioboo-Sintoo, a Sintoo sect	21
Rio-shen-zhi, a Buddhist temple, Simoda	409
Rocks, remarkable masses of, Lew Chew	168
at entrance of the bay of Yedo	325
Rock island, near the bay of Yedo	231
Simoda harbor	415, 416
near Simoda	489
Rodgers, Commander, letter to Messrs. Reed and Dougherty	391
Roman Catholic missionaries at Lew Chew	225
Japanese dislike of	446
Roofs of dwellings, Simoda	404
Roquemaurel, Commodore, of the French navy, pleasant intercourse with	133
Rozario, identity of, with Disappointment island	213
Rouge, applied by Japanese women to their lips	395
Russia apparently desirous of sharing the honors of the Japanese expedition	62
Russian intercourse with Japan	44
possessions adjacent to Japan	44
advantages to her from the possession of Japan	45
visit to Japan in 1853	62

INDEX. 533

	Page.
Russian temporary possession of the Bonin islands	200
ambassador, application of the expedition to Nagasaki	350
	365
treaty with Japan similar to the American expedition at Simoda	388
	511
Russians, intercourse of the, with Japan	4
Saboroske, impertinent curiosity of, on board the Susquehanna	264
Saddles islands, near Shanghai	149
Sagami, cape	231
shores of	232
Sago palm, Peel island	204
Sail-boats, Lew Chew	179
Sailing directions for Simoda	416
Sailing-fish of Singapore	131
observations	229, 272
Sailor epitaph, Japan	476
Sailors of the expedition, misconduct of three of, at Lew Chew	493
Sakee	191
Sakee, Lew Chew	317
Saki, Lew Chew	219
Saki	380, 396
Saltness of sea-water, Lew Chew	175
Salute, Chinese, three guns	147
"Sam Patch," a Japanese	340, 450
before the Japanese officials	342
the Japanese	485
Samuns, the, teachers in Lew Chew	224
Sandwich islands, expedition to the Bonin islands from	200
islanders on the Bonin islands	204
Sangar, straits of, fogs about	429
strait of, navigation of	430
San Kolp Tsoir Ran To Sits, a Japanese writer, account of the Bonin islands	198
Santa Mesa, Philippine islands, murder of an American at	501
Saris, John, an English sea captain, visits Japan	34
has an interview with the Emperor	34
his visit to Japan in 1613	369
Satskai, the rainy season of Japan	8
Satsuma, prince of Lew Chew, a dependency of	151
Japanese prince of, his revenue	325
Savory, Nathaniel, an American resident at the Bonin islands	200
robbed by sailors under the American flag	200
an early settler of the Bonin islands	305
Sayka-Sinka, founder of Buddhism	21
Scientific knowledge of the Japanese	54
men, not of the navy, applications of to join the expedition declined	78
Scott, Mr., his intercourse with the Lew Chewans	194
Screens of cloth set up as mock fortifications by the Japanese	237
of painted cloth, Japanese	252, 265
of cloth, Japanese	336

	Page.
Scribe, Japanese	347
Sculling, Japanese	450
Sculls and oars	336
Sculpture, Japanese	463
Simoda	407, 409, 410, 411
Scurvy in Yesso	454
Sea-weeds of the Kurosiwa	429
Sedan chair of Commodore Perry	188
at Lew Chew	279
Sedgewick, Mr., a writer on hurricanes	113
Sennimar, founder of a fraternity of the Japanese clergy	20
Serofama, Cape	427
Serpents of Ceylon	119
Shah bay, Lew Chew, coal at	311
Shanghai, visit to	146
Commodore Perry on commercial importance of	212
Shang Hung Hiun, new regent of Lew Chew	215, 217, 218
regent of Lew Chew	279
Shang Ta-mu, regent of Lew Chew, letter of, to Commodore Perry	159
Sharks taken by dogs, Bonin islands	202
Sheude, capital of Lew Chew	163
Shiomio-zhi, a Buddhist temple, Hakodadi	443
Ship-yards, Hakodadi	457
Shipwrecked sailors, American, in Japan	382
Shira-hama, Simoda	411
Shirasawaki, near Hakodadi	448
Shoes, Japanese, of straw	51
Sho-Ho-Yé, or Chess	465
Shops, Simoda	404
Shrines, Simoda	404
of temples, Simoda	406
roadside, Hakodadi, frequent genuflexions at	445
Shrubs, new varieties of, Lew Chew	167
Shui, a "University" at	223
Shunteen dynasty rulers of Lew Chew	221
Shutters, Simoda	404
Siamese naval commander visits Com. Perry	120
Sida, or Indian gooseberry, Peel island	205
Siebold, a writer on Japan	4, 7
his comparison of the language of Japan with that of the adjacent shores	10
remarks on the Siktoo worship	19, 20
remarks on Japanese teas	52
his opinion of the Japanese expedition	61
story of his banishment from Japan	69
desirous of joining the Japanese expedition	70
his pamphlet	70
letter to an officer of the Japan expedition	71
remark on Gutzlaff and Foreade, missionaries	72
account of Oho-sima, or Tatao	229
inaccuracy of his map of the bay of Yedo	326
account of whale-ships, Japan	151
on Japanese mining	483

534 INDEX.

	Page.
Signs of shops, Simoda	404
Sikai, or "ten counsels" of Buddhism	21
Silks, Japanese	268, 458
woven by criminals	51
Sillibaboos, picked up at sea by the Southampton	501
surgical examination of the	503
left to be sent home from Manilla	504
Silver, abundant in Japan	60
Simoda, opened to trade by the United States	69
discussion relative to opening the port of	364
approval of as an American port	377
Japanese proclamation to the Americans at	390
Japan	401
beauty of the environs of	402
its antiquity	402
docks, streets, sewers of	403
houses, shops	404
officials, baths, diet, vegetables	405
rice, religion, temples, monasteries, shrines	406
sculpture, pictures, demons, grave-yards	407
festivals, "Mariners' Temple"	410
environs of	411
its topographical characteristics	413
government of	414
harbor of	415
Commodore Perry's return to	477
regulations respecting American vessels at	487
earthquake at	510
harbor unaffected by the	512
Simpson, Alex., letter respecting the Bonin islands	305
Sinagawa, a suburb of Yedo	267, 343
Singapore, visit to	125
Sintoo, the priests of	13
religion of Japan	19
its deities	19
idols	19
temples	19
priests, question of their marriage	20
pilgrimages	20
duties	20
festival services	20
sects	21
temple, Simoda	406, 409
shrines, Simoda	410
Siutoo, a Japanese belief; its rules	22
Sira-hama, bay of, near Simoda	416
Sirija Saki, Nippon	430
Sirocco, the, compared with the Harmattan	89
Sitkokf, an island of Japan	7
Slave, value of a Lew Chewan	226
Slavery, system of, in Lew Chew	226
Sledges, carriages drawn on, at Funchal	84
Smith, Sir Thomas, licensed, as governor of the East India Company, to trade with the Japanese	34
Society in China	296
Socks, Japanese	347
Sorghum, or millet, Lew Chew	173

	Page.
Sotowra, near Simoda	411
Soundings bay of Uraga	232
Southampton rock, near Simoda	417
Southeast bay, Peel island	208
Southern Head, Bonin islands, natural tunnel at	20
Sovereignty of the Bonin islands	213
Sowas, a metal made by the Japanese	50
Spaniards, intercourse of the, with Japan	4
Spaniel, an English species of, possibly introduced from Japan	369
Spars, purchase of, at Simoda	484
Spectacles, Japanese	462
Speiden, W., purser, report on Japanese currencies	478
Sphynx, her British Majesty's ship, visit to Napha, Lew Chew	215
Spies	193, 194, 217, 423
at Lew Chew	157, 160, 172, 176, 192, 219, 220, 226, 280
in the bay of Uraga	236
vigilance of, relaxed at Lew Chew	284
bad effects of the system of	285
Japanese	328, 347, 359
follow American officers in Japan	418
Spooner, Mr., hospitality of	139
Springs, Peel island, brackish	209
Squadron, disposition of, for the return voyage	491
St. Geran, shipwreck of the French vessel, the foundation of the story of Paul and Virginia	112
St. Helena, visit of the expedition to	91
military strength of	94
greediness for money of the people of	94
St. Pierre Bernardin	111
St. Thomas, said to have preached in Ceylon	120
Standards, Japanese	252
Stapleton island, Bonin islands, goats on	203
Steam-engine, astonishment of the Japanese at	155
not unknown to the Japanese	248
Steel, Hakodadi	456
Stirling, Admiral, makes a treaty with Japan	63
copy of his Japanese treaty	388
Stone worked by Japanese	400
Storms off the Cape of Good Hope	104
Streets of Simoda guarded by gates	403
Styx, her British Majesty's steamer	105
Subscription list in a Sintoo temple	410
Sugar-cane, Lew Chew	173
Sugar crop at Mauritius	109
Sugar-loaf island, Lew Chew	178
Sugar mills, Lew Chew	313
Sugar, use of, Lew Chew	313
Sulphur in Japan	60
spring, Peel island	209
Sunday, observance of, by the expedition	240
Supplies for whale ships at the Bonin islands	203
for American ships in Japan	356
cost of, Simoda	484
Supply rock, near Simoda	417
the, nearly wrecked	144
Suraga-no-kami, Japanese commissioner	477
Surro-kubo, or Cape Blunt	430, 431
Survey of the bay of Uraga	238, 241, 267, 268, 270

INDEX.

	Page.
Survey of the bay of Yedo	332
of the bay of Yedo, signals for the	355
of Volcano bay, Endermo harbor	468
Surveys, Kelung	501
of the Japanese harbors, copies of presented to the Japanese government	351
Susaki, Simoda	411
Cape	427
Susquehanna bay, Japan	268
Swell from the northwest at sea	88
Swords, Japanese	248
Japanese	456
Syakfdo, a species of enamel work	59
Table bay, visit to	98
Table-cloth, a cloud on Table mountain	99
Table mountain	99
Tailoresses, street, China	292
Takahasi, his connection with Siebold	70
Take-no-uchisetaro, Japanese commissioner	477
Talipot tree of Ceylon	118
Tanka boats	294
boat girls	294
boats at Macao	140
Taoutai, commander-in-chief of Chinese fleet	504, 505
Taoutai, or governor of Shanghai	146
Taro plant, Peel island	205
Tatao, one of the Lew Chew islands	229
Tatznoske, Japanese interpreter	244
interpreter, his facility in the acquisition of languages	251
his conviviality and shrewdness	269
Tayko, opposes the Portuguese	26
Tayko-sama, his history	12
Taylor, Bayard, his manuscript journal	iv
description of Lew Chew from the sea	152
joins the expedition	152
account of the harbor of Napha by	154
first landing on Lew Chew	156
exploration of Peel island	204
Tea and pipes served to guests in Lew Chew	158
culture of, by the Japanese	52
drinking, Lew Chew	219
Teén-sun, the first ruler of Lew Chew	221
Teeth dying in Japan	395
Telegraph, magnetic, in Japan	357
Telescope, Japanese	417
Temperature at sea, near Japan, in July	230
bay of Uraga	239
of Simoda	413
Temple at Lew Chew, visit to	158
Teneriffe not seen	87
Ten Fathom Hole, Port Lloyd, Bonin islands	202
Ten-sio-dai-zin, the patron divinity of Japan	19
the most sacred of Japanese shrines	20
Testacea, Bonin islands	202
Theatrical performances by sailors of the expedition	470
Thermometric range at Point de Galle, Ceylon	115
Thieves, Chinese	138
Thom, Dr., a writer on hurricanes	113
Thunberg, a writer on Japan	4, 7

	Page.
Thunberg, his account of Japanese rouge	395
Tides in the straits of Malacca	123
of Cochin China	132
at Shanghai	144
at Napha, Lew Chew	195
bay of Yedo	272
Tigers, ferocity of, at Singapore	130
Tima-gusko, ruins of the castle of, Napha	280
Tin, in Japan	60
Titsingh, a writer on Japan	4, 7
account of the operation of the Dozia powder	56
Toasts, drinking, in Lew Chew	191
Tobacco, Peel island	206
smoking, Lew Chew	219
Toda-Idzu-no-kami, Japanese commissioner	251
Todo, Japanese commissioner	255
Togirasaki, a Japanese village	268
Tomatoes, Peel island	208
Tombs, Lew Chew	167, 168
called "houses of the devil's men," Lew Chew	173
Lew Chewan	226
Tomes, Robert, his share in the authorship of this publication	iv
Torigasaki, village of, bay of Yedo	328
Town hall, Tumai, Lew Chew	158
Trade winds, northern boundary of	88
encountered by the expedition	90
Trades	97
Treaty between Japan and the United States	350
of commerce, terms proposed by the Japanese	361
Commodore Perry's replies to	362
conversation between Yenoske and Commodore Perry respecting the	372
conference respecting the	376
between the United States and Japan	377
objects secured by the	380
difficulties incident to its formation	380
progress of the formation of the	383
discussion as to when it shall go into effect	384
patience required for its negotiation	386
qualifications of the, inserted by the Japanese	386
advantages secured by	388
the, sent to the United States	393
ratified by the Senate	509
time of ratification of, in Japan	513
"Treaty-house," Yoku-hama	344
Treaty Point, near Hakodadi	430
Trees of Japan	61
Trials, mode of conducting among the Japanese	18
Tsuki Point, near Hakodadi	432
Tuchara, island of	222
Tunnels, natural, in the Bonin islands	201
Turcomans of Asia Minor use ladles similar to those of the Japanese	157
Turtle, Peel island	205
green	202
Turtles from the Bonin islands	424

INDEX.

	Page.
Typhoon near Formosa	500
Typhoons felt at Lew Chew	311
Tzudsuki, Japanese commissioner	477
Udono, Japanese commissioner	347
Ukona rocks, near Simoda	417
Uniform, Japanese	237, 243
United States commercial agent at Point de Galle, Ceylon, imprisoned for debt	115
correspondence of the, with Holland, relative to Japan	66
intercourse with Japan, expedition of 1846	47
priority of their treaty with Japan	74
seamen imprisoned in Japan	48
forced to trample on the cross	48
released	48
the "Middle Kingdom"	75
Un-na, Lew Chew	180
Uraga, Japan	231
bay of, Japan	232
city of	232
vice governor of, received on board the squadron	234
picturesque shores of the bay of	237, 265, 267
survey of the bay of	268, 270
proposed as a place of negotiation	328
discussion respecting a meeting at	336
Vandalia, voyage of the, to Lew Chew	286
Vandalia bluff, Simoda harbor	416
Van Twist, Duymaer, letter to Com. Perry announcing the death of the Emperor of Japan	322
Vegetables, Simoda	405
Vegetation, peculiar, of the Bonin islands	209
luxuriant, of the bay of Yedo	394
Vessels, sea, of the Japanese	53
Victoria, Hong Kong	134
Victoria, the English bishop of, and his account of his official visit to Lew Chew in 1850	223
Victoria, the English bishop of, remark on the writings of Confucius	224
Victoria, the English bishop of, account of Dr. Bettelheim	225
Village, Lew Chew, description of	218
Villages, Lew Chew	173
Virgin and child, image of, found in a heathen temple in Singapore	128
Vocabulary of Lew Chew and Japanese words	315
Volcanic formation of Peel island	209
Volcano bay, survey of	468
Volcanoes	7
in Endermo harbor	469
Vries island, or Oo-sima, bay of Yedo	231
Japan	271
Vulcan island, Japan	271
Wages of laborers, Lew Chew	220
Walls of coral in Lew Chew	156
Wampon river	144
Wardenaar, his connexion with the expedition of Raffles	42
Washington, George, remark of Lew Chew official on	159

	Page.
Washington, "very great mandarin"	192
known to the Japanese	333
styled the great mandarin at Lew Chew	496
monument, Japanese stone for	485
stone contributed to, from Lew Chew	497
Washington's birth-day, celebration of, by the American squadron in Japan	333, 334
Watch, a curiosity in Lew Chew	175, 176
Water buffalo of Singapore	131
Wax plant, Lew Chew	168
Webster island, Japan	353, 399
We-dae-o-gang, or smaller officials of Lew Chew	226
Weirs for fish, Lew Chew	168
Whale ships, supplies for, Bonin islands	203
fishery off Japan opened by the treaty	212
fishers, protection to shipwrecked, demanded of the Japanese	257
Whaling depot, Hakodadi	451
Whampoa, a Chinese merchant at Singapore, his hospitality	128
anchorage at	135
pagoda	135
Wharf, temporary Japanese, of bags of sand and straw	254
Williams, Wells, interpreter	154, 155
Wind, direction of	89
Winds, encountered off the Cape and in the Indian ocean	103
Winter, severity of, Japan	342
Women, seclusion of, Lew Chew	193
industry of, Lew Chew	219
position of, Lew Chew; dress	316
foreign, not wanted in Japan	385, 386
American, at Simoda	390
driven away on approach of Commodore Perry	394
Japanese, visited by Commodore Perry	395
Japanese, work in the fields	396
social position of, in Japan	397
Wood, dense, Lew Chew	177
Wood-cuts, Japanese	459
Woosung, village of	144
Wives, importance of the number of, in China	296
Woven fabrics of the Japanese	51
Wrecks of American vessels, Japan, communication respecting	471
Wrestlers, Japanese	369, 370
Japanese, drawings of	461
Wrestling match, Japanese	371
Writing, hand, Lew Chew	224
Xavier, his mission in Japan	24
establishes Christianity in Ceylon	120
Yang-tse-keang river	144
Yedo	6, 7
town observed on the bay of	241
plan of, shown to Japanese officials	251
port of, in sight	267
advantages of the survey of the bay of	273
shores of the bay of, in winter	326

INDEX. 537

	Page.
Yedo, bay of	327
Japanese refuse to receive the expedition at	330
bells of, heard by the American expedition	337
surveying boats of the expedition approach within four miles of	340
populousness of the bay of	343
an American officer on his way to	359
glimpse of, through a fog	398
Commodore Perry's reasons for not visiting	399
scurvey, Ainos	454
Yenoske, a Japanese interpreter	340, 348, 417
reply to the letter of the President of the United States	350
visits Commodore Perry	372
duplicity of	395
readiness to assume blame	485
his farewell visit to Commodore Perry	486
Yezaimen, governor of Uraga, visits Commodore Perry	237
his second visit	240
his third visit to Com. Perry	244
bearer of a letter from the Emperor of Japan to Com. Perry	249
visit to the Susquehanna on the day of the reception of the letter of the President	253
conversation with Captain Buchanan	263

	Page.
Yezaimen, his examination of the engine of the Susquehanna when in motion	264
his visit of expostulation on the advance of the squadron	265
his appreciation of good cheer	266
brings presents to Com. Perry	268, 269
his friendliness	269
parting health to the Americans	270
visits the squadron	337
visits the Powhatan	340
takes charge of a letter from "Sam Patch," of Japan	340
conversation with Captain Adams	341
makes arrangements for the delivery of the Emperor's letter	342
Yokuhama, Japan	343
Yomi, the pure Japanese dialect	9
Yoritimo, his history	11
Ynitz, a Sintoo sect	21
Zhetsa-zhi, a Buddhist monastery, Hakodadi	443
Zhiogen-zhi, a Buddhist temple, Hakodadi	442
Zhi-zo-bozats, a Japanese deity	442
Zingoons, or temporal sovereigns of Japan	11, 13
Zin-mu-ten-woo, the founder of the Japanese sovereignty	11
Ziogoon, now dethroned	15
Zipangu	4

68 J

Milton Keynes UK
Ingram Content Group UK Ltd.
UKHW021106270324
440143UK00004B/121